Living with Jazz

Living
with
Jazz

DAN MORGENSTERN

A reader edited by Sheldon Meyer

PANTHEON BOOKS
NEW YORK

Grateful acknowledgment is made to Oxford University Press, Inc. for permission to
reprint "Recorded Music" by Dan Morgenstern, from *Oxford Companion to Jazz*, edited
by Bill Kirchner. Copyright © 2000 by Oxford University Press, Inc. Reprinted by
permission of Oxford University Press, Inc.

All articles that were previously published in *Down Beat Magazine* appear
courtesy of *Down Beat Magazine*.

Library of Congress Cataloging-in-Publication Data

Morgenstern, Dan.
Living with jazz : a Dan Morgenstern reader / foreword by Sheldon Meyer.
p. cm.
ISBN 0-375-42072-X
1. Jazz—History and criticism. I. Title.

ML3507.M67 2004
781.65—dc22   2004043432

www.pantheonbooks.com
Book design by Virginia Tan
Printed in the United States of America
First Edition
2 4 6 8 9 7 5 3 1

To Adam and Josh

Keep Listening!

Contents

LINER NOTES

RECORD REVIEWS

CAUGHT IN THE ACT

Foreword

Dan Morgenstern has been a major figure on the jazz scene for more than four decades. During the 1960s and into the 1970s, he was the editor of *Down Beat*, then the premier jazz magazine. His comments, criticisms, reviews of records, and reports on live jazz activities were central to the discussion of jazz at the time. Since 1976, he has been the director of the Institute of Jazz Studies at Rutgers University, Newark, New Jersey, which he has made the central repository of jazz archives and research in the world. With his wide experience and knowledge, he has advised and directed a generation of jazz scholars and broadened the discussion and range of the discipline.

I have known and respected Dan Morgenstern throughout my career as a book editor at Oxford University Press and have long been eager to publish a book by him. Indeed, Dan and I have talked about doing so on many occasions, but his busy schedule never enabled us to pull something together until now. Fortunately, Robert Gottlieb, another editor who loves jazz, was able to find a way. Gottlieb suggested that a book be published that brought Morgenstern's significant writings into one volume, and since he knew I had recently retired as a full-time editor, he asked if I could help Dan put the definitive collection of his work together. Both Dan and I jumped at the chance to collaborate on this important project. So began one of the happiest experiences of my working life.

Dan Morgenstern is perhaps the only significant jazz critic whose writings have not been readily available in book form, which is why this definitive, substantial collection represents an important jazz event.

We started our collaboration with Dan sending me photocopies of all of his writings. We then indulged in a friendly debate about which pieces should be included and which left out. Then we realized that we needed to create a framework for the book. Mere chronology would not work, so we divided the book into a number of categories that would bring subjects together and provide a proper context for Morgenstern's essays. Our editorial work then developed in this context.

In the charming memoir "Reminiscing in Tempo," which opens this volume, Dan describes his early years, first in Vienna and then, when he and his mother were forced to flee because of the Nazi takeover, in Denmark and later in Sweden. The main source of music for him in his childhood was the phonograph, through which he was introduced to jazz. Except for occasional live encounters in Copenhagen (mainly with Fats Waller and Django Reinhardt), he developed his passion for the music through records. In Vienna, at age six, though, he had his richest early music experience when one of his father's closest friends, the great composer Alban Berg, presented him with a recording of Mozart's *Eine Kleine Nachtmusik*. Throughout his life, jazz has always been part of a wider musical horizon.

Morgenstern begins by bearing testimony to the great figures in jazz history. He bestows his greatest love and attention on Louis Armstrong, jazz's greatest figure. No one has written about Armstrong with greater understanding and brilliance. For him, Armstrong "spread love, happiness, and beauty," and Morgenstern stresses "the prodigious quality of effort and energy" that he put into his life's work. He speaks of Armstrong as "the spirit incarnate of the music he did so much to create." His trumpet produced a "golden sound, unlike any other coaxed from the instrument." Armstrong is the "old master, making each phrase a gem, distilling the essence of his music, bringing each melodic contour out in relief."

Morgenstern himself has had a profound effect upon the way Armstrong is perceived today. The traditional view of Armstrong's career acknowledged him as the first major voice of jazz in the 1920s, as revealed by his revolutionary series of Hot Five and Hot Seven recordings. But in the 1930s and 1940s, when Armstrong fronted a big band, critics felt that his playing became repetitive and formulaic, and they condemned him for striving for commercial success. In a liner note for the reissue of Armstrong's early 1930s big-band recordings—entitled "VSOP" (Very Special Old Phonography)—Morgenstern effectively demolishes these clichés about Armstrong. He decisively demonstrates how Armstrong's playing with his big band revealed the way his "mastery of his instrument and musical imagination continued to grow. What we encounter here is jazz's first and greatest virtuoso and master improviser in the process of flowering and self-discovery." Morgenstern points out how his playing on these records is "unparalleled . . . he executes some of the most fantastic instrumental passages." In some instances it is "sheer bravura playing," but, as Morgenstern points out, wasn't this what great virtuosos in music always showed? In these solos Armstrong's "sense of form and proportion are infallible." In fact, Morgenstern turns most jazz criticism on its head—for jazz critics, small-group music is usually preferable to that of big bands—by declaring that a big band "was the best backdrop" for Armstrong's trumpet in this period: "A full band, with appropriate arrangements especially designed for the purpose, set off his playing and singing more dramatically than a small group ever could have."

Morgenstern's other telling insight into Armstrong's greatness focused on the fact that, in approaching Armstrong, one has to embrace the man in all the fullness of his being—not only in his incomparable trumpet playing and singing but also in his writing (as Morgenstern demonstrates in his perceptive introduction to Armstrong's memoir *Satchmo: My Life in New Orleans*), his great ability to communicate with an audience, and his overwhelming wish to please and entertain. Morgenstern vehemently derides the "fallacy that Louis had sold his birthright of 'authentic blues and stomps' for Tin Pan Alley pottage" (just because he began playing the Great American Songbook). And, finally, Armstrong, in his actions and his playing, refused to recognize the dichotomy between art and entertainment that has plagued jazz since its early days. For Armstrong, there was no such dichotomy. As he said, "I don't think musicians should type themselves." And he certainly never did.

There is a knowing and insightful portrait of Duke Ellington, jazz's other central figure. Morgenstern brilliantly assesses Ellington's recording career from the later 1920s to the mid-1940s. Especially valuable are his perceptive reviews of two 1960s Ellington LPs—*The Far East Suite* and ... *And His Mother Called Him Bill* (a memorial to his great collaborator, Billy Strayhorn)—in which he captures the unique qualities of Ellington at his best.

In the "Profiles and Portraits" that follow, he brings to life a whole range of major jazz performers. No one has so imaginatively defined the greatly influential tenor player Lester Young. "Lester was a dancer, a dreamer, a master of time and its secrets. Foremost among them was equilibrium. He never stumbled on the tightrope of swing. He is a juggler, a high-wire artist without a net, a diver, a gambler, a gamboler." And his characterization of the incomparable Miles Davis as an innovator has the ring of truth. "In today's world, there are many seekers of new ways. Often the searches seem forced, and the results not natural. Miles Davis, however, has that rare gift of being able to give birth and life to new ways which, no matter how startling, always seem natural and logical, and open new roads for others to travel after he has moved on."

Among the particularly memorable "Profiles" are in-depth interviews Morgenstern conducted with major jazz figures. Such interviews represent a whole subgenre of jazz criticism, a form at which Morgenstern was a unique master.

Then come "Liner Notes," an art at which Morgenstern was a true practitioner. With the arrival of LP records, it became necessary for record companies to provide copy to describe the music on the disks. Most of these notes for jazz records were sheer hype, but many of them—especially those written by jazz experts or critics—could be quite illuminating. Morgenstern's notes certainly were in this category. As I have mentioned, his note on the Armstrong "VSOP" reissue represented a major jazz statement. He has written liner notes on a huge range of jazz figures from the early 1920s to the present. For his liner notes, Morgenstern has received six Grammy awards. This whole section contains keen musical assessments of many important jazz figures and their key recordings and shows how actively and understandingly Morgenstern responds to what his ears hear.

Much of the "Record Reviews" and "Caught in the Act" pieces represent Morgenstern as a working journalist while he was editor of *Down Beat.* His memoir, *Reminiscing in Tempo,* describes how, when he first arrived in America in 1947, he immediately gravitated to Fifty-second Street and heard such jazz giants as Sidney Bechet, Charlie Parker, and Billie Holiday in clubs, often while standing in the street outside the club engulfed in traffic noise. There he met the jazz trumpeter Hot Lips Page, who brought him uptown to the after-hours places in Harlem. The experience affected him in crucial ways as a jazz critic later on. As he says: "What has served me best is that I learned about the music not from the books but from the people who created it, directly or indirectly."

"Caught in the Act" reveals Morgenstern's great understanding of the jazz musician as an active performer. In four separate assessments of the controversial modernist Ornette Coleman, he sets out the unique qualities that make Coleman such an essential but complicated jazzman. It reveals that Morgenstern was really aware of jazz people and what they were doing.

"Festivals and Events" shows Morgenstern responding in stirring fashion to a number of special jazz events. The section begins with his presence at the 1960 Newport Jazz Festival. He actually covered every Newport Festival from the halcyon days of the late 1950s through 1970. The 1960 festival had a particular dramatic flavor—not only the infamous "riots," which almost stopped the festival in its tracks, but a particularly rich mixture of the blues and some old-time performers. Given the space limits of the book, 1960 will have to stand for the series of fascinating chronicles Morgenstern presented on Newport, where he deals in turn through the years with a whole range of famous jazz players. Especially memorable in "Festivals" are his wry and insightful accounts of jazz events in and around the White House in Washington, as well as a touching re-creation of the famous club Birdland, both in its early days and in its later life.

In his childhood Morgenstern began what he calls his "lifelong love affair" with the phonograph. Several of his extended liner notes in the "Recording Jazz" section are highly informative histories of individual record labels. Morgenstern believes that "jazz and the phonograph were made for each other." Without the phonograph, he asserts, jazz's spontaneity, special sound, and rhythmic complexity would probably have remained a special taste; it is unlikely that the music would have been widely dissemi-

nated, and it certainly might never have achieved its popularity or significance. To recall his "love affair" with the phonograph, Morgenstern closes
this section with the definitive history of the entire subject of "recording
jazz."

There follows an in-depth assessment of "Jazz and the Arts"—dance,
film, and television in turn. Then, while Morgenstern is in many ways a
most modest, even-handed, and objective critic, he makes a point of in-
dulging in controversy and expressing some strong opinions. In addressing
"commercialism" and jazz, he further develops a point he first raised about
Louis Armstrong. He talks about how jazz critics and fans have had "an innate suspicion of success." For Morgenstern, art and entertainment are indivisible. In a "Caught in the Act" review of Erroll Garner, he defends
Garner for committing "the sin of being accepted by the general public"
and praises him as "unashamedly and nakedly romantic," a player who obviously enjoys what he is doing and responds to the public. He sums up his
view in a final piece labeled "In Defense of 'Commercialism.'"

The book stands as a monument to Morgenstern's immense contribution to jazz. It reveals his incomparable insights into the entire course of
jazz history. What makes him especially important is his great awareness of
jazz people, what they are doing, and how they pursue their art. An enormous breadth of knowledge, deep cultural roots, and an overwhelming fair-
mindedness pervade every page of this book. The entire jazz world is in
Dan Morgenstern's debt.

Sheldon Meyer

Acknowledgments

Most writers would consider themselves lucky to have one great editor. Well, I am doubly blessed: this book was made possible by not one but two brilliant editors. I first became acquainted with Robert Gottlieb when he began work on his monumental *Reading Jazz*, in the course of which he kindly pointed out that my writings were largely inaccessible.

Among those who, over the years, had suggested that I put together a selection of my stuff was that paragon of jazz editors, Sheldon Meyer, whom I first met ages ago through our mutual friend Martin Williams. But there never seemed to be time enough, and getting a handle on all that scattered output became more daunting as it kept accumulating.

Then, one fine day, Bob Gottlieb invited Sheldon and me to lunch, at Kean's Chophouse, Sheldon's favorite watering hole, and then and there he unveiled the idea for this book. Needless to say, it seemed marvelous to me, and to my delight, Sheldon accepted. No lunch ever tasted better!

It was Sheldon who imposed structure and order upon the massive amount of material that I extracted from a wide variety of sources—something I could not possibly have accomplished on my own—and gently but firmly helped me separate the lasting wheat from the fading chaff. With the extraction and formatting of all that material, I had the invaluable assistance of my son Josh, who thoughtfully graduated from the University of Chicago, where he had been editor-in-chief of *The Maroon*, in time to be back home and available to be imposed upon by his father.

When Sheldon and I feared that we had given birth to a monster, Bob Gottlieb cast his objective and vastly experienced eye on the draft manuscript and guided us to the finish line.

During my many years of working for periodicals, I was my own editor—not always an ideal situation—and the same holds true for most of the liner notes. But I learned much from the late Don DeMicheal, my mentor and predecessor at *Down Beat* and one of the fairest and most decent men I've known (as well as a first-rate drummer and vibist). And if some of my liner notes read better than others, the fine hand of Orrin

Keepnews no doubt was involved—he was an editor before he became a record producer.

Lastly, for understanding and encouragement, I thank my patient colleagues at the Institute of Jazz Studies, Ed Berger especially. And also Lynn Mullins, Larry Kart, and Daryl Sherman.

Living with Jazz

Introduction: Reminiscing in Tempo

T hough I was born in Europe, I'm a child of the swing era. Even in Vienna, home of the waltz, where I spent my earliest years, the sound of American popular music was heard. For me then, the main source of music was not the radio, which was for grown-ups to listen to news on, but the phonograph, with which I began a lifelong love affair as soon as I was old enough to master the mechanics of winding up the spring-driven motor and making the turntable start and stop.

The world has long since become spoiled in its easy consumption of recorded music, but I had to work for my magic sounds. My mother's portable phonograph had to be rewound after every three-minute 78 side—unless you liked the effect of the music gradually slowing down, which could be fun, especially when it came to the human voice. And 78s, made of shellac, were quite heavy for a small child to handle—and breakable. Before I began to make my own acquisitions, the "libraries" at my disposal consisted of the records my mother and her younger siblings had danced to as teenagers, from the early '20s through the mid-'30s, when I began to get interested.

In retrospect, there wasn't much that could qualify as real jazz. The closest was "Georgia on My Mind" by the British trumpeter, singer, and Armstrong acolyte Nat Gonella—my first, indirect connection with the master. There was "Crazy People" by the Boswell Sisters, which I liked, and "The New St. Louis Blues" by Abe Lyman's Californians, which I didn't (and I was right—it's corny and loud). Early favorites were "Singin' in the Rain" and "Nobody but You" by Fred Rich's orchestra. As I discovered much later, this was a studio group including the Dorsey brothers, who were responsible for the good if brief jazz solos after the inevitable vocals that conditioned my young ears to English with an American accent.

There were a few classical records as well, and from an early age I was taken to Sunday symphony concerts for young people. But it wasn't until one of my father's closest friends, the great composer Alban Berg, presented me, on my sixth birthday, with two beautiful, shiny 12-inch discs of Mozart's *Eine Kleine Nachtmusik*, performed by members of the Berlin Philharmonic under Erich Kleiber, that this kind of music got through to me. I loved this piece, soon knew it by heart, and was shaken by Berg's sudden death just two months after he gave me this gift.

About a year later, much against my will, I started violin lessons. Like most kids, I'd been banging on pianos and enjoyed the effect, but Nathan Milstein had come to visit and proclaimed that I had the hands of a violinist. And our grand piano was no longer available to me. My father had lost his job as Viennese cultural correspondent for a major German newspaper in the wake of the Nazi takeover, and we had to take in a lodger—a famous but ill-tempered cellist, who needed the piano to rehearse and teach. Maybe it was because our tenant played a stringed instrument that I didn't take to the fiddle, but in any case, we soon had to leave Vienna. One of the ugliest and most unmusical sounds I'd yet heard was that produced by the crowds greeting the arrival of Hitler in the city where he had learned to hate Jews.

For years I was certain that my first taste of live jazz had been in Denmark, where my mother and I found a haven after the Anschluss (my father wound up in France). But when I heard a record by Jack Hylton's band (Hylton was England's Paul Whiteman) called "Ellingtonia," I suddenly recalled that I had seen them in Vienna and heard this medley of "Black and Tan Fantasy," "It Don't Mean a Thing," "Mood Indigo," and "Bugle Call Rag." It was "Mood Indigo" that triggered my memory. For this number, the houselights had gone down and pin spotlights had picked up three instrumentalists at center stage: trumpet, trombone, and clarinet. The two brass horns had sparkling mutes in their bells, and the effect, combined with that haunting melody, was magical.

The jazz I heard and saw in Copenhagen, however, was something else. It came in the person of none other than Fats Waller, who gave a series of concerts in the Danish capital in the fall of 1938. My mother, bless her, took me to one of them, and I was fascinated by this huge black man who played the piano and sang, moved, and talked with such enormous energy and good humor that it was impossible to keep still (it mattered little that I understood only a word or two of his lyrics and patter).

Of course I had to have some Waller records, and by then I'd also taken a liking to Ella Fitzgerald and the Chick Webb band—in particular, the song "The Dipsy Doodle," which had a childish vocal that I enjoyed, though less than the Sandy Williams trombone solo that followed it. In those days, we listened to records in a different way than we do now. They were usually acquired one at a time, and one would listen again and again to each three-minute side. It was, I think, a good way to learn how to appreciate nuances.

In addition to Waller, I also got to see the Mills Brothers, that unique vocal quartet which then still had considerable jazz in its repertory. I was particularly taken with "Tiger Rag." And while they were not American, the Quintette du Hot Club de France, which I also saw in concert, had jazz of high order to offer in the persons of Django Reinhardt and Stephane

Grappelli. Though I admired Grappelli's supple fiddling, it was the Gypsy guitarist Django, with some of the same rhythmic vitality that Waller gave off, who got to me.

Soon afterward, World War II broke out, and there were no more foreign visitors. By then, I'd been in a boarding school outside Copenhagen for some time. It was run by a progressive educator who had a warm personality and all sorts of ideas about teaching kids, but no business sense whatever. The turnover of students and teachers was fairly constant and the food pretty awful (a rarity for Denmark), but I had a good time. Discipline was lax, and the older kids liked me because I had my little record collection, by now including Benny Goodman and Artie Shaw, which I let them borrow to dance to, provided they let me kibitz. There was an older boy who knew a lot about jazz and had many more records than I; he had almost all the Goodman small-group sides and also liked the great Danish violinist Svend Asmussen. He was a loner, but sometimes invited me to his room to listen. He chided me for letting other kids borrow my records—he was my first encounter with the odd species called the collector.

The boarding school came to a sudden and dramatic end during the war's first winter, which was uncommonly cold. There was no money for heating, so all classes were held in the big dining room, which had a fireplace that was fed by chopped-up furniture. Eventually the septic tank burst, and when a huge mound of frozen sewage decorated the backyard, the authorities swiftly closed the place. I was back in Copenhagen by early April when, for the second time in my short life, I was awakened by Nazi-generated noise. This time it wasn't hysterical screaming but airplanes filling the sky. I had a good view of them from my slanting bedroom window: they were flying low enough that the swastika tail emblems were clearly visible. Fortunately they were dropping leaflets, not bombs, and despite my mother's entreaties, I rushed out to read the message. In very bad Danish, the leaflets informed the populace that the Germans had arrived to "protect" them.

As an unintended result of the Nazi occupation, jazz became more popular than ever—a phenomenon universal to countries under the Hitler jackboot. In France, Django Reinhardt enjoyed the greatest acclaim of his career, and even in Germany there were clandestine groups of jazz fans who'd meet to listen to records. Jazz was anathema to the Nazis, who considered it a mongrel affront to Aryan "culture," the product of an unholy alliance between Africans and Jews. But to those who hated the Nazis, jazz stood for freedom, for democracy, and for the spirit of America, which, especially after Pearl Harbor, seemed to embody hope for a better future. In Denmark, Asmussen became so popular that the Gestapo arrested him and took him to Berlin for questioning. When they eventually released him, he soon fled to Sweden, where I also wound up after the Danish underground had ascertained that the Nazis were about to round up all Jews for deportation. The story of our rescue has been told often (if not often enough); what seems most remarkable about the experience is that the Danes who risked their lives to save strangers did so as if it were the most natural thing to do—a ray of light in the darkness of the twentieth century.

Sweden had no blackouts, as we'd had in Denmark, and there were new American movies and recent jazz records by way of England. Along with a bunch of other refugees, Danish and Norwegian, I soon found myself at a boarding school outside Stockholm that specialized in teaching kids from upscale broken homes. One of my roommates, luckily, was a jazz fan with a small but distinguished stash of records. One of the best was "Bugle Call Rag" by a group generically known as the Rhythmmakers. Assembled by the enterprising Eddie Condon in the depth of the Depression, this joyful, integrated band featured Red Allen's trumpet, Pee Wee Russell's clarinet, Joe Sullivan's piano, and a super-caloric rhythm section anchored in Zutty Singleton's drums. Whoever woke up first would activate the turntable, and those swinging sounds would promptly dispatch any cobwebs. They were still lingering in my ear when on June 6, 1944, the morning's first class was interrupted to bring us news of D-day.

I spent that summer in the home of a hospitable, wealthy Swedish family. Their young son, my junior by a few years, was such a jazz fan that his room was decorated with photos of musicians—most prominently Benny Carter, whose visit to Sweden in 1936 was still fondly remembered. The boy's records were my introduction to Carter's marvelous music. That fall, a special school for Danes was set up in Goteborg, and I found fellow jazz fans there as well. But I had now become passionately involved in all things American; my father had made his adventurous way to the United States in April of 1941, and I knew that I would join him there after the war. Movies, which I was crazy about, were not just a diversion but a learning tool, for I would force myself not to read the Swedish subtitles. Neglecting math and Latin, I devoured American literature, from Hemingway, Faulkner, and Erskine Caldwell to mysteries with slangy dialogue and a discovery, Horace McCoy, a screenwriter who wrote novels in a tough, Morse-code style (he turned out to be a jazz fan). And of course, I loved to hear jazz singers, who weren't always easy to decipher.

Much of our spare time, however, was spent listening to war news on the radio. There was the BBC, of course, but also clandestine stations broadcasting anti-Nazi propaganda in German, and Radio Moscow, in English and German. Not long after V-E Day, I was back in Denmark, where our neighbors had preserved our apartment and its contents—not a fork was missing, and the plants had been watered—again, as if that were simply the natural thing to do.

Though I was delighted to be back in Copenhagen—a city I still love—
my thoughts for the future were focused on America. It would be a while;
my father had to become a U.S. citizen before my mother and I could be
admitted. Meanwhile, my thus far rather scattershot interest in jazz began
to become a bit more directed. I read a somewhat slanted overview by
Hugues Panassié; unfortunately, no one turned me on to a remarkable
Danish book—Sven Moller Kristensen's *Hvad Jazz Er* (*What Jazz Is*), published in 1938—that was far better than Panassié or, for that matter, anything by then published in English. I also started to collect records
seriously. I couldn't afford the specialist stores, but I found a basement shop
that was a marvelous jumble of secondhand records, books, and magazines.
Not having yet discovered Charles Delaunay's *Hot Discography*, I was pretty
much on my own, and would certainly have passed up a disc by the Mound
City Blue Blowers if not for a notation, in white ink, on the label that said
"Coleman Hawkins," a name I was aware of, mainly from the beautiful
"Heartbreak Blues" I had already acquired. The Blue Blowers included not
only Hawkins, whose "Hello Lola" and "One Hour" solos were landmarks
in his career, but also Pee Wee Russell, already known to me from that
"Bugle Call Rag," and its flip side, "Spider Crawl."

The first individual artist I collected was Duke Ellington, starting with
the OKeh "Black and Tan Fantasy." Every Ellington record seemed to be
different; nothing was predictable. My first Armstrong was a good one: the
Hot Five's "Basin Street Blues." That, of course, is a blues in name only, but
Muggsy Spanier's "Relaxin' at the Touro" was really the blues—one of my
great early favorites. On occasion, I'd buy some new records—British imports—at a fine, big music store, where a friendly jazz-minded salesclerk
would give me some guidance (and in those days, of course, you could listen
to a new record before you bought it). One fine day he persuaded me to
purchase a book, American and very expensive but a good investment. This
was *The Jazz Record Book*, published in 1942, which not only was an annotated guide to hundreds of records, from country blues to swing bands, but
also contained a concise and well-written survey of jazz history. (Years later
I came across a contemporary review by Barry Ulanov in *Metronome*, already the leading journal of jazz modernism, which castigated it for prais-
ing the music of Jelly Roll Morton and, in particular, Sidney Bechet. But in
Denmark I was still blissfully unaware of journalistic infighting in the jazz
world, and in any case had found out about Bechet on my own, via a friend
from school who owned the gorgeous "When the Sun Sets Down South.")

There was good Danish jazz as well—from Asmussen, still very popular,
and from trombonist Peter Rasmussen, who could hold his own with the
best Americans. I was still too young—and too broke—to hear live jazz in
nightclubs, but there was the occasional jazz concert, and also some fine

programs of jazz films. The biggest event of my European phase, however, was the first visit of an American jazz band to Copenhagen since the pre-war years. This occurred in the fall of 1946, and the band was Don Redman's; the last to be fronted by this big-band pioneer who'd made history in the 1920s as Fletcher Henderson's chief arranger. It had been put together mainly to perform for the U.S. servicemen and women still stationed in Europe, with the assistance of Redman's friend, the Danish jazz baron Timme Rosenkrantz.

The star soloist was Don Byas, a master of the tenor sax, who remained in Europe for the next twenty-six years and as a result did not achieve the wider critical recognition he deserved. Byas had been a member of the first group to play bebop on Fifty-second Street, but he was not stylistically a bopper. Nor were the other Redman stars—trombonist and vibraharpist Tyree Glenn, trumpeter and singer Peanuts Holland, and the twenty-five-year-old pianist Billy Taylor—but they were certainly at the cutting edge of swing. The band's two genuine boppers, interestingly, were its only white members, trumpeter Allan Jeffreys and trombonist Jack Carmen. The singer was Inez Cavanaugh, Rosenkrantz's companion and also an accomplished journalist.

I attended two of the four standing-room-only Copenhagen concerts and was swept away by Byas's huge tone and show-stopping balladeering on "Laura," the band's punch and swing on up-tempo numbers, and Holland's playing and singing, influenced by Armstrong and Hot Lips Page. One of the band's most interesting pieces was "For Europeans Only," commissioned from Tadd Dameron, staff arranger for the Billy Eckstine and Dizzy Gillespie bands, whom Redman hailed as "a young man you'll be hearing from." But it was the total impact of this genuine American jazz orchestra— with its rhythmic drive, individual virtuosity, and showmanship (the big production number was "Stormy Weather," featuring Cavanaugh, trombonist Quentin Jackson, the band as a glee club, and several tempo changes; it brought down the house)—that was a taste of things to come.

On April 22, 1947, my mother and I arrived in New York. I hadn't seen my father since early 1939, when I'd briefly visited him in Paris. He had a little radio, and on my first night in New York, when I couldn't sleep, I turned it on in search of what I expected to find in abundance: jazz. It took quite a while. There was lots of talk, not all in English, and much pop music, but no jazz. Finally, near the end of the dial (strictly AM in those days, of course), I caught the last notes of something jazzy, followed by the husky, black-sounding voice of the disc jockey, which I found hard to fully understand. He referred to himself by the unlikely name of Symphony Sid. What was even harder to comprehend was the music that followed: a version of a tune I gradually came to recognize as "I Can't Get Started," which

I knew from Bunny Berigan's famous, triumphantly accented record. This version also featured a trumpet, but it was dirge-like, with an oddly mournful backdrop, and, to my naive ears, out of tune. (I knew dissonance from modern classical music but was unaccustomed to it in jazz.) This, of course, was Dizzy Gillespie's unique interpretation—an appropriate introduction to jazz in 1947 New York.

But I hadn't finally reached Manhattan to listen to jazz on the radio—or on records. While most first-time visitors wanted to see the Statue of Liberty (arriving by ocean liner, I'd already seen it) or the Empire State Building, I wanted to go to Fifty-second Street, that legendary block of jazz clubs I'd read so much about. It wasn't much to look at from the outside, though the names on the various marquees and sandwich boards made me drool. History tells us that by the spring of 1947, the street was well into its decline and fall, and to be sure, there were signs touting strippers and comedians. But having Sidney Bechet, Charlie Parker, and Billie Holiday all on the same block wasn't shabby.

I soon discovered that it was possible to hear a lot of music from outside the clubs, if there wasn't too much traffic noise and the doormen didn't chase you away. Eventually I learned how to nurse a beer through several sets of music by drinking from the bottle, which was opaque, instead of from a glass, which the bartender could easily spot when empty, or, if I wanted to stick around all night, to tip the bartender well on the first transaction, after which he'd leave me alone with my empty bottle.

I learned these tricks from a man who became my jazz Virgil—an unsung trumpeter named Nat Lorber, whom everyone knew as "Face." Nat did indeed have a striking visage: a big head with the broad features of his Russian-Jewish peasant ancestors. Both his parents were born in the old country and still spoke Yiddish at home. Nat, the oldest of three siblings, was born in 1920—in Harlem, as he liked to point out—and reared in the Bronx (where a neighbor was fellow trumpeter Milton Rajonsky, later known as Shorty Rogers) and then Brooklyn, where his father, a garment cutter, rented a modest house near Coney Island. Nat knew New York—all of it—like the back of his hand, and he knew where to find jazz off the beaten path.

I met Nat just off Fifty-second Street at the White Rose, a bar where drinks were cheap and there was a so-called free lunch—pickled herring, beets, onions, cheese, pickles—and where the musicians hung out between sets when working or just anytime. We were introduced by a pretty girl who'd befriended me at a Greenwich Village left-wing gathering and had taken me on my first visit to Harlem, to the Lenox Lounge, and to see Dizzy Gillespie's big band, with Chano Pozo, at the Apollo Theater—an unforgettable event. Pozo, who would soon die, was something to see as well as to hear. She also took me to the Royal Roost, predecessor of Bird-land as the home of bebop in New York. There I got to tell Tadd Dameron, whose band included Fats Navarro on trumpet, that I'd heard his music performed in Denmark. Tadd was the only musician in his group who was interested in and nice to me—the others were attentive only to the ladies—and he and I became lifelong friends.

That same girl also introduced me to Randy Weston, the world's tallest pianist (and one of the best), who, happily, is still around. In those early days, he was still managing his father's luncheonette in the Bedford-Stuyvesant section of Brooklyn, where I spent a fabulous New Year's Eve at a local dance, with Randy's band supplying the music. It included the excel-lent guitarist Rector Bailey, never heard to advantage on records—the first of many musicians I was to encounter who don't show up in the history books but could outplay many who do.

Nat Lorber was such a one. He couldn't read music and his harmonic knowledge was rudimentary. He was mainly self-taught, though he took a few lessons from Charles Colin, a renowned trumpet teacher. Nat had one of the biggest sounds ever coaxed from a trumpet, and it was a pleasing sound. He adored Louis Armstrong and knew everything there is to know about his records. When I met Nat, he was the protégé of another of his idols, Hot Lips Page, who always tried to find him jobs though he had a hard enough time getting decent gigs for himself.

Lips was not tall, but had an inch or more on Nat, whom he affection-ately dubbed "Shorty" (in Lips's Texas accent, it came out "Shawty"). Lips, whom I came to know through Nat, was the veritable incarnation of the spirit of jazz. A master of the blues instrumentally and vocally, he would, I'm sure, have found the fame he so richly deserved in the wake of Ray Charles's success, but it was too late for Lips by then—he died of a heart at-tack in 1954, at the age of forty-six. Though he was a consummate show-man in the Armstrong mold (Lips came closer to Louis in certain ways than any other trumpeter-singer) and knew how to put together swinging bands, big or small, his true métier was the jam session. He was a master at setting riffs, a skill he no doubt had honed in Kansas City, and at beating off the right tempos. When challenged, he could outblow all comers. "When it comes to the blues, don't mess with Lips," said Dizzy Gillespie, "not Louis, not Roy [Eldridge], not me, not anybody." Truth be told, it wasn't just the blues. Lips knew his changes, though he was anything but orthodox. And he was a great teacher of session etiquette. Bandstand boors would get their comeuppance in various ways, all designed to let them make fools of them-selves. But he could also be kind and patient when it was called for.

Going uptown with Lips and Nat was a treat. Between them they knew every joint where there might be some music. The wide variety of venues ranged from the Lotus, a workingman's bar equipped with a turnstile so no one could leave without having paid (Lips referred to it as "a bucket of blood," but I never witnessed any mayhem there), to the glamorous after-hours place in the basement of the Braddock Hotel, adjacent to the famous Minton's. Perhaps my fondest memory is of a so-called social club, after hours but semi-legitimate. You had to sign up at first visit and receive a membership card, and only then would a door leading down a flight of stairs be opened. Greeted by the good uptown smell of chicken in the basket, we spotted Billie Holiday at a table consuming some of it as she listened to Art Tatum, seated at an upright piano. On the floor, sitting cross-legged, were Charlie Shavers and Joe Bushkin, gazing up at Art, who taunted Charlie: "Any note you can play, I'll play figure eights around it!"

When the music and the socializing ended, often after dawn, one might repair to Jenny Lou's (immortalized in Louis Jordan's "Early in the Morning"), a sparkling little restaurant appointed in Southern style, where such simple things as eggs with grits and biscuits tasted like manna from heaven and the coffee too was out of this world. Harlem was also the home of marvelous ribs and the best potato salad I've ever tasted.

The Apollo was a trip. No other audience was so attuned to what transpired on stage, be it music, dance, or comedy. When B. B. King gave out with one of his long, suspended guitar notes, a perfectly placed comment from the audience rang out: "Take your time—this is my day off!" Pandemonium. When the Ellington band was in residence, one waited for the moment when Duke would introduce Johnny Hodges. The always expressionless alto genius would slowly make his way to the solo mike (not that he needed it). When that first golden, glissandoed note issued forth, all the ladies present would utter a collective sigh. And then there was the time when Dinah Washington and party were in the house, front row center, and we were seated right behind them, having come early to catch Redd Foxx in his favorite lair. Don't ask me to recall the repartee (in any case not printable, even today), but I do know that my gut was sore for days from laughing so hard.

Except for an occasional elbow at the bar, I never experienced any hostility in Harlem, even in later years, when the music scene, or what was left of it, had changed and the Apollo no longer was what it used to be. For a while, starting in the later '50s, there was a little bit of Harlem in midtown Manhattan. The Metropole on Seventh Avenue between Forty-eighth and Forty-ninth Streets, which previously had featured Gay Nineties–style entertainment, gradually switched to jazz. At first, it was Dixieland, but then, starting with Max Kaminsky and Sol Yaged, it veered more toward what by then was called mainstream jazz; that is, latter-day swing. Red Allen was soon ensconced on the world's most peculiar bandstand, running above the nearly block-long bar (I never figured out how they got the upright piano into place; it was hard enough for the drummers), with mirrors both behind and across from the band. Music was continuous from three in the afternoon, when a trio (a horn, piano, and drums) began playing for five hours; after that, two bands (six or seven pieces) would alternate until closing time, between three and four in the morning.

Aside from Allen's resident band, which most often included Buster Bailey on clarinet, J. C. Higginbotham on trombone, and the great Cozy Cole on drums, there might be Roy Eldridge and Coleman Hawkins, when they were not touring with Jazz at the Philharmonic, or Charlie Shavers and Budd Johnson, or any of a host of great musicians. Once, Shavers sent Dizzy Gillespie in as a sub, and it was a kick to hear Diz with the New Orleans veteran Tony Parenti on clarinet—they got along just fine. Twice each night both bands would play; this was the so-called jam session, and mostly it would be a fairly routine run through "When the Saints Go Marching In," on which each hornman was supposed to sing as well as play a chorus—something Hawkins steadfastly refused to do. On occasion, there'd be some sparks, such as when Red got ambitious and challenged Roy, who smote him. But the most memorable jam was when Dinah Shore was in the house, Roy and Charlie Shavers were leading the bands, and "Dinah" was aptly chosen as the jam vehicle. Roy had his fluegelhorn that night, and when he and Charlie got into trading eights and fours—look out!

Though the Metropole was kind of funky, such celebrity visitors were not uncommon. And there were always musicians in the crowd. Miles Davis came by more than once to dig Roy and Hawk, and Roy insisted that this was where Miles picked up on the fluegelhorn. John Coltrane came to check out Hawk and stayed all night. And Benny Goodman dropped in to visit with his old friend Buster Bailey; they'd shared the same clarinet teacher in Chicago decades before.

Between sets, one would repair across the street to the Copper Rail, a bar where the drinks were bigger and cheaper than at the Metropole, and where on a given afternoon and night one might encounter a veritable who's who of jazz. This was especially so after the Rail began to feature soul food, cooked up by a sweet lady named Della, who, according to far better-versed experts than I, was an artist without peer. Having been introduced in my early New York period to chitterlings—by a friend who cleverly didn't tell me what they were until I'd decided that they tasted good—I was ready to experiment, though my standbys were such things as chicken and dumplings, or smothered pork chops. Once, when I was checking out pig's tails, Ben Webster walked in, looked at my plate, and picked me up from my stool, holding me in the air and announcing to all present what I was dining on. (I also remember Ben, who himself had a reputation for being difficult when inebriated, trying his level best to restrain Oscar Pettiford, who was four sheets to the wind.)

Perhaps the most glorious night at the Copper Rail was when Louis Armstrong's All Stars did a one-night stand at the Metropole and the musicians threw a party for Pops across the street. This was just after "Hello, Dolly!" and there was a banner that read: "You Beat the Beatles!"

My first encounter with King Louis had come about fifteen years before, also through my friendship with Nat, who'd introduced me to a very special lady named Jeann Failows. (Incidentally, in those days, women on the jazz scene were generally much hipper than the men—musicians, of course, excepted.) Jeann, who'd been a WAC during the war and worked in publicity (she promoted a now exceedingly rare paperback called *To Be or Not to Bop*, an informal history of bebop by a young man named Nard Griffin; had done work for Musicraft Records, and produced jam sessions at various venues, including the Club Harlem on 145th Street), was a member of Armstrong's inner circle. At the time I met her, she was entrusted with Louis's voluminous fan mail from all over the world, which she would answer with Pops's personally autographed diet pointers, responding, if need be, to often arcane questions.

Louis and the All Stars were appearing at the Roxy, a long-gone Times Square landmark, the city's biggest movie-and-stage-show palace after Radio City Music Hall. Nat and I met Jeann at the backstage entrance and were escorted to Louis's star dressing room. Wrapped in a white bathrobe, with that famous handkerchief tied around his head, he greeted us warmly. Jeann had to repeat my name, adding that I'd recently arrived from Denmark. Louis weighed "Morgenstern" and "Scandinavia," coming up with "Smorgasbord," his name for me from then on. But when he signed a photo for me, he made it out to Dan; it was the first of many. He had an astonishing knack for making you feel at ease in his presence; it soon seemed as if you were an old friend. Someone who really was now dropped in: Joe Bushkin, who presented Pops with a long-stemmed red rose, a gift from Tallulah Bankhead, sent with love . . . and something else as well. Pops smelled the rose, broke into a smile, and extracted from the yet unopened blossom an elegantly rolled large reefer. Also present was an even older friend, June Clark. Of Louis's age, June had been a prominent trumpeter on the New York scene in the 1920s, but tuberculosis put an end to his playing career, and, as he often said, there was no reason for him to go on with the trumpet anyway after what Louis had accomplished. For a time, he'd been Louis's road manager; later he became Sugar Ray Robinson's right-hand man.

Louis now excused himself, explaining that he wanted to catch a nap before the next show. He and June disappeared behind a partition, and Jeann gestured to us to be quiet. Soon we heard the most beautiful whistling: it was Louis's solo from the 1930 recording of "Sweethearts on Parade," note-perfect, with all the right inflections. June emerged, saying, sotto voce: "He's asleep." It was a very special lullaby. Jeann informed us that June could whistle almost all of Louis's famous solos.

Half an hour later it was time to wake Louis, who demonstrated his life-long talent for going to sleep in seconds and waking up alert and refreshed regardless of the length of the nap. While Pops was getting dressed, Jack Teagarden dropped in to discuss a musical point. The rapport between the two was evident, but I was amazed at Jack's eyes; in the words of a famous blues song, they looked like cherries in a pool of buttermilk. The stage manager arrived to give the five-minute warning, and Pops promptly entrusted us to him, with firm instructions to find us places from which we could see well, leaving us with "Enjoy the show!" As you may well imagine, we did. As Mezz Mezzrow put it, "Them first kicks are killers." I would, thankfully, share many more moments with Louis Armstrong, and the magic never wore off.

Like the Ancient Mariner, I could go on and on. When I was "hanging out," I had no intention of becoming what people call a jazz "critic" (most who write about jazz aren't critics but at best reviewers, or reporters, editors, etc.). Since I was friendly with musicians, I shared their often jaundiced view of that other breed, very few of whom I ever encountered in my nocturnal pursuits of the muse. I haven't told much about encounters with a more modern breed of players, such as the time when I had a one-on-one with Charlie Parker in the little bar next to Birdland called the Magpie. It was early evening; nobody in the joint; waiting to meet a friend. In walks Bird; it was the time when, briefly, he was using a cane, but he looked well and rested. He sat down next to me—a nice gesture, since there were many empty stools. "Mr. Parker," I said, "can I buy you a drink?" "Let me buy you one," he responded, and I noticed, as I had before when hearing him speak, how much he sounded like my main men, the guys from the generation before him. Not knowing what to say, I brought up Hot Lips Page, who often talked about Bird and loved his playing. His face lit up at the mention of Lips's name, and he asked when and where I'd last seen him and said to give Lips his best. I wish I could remember the rest, but there wasn't much. Bird's date soon arrived and we said goodbye. I never had a chance to buy him that drink back.

Life moves in strange ways, and sometime after embarking on a journalistic career, I was urged by Stanley Dance (who was then visiting the United States and kept encountering me at the Copper Rail and at recording sessions I was attending at the musicians' invitations) to send a monthly news column to the British magazine *Jazz Journal*. "They can't pay," he explained, "but they'll send you records and books, and it'll be a service to the musicians." I'd written a bit about jazz in the college paper I edited at Brandeis University, mainly to make propaganda for some jazz concerts we were producing on campus—most memorably, a solo recital by Art Tatum (who told us, when we drove him back to Boston, where he was appearing with his trio, that this had been the first time he'd done a concert all by himself, and he thanked us, which floored me, though I'd soon enough learn more about such injustices)—and a short review or two in the *New York Post*, where I was an editorial assistant, but this was a challenge.

My most enthusiastic early readers were my musician friends, and one thing led to another. What has served me best, I hope, is that I learned about the music not from books but from the people who created it, directly and indirectly. The greatest compliment I ever got was from Louis Armstrong. I had sent him an advance copy of the special issue of *Down Beat* we had prepared for his seventieth birthday, and for which we had gathered warm greetings from more than eighty musicians, spanning the length and breadth of the music. Within days, a letter arrived in that familiar hand (Pops always addressed his personal envelopes himself). "I received the magazine," it began, "and it knocked me on my ass!" No raves from critics could ever top that.

(2000)

Armstrong and Ellington

Portrait of the Artist
as a Young Man

"What would we have done without Louis?"

—Benny Morton

*"You can't play anything on the horn that Louis hasn't
played . . . even modern."*

—Miles Davis

He never was billed as the King of Jazz, but Louis Armstrong is the sole legitimate claimant to that musical throne. Without him, there would still be the music we call jazz, but how it might have developed is guesswork. He was the key creator of its mature vocabulary, and though nearly three-quarters of a century have passed since his influence first manifested itself, there is still not one musician partaking of the jazz tradition who does not, knowingly or unknowingly, make use of something created by Louis Armstrong.

For those who basked in the living presence of Armstrong, it is sobering to contemplate that we are at a point in the history of jazz where many among us know him only in his posthumous audiovisual incarnation, and many, alas, not even that well—unable instantly to recognize that voice, that

trumpet sound, that face, that smile. Our age consumes even the most consummate art at such a pace that Armstrong's universality is no longer a given.
Yet the infinite reproducibility of his recorded works ensures his immortality, and future generations will surely come to know that jazz and Louis
Armstrong are synonymous. The language he created is a marvelously flexible and expandable one that can be spoken in ever so many accents, and as
long as it remains a living tongue, it will refer back to its creator.

So if you are someone who is hearing the music in this collection for the
first time—and that is an enviable way to discover what took some of us
years of searching for rare old records, a few at a time—it will be most surprising if there are not familiar strains in it. Miles Davis knew what he was
talking about.

By all odds, Louis Armstrong, born out of wedlock on August 4, 1901, in
New Orleans, raised in the city's poorest quarter, out of school and working
for a living before he'd finished fifth grade, was not slated to become world-
famous. Yet against all odds, he not only survived but thrived. Sent to reform school at age twelve, he learned the fundamentals of music there and
by the time he was sixteen was able to supplement his income from work as
a longshoreman or day laborer by playing his cornet on weekends in such
rough joints as the Brick House, where, as he tells us in his autobiography,
Satchmo: My Life in New Orleans, "Levee workers would congregate every
Saturday night and trade with the gals who'd stroll up and down the floor
and into the bar. Those guys would drink and fight one another like circle
saws. Bottles would come flying over the bandstand like crazy, and there was
lots of just plain common shooting and cutting. But somehow all that jive
didn't faze me at all, I was so happy to have some place to blow my horn."

Indeed there was not much that ever fazed Louis Armstrong. He was
blessed with a perfect physique for blowing that most demanding of instruments, the trumpet (actually a cornet for the first decade or so, but as we
shall see, the difference is slight), and with a perfect disposition for making
his way in the toughest of environments. "Little Louis," the first nickname
he was known by, could be tough when required but mostly made friends
wherever he went. He credited his maternal grandmother—the one permanent adult presence in his early childhood years—with instilling in him the
system of values that would carry him through his extraordinary life and enable him to confront with equanimity situations and experiences he could
not have imagined in his youth. As he describes them, these fundamentals
seem deceptively simple: "I didn't go any further than fifth grade in school
myself. But with my good sense and mother-wit, and knowing how to treat
and respect the feelings of other people, that's all I've needed through life."

Armstrong's "good sense and mother-wit" covered a lot of ground. He also had, in abundance, what used to be called character—a currently unfashionable concept, since we are all supposed to be molded by environment. Of course, New Orleans was and is a very special place, and at that time it had a unique musical culture-in-the-making, something that gave young Louis inspiration. But even early on, his love of music and of life was combined with an extraordinary sense of responsibility, toward himself and what he very soon conceived of as his work. We speak of "playing" music, and young Louis certainly found exhilaration in playing his horn. But he also quickly noticed that musicians who didn't watch their intake of alcohol or take care of their health in other ways were less likely to play consistently well.

Armstrong was never a puritan, but he was a firm believer, early and late in life, in the separation between work and play. Thus he never tablehopped between sets, always warmed up before taking the stand, and reserved his pleasurable indulgences for after working hours. But, as we learn from his autobiography, he certainly did not practice deprivation of the senses. He writes of a musician on board the Mississippi riverboat that carried the band, led by Fate Marable, in which the young cornetist honed his playing and reading skills. This man nearly starved himself in order to invest all his earnings in cotton farming, but the boll weevils devoured his cotton and he became near-suicidal. "I'll never be rich," Armstrong concluded from observing this, "but I'll be a fat man." He did become rich, however (and sometimes fat as well), but never spent much on himself. His wives were well provided for, but he had no need for "a flock of suits," and perhaps because he never forgot the generous tips his early playing had inspired from his audience of whores, pimps, toughs, and hustlers, he gave away what he could afford as long as he lived, without the slightest ostentation.

Sharp powers of observation also led Armstrong to let others handle the business side of bandleading, including hiring and firing. This decision was often misunderstood, but he explains it perfectly well in *Satchmo:* "I never cared to become a bandleader; there was too much quarreling over petty money matters. I just wanted to play my horn as I am doing now [1954]. I have always noticed that the bandleader not only had to satisfy the crowd but that he also had to worry about the box office." Of course Armstrong did not leave all bandleading decisions, especially hiring, to his musical directors or managers; he simply did not want to take energy away from his playing in order to deal with the everyday banalities of music as a business. Making the music was a full-time job; he let others count the house.

Throughout his long career, Armstrong looked back on his New Orleans apprentice years with the greatest warmth and respect for his peers. First, of course, came King Oliver, who had treated him somewhat like a son, given him pointers, and groomed him to take his job with trombonist Kid Ory's band when Oliver left in 1919 for Chicago. Then came such other influential cornetists as Buddy Petit, Bunk Johnson, and Freddie Keppard, and a host of other musicians: clarinetists, drummers, bass players, guitarists. And most of all, there were the brass bands with which Armstrong loved to march, and to the strains of which he had "second-lined" (danced in the streets) as a child.

It was in New Orleans, too, that he'd heard the strains of European music, not only the marches, quadrilles, and waltzes so inventively transformed by the early jazz players, but also the operatic arias popular in the city that took such pride in its French Opera—the center of New Orleans social and cultural life. Operatic themes were also prominent on the programs of the concert bands that played on Sundays in the park band shells and featured cornetists as their star soloists, and on a lesser scale, these themes were also ground out on barrel organs.

And there was yet another, strictly modern, influence: the phonograph. Armstrong first acquired one after his marriage (at seventeen) to Daisy Parker, whom he'd first met when he was her customer. (The marriage didn't last long, for reasons well described in *Satchmo*.) In 1966 he recalled those early records: "Most of my records were the Original Dixieland Jazz Band—Larry Shields and his bunch. They were the first to record the music I played. I had Caruso records too, and Henry Burr, Galli-Curci, Tetrazini—they were all my favorites. Then there was the Irish tenor, McCormack—beautiful phrasing."

Many ingredients went into the making of Armstrong's musical mind. Early writers on jazz emphasized ragtime, spirituals, blues, marches, and dance music; few, if any, mentioned opera. More recently musicologists have been taking some notice of the parallels between Armstrong's formal solo structure (including such elements as opening and closing cadenzas) and operatic arias. As we shall see, Armstrong not only listened to such material, he later played it as well.

When he joined the Fate Marable orchestra aboard the steamer *St. Paul*, which cruised up the Mississippi as far as Davenport (where a young man with a horn, Bix Beiderbecke, first encountered Armstrong), the repertory included the latest popular hits. These were learned from sheet music, and Armstrong's reading knowledge was rudimentary. Marable thought so well of his playing that he hired the young man nonetheless, with the understanding that he would apply himself diligently. David Jones, who played saxophone and tenor horn in the band, took Little Louis under his wing and taught him to read (and write) music; the pupil caught on quickly. Also in the band were such stellar players as the brothers Dodds, clarinetist Johnny and drummer Baby; the bassist Pops Foster; and the guitarist

Johnny St. Cyr, all of whom would become Armstrong associates in the next decade.

About this time Armstrong also showed his first gifts as a songwriter. He whipped up a little number called "Get Off Katie's Head," and sold it outright for $50—a good deal of money in 1920—to society bandleader A. J. Piron and pianist Clarence Williams, partners in a publishing company. The song became a big hit under the more saleable title of "I Wish I Could Shimmy Like My Sister Kate," and thus Louis learned a lesson: on the business end of music, nobody could be trusted very far. Williams soon moved his organization to New York, where he prospered, though not always with the methods he had applied to Louis. Their future collaborations would be more equitable.

We know little about Armstrong's playing at this point, other than what musicians have related. Sidney Bechet, four years older, confirmed that Louis started to play around age ten, and recalled that the kid stunned him a bit later by playing the famous "High Society" clarinet solo on cornet, something quite unheard of. This alone tells us that a very young Armstrong (Bechet left New Orleans in 1917) already had the technique to execute a passage that would have challenged the best cornetists of the day.

Reliance on recordings is at once jazz's blessing and curse. Without this evidence, we would have no case on which to build a sensible history of the music, yet it is only circumstantial. The annals of oral jazz history are filled with players and bands that never encountered a recording device. In Armstrong's case, we have been fairly lucky, though it's a pity he didn't get to record before March 31, 1923—some seven months after he came to Chicago at King Oliver's beckoning to join the King's Creole Jazz Band at the Lincoln Gardens. That move would forever remain in Armstrong's mind as the key step in his career, the one that made him.

The year 1923 was a watershed in jazz recording. Black bands and singers had been recording for some time: James Reese Europe's was the first, in late 1913, that was remotely jazz related; Mamie Smith's 1920 "Crazy Blues" started the business of "race records"—recordings specifically made for the African-American market, which turned out to be considerable. And of course the first "real" jazz records, by the white New Orleans Original Dixieland Jass Band [*sic*] were made in 1917 (and bought by Armstrong along with his first Victrola in 1918). Kid Ory, who'd moved to California, made records there in 1922, but they hardly circulated outside that state. But in 1923 King Oliver, Bessie Smith, and Jelly Roll Morton all made their first records—a major breakthrough.

Oliver's Creole Jazz Band has gone down in history as a true New Orleans band, but it is more accurate to see it as a development of the parent style. Though its best records feature two cornets, trombone, and clarinet with a rhythm section of piano, banjo, and drums, there are frequent additions, such as C-melody or bass saxophone, and changes in personnel that do not quite measure up to Armstrong, Oliver, and the Dodds brothers. Be that as it may, the band's recorded legacy became the sacred texts of the 1940s traditional jazz revival that coincided with the coming of bebop—which is another story.

From the testimony of musicians (and fans) who heard the 1922–24 Oliver band live, its most potent attraction was the unique two-cornet team. Oliver and Armstrong worked out fancy double-cornet breaks that seemed to be miraculously harmonized and synchronized, of which we get an echo on such records as the two versions of "Snake Rag." Though they seemed purely spontaneous to the listeners, these breaks were in fact worked out in a most ingenious way: at a given point in the preceding collective band chorus, Oliver would play what he intended to use as his part in the break, and Armstrong, lightning quick on the uptake, would memorize it and devise his own second part—which always fit to perfection. No doubt some of the most successful breaks became standardized in the band, just as Oliver's famous three-chorus solo on "Dippermouth Blues" became what is known as a "set" solo, repeated not only by its author but by others playing the piece—which, incidentally, was co-composed by the two cornetists. (Dippermouth was Armstrong's first nickname among musicians, often shortened to "Dipper.")

Armstrong played his first recorded solo at the first Oliver studio session, on "Chimes Blues." It sticks close to the attractive melody but, in its sound, phrasing, and swing, stands out like a little gem that blends with its plainer setting. What isn't discernible to the listener on these recordings is that Armstrong was so much more powerful in tone that he had to stand much farther back from the recording horn than Oliver. On "Tears," a tune composed by Armstrong, his solo breaks are the strongest indicators of the future in his recorded work with Oliver.

In early 1924, Armstrong married the band's pianist and best reader, Lillian Hardin. She was certain that Oliver had hired her man to keep him under wraps as a potential rival to his crown. She was aware how far superior Louis's playing was to Oliver's, something the modest young man would not admit without constant hectoring. Eventually she succeeded in cutting Armstrong loose from his mentor, not least, perhaps, because the King was caught holding out money from his men—the bane of many bands in the history of the music. In a charming recorded memoir, *Satchmo and Me*, Lil describes how, after she left the band, she would hear her husband whistling on his way home, inventing the most beautiful music. One night she asked him why he didn't play like that, since he could whistle it. Reluctant at first, he eventually came around, of course. This story raises the issue of what kind of music the Oliver band played outside the recording studios.

We know, for instance, that they could play so softly that the *woosh* of the dancers' feet could be heard above the music in a slow drag number. And from recently discovered deposits in the Library of Congress copyright files, we also know that Armstrong conceived and wrote down (in his own already quite accomplished hand) the piece "Cornet Chop Suey," which he would not record until February 26, 1926, with his own Hot Five. The deposit bears the stamped registration date of January 18, 1924.

This discovery tells us once again that recordings are not an accurate reflection of musical reality. In reality, Louis Armstrong was capable of conceiving (and certainly of playing) the innovative, even virtuosic ideas of a piece that seemed fresh and surprising when recorded more than two years later—and at that stage of jazz history, two years is a considerable span of time. Where, if anywhere, was Armstrong performing "Cornet Chop Suey" in 1924? Not within the Oliver band as it comes to us on records, but perhaps on a night off with Lil and a pickup band? Maybe. But also not with the New York band of Fletcher Henderson, Armstrong's next musical berth.

Henderson had heard Armstrong in 1921 while Henderson was touring with singer Ethel Waters and had tried to hire him for her small group then. Now that Henderson's own much bigger dance band had a permanent and well-paying job at the Roseland Ballroom on Broadway, he tried again to lure Armstrong to the big town. With Lil's help, it worked.

Just as he had been nervous about joining Oliver and had shyly remained outside the Lincoln Gardens doors when first confronted with the impact of the band, thus Armstrong now felt somewhat intimidated by the New York swells on Henderson's bandstand. He arrived during a rehearsal already in full swing, causing some amusement with his wardrobe, his thick-soled "policeman's shoes"—by his own account sharp in Chicago, perhaps, but rube-like in Manhattan. Also by his own account, he committed a gaffe by blowing lustily through a passage marked *pp* (*pianissimo*, "very softly"), whereupon Henderson stopped the music and asked him what the mark meant. "Pound plenty," the always inventive Armstrong answered, provoking laughter all around. There was no laughter, though, when the new kid took his first solos. Before long, New York jazz trumpeters were wearing policemen's shoes.

Henderson's 1924 music was far removed from the lilting New Orleans rhythms of King Oliver. Though the band contained some gifted players— and at least one who could play real blues, trombonist Charlie "Big" Green—its arrangements, designed for Roseland's white dancing public, were rhythmically stiff, its players stilted in phrasing and only technically, not musically, adept in solo work—Green aside. As Armstrong begins to contribute to the band's recordings, his solos—often no longer than 8, 12, or 16 bars, seldom a full chorus—stand out not like gems in a fitting setting as with Oliver, but like poetry in a sea of doggerel. Even so accomplished a saxophonist as Coleman Hawkins sounds like a stumblebum behind Armstrong. By the time Louis leaves the band fourteen months later, the changes that have been wrought are substantive. A case in point is "Sugar-foot Stomp," arranger-saxophonist Don Redman's setting of Armstrong and Oliver's erstwhile "Dippermouth Blues." The rhythm is smoothed out to an Armstrongian 4/4 feel; the sections phrase much more smoothly; and the centerpiece, Armstrong's three-chorus tribute to his ex-leader, is set in a fitting context. That solo (played, incidentally, with a straight mute where Oliver used a plunger mute) reveals the pupil's rhythmic and tonal superiority to the teacher.

There are other noteworthy Armstrong solos with Henderson, and the gradual improvement in Hawkins's playing is remarkable. (His subsequent rise as the first great soloist on his instrument is most certainly due to that year of proximity to Armstrong, combined with his own superb musical gifts.) But the finest recorded work by Armstrong during his first New York period can be found on a series of small-group recordings made outside the Henderson fold and in accompaniments to blues singers. The small groups were led by the New Orleanian entrepreneur Clarence Williams, then the leading producer of race records. (That term, by the way, is not pejorative; it was widely used by the black middle class. Nor did it represent a racist or segregationist attitude by record companies, then accustomed to catering to various ethnic groups with special catalog series, including all sorts of European, Eastern, and Asiatic musics and the native idiom called "old time" or [unflatteringly] "hillbilly.")

What was most special about the Clarence Williams Blue Five recordings was the teaming of Armstrong with the only other horn player then capable of giving him real competition: fellow New Orleanian Sidney Bechet, who had already been to Europe and there had added the soprano saxophone to his formidable clarinet. When these two, the only true jazz virtuosos of the day, get together on "Cake Walking Babies (from Home)," sparks fly. They engage in actual rivalry, each man soloing and presenting a sequence of slashing breaks. It's almost a draw, but what wins Louis the prize is his superior rhythm; even Bechet, a powerful swinger, cannot match the Armstrong juggling of almost subliminal time shifts. Like a great tightrope walker, Louis never makes a wrong move. In 1924, jazz here reaches a first plateau of maturity, balancing instrumental mastery and what would later become known as "soul." These two men had taught themselves how to tell a story in music.

Among the blues singers with whom Armstrong collaborated, Bessie Smith stands out. She presumably preferred Joe Smith (who rejoined Henderson's band shortly before Armstrong left), and from her point of view this may have made sense: Smith was a perfect foil, while Armstrong was her equal. Yet Louis's fills and counterlines consistently enhance the singing, and as far as he was concerned, Bessie was the greatest. "Everything I did with her, I *like*," he said years later.

Of course Armstrong already considered himself a singer, and this was one of his reasons for leaving Henderson. The few half-spoken breaks at the end of one of the two issued takes of Henderson's "Everybody Loves My Baby" are Armstrong's first recorded vocal efforts, but he seldom sang with the band in person, and there were no other recorded vocals. This still rankled him years later. During my last visit to his home, in December 1970, he was in a feisty mood when the conversation brought up Henderson. We already knew some things. There was a weekly talent contest at the Roseland, and sometimes when the customers proved shy, the bandsmen would offer some specialty numbers—comedy and so on. On one occasion Armstrong sang and brought the house down, but Henderson did not respond; at most, he sometimes let Armstrong sing when the band performed for black audiences.

This we knew, but now Armstrong, who seldom uttered an unkind public word, let go. Henderson, he said, was a light-skinned, college-educated Negro who'd never accepted the darker Armstrong for what he was and could do. Louis didn't mind sharing trumpet solos with Howard Scott, who could play, but resented getting barely more solo space than the third member of the section, Elmer Chambers, a Henderson favorite, "with his nanny-goat sound and ragtime beat" (here Armstrong gave a devastating vocal imitation of Chambers's corny phrasing and tone). Fletcher wouldn't let him sing, he said, because his gravel voice actually embarrassed the "dicty," high-toned bandleader—though he did let Armstrong do a Bert Williams imitation! It was clear that Armstrong had never forgiven Henderson, and it is also clear that he was right: for more than a year, Louis Armstrong sat in Fletcher Henderson's trumpet section at one of New York's most famous ballrooms, and apparently the only people aware of his presence were fellow musicians, black and white. It wasn't the last time Henderson missed the boat: ten years later, he turned down a chance to hire young Ella Fitzgerald.

It wasn't just the issue of singing that caused Armstrong to return to Chicago: "After a while, the cats in [the band] would drink so much, and they'd come out on the stand and goof, wouldn't keep time, didn't hit notes on time . . . I didn't appreciate that. I was always serious about my music."

His wife had a band at Chicago's Dreamland Ballroom, and when he returned she had prepared a banner that read "The World's Greatest Trumpet Player." Louis was embarrassed, but the banner stayed up and nobody questioned it. Soon he was doubling with Erskine Tate's big band at the prestigious Vendome Theater, the South Side's first-run movie palace, where the stage shows included semi-classical features for Armstrong, such as the Intermezzo from *Cavalleria Rusticana*, as well as jazz specialties.

We must remember that much popular music in the first two decades of this century was still rooted in "the classics." Paraphrases of operatic arias were a regular part of the concert-band repertory, and not just in New Orleans. (When I asked trombonist Vic Dickenson, born in 1906, about early models for his instrument, he pulled out an ancient disc of "Celeste Aida" performed by Arthur Pryor, who'd been John Philip Sousa's star trombonist before starting his own concert band.) Ragtime was rooted in the classical piano tradition; its star performers had in their repertory the sort of operatic paraphrases that Liszt had specialized in.

Armstrong's work at the Vendome included performing special scores written for major silent pictures, and overtures such as "Poet and Peasant." He now perfected his sight-reading skills and became a full-fledged virtuoso of the trumpet, which he had taken up in place of the cornet. The trumpet's greater range and tonal brilliance suited his rapid development as an executant.

Most significant for the future of jazz, Armstrong now began to make records as leader of his own group, the Hot Five. This was strictly a studio combination; it performed in public only once (at a benefit concert) during its two-year existence. It also reflected the record company's needs: the main market for race records was the South—via mail order—and the public there was still fond of the New Orleans ensemble style. Armstrong was the youngest member of his own band, which otherwise included Lil (two years his senior) on piano; his former boss, Kid Ory, on trombone; and two riverboat and Oliver bandmates, Johnny Dodds, clarinet, and Johnny St. Cyr, banjo. The absence of bass and drums was not so much an artistic or economic decision as a technical one: the OKeh company was still recording acoustically in late 1925 in Chicago, and these two instruments could not be reproduced well. In fact, by May 1927 the Hot Five had become the Hot Seven, with drummer Baby Dodds and a tuba player added for the now electrical recordings.

Traditional-minded jazz commentators used to argue that the Armstrong groups destroyed the wonderful collective New Orleans style, but this manner of ensemble playing was on its way out anyway, what with ever-larger bands, the rise of the saxophone, the changing jazz repertory, and other factors. In fact, the Hot Five/Seven more likely helped to keep the parent style alive for a while, though clearly Armstrong's was increasingly the dominant musical voice. Even though this Hot Five and Seven music did not represent what he was playing day by day (or rather, by night), it gave him his first opportunity to play extended solo passages regularly on records, and to display fully his powerful lead work. For most musicians (as distinct from critics, who came to jazz about a decade later) the work of the other players was simply something to sit through, but we should not be as hard on Ory, Dodds, et al. as critic André Hodeir is, who barely allows them standing as professionals. Dodds had a beautiful clarinet sound and deep feeling for the blues, and Ory was a past master of the New Orleans "tail-gate" ensemble style for his instrument; in fact, he had probably played a major part in shaping its role. Yet only Armstrong's work on these records remains undated—the difference between genius and mere talent.

The more room Armstrong gave himself on these records, the better were the results, and when we arrive at such masterpieces as "Big Butter and Egg Man," "Potato Head Blues," and "Hotter Than That," we are fully in the presence of the revolutionary young Armstrong. With solos such as these, he created a vocabulary of phrases that would echo in the music for decades, even unto this day, in the work not only of such older players as Ruby Braff (born 1927) but also that of Wynton Marsalis and other young neo-traditionalists (or post-modernists—whatever your favorite nomenclature). He now proceeds with utter fearlessness and freedom, crossing bar lines; extending the working range of the horn; mastering breaks, stop-time, and other rhythmic devices; and creating lovely melodies and phrases that linger in the mind and stir the emotions. Hundreds upon hundreds of musicians, not only in America but wherever records were sold (it was possible to special-order race records in white stores, but clever store owners began to stock whatever was in demand, and OKeh's overseas affiliates soon ordered the Armstrong masters for domestic pressing), studied these solos note by note—to memorize if not actually to play, for the technical demands, not to mention the rhythmic and harmonic ones, were well beyond the capacity of most musicians of the day.

Armstrong's phraseology began to enter the mainstream of the music; it would remain a cornerstone at least until the advent of bebop—and a close analysis of Charlie Parker's vocabulary clearly shows that he, too, was steeped in Armstrong. In a 1986 *Down Beat* "Blindfold Test," in which records are played for musicians without identifying them, veteran tenorist Bud Freeman (born 1906) commented about the Jimmie Lunceford band's 1942 recording of "Blues in the Night" as follows: "It was all Louis. That arrangement was all taken from Louis Armstrong phrases. Louis created every bar in that thing. Whoever it was really idolized Louis, even to the singing." This would hold true, more or less, for more than 50 percent of the records made in that or any other year between 1930 and 1945. In this instance, it's interesting to note that the arranger was Sy Oliver, an

Armstrong-inspired trumpeter and singer who in the 1950s was musical director for many Armstrong studio sessions. The Lunceford singer-instrumentalists included Trummy Young, a member of Armstrong's All Stars for twelve years in the '50s and '60s.

Armstrong also sang on the Hot Five/Seven discs, at first in a pre-microphone style that sounds bucolic compared with his later work but already reflects his playing. It is probably more accurate to say that Armstrong sings like he plays than vice versa, there being so many trumpet-like aspects to the voice, among them, as English critic Eric Thacker said, "using dentals, labials, and gutturals as he would use tonguing in a cornet solo, and enlivening the vowel colors with abrasive flutterings of the throat." Be that as it may, Armstrong's singing had a profound effect on his listeners. On the 1926 "Heebie Jeebies," he claimed that he dropped the lyric sheet while recording and substituted "scatting" for the words; chances are that this was a bit of deliberate legend-making—and there are earlier examples of scat. Yet it was this record that made scatting catch on, with among others the Paul Whiteman Rhythm Boys (young Bing Crosby; Al Rinker, the brother of singer Mildred Bailey; and Harry Barris).

The repertory of the Hot Five/Seven consisted, in the main, of original compositions by the members. Armstrong himself, as we have seen, was showing gifts as a composer, and Lil was no slouch.

The old Hot Five/Seven bowed out with a December 1927 date. A new Hot Five (really Seven), sometimes known as the Savoy Ballroom Five, made its debut the following June. It included members of the band with which Armstrong was now working at Chicago's Savoy Ballroom, led by Carroll Dickerson, and was a much more "modern" unit than its predecessor. Its second star was pianist Earl Hines, a key representative of a new breed of players to whom the Armstrong vocabulary was second nature. Also on hand was Armstrong's New Orleans buddy, drummer Zutty Singleton, perhaps the best player on his instrument in 1928. The trombonist and clarinetist were merely competent, lacking the personality of Ory or Johnny Dodds, and the banjoist, Mancy Carr (whose name has been misspelled *Cara* since time immemorial), was serviceable. The group was sometimes augmented by Don Redman, then the musical director of McKinney's Cotton Pickers, who provided excellent arrangements.

The most famous by far of the "new" Hot Five sides is "West End Blues," a jazz landmark largely because of Armstrong's dazzling introductory cadenza. This masterful creation, with its "spectacular cascading phrases" (Gunther Schuller), has often been imitated but never successfully; its rhythmic pitfalls are not really negotiable, and reading won't help the player much. Cootie Williams came closest, but he simplified matters cleverly. The first and most disastrous attempt came not long after the appearance of the original, when Louis Metcalfe, recording with a band under

King Oliver's leadership, made a travesty of his attempt to copy Armstrong. (Poor Oliver was credited with this mishap as recently as 1991, on a CD reissue.)

Other works by this band come close, including a lovely "Basin Street Blues" with another wordless vocal, backed by a glee club of band members, and a concluding solo that is a dramatic example of the operatic influence on Armstrong—as is the "West End Blues" cadenza. Musicologist Joshua Barrett, who has made a study of Armstrong's relationship to opera, has traced that cadenza's genealogy, making use of Lewis Porter's discovery of its 1924 germ cell in a break behind singer Margaret Johnson on "Changeable Daddy of Mine." What such discoveries imply is that, far from being as gloriously spontaneous as it sounds, Armstrong's "West End Blues" opening was the result of years of refining an idea that is spectacular even in its embryonic form. (This is yet another demonstration of the need for stringent reconsideration of the concept of jazz improvisation—always nebulous at best.)

The Hot Five/Seven/Savoy Ballroom Five stage of Armstrong's recordings ends with further masterpieces, among them "Beau Koo Jack," with a concluding Armstrong invention that quickly found its way to transcription for whole trumpet sections. It was surpassed, however, by a piece performed by Armstrong and Hines alone, "Weather Bird." The piece comes from the Oliver Creole Jazz Band canon; that band's recorded version on some labels credits Armstrong and Oliver, but the earlier Library of Congress deposit (in his own hand) credits Armstrong alone. The duet is among the all-time masterpieces of recorded jazz, stunning in its almost symbiotic teamwork and joint virtuosity. In his seminal book *Early Jazz*, Gunther Schuller devotes nearly three pages of analysis to the piece, in the course of which he states that "the cohesiveness of this performance is at a level we usually attribute to consciously premeditated composition. When we realize that it is the result of spontaneous creation born of the passing moment, we can only marvel at the musicianship displayed." But years of listening have convinced me that this is by no means an unpremeditated "first" spontaneously created in the studio. The piece is in three strains, and there is no way Hines could have familiarized himself with its structure on the spot. A far more likely scenario is that the two by then inseparable friends, who by their own testimony often got together to play without others being involved, had fooled around with this piece until they felt ready to record it. They certainly hit upon fresh ways of playing in the studio, but there can be little doubt that they knew where they were going—which does not in the least detract from the magnificence of their work.

The Hot Five era extended from November 12, 1925, to December 12, 1928—three years, within which this specific recording activity adds up to about three weeks of real time. During the same period, Armstrong also recorded with various singers, mostly of the blues but also of popular songs; twice with other leaders; and on a mere three occasions with actual working bands. These produced the only recordings made by him with Erskine Tate; a 1927 session by Louis Armstrong and his Stompers, the band he led at the Sunset Café, from which just one side, Jelly Roll Morton's "Chicago Breakdown," survived, not issued until 1942; and two 1928 sides by Carroll Dickerson's band from the Savoy.

These few glimpses suffice to show us that the music of the Hot Five was a far cry from what Louis was playing outside the studio. All three big bands have a typical 1920s approach to orchestral jazz, with the earliest (Tate) being the most explosive. In any event, this handful of items can do no more than dimly illuminate what Armstrong himself and other contemporaries have told us. For instance, pianist Art Hodes spoke of hearing Armstrong improvise at the Sunset for half an hour on "Poor Little Rich Girl," a sophisticated Noel Coward tune. Nothing remotely like that survives for us to hear, but the statement tells us that the switch from New Orleans–type originals, so-called stomps and blues, to popular songs of the day (the jazz critics' bêtes noires, at least until Broadway composers gained cultural stature) took place much earlier in his working repertory than in his recorded repertory. In fact, such late Hot (or Savoy Ballroom) Five pieces as "Squeeze Me," "Save It Pretty Mama," and "Basin Street Blues," all by black songwriters, already presage this change, but since they were recorded with small groups, they have escaped critical censure.

The breakthrough recording for Armstrong took place during a brief visit to New York in March 1929. He joined the Luis Russell band on a Jimmy McHugh–Dorothy Fields song, "I Can't Give You Anything but Love," performing it at a very slow tempo. He opens with a muted trumpet solo (Armstrong seldom used a mute, and when he did, from 1926 on it was never anything but a straight mute, the kind that least alters the tone of the open trumpet) backed by chords from the band, then sings a passionate vocal and, after a trombone break, constructs an aria-like open horn solo, ending with a climb to the top. Schuller doesn't even discuss this record, other than to dismiss it as "insipid"; nevertheless, it represented something rare in jazz recording: letting a black artist sing a standard pop song. Only Ethel Waters, the much lesser Lillie Delk Christian, and the McKinneys Cotton Pickers' popular vocalist George Thomas had done so before, with far less of an "African retention" than Armstrong's voice displayed. On that very morning, he had made another kind of breakthrough, recording an impromptu blues, "Knockin' a Jug," with a racially integrated group.

A few months later Armstrong went to New York to stay. He had been invited by Tommy Rockwell, OKeh producer and booking agent, to come alone to try out for a new Vincent Youmans musical, *Great Day*, but couldn't bear to leave his band behind (knowing that without him they'd soon fall apart). The bandsmen ventured east in a fleet of more-or-less dilapidated cars and were surprised to find, on their stopovers, that Armstrong had become a celebrity through his records. Rockwell was aghast that the band had come along but found them a job at Harlem's Connie's Inn—a good move, since *Great Day* (which in any case became a costly flop) had no place for Armstrong.

The nightspot was the chief rival of the Cotton Club and, like it, a venue for elaborately staged, specially written and choreographed floor shows featuring singers, dancers, and specialty acts. As luck would have it, the 1929 edition of Connie's revue, *Hot Chocolates*, was so good (with a score by Fats Waller and Andy Razaf) that it moved to Broadway, where it earned rave reviews and a respectable run.

Initially, Armstrong was in the pit band, standing up only during the entr'acte, playing and singing the show's prime hit, "Ain't Misbehavin'," already introduced by the romantic male lead. Soon Louis had to be moved up on stage and was also given a spot in a trio billed as "One Thousand Pounds of Rhythm," which included Waller and the show's female lead singer, Edith Wilson. After each night's show, Louis taxied uptown to lead his band (still the Dickerson crew from Chicago) at Connie's, where it was subbing for the regulars now ensconced in the Broadway pit. He was in such demand that for a while he also did a spot in the late show at the Lafayette Theater next door to Connie's. "Had to get my sleep coming through the park in a cab," he recalled years later. "I was only 29 years old [actually 28]. Didn't exactly feel I had the world at my feet, but it was very nice that everyone was picking up on the things I was doing, and all the bandleaders wanted me. Pretty soon I had to get in front of my own band. Nothing else I could do."

"Ain't Misbehavin'" was Armstrong's first real hit record, backed with another song from *Hot Chocolates*, "(What Did I Do to Be So) Black and Blue." In the wake of a 1993 biography of lyricist Andy Razaf, it needs to be reiterated that it was Armstrong who turned this song (which in the show functioned as a dark-skinned lady's lament about being a loser in the game of love, as compared to lighter rivals) into what has long been regarded as a protest song. (Indeed, as such, it [and Armstrong] are made emblematic of the hero's plight in Ralph Ellison's masterful novel *Invisible Man*.) By stripping it of the verse and singing it in a male voice, and with such dignity and passion as to gloss over some of the lyrics' less fortunate turns of phrase and turn them into poetry, Armstrong forever transformed the song, adding some majestic opening and closing trumpet passages for good measure.

The success of this record established the pattern for Armstrong's recordings through the next two decades. Henceforth, his material would

be popular songs, often of high quality and sometimes written especially for
him, with a smattering of novelties. And he would perform them with his
own big bands, whose task was very specific: to back the leader's playing and
singing. Record buyers wanted Armstrong, and most of his bands served
competently in their self-effacing role.

What is significant is the repertory: Armstrong was the one who turned
many Tin Pan Alley tunes into jazz evergreens. He had a special relationship with Hoagy Carmichael, who shares the vocal on the first recording of
his "Rockin' Chair" with Louis, in 1929. In 1931 Armstrong found inspiration in Carmichael's masterpiece, "Stardust," cut a definitive version of
"Georgia on My Mind" (Ray Charles wasn't the first African-American to
put his distinctive imprint on this song), and made "Lazy River" (a collaboration between Carmichael and New Orleans clarinetist Sidney Arodin) his
own for keeps—this piece remained in his repertory to the end.

Armstrong also showed a special affinity for songs by Jimmy McHugh
and Dorothy Fields, starting with "I Can't Give You Anything but Love."
Both "Exactly Like You" and "I Can't Believe That You're in Love with
Me" were three years old when Louis recorded them in 1930; they've been
jazz standards ever since. "On the Sunny Side of the Street" entered the
working Armstrong repertory before he first recorded it in Paris in late
1934; one of his sincerest imitators, trumpeter-singer Taft Jordan, beat him
to it by almost a year. (From 1929 on, record companies tried to groom
rivals to OKeh's Armstrong: Brunswick had the fleet and inventive Jabbo
Smith, Vocalion the lesser-known Ruben Reeves, and Victor the brilliant
New Orleanian Henry "Red" Allen. Not one proved viable competition,
creatively or commercially, though Allen showed a remarkable grasp of
Armstrong's musical essence.)

As early as 1930, Armstrong pioneered in what the record industry
would later call "crossovers." At the special request of Jimmie Rodgers, accurately described as the father of country music, Louis and Lil joined him
in recording "Blue Yodel No. 9," incidentally the last in a string of brilliant
blues accompaniments by Armstrong that had begun with Ma Rainey in
1923. Louis also crossed over to Hawaiian music, recording (with three violins added to the Luis Russell band) "Song of the Islands." And with his
1930 version of "The Peanut Vendor," a Cuban specialty, Louis can be said
to have initiated Latin jazz.

This last was recorded in Los Angeles, where Armstrong was appearing
at Frank Sebastian's New Cotton Club, a nightclub catering to the movie
colony. During his eight-month stay, the young drummer in both bands
that Armstrong successively fronted was Lionel Hampton, who credits the
trumpeter with getting him started on the vibraphone. He plays it on the
memorable recording of Eubie Blake and Andy Razaf's "Memories of You,"

yet another song made a jazz classic by Armstrong. Other key recordings from this California sojourn include "You're Driving Me Crazy," which directly inspired arranger Eddie Durham's "Moten Swing," based on the chords of the Walter Donaldson song and considered the anthem of Kansas City jazz; "Sweethearts on Parade," which constitutes a kind of summation of Armstrong's vocal and instrumental artistry at this point in his career; and "I'm a Ding Dong Daddy (from Dumas)," with its remarkable stop-time breaks, including one that contains the riff later expanded into the bebop classic "Salt Peanuts."

In Chicago in early 1931, Armstrong and his new manager Johnny Collins formed the first Armstrong big band proper—not a pre-existing unit fronted by the trumpeter but a specially assembled crew. It contained several New Orleanians and was later described by its leader as the happiest band he ever led. With it, he made his first trip to his hometown in nine years.

The tour of the South that culminated in that visit was unplanned, a spontaneous reaction to an unwelcome backstage visit by a notorious New York gangster, who brought Louis a message from his former employers at Connie's Inn, that he was to return there promptly. Collins's response was to take Louis and the band immediately to points south.

In New Orleans, Louis received a triumphant welcome, including a parade (not an honor commonly accorded blacks in 1931); had a cigar (the Louis Armstrong Special) and a baseball team (Armstrong's Secret 9) named for him; and, in a typically quick response, became the first performer of his race to do his own announcing on radio when a bigoted announcer refused to introduce him on opening night. The man was fired, but Louis had been so effective that he continued to fill the role for the duration of the long engagement.

Before and after this historic visit, which included a sentimental journey to the Colored Waifs' Home (his old reform school), Armstrong recorded some of his biggest hits to date with this "happy" band. Among them: his theme song from then on, "When It's Sleepy Time Down South," and the humorous novelty "You Rascal You," which, though recorded by many others, became permanently identified with Armstrong.

There was also room for trumpet specialties like "Chinatown, My Chinatown," with its "battle between the trumpet and the saxophones"—no other instrumental virtuoso created such miniature skits within which to frame his flights—and "New Tiger Rag," in which he announces that it will take eight choruses to catch the big cat. (This was nothing compared to Armstrong's live performances of the venerable "Tiger" during the period, as a climax to which he would offer as many as 200 high C's, topped by some F's. This kind of display of course gave rise to grumblings from the

budding esthetes of jazz, and Armstrong himself later disowned such acro-
batics, saying he was just trying to impress his fellow musicians. Which he
certainly did.)

This period also finds Armstrong's first recorded encounters with
Gershwin ("I Got Rhythm," the anthem of jazz to be) and Arlen ("Between
the Devil and the Deep Blue Sea," extant in two takes, of which the slower
contains a muted trumpet passage that, in its mastery of melodic double
time, presages Charlie Parker). And in his vocal on "When Your Lover Has
Gone," Louis sets the stage for the kind of impassioned crooning sometimes identified with singers of Italian-American background. There were
many strings to Armstrong's bow.

It should not be forgotten that the years 1931–32 were the absolute
nadir for the record business in the U.S. The fact that Armstrong did so
much work in the studios at this lean time speaks volumes for his popularity,
growing apace among blacks and whites. During this period he also made
his first appearances in films, including a surrealistic Max Fleischer cartoon
that mixes animation and photography as Armstrong's disembodied head,
singing "You Rascal You," chases a creature through the jungle, and a comedy short in which he appears dressed in a leopard skin. The social implications of these films may be debatable, but the music is outstanding.

In July 1932 Armstrong made his first transatlantic foray. Of course
there had been many jazz-related American performers in Europe already,
starting in 1919 with the white Original Dixieland Jazz Band and the black
Southern Syncopated Orchestra, led by Will Marion Cook and featuring
young Sidney Bechet (who would spend much of the 1920s touring all over
Europe with various bands, including his own). But Armstrong was the
first jazz artist to appear as an individual star, not a bandleader or member.
He did not bring his own accompanists but was featured first with a band
of black musicians of various nationalities (including some Americans) assembled for him in Paris, and then, in another Armstrong first, at the helm
of a group made up of some of Britain's best white jazzmen.

Reception was mixed: enthusiasm from musicians and jazz fans (there
was a substantial number of the latter by 1932, and thirty-eight Armstrong
performances were available on record in England by that date), and
puzzlement and sometimes outrage (primarily among older attendees at
the London Palladium) from others. Among the more amusing sidelights
was a delegation of musicians asking to examine Armstrong's trumpet to ascertain that it, and his mouthpiece, had not been doctored in some odd
fashion. His virtuosity was still something not quite credible.

If nothing else, this first three-month European visit made it clear to
Armstrong that there were people of means who took his music quite seriously, and that (though London and the British hinterlands of 1932 were far

from free of prejudice) there were places where racism was not a constant factor. He would return soon, and for a considerably longer stay. A non-playing visit to Paris topped off the first trip abroad.

Back home, Armstrong toured with a new *Hot Chocolates*—far from the first in quality—accompanied by the Chick Webb band, with which he recorded in December. By then he was increasingly plagued by lip problems (he used the pressure system, and the abundance of high notes was taking its toll), but the date produced fine results. He was under a new contract with Victor, then the most prestigious record label, and the famed Camden studios captured his sound in all its awesome beauty better than any previous recording environment had.

By January 1933 a new band had been assembled in Chicago, in some ways the best of the Armstrong big bands yet. The brilliant young pianist was Teddy Wilson (who made his recording debut with Armstrong), and the Johnson brothers—Keg on trombone, Budd on tenor sax—were first-rate soloists. Recording sessions on three consecutive days were taxing on the embouchure, yet Armstrong is in brilliant form on such wonderful Arlen tunes as "I've Got the World on a String" and "I Gotta Right to Sing the Blues" and creates a new and very special "Basin Street Blues."

When a projected summer engagement for the band fell through, Armstrong told his manager, Johnny Collins, that he wanted to return to Europe. He opened in London in August 1933 at the helm of a band that included several of the members of the previous year's Paris-based group. He soon rid himself of the unsavory Collins, who, after being dismissed, left with Louis's passport (quickly replaced, of course) and dire threats that the trumpeter would never work in the U.S. again. Under new management (British bandleader and entrepreneur Jack Hylton), Armstrong toured Denmark, Sweden, Norway, Holland, and Belgium. By a stroke of luck, the Danes were making a musical film at the time of his visit and included a set of three tunes with him and his band in a straightforward performance on the concert stage, without gimmicks. The sequence also benefits from the fact that it was filmed "live," not with the customary synchronized sound. And from Sweden, there survives a partial transcription of a concert broadcast. Since Armstrong would not record in a studio again until a full year later, these performances are doubly important.

Armstrong's reception in Copenhagen, incidentally, was the most enthusiastic he had yet received. A crowd estimated by the un-hyperbolic Danes at some ten thousand awaited his arrival inside and outside the train station; there was a band, a sea of flowers, and a motorcade. Not until after World War II would there be anything comparable in the way of a public demonstration of affection for Armstrong, and he was very moved—at first he thought all those people were waiting for someone else.

After more performances in England, Armstrong, accompanied on this trip (as on the 1932 one) by Alpha Smith, whom he would eventually marry, took what was to be the longest vacation of his life, from April to October 1934. In an interview that January, he had made the point that he'd had very little time off during the past ten years. He rented an apartment in Paris, and he and Alpha did much "hanging out" with musicians: fellow Americans and locals, such as Gypsy guitarist Django Reinhardt, who idolized Louis. (It was an Armstrong record, "Dallas Blues," that first led Django to jazz.)

With yet another manager—N. J. Canetti, who had ties to the record industry—Louis reorganized a band, again with some of the same players who'd been with him before. This time there were records, made in Paris prior to a series of Salle Pleyel concerts in early November. Though there'd been all sorts of rumors about lip problems, Louis sounds just fine on these discs, and at his first Paris concert he had to take so many curtain calls that he'd changed into his bathrobe by the time of the last one. There were further concerts in Belgium, Switzerland, and Italy, but then Armstrong quarrelled with Canetti and abruptly decided to return home, arriving in New York in late January 1935. He'd planned to front Chick Webb's band again, but Johnny Collins threw a wrench into the contract; to make matters worse, Lil sued for sizable back maintenance. The old lip trouble was the official excuse for the ensuing six months of inactivity, but trouble with Collins (and perhaps with other gangsters from the past) was certainly a factor.

At this low ebb in his career, Armstrong contacted an old acquaintance from the Sunset Café days, Joe Glaser. There was a tie between Glaser and Tommy Rockwell, who had played a central role (if from the sidelines) in Louis's 1931 Chicago gangster trouble and had been an executive of OKeh Records during Louis's tenure there. Glaser proved the right man at the right time: he solved the gangster problem.

The relationship with Glaser was unique. Nothing was signed; a handshake sufficed. Glaser took a desk in the Rockwell-O'Keefe booking agency's office, at first with Armstrong as his sole client. In June, Louis was back in front of a band, again organized in Chicago, with Zilner Randolph (of the '33 band) as musical director. With this group, said by some to be an excellent one, he returned to New Orleans for another welcoming parade and then proceeded to break attendance and salary records at Harlem's new Apollo Theater. A long-term booking at Connie's Inn (again, shades of the 1931 gangster trouble) was obtained, but Louis's Chicago musicians could not get the union's approval to play a regular New York club engagement. Thus it was arranged for Louis to front, once again, the Luis Russell band. This time the collaboration stuck (until late 1942); it also inaugurated a contract with the newly formed Decca Records.

This began auspiciously with yet another Jimmy McHugh song, "I'm in the Mood for Love," and an interpretation of "You Are My Lucky Star" that contained a startling trumpet solo that introduced the "new" Louis Armstrong of the swing era. This was a much more controlled and sober Armstrong than the one heard prior to the second European stay, or even the one from just the year before, captured in Paris—though the two-part 1934 "On the Sunny Side of the Street" hints at the new sobriety. Along with more measured cadences came an almost majestic phraseology, utterly relaxed and rhythmically secure. And the tone, burnished and mellow, was also imbued with new maturity. All this is not to say that there were no further flights of high-note fancy or startling ideas: there was the double-timing on "Lucky Star," for instance, and that solo's oblique approach to harmony.

The singing, too, was new, in that Armstrong now took greater care to convey the lyrics clearly. To be sure, he still throws in the "mamas" and the hummed or scatted asides and fills of yore. But there is a new clarity of diction—without, however, a trace of affected "correctness." This is Louis's own voice, as always the most natural medium, but with a new discipline.

The Decca repertory was in the main oriented toward the desires of song publishers, but because Louis was now entering a new phase of popularity, he could be a bit more choosy than other artists, black or white. He also began to write songs again, as he had in the '20s. "Old Man Mose" was a hit for him and for Eddie Duchin; "If We Never Meet Again" was a fetching ballad; the 1936 "Swing That Music" was launched to coincide with the publication of his first book, the rather heavily ghostwritten but not uninformative "autobiography" of the same title. Later came "Heartful of Rhythm," "What Is This Thing Called Swing?," and several others.

Hoagy Carmichael weighed in again with special material. One of his best was the rustic "Eventide," but the most spectacular was "Jubilee," written for the 1937 film *Every Day's a Holiday*, a Mae West vehicle in which Armstrong appeared. The previous year had seen his first major feature film, *Pennies from Heaven*, produced by and starring Bing Crosby. Louis's showstopper, "The Skeleton in the Closet," found him doing, in an old minstrel stereotype, the black scared of ghosts: Louis smites the skeleton with his trumpet. A cameo in another Crosby feature, *Dr. Rhythm*, wound up on the cutting-room floor, while his long sequence with a lightly blacked-up Martha Raye in *Artists and Models* was removed by many Southern exhibitors. There was no controversy about Louis in *Going Places*, an amiable comedy in which Ronald Reagan had the junior male lead (Dick Powell was the star). Here Louis launched a perennial, "Jeepers Creepers," sung by him to a horse, which was apparently acceptable to the South. The song was nominated for an Academy award.

An unusual collaboration was that between Louis (music) and Ben Hecht (words) on the song "Red Cap," a celebration of the members of A. Philip Randolph's powerful Pullman porters' union. The now largely forgotten Hecht was a man of many parts: novelist, playwright, screenwriter, director, muckraking journalist, and political activist. We don't know how he and Louis got together, but it's sort of nice that they did. (The tune is charming.)

Periodically, Louis also revisited some of his landmark recordings. Best of these is the 1938 "Struttin' with Some Barbecue," with an excellent arrangement (by Chappie Willet) and a trumpet solo that first states the melody with matchless accents, then transforms it into something new and startling, and concludes with a cadenza in which fingering and tonguing combine uniquely. (It was through musicians that I was made aware of this and other Armstrong masterpieces not mentioned in the jazz literature. In a late 1950s *Down Beat* panel on Armstrong, two trumpeters as stylistically and esthetically polarized as Bobby Hackett and Maynard Ferguson both cited the Decca "Barbecue" as a special favorite.)

Decca experimented with bringing together in the studios various contract artists—a kind of precursor of the LP-era sampler. Sometimes the results were excellent, as with Louis and the Mills Brothers, in several encounters; their "Darling Nellie Gray" is a little masterpiece. At other times, things got a bit far-fetched, as when Louis joined Andy Iona and his Islanders for "On a Little Bamboo Bridge." He was also teamed, as a singer only, with the Lynn Murray Mixed Choir in some spirituals. A special moment occurs on "Going to Shout All Over God's Heaven" when the chorus (white) repeatedly sings "hebben" and Louis responds each time with a clearly articulated "heaven."

One of Louis's Decca milestones was another spiritual, "When the Saints Go Marching In." The 1938 record was a hit, yet it is seldom noted that this tune's entry into the jazz repertory dates from that release. Had he been in a position to copyright the piece, Louis would have died even richer than he did. To some Armstrong fans, his 1941 remakes of "Sleepy Time Down South" (without vocal) and "You Rascal You" are superior to the originals, not least due to the presence of the great Big Sid Catlett on drums and the excellence of the Russell band at that time. Another gem was the 1939 all-instrumental "Wolverine Blues," with its climactic Armstrong-Catlett collaboration.

During the 1930s Armstrong succeeded in desegregating many motion picture theaters in the downtowns of many major American cities outside the South. In those days, theaters featured stage shows along with first-run movies, and big bands were favorites in these shows. Armstrong was the first black bandleader to perform in many of these venues, as can be gleaned not from histories of jazz but from a perusal of black newspapers, such as the *Chicago Defender* or the *Pittsburgh Courier*. He was also the first black performer, in 1936, to have his own sponsored radio program, when he and his band substituted for several months for singer Rudy Vallee on the Fleischmann's Yeast Show. (Vallee was one of many Armstrong fans in show business; Louis's artistry had long since transcended categories.)

World War II took its toll on Armstrong's band, as it did on all the big orchestras. The recording ban imposed in 1942 by the musicians' union didn't prove helpful to jazz and contributed to the already rising popularity of singers as compared with big bands. But Armstrong, like many other leaders, hung in. He did a record number of engagements at military installations during the war. These jobs didn't pay as well as civilian ones, and often travel and accommodations were problematic. But Armstrong and Glaser shared a patriotic spirit; the trumpeter was especially keen on entertaining black men and women in uniform.

Glaser, meanwhile, had become an empire builder. He had long since established his own talent agency, Associated Booking Corporation, and expanded his roster from one to dozens of clients. Armstrong always came first, but Glaser was now the leading booker of black musical talent. In the early days he had gone along on every Armstrong road trip himself; now he delegated such responsibilities but still saw to it that Armstrong was shielded as well as possible from the pervasive problems of racism. Still, the Armstrong band was not as well off on their frequent Southern trips as the Ellington orchestra, which traveled in its own Pullman car. Armstrong shared the tribulations of his men—unlike some other leaders who traveled separately. And while he gladly left everyday business matters and even most personnel and salary decisions to Glaser and his staff, he was far from a passive leader.

For example, Armstrong himself hired one of the outstanding members of his 1944 band, tenorist Dexter Gordon. He heard him at a Los Angeles jam session and invited him to join the band then and there, according to Gordon himself. And when Gordon eventually told him he wanted to quit, Armstrong immediately offered him a substantial raise. Clearly, the picture of Louis Armstrong as someone who let others run his band is distorted, as is so much else said and written about this man—especially when we come to the period from 1945 on, when bebop, later called modern jazz, gradually became dominant. Initially, as his hiring of Gordon (the premier modern tenor sax stylist) indicates, there was no hostility from Armstrong toward the "new sounds," as proponents soon called them. But bebop was as much an attitude as a music, and that attitude, too complex to analyze in detail here, triggered a war of words between traditionalists and modernists that tore the world of jazz apart.

Not that the boppers were the only sinners. By some twist of irony, the advent of modern jazz coincided with a rising interest in pre-swing music, specifically New Orleans style, as symbolized by the rediscovery of Bunk Johnson. A legendary New Orleans trumpeter who had left music around 1931, Johnson was rumored to have played in Buddy Bolden's band and said to have taught young Louis Armstrong. Louis himself aided in Johnson's rediscovery and presented him with a trumpet. He didn't protest when Bunk began to tell eager critics how much he had taught Louis when he was a boy, and it wasn't until after Johnson's death in 1949 that Louis took the gloves off and corrected the record: Bunk was too busy drinking port wine and chasing women to pay attention to a kid wanting to learn to play trumpet, he said. Bunk did have a lovely tone, and little Louis had enjoyed listening to him. But a teacher? That had been King Oliver, not Bunk.

Bunk told a lot of bunk, in fact, but while he was alive, his personality, imagination, and historical aura made it all seem convincing. We know now that he was younger by some considerable years than he gave out, that he had never played with Bolden, and that much of what he had to say about early New Orleans music was learned or imagined; however, Bunk did have a fertile imagination, and he cut a dashing figure. He was also a much more sophisticated musician than the players his sponsors surrounded him with, and whom he privately dubbed "emergency musicians." When left to his own devices, he hired men who could read music well, taught them arrangements from the *Redback Book of Rags* and asked them to play things like "Out of Nowhere" and even "Marie Elena"—enough to give traditionalists heart attacks.

Bunk was a symbol; the traditional movement would have happened without him. In fact, the seeds were sown as early as 1938, when Tommy Ladnier, Sidney Bechet, and Mezz Mezzrow recorded in New York under the aegis of visiting French critic Hugues Panassié. Though Panassié also idolized Armstrong, that worthy was often blamed for having destroyed the intimate ensemble fabric of New Orleans style with his egocentric solo excursions, as early as with the Hot Five.

The traditionalists were dubbed "moldy figs" by the moderns, to whom Armstrong increasingly became a symbol of the past—if not entirely from a musical standpoint, then certainly from a social one. Journalists fanned the fires, and pretty soon ugly statements found their way into print, triggering equally ugly responses. Stung by the boppers' accusations of Uncle Tomming, the man who'd so long been idolized by his fellow musicians and opened so many doors for jazz now spoke of "the modern malice," called bop "jiujitsu music," and warned that young trumpeters would quickly ruin their embouchures by attempting to follow in Dizzy Gillespie's musical footsteps. (Louis exempted Dizzy himself from criticism. They were then neighbors and on good personal terms, and their wives had been dancers together in nightclubs years before. Aside from that, Louis was quite right when he called Dizzy "an old fox" and said that the trumpeter knew exactly what he was doing instrumentally.)

Ironically, Louis himself and his own big band were not at all immune from "modern" influences. Thus, on his first issued post-recording-ban session, from early 1945, one hears long-lined, harmonically complex trumpet playing on both the sinister "Jodie Man" and the beautiful "I Wonder," a rhythm-and-blues ballad composed and recorded by the short-lived singer-pianist Cecil Gant. In a more traditional vein, Armstrong is in wonderful form on a V Disc (a record made for the Armed Forces) dated a month before, which brought him together with Jack Teagarden and Bobby Hackett, among others, and was a kind of preview of the Armstrong All Stars to come. In any case, Louis was much more comfortable here than at a public event in early 1944, the much-touted First Esquire All-American Jazz Concert, held at New York's Metropolitan Opera House. While Teagarden was on hand there as well, so were Coleman Hawkins, Art Tatum, and Louis's chief trumpet rival of the day, Roy Eldridge. It never came to a "battle" between the two, though Eldridge later admitted he'd have loved to lock horns with his erstwhile idol, who wasn't having a very good night.

Such encounters with smaller groups not only offered interesting contrast to Armstrong's everyday big-band work but also pointed toward the future. So did a 1946 film, *New Orleans*, in which Armstrong was prominently featured. Unlike the several films he'd appeared in during the war years (*Cabin in the Sky, Jam Session, Atlantic City, Pillow to Post*), this one gave him acting as well as playing opportunities. The rather hokey script dealt with New Orleans at the time of Storyville's closing. Billie Holiday was cast as a society lady's maid, and Armstrong was seen at the helm of a band made up of Crescent City veterans like Kid Ory, Bud Scott, and Zutty Singleton, performing traditional material as well as the film's hit song, "Do You Know What It Means to Miss New Orleans." At the end, Louis is seen at Carnegie Hall (where else?) with his 1946 big band, but the film's musical message clearly was that the good old days had been the golden ones.

The making of this film provided an opportunity for the critic, record producer, songwriter, and promoter Leonard Feather to organize a record date in Los Angeles that surrounded Louis with some of the players from the film's small group but substituted the swing trombonist Vic Dickenson for Ory and ex-Goodmanite guitarist Allan Reuss for Scott. It was a delightful session, with Armstrong in a relaxed mood, vocally and instrumentally, on "Sugar" and "I Want a Little Girl." The film band also recorded, and in between there was a session with Louis's big band, which had been brought to California for some dates between shooting sessions.

Feather kept nudging Louis and Glaser to present the trumpeter in New York in a small-group setting. (Like most critics, Feather hated Louis's big band, and though he was a champion of bebop, he also greatly valued Armstrong.) Eventually Louis agreed, with the proviso that it be a two-part concert, with his big band also included. The event took place at Carnegie Hall on February 8, 1947. Armstrong appeared with a working sextet led by a fellow New Orleanian, clarinetist Edmond Hall, in a program of tunes long identified with Louis, among them "Lazy River," "You Rascal You," "Muskrat Ramble," "Struttin' with Some Barbecue," and "Dippermouth Blues." Though Big Sid Catlett was brought in to beef up the big band, and Billie Holiday made a second-half cameo appearance, the press (both jazz and lay) waxed ecstatic over the small-group half and generally panned the second.

Esthetics aside, Armstrong's big band had fallen on lean days. There was a recording contract, to be sure, and some of the recent records ("I Believe," "You Don't Learn That in School," and "Back o' Town Blues") were quite good and even modestly successful. But the asking price for the band had gone down to $750 for a one-nighter, and while Louis was loathe to let sixteen men and one woman go, the handwriting was on the wall.

The decisive instance was the concert (actually concerts: a second event at midnight had to be added, so great was the demand for tickets) at New York's Town Hall on May 17, 1947. This time there was no trace of the big band, though Sid Catlett shared drumming chores with George Wettling. The rest of the handpicked cast included Teagarden and Hackett. There was a recording device on the premises, and a portion of the concert was issued a few years later on Victor. (Other portions had to wait more than thirty years.) What one hears is Armstrong in magnificent form, clearly inspired by the love that surrounded him on the bandstand and in the packed house.

The big band was put on notice, and Glaser and Louis began to make plans for a small group. Three weeks later, Teagarden, Hackett, and some others joined Louis in the Victor studios for a session that produced a lovely first recording of Louis's own "Someday" and a caloric "Jack-Armstrong Blues," on which Louis's long concluding solo shows that he'd been cocking an ear in the direction of Charlie Parker and Dizzy Gillespie—not obviously, yet clearly, if one wanted to hear. A week later, there was another public event, the opening of the film *New Orleans*, with Louis fronting a small group.

Soon thereafter, he was off again to Hollywood to participate in the making of a bigger film, the Danny Kaye vehicle *A Song Is Born*, which also had parts for Benny Goodman, Tommy Dorsey, Charlie Barnet, Lionel Hampton, and other notable jazzmen. Not long after shooting ended, the Louis Armstrong All Stars made their debut at Billy Berg's club in Los Angeles. A new chapter in the Louis Armstrong saga had begun.

Glaser had not been idle. First, seeing how well Louis and Jack Teagarden worked together, he had persuaded the trombonist-singer to get rid of *his* big band—a veritable millstone around his neck which had gotten him deeply into debt. Clarinetist Barney Bigard had been with Louis in *New Orleans*, and though he'd left Duke Ellington in 1942 to venture out on his own, he had most recently been a sideman in Kid Ory's band. It didn't take much persuasion to make him join his fellow New Orleanian. Big Sid Catlett was doing well, freelancing on Fifty-second Street and in the recording studios, where recent associates had included Charlie Parker and Dizzy Gillespie, but he loved Louis and was ready to give him that special beat once again. On piano, the nod went to Dick Cary, who'd been involved in the Town Hall concert, sketching out arrangements, doing a fine job as accompanist and occasional soloist, and generally making a good impression. Louis knew whom he wanted on bass: a youngster who'd been in his big band long enough to impress the leader with his solid time, big sound, and showmanship. Arvell Shaw was the baby of the All Stars in age only. The girl singer, as they said then, was also a given: Velma Middleton had been in Louis's big band since 1942, and they had a special relationship, working and personal.

It only took a short while for the All Stars to find their groove. The first recording session, in October 1947, yielded four current numbers: one the title tune from Louis's latest film, another a charming ballad by Catlett, "Before Long," and two rather lightweight novelties. None of these numbers was in the program at a concert recorded live in Boston that December and eventually issued on Decca. The mixture performed there, of individual features, ensemble numbers, Armstrong-Teagarden and Armstrong-Middleton duets, and evergreens from the Armstrong annals, pretty well defines the musical profile of this most durable group, which lasted until the end of Armstrong's life.

The initial success of the All Stars was great when compared to the final years of Armstrong's big bands, but it wasn't an overnight smash. There were ample bookings in leading jazz clubs and a first visit to Europe in the winter of 1948 for a star turn at the world's first international jazz festival, in Nice. (History generally assigns that distinction to the Paris event of the following year, which starred Charlie Parker and Sidney Bechet, but Nice was first.) By now the All Stars had become even more so: one of Joe Glaser's prime clients had decided to give up *his* big band, and thus Earl Hines was reunited with his old friend from the Chicago years.

Musically this reunion didn't quite draw the sparks one might have hoped for, though Hines was even more brilliant at the keyboard than in the '20s. Years of big-band work had clearly affected all the players in the group, and in a sense it was more a collection of soloists than a band with a style of its own. But when Louis played lead, there was a special sound and feeling. There was never any doubt that he was in charge. In fact, as the drummer who replaced the ailing Catlett, the powerhouse Cozy Cole, once stated, Louis was active in the All Star performances "at least 80 percent of the time." He was featured on his own specialties, partnered the two other vocalists, led the ensembles on the other instrumentalists' features, and did all the announcing. This was different from the big-band era, when, at least for dance dates, the band would open without Louis, who would be featured in a show segment after the set. And when the big band did a stage show, it would not be nearly as long as a nightclub set by the All Stars.

As the All Stars settled into their routine, it became clear that this was one of the hardest-working bands in jazz history. Louis had been consumed by the work ethic all his life, and Glaser was a man to whom turning down a solid booking was a crime against nature; consequently, the more in demand the All Stars became, the more they worked. If either man had been less obsessive, there could have been a much easier life for the band than the constant travel, work, more travel, and more work that was the rule for more than twenty years.

But the public was blissfully unaware of how tired the All Stars might be when they hit the stage, because when Louis Armstrong hit, he put on a show that never let his audience down. "We got to keep it moving," he'd say periodically, and keep it moving he did. Certain things, after the first few years, became set. The opener—after the theme, "Sleepy Time Down South"—was always "Indiana," a fast-paced instrumental. (It got to be so that Armstrong fans were able to tell from his trumpet solo on this number whether Louis was in great or just good form.) From then on until the closing "Sleepy Time" reprise, the order would be whatever the leader felt was right under the specific circumstances—he had an acute sense of what an audience wanted. The band's repertory was always large (much larger than that of most organized jazz groups, though the critics always harped on Armstrong's playing "the same things"), and often numbers were added or dropped. While there were many warhorses, surprises were also frequent. And always there was the pacing, at which Armstrong was a master. There were no dull spots, even when the sidemen were not of the highest caliber.

.   .   .

Personnel was surprisingly stable during the All Stars' first decade. Catlett left for health reasons; Earl Hines left because he wasn't cut out for a side-man role (after all, he'd led his own bands from 1929 on) and accepted it solely with Armstrong; Teagarden gained so much exposure from his All Stars tenure that he would have been foolish not to seize the opportunity to front a similar group of his own (as he did until his death, though reunions with Louis were frequent and always warm). The new permanent trombon-ist (after the short-timer Russ Phillips) was Trummy Young, who stayed for twelve years and was Armstrong's closest friend and strongest musical sup-porter among the All Stars. He was replaced by Big Chief Russell Moore, an Armstrong big-band alumnus, and then, for the duration, by the de-pendable Tyree Glenn. Hines's permanent replacement, Billy Kyle, was an-other twelve-year man; unfortunately, it was sudden death that ended his tenure. Bigard, the charter clarinet, remained until late 1956. His successor, Edmond Hall, was the best clarinet in All Stars history; after him came the able but somewhat bland Peanuts Hucko and the excellent Buster Bailey; the final incumbent, Joe Muranyi, knew what Armstrong represented and gave him all he had. Arvell Shaw left often but always came back. Among the other basses, Buddy Catlett was the most gifted, Mort Herbert the most reliable. Drummers included Barrett Deems, in for several key years and much better than the critics said, and Danny Barcelona, who stayed from the late '50s until the very end. No matter what the weak spots, the All Stars were held together by the leader, who in a very real sense could be the whole show when he had to.

That he sometimes did have to was probably unavoidable. Great players who'd have loved to work with Armstrong refused to risk their health by undertaking the All Stars' notoriously grueling pace, though the pay was good. The examples of Kyle and Bailey, who succumbed to the road—or at least so it seemed to their colleagues—were not encouraging. Perhaps even more poignant was the fate of Velma Middleton, whose devotion to Arm-strong was legendary. She suffered a stroke during the All Stars' tour of Africa in 1961 and had to be left behind in a Sierra Leone hospital, where she died three weeks later. Louis was an iron man, but even he could fall ill, as the 1959 Spoleto episode demonstrated. It is by now nearly certain that this bout with "indigestion" was a heart episode that both patient and doctors deliberately misidentified. It was an indication of Louis's fame that his collapse made front-page news throughout the world. Aside from China and the USSR, there was hardly a country the All Stars hadn't per-formed in.

He was "Ambassador Satch," and, mainly through his international suc-cess, jazz had become a valuable commodity in the cultural cold war. It was through his example that other jazz artists soon were enlisted by the U.S. Department of State to make goodwill tours all over the world.

. . .

The All Stars was Armstrong's everyday musical environment, yet much of the group's repertory was born and bred outside of it. Starting in 1949, Armstrong often recorded with augmented All Stars personnel, or entirely without them—with big bands, with strings, with choirs, and as in earlier days, in partnership with other stars. The All Stars' own records, many of them live, almost never gained the popularity of such items as the 1949 "Blueberry Hill" (a revival of a 1941 Gene Autry hit and a direct inspiration for Fats Domino's hugely successful 1956 version) or the 1951 "A Kiss to Build a Dream On," even bigger in Europe than at home. His versatility expressed itself in a beautifully tender "La Vie en Rose"; another French hit for Louis was "C'est Si Bon." From an All Star studio date came the astonishing "That's for Me," with a vocal in the upper part of his range that ranks with his greatest. Teamed with Ella Fitzgerald (they first met on records in 1944), he came up with "Can Anyone Explain?" and the sublime "Dream a Little Dream of Me." When producer Norman Granz got Ella away from Decca and onto his own label, Verve, there were the marvelous LPs *Ella and Louis* and *Ella and Louis Again* and the spectacularly packaged and lovingly produced *Porgy and Bess* with these two matchless voices in the title roles. (Louis's trumpet took no backseat in these enterprises, by the way.) The 1956–57 *Autobiography* was a four-LP box of re-creations, on some of which Armstrong surpassed his early masterpieces.

Granz also paired Louis with Oscar Peterson in a thoroughly mainstream repertory, including some fine songs the great man hadn't previously tackled, like "What's New?" and "Moon Song." On the other side of the musical coin, there were recorded meetings with the hugely popular Dukes of Dixieland; the results were surprisingly good for Louis, since this New Orleans–based group treated him with profound love and respect. In 1960 he got together with old fan Bing Crosby for an album of relaxed duets. But it was 1961 that saw some spectacular get-togethers.

Louis had a small but prominent role as a trumpeter named Wild Man Moore in the film *Paris Blues*, for which Duke Ellington scored the music. Duke didn't have his band at hand for a jam session scene starring Louis, but he made a group of French players and American expatriates sound very Dukish. The two stars had fun, and a few months later record producer Bob Thiele had the bright idea of bringing them together for the first time in a recording studio.

Since the protagonists were signed with different companies, he had to act quickly, and there was no time for rehearsals. Also, the budget only allowed for Ellington to take the piano chair in the All Stars, to which ex-Ellingtonian Barney Bigard had briefly returned. Made in two sessions—

one late at night, the other the following afternoon; then the All Stars hit the road that evening—the results (though Louis's lips were sore throughout the second session) were remarkable, not least because Louis learned new material on the spot and then performed it as if it had been in his repertory for years.

Six months later came an encounter with another pianist-composer, Dave Brubeck, who in collaboration with his lyricist wife, Iola, had composed a kind of jazz oratorio intended for the concert stage: *The Real Ambassadors*, a paean to jazz starring Armstrong as the music's incarnation. In the company of the All Stars, singer Carmen McRae, and the popular vocal trio Lambert, Hendricks & Ross, Armstrong again mastered brand-new material in record time and deeply impressed Brubeck with his dedication and professionalism. (Much nonsense has been written about Armstrong as an "intuitive" artist. Having had the privilege of seeing him work on new material [such as on the two above-mentioned occasions], I can assure the reader that this was a man who combined remarkable natural gifts with thorough discipline, and that he was able to sight-read highly sophisticated music and absorb it instantly.)

An example of the Armstrong ability to transform unexpected material was his 1955 encounter with Kurt Weill's "Mack the Knife," also known as "Theme from the Threepenny Opera." This became a big Armstrong hit, and Louis noted that his New Orleans childhood made it easy for him to capture Mack's unsavory essence. But hits like this or "Blueberry Hill," or the success of such album concepts (with the All Stars) as music by W. C. Handy (hailed even by professional Armstrong detractors) or Fats Waller (for whose music Armstrong had a genuine affinity), were dwarfed by the totally unexpected success of Louis's version of the rather unsophisticated but good-natured title song from a new 1963 Broadway show, *Hello, Dolly!* It was another tune from the Jerry Herman score, "I've Got a Lot of Living to Do," that was considered the more viable of the two tunes recorded at a hastily arranged session for a new label, Kapp.

To give proper early 1900s period flavor, a banjoist was added to the All Stars for the occasion, but Louis's main concern was that his dear friend Trummy Young was leaving the band—indeed, this was his final All Star recording session. The two sides were soon made and had almost been forgotten by Louis when the disc, a single, was released in early 1964, with overdubbed strings. It was one of those things that can't be planned or manufactured: an instant smash hit, soon heard on the radio, in the street, everywhere. It knocked the Beatles from the number-one perch on the Top 40 list, which they had occupied for months, and it gave Armstrong tremendous pleasure as well as plenty to put in his bank account. No one else, not even Barbra Streisand, could do much with the song, as demonstrated in the film version of the musical, in which she and Armstrong appear together. Only he knew how to make that song sound good, and he was stuck with it from then on—which bothered him not one bit. The *Dolly* cameo was his final film role; his next-to-last, in a Sammy Davis, Jr., vehicle about a bebop trumpeter, *A Man Called Adam*, gave him some moments to show what an actor he was, and contained some good music as well.

In 1967 a new song, "What a Wonderful World," became a number-one hit for Louis in England and on the Continent, and did nicely at home. Another title song from a Broadway musical, "Cabaret," also did well for him that year, and in 1968 he proved once again that he could work wonders with unlikely material, on an album of Disney-related songs, notably the dark and oddly ominous "Chim Chim Cheree." (His trumpeting was, by earlier standards, somewhat impaired on this, but the musical message was almost overwhelming.)

By September 1968, Louis was seriously ill and hospitalized; he was released the following January but back within a month. Not long after, Joe Glaser, who'd been considering urging Louis to retire, suddenly suffered a massive stroke and was taken to the same hospital. The news was kept from the recuperating trumpeter, but he found out and was devastated that Glaser, in a deep coma, didn't respond to him. Glaser died on the sixth of June without regaining consciousness. By then Louis was well enough to sing at a benefit for Louis Metcalfe, a veteran trumpeter who'd challenged Armstrong when he came to New York in 1929. In October 1969 he returned to the studios, recording (vocally only, the trumpet forbidden by doctors) the theme song "We Have All the Time in the World" for a new James Bond film.

Remaining time for Louis was considerably less, but it was filled with a long-overdue outpouring for him by the so-called jazz community, which for once acted as such. In May 1970 a recording session brought into the studio (in addition to a large complement of playing musicians) an unusual group of backup singers: Miles Davis, Ornette Coleman, Chico Hamilton, Tony Bennett, Eddie Condon, Bobby Hackett, Ruby Braff, and even a bunch of jazz critics.

For his seventieth birthday (really only his sixty-ninth), *Down Beat* magazine (then edited by this writer) gathered tributes from eighty-six musicians covering the entire spectrum of jazz, including some who decades before might not have been quite so forthcoming. Perhaps most interesting were the statements of Kenny Dorham, Cal Massey, and Thad Jones that it was Armstrong who'd been the cause of their taking up the trumpet. Critics had been saying that his active influence had ceased by the early '30s, and current academic wisdom perpetuates that fable.

There was a star-studded pre-birthday party in Hollywood, at which Louis's old friend and collaborator Hoagy Carmichael cut a giant cake. And at the Newport Jazz Festival in July, a red carpet was spread for Louis. There was a night of musical tributes from trumpeters, including Hackett, Ray Nance, young Jimmy Owens, Joe Newman, Wild Bill Davison, and Dizzy Gillespie. The Eureka Brass Band came up from New Orleans to march for Louis, and Mahalia Jackson (a hometown girl) duetted with him on "Just a Closer Walk with Thee." The event was filmed, including back-stage and rehearsal sequences, and later, interview passages with Armstrong were inserted. And of course there was "Hello, Dolly!"

Armstrong still wasn't allowed to play trumpet, though friends knew he was practicing at home. But by September, the All Stars were reactivated for a two-week Las Vegas stand. At their first rehearsal, according to Joe Muranyi, Louis played like a man possessed. In October he flew to England for a charity concert, and in late December, after a rare Christmas celebration at home, he was back in Las Vegas. In February 1971 he and Bing Crosby were reunited for the last time on the David Frost television show, doing "Blueberry Hill" together. There wasn't much trumpet playing on the show, but in his dressing room Louis warmed up, with a mute in the bell, on "Pennies from Heaven." I won't forget that.

The All Stars played their final engagement in March, at the Waldorf Astoria's Empire Room. Louis clearly was ill by the end of that two-week stint, and he then suffered a heart attack. Released in May, he recuperated at home. On his birthday he was seen on a television newscast with trom-bonist Tyree Glenn of the All Stars at his side. Frail but smiling, he ven-tured a few notes of "Sleepy Time Down South" and told the visitors (and of course the world at large) that he would be back to entertain them soon. In the early morning of July 6, 1971, Louis Armstrong died peacefully in his sleep.

It was a young trumpeter from Louis's hometown who, having come to sudden fame in the 1980s for his unique combination of great jazz and clas-sical skills, began to change fundamentally the perception of the master among contemporary jazz musicians. Wynton Marsalis, by speaking of Armstrong always in reverential tones, and even more by his example of performing Armstrong music and by his insistence that the jazz tradition must be honored in more than just words, brought about a new image of Louis Armstrong and spawned some even younger acolytes. It is today no longer surprising that a Byron Stripling or a Nicholas Payton can perform almost note-perfect Armstrong simulations (Stripling also sings à la Louis), or that Marsalis and the somewhat older Jon Faddis (well versed in Arm-strong before it became *de rigueur*) shared the excruciatingly difficult Armstrong solo from 1936, "Swing That Music," at a 1993 JVC Festival concert. But the man himself had some surprises left in store for us.

As if there hadn't been enough Armstrong firsts during his lifetime, he came up with a posthumous encore. In the 1989 film *Good Morning, Viet-*

nam, the star disc jockey plays many records, among them Armstrong's "What a Wonderful World." The artist's name isn't mentioned, nor is his face seen. There is no trumpet, just that voice. On the strength of this unannounced performance, the quickly reissued record "charted," as they say in the music business, staying on *Billboard*'s Top 100 for many weeks and reaching the number 33 spot.

Louis would have been pleased. He didn't realize he was immortal.

(1994)

Introduction to *Satchmo: My Life in New Orleans*

E ver since I was a small kid," writes Louis Armstrong in these memoirs, "I have always been a great observer." Indeed, it is a vivid picture Armstrong draws for us of life as he experienced and witnessed it during the first two decades of this century in New Orleans.

By contemporary Western standards, this life was one of deprivation and extreme poverty, but the tone of *Satchmo* is far removed from, say, Orwell's *Down and Out in Paris and London*. But then, Armstrong was not an educated man, and there was no distance between him and those with whom he shared his early lot in life. He was different from most of them, and the key difference was character. While he doesn't pass judgment on the "gamblers, hustlers, cheap pimps, thieves [and] prostitutes" among whom he was raised, it is clear throughout this book that his values, from a very early age on, differ from theirs.

This is perhaps most poignantly revealed in a passage toward the end of the narrative. Armstrong has just returned home from a six-month stint on the Mississippi steamer *St. Paul*, with more money in his pockets than ever before. He heads straight for the old neighborhood, and the first familiar face he encounters is that of Black Benny. This hustler and gifted part-time drummer is one of the most strongly drawn figures in *Satchmo*, an older man of great physical strength and real courage who early on becomes one of "Little Louis's" many protectors, and whom the youngster clearly admires.

Benny is happy to see his young protégé again, but immediately makes him aware that he knows about the money:

He asked me to stand him a drink, and who was I to refuse the great Black Benny. . . . Nobody else ever did. When the drinks came I noticed that everybody had ordered. I threw down a twenty dollar bill to pay for the round which cost about six or seven bucks. When the bartender counted out my change Black Benny immediately reached for it saying, "I'll take it." I smiled all over my face. What else could I do? Benny wanted the money and that was that. Besides I was so fond of Benny it did not matter anyway. I do believe, however, if he had not strong-armed that money out of me I would have given him lots more. I had been thinking about it on the train coming home. . . . But since Benny did it the hard way I gave the idea up. I sort of felt he should have treated me like a man, and I did not like the way he cut under me. . . . So I disgustedly waited for an opening to leave, and did.

Though Armstrong doesn't comment further, one senses that this experience, almost as much as his newfound confidence in his own musical abilities and his growing estrangement from his wife, is his "opening to leave" his hometown and his old environment for good. Armstrong was not immodest in his claim to be a great observer of human nature.

Armstrong credits his maternal grandmother, who raised him to the age of five, and his mother, to whom he was deeply attached, with instilling in him the system of values that would carry him through his extraordinary life and enable him to confront with serenity experiences and situations he could not have imagined in his wildest childhood dreams. As he describes them, these values seem deceptively simple:

I didn't go any further than fifth grade in school myself. But with my good sense and mother-wit, and knowing how to treat and respect the feelings of other people, that's all I've needed through life.

And, in a variation on the same basic theme (variations, after all, are of interest in the work of a great improvising artist): "I managed to teach him [his adopted son, Clarence, a second cousin] the necessary things in life, such as being courteous, having respect for other people, and last but not least, having good common sense."

How does a man who didn't finish fifth grade come to write a book? Before we attempt to answer that question, we must deal briefly with the doubts that have been cast on the authorship of *Satchmo* by James Lincoln Collier in *Louis Armstrong: An American Genius*, which does not fulfill the promise of its title. Lumping together two very different books—the one to hand and the 1936 *Swing That Music*—Collier states: "The two books

Armstrong signed—one of which he probably wrote, in the main—are un-reliable." The attack on Armstrong's veracity is unworthy, while "probably" and "in the main" can be easily disposed of. A copy of the typescript of *Satchmo* (the author's working title was *The Armstrong Story*) resides in the archives of the Institute of Jazz Studies at Rutgers University, and I have carefully compared it to the published text. Though substantial editing was done, it was mostly a matter of changing Armstrong's three-dot style to conventionally punctuated sentence structure. The words are essentially Armstrong's own, and nothing of importance he did not write has been put in his mouth. Anyone at all familiar with the editing process as applied to many famous works of fiction, not to mention non-professional autobi-ographies, should consider Collier's qualifying "in the main" wholly irrele-vant. (If anything, the original version reads better.)

As for Collier's "probably," only Armstrong could have typed that man-uscript. His approach to language, spelling, and syntax—even his touch on the typewriter—is inimitable, and as distinctive as his handwriting. The authenticity of *Satchmo* is not in question. (*Swing That Music* is heavily ghosted and in any event as much—or more—a paean to swing and an at-tempted introduction to its musical methods as an autobiography. Yet it has the distinction of being the first book published about a jazz musician, un-less Paul Whiteman and Vincent Lopez fit that description.)

How, then, did this "uneducated" and "deprived" man come to be a writer, and a real one, with a clear and distinctive voice of his own? We know that Armstrong already owned a typewriter and knew how to use it when he first arrived in Chicago to join King Oliver's band—the climactic event in *Satchmo*. The earliest surviving typed letter by Armstrong I've seen is dated September 1, 1922, and it contains complaints that three previous letters (one to the recipient, two to other friends) have gone unanswered. Armstrong left New Orleans on August 8, so we can conclude that he was already a fairly prolific correspondent. Some twenty years later, he was ca-pable of tossing off a thirteen-page single-spaced missive, though most of his known letters average a page or two. (Short greetings and strictly per-sonal messages were always handwritten, preferably in green ink, but the Institute's archives also contain a biographical sketch of some ten thousand words penned in this manner, dating from 1944. It was written "on the road," probably while the typewriter was packed away. Incidentally, insofar as its subject matter overlaps with *Satchmo*'s, the facts are consistent.)

Clearly, Louis Armstrong loved to write, and, given stylistic and lin-guistic idiosyncrasies, he wrote exceptionally well. Writing was a natural extension of his gift for the spoken word, his love of storytelling, and his ceaseless fascination with the foibles of human beings. Graceful, effortless, unselfconscious, but always at pains to make his meaning clear (the *Satchmo* manuscript contains many parenthetical explanations to the potential uninitiated reader), Armstrong's prose style reflects structural and emotional aspects of his musical expression. It is, of course, much more down-to-earth, but after all, Armstrong wrote for relaxation. Music, as even a superficial reading of this book reveals, was work.

The work ethic was fundamental to Armstrong's outlook on life. In this respect, he was most certainly a moralist, though his tolerance for a broad range of behavior was vast. His sense of humor combined with this tolerance prevents him from striking a self-righteous pose, as a writer and a man. Nothing human was alien to him, yet the standards he applied to his own behavior were quite strict, from an ethical standpoint. Collier, ever the puritan, finds Armstrong's fondness for eating "obsessive," yet Armstrong explains succinctly in these pages why he is against self-deprivation. A fellow musician aboard the *St. Paul* nearly starves himself in order to invest all his earning in cotton farming. But the boll weevils devour his cotton, and he almost becomes suicidal. "I'll never be rich," Armstrong concludes from observing this nasty trait, "but I'll be a fat man." He did become rich, of course, but never spent much on himself. His wives were well provided for, but he saw no need for "a flock of suits." And, perhaps because he never forgot the generosity his early playing had inspired from his "deprived" audiences of whores, pimps, and hustlers, he gave away all he could afford as long as he lived.

The music always came first, but even in this, Armstrong has often been misunderstood. Why, it has been asked, did he leave the direction of his bands, especially the big ones from 1929 to 1947, mainly to other (and, needless to say, lesser) musicians? The question is answered perfectly well in these pages:

"I never cared to become a band leader; there was too much quarreling over petty money matters. I just wanted to blow my horn peacefully as I am doing now. I have always noticed that the band leader not only had to satisfy the crowd but that he also had to worry about the box office." Armstrong let others count the house and mind the payroll; he had more important things to do, such as making music. Others (Duke Ellington, for one) found more ingenious and sophisticated ways of confronting this dilemma, but Armstrong knew that when he picked up his horn or opened his mouth to sing, the relative quality of the accompaniment became strictly a secondary concern.

Many other themes struck up in this book are recurrent in Armstrong's comments, written or spoken, about his music. There was his love and respect for King Oliver (his mentor and first and lasting idol) above all, and then for all the music and musicians he'd grown up with. Though he would go far beyond what they had accomplished, to him they remained the best of all time. Was this nostalgia? Perhaps; this book makes it evident that while Armstrong quickly outgrew his native environment, he retained a strong empathy for it all his life. But it was more than simply that, or even the displeasure with newer trends in jazz that had become apparent in his attitude by the time he began to write *Satchmo*. It was, I think, the feeling and the originality that the musicians he admired in his youth brought to their art and craft. It was truly new, and they had made it up; nothing like it had been heard before. And even as he went on to create what seems to us far more remarkable and adventurous music (from which what he later came to disdain so clearly sprang), he remained a traditionalist at heart, a man who played and sang pretty or funny songs to make people feel pleasure.

Today, we say that Louis Armstrong saw himself as an "entertainer," and understand this term to mean something less than "artist." Paradoxically, what Armstrong created to entertain happens to surpass in artistry a great deal (if not most) of what self-styled artists have to offer. This paradox never interested or concerned Armstrong himself. He did what he did; he was who he was. And what he did and was eludes analysis and explanation. Reading this little book without preconceptions, and above all without the blinding burden of modernistic sociological and psychological notions about class, race, "intellect," and high versus popular culture, will bring you a bit closer to the mysterious wellsprings of Louis Armstrong's art, and to one of nature's noblemen—in the truest sense of the poet's term.

(1986)

A Sixty-fifth Birthday Interview

There can be little doubt that Louis Daniel Armstrong is one of the best-known and best-loved personalities in the world today. His smiling face and unmistakable voice are familiar to millions, many of whom may have only the most nebulous conception of jazz—the music of which he is the very incarnation, but the confines of which he has long ago transcended.

Forty years ago, this remarkable man revolutionized jazz with the first records made under his own name—records that mesmerized musicians, young or old, who heard them. And there were few who didn't. Seven years later, Armstrong paid his first visit to Europe, becoming the first jazz musician to play before royalty, to be reviewed by first-string music critics, to be recognized officially as an artist in a music that had hitherto been considered little more than entertainment.

A few years later, he became the first performer of his race to be consistently featured in class-A movies. After World War II, the trumpeter began his phenomenally successful travels to nearly every corner of the globe, spreading the gospel of jazz to people of all ages, from all walks of life, and of every race, nationality, and creed.

And a year ago, Armstrong had the biggest record of his career, squeezing the Beatles from the number-one spot on the Top 40 list and spawning a new generation of fans.

There are those (oddly, almost entirely to be found within the world of jazz) who envy Armstrong his achievement. They are to be pitied, for that achievement can be measured only in terms of spreading love, happiness, and beauty—and to be envious of such qualities and feelings is to have a barren heart. Nor can such people have any conception of the prodigious quantities of effort and energy that this man has put into his life's work. For there can be no question but that Armstrong is the most dedicated and hardest working of the great artists in what is so aptly called "show business."

On July 4, Armstrong celebrates his sixty-fifth birthday. Characteristically, he will celebrate it by being on the job—for the opening night of a one-week stand at Atlantic City's Steel Pier. "From there," he said recently, "we go to do a TV show from the Hollywood Bowl, and then on to Las Vegas with Abbe Lane. . . ."

Armstrong was sitting behind the desk in his den, a comfortable room on the top floor of his comfortable house in Corona, New York, on Long Island. Rested and relaxed after an unusually long period away from his work (most of it, however, spent having dental work performed), he graciously shared with his visitors a sunny late-May afternoon perhaps better spent in his pleasant garden.

"I'm feelin' fine," he said with a smile. "Chops are all repaired—I've been blowin' a few notes in the house, and it's comfortable. Lucille [Armstrong's wife of twenty-three years] is packing—we're getting ready to go to Europe this time; Denmark first, then England—for broadcasts, TV, and some concerts in London and a few of the provincial cities."

Not long before, the trumpeter had made an unprecedented tour of Eastern Europe, playing in several Communist countries where no major U.S. artist had performed since before World War II. Wherever he went, the reception was tumultuous, but Armstrong spoke of the experience with typical lack of vanity.

"We had a nice trip behind the Iron Curtain, and the people—well, they seemed pretty happy," he said. "Like they say, you can adjust yourself to anything. They seem to have everything they want—it's just that they can't come out to this side. . . .

"The concerts were sold out every night," he continued. "Mostly, it would take about five minutes on stage before we even got to play that first note."

After the concerts would come a time-honored Armstrong ritual: the signing of autographs for hundreds of fans.

"I'd get dressed," Armstrong said, "they'd put a table at the door, and I'd autograph everyone's program who was in the hall—or that's what it seemed like. Some of them wanted eight or nine autographs—one for the family, and this and that, and I'd let them go . . . some of those names were rough!

"They gave us a lot of presents. In Prague they gave me a trumpet— a beautiful horn. I played it for them, of course. I'll keep that as one of my cherished possessions. And beautiful Polish and Czech crystal. In East Berlin they gave us a lot of things, too. They also found out that I like Eisbein (we call 'em pigs' knuckles over here), and everywhere I went in Germany they had it waiting for us."

Politics were not discussed, according to Armstrong. "We met on a common ground: music," he said. "We came to liven up the situation—not to depress anybody."

Armstrong's visit to Russia—long discussed and long awaited—did not materialize in this opening round. But he said, "a couple of Russian ministers came to see us in Prague, and I met them, and they said we should do the same thing there. For a while, I thought we were going to go." Armstrong is confident, however, that he will someday play in Russia.

The Armstrong All Stars played more towns in East Germany than anywhere else on the tour and thus had to travel by bus as well as plane. One of these side trips was the occasion for a revealing incident.

"The Army was maneuvering," Armstrong recalled, "so we had to go an around-about way and saw a lot of towns we weren't really allowed to see, but they had put us off the autobahn. Still, we got caught in a convoy, and it was just like being in parade all day. The soldiers would be standing up there all stiff and everything, but then one would recognize us and they'd start to wave . . . 'Satch,' you know.

"The bus driver got hip while we were going through some small town with a little square—the convoy was turning to the left—to turn right about a block away, and he went to the right to turn left, figuring he could cut them off. But he ran right smack into them, and we had to stop and wait for the whole thing to pass! I got out to look for one of those German beers, and found out that we were going to stay for a long time, so I commenced looking for a delicatessen—and what did I do that for?

" 'Cause a lot of students who were sitting in these beer parlors recognized me and wanted autographs, and once I got started I was hours signing them, for they were coming from every angle of the town. The whole town came out for autographs. . . . Some cats were saying 'Supposing they keep you over here?' And I said, 'Well, as long as I can blow. I'd wait till they got together on it. . . . What else could you do?'

"We finally found an opening and made a beeline to the town where we were booked. Got there about a half hour before the concert. The place was loaded—everyone was waiting. But it turned out all right. You throw a little water up and run from under it, grab a sandwich, and go to the concert. And afterwards—oh boy, did I sign autographs! But I don't mind. You adjust yourself to it."

From time to time, rumors of retirement plans surround Armstrong, but he always nips them in the bud. There are things he would like to do, but, as he says, "you're still in business and you can't do everything at once." And there isn't much time to relax.

"When there are a few days off," Armstrong said, "Lucille and I kind of cool it at home. It's rough . . . mail stacked up here and there, records and tunes they want me to listen to. Sometimes I have time to do things and sometimes I don't. I must have a thousand records down in the basement— but I know where they are, and someday I'll listen to them all. I'll get to things."

At one time, there was talk of Armstrong's opening a club in his neighborhood.

"There's a place on the corner," he said. "We could go up there and have cats come from everywhere. But what would be the outcome? Stickups . . . handouts . . . IOUs . . . nothing to put in the cash register. Cats ain't going to tell you anything until they've drunk up all your whisky. Then what are you going to do? You can't siphon it out of them!

"If you don't know business, you're in trouble. And if it was my club, I feel I should be there. You can't go into that kind of thing unless you're at least there to greet the people. But maybe there'll be a day—when perhaps I'm not blowing anymore, just hanging around to sing on a record and stuff—when I'll open up a little 'hostel.' It won't be one of those big elaborate things in competition with places that are already in session—just something that will interest my fans."

Armstrong holds no brief with those who say jazz is dying. "As I see it," he said, "there's always some place to work, to exercise your music. That's how it was in the olden days—always some place to blow. Naturally, there are new styles in music today, and they display them on radio and TV, so the jazz musician doesn't get the chance to record the way he used to. Something is bound to get lost. But the main thing is to stay before the public. That's what the old-timers always told me."

Armstrong knows that "staying before the public" is not always easy. "The trouble is that all the good jazz players aren't getting the chance to prove that they can still play something good," he said. "It's not that they can't play anymore, but the public can forget you in a minute. It doesn't take long. . . ."

But if it should ever get to the point that people in general come to believe "that jazz is finished," Armstrong would not be at a loss: "I'd get me a record company and record nothing but what people said was finished—and we'd make a million dollars. You get those boys blowing out there—waitin' for that one gig, that one recording session, and we'd get together and set up, you know—we wouldn't go wrong. Everybody's looking for that top banana, but they're asleep on the good music that started all this."

Another pursuit that Armstrong has in mind when the time comes is the completion of his autobiography. (His first volume, *My Life in New Orleans*, was published in 1954.) He has accumulated considerable material, but so far only on the run.

"Someday," he said, "I'll write it all and let you read it and say, 'There it is.' There'll be days when I can just sit around and lay around and dictate. It might be to a young chick," he said with a twinkle. "But it could be a young boy, too . . . as long as they can scribble in shorthand. You know, you run your mouth so fast!

"It's got to be done someday—maybe that'll take care of my old age. Then they can pick up on old Satchmo and see what he's got to say."

In the meanwhile, there is still playing to be done. Throughout his long career, Armstrong has taken care of business to a degree matched by few, if any, in his profession. "The music comes first" is one of his golden rules, and he lives by it.

"Now, I never professed to be a saint," he said, "but I've always tried to do my work to the extent that I can have a ball when I finish. I don't know," he laughed, "if I'll have a ball too long after I finish for the next engagement—but I'll have a better chance, anyway. There are very few gigs that I've ever missed."

Until this day, Armstrong doesn't table-hop with his admirers during intermissions. "I never go to the tables—I never did believe in that. If they want to see me, they can come to the dressing room."

Not that the trumpeter doesn't like to socialize. He loves it, and people love to be around him. So much so that the mere act of going out in public, even if the aim is only to relax and enjoy himself, can become problematic.

"When I go out to some joint—well, I won't call them joints; they are 'lounges' now—I seem to know everyone that frequents them," he said. "I can't even drink my drink for shaking hands. And right where we sit, that's where we stay, with the table crowded with our disciples and our cats. Now, if some other people want to say hello, I can't get over there. That's another reason why I don't go to tables during my intermission. If you go to one table, you've got to go to the next one, and then, where's your intermission?

"And don't start that autograph thing. . . . I was going to my doctor's the other day (he's on Fifty-fifth Street between Sixth and Seventh Avenues) from my dentist (who's on Fifty-fourth and Fifth), so we go to Fifty-fifth and walk straight down, and on Sixth Avenue there are about twenty kids with two Sisters. One turns around, does a double take, and says: 'There is Satchmo!' And there I was, autographing and autographing, and finally the two Sisters come right up, look at me, and say: 'Love that man.' Naturally, some people have gathered to see what's happening, and now *they* have me scribbling, writing on shopping bags, anything that's handy. And you can't say no. Who wants to say no?"

Certainly not Armstrong. And that, he said, "is one reason why you don't see me out so much. If I go to the World's Fair and take that walk, I don't get to see anything. None of the exhibits. I go to a ball game [he loves baseball], and people start jumping over seats. 'You've got to autograph this for my little boy. He's your fan. He loves your "Hello, Dolly."' Okay, you've got to do it. When I went to Freedomland—I was just a visitor there—I went just to see things for myself, like a kid would, you know? But I didn't get the chance.

"The night I went to see the first Liston-Clay fight, at a movie theater in Flushing, the people were so busy getting my autograph they didn't even see the fight. I didn't either. And after they turned on the lights, they had a line from here to around the corner for autographs. It's wonderful—to an extent. They say when they stop asking for autographs, you're in trouble. I wonder how it would feel to know that they'd stopped? Do you think I'd be lonesome for it?"

Lest anyone doubt Armstrong's sincerity in asking this, let it be said that it simply does not occur to him that people would not stop even if he were to retire. He sees himself as a performer whose popularity is based in what he does, not as a celebrity whose popularity is synonymous with who he is. His fame has never gone to his head; perhaps this is one of the secrets of his fame. And he has not become blasé.

"I went to see *Hello, Dolly!* . . . the whole show was for Lucille and me. I went on stage just to take a bow with Carol Channing, and you'd have thought the walls would come in. . . . It's wonderful—but nobody lasts forever. But after fifty-two years of playing, I had a wonderful experience for a man who came up from New Orleans selling newspapers and who just wanted to blow the horn. . . . The people put me in my seat, and I'll never let them down. And there's no problem: they love music, and I love music, too."

Armstrong's love of music as a form of communication between artist and audience is expressed in his attitude toward playing music "right."

"If a cat can play a beautiful lead nowadays, he's in business," he said. "He doesn't have to stand on his head—just play pretty. That's what bands need: a trumpet man with a tone who can phrase pretty. Anybody can stand up and squeal out a high note, and things like that. But when a cat can play a beautiful lead, he's in business at all times. You don't have to worry about his age."

Though he is one of the greatest improvisers jazz has known, a man who, when he just "plays that lead," puts his own indelible stamp on every note, the lead is what he believes in.

"That's the first thing Joe Oliver told me when he listened to me play," Armstrong remembered. "He used to come around the honky-tonks where I was playing in the early teens. 'Where's that lead?' I'd play eight bars and I was gone . . . clarinet things; nothing but figurations and things like that. Like what the cats called bop later; that was just figuration to us in the early days. Running all over a horn. Joe would say, 'Where's that lead?', and I'd say, 'What lead?' 'You play some lead on that horn, let the people know what you're playing.'"

Speaking of Oliver, his first idol, and the man who gave him his start in what was to become the big time, Armstrong remembered others from those early days.

"We lost a lot of good boys who will always be remembered when a story comes up about music," he recalled. "Like Sidney Bechet. You know, way back when in New Orleans, just he and I and a drummer would advertise the fights from the back of a furniture wagon—we had some good sounds. He did a lot for music, but in his way. He was very much loved in France. Oh, I'll always remember Bechet, Big Eye Louis Nelson, George Bacquet, Freddie Keppard, King Oliver. . . . I loved those boys. All soul musicians. And it was something nice for a kid to listen to.

"I remember them all, and others that you wouldn't know if I mentioned their names. . . . I heard them all when I was a kid, second-lining in the parades, before I started blowing a horn. Those people *moved* me. Buddy Petit, Buddy Johnson, Mutt Carey, Jack Carey, Bunk Johnson. I thought that was a wonderful thing when they found Bunk and let him have a little more fun before he died. And he could have cooled it and probably lasted a little longer, but he was so happy and carried away over the things he'd missed even when he was in his prime. Life is a funny thing. . . . He came up on the stand the night I was playing in New Iberia, in 1949, the night before going to New Orleans to be King of the Zulus. He picked up that horn and played for hours. And Kid Ory. He still looks good. . . ."

Kid Ory—who alone of all the famous pioneers is still around, who was the trombonist on the famed Hot Five recordings of 1925–27, and whom Louis does not in the least begrudge the fact that he is credited with a famous jazz standard that Armstrong claims is his own.

That piece of jazz lore was revealed when Louis was asked if he had written any tunes since his lovely "Someday" from the mid-'40s. "I haven't really had the time," he answered, "but if anything comes to my mind, I just jot it down. I've got a few scripts and little scratches here and there. And there's always a time when you can sum them up and blow them up. You don't know whom to go to now when you do those things.

"Of course, in the early days," he continued, "we had no knowledge of royalties and things like that. I used to take a tune down to OKeh Records and sell it right out, like Fats Waller did. I'd get a little change, so Zutty [Singleton] and I could go somewhere and ball. We were running together at the time. Just give me a little taste now—that was the way we looked at it. I wrote 'Muskrat Ramble.' Ory named it, he gets the royalties. I don't talk about it. A whole lot of things like that. . . . 'Sister Kate' [which he wrote and sold to A. J. Piron]."

But Armstrong is stoical about such things. "You can't have everything in life," he reflected. "You can get yourself all riled up, but what good is it? I wasn't brought up to educate myself in that kind of business, like some cats were. But there will be other tunes. There's always another one coming along—like a streetcar. We can't get everything that's coming to us. . . ."

Such as a proper reception in one's own hometown, for instance. Louis has steadfastly refused to play New Orleans for the last decade or so—not until it can be done right. But he remembers with some pride his triumphant return to New Orleans in 1931—nine years after he had left for Chicago to join King Oliver at the Lincoln Gardens.

In New Orleans, he played the Suburban Gardens. Armstrong, with his first big band (the previous ones had been Carroll Dickerson's and Les Hite's), stayed there for a couple of months.

"We were the first band on the radio down there—every night," he said. "I did my own announcements—that was the first time, too. Cats were buying radios to dig my program, and, quite naturally, I would dedicate this one to old so-and-so and to places like the Alley, where Bechet came up from, and the Colored Waif's Home, and the Zulus. I walked down Rampart Street one day, and a cat hollered from across the way, 'Man, *delegate* one for me tonight.' That first night, the ovation was something—fifty thousand Negroes were out on the levee listening. The place was right near the levee, so they could hear. . . ."

The only sour note of that visit came at the end. It had been planned that the trumpeter would play a giant concert in a big armory—for Negroes only. They came from miles around; some even came in horse-drawn wagons. "But the promoters pulled out on a technicality at the last moment," he recalled. "Seems there were some people in town who didn't want it to come off. So we left at midnight. To this day, there are people who think that I didn't want to play—that *I* pulled out. How about that?"

In Texas, things were better. "We arrived in Houston the next morning, and there were eight thousand people waiting for us. And they let everybody in. One dollar a head—no taxes. We played through all the states down there. One dance, in Arkansas, I'll never forget. Some little town down there—no roof on the place. Packed with people—and then the rains came. And cats were dancing around with umbrellas, us standing right out there blowing with them. And they were dancing—just as if nothing had happened."

If he had to play standing in the rain today, Louis probably would. He hasn't lost his dedication to his art and craft. And while he likes to reminisce, his eyes are on today and on the future.

"I admire the youngsters and their way of life," he stated, "just the way they feel it. They're vivacious—with the Watusi and things like that. We can do a little of it, but not as long as they can. But it's nice to watch. I'm not going to do everything that they do, but I'm going to stay in there with them."

About criticism, Armstrong is again stoical—and quite perceptive. "I say, well, all right; at least they spell my name right. That's more than the other cat got—they didn't even mention him. If you perform, you're going to have your ups and downs, but what is said about you, good or bad, is forgotten tomorrow. The public is ready for tomorrow's news. That's how fast our America is.

"I don't try to do the impossible," he said. "You know, we have a lot of greats out there, and they take care of their end of it. I just do the things I like and the things the people like for me to do, and I think there is a lot of room out there for everybody."

Not that he is taking a backseat yet—and he never will. "There isn't a thing anybody can sing or do with music that I can't do," he said. "But

I say, there's time to show that. I don't want to be egotistic. I just want to be among them. As long as you're among them, you can do good things. . . ."

And Louis is still among them, though he may say a bit wistfully: "The time will come when I'll just be a musical citizen—I mean, help some youngsters, and grab a little gig here and there. Probably I'll stop traveling so much—that's the main thing. I can always do something in New York, musically. There are a lot of songs, and a lot of things. . . ."

As for now, Armstrong is still out there, on the road, where he has spent so much of his life, bringing happiness to people who can take it home with them while he travels on. And he has no regrets, after fifty-two years of blowing.

"It's wonderful," he sums up at the threshold of sixty-five, "to be around and to see so many things happening with the youngsters. And you're right in there with them. Today. That's happiness—that's nice. I don't regret anything. I still enjoy life and music."

(1965)

Chicago Concert

Step right in . . . the show is on! And what a show it is: Louis Armstrong is performing with his All Stars—ready to entertain you royally. To be entertained by a king is not an everyday event. Show. Entertainment. Those are the terms which, when Louis was making the music heard herein, jazz critics were wont to hurl at him, as if they were invective. And to the hurlers, they were. By 1956, jazz had become an art form, serious business. (The more serious, the less business, but the gentlemen of the pen couldn't care less.) After all, hadn't they decreed that jazz was A Serious Art Form? Louis Armstrong, of course, had been A Serious Artist in the 1920s, when he recorded with his Hot Five, playing The Real Jazz. But then Louis became a star. He fronted big bands (bands of which the critics disapproved even when other big bands were in). He sang and played pop tunes. He appeared in films. He had fallen from grace.

Never mind that musicians admired him more than ever, that he continued to refine the astonishing creative and instrumental powers that had stunned all within hearing of his horn from the time he'd come to Chicago to join King Oliver. Never mind that his magic ways with an ordinary song had enraptured a generation of singers, starting with Bing Crosby, and changed the way everybody in America sang, whether they knew where the new way came from or not.

Never mind all that: Louis Armstrong had become an entertainer. It could not be denied that he still played the trumpet well—but all that other stuff. Good heavens!

Today almost everyone with access to print fawns over Louis Armstrong's memory, including those who jabbed and jived him when he was around. Not that it bothered him much. He had the love of his audiences, and those audiences outnumbered and outloved those of any other living artist. Only Charlie Chaplin could rival his worldwide fame, and Chaplin did not perform in person. Yet it did get under his skin, and sometimes he fought back—Louis was a counterpuncher from the start; had to be in order to survive.

It didn't rub him that he was criticized. "As long as they spell my name right and keep it before the public," he used to say to friends. And though he was held responsible for such presumed flaws in his "act" as the unchanging repertoire (a canard: what working jazz group doesn't have a set repertoire?); the "tasteless" jokes (Louis had the capacity to genuinely enjoy his ability to make people laugh, and besides, his timing was superb); the flashing teeth and rolling eyes (judged suspect, though they came naturally to Louis: could or should he have hidden those magnificent teeth that supported his horn for all those blowing years, or those battle-scarred lips he cared for so tenderly with the special salve made for him by a German master craftsman, an instrument-maker who understood what went into playing the most demanding horn yet devised by man?), so clearly reflected in the expressions and mannerisms of the people of West Africa (the former Gold Coast), whence he proudly traced his ancestry, long before *Roots*, always ahead of his time, and in every way—he didn't let all that get him down. Not even when some whites (who had no right to) and some blacks (who had no right to) called him Uncle Tom, aggressively or apologetically, maliciously or misguidedly, did he let it frustrate him, though it hurt him deeply. (He spoke of "the modern malice" and was misunderstood.)

No, it was when the musicians in his band were disparaged, that was when he became furious. Not only because it was unfair: his people did their job, or they left the band. But because it destroyed morale, and in a band that traveled and worked like Louis's did—more than any other organization, perhaps with the exception of Duke Ellington's orchestra—morale was a crucial factor. Steady work and good pay made up for a lot of barbs, as did the sheer fact of working with Louis and basking in his glory, but musicians are not the world's most thick-skinned people.

Newport, July 4, 1957: Louis Armstrong's and the nation's birthday. Louis Armstrong Night. Louis and his group arrive at Freebody Park in mid-afternoon, straight from a one-nighter somewhere in New England. That they're used to; routine. Sometimes they go on within hours after a flight of thousands of miles, in places they've never been to before. All in a year's work: get on, do the show (always a hell of a show; nothing less than all you've got with Louis, who never gives less than his all). But this time, in the tent behind the stage that is the Newport Festival's star's "dressing room" at this stage of the game, Louis hears from the producer, and the producer's advisory board, and his own manager, that he is to appear with almost every act on the bill except his own group, with people he hasn't played with in years, a parade of figures from the past: Henry "Red" Allen, once or twice in his band; Buster Bailey, a 1924–25 colleague from Fletcher Henderson's band; J. C. Higginbotham, who was with Louis's big band in the '30s; and Jack Teagarden and Cozy Cole, alumni of his All Stars. Plus special guest Kid Ory: the septuagenarian trombonist who gave Louis his first important gigs and was in his Hot Five recording group. And with Sidney Bechet, a boyhood acquaintance and 1924 and 1940 recording partner. Then with Ella Fitzgerald, friend and recording partner. Then with everybody for a "Happy Birthday" jam.

Louis, who never in his career has favored unrehearsed public performances, especially on stage before thousands, is stunned. While press and musicians and backstage hangers-on mill about, he considers a compromise. "Maybe a number [or] two, but I go on with my band to close the show—no other way." Meanwhile a telegram from Bechet (the one he might have secretly wanted to play with; they are old rivals, and Louis has not had many such): "Sorry, but unable to come to America. Happy birthday to Louis." Now there is room for Louis's band—even a need. Okay, the band will close the show ("We don't do less than an hour," says Louis), but—without Velma Middleton, the All Stars' singer. Louis can't believe what he hears. Velma has been with him almost uninterruptedly since 1942. He knows the critics find her distasteful. (Many men have problems with fat women, especially if they are attractive. Velma has a pretty face atop her robust 250-pound body, and she's light on her feet. Before she joined Louis, she was a solo turn—singing and dancing. She does a mean split. She also sings nicely, with feeling, and is a perfect foil for Louis's comedy—perfect because she is funny but not ridiculous.) The rationale, of course, is that Ella is on the bill and one female singer should be enough.

Louis has had it by then, and he withdraws behind the tent flap that contains his "private" area. Soon Velma hears the news, and bursts into tears. Louis, who has fantastic ears, hears her crying. Suddenly he appears from behind the flap, wearing nothing but a handkerchief tied around his scalp.

Shouts and alarums. Women shriek, grown men flinch, and everyone scatters to the winds, Louis's curses in their ears. Like an ancient African king, he smites them with his righteous wrath.

A special Newport society dinner party has been arranged, with Louis as guest of honor. (That it would take the place of his only chance to rest before the performance did not occur to the well-bred planners.) Louis does not appear, nor does he play with any act but his own. Velma performs. The show goes down in style; no one not in the know senses anything wrong. At the end of Louis's set, a giant birthday cake is wheeled on stage, and Ella and Johnny Mercer sing "Happy Birthday." Louis has fine manners; he joins in, backing them up on his horn. As Ella cuts the cake, someone (perhaps the producer himself) whispers to Louis that Ory and the other musicians are waiting to come on stage with him for a jam-session finale. "No one hangs on my coattails," says Louis, and intones the national anthem. his band falling in behind him. He doesn't taste his cake. That night, Louis Armstrong didn't eat anything they were dishing out.

The next day, Murray Kempton, then an influential newspaper columnist, who—like so many members of the press—had discovered jazz when Newport became a fashionable media event, wrote a piece attacking Louis for his boorish behavior. His sentiments were echoed by other writers. The musicians knew better. "Some of these people seem to be trying to crucify Pops," said Jack Teagarden.

Louis never bore a grudge. . . . At next year's Newport, he played with the Youth Band (they had rehearsed that afternoon), and Teagarden and Bobby Hackett guested with the All Stars—as those two good friends were always welcome to do. The press was cautiously laudatory.

All this to say that Louis Armstrong was a complex and proud man, who gave his life's work (I should say his calling) everything he had—a reasonable man, but not one to be pushed around, and a tiger when his special people were pushed. And also to say that Louis Armstrong was the greatest musician of his day (which means our time) and one of the greatest entertainers of his day, both things (not contradictory, fashionable esthetics to the contrary notwithstanding) rolled into one. To know Louis was to understand that, and those who knew could find untold joy in hearing, yes, again and again, how he had perfected those same pieces—the way you could tell, from the way he kicked off the opening "Indiana," or even the way he intoned his theme song (written especially for him by a team of black songwriters including the famous actor Clarence Muse, and a thorn in the side of confused liberals), "Sleepy Time Down South," if this was going to be an extraordinary night or just (just!) an ordinary very special one. Every encounter with Louis Armstrong, every note from his horn or vocal cords, was special—from first to last.

So come on in—the show is on!

Louis Armstrong's official, certified jazz-historical fame rests chiefly in his seminal recordings of the 1920s with his small studio groups, variously called Hot Five or Hot Seven or Savoy Ballroom Five. These are supposed to be representative of his work in the mid- to late 1920s, but it is seldom considered that the small groups were strictly studio units, and that from the time he left King Oliver's Creole Jazz Band in 1924 to join Fletcher Henderson, his day-to-day work was with big bands, including his own. The small-group records represent some twenty-five days of his musical life in the years between 1925 and 1929. And not complete days at that, just a few hours before starting the night's work.

The more incongruous, then, that because he ceased to make such small-group records in 1929, he should have been judged to have radically changed his approach to music. The fact is that Louis Armstrong did not head up any working small group until the first All Stars were formed in late 1947. By then, big bands had fallen on evil days economically. Even so, it took all of manager Joe Glaser's persuasive powers to convince Louis to lay off his sixteen men and one woman. He knew that he was their meal ticket, and he was a compassionate man.

The All Stars grew out of some New York concerts in 1947 with hand-picked small groups that were ecstatically received by press and public. According to the scribes, Louis was returning to his proper element. In truth, he was going through a major adjustment. Long accustomed to the role of featured soloist and singer backed by scores devised for a big band, he now found himself playing ensemble lead, as with King Oliver. The music he had played for more than twenty years had moved with the times, and by the mid-'40s was by no means untouched by "modern" tendencies. Not that Louis played bop. But his 1944–45 band featured a young tenor player named Dexter Gordon. The New Orleans revival that was also an aspect of the jazz world of the day had not reflected itself in Louis's music, except when he was featured in a 1946 Hollywood epic called *New Orleans*.

Yet he had never lost his love for the music of his hometown, and the All Stars, at first more or less a swing group, gradually moved toward incorporating traditional pieces into its repertoire. It never became a "Dixieland" band, however. On records, Louis continued to work with groups of all sizes, sometimes with strings, playing current material. If the results became successful sellers, they were incorporated into the All Stars' book. ("Blueberry Hill," for example; or "La Vie en Rose" and "C'est Si Bon.")

The core of the first All Stars was the empathy between Louis and Jack Teagarden, and the superb drumming of Big Sid Catlett, who'd been in Louis's big bands. Earl Hines, with whom Louis had collaborated so excitingly in the late '20s, came aboard for a while, another victim of the declining market for big bands, but he'd been a leader too long to play second fiddle, even to Louis. Teagarden had been a leader, too, and he also left, after some four years. Clarinetist Barney Bigard, from New Orleans, and Duke Ellington, stayed longer, though his style was not ideal for the group.

The All Stars visited Europe for the first time in 1948—Louis hadn't been there since early 1935—and made other long journeys from time to time. But it was not until 1954 that the constant worldwide touring began in earnest. Louis now stood on the threshold of his greatest fame, and 1956 was the year in which he crossed it.

First, there was a tour of Great Britain, where he had not appeared since 1934. The warmth of his reception was overwhelming. The tour climaxed in a typical Armstrong escapade. Performing in London's Empress Hall before an audience including Princess Margaret, he "broke all rules of theatrical protocol," according to the Associated Press report, by acknowledging the presence of a member of the royal family. "We've got one of our special fans in the house," he announced, "and we're really going to lay this one on for the princess." The audience gasped, and the object of Louis's affection applauded enthusiastically. It was further reported that she "started to beat her feet up and down in full view of hundreds" as the All Stars swung into "Clarinet Marmalade"—another breach of protocol. Such things made worldwide news.

It also made news when Louis played in West Berlin and a sizable contingent of fans crossed over from the Eastern sector, including a number of Russians. And it made more news still when, in May, Louis made his first visit to Africa, to what was then still called the Gold Coast, soon to become part of Ghana and already run by Nkrumah. Tens of thousands received the All Stars at Accra airport, and at an outdoor concert, a crowd estimated by *Life* at half a million turned out to hear and see them. Louis was more than pleased to find traces of his ancestry here, and was particularly moved by a dancer who strongly resembled his mother, in features and movement. Black had not yet been officially declared beautiful, but Louis knew.

The All Stars, accompanied by Edward R. Murrow and his CBS-TV crew (shooting the documentary later theatrically released as *Satchmo the Great*), left Accra on May 28. On June 1, they were in Chicago for the concert captured on this album. Billed as "50 Years of Jazz," it was a benefit for the Multiple Sclerosis Society, narrated by Helen Hayes, and "illustrating the development of American jazz from New Orleans to Chicago, New York, Europe and back to America again," according to a contemporary newspaper account.

Louis had little patience with such gimmicks. Basically, he and his band just did their show—a long and full one—with a few token gestures toward the format. Apparently, the concert opened with the band marching through the hall (Medinah Temple) to the strains of "Free as a Bird" and

"Didn't He Ramble" (part of the group's standard repertoire). We pick them up as they reach the stage, playing a single chorus of "The Memphis Blues," pianist Billy Kyle reaching the keyboard *in medias res*. In medley style, "Frankie and Johnny" and "Tiger Rag" follow. Miss Hayes's stilted narration has mercifully been omitted, so what we hear is an unadulterated Armstrong show by what was arguably the best edition of the All Stars.

On board were trombonist Trummy Young, the erstwhile star of the Jimmie Lunceford band, who had joined in 1952. Favored by the critics during his Lunceford days and later when he worked and recorded with Dizzy Gillespie on Fifty-second Street, his playing with Louis often came in for critical knocks as overly emphatic and crude. But Trummy had always been an extroverted, blustery player, and he did what Louis wanted and needed. He soon became Louis's mainstay in the group, musically and personally, and it was a sad day for both men when he left in early 1964 to return to Hawaii, his wife's native state, at her request.

Trummy loved Louis, and understood his role in the band even better than Teagarden had. Like Jack, he also sang and entertained.

Clarinetist Edmond Hall had joined in the summer of 1955. From Louisiana, and just a year younger than Louis, he was a man with his own style and his own mind. He never called Louis by anything but his first name, with a sibilant "s," and referred to him as "Armstrong." That was very much old New Orleans, and so was the Albert system clarinet he favored. He fitted into the band and was an inspired and inventive soloist. But he was restless and quit in 1958, using the band's fixed repertoire as a convenient excuse.

Pianist Billy Kyle had been aboard since 1953. A brilliant stylist (and a favorite of Bud Powell), he also knew a thing or two about arranging, and was a flawless accompanist. He stayed with Louis until, in his fifty-second year, he died on the road in early 1966. During his thirteen years with Louis, no record company offered him a date outside the All Stars—a great pity and a symptom of the benign neglect in which the jazz establishment held Louis's sidemen (Trummy had no offers, either).

Bassist Dale Jones, the least known of these All Stars, was also an old-timer, born in Nebraska in 1902. An early associate of Jack Teagarden, he came to the All Stars in 1951, when Arvell Shaw took a sabbatical, and rejoined from time to time in ensuing years, not willing to stay on the road. A sturdy player, he led his own groups in California and Las Vegas.

Barrett Deems had been billed as "the world's fastest drummer" when he broke into the big time with Joe Venuti's band in 1938, at the age of twenty-four. With Louis from 1954 to 1958, he was a special target of the critics. Being white, he was fair game for white critics, with their prejudices bred of guilt and insecurity. Still active in Chicago in 1980, Deems is a brilliant technician with a firm beat who counts Tony Williams among his fans.

Barrett played loud and strong when Louis wanted it that way, but was a good man with brushes, too—as on "Perdido," Billy Kyle's feature, and, more unexpectedly, on Hall's fiery "Clarinet Marmalade."

As for Louis, he had long since taken to heart King Oliver's advice to play the lead and let a good melody speak for itself. Gone were the striking flights of fancy from the days when, by his own account, he was more interested in impressing "the musicians in the house" than in playing for the public's benefit. With Louis, there was never any doubt about what tune was being played. His majestic phrasing and matchless gift for melodic construction enhanced the most banal material, and when he sang a lyric, the words attained poetic loftiness and weight. (For one example, hear what Louis does with the word "else" in "The Gypsy," a song which he and Charlie Parker were the only jazzmen to favor.)

No wonder Billie Holiday loved him—and not just as a girl. As he became more stylized, more deliberate, so did she. Fittingly, her very last album contains a beautiful version of "Sleepy Time Down South."

A Louis Armstrong show was a masterpiece of pacing. As he says somewhere along the way, "We've got to keep it rolling." Which he did. Changes and contrasts in mood and tempo abound, and the variety of material is astonishing: from "Bucket's Got a Hole in It" to "Tenderly," from "Black and Blue" to "Ko Ko Mo," from "West End Blues" to "You'll Never Walk Alone." About that last tune: played as a medley with "Tenderly," with a strictly New Orleans beat, slow and stately, yet great for dancing (this medley was always a highlight of Louis's dance sets), it is transformed by Louis's respect and artistry from Broadway bathos to true pathos.

As he told a young journalist named David Halberstam, who spent a few days on the road with the All Stars in 1957: "When we hit Savannah we played 'You'll Never Walk Alone' and the whole house—all Negroes—started singing with us on their own. We ran through two choruses and they kept with us and later they asked for it again. Most touching damn thing I ever saw. I almost started crying right there on stage. We really hit something inside each person there."

(Louis had a way of "hitting something" inside people. At Newport in 1958, I was listening to Louis's set with James Baldwin. As always, Louis concluded with the National Anthem. It was early in the morning—the show had run very late—and the music carried beautifully in the damp air. The crowd had roared for more, but now they were still. After Louis's final golden note had faded, Baldwin turned and said: "You know, that's the first time I've liked that song.")

Forget all the nonsense about this or that stage of Louis, about commercialism and redundancy, and hear Louis Armstrong imbue each note he plays with the essence of music and life. Hear his ensemble variations in the several da capo sections of "Bucket's Got a Hole in It" (in perhaps its best versions ever here) and hear a master of the blues, and of spontaneous, amazing invention. Never mind that his "West End Blues" doesn't (couldn't, and shouldn't be expected to) measure up to the 1928 version. Never mind the brief confusion on "Manhattan," put in strictly for this concert. But do hear Louis's lead and solo on "Struttin' with Some Barbecue," hear the background riffs and obbligati (how about "That's My Desire"?) he fashions throughout, and hear how he knows to build to a climax.

And since it comes last, hear him take "Ko Ko Mo" from Harlem through the Caribbean to Africa, quoting "The Peanut Vendor" and singing the blues, free as a soaring bird. Then you'll hear the father of all that is good and great in this music called jazz, one of nature's true noblemen, and one reason why this sad, monstrous century will be remembered well.

And then, listen to some more Louis Armstrong music. I've been doing that for more than thirty-five years, and I still discover new and magic things about the mystery of Louis Daniel Armstrong.

(1980)

Satchmo and the Critics

Now that Louis Armstrong has achieved the iconic stature he deserves, it seems passing strange to recall the days when Satchmo was not just fair game for the critics, but when his relationship with them resembled the fox and the hounds. The attitude, rooted in the fallacy that Louis had sold his birthright of "authentic" blues and stomps for Tin Pan Alley pottage (the contempt in which most jazz critics once held the Great American Songbook is another fascinating subject), can be traced back to the '30s, when the great man's recordings as a leader changed from small to big bands and his recorded repertory stressed popular songs. In truth, Louis had from the very start of his musical activities sung and played all manner of music, and even when he was featured on records with his Hot Fives and Sevens in the 1920s, his bread-and-butter work was with large ensembles. The critics had, of course, routinely complained about the poor quality of Louis's big bands, and they were indeed unanimous in cheering the advent of the Armstrong All Stars, born in 1947. But the honeymoon was brief, and by mid-1950, when the jazz world was about to celebrate Louis's fiftieth birthday, or what he and the rest of the world thought was his fiftieth, George Simon, editor of *Metronome* (a magazine as important at that time as *Down Beat*), found it necessary to construct his tribute around the theme of disrespectful criticism. Typically, Simon (who, at the time of his death this past February, was the dean of jazz critics) was conciliatory in tone: "To belittle his playing today is like minimizing the impact of, say, Lincoln's Gettysburg address because it wasn't delivered in *Time* magazine's terse, modern, unemotional style. To some, Louis Armstrong may appear old-fashioned, but to many of us he is the man who set the fashion in jazz, who gave it warmth and musical stature, and who made it possible for jazz to go ahead as far and as handsomely as it has." He also noted the irony of a birthday celebration being planned at Bop City, the nightclub where the Armstrong All Stars were currently in session. (Armstrong was the only attraction to fill the cavernous space of the club, which soon folded.)

Let's modulate to 1956, a key year in Armstrong's career, the one in which he first visited Africa, where he received a tremendous reception; in which he had perhaps his best film role, in *High Society*, with Crosby and Sinatra (and Grace Kelly, whom he absolutely charmed); and in which he was featured on television in Edward R. Murrow's *Satchmo the Great*. He had already been dubbed "Ambassador Satch," and the All Stars were, by a long shot, the highest-paid (and hardest-working) jazz attraction. But success has never sat well with critics.

When the All Stars appeared at the Newport Jazz Festival, then in its third year, here's what Jack Tracy, editor of *Down Beat*, had to say: "Too much Louis . . . marked the second night . . . the only reign to fall [it had poured the night before] was that of King Louis Armstrong. He demonstrated with finality that it takes more than rolling eyes, handkerchief on head and chops, and the same old Paramount theater act to warrant using an hour's time at an American festival of jazz." Tracy mentioned flashes of "the majestic tone and ingrained feeling that has made him an undeniable great in jazz," but thought they came too seldom. Armstrong, he complained, was playing "the same old tunes and fronting the same indifferent band he's been working with for too long." His "appearance seemed commonplace . . . an insult to an audience that was there to hear the best from everyone."

Hindsight, provided by Columbia Records, which issued part of Armstrong's set on an LP, reveals just how insulted the audience was, roaring its approval when Louis announces "Mack the Knife," which at the time he had not been playing for very long. We also get to hear the "Indiana," on which Tracy found "Louis running into some difficulty on his solo which he barely works his way out of "—utter nonsense.

Tracy's tone and content didn't arouse much response on this side of the pond, but it was also printed in Britain's *Melody Maker*, where Max Jones and Sinclair Traill suggested it was possibly an example of modernist bias (they also defended drummer Barrett Deems, the critics' favorite All Star whipping boy). Tracy responded with "strenuous objections" to their "ridiculous assertions," but the two Brits had the last word, asking if Tracy knew "of a better small group playing hot jazz today." (This "indifferent" edition of the All Stars had Trummy Young, Ed Hall, and Billy Kyle; it was my favorite lineup, with the Teagarden-Catlett band a close second.)

But Tracy (a nice man who went on to produce some of Woody Herman's best LPs) was not alone. Here, still in the same year, is the present dean of jazz critics (like Tracy, no longer active), the *New York Times'* John S. Wilson, on the occasion of the first ever jazz concert at New York's thirty-nine-year-old Lewisohn Stadium, the one where Louis and the All Stars joined Leonard Bernstein and the New York Philharmonic in the grandiose "symphonic" arrangement of "St. Louis Blues" captured in *Satchmo the Great:* "[This collaboration] was a welcome event for those who had gone to the stadium in hopes of hearing Mr. Armstrong play with some suggestion of the jazz artistry of which he is capable. His solo . . . was movingly expressed and beautifully developed . . . a refreshing change from the Armstrong performances that have been heard here recently . . . [and were limited] to repetitions of a program that rarely varies." Wilson acknowledges that the audience responded enthusiastically "and even made a brief attempt to dance in the aisles." But, undeterred, he goes on to say that "it is somewhat disturbing to realize that the Armstrong group's performances are being seen all over the world and are widely publicized as outstanding examples of the propaganda value of American jazz. . . . Except for occasional instances, it would be misleading if the antics of Mr. Armstrong and his colleagues were to be accepted as representative of well-played jazz."

I've quoted Wilson at length because his review is such a clearly stated position (unusual in the amount of editorializing) of the mind-set that reveals a deep-seated dichotomy between art and entertainment that, in the case of Armstrong, was prevalent.

To Louis, this was a no-brainer. And to musicians who appreciated him, this dichotomy was nonexistent. In 1964, the great Chicago tenorman Bud Freeman, nurtured on Armstrong, whom he first encountered at the Lincoln Gardens with King Oliver, said that "to me, Louis swings more telling a joke than most others do playing a horn." In that same year, Ann Baker, who'd sung with Louis's big band, was present when the All Stars performed in West Virginia, bringing the house down, as always. She hadn't seen Louis in years and was moved to tears when he introduced her. Afterward, she told a reporter: "You don't know how great he really is until you've worked with him."

For me, reading stuff like the Wilson piece and worse brought me closer and closer to finally deciding that I should write about jazz and become part of a breed from which I felt profoundly alienated. There wasn't much else to be done when you had to put up with such Wilson comments as this, concerning a Brooklyn Academy of Music concert: "All things considered, it scarcely seems proper to book Mr. Armstrong's group in a jazz series such as the Academy is offering. For this troupe is less a jazz band than an 'attraction' and, as such, its appeal—which is undeniable—is primarily to people who have little, if any, interest in jazz."

Of course there were exceptions. Leonard Feather, no paragon of critical virtue, was always a staunch defender of Louis, who had befriended him long ago. In 1959, for instance, he complained about "musicians and fans [who] tend to be condescending and supercilious about a man who has done more for jazz and, in his oblique way, more for brotherhood than any of those who have belittled him." But even he complained about "crude humor" (clearly there were no Redd Foxx fans among white critics) and "insensitivity" to the contemporary psyche. Martin Williams was another who could see how much Armstrong still had to offer and often praised the man's trumpeting. But Martin had a blind spot for his marvelous singing, hearing it as "one-sided" and filled with "surface geniality, like his stage manner." He even went so far as to say, in 1964, that Louis "has learned, like many jazzmen of all schools, how to coast and shuck his way through several nights." Coasting was something Louis was absolutely, constitutionally incapable of doing—even when he was exhausted and unwell.

The general press was usually more aware of the virtues of the Armstrong All Stars, but even here there were exceptions, often from those endangered by the little knowledge they had of jazz. One such was the much admired Murray Kempton, whose reporting of an incident at the 1957 Newport Jazz Festival was bizarre. He led off his column with a dire prediction: "Louis Armstrong, jazz's greatest figure, is unlikely ever to be asked to appear at [Newport], the major showcase of the medium he helped so much to raise to international stature. The 57-year-old master tore the patience of his hosts to shreds . . . by turning what had been planned as a sentimental birthday party for him into a massive display of the sulks." Kempton misreported almost everything that had led to Armstrong's fully justified decision not to serve as anchorman for a parade of performers at the expense of his own group's self-respect. Kempton described him as "insecure, infrequently happy, in constant need for reassurance as to his stature . . . reluctant to learn new things or even to revive all but the most familiar of the old, jealous of his billing, and distrustful of his juniors. The mask of the clown is only a mask." (It just occurred to me that

Kempton wrote the script for James L. Collier's odious biography.) The term "hosts" is nice—Louis's band had not been invited to a party. It had a gig to play and had just come from one of hundreds like it. And of course, their "hosts" had him back next year.

Kempton wasn't the only one to dump on Louis, who, as always when he was angry, played superbly that night. His old friend Jack Teagarden, who like this writer was there, said, "It seems like they want to crucify Pops." But like the many scribes and fellow performers who jumped on Louis when he attacked Faubus and Eisenhower and predicted that he had jeopardized his career, they had to eat their words.

To the man himself, all such things were of little import, especially the barbs of critics. "A note or a good tune will always be appreciated if you play it right," he said in his sixties. "I appreciate all kinds of music and play all kinds. I don't think musicians should type themselves. . . . If you perform, you're going to have your ups and downs, but what is said about you, good or bad, is forgotten tomorrow. That's how fast our America is."

Right, dear Louis. But not so fast that what you've left us will ever be forgotten.

(2001)

V.S.O.P.

In this age of violated words, when even toothpaste is claimed to be "created," it no longer means very much to call an artist a genius. Especially not on album liner notes, where geniuses are spawned with alarming frequency.

The semantic fog that thus obscures meaning is symptomatic, the handmaiden of beclouded comprehension, of the inability (sustained) to see the present and the recent past in proper perspective. In the case of the music we call jazz, a consensus of so-called informed opinion would confirm that Louis Armstrong is the single most significant and influential creative artist in its brief but substantial history.

Such acknowledgment, however, unfortunately does not represent a true understanding of Armstrong's contribution, which has been thoroughly fragmented by a variety of nitpickers—critics and historians and journalists and even musicians—who have brought to their investigations of Armstrong's art an entirely irrelevant set of criteria.

Even as learned and insightful a student of jazz as Gunther Schuller, in his monumental *Early Jazz: Its History and Development*, concludes his first-rate chapter on Armstrong in the 1920s with a summation that reveals gross misconceptions of the subject.

In early 1929, you see, Armstrong abandoned the small-group format within which he had done most of his important recording work and began to work only with big bands. (In fact, he had been doing so *off records* since 1925; the small bands were recording units only.) By the peculiar standards of jazz criticism, there is (save Ellington) something intrinsically superior about small groups as opposed to larger ensembles. Furthermore, Armstrong committed a second unpardonable sin. He gradually shifted his repertoire toward popular tunes of the day, which by some standards are considered inferior to traditional jazz pieces and originals. And to compound the felony, he began to feature his singing more prominently.

Thus, Schuller can say in speaking of Armstrong's work in the '30s: "The records of the next decade, though numerous and commercially successful, added nothing to Armstrong's stature as one of jazz's greatest innovators and musical giants. . . . His conceptions . . . became set and firmly embedded in his mind and lip . . . through constant repetition and the elimination of all but sure-fire formulas."

Though he singles out a few performances as surmounting this evaluation (among them, the second "Stardust" and "Between the Devil and the Deep Blue Sea" on this album), Schuller has fallen squarely into the trap dug by thirty years of nonsense. Perhaps the reissue of Armstrong masterpieces of the early '30s begun with this album (backed with later works from the decade available on other labels) will serve to scatter the fog, since the music speaks for itself. In view, however, of the absurd review of a recent Armstrong reissue that appeared in the *New York Times*, this is a feeble hope.

In fact, Armstrong's mastery of his instrument *and* musical imagination continued to grow, far beyond the threshold of the '30s, and what we encounter here is jazz's first and greatest virtuoso and master improviser in the process of flowering and self-discovery. The ease with which he executes some of the most fantastic instrumental passages in the history of music is unparalleled, and it is far removed from mere virtuosity in its wedding of technique to uncanny musical and rhythmic sensitivity.

There are, of course, passages that *are* sheer bravura. And why not? All virtuosos, from Liszt and Paganini to Kreisler and Rubinstein have indulged themselves in such celebrations of skill for skill's sake, for art is by nature playful and takes joy in flexing its muscles. There are, too, musical shortcomings in the accompaniments. Again, why not? Plato to the contrary notwithstanding, art and ideal standards of perfection are by no means synonymous; especially not in functional art, art created not for its own sake and as its own end-all and be-all, but for the sake of entertainment, and in the cases here on exhibit, for the sake of selling records.

Perish the thought, eh? Well, one could make a good case for high art as "entertainment" in almost any time until the nineteenth century. We haven't time for elucidation here, but Shakespeare was concerned with getting people to come to the Globe Theatre, and Bach was supposed to get the congregation to church, etc., etc.

At the time Louis Armstrong made these records, there were very few people—aside from himself and those he had inspired—who had any notion at all that jazz was an art and the great jazz musicians artists. They were performers, entertainers making their way in life playing for people to dance. Louis made them listen.

The band heard with Louis on these selections was really the first big band of his own he'd fronted. (The ones he'd worked with previously were led by Carroll Dickerson, Luis Russell, Les Hite, and other men.) It was a relatively small band—ten pieces, including Louis himself—and it contained a goodly number of the leader's "landsmen": cats from good old New Orleans.

Among these were three members of the powerful rhythm section: pianist Charlie Alexander, who'd worked with Johnny Dodds; bassist John Lindsay, already a seasoned veteran, six years Louis's senior, known for his work with Freddie Keppard, King Oliver, and Jelly Roll Morton; and drummer Tubby Hall, who played in the tradition of his great predecessors with Louis, Baby Dodds and Zutty Singleton.

Also from New Orleans was trombonist Preston Jackson, not featured much but a good, solid man. The others were from, or had worked in, the second great jazz center, Chicago. Trumpeter Zilner Randolph had been touring the West with such bands as Bernie Young's, and was Louis's arranger and musical director. Guitarist Mike McKendrick (discographies notwithstanding, he plays guitar here, not banjo—probably a metal guitar with a resonator and special strings) was the "straw boss," i.e., chief disciplinarian and organizer, a role he would fill again for Louis in 1933. He was a big man with a powerful beat.

Of the saxophonists, tenorist Al Washington is most prominently featured. He later worked in Chicago with Richard M. Jones and various other bands that in today's parlance would be classified as rhythm-and-blues. George James, who led the section on alto, later worked with such bands as Benny Carter's, Lucky Millinder's, and Teddy Wilson's. Lester Boone, the second alto man, had been with Earl Hines, Al Wynn, and other good bands; he later settled in New York and is still active in Brooklyn at this writing.

Then as today, a leader didn't exactly have his pick of men to take out "on the road" with a band, and Louis's was a working and traveling band.

The men must have been chosen well, for the band remained together without a personnel change for more than a year, until Louis broke it up to make his first trip abroad, to England in 1932.

By today's stringent standards, the band's Guy Lombardo–patterned sax section sounds dated, but then the Lombardo "moan" was the first wholly identifiable sax-section sound in popular music, and Louis liked it. Randolph was a good arranger, and many of his charts wear their years well. The task of writing for (and playing in) a band led by Louis Armstrong was not routine and could not lean heavily on other models. The band was there to back Louis, to set him off well; the rest was immaterial. Randolph did this musically and sympathetically, and the rhythm section always swung, with Lindsay particularly good and prominent. Riffs were developed to a fine art, and Louis certainly doesn't seem uncomfortable. At times, when the going gets heavy, he unabashedly exhorts the players (as on "Love, You Funny Thing": "Come on, saxophones . . . bring it on out there!").

Such comments were left in the record; had anyone else acted so spontaneously when a "master" was being made, it would certainly have been scrapped, but Louis's informality had already become established procedure. At any rate, many years later Louis himself referred to this band as the happiest he ever led, and the evidence bears him out.

A word about the material: Many of these songs were introduced into the jazz repertoire through these recordings and went on to become standards. Others were already established pieces ("Home," "Tiger Rag," "Stardust"), while others yet were hits of the day that did not survive as jazz pieces ("Love, You Funny Thing"; "Kickin' the Gong Around"). In all cases, the Armstrong treatment is definitive—comparison of his "Lawd, You Made the Night Too Long" with, for example, Bing Crosby's, is interesting.

Take "Stardust." Written in 1927, it had already been recorded in "jazzy" versions by Hoagy Carmichael himself, McKinney's Cotton Pickers, Fletcher Henderson, and a studio group including Pee Wee Russell and Jimmy Dorsey. But Louis's treatment of the song gave it further definition. (Years later, Carmichael searched for the rare alternate take on which Louis repeats the words "Oh, memory" three times, because he liked it so much.)

Both takes are presented here (the rumored existence of a third master, supposedly issued on Italian Parlophone, has not been confirmed; it was scheduled for this album, in keeping with the concept of reissuing all known alternate takes in the Armstrong series, but could not be found).

The two versions bear close study, which will reveal how absurd Schuller's proposition about "set" playing really is. There is a pattern, of course—Armstrong's sense of form and proportion is infallible, and when he works out a framework for a piece, he sticks to the outline. But there is no end of variability within this framework, not just in nuance, but in overall design. It's Louis all the way, excepting the pickup for his vocal and the backdrop for the instrumental passages, which consists entirely of ensemble chords. The opening trumpet solo is already a very sophisticated paraphrase of the melody; the concluding solo is pure improvisation on the melody and the changes. Both vocals are gems; in his singing, Louis perfectly mirrors the subtle inflections and rhythmic shifts of his trumpet playing; in addition, his wholly engaging personal ambience is transmitted with immediacy.

Most of the time, Louis plays open trumpet, letting his ravishing sound flow unencumbered. But two masterpieces contain muted gems: "All of Me" and "Between the Devil and the Deep Blue Sea." The only mute (there are many kinds) Louis ever uses, then as now, is a straight mute—the type that least alters the trumpet's natural sound. On "Devil," after the vocal, he plays a full chorus muted, incredibly subtle and "modern"—there are Charlie Parker phrases here—then removes the mute in midstream for the climax.

The two versions of this piece, to me, are even more rewarding as studies in comparison than the "Stardusts." The second, rarer take is a bit slower in tempo, and the muted solo even more poised. On "All of Me," his muted opening solo employs double time in a manner then far beyond the grasp of others, and the last six bars of the solo (the saxes finish the chorus) are a forecast of Lester Young. The vocal is perhaps one of Louis's greatest.

But such opinions are of the moment; certainly, it is closely rivaled by "Love, You Funny Thing." This is a perfect example of Louis's ability to transform the rather tawdry sentiments of a typical pop-song lyric into genuine emotion. His embracing of the song makes it beautiful. Please don't miss the trumpet bridge in the final chorus, with its unusual multiplicity of notes and that startling glissando to an even more startling high note—as complex and abstract a piece of musical design as you will find in jazz of any vintage.

"Home" would scarcely be considered a jazzman's first choice (only Jack Teagarden, to my knowledge, has followed in Louis's footsteps in this case), but the treatment makes it seem ideal. This is a good arrangement, opening with a few fast bars of "There's No Place Like Home" before the rubato piano interlude brings on Louis, vocalizing in slow tempo. Again, he makes a trite lyric believable—perhaps because he approaches it in the best of faith. Dig his emphatic delivery of the first word—it assures undivided attention for what follows. In the bridge, an object lesson in what Louis does with the time can be gleaned by listening to the saxophones playing the melody in the background, straight and on the beat. The cadenza, starting with stop-time breaks, is glorious.

"I Got Rhythm," little more than two years old at the time, was the first example of a big-band tradition kept alive to this day by Duke Ellington in "Jam with Sam." On it, Louis introduces all the members of his band by name as they take short solos. This is preceded by some Armstrong patter in a mock-serious manner. The tempo kicks (fine work by the rhythm section), and when Louis picks up the horn, the band joins in, playing in a polyphonic ensemble style redolent of, but quite different from, old New Orleans. Louis combines a freestyle lead part with unfettered soloing in a remarkable way, *improvising* in the truest sense of the word. The gag ending is just that—for laughs, and it will take you by surprise.

"Kickin' the Gong Around," not quite as memorable an effort by Arlen and Koehler as "Devil and the Deep Blue Sea," is one of those opium ditties brought on by "Minnie the Moocher." Minnie herself, in fact, is the object of the singer's search in Chinatown after dark. If nothing else, it proves that drug songs aren't particularly new (there's a treasury of pot songs from the '30s, kiddies), and the lyrics almost break up Louis at one point. The trumpet work also reflects his high good humor that day.

"Georgia on My Mind" shows that Ray Charles was not the first to bring soul to this Hoagy Carmichael classic. There's a bit more arrangement and less trumpet solo work than customary, and the verse is played twice. (Today, the verses to popular songs are hardly ever sung or played; most of the newer songs don't even have any. Here, they appear quite often, as on "Devil" and "Keepin' Out of Mischief Now.") George James's sweet alto quotes from "Rustles of Spring" in the coda, after the sudden change in time and tempo. Note here the difference in the sound of the ensemble when Louis joins in. Washington's tenor is worth a listen.

Even more arranged and less soloistic is "You Can Depend on Me," a fine song. Louis leads the brasses, or rather the whole band, which plays as a choir, not in sections. This chart already has a swing-era flavor, not least in the concluding passages, where Lindsay's bass comes into focus. Randolph's obbligato to the vocal is idiomatic.

"The Lonesome Road," made the following day, had in the studio audience the composers of "You Can Depend on Me," introduced by Louis among the members of his impromptu congregation as "two little songwriters, Louis Dunlap and Charles Carpenter." The reference to their "smoking a Louis Armstrong Special Cigar" is not a euphemism for something other, but the *Ding an sich*, as the German philosophers say. There was indeed such a brand of cigar—it was a by-product of Louis's triumphant return to his hometown earlier that year. The reception he was given, one can safely say, was a first in the history of the American Negro. The first night he played in town, at a prominent nightspot, ten thousand black New Orleanians lined the levee to catch the sound of his golden horn, and there was a network radio spot during his stay, contributing greatly to the increase of his nationwide popularity.

"The Lonesome Road" is comedy, and there are some who take offense at that sort of thing. For them, the beauty of Louis's half chorus, emerging suddenly from the levity of this mock revival meeting, should have redemptive power. The rest of us may laugh with Louis as he takes up a collection to get his shoes out of pawn in his best Bert Williams manner.

Another kind of showmanship is displayed on "Tiger Rag," which was Louis's second waxing of this already venerable display piece. He introduces it as "a little novelty," but takes it far beyond this category in eight solo choruses of fireworks, including interpolations from everything from "Singing in the Rain" and "Stars and Stripes Forever" to *Pagliacci*. The practice of "quoting" is frowned upon by the higher estheticians of jazz, but they would probably dismiss the entire piece as "grandstanding." In point of fact, Louis was taking it easy; at the time, he was fond of serving up several hundred (literally) high C's on "Tiger Rag" at in-person performances, "for the musicians in the house."

"Chinatown, My Chinatown" was also a favorite display piece for Louis in that period, another "little novelty." It takes the form of a "battle" (or rather, a race) between the trumpet and the saxophones, and guess who is the winner? During his patter, Louis has a conversation with his trumpet, which he calls "a little devil." Amiable nonsense, you may think—and yet, also a touching glimpse of the enormous pleasure Louis derived from playing his horn, and of his love for it. Musically, they were indeed one and the same, as the series of four astonishing choruses here well proves. Pay attention to what Louis does with one note in the second chorus, and study the first for a supreme example of relaxed playing at fast tempo—another of Louis's inventions.

By contrast, "Keepin' Out of Mischief Now" is restrained. The arrangement again plays a considerable role, but there is a mellow vocal. And after George James's convoluted alto solo, we have the pleasure of hearing Louis in four-bar exchanges with tenorist Washington. (The Fats Waller tune, by the way, is not of regular pop-song construction and has only 20 bars rather than the customary 32.) At the end, Louis plays over as well as in the ensemble, and tosses off a lovely solo passage for good measure.

"Lawd, You Made the Night Too Long," one of those pseudo-ethnic songs of plight, was very popular in its day; so popular, in fact, that it gave rise to a parody, entitled "Sam, You Made the Pants Too Long." But again, Louis takes the song at face value and transmutes it. The opening trumpet work here carries echoes of the classic "Tight Like That." The impassioned vocal is enhanced by Louis's pronunciation of the word "earth" in his best New Orleans manner (surprisingly similar to Brooklynese). There is a breathtaking trumpet break in the final chorus, and the brief cadenza is masterly.

Well, there you have it: a choice sixteen; some gems from the Armstrong collection. It is good to have them on display once again, one hopes permanently. One of the biggest drawbacks to a clear perspective on jazz is the general unavailability of the jazz heritage in sound. To be sure, what was recorded is but a glimpse, but even a glimpse of the truth is illuminating. Never mind the occasional imperfection of the settings; the essence is the thing. And what an essence!

(1969)

Review of *Louis Armstrong: An American Genius* by James Lincoln Collier

In spite of its promising title, this critical biography is a deliberate attempt to overthrow the established view of Armstrong. In his preface, the author states that "much of what [has] been published about Armstrong was simply a rehash of the old myths," and some of it "sheer fiction. . . . The body of reliable writing about [him] was surprisingly small."

It is true that book-length studies of the most influential (and arguably the greatest) of all jazz musicians are few in number and less than scholarly in approach. The earliest, Armstrong's own *Swing That Music* (1936; the first biography of a black jazz figure), was heavily ghosted. Next came *Satchmo: My Life in New Orleans* (1954; the first installment of a full autobiography on which Armstrong continued work throughout his remaining years; the fate of the manuscript is unknown). This was definitely by Armstrong himself, if somewhat pedantically edited, and Collier's attitude toward it is revealing. He states that Armstrong "probably" wrote it "in the main," though no one acquainted with Armstrong's writing can doubt that the voice is authentic, and also claims that the book is "unreliable." He quotes much more extensively from Richard Meryman's *Louis Armstrong: A Self-Portrait*, published in 1971 and based on an extensive interview in *Life*. While often revealing, this little book contains frequent mishearings and garblings of Armstrong's transcribed spoken words. Hugues Panassié's *Louis Armstrong*, published in France in 1969 and in English translation two years later, contains much valuable information about the recorded works but can be regarded as idolatrous. Max Jones and John Chilton's *Louis*, published in 1971, is journalistic and not well organized, but contains many interesting facts, prodigious quotes from its subject, and an excellent essay on Armstrong the musician by Chilton, a professional trumpeter. One must agree with Collier that Robert Goffin's *Horn of Plenty* (1947) is fiction rather than biography. There are several Armstrong biographies for the juvenile market (a field in which Collier has been active), but these are of little significance.

Some of the best writing on Armstrong's music, however, is contained in more general works, notably Gunther Schuller's *Early Jazz*, Martin Williams's *The Jazz Tradition*, André Hodeir's *Jazz: Its Evolution and Essence*, and Humphrey Lyttleton's *The Best of Jazz*. While Collier analyzes Armstrong's playing at some length, it can fairly be said that he adds nothing to what can be learned from these sources.

But then, musical analysis is not the focal point of Collier's book, which is biography first and foremost. As such, does it tell us anything new? Collier has organized and presented his considerable research well and gives a detailed account of Armstrong's life and career, bringing together many facts and minutiae hitherto scattered among numerous sources. In this he has performed a valuable service. Unfortunately, he also insists on psychoanalyzing Armstrong at every turn.

In that respect his ideas are decidedly novel. Early on, he tells us that Armstrong was "clearly afflicted with deep and well-entrenched insecurity, a sense of his own worthlessness so thoroughly fixed that he was never to shake it off." Further, Armstrong was driven by an "insatiable, visceral lust [*sic*]" for applause, and eventually applause became the only balm that could "quench that relentless, sickening interior assault on his self-respect," and, if only for the moment, push "away the feeling that nobody liked him, that he was basically no good."

Strong stuff, more from Adler than from Freud, and a view of one of the most beloved men of our age that is, to say the least, bewildering. If accurate, it would make Armstrong one of the most successful dissemblers in history—a man who craftily managed to hide his true, stunted self not just from the world at large but also from those closest to him. (As if to guard against any nagging doubts, Collier insists that Armstrong had no "truly" close friends.)

To this reader, who knew Armstrong personally and professionally for some twenty-four years, this interpretation of his personality (Collier trots out every cliché regarding absent fathers and neglectful mothers a fan of *Psychology Today* could ask for) seems absurd. But like any writer possessed by a preconception, Collier selects his "facts" to fit the model. Thus he gives us liberal doses of "insights" from Marshall Brown, who for a few days occupied a dressing room adjacent to Armstrong's and only worked with him for a few hours, but fails to consult such close associates as Trummy Young, Armstrong's right arm for twelve years, or bassist Arvell Shaw, whose long tenure with Armstrong, starting with the last big band and stretching over two decades, he totally ignores. And, convinced that Armstrong had no real friends, he didn't bother to look for putative ones.

On the other hand, he presents the negative comments of such New Orleans contemporaries as Pops Foster (whose reliability may be gauged from his straight-faced claim that Jelly Roll Morton employed a second pianist on his solo recordings because he had a weak left hand) and Zutty Singleton, with whom Armstrong had a lifelong, complex relationship. Collier makes much of the conflicts between these proud, stubborn men as seen from Singleton and his wife's point of view. Clearly, Collier has no understanding of the peculiar ways of elder New Orleans musicians.

Collier's relentless pursuit of his slanted view of Armstrong frequently overwhelms his sense of reality. A revealing example on which I must dwell at some length is his surreal interpretation of the recording sessions made by Armstrong and his band for Victor in January and April of 1933. Twelve sides were cut over a three-day period in January; a further two on April 24 and 26. To Collier, this level of output is evidence that Armstrong was "held in contempt" by "the white men who were overseeing his career," in particular manager Johnny Collins. "It is doubtful," Collier claims, "that any important show-business figure, much less a major artist, has ever been so driven like a pack mule as Armstrong was at this time." Characteristically, he adds that Armstrong "of course should have stood up to Collins."

Collins was indeed an unsavory man, as has been well documented by others, including Armstrong himself, who eventually fired him. But it is nonsense to present these recording sessions as paradigmatic of Collins and others being "callous to [Armstrong's] needs to the point of cruelty." There was nothing unusual about marathon recording sessions, which were scheduled when performers were available in cities with studio facilities; since prolonged touring was part and parcel of any band's working life, the most was made of such opportunities. The all-time record for a single day's jazz output in a studio is held by Benny Goodman, whose band, on June 6, 1935, cut fifty-one tunes—for which the sidemen were paid the munificent sum of one dollar per song!

Having set the stage with such misleading melodramatics, Collier must now find supporting evidence in the records themselves. Of "Dusky Stevedore" he hallucinates that Armstrong "barely gets through" the performance "at all," though that record is filled with trumpet pyrotechnics. Here and elsewhere, a problem seems to be that Collier mishears Armstrong's imaginative use of space and his stretching or contracting of the time values of notes—stylistic traits especially in evidence at this period—for pauses caused by the need to rest sore lips. Thus he says about "Son of the South" that "Armstrong leaves gaps after each high note . . . to steal a couple of seconds rest," and elsewhere in his comments on these records points to "thin" tone and "faltering upper register." Trumpeter-critic John Chilton, however, has this to say about "Son of the South": "A master of the unexpected, [Armstrong] unites stamina and skill . . . again takes the first trumpet part [Collier fails to state, or cannot hear, that Armstrong plays lead in addition to solo on most of these discs] and tops a fine performance with a spine-tingling coda." Listening to these sessions, Collier works himself up to the point of tears as he fancies how Armstrong "was jamming the sharp circle of steel of the mouthpiece deep into the flesh of his lips to give them enough support to reach the high notes." Collier, a trombonist, at least ought to know that mouthpieces are made of brass.

Collier further imagines that for these sessions, "Victor supplied Armstrong with commercial rubbish: mediocre pop tunes, nonsensical jive songs, and worse," the "worse" being one of Collier's pet peeves—what he chooses to call "coon songs." (In this instance, one such is Hoagy Carmichael's "Snow Ball," also recorded by that notorious Uncle Tom, Paul Robeson.) The "mediocre pop songs" include two brand-new Harold Arlen pieces, which these recordings helped make jazz standards ("I've Got a Right to Sing the Blues" and "World on a String"), and a couple of more-than-decent tunes of the day. Almost all the other material is the work of black songwriters and composers, such as "St. Louis Blues," "Mahogany Hall Stomp," and "Basin Street Blues" (the latter an Armstrong masterpiece which Collier inexplicably fails to mention); two songs written especially for Armstrong by the noted Anglo-African composer-arranger Reginald Foresythe ("Son of the South" and "Mississippi Basin"); and other special Armstrong material, including "Laughing Louis," to Collier no doubt a "nonsensical jive song," to others, like Stanley Crouch and this reviewer, a magical performance that must have mystified the Victor executives as much as it does Collier, who evades it. (In any case, humor is not Collier's strong suit, a handicap when it comes to Armstrong.) He does pounce on "Don't You Play Me Cheap," but this was written by the drummer in the band, Harry Dial, and recorded by Armstrong as a favor to him. And does Collier really assume that the "viper's chorus" on "Sweet Sue" was mandated by white exploiters?

The incontrovertible fact is that Victor, Collins, et al. had little or nothing to do with choosing this repertory, which was intrinsic to Armstrong and his band, and that the flaws Collier hears in the trumpet playing on these records simply do not exist—esthetic judgments aside.

Collier's incessant harping on Armstrong's presumed failings as a man result in tainting even the praise he frequently (and sometimes fulsomely) heaps on Armstrong's music. He is at home with the Hot Five and Hot

Seven series and other works from the 1920s, but finds the mature Armstrong solo style less to his liking. *De gustibus non est disputandum*, but it is peculiar that Collier fails to see that Armstrong's solo architecture and sense of the dramatic stem straight from nineteenth-century vocal traditions, notably Italian grand opera—which also influenced Sidney Bechet. Approval is not required; understanding is.

By the time Collier arrives at Armstrong's post-1946 music, he is as exhausted as he perceives Armstrong to have been on those 1933 sessions. He identifies a few highlights, such as the superb 1957–58 *Autobiography* dates, but omits mention of the significant collaborations with Duke Ellington, Ella Fitzgerald, and the Dukes of Dixieland, among others. His avoidance of the Fitzgerald albums might well be deliberate, since the superior quality of the repertory (the cream of American popular song) and the excellent production values (notably the luxurious original edition of *Porgy and Bess*) contradict his claim that unworthy and/or redundant material and shoddy production marred Armstrong's later recorded work. Since Collier quite clearly comes to the later Armstrong as an outsider, he can't be blamed for merely having skimmed through the enormous recorded output of the All Stars, which he nevertheless dismisses rather cavalierly. He is also puzzled by the great success of the All Star format in live performance, and one cannot avoid the suspicion that he never witnessed one himself—or never encountered Armstrong in the flesh.

Among the many gaffes in the text is the resurrection of the old canard that Don Redman composed the verse to Carmichael's "Stardust." To add spice to the opening of his Chicago chapter, Collier would have us believe that the white clarinetist Don Murray was beaten to death in that city for having associated with a gangster's moll. Murray, of course, died in Los Angeles, after a fall from the running board of a friend's car. Minor errors often are caused by lack of proper background knowledge: Armstrong did not switch from the OKeh label to Victor due to a dispute with Tommy Rockwell, but because OKeh was going bankrupt; the band that made the *Medley of Armstrong Hits* was not "a pickup group, hastily put together," but the pit band of the Philadelphia theater where Armstrong was appearing when making the record; and he recorded with Chick Webb's band in 1932 during a joint tour with *Hot Chocolates*. For dramatic effect, Collier states that Armstrong and Zutty Singleton never worked together again after their 1930 parting, but they recorded in 1946, the year they also appeared in the film *New Orleans* (which Collier inexplicably claims starred Bing Crosby).

Technically, Collier seems no more secure. Reams of conjecture concerning embouchure problems rest in the main on wisdom gleaned from the aforementioned Marshall Brown. It is astonishing that, as a brass player,

Collier mislabels Armstrong's frequent use of the glissando as "half-valving," which he condemns. Armstrong hardly ever used the half-valve device, yet Collier claims that Rex Stewart picked it up from Armstrong. But then, he is rather weak on Armstrong's influence on specific trumpeters, lumping Bobby Hackett in among "Dixieland" players. The statement that Armstrong's direct influence as a trumpeter had ceased by the early 1930s is astonishing, but par for Collier's idiosyncratic course.

Collier makes much of his suspicion that Armstrong was born several years before 1900 and not on the Fourth of July, mainly to set up his subject's "unreliability" as a witness to his own life. But mere suspicion it remains, as only circumstantial evidence is offered. (Collier of course ignores Armstrong's remark that his mother called him her "firecracker baby" due to the events surrounding his birthday.) He also intimates that shooting off a pistol loaded with blanks was not the true reason for Armstrong's commitment to the Colored Waifs' Home. Throughout the section on the early life, Collier paints a doleful picture of physical and spiritual deprivation that runs counter to Armstrong's own sunny view of his upbringing.

In doing so, and in (for one telling example) defining the Harlem of 1930 as a "virulent slum," Collier reveals the cultural preconceptions that permeate his book, culminating in the astounding observation that "we cannot perceive Louis Armstrong as we might Ralph Ellison, James Baldwin. He was, by the standards of middle-class America, rough, uncivilized, naive, and ignorant." Clearly, these are also Collier's standards. (Neither Baldwin nor Ellison appears in the index; the reader is referred to page 74.)

Whose perception of Baldwin, born in Collier's "virulent slum," the son of a storefront preacher and one himself before his teens? And *whose* of Ellison, a jazz trumpeter in the image of Oran "Hot Lips" Page (who idolized Armstrong) long before he became the writer who made Armstrong emblematic of his masterpiece, *Invisible Man*? In Ellison's terms, Collier's book proves Armstrong's invisibility. I recall no references to Armstrong in Baldwin's work. But at the 1958 Newport Jazz Festival, as Armstrong concluded a long set with the National Anthem, Baldwin turned to me and said: "You know, that's the first time I've liked that song."

Perceptions may differ, but Collier's are consistent. He believes that as late as 1929, "many blacks, perhaps the majority, however much they might deny it, truly felt they *were* inferior" (Collier's emphasis). And he goes on: "Even when blacks were beginning to be successful, in show business especially, it was hard to prove that they were 'better' at it than whites." (Note the quotes around "better.")

Prove it to whom? To themselves, as Collier clearly implies? The presumption that black artists and entertainers, at that late a stage of the game, could be unaware of their superiority to the white stars who came in droves to learn and "borrow" from them goes beyond disingenuousness. But it does help us understand Collier's peculiar perception of Armstrong.

Always at pains to place events in their proper context, Collier neatly explains away every forceful act performed by Armstrong on behalf of himself or others by dint of psychosocial rationalization. Even Armstrong's legendary generosity becomes a guilty reflex conditioned by childhood deprivation. Facts that can't be neutered in this fashion are simply ignored. Nowhere does Collier mention that this "ignorant" and "uncivilized" man, who had barely finished fourth grade, was a virtuoso letter writer. In 1922, he acquired a typewriter, fell in love with it, and from then on produced a ceaseless stream of correspondence with friends and associates, old and new, close and distant, expressing himself in a unique style remarkable for its playful approach to the rhythms, rhymes, and patterns of speech and prose. Conveniently, this omission enables Collier to ignore what the content of the many published (and unpublished but accessible) Armstrong letters might reveal about their author.

But I do Collier an injustice. He does mention that Armstrong wrote letters, if only to dwell on that he signed them "red beans and ricely yours," proof to Collier that he was "obsessive" about food. Armstrong's favorite dish is dismissed by Collier, who has already demolished gumbo and fishhead stew, with "and red beans and rice are—well, beans and rice." Quite so. And wine is fermented grape juice.

In the course of his summation, Collier grapples with larger issues, such as changing perceptions of art and artists. Ultimately, he has to confess that he "cannot think of another American artist who so failed his own talent. What went wrong?"

It is easier to guess what went wrong with Collier. The first thing required of a good biographer is empathy with his subject. In taking what he doubtless considers a hardheaded, unsentimental approach to the legend of Armstrong, Collier succeeds only in creating a phantom. Armstrong, the man, eludes Collier because he is unable, from his white, middle-class, and essentially puritanical perspective, to identify with the culture and environment in which Armstrong's psyche is rooted. Armstrong, the creative artist, remains a puzzle to Collier, whose sober, serious, rational, and essentially classicist esthetic is in constant conflict with Armstrong's passionate, playful, intuitive, and essentially romantic gift for transformation—indeed alchemy—that transcends (or simply bypasses) the bourgeois conventions of Western European "high" culture.

So deep is this gulf that Collier the listener, having arrived at 1947—Armstrong's twenty-fifth year of recording—can't tell Armstrong's playing from that of Irving "Mouse" Randolph, though he is surprised that the solo he thus misattributes is played, uncharacteristically, with a cup mute.

Alas, given our undue respect for appearances, what seems to be the first scholarly book about Louis Armstrong has predictably been hailed as authoritative. Armstrong's music, of course, is the best answer to this attempt to reduce a great artist's humanity to the scale of rat psychology and "explain" his art in terms of sociocultural stereotypes. In lieu of a vintage Armstrong cadenza, I offer the words—not to be found in Collier—of two great musicians.

First, Teddy Wilson: "Every musician, no matter how good, usually has something out of balance. But in Armstrong everything was in balance. He had no weak point. I don't think there's been a musician since Armstrong who has had all the factors in balance, all the factors equally developed."

Next, Jaki Byard, on his first meeting with Armstrong: "As I watched him and talked with him, I felt he was the most *natural* man. Playing, talking, singing, he was so perfectly natural the tears came to my eyes."

To Collier, of course, it was all an act.

(1985)

Review of *Louis Armstrong: An Extravagant Life* by Laurence Bergreen

L ouis Armstrong is a biographer's dream. Not only is the life of the most influential figure in jazz history a classic rags-to-riches story (as Duke Ellington put it, "He was born poor, died rich and never hurt anyone on the way"), but he also left us a mother lode of autobiographical material. This fifth-grade dropout was twenty-one when he acquired his first typewriter, and he soon became an enthusiastic correspondent who, for the remainder of his life, favored friends and acquaintances with epistles ranging from a dozen lines to as many or more pages. In addition, he published two autobiographies (the first, *Swing That Music*, was heavily ghosted; the second, *Satchmo: My Life in New Orleans*, was written strictly in his own inimitable words) and several lengthy articles.

Armstrong also made considerable contributions to two biographical works, Robert Goffin's somewhat fictionalized *Horn of Plenty* and *Louis: The Louis Armstrong Story*, by Max Jones and John Chilton. Additional autobiographical writings have posthumously come to light and were first made good public use of by Gary Giddins in his 1988 biography, *Satchmo*.

Laurence Bergreen, whose previous biographies were of James Agee, Irving Berlin, and Al Capone, has drawn deeply from these autobiographical writings for his affectionate but flawed portrait of the man he sees as a "character of epic proportions." That alone would set him miles apart from James Lincoln Collier, author of the deceptively named *Louis Armstrong: An American Genius*, who considered Armstrong an "unreliable" witness to his own life, but there is much more.

Unlike the puritanical and judgmental Collier, whose sensitive nostrils recoiled from the pungent odors of Armstrong's youthful environment and who saw the man and the artist as fatally flawed by feelings of inferiority, Bergreen makes himself at home in Storyville, the New Orleans red-light district where Armstrong was reared. With great relish, he conjures up images of brothels and whores and accuses historians and scholars of efforts "to place a fig leaf over the origins of Jazz," when it is obvious to him that the music "was born in whorehouses and on the sidewalks in front of whorehouses" and thrived in "down-and-dirty honky-tonks, dives, brothels [and] gambling and dope dens." Furthermore, this "was precisely why [early jazz] was so lively."

That such a view, curiously old-fashioned, is overthrown by what Bergreen cites from Armstrong himself and other New Orleanians—street parades, funerals, picnics, white social events, riverboat excursions, etc.— bothers him not one whit. And he is consistent, viewing both swing and bebop as weakenings of the potent genetic essence of jazz and defining Armstrong as a "profoundly intuitive musician." Even his ability to read music is considered slightly suspect.

But Bergreen would have been much better off, and his subject much better served, if he had refrained from introducing his own opinions and musical descriptions of jazz and had spent a bit more time acquainting himself with its history. He cites and quotes from Donald Marquis's book on Buddy Bolden, yet tells us that the cornetist was also a barber and publisher of a scandal sheet—two myths that Marquis indisputably overthrew. He has no inkling that Sidney Bechet, whom he consistently describes only as a clarinetist, played soprano saxophone on the recordings with Armstrong that he attempts to analyze. He has Armstrong playing "Basin Street Blues" a full decade before it was composed. He tells us about Don Redman's arrangements for the Fletcher Henderson band and says that "when he [Redman] played the sax section off the rest of the brass, the effect was electric" (a choice bit of gibberish, that!). He identifies Dave Brubeck as "the apostle of cool jazz" and claims that the *New York Times* did not print an obituary of Charlie Parker ("the only memorials were graffiti")—sentimental nonsense that a copy editor should have squelched, along with dozens of other anachronisms, errors, and simple misperceptions. When one reads that

"[Norman] Granz presented his musicians in austere settings" and that Benny Goodman gave "concerts" at the Palomar in Los Angeles in 1935, one must wonder how Bergreen's five research assistants spent their time.

The more's the pity, since Bergreen has the ability to spin a good yarn. He has uncovered much ancient dirt about Armstrong's longtime manager and *éminence grise*, Joe Glaser (though the essence of that strange man eludes him), and is most enlightening about his hero's relationships with women. Armstrong's first wife, Daisy, whom he married when he was seventeen, is brought into full view, and there is a balanced portrait of her successor, Lillian Hardin, using both her own and Armstrong's accounts. Wives Nos. 3 (the acquisitive Alpha Smith) and 4 (the steadfast Lucille Wilson) also get their dues, though the latter was more controlling than Bergreen seems to realize.

But then, the book is heavily weighted in favor of the earlier and more "extravagant" years of Armstrong's life. Almost four hundred pages have passed before we reach 1940, and only some of the highlights of the next thirty years are covered. This is, at least in part, because Bergreen believes that his subject did his best work before the 1930s, that swing passed him by, and that the famous Armstrong All Stars, assembled in 1947, represented a return to the trumpeter's roots. It is also because once Armstrong settled in New York in 1929, the backdrop was no longer as colorful as brothel-laden New Orleans and gangster-dominated Chicago. The trouble Armstrong had with gangsters until he hooked up with Glaser in 1935 is grist for Bergreen's storytelling forte.

Unlike Collier, Bergreen is able to deal sensibly with Armstrong's involvement with marijuana, though he overestimates the extent to which his subject made use of it in a working context. But he refrains from moralizing or finger-pointing. He's also quite sensible about Armstrong's addiction to laxatives, though, again, he exaggerates the amount of the stuff actually consumed. And Armstrong did not use that famous (or infamous) photo of himself on the potty, holding up a package of Swiss Kriss, the herbal purgative he swore by, on his stationery, nor was his den, where he loved to spend what little time he had at home, decorated with images of himself. The collages he created included pretty women and famous men, mostly African-American, but Winston Churchill as well.

Bergreen gives Armstrong due credit for his strong public stand on school desegregation in Little Rock, Arkansas, in 1957, when, among other things, he said that President Eisenhower had "no guts" and called Arkansas governor Orville Faubus an "uneducated plowboy." Yet he underestimates Armstrong's less public role in breaking the color barrier, especially during the 1930s, when he was the first of his race to perform in dozens of venues all over the land.

But then, Armstrong's life and art was, in and of itself, a triumph over racism or, more accurately, its obversion. Bergreen senses this but seems to believe that Armstrong's main weapon was accommodation, a tactic that came to him naturally through his love for people of all kinds and complexions. That's only part of the story, just as the music Armstrong created was much more than what Bergreen says it is: "It was all so much fun, more fun than any other music." Serious fun—very serious!

If Bergreen realized just how serious, he would probably not have undertaken the task at hand. Clearly, he is not alone, for the publication of this book is proof that jazz, with all the recognition, tributes, and honors by now bestowed upon it, is still not taken as seriously as it merits. Would a major publishing house accept a manuscript about Mozart as shorn of elementary knowledge of music as *Louis Armstrong: An Extravagant Life*? This is a well-intentioned book, but good intentions are no longer enough when it comes to one of the greatest figures the twentieth century has brought forth, the fountainhead of, arguably, its most original form of musical expression. As the old blues lyric put it: "How long, baby, how long?"

(1997)

Louis and Duke: The Great Summit

It should have happened sooner. It should have been better prepared. It should have involved Duke's other "instrument," his orchestra. But in this not-best-of-all-possible-worlds, we must be grateful that the meeting of inarguably the two greatest figures in the history of jazz took place at all.

That it came about is due to the enterprise (or chutzpah) of the late Bob Thiele, one of the truly legendary figures among jazz record producers, though you wouldn't know it from reading his guarded autobiography (which mentions this grand encounter only in passing). A fan and friend of Ellington since his teens, and on good terms with Armstrong's feisty manager, Joe Glaser, Thiele seized the rare opportunity presented by the simultaneous availability in New York of the two masters, Duke having recently returned from post-production work in Paris on the film in which he had worked with Armstrong, *Paris Blues*, and Louis taking a much-needed break (interrupted by some television shots) after a strenuous tour of Africa and Europe.

Both legends would soon be on the road again (the Armstrong All Stars were set for their first gig following the layoff on the day after the second of these recording sessions), but Thiele, having persuaded Morris Levy of Roulette Records to bankroll the project, managed to put all the pieces together. Thanks to the genius and professionalism of the co-stars, some twelve hours of dedicated work yielded superb results. Excepting a 1946 all-star session concocted by Leonard Feather that allowed for minimal interaction, Louis and Duke had not been in a recording situation before. Indeed, there had been remarkably little collaboration between them. Even when both were managed by Glaser, nothing was concocted. But during the two years just preceding this encounter, they had crossed collaborative paths. On January 7, 1959, the Ellington band and the Armstrong All Stars were both on hand, among many other performers, in a New York television studio for the rehearsal and broadcast (no videotaping then) of a Timex-sponsored jazz spectacular. Since I was there, I can state with some authority that a marvelous opportunity was aborted. During rehearsal, Duke opened up a chart (as I recall, a blues) for interplay between his trumpets and Armstrong, with marvelous results. But the program was so overloaded with acts that what would have been a matchless climax was scrapped, and instead a truncated version of "Perdido," with Satch riding over the ensemble, was heard mainly over the closing crawl—the only known audio capturing these two majestic sounds: the Armstrong horn and the Ellington orchestra. An approximation came about for the aforementioned *Paris Blues*, far from the worst film with a jazz theme, if no masterpiece. The Ellington and Strayhorn score, however, is masterful, though most of it is performed by non-Ellingtonians, as is the case for the two numbers involving Louis: the brief "Wild Man Moore," with a small group, and the extended "Battle Royal," with a big band of mostly French musicians, whom Duke manages to make sound quite Ellingtonian. But that is it. When Louis, near the end of his life, sat in with Ellington at New York's Rainbow Room, Duke was at the helm of an octet, and the one time they got together on *The Ed Sullivan Show* (in December 1961), it was Duke sitting in with the All Stars.

But of course, starting with Freddie Jenkins in 1928 and ending with Money Johnson in 1974, the Ellington band was never without an Armstrong voice, and more often than not the entire trumpet section had its own bona fides. Lawrence Brown was Armstrong transposed to trombone, and one need only cite a few masterpieces—"Daybreak Express," "Braggin' in Brass"—to illustrate the profound Armstrong influence on Ellington's music, something rarely noted in the by now burgeoning literature. Louis, on the other hand, had recorded (and, most likely, performed) very little Ellington material. An outstanding 1935 "Solitude" (three extant takes) is all from that decade; the mid-1940s big-band repertory included "Perdido" (a couple of airchecks, one with a Dexter Gordon solo), and there was a most peculiar 1945 broadcast for which Louis (in New Orleans) and Benny Goodman (in New York) joined the Ellington band (in Los Angeles) for "Things Ain't What They Used to Be." And the early All Stars did "C Jam Blues" as a Barney Bigard feature. There's a one-time-only "Take the A Train" from a 1952 concert, but when Billy Kyle joined the All Stars the following year, "Perdido" re-entered as one of his showcases. In 1957, Louis recorded "Don't Get Around Much Anymore" and "Do Nothing 'Til You Hear from Me" with a big studio band. And that, plus the Timex "Perdido," was it.

The first session was called for 6 p.m. at RCA Victor's Studio One, on East Twenty-fourth Street between Lexington and Third avenues in Manhattan. According to Stanley Dance, who came early, everyone was on time, and Duke joked that Billy Kyle, though convalescing, had complained that he had "stolen his gig." Thiele had decided on a program of Ellington tunes, and what quickly became evident was how surprisingly familiar Louis seemed with the pieces Duke proposed. As Dance noted in his report on the event for Britain's *Jazz Journal*, the trumpeter was "so quick to grasp the whole conception of an interpretation [and] on several numbers, notably 'Black and Tan Fantasy,' he seemed to know the Ellington routines better than Barney."

The ex-Ellington clarinetist's presence (he had rejoined the All Stars after a five-year absence in 1960 and would soon leave again) added a special flavor to the occasion. There could have been tension—after all, Barney's departure almost twenty years before had not pleased the bandleader—but Duke greeted Barney warmly, as Dance observed. And while Barney was not in top form, there are moments when he seems inspired by the old tunes. In his autobiography, *With Louis and the Duke*, he writes that "it was fun to be recording with the two most important bandleaders in my career at one session . . . but the main thing was that Louis got along so great with Duke . . . two prominent leaders on one date could have been rough, but we had no problems."

That first session lasted until 1:30 in the morning, yielding no less than ten numbers, concluding with an on-the-spot Ellington original. As Dance observed, Ellington sang a few phrases and had Barney play them; wrote them out for the horns, decided to mute Trummy Young's trombone with Barney's beret, "and they were off." Louis does some of his finest blowing on what was called "The Beautiful American," after Dance, a Graham Greene fan, had suggested "The Unquiet American."

Trummy Young's contribution here, and throughout both sessions, was emblematic of his role with the All Stars. Dedicated to Louis, his original inspiration (just listen to "Margie," his star turn with the Jimmie Lunceford band), he was the leader's right arm, musically and personally, the closest friend Pops had had in the group since Jack Teagarden, and perhaps even closer. When he left in early 1964, after almost a dozen years (in response to an ultimatum from his wife: him or me), the gap he left was never truly filled. He's in fine fettle here; the critics never tired of faulting him for being too boisterous (he always was an extroverted player) or lamenting that he had "abandoned" modern jazz (since he was present on some seminal bebop sessions). And no A&R man offered him a date (as was the case for Billy Kyle, the All Stars' brilliant pianist). Bassist Mort Herbert acquits himself well here; bassists always thrived in the company of Ellington. This was his last record date with Louis; he subsequently passed the bar and for a while was a deputy district attorney in Los Angeles. Danny Barcelona had worked with Trummy in Hawaii and was recommended by the trombonist to Armstrong, with whom he stayed from 1958 until the last gig. The youngest member of this cast, he is its sole survivor, making his home in California—this may be his finest work.

The second session commenced at 2 p.m. the next afternoon, and this writer was now on hand, noting, when greeting Pops, that he was dabbing his lips with cotton balls dipped in spirits of nitrate. He'd blown hard the night before, after an unaccustomed layoff, and now the chops were a bit tender.

But that didn't dampen his spirits, or cause him to hold back. And the new (and improved) lyric he devised for "Drop Me Off in Harlem" put everyone, including Duke (who'd complained of a headache), in a happy mood, and that horn was as strong as one could ask for. (No one ever made, or ever will make, a trumpet sound like that, and while the sound here is markedly better than ever before—even better than on the audiophile vinyl edition—no reproductive device can fully re-create what Louis Armstrong sounded like in person, or recapture the aura he gave off.) As much in evidence as Ellington the musical director (always in consultation with Louis, by word, gesture, or eye contact) was Ellington the pianist. It's become accepted wisdom by now, but in early 1961, his stature in this role was not yet fully understood. Suffice it to say that Duke Ellington may well have been the greatest band pianist of them all, and that he is in brilliant form here. Just dig him on "Lucky So and So," virtually a duet with Louis (who sings sublimely), for one standout example. And what introductions and transitions he creates! This intimate setting, by the way, also demonstrates, time and again, how big an impact Duke had on Thelonious Monk. The late Don DeMicheal (my mentor and friend, and underrated both as a critic and a drummer and vibist) pointed this out in his *Down Beat* review of 1961, adding that someone should record Ellington the pianist as Norman Granz recorded Art Tatum—alas, no one did.

Every piece here is a joy, with discoveries to be made at each repeated hearing (and if you don't listen to this music more than once, later for you). "Mood Indigo" (on which Barney, who had a hand in composing it, is at his best) has another fabulous vocal (dig Pops's aside to Trummy) and eventually became an Armstrong staple; I'll never forget a late-in-life TV spot when Pops, leaning back in a comfortable chair, did some unearthly scatting on it. And how about his scatting on "Cotton Tail," and that trumpet bit—this was the conclusion of the session, the icing on the cake. But to me, after all these years and who knows how many listens, the biggest kick is still "Azalea," the most unanticipated of all the selections here. According to Dance, Duke wrote this bit of Southern romanticism twenty years before with Louis in mind. He'd previously attempted it in the studio with two hapless singers—Chester Crumpler in 1947 and Lloyd Oldham in 1951. Both efforts remained unissued, and indeed the extravagant lyric (Dance calls it "very lofty"; it includes such devices as rhyming the title with "assail ya") is practically unsingable, the more so when coupled with a not exactly simple melody.

But after "Lucky So and So" had come off so well, Duke mustered up the courage to dig out a lead sheet for "Azalea." He pulled up a chair, sat down facing Louis, and held up the words and music. Louis donned his horn-rimmed glasses, smiled that matchless smile, and began to hum and sing. An expert sight-reader, he soon had the melody down. The lyric, even with Duke having moved to the piano, was a bit more challenging, but it too fell into place. As all this was taking shape, Ellington was positively beaming, and when a take had been made, he was ecstatic. If indeed he'd had Louis in mind when he created this hothouse conceit, he had chosen properly, for no one else could have made it credible but the incredible Mr. Strong.

Louis then proceeded to upstage, quite unintentionally, Barney on the routining of "Black and Tan Fantasy," which, to the best of anyone's knowledge, he'd never played before but knew so very well. On this, he uncorked one of his favorite blues, the one heard in 1928 on "Muggles" by the second Hot Five. The majestic sound and noble accents he clothes it in here should serve as a lesson to those who—still—speak of his decline. But then, we need no intermediaries to enjoy this wonderful music. Here's what I wrote in 1961: "The easy, warm rapport between these two great artists, their understanding of each other's needs and purposes, their mixing of high seriousness and frivolous banter, were a unique personification of jazz, at its warmest and tightest. It was a joy to be there, and a wonder to reflect on and bask in the youthful presence and spirit of these two men in their seventh decade of life, still finding challenges and discovering joy in their work."

The wonder still works.

As a postscript to this historic get-together came another grand encounter. Because Thiele had used Duke without permission from Columbia, that label got its quid pro quo by obtaining the entire Basie band from Roulette to record both bands together. Morris Levy wasn't such a tough guy after all. And in that session's repertory, the two Louis-related items from the *Paris Blues* score, "Wild Man Moore" and "Battle Royal," became centerpieces. God bless 'em all!

The Making of *The Great Summit*

The discovery, by the intrepid jazz explorer Michael Cuscuna, of hitherto unknown and unsuspected outtakes from one of the most famous summit meetings in recorded jazz is an occasion for rejoicing. It not only brings us additional doses of vintage Pops and Duke, but also sheds light on how these two giants worked together during that singular encounter.

What is surprising, as we listen to these workouts on ten of the seventeen numbers completed at the two sessions, is how quickly and effectively each tune took shape for satisfactory performance. Or maybe not, since the greatest and most experienced arranger in jazz was there, and the material was of his own devising; and the star was one of the quickest studies ever to set foot in a studio.

Digression: A bit later, I again had the pleasure and privilege to observe Louis Armstrong at work in the studio, this time with brand-new material. This was part of the "Real Ambassadors" sessions that joined the All Stars with Lambert, Hendricks & Ross, Carmen McRae, and the composer-and-lyricist team of Dave and Iola Brubeck. Perhaps the finest piece in that score was "Summer Song," and it was evident that Dave felt a bit awkward, having to present it to Armstrong sight unseen. Dave gave Louis the lead sheet, sat down at the keyboard and outlined the melody and changes while Louis looked things over, and then hesitated until Louis said, "Let's try it." A tempo was chosen, the composer played a brief introduction, and the singer proceeded to offer not the anticipated first attempt but what amounted to an interpretation, and a moving one at that. In what seemed like little more than an instant, this great artist had grasped the essence of a sophisticated piece of music and given it perfect life and shape. Tears came to Brubeck's eyes, and this bystander had witnessed yet another Satch miracle, comparable to the "Azalea" one. Here, you're invited to listen in as things take shape; not much has been edited out in terms of studio banter, false starts, comments from the booth (Bob Thiele certainly wasn't awed by the company he kept; there are times when he sounds a bit rude, but that's the way producers tend to be when the clock is ticking), and various, inevitable goofs. Some routines fall into place almost instantly (no problems with "In a Mellotone"), while others take longer. There are priceless moments, and there are marvelous vocal and instrumental passages (hear Duke's full chorus on take two of "Don't Get Around" or Pops's second vocal chorus on the first complete run-through "Beginning to See the Light" for just a couple of random choices). Always, even when he makes mistakes (most of which are miscues or verbal mix-ups and none of which involve wrong notes, only missed or messed-up ones), Satchmo plays and sings with compelling authority and flawless timing, and even when a take is clearly not going to be mastered, he hits those high ones at the end. This man just didn't know how to coast or stint. And while we can't see it, take my word (and Stanley Dance's—he was surprised 'cause he'd seen Pops in the studio less often than I) when I point out that he delivered all his vocals with the gestures and expressions we know from his public performances— proof positive that this was his natural way of getting into his material, not an act or an affectation.

As impressive in its own way is Duke's pianistic authority—he conducts from the keyboard, he cues, he prods, he eases, he polishes. And what a touch. Want to hear Duke bop a little? Dig the solo on take five of "Duke's Place" (otherwise known as "C-Jam Blues"). Want to hear a little Monkishness? Try "Drop Me Off in Harlem" (after a nice one by Trummy), both the piano solo and the backdrop to Mort Herbert's bass spot. Louis's singing on "Lucky So and So" (which begins with some fine conversation and a funny breakdown, turns into a rehearsal, and features a classic mess-up of "confidentially") is a lesson in how a masterpiece takes shape—follow up with the master take and you'll see what I mean. "Azalea" reveals that the master, though called take seven, must be a composite. The opening trumpet work is lovely here—more secure than on the master—but the vocal (what impossible lyrics!) gets messed up on the first attempt. The second attempt, however, is perfect—and how about that tag!

As Dance pointed out, Pops seemed to know the "Black and Tan Fantasy" routine better than Barney Bigard. Pops dons his straight mute (only one he ever used) for the theme, with Trummy plungered. Barney deserves to have his part trimmed down, but he swoops pretty good later on—he's mad! We get a tango beat on the theme by take six, and then Duke plays the shit out of the second strain. The two blues choruses by Pops again pick up on "Muggles" and have great velocity, while Trummy growls in the best Ducal tradition. Those splendid trumpet breaks were incorporated into the master, and hear how Louis responds to Barney's flat ensemble part by putting in some dissonance to make it sound better. "Cotton Tail" is just a smidgen of studio chatter.

(2001)

Ellington at Philharmonic Hall

This concert, part of Lincoln Center's Great Performers series, afforded an interesting and unusual opportunity to witness Ellington's wizardry with a small ensemble—an interest heightened by the fact that he restricted himself to a palette of woodwinds.

The Ellington reed section (complete except for the omission of Johnny Hodges) is a noble institution. Seldom has its versatility and unique togetherness been better demonstrated than on this occasion, which also served to introduce several new works by Ellington and Billy Strayhorn.

Ellington began with a new piece for solo piano, "Wild Cherry," a rhapsodic evocation of romantic nostalgia, with an improvised quality explained by the composer with the comment that it "was not written yet." There followed two excerpts from the suite dedicated to Queen Elizabeth of England, "Le Sucrier Velour" and "Single Petal of a Rose." On the latter, John Lamb's softly bowed bass joined with the piano. The harmonic language of these three pieces was that of late romanticism and impressionism but with a distinct Ellington touch.

The jazz beat, until now barely implied, was fully present on "Tune Up," with drummer Louie Bellson added. Ellington shook out of his reflective mood with beautifully shaped and swinging phrases. A half chorus here could have passed for Thelonious Monk, though the Ellington piano sound is rounder and less percussive.

Ellington then invited the reeds to join the party with "a suggestion, much to their surprise," of "Creole Love Call." This lovely evergreen (written in 1927) was given a gentle, haunting interpretation by the two clarinets and Harry Carney's bass clarinet, with a full-toned solo by Russell Procope. Ellington's fills behind the trio passages—no two alike—were delightful.

A Latin feeling was predominant on something described by Ellington as "a little thing in B-flat," the highlight of which was a Paul Gonsalves solo in 4/4. The tenor saxophonist remained front and center for "Happy Reunion," one of his finest showcases with the band. Here it was more relaxed than customary, with the soloist in his best ballad form. It was a moving performance and received the most applause up to then.

Always alert to audience response, Ellington called Gonsalves back, beat off a swinging tempo, and gave a piano cue to "Tea for Two." Gonsalves, now thoroughly warmed up, delivered a series of voluptuous, serpentine choruses, the rhythm section stoking the fire beneath him. For the final chorus, his section mates created an appropriately climactic riff.

Gonsalves, a player sometimes overlooked when the roll of great tenor saxophonists is called, emphatically confirmed his place in their ranks. When he is right, Gonsalves has few peers.

Now the magic of the four reeds was brought into full play, in a charming, new, and as yet untitled Strayhorn blues.

Jimmy Hamilton's flawless clarinet had the leading ensemble role, weaving in and out. Gonsalves returned for a very blue solo, followed by Carney on baritone—with that sound that makes all other baritone saxophonists sound like hoarse children.

Ellington now introduced the pièce de résistance of the afternoon, a four-part suite, *A Blue Mural from Two Perspectives*, co-written by Strayhorn and Ellington, and, according to the latter, "just finished today." This being an afternoon concert, there had obviously been little if any time to rehearse the piece, and though Ellington warned of impending clinkers, they were notably absent.

The opening section, soft and mysterious, was scored for only three instruments: Hamilton's clarinet, Carney's bass clarinet, and Bellson's drums—the latter a mere suggestion of rhythmic backdrop played with the hands only, while the two woodwinds conversed.

An interlude for piano with gentle tom-tom backing followed, moving gradually into 4/4 and tempo. A gorgeous all-saxophone ensemble now took up a singing melodic line, with an eight-bar spot for Procope's bright alto. This segment ended with a piano-and-bass duet, highlighted by Lamb's deft slides.

A bright section followed, a catchy 32-bar song, scored for three saxes, with Hamilton's clarinet lead an octave above. The final segment of the piece, an example of exotic Ellingtonia, featured a long piano solo, with effective double octaves. The suite ended as it had begun—on a subdued note.

Ellington will seduce the listener with gorgeous sounds, and the reeds supplied a truly amazing variety of such throughout the piece. But the suite is not merely a matter of magic sounds; it is also substantially structured and plumbs a wide range of moods and feelings. The opening section is a prime example of Ellington's (and Strayhorn's) ability to create with a minimum of instrumental resources and, one might add, to create music beyond categorization.

The concert's second half provided a less challenging context for the players, who certainly deserved a rest on their laurels after the taxing baptism of the suite. However, what transpired could hardly be described as resting, though the musical territory was familiar.

It was, in fact, a series of showcases. Ellington and Lamb led off, with the first part of "Ad Lib on Nippon," the bassist displaying, as he did throughout, a masterly instrumental technique and great musical sensibility. Lamb certainly merits the title of discovery, and there is no doubt that his name will be mentioned with increasing frequency.

Hamilton was featured on "Tenderly," and just as several hardened Ellington followers were about to register a "what?—not again" reaction, the clarinetist squelched such thoughts with a perfect introduction. The hall, still an acoustic nuisance, favors the clarinet, and Hamilton's beautiful, clarion sound filled its spaces.

Carney, up next with his familiar "Sophisticated Lady," also managed to turn the tried-and-true into something refreshing and spectacular. A great virtuoso is never boring, and the tune, to say the last, bears rehearing. The held-note ending elicited the expected response from an audience that contained a not inconsiderable portion of surprisingly well-behaved and appreciative children.

Bellson climaxed the show portion of the concert with a rousing solo on "Take the A Train." With his eye-catching display of equipment (five cymbals of varying sizes, hi-hat, two bass drums, two floor tom-toms, and snare), Bellson is the most glamorous Ellington drummer since Sonny Greer. But he is no show-off. Throughout the afternoon, he had distinguished himself with unselfish musical support. Now it was his moment, and he was ready.

With a firm sense of contrast and construction, Bellson built his long solo, first from a single-stroke roll to a snare-and-bass-drum crescendo, down again to almost inaudible brushstrokes, and then back up, from a stint with sticks that had bells attached, to a roaring climax with all his equipment in action.

A few perfunctory encores, the Ducal finger-snapping ritual, and it was over—a most rewarding afternoon with the two sections that constitute the real backbone of the current Ellington band.

It was, among other things, a demonstration of the ultimate in musical unity. Every man on stage was an artist and an individual, but together they formed a *unit*. It was truly an afternoon with the great performers.

(1966)

Billy Strayhorn in Concert

As composer, pianist, arranger, and trusted friend and collaborator, Billy Strayhorn has been an integral element of the Duke Ellington organization since 1939. Throughout these many years, Strayhorn has never sought the spotlight, and while knowledgeable students of Ellingtonia are well aware of his tremendous contributions, his self-effacing role has meant little publicity for him.

This New School Auditorium concert—the fifth event in an annual series sponsored by the Duke Ellington Jazz Society—afforded a rare and welcome opportunity to hear and see Strayhorn in a full-fledged showcase of his multiple talents. It indicated, among other things, that Strayhorn is much more than Ellington's alter ego (though that in itself would be no mean accomplishment).

Strayhorn's distinctive musical personality unfolded in a well-paced program of eighteen originals, including well-known as well as rarely heard pieces.

The concert began with Strayhorn in the role of solo pianist. His opening selection was a new composition, "Love Passed," a gently romantic ballad typifying one of the characteristic Strayhorn moods: reflective nostalgia. It was followed by "Lotus," a charming waltz ("named by a young friend of mine who leads a band and plays the piano," Strayhorn commented), and then the first recorded Strayhorn contribution to the Ellington library, the 1939 "Something to Live For," a piece not in the least dated and still a challenge to any singer (or player). This performance included the rarely heard verse.

Strayhorn's approach to the keyboard is marked by the arranger's orchestral conception. His chords are full and rich, often suggesting more varied and sophisticated sounds and voicings than the piano is capable of reproducing—the point is that he suggests these possibilities convincingly.

His touch, however, is certainly pianistic, and while his technique is not that of a virtuoso, he is more than competent. Moreover, everything he plays is invested with a rare sense of form and development, and there is none of the empty rhapsodizing to which some of his melodies and harmonies lend themselves in lesser hands.

Other solo pieces included the bouncy "Clementine," with a happy passage reminiscent of Willie "The Lion" Smith, the highly chromatic "All Heart" (for Ella Fitzgerald), "Orson" (for Orson Welles), and "Drawing

Room Blues," an impressionistic improvisation originally conceived for two pianos by Strayhorn and Ellington. On the latter, Strayhorn revealed a genuine gift for improvising, and his dissonances in the last chorus were striking.

Joined by Wendell Marshall (bass) and Dave Bailey (drums), Strayhorn picked up the tempo for a sprightly "Smada," followed by "A-Sittin' and A-Rockin'," a famous piece that Strayhorn did not claim, though his inclusion of it in the program speaks for itself. The trio portion concluded with a shimmering performance of the haunting "Daydream."

Some of Strayhorn's earliest work for Ellington was done with small groups from within the band. His arrangements for the group he introduced as the Riverside Drive Five showed that years of big-band writing seem to have heightened rather than lessened his ability to produce fresh and provocative scores for small ensembles.

A clarinet lead blending with muted trumpet and soft French horn brought lovely hues to "Upper Manhattan Medical Group," a tune with sufficient melodic profile to survive the reduction from full-band treatment. Bob Wilber, a gifted musician, contributed a lithe and elegant clarinet solo, and Clark Terry played a swinging, stinging two choruses with Harmon mute. Then followed chases between the two horns.

The theme statement of "Chelsea Bridge," surely one of Strayhorn's loveliest pieces, was given to Willie Ruff. The sound of the French horn was entirely suited to set and sustain the soft and warm mood. (In his spoken introduction, Strayhorn revealed that the piece was originally called "Battersea Bridge," inspired by the Whistler painting—"Chelsea" was a slip of memory at the recording session.)

"Raincheck," a happy tune, was introduced and concluded by *a cappella* French horn (Ruff did not play any improvised solos, but his ensemble contributions were essential). Wilber played his curved soprano here, very much in a Johnny Hodges groove, and Terry broke loose with a rousing, shouting solo.

Singer Ozzie Bailey, featured with the Ellington band some years ago, then joined the group to do "What Else Can You Do with a Drum?" (from *A Drum Is a Woman*), followed by "Your Love Has Faded," a pretty ballad from the late '30s with an interesting bridge and good lyrics.

Bailey, a silken-voiced singer with faultless intonation, is the ideal interpreter of Strayhorn the romantic, as he proved with "Multicolored Blue," highlighted by an extraordinarily mean and funky Terry plunger solo. The romantic groove was maintained with "A Flower Is a Lovesome Thing," an encore for the singer.

The performance of the famous "Passion Flower" (according to the composer, "a frame of mind rather than a bloom") was a surprise.

After a flowery out-of-tempo piano introduction, Strayhorn brought in the rhythm section with a pickup into fast, bright tempo, and the solos (Wilber's frisky clarinet and Terry's joyful plunger) also jumped. Had any other arranger dared to meddle with the established groove for this piece, he would have been denounced by the critics for his lack of understanding of the composer's intentions. But the novel treatment worked perfectly, revealing this erstwhile near-decadent and ripely sensual line as excellent blowing material.

After a reprise of "Love Passed," this time with a Bailey vocal, the famed "A Train" rolled in, with a rhapsodic piano introduction, followed by Ray Nance's recorded trumpet solo scored for ensemble, a knocked-out scat vocal from Terry, a taste (too brief) of Wilber's soprano, and a flying finish.

On these, as throughout, bassist Marshall and drummer Bailey contributed a firm and springy foundation. On the slower pieces, Marshall distinguished himself with remarkable fills and counterlines. And Strayhorn made a perfect emcee.

(1965)

Early Ellington

To be sure, this is early Ellington. The six-year span represented here rounds out the first decade of recording activity by the phenomenally gifted composer-arranger-pianist-bandleader, which had begun late in 1924 and was to continue for a total of fifty years. But in Ellington's case, "early" does not imply that the music is of interest merely as a prelude to things to come. Had Ellington through some misfortune ceased to record in 1934, he would nonetheless be a figure to reckon with in the annals of jazz. This music needs no historical footnoting to be appreciated; like all art worthy of the name, its message is direct and valid in its own right.

Clearly, by late 1927 Ellington was making his own music and shaping his band into its unique voice. And he was already, as he would be until the end, reworking his favorite pieces. Thus, the earliest composition in this collection, "East St. Louis Toodle-Oo," is heard in its fourth recorded incarnation, the first having been waxed one year and three weeks earlier. (Even that version reached out to, among others, a sixteen-year-old trumpeter, Sy Oliver, who became one of the swing era's most brilliant arrangers. Hearing it, he said almost fifty years later, "actually changed my life . . . it sounds almost too simplistic, but it's true." Already Ellington was making music unlike anything else—in jazz-and-dancedom or in the concert hall.)

And why not? Our common perspective on jazz, which adversely affects our openness to the music's rich heritage, is so reflexively historical that we hear the past not for its own sake, but merely as an overture to the present. In late 1927, however, Ellington was in his twenty-ninth year; older than most members of his band, he was a leader and molder of musicians, a professional secure in his craft. If his eye was on the future, it was surely the immediate one: on December 4, 1927, eight days before his second studio session for Victor, his band opened at the Cotton Club.

This opportunity to work at a venue known as (*pace* Francis Ford Coppola) "the aristocrat of Harlem"—where shows were produced by a crack team of directors, songwriters, choreographers, dancers, and singers unmatched by any other nightclub, and where audiences included the cream of Broadway and Hollywood—was a golden one. Ellington seized it with alacrity.

His band had to play for elaborate floor shows that changed quite frequently; this meant backing singers, supporting solo dancers and chorus lines, and working behind all sorts of specialty acts. The band members had to be quick studies, be presentable showmen, and stay on their toes. And of course they also played for dancing by the patrons, which called for still different skills. Some bands were great show bands, some were great dance bands; Ellington's was one of the few to be both.

While he was frequently called upon to arrange other people's music (Jimmy McHugh and Dorothy Fields were the incumbent writers), he soon got the chance to add his own material to the shows. And the Cotton Club had a network radio wire, still a relative rarity, especially for black bands. Ellington and his shrewd and dedicated manager, Irving Mills, knew the value of that in building a national audience for the band. And they also understood, better and sooner than anyone else in the realm of jazz, that making phonograph records (a chance to build an audience not just at home but abroad as well) was an entirely different proposition than playing "live."

Reams have been written about Ellington and his music, but it has seldom been emphasized how well he grasped that the record, especially with the advent of electrical technology, was a wholly new medium for music. In the 1920s, most performers, classical as well as popular, thought of records as a means to publicize in-person appearances and plug hit songs (in those days, a song's hit status was based on how much sheet music it sold). Amazingly few seem to have noticed that Caruso became a star way beyond normal operatic magnitude via the phonograph, or that jazz itself had spread much faster and more effectively via recordings than would otherwise have been possible.

Ellington (and Leopold Stokowski) knew this, and he also knew that engineers were not musicians, or necessarily good listeners. Take any 1920s record by Fletcher Henderson and compare it with a contemporary Ellington disc, and you will hear that Henderson didn't care about studio balances or (except on very rare occasions) tailor his recorded performances to best fit the time limit imposed by the 78-rpm format. Paul Whiteman was well ahead of Henderson in this respect, but even he lagged behind Ellington. Ironically, the only other jazzman to grasp the true nature of the medium was the fellow composer, arranger, pianist, and bandleader for whom Ellington had no kind words, Jelly Roll Morton. But Morton lost his touch after 1927, while Ellington perfected his, and eventually even knew how to adjust it to the coming of long-playing records—a whole other ball of wax.

Listen to a piece like "Black Beauty," clearly one of Ellington's 1920s gems. Granted that Victor, then the world's leading record company, had the best engineers, and technicians whose mastering and pressing skills could handle well over three minutes of music on a 10-inch disc. But what other band, in early 1928, comes across with such presence and impact? Where else do we hear the string bass in such a forward position in the sonic spectrum? Where else are the piano and the drummer's kit so well balanced with the horns, and the particular sounds of those horns, in concert and in solo, so strong and true? Obviously, the same engineers in the same studios recorded other orchestras and performers. But only Stokowski's Philadelphians can compare, and we know from his own testimony that Stokowski made it his business to understand recording technology.

To continue with the specific example of "Black Beauty," this is a complete and extraordinarily shapely piece of music. We do not, as with so many Henderson discs, wish that the soloists had more time to "stretch out." What we hear from Arthur Whetsol's pretty trumpet, Joe Nanton's raucous (but knowing) trombone, and Barney Bigard's luminous clarinet is enough. These are complete statements that function within the piece as a whole. And then the charming and completely original conversation between piano, bass, and drums that is at the center, contrasting with and complementing the orchestrated passages. This is a composer's mind at work, and it's good to know that a classically trained and oriented critic, R. D. Darrell, realized this when the record came out and accorded it (and Ellington) high praise in a small but distinguished publication—fittingly enough aimed at serious collectors of phonograph records.

There are many other delights in this collection, which is focused on pieces that became Ellington standards ("East St. Louis Toodle-Oo,"

"Black and Tan Fantasy," "Creole Love Call," "The Mooche," "Mood Indigo," "Rockin' in Rhythm," "Solitude") and remained in the "book" (but constantly changed accoutrements) until the end, but also includes less enduring but equally enjoyable works, the quite staggering "Daybreak Express" among them. This train piece to end all train pieces (Ellington would score again in this vein with "Happy-Go-Lucky Local") is based on the chord structure (and melody) of "Tiger Rag's" main strain, but completely transforms that venerable jazz favorite. Likewise, the masterly "Old Man Blues" (from Ellington's first Hollywood feature, the 1930 *Check and Double Check*) is, as the title tells us but few musicologists seem to have heard, Ellington's answer to "Ol' Man River"—a hip message indeed to insiders, since the film itself starred Amos 'n' Andy!

We are also treated to Ellington's first extended work, "Creole Rhapsody," or more accurately, his revision of it, since he'd first waxed it for the Brunswick label some five months earlier. Victor gave him both sides of a 12-inch disc, while Brunswick had only two times 10 inches to spare. (Most notably, the Victor version has a principal theme, introduced by Whetsol's trumpet at its most lyrical, which is absent from the earlier score.) If one dares to say so, it shows the influence of Whiteman, or rather of Gershwin and Ferde Grofé, and thus is more a period piece than anything else offered here. Yet it is also very much Ellington, in his disarmingly grandiose manner.

The great individual voices in the band include trumpeters Bubber Miley (co-composer of several Ducal milestones and master of the growl), Cootie Williams (majestic on open horn in the Armstrong mold, as on "Solitude," or growling in his own masterful way, as on "Ring Dem Bells"), and the underrated Arthur Whetsol; "Tricky Sam" Nanton, undisputed master of plunger trombone, and the contrastingly romantic Lawrence Brown; the young but oh-so-agile and poised Johnny Hodges, making his alto sax sing; Barney Bigard from New Orleans, never better than with Duke; Wellman Braud, from the same town and the first true solo voice on the bass, logical predecessor of Jimmy Blanton; Sonny Greer, colorist supreme, but also a fine tempo man; and Harry Carney, who spent most of his life with Duke and was a key voice in the sound of Ellingtonia. And not least, Ellington the pianist, perfect on introductions, interludes, and fills (not to mention accompaniments) and no slouch in the solo spotlight. Like all he touched in music, his piano had that sound.

Early or late, Ellington music is music at its very best. By 1932, his label billing began to read "Duke Ellington and His Famous Orchestra." It was a credit that rightly remains unique.

(1989)

The Ellington Era

For many years jazz had to fight an uphill battle for official recognition as a bona fide "art form." In light of the current state of affairs in the jazz world, this recognition might well appear to some observers as a mixed blessing indeed. It has largely removed jazz from its original context—the functionality of entertainment and dance music—and has placed this music and its creators adrift in the esthetic, philosophic, semantic, and economic miasmas that constitute the contemporary environment of art and "art appreciation."

Though it is a very young art, jazz has already been tightly strapped into the rigid bed of formalistic "history" and evolutionary theory. This framework—often sloppily and haphazardly erected—has supplied the intellectual justification for the demand for constant "innovation," which goes hand in hand with the promotion of all forms of art in this country. This need for novelty—commercial in nature but beefed up by the prattling of befuddled "spokesmen" for the arts—results in the swift condemnation to obsolescence of all but the latest style and mode.

In this atmosphere, jazz history becomes nothing but a tracing of influences pointing to the latest genius, and the searching jazz musician is confronted with a process of evaluation that equates music with technology and robs him of the benefits of a viable tradition.

The more's the pity, since jazz is the possessor of an exceptionally strong and durable tradition that counts among its pillars a number of artists still active and still in full command of their creative resources.

Outstanding among these "old masters" is the sixty-four-year-old orchestra leader-composer-pianist-arranger Duke Ellington, who, alongside the indestructible Louis Armstrong, could well be called the greatest living exponent of jazz. Ellington's career as a bandleader dates back forty years and is exceptionally well documented on phonograph records.

Columbia Records—the only American record company aware of its responsibilities to the present as curator of past treasures—has now made available, in a handsomely boxed and annotated set of three long-playing records, forty-eight pieces of Ellingtonia dating from the period 1927–40, under the title *The Ellington Era, Volume 1*. Some of the music—very little—sounds dated. But the impact of the freshness, vitality, and beauty of these "old" works constitutes a most effective refutation of the progressivist theory of jazz.

Newcomers to the world of Ellington's music might well assume that this collection is a carefully chosen sampling of "the best" from the period in question. Not so. Not counting his small-group efforts, Ellington recorded more than four hundred selections in those years, and Columbia is readying another collection to follow. It is a representative sampling—nothing more or less. In fact, every Ellington collector will miss more than one of his favorites—and there are many such collectors.

These remarks are made only by way of indicating the richness of Ellington's contribution to jazz, which began around 1925 and by no means ended in 1940. In fact, it seems a bit arbitrary of Columbia not to have broadened their perspective and included some of the works from 1947 to 1952, when the band was once again under their banner, or, for that matter, from 1956 to 1962. But these, one hopes, will come later—the "Ellington Era" is still in full swing.

Ellington is one of the few jazz veterans who has escaped from the prevalent theory of obsolescence—though there was a time, in the late 1940s and early '50s, when it was considered "in" to label him as "passé." Yet, the continuing appreciation of Ellington has, as often as not, been mainly based on his current work. Even in the booklet accompanying this collection, one finds a reflection of this attitude. Leonard Feather—never a man not to keep up with the demands of the times—talks of "seemingly primitive exercises" and "the tremendously advanced sensitivity of present-day ears." In view of the staggering amount of pretentious trash that these "sensitive" ears have so readily accepted, this seems a peculiar apologia—when none is needed. Happily, Stanley Dance does not water down his appreciation of the music in the informative program notes.

What strikes the listener first about Ellington's music is his mastery of form. These recordings were all made at a time when the limits of 78-rpm techniques still applied. The average length of the pieces is three minutes (only the two-part "Diminuendo in Blue/Crescendo in Blue" is an exception). But though seeming to be a limitation, this time stricture actually provided a disciplinary framework for Ellington's imagination. It coincided with a truth about the nature of jazz that has often been forgotten: jazz is an immensely concentrated music. Western—late Western—assumptions about the superior value of large, complex, and time-consuming structures in music gave jazz an inferiority complex. But no jazz composer—including Ellington himself—has yet created a "large" work of merit and stature comparable to the three-minute masterpieces of classic jazz. (It needn't be *three* minutes—six or seven will do, too. I have in mind the jazz suites and such.) In his most successful longer works, Ellington still remains the master of the cameo form—in *Such Sweet Thunder* and *Suite Thursday* it is the individual segments one returns to.

The three-minute form also coincided with the function of jazz, if one may be allowed to introduce such a concept. The conditions that made possible Ellington's development as an artist are interwoven with the "function" of his orchestra. For almost five years, from late 1927 until 1932, Duke Ellington and his orchestra performed at the Cotton Club in Harlem, playing for floor shows and dancing. The "jazz concert" was not a workaday reality then. Even today, the band still plays for dancing. But dancers don't stay on the floor for more than a few minutes at a time, nor do nightclub acts occupy the stage for the length of a symphony. And many an Ellington classic had its origin as "special material" for a dancer, or background to a juggling act. To imply that such origins reduce the "artistic" stature of these works is to demonstrate gross ignorance of the history of art, which has always—until it became a commodity in itself—had "functional" roots.

Ellington thus made a virtue of a necessity. He didn't invent the jazz orchestra, either. The basic instrumentation was given, and the development of Ellington's band (from two trumpets, one trombone, and three reeds plus four rhythm to a proportional increase in all but the rhythm section) followed that of jazz bands in general. His originality expressed itself in what he did with this format and instrumentation, which was to imbue it with an unprecedented (and still unmatched) richness of timbre, texture, and expressiveness.

One of his chief means for so doing was to cultivate a steady personnel. Throughout the years, there have been remarkably few shifts and changes in the Ellington band, and during the '30s there were only three defections (two due to illness) from the ranks. The remaining changes were additions. No orchestra in jazz history can point to a similar record. But the Ellington men were not just steady employables. Each member of the ensemble was an individual voice, each had a special gift, each contributed to the totality of what could well be called an organism as well as an organization.

The orchestra thus soon became a continuous workshop in which ideas could be introduced, amended, polished, and reworked; an interpretative instrument unique both within jazz itself and in music as a whole. Indeed, the conception of the band as an "organism" became so rooted in the consciousness of its admirers during the '30s that it was considered a major and unamendable catastrophe when such key men as trumpeter Cootie Williams (who left in 1940 and rejoined last year) and clarinetist Barney Bigard departed from the fold. But these critics underestimated Ellington the catalyst. The band never lost its personality.

In addition to his seemingly inexhaustible gifts as a melodist and composer, his talents as a pianist (which only recently have been duly appreciated by jazz critics), his organizational capacities, and his personal charm and urbanity, Ellington is one of the great orchestrators of all times. The unique sound of his orchestra—it has never been duplicated, though often imitated—springs in large degree from his profound understanding of harmony and, as Sidney Finkelstein (one of the few musically perceptive writers on jazz) has pointed out, harmony related to instrumental timbre. He is a veritable poet of sounds, and the range of his sensibility is astonishing. He can be tender (what band ever sounded sweeter than Ellington's in "Blue Tune"), brash, biting, sly, humorous, nostalgic . . . whatever the mood, there is an Ellington piece to fit it.

In his understanding of the overwhelming importance of sound can be found the secret of Ellington's success as a recording artist. (The history of jazz runs parallel to that of the phonograph; more than likely, one would have been impossible without the other.) From the beginning of its career, the Ellington band recorded better than any other (its chief early competitor, Fletcher Henderson's orchestra, never came through on records), and one might well say that Ellington was the first A&R (artist and repertory) man in jazz, for there can be no doubt that he was the one who saw to it that the balance was judiciously adjusted, the soloists properly placed, and the atmosphere relaxed and congenial.

Thus, Ellington's records, in contrast to most jazz discs, do give a good reproduction of the music itself. And what music it is! Among the best of these forty-eight pieces, one might cite, in chronological order, the joyous "Old Man Blues" (with its striking use of polytonality); "It Don't Mean a Thing" (after thirty-one years still the definitive version, including Duke's own later attempts); "Harlem Speaks" (with a brilliant contribution from trombonist Tricky Sam Nanton); the amazing "Clarinet Lament" (with its unearthly opening fanfare); the playful "In a Jam"; the aforementioned "Diminuendo/Crescendo in Blue" (a startling study in dynamics, displaying the virtuosity of the orchestra to the fullest); the poignant "Subtle Lament"; "Portrait of the Lion" (first in the Ellington portrait gallery, dedicated to the great Harlem pianist and early influence on the composer, Willie "The Lion" Smith), and "The Sergeant Was Shy" (a demonstration of humor and swing).

There are, of course, the famous "hit" numbers: "Mood Indigo," "Solitude," "I Let a Song Go Out of My Heart," "Caravan," and "Sophisticated Lady," proving that as a "songwriter" Ellington can hold his own among the best. (Though it must be noted, in all fairness, that some of the band's sidemen had a hand in several: Barney Bigard in "Indigo" [originally recorded as "Dreamy Blues"], Juan Tizol in "Caravan," and Otto Hardwick and Lawrence Brown in "Sophisticated Lady.")

A few words about the great sidemen. Of the featured soloists, Johnny Hodges, on alto saxophone (and occasionally soprano sax as well), and trumpeter Cootie Williams (as fine on open horn as in his well-known role of "growl" specialist) are outstanding. The late trombonist Joseph "Tricky Sam" Nanton was a unique musician; like Williams, he specialized in the use of the plunger mute, with which he produced a sound closely approximating the human voice, yet wholly instrumental—it could be either humorous or deeply moving. Harry Carney, unquestionably the greatest baritone saxophonist in jazz, has been with Ellington uninterruptedly since 1927. A tower of strength in the ensemble, he is a warm and affecting soloist. Trombonist Lawrence Brown, who joined in 1932 and is back in the fold once again today, has a big, ripe sound and brilliant instrumental technique. Barney Bigard, one of the great New Orleans clarinetists, never regained the heights he reached during his Ellington tenure. His sound is unequaled.

These were the stars. Trumpeter Bubber Miley, who left the band in 1929 and died in 1932, was the most important early member. He was a gifted writer as well as a very personal soloist, and his "Black and Tan Fantasy" and "East St. Louis Toodle-Oo" remain in the Ellington repertoire as his legacy. Arthur Whetsol, also a trumpeter, was a sensitive and lyrical player, who, like Miley, died young. Sonny Greer, the band's drummer from the start to 1951 (he met Ellington in 1919 and worked with him from then on), was an integral part of the Ellington sound, and no drummer since Greer has quite filled his shoes. Bassist Wellman Braud, from New Orleans and the oldest musician in the band, has often been maligned by critics of modernistic persuasions. But Ellington featured him as no other bandleader had ever featured a bassist, and his big tone and propulsive swing were the rhythmic foundations of the band in its early years. The great Jimmy Blanton only appears on two selections, and not in a featured role. The late Ivie Anderson, the vocalist, was as different from the average band singer as the orchestra she sang with was different from the average swing band. She appears on three selections, and one would like to hear more of her.

Alongside such RCA Victor albums as *The Indispensable Duke Ellington*, *At His Very Best* and *In a Mellotone* (among the few reissues in the Victor catalog), this set belongs in every jazz library. Even so, in terms of Ellington's total contribution, it is, to quote an Ellington tune, "just scratchin' the surface." Edward Kennedy Ellington is more than a great jazz musician—he is one of the greatest musicians of our time, and the greatest American composer yet to appear. His name and his music will long outlive the tortured products of our avant-garde experimenters. Few musicians—living or dead—have worked as long and as hard as he, and he has never received a foundation grant. But his music is loved throughout the world, and no grant can buy that kind of success.

(1963)

Ellington: 1927–40

This is an exceptional set of records—as any documentation of authentic Ellingtonia must needs be. It bears eloquent witness to the art and craft, the stature and scope of one of the greatest figures—and the greatest ensemble—in jazz. In a jazz publication, there is no need to recite the historical facts pertinent to the music contained in the package, or to list in detail all the brilliant sidemen and their accomplishments. Let's assume you know about Rabbit and Cootie, Bubber and Tricky Sam, Harry and Barney and Lawrence, and proceed to specifics.

During the thirteen years encompassed by this collection, the Ellington orchestra recorded some 370 selections—not counting the small-group work issued under the names of various sidemen. It stands to reason, therefore, that forty-eight samples—to quote an Ellington title of more recent vintage—are "just scratchin' the surface." Columbia has promised at least one other volume covering these years, and so one must suspend judgment on the choices made until a later date. Suffice it to say that every Ellington admirer will find many favorites included here—and just as many missing. The sequence is pretty much chronological, but for no apparent reason not strictly so; most annoyingly in the instance of the 1930 "Rockin' in Rhythm," which ends the first side on the heels of a 1928 selection and is followed, on side two, by a 1929 tune—in each case, the recording date took place in November, so the separation is neat indeed. The bulk—thirty-two selections—stem from the years 1932 to 1938, which does give the set a certain unity.

Jazz history, with its obsession for developmental theories, tends to handle music with hindsight and has categorized most pre-1940 Ellingtonia as "leading up to" the indisputable plateau of "Ko Ko," "Main Stem," etc. But to someone like myself, who first heard many of these pieces without knowing all this, and who was in many ways enticed into jazz by listening to them just as *music*, this approach seems regrettably limited. Indeed, what strikes me most forcibly upon rehearing all this music in bulk, so to speak, and in a sequence that differs so markedly from that followed when sampling one's own collection, is how much each individual piece has to offer just in itself . . . not, say, as an example of the "jungle style," or a specific instance in the maturation of Johnny Hodges's musical personality, or the use of the concerto form, but just as a piece of jazz music called "Old Man Blues" or "Clarinet Lament" or "The Mooche" (I like the old spelling) that captures and reflects a certain mood or paints a certain picture, and stands the test of time without need of footnotes or *explications de texte*. To me, it is the greatest possible tribute to the genius of Ellington and his famous men that this should be so, for after all, at each given moment of playing, they were making music and not writing chapters in the history of jazz.

This is not to say that one should not use the past to illuminate the present, or that jazz history is without its virtues and purposes. It is, of course, impossible to do without it. But it should not reach the point where it gets between the music and the ear, and it seems to me that today it very often does. A package like this, with full discography, critical essay, and nostalgic photos, fairly reeks of history and could conceivably intimidate the willing but hitherto uninitiated listener. Leonard Feather, in fact, finds it necessary to apologize for most of the pre-mid-1930s pieces here, describing them, in the course of an otherwise excellent article, as "primitive exercises" and "treasured museum pieces." They are nothing of the kind; if you can't feel the terrific drive and swing of Wellman Braud's bass just because he's playing four beats (or sometimes only two—oh heresy!) to the bar, you are not, my friend, an example of "the tremendously advanced sensitivity of present-day ears," but a victim of the history virus, which deprives you of the joys offered so graciously by a vital and friendly past. What's to keep in mind when listening to the older things at hand is not how much we have progressed (have we?) but rather how much we have accomplished—how many different ways jazz has found to speak emotions and attitudes, and how freshly the horn of Bubber Miley, dead all these many years, comes through to us out of times gone by but captured for all time. Thanks for that, and no apologies needed. These are stories being told, not lessons recited, and no trombonist will ever match old Tricky Sam Nanton's special things. New things or old things—what matters is good things, and there are plenty of those right here.

Such as: the joyous saxophones (historically: the beginnings of a "section") on "Hot and Bothered," one of Duke's many paraphrases of "Tiger Rag" (and it's a pity they didn't put "Braggin' in Brass" on here with it so we could see what happened to the "Tiger" in ten years . . . history without tears); the utter relaxation of the whole band on the lovely "Drop Me Off in Harlem," soft, supple, and sexy; or the sad beauty of "Subtle Lament," with one of Rex's most moving messages; or the incredible variety and excitement packed into the two minutes and fifty-eight seconds of "Old Man Blues"; or the unearthly fanfare that opens "Clarinet Lament" (or: what a master can do with "Basin Street Blues"); or the way the band backs Johnny Hodges when he comes up for his solo on "Harmony in Harlem" (how can you miss when it's tight like that?); or the way Ivie Anderson handles "Rose of the Rio Grande," supposed to be Lawrence Brown's record, but to me Ivie's for sure . . . there's something on every one: Duke playing piano like

James P. on "Jubilee Stomp" (which Jimmy, much later, recorded as "Victory Stride" . . . who had it first we'll never know); Cootie paying his respects to Louis on "Blue Harlem"—and all over the place—sometimes the whole band comes on like Pops; Tricky Sam on top of the growling ensemble at the end of "Harlem Speaks," growling like a possessed prophet but knowing what he's doing all the while; how everybody on "Bundle of Blues" speaks his own piece but yet the whole thing ties up with a ribbon into a musical entity; Bubber on "Blues with a Feeling," playing such a lovely little melody of his own, stretching out to tell his story; Johnny's soprano on "The Sheik" . . . well, pick out your own Arabian delights, and come back to them: that's half the fun . . .

A few words on behalf of the not so frequently praised members of the congregation: Arthur Whetsol, trumpet, who played with such melodic grace, taste, and nostalgia, and who brings Bix to mind on "Mood Indigo"; Freddie Jenkins, real firecracker, not often up front on this set, but very nice on "Harlem Speaks" and in his Louis spot on "Old Man Blues"; Otto Hardwick, of the creamy lead alto, who could really get around on his horn when given the chance, as on "Hop Head" (the closing ensemble of which shows that early Duke was on familiar terms with New Orleans cooking); Freddie Guy, Duke's F.G., who had a fine, dry, even stroke on first banjo and then guitar and always made himself felt, and Wellman Braud, the senior cat in the band, who always seemed to me every bit as fine a bassist as Pops Foster, though nobody talks about him. Duke must have liked what he did, for he featured him more than any bassman had ever been featured in a band. Dig him behind the "vocal" on "Hot and Bothered," when the tempo picks up, and in his struttin' solo on "Blue Harlem." Sonny Greer is perhaps not as underrated now as he was (by the hip critics) in the '30s and '40s, when it was fashionable to say that he didn't swing. Well, Duke never had another drummer like Sonny, who used his set (and a big one it soon became) to color and underline and bring out nuances in the scores with incredible skill and fancy, and never dropped the beat while he was painting.

Some factual notes to wind up: the discography errs in attributing "Lazy Duke" to the full band; it is played by trumpet, trombone, clarinet, and rhythm only. The fact that Otto Hardwick also doubled on bass saxophone is nowhere indicated, but in the big center spread of the band, you can espy the monster's neck right up in front of Duke's outstretched arm. Some discographies list one Fred Avendorf as drummer on the date that produced this (by the way, inferior to the previous) version of "Merry Go Round," and it doesn't sound like Sonny. Anybody know for sure? And to inject one carping note: no excuse for that horrible *wow* on "Sophisticated Lady," which isn't a rare disc, or for the clicks on "Clarinet Lament," which is a bit rarer but not *that* rare. Otherwise, thanks Columbia, sole keeper of the faith in the jazz past, and may you prosper! Bring us, please, soon a package of small-group Ellingtonia, among which there is some of the very finest of the vintage crop. And thank you, Duke Ellington and ever-famous orchestra, for bringing beauty into the world, then and now and for all time.

(1964)

Ellington: 1944–46

When Duke Ellington entered RCA Victor's New York studios on December 1, 1944, for his band's first commercial recording session since the summer of 1942, his first concern was to quickly prepare for release the best possible version of a song he had recently written with lyricist Don George, "I'm Beginning to See the Light." Convinced of its hit potential, the energetic George had already brought the song to Harry James, and the trumpeter had liked it so much that he had recorded it for Columbia a week earlier. That label had also just come to terms with the American Federation of Musicians. The third major label of that era, Decca, had settled in the fall of 1943. A two-year recording ban had ended. Now Ellington had to hurry to avoid being beaten to the punch with his own material.

The James version of the song rose to first position on the charts, Ellington's climbed as high as sixth, and both stayed in the Top 10 for several months, while sheet-music sales ranked fifteenth for the year. In all, it became one of the biggest hits of Ellington's career as a songwriter, and James got his name on the song—published by the company with which he was affiliated—in recognition of his role in having made it so. No doubt this success spurred Ellington to write more popular-styled songs during the next few years than in any other period; no fewer than fifteen of them are included in this compilation, only two of which had a prior identity as instrumentals ("I Didn't Know About You" is "Sentimental Lady"; "Just Squeeze Me" is "Subtle Slough"). And perhaps not coincidentally, the band had a larger complement of singers at this time than at any other.

It is important to keep such things in mind to counterbalance the picture painted by many jazz scribes of Ellington contemplating with furrowed brow the task of following what is often considered the peak of his career, the 1940–42 span of the so-called Webster-Blanton band. For one thing, few artists allow themselves to think in such terms; to be constantly confronted with one's own past is inevitably counterproductive. For another, although Ellington was more keenly aware than most of his fellow artists of the importance of phonograph records, and much better at making them than almost anyone else, he never valued records more highly than live performances. His main objective was always to keep the band working so he would have it at his disposal to lead and write for. That—not making records for posterity—was his life.

Although Ellington had been entirely out of the studios from the start of the recording ban until November 1943 (when the union first permitted the making of transcriptions solely for broadcast use), his activities are well documented by private recordings of concerts and airchecks of many broadcasts. Although World War II was on, it was a busy and fertile period for the band. They were seen in two full-length films (*Cabin in the Sky* and *Reveille with Beverly*) and several shorts, and from April through September of 1943 appeared in the heart of Manhattan at the Hurricane, a nightclub at Forty-ninth Street and Broadway. This unprecedented twenty-five-week run was made all the sweeter by being the band's first New York location date in five years, and sweeter still by offering no fewer than six weekly radio spots.

One of these, a half hour on Sunday nights at seven, was fashioned by Ellington as "The Pastel Period." With the dreamy "Moon Mist" replacing their usual theme, "Take the A Train," to set a romantic mood, the show specialized in mellow music and was very well received. The year had begun with much attention to Ellington. The week of January 17 to 23 was proclaimed "National Duke Ellington Week" by his management, the powerful William Morris Agency, and a flood of ads, articles, and radio spots (music as well as interviews) helped to set the stage for the band's first Carnegie Hall concert, on January 23.

This, of course, was the event that introduced Ellington's most ambitious work to date, *Black, Brown and Beige*, and while the critical reception was quite mixed and unquestionably disappointing to the composer, the concert itself was an unqualified success, with the hall filled to capacity, an overflow of some two hundred persons seated on stage, and more than $5,000 raised for Russian War Relief, for which the concert was a benefit (with Benny Goodman as chairman). Until the decade's end, Ellington's Carnegie Hall concerts became annual events.

As for *Black, Brown and Beige*, it had been performed at its full forty-five-minute length the night before at a sort of dress rehearsal at a high school auditorium in Rye, New York (attended by a crowd of 1,000), and five nights later in Boston, where 1,200 were turned away despite a blizzard. It is believed that Ellington never again performed the work in its entirety.

Fortunately, recordings of the Carnegie Hall and Boston Symphony Hall concerts combine to preserve it in full, and Ellington continued to tinker with parts of it for the rest of his life.

When he came to record it for the first time, almost two years after its premiere, Ellington decided to pare down the work to a mere eighteen minutes. Even so, it was an uncommon recording venture for a jazz orchestra in an era when even single 12-inch discs were a rarity, with Ellington among the few who had previously merited such treatment ("Creole Rhapsody" parts one and two, and the long-playing "Medleys" of 1932). Now he became the first to rate two 12-inch discs, encased in a four-color double cardboard sleeve, presented as an "RCA Victor Showpiece," and described, not quite accurately, as "a Duke Ellington tone parallel to the American Negro as played by the composer and his famous orchestra at his Carnegie Hall concerts." The term "tone parallel" was Ellington's own invention, and the plural "concerts" was somewhat of an overstatement, since the band had only included a couple of excerpts in its second Carnegie Hall concert on December 11, 1943.

The back cover sported a biography and a photo of the Duke, attired in a yellow robe over an open-neck white shirt, and a splendid pair of slippers, listening to his own RCA Victor records on a fancy radio-phonograph combination. The inside gatefold presented annotation uncommonly good for its day, along with photos of some of the principal sidemen. The text was the work of Inez Cavanaugh, a young African-American woman who had worked for the *Amsterdam News* and the jazz press, recorded as a singer, and later would operate a jazz club in Paris. She intelligently paraphrased Ellington's comments about the music. On the whole, it was another Ellington "first," as far as presentation of records is concerned.

During the recording ban, there had been many changes in the band's personnel, in sharp contrast to the incredible stability that had been the rule between 1932 and 1942. Barney Bigard was long gone, and Jimmy Hamilton, his permanent replacement, came on board in May 1943. Hamilton brought an entirely different clarinet voice to the band, in the Goodman tradition rather than New Orleans–flavored, with superb execution and intonation. He also doubled effectively on tenor sax and was an excellent arranger. Not much later, Ben Webster vacated the tenor chair he had himself inaugurated. His temporary replacement was the able Skippy Williams, but it was Al Sears who made himself surprisingly at home in Big Ben's role after joining in the summer of 1944. Robust in sound and with a rhythm all his own, Big Al was a soulful and swinging soloist, unjustly neglected by the critics. A bit earlier, Juan Tizol had left to join Harry James, who offered less travel and more pay. First Claude Jones and then Wilbur De Paris took his chair but could not replace his unique sound; he returned in 1951. The underrated Junior Raglin was replaced by the famous Oscar Pettiford in late 1945. An equally famous but temporary substitute for Sonny Greer, Sid Catlett, appears on a single session here. One of Ellington's earliest associates, lead altoist Otto Hardwick, left quite suddenly during a stand in his hometown, Washington, D.C., in the spring of 1946; he was replaced by Russell Procope, who would remain until Ellington's death.

The trumpet section at one point swelled to no fewer than six, due to the leader's famous unwillingness to fire a good musician. Taft Jordan had come in as a temporary replacement for vacationing Rex Stewart, but remained when the cornetist returned. The stratospheric and versatile Cat Anderson came on board in September 1944, filling the fifth trumpet chair that had been vacant since Harold "Shorty" Baker had been drafted into the armed forces earlier in the year. Also in 1944, lead man Wallace Jones was replaced by Shelton Hemphill. Francis Williams, who could play lead and high notes as well as solos, was brought in to replace Stewart when that veteran left for good in late 1945. When Baker got back from military service, there were six trumpets on hand. (Stalwart Ray Nance had also been temporarily absent to try his luck as a single, but soon returned.)

Other big bands certainly underwent more frequent changes in a period when military service and economic factors affected the band business, but because Ellington's personnel had been so stable, every change tended to be viewed as potentially significant. Actually, the unique sound of the ensemble remained intact, not least because of three constant factors: the incomparable anchor of the reeds, Harry Carney; the matchless poet of the alto sax, Johnny Hodges; and the grand romantic of the trombone, Lawrence Brown. These three, and the band itself, were taking first place in the *Down Beat* poll throughout these years. Perhaps no less important were the unique triple-threat man, Ray Nance, whose mastery of both trumpet and violin, plus his vocalisms, made him a key ingredient in the Ducal mix; and the master of the plunger trombone, Tricky Sam Nanton, whose last recordings are heard in this set. Apart from Hardwick, the band's most senior members were in the rhythm section: Ellington's boyhood friend Fred Guy, whose presence on guitar was usually felt rather than heard (but check him out on "I'm Just a Lucky So-and-So"), and the last remaining member of the original band, Sonny Greer. Much maligned by certain critics, Greer's approach to big-band drumming was *sui generis* and, for a very long time, uniquely suited to the Ellington conception. He called himself "the mix-master" and was as conscious of sound and timbre as he was of time. Because years of heavy drinking were beginning to affect his reflexes, his days with the band were numbered. (Ellington was surely relieved when his old friend and one-time mentor left voluntarily in 1951, along with Lawrence Brown, to join the small group Johnny Hodges had decided to form—although the latter two were departures that Duke definitely did not relish.) Greer can be heard at his later best on the trio performances here and on such big-band pieces as "Swamp Fire" and "My Honey's Lovin' Arms."

Billy Strayhorn's presence is felt throughout this period. He was still handling his original assignment, to craft the vocal settings, and this he did to perfection. We've mentioned the large cast of singers, and they were a varied lot. The charming Joya Sherrill, only seventeen when she joined just prior to the end of the recording ban, is surprisingly secure even in her first efforts, and surely Strayhorn's skill and tact had much to do with that. Al Hibbler, the temperamental "tonal pantomimist," as Ellington once called him, was a special favorite of the leader's, who himself tailored pieces to suit the blind singer's special talents. He was also a crowd-pleaser, especially with African-American audiences throughout the country, although white critics almost invariably failed to appreciate him. Hibbler is an acquired taste, but once you've caught on, chances are that you'll be a fan for life. Almost every song he touches here he makes his own and, aside from the very different Herb Jeffries and the little appreciated but very musical Ozzie Bailey, Ellington never had another male singer of such appeal. Marion Cox, who replaced Sherrill, is unspectacular but musically secure, with a pleasant sound; Strayhorn does well by her also. Kay Davis, used as a vocal color rather than as a singer per se, had a rich voice and good intonation; the jewel in her crown is "Transblucency." That piece is a highlight for the leader (and for Lawrence Brown), while Strayhorn's masterpiece in this batch is "Midriff" (and not just in this batch—it's one of his all-time best in a swinging vein). Strayhorn also shines in the piano duets, where the closeness between him and Ellington is illuminated from a very special angle.

That leaves the piano player, as Ellington was fond of introducing himself. His keyboard skills, though much in evidence from the very start, were not widely appreciated until much later, but musicians always knew his worth, not least as an accompanist and rhythm-section player. As can clearly be enjoyed on so many of these pieces, he was a master at creating introductions and interludes—to inject an appropriate baseball term, he was a "set-up man" beyond compare. He solos sparingly at this point in his career, but can make just four or eight bars tell a story. And he does give himself some featured space on the trio and duo pieces. "Frankie and Johnny" is something of a masterpiece of constraint and construction, and "Dancers in Love" became a staple for the rest of his life; it was one of those special ways in which he involved his audience directly, and he relished that kind of interaction.

There are several distinct kinds of Ellington music in this compilation, and it may be helpful to have it sorted out by categories. There is the previously noted substantial body of Ellingtonian popular songs and novelties (fifteen), and the related segment of pop tunes and standards (including instrumentals) from other sources (eleven). There is a fascinating component that can be called "Ellington classics reconsidered" (ten), and an equal number of new Ellington instrumentals (this group includes what amounts to the first full-band version of the 1941 small-group piece "Things Ain't What They Used to Be," as well as the feature piece constructed for Tommy Dorsey's guest appearance). Then there are the various piano features, including the duets with Strayhorn and the guest shot with the Dorsey band.

Last but certainly not least, we have the extended works *Black, Brown and Beige* and the *Perfume Suite*. I've already noted some aspects of the former. Even in this severely abbreviated form, it is a fascinating effort. In the opening "Work Song," leading roles are assigned to three "elders"—Carney, Hardwick, and Nanton—with the latter the undisputed star. The pathos with which Nanton imbues his plunger-muted statements has never been even remotely approached by other practitioners of this very special art. "Come Sunday" would become a freestanding Ellington standard; here, Nance's pizzicato and arco violin, joined by Claude Jones (giving a fine impersonation of Tizol), prepare what is perhaps the high point of the entire composition, the entrance of Hodges with the beautiful melody. Too much can never be said in praise of Hodges: to call him, as one admirer has done, "the Heifetz of the saxophone" is no exaggeration, and we know that Charlie Parker loved his playing. (Throughout this compilation, there is a special aura whenever Hodges makes a solo appearance, but his contributions to the ambience of the band's incomparable saxophone section should not be underestimated.)

"The Blues" finds Sherrill sounding surprisingly mature (like all Ellington singers, including the blues-bred Hibbler, she had excellent diction) and Sears manages to evoke Ben Webster's blues authority. Note the *a cappella* trumpet-section interlude that would be expanded into "Carnegie Blues." All of "The Three Dances" are abridged, but they find Nanton in superb form, while Taft Jordan, an expert mimic, replicates Rex Stewart's original contributions. The concluding "Sugar Hill Penthouse," all that remains of the "Beige" segment, finds Harry Carney on clarinet, leading the creamy reeds in this snippet of a charming waltz celebrating the section of Harlem where Ellington once made his home. In Duke's own words: "If you ever sat on a beautiful magenta cloud overlooking New York City, you were on Sugar Hill."

The *Perfume Suite*, premiered at the band's third Carnegie Hall concert, is a lesser work; as previously noted, only "Dancers in Love" found its way into the band's permanent repertory. The suite is mainly the work of Strayhorn; the opening "Balcony Serenade" offers some of his splendid reed scoring and has effective trumpet contributions by Nance and Anderson.

Hibbler relates well to the melodramatic mood of "Strange Feeling"; the piece builds to an effective climax. The sunny and playful "Dancers in Love" is quite another story, but melodrama returns with "Coloratura," the first of many showcases for Cat Anderson, who shows a more than passing Harry James influence. (An unissued first take is included here, but the re-make finds both band and soloist in firmer form.)

Though not an extended work in the same sense, the Ellington-Strayhorn settings of three famous W. C. Handy blues pieces were a feature of Ellington concerts during this period, sometimes introduced as "The Handy Trilogy." Composed of "Beale Street Blues," "Memphis Blues," and "St. Louis Blues," they are highly imaginative "recompositions" of these familiar themes and strains. "Beale Street" moves along at a marvelous pace (Ellington could make any tempo swing, and his band had more variety in this respect than any other) and has some remarkable work by Hamilton. "Memphis" opens wonderfully with unaccompanied Hodges. It has a neat scoring touch in Carney's subtone baritone voiced on top of the trombones; Hamilton is fine here as well, and he brings on "St. Louis," in which Marion Cox keeps her head above some very active goings-on while Al Sears fashions a solo that includes the germ cell of his later hit, "Castle Rock."

The reconsiderations of Ellington standards offer a host of felicitous touches. Carney is everywhere; majestic on "Prelude to a Kiss," "Sentimental Mood," and "Black and Tan Fantasy." (The last-named is closest to the original and can serve as Tricky Sam Nanton's swan song—it includes his last studio-recorded solo, although it was made more than a year before the great trombonist died in his sleep on July 21, 1946, aged only forty-two.) Carney also plays marvelous bass clarinet on both takes of "I Let a Song Go Out of My Heart" and on "Black Beauty." On the latter piece, Lawrence Brown also shines; the veteran trombonist, whose personal relations with Ellington were not always the best, was particularly well featured during this period. He is in fine fettle on "Caravan," perhaps the most intriguing of this whole bunch of reinterpretations, which also spots some striking Nance violin; that instrument is heard as well on "Black Beauty" and "Prelude to a Kiss." The singers are effectively employed in this segment both as tonal coloration and with lyrics to deliver. All three female singers are deployed on "It Don't Mean a Thing," enhanced by Sears's tenor, and Kay Davis does her thing on a somewhat tentative "Mood Indigo," a kind of preliminary sketch for the extended Columbia version recorded in 1950. Sears here sounds surprisingly like his successor, Paul Gonsalves.

Among the new instrumentals, "Transblucency" is the most intriguing. Based in part on Brown's great trombone solo on the 1938 "Blue Light," it first presents the trombonist, Hamilton's clarinet, and the voice of Kay Davis in counterpoint (it's a wonderful blend of sonorities), then Brown in solo, and then another unique blend of tonal colors, interweaving clarinet and soprano voice by virtue of sheer Ellington magic! "Mood to Be Wooed" is one in an ongoing series of Hodges showcases, with effective rhythmic shifts and thematic variety. (David Hajdu's biography of Strayhorn, *Lush Life*, suggests that his subject had more of a hand in creating this piece than the credits imply.) Hodges is also to the fore on "Rockabye River," on which Cat Anderson dons a plunger to good effect. That trumpeter's versatility included both composing and arranging skills, displayed on "Gathering in a Clearing," a kind of gospel meeting at which the Reverend Sears preaches soulfully. "Blue Cellophane" is Ellington's gift to Lawrence Brown; strangely, it had to wait until well into the LP era to be heard. "Carnegie Blues," the spin-off from the blues movement of *Black, Brown and Beige*, offers additional sterling contributions from Brown and Sears. One of the trombonist's finest moments here is the vigorous blues statement on "Things Ain't What They Used to Be," with Ellington's piano in rocking support. Brown excels in a quite different vein on the previously noted "Midriff." This, it must be admitted, is one of the very few Ellington-Strayhorn pieces to suffer from the time limitations imposed by 78-rpm technology. It's the ending that is adversely affected, but the band and Brown are in such splendid form that it almost doesn't matter. Hodges is the star of "Esquire Swank," which he had a hand in writing. This, incidentally, was part of a never-fully-recorded *Magazine Suite* that also included "Metronome All-Out" and a piece entitled "Downbeat Shuffle."

We have already touched on the piano pieces. "Frankie and Johnny," with its shifts in tempo and rhythm, is a marvelous display of Duke's keyboard prowess, while "Jumpin' Room Only," in contrast, sounds as if it had been invented on the spot, but nevertheless features great interplay with bass and drums. The duets with Strayhorn were recorded as the two were wont to perform them at private parties: on a single keyboard. On the reflective, romantic "Drawing Room Blues," they take turns, Strayhorn leading off, while "Tonk" finds Strays at the treble, Duke at the bass end. Then there's the visit with Tommy Dorsey's great band, a piano showcase crafted by Sy Oliver, with the descriptive title of "The Minor Goes Muggin'." The famous Dorsey trombone is heard from, and Buddy Rich gives firm support throughout. The Dorsey visit with the Ellingtonians showcases his expert ballad playing (compare his sound with Brown's) on a fine and little-known Ellington tune discovered by Stan Getz during the final decade of his life, "Tonight I Shall Sleep." There's a spot for Hodges, and don't miss Tommy's ever-so-smoothly executed ascending coda.

Last but not least, a look at the popular tunes. Some may be ephemeral, but even those are so well crafted and executed that they offer all kinds of joys to the discerning ear. And others are substantial offerings, such as

"Everything but You," with one of George's best lyrics and a marvelous conclusion spotlighting Carney at his robust best, and the delightful "Squeeze Me," with Nance showing off his vocal stuff. Among the Hibbler features, "I'm Just a Lucky So-and-So" and "Pretty Woman" stand out; the former just about perfect of its kind, with piano touches that make the whole thing cohere, and great Hodges; the latter with those ominous overtones that Hibbler could create, and a fine trumpet invention by Shorty Baker. Nance also scores vocally on "Riff Staccato," with an unusual lyric all about musical terms; the composer here is Milt Orent, a friend and collaborator of Mary Lou Williams, then on Ellington's arranging staff. There's some really swinging riffing in that last chorus, with Sears hollering. And what is there to say about the almost overripe lushness of "(All of a Sudden) My Heart Sings"? Is there any other band that had so many strings to its bow, so many hues in its tonal palette?

The answer, needless to say, is a resounding "no." There never was, and never will be, another band like Duke Ellington and His Famous Orchestra.

(1999)

Far East Suite

If you have been saving a vintage bottle of Chateau Lafitte Rothschild or some other kind of ambrosia, the advent of this new chapter in Ellingtonia provides that special occasion you have been waiting for.

There are nine parts to this new work, and if, as in the old days, they had been issued two by two, each would have been hailed as a masterpiece. They can be savored separately or *in toto*, and the music lover who acquires this record may expect it to come to live with him.

Periodically, impatient voices clamor for new Ellington music, little knowing that Ellington's music is constantly new and constantly renews itself. Besides, through the clamor, Ellington is usually at work on something *all* new, and when he is ready, it is performed and, if it meets his standards and the moment is opportune, recorded.

Sometimes, the growth is organic. Portions of this suite have been around since 1963, others have been added in the intervening years, and some, at least to these ears, are brand-new. Together, they add up to the most remarkable Ellington achievement in quite some time, perhaps since *Such Sweet Thunder*; though there have been many morsels in between, this is a veritable banquet, a feast.

At the point in a career that Ellington has reached, most artists are not expected to compete with their own past. But Ellington is a special case, and, as an artist whose lifelong body of work has achieved permanence through recording and whose past lives on side by side with his present, he is in what to a lesser man might be an unenviable position.

Over the long years of continued creativity, there have always been critical voices who have announced the beginning of the end. The first one, as long ago as 1933, was that of British critic, musician, and Ellington admirer Spike Hughes, for whom the knell of doom was the addition of Lawrence Brown's trombone to the band. It didn't belong, he said, and would destroy the character of the Ellington ensemble. There were a lot of appropriate answers to that, not least among them "Slippery Horn."

A few years later, the doubter was none other than John Hammond, who was led, by the appearance of "Reminiscing in Tempo," to declare that Ellington had become pretentious—or words to that effect. That was some five years prior to "Ko Ko." More examples could be added, among them reverse accusations of living in the past. Wisely, Ellington has ignored them all, and made them all obsolete.

As Sonny Greer points out, Ellington has always perfectly understood his obligation to his public as well as his obligation to his art, and has discharged both in a supreme manner. Still, even his staunchest admirers might marvel at the freshness, vitality, and creative force of the *Far East Suite*. It is an achievement which would allow him to perform nothing but the "Medley of Hits" for the next ten years without legitimate objection.

To describe this music in detail, to subject it to analysis, is a task for which this reviewer is not suited and toward which he is not inclined. It speaks for itself, and it must be heard. The ensuing program notes are offered only to whet the appetite.

The genesis of the *Suite* in the aural and visual impressions gathered on tours and travels is well described in Stanley Dance's excellent notes, which include many direct quotes from the composer. (If any critic has earned the right to annotate Ellington albums, it is Dance, who has never wavered, or bowed to fashion.)

As is usually the case with Ellington, the extra-musical theme is of secondary importance. *Such Sweet Thunder* was most certainly a Shakespearean suite, and the music was related to specific characters and dramatic actions. Yet, one's enjoyment of the music was not at any moment predicated on previous knowledge of these details of inspiration; the music always existed for its own sake, with no hints required.

The same holds true for this new work. To be sure, there is wide usage of exotic and "Eastern" colors and devices, but "Isfahan" is Ellington and Billy Strayhorn (and Johnny Hodges) much more significantly than it is Persia, while "Ad Lib" is on Ellington more than on Nippon. But if the music moves you to wax romantic about the mysterious East, that's perfectly fine, too. The current vogue for Indian music makes it quite timely.

Just don't expect any tampering here with the basic Ellington idiom. There are no sitars, no ragas, no signs of a Ravi Shankar influence. The language is that of classic jazz and Western music, glory be, and what is Eastern is a spice, a color, a hint—not a graft or affectation.

This is not to say that Ellington did not listen to the fascinating musics of the countries he visited. He did, and very well. But he has not allowed this to influence him into attempts to be "authentic," or any such detours. The music is authentically Ellington; the experiences have furnished a new perspective without fragmenting the unified vision of a personal conception.

The sounds in which this work abounds are the gorgeous sounds of Ellingtonia, realized by the unique voice of the orchestra. There are no other sounds like them, and one could easily become ecstatic in attempting to describe them. But their warmth, density, seriousness, and beauty have no equivalent in words.

Suffice it to say that the reeds have never blended more rapturously than, for one example, behind Hodges's matchless singing on "Isfahan," a lovely theme. And these reeds, together for so long that they think and breathe as one, are the crowning glory of this edition of the Ducal instrument.

The section's individual components are well displayed: Harry Carney, the absolute and undisputed master of the baritone, is his noble self on "Agra," a stately song; Paul Gonsalves, whose status as one of the truly great tenor saxophonists is undisputed, is inspired on "Tourist Point of View," with its arresting changes, and on "Mount Harissa," with its gentle swing.

Jimmy Hamilton's clarinet, with its beautiful tone and impeccable execution, is the voice of the "Bluebird of Delhi," a charming piece that bears the stamp of Billy Strayhorn; the clarinetist is also much in evidence on the grand finale of "Ad Lib on Nippon." The nonpareil Hodges, in a blue mood quite different from "Isfahan," is featured also on "Blue Pepper." And let us not forget Russell Procope's sterling lead voice.

There is not much featured work by the brasses: Brown has the concluding statement on "Amad," which is Arabic in mood; Cat Anderson's striking presence is felt on "Tourist" and "Pepper"; and the majestic sound of Cootie Williams rises briefly to the surface on "Bluebird." The trumpet section has been stronger, but its occasional unsureness is a blemish so minor that it can easily be overlooked. (Perfection is not a necessary virtue in art, while spirit is, and that prerequisite is present.)

John Lamb is an exceptional bassist, and he knows how to play Ellington music. He is in the spotlight on "Nippon," but his contribution is felt throughout. Rufus Jones is not the colorist that Sam Woodyard is, but he is a good musician, and works hard and conscientiously.

One major soloist remains to be mentioned: the pianist in the band. He does not tease us here, but gives generously of himself. "Nippon," until the last third, is in fact a little piano concerto, or rather, a rhapsody for piano and orchestra, with the emphasis on the former. The theme and opening passages will delight Thelonious Monk; further on, there is piano playing in the grand tradition such as one rarely hears today—not just the special tradition that evolved into jazz, but the great, expansive, full-bodied classical tradition that began with Lizst and Chopin, ended with Horowitz, but lives on in Rubinstein. It is a matter not so much of virtuosity (though Ellington has the grand gesture) as of sound and touch. He makes the piano ring and sing, and "Nippon" is an outstanding example of Ellington the pianist.

There is more, too. On the infectious "Depk," inspired by dancers and an invitation to the dance, Ellington's piano is pitted against the ensemble in a different key, with effervescent effect. His introduction and theme statement on "Harissa" are rich and warm, and he also spices "Pepper" expertly.

(A historical footnote: in the early days of the band, Ellington's piano often swung less than the ensembles or other soloists; today, he can outswing most piano players, hornmen, and rhythm sections.)

Hail, then, to the Duke of Ellington, who has added the colors and textures of the Orient to his brilliant palette, and has given us new riches on top of riches. Hail, also, to Billy Strayhorn, who has enriched his legacy. It is encouraging that music of such strength and beauty can be created in our troublesome times: music that fulfills the uplifting purport of true art.

(1967)

" . . . And His Mother Called Him Bill"

Duke Ellington's tribute to his fallen comrade-in-arms, Billy Strayhorn, is the perfect tribute to an artist: the breathing of new life into his work. No testimonial could be more fitting.

Ellington and Strayhorn were collaborators for almost thirty years, and the word "collaborator" does not even begin to express the closeness of their working relationship. Thus it is not surprising that the Ellington repertoire includes work that is so unified, so "one," that it is impossible to attribute it to one or the other.

But there is also much that is all Ellington, and much that is all Strayhorn (always bearing in mind that they were writing for the same living instrument). The pieces Ellington has chosen here are among the latter. Some of the most famous ("Take the A Train," "Chelsea Bridge," "Passion Flower") are missing, but not missed—this is not a collection of Billy Strayhorn's greatest hits.

Rather, it is a selection from his finest work; inevitably, one must conclude that these are among the pieces of which Ellington is most fond. Lovingly interpreted and beautifully recorded, they reveal the creative scope and emotional range of Strayhorn: one of the supreme melodists and orchestrators of our time.

Some have rarely been heard since their introduction on record, others have undergone several transformations, still others are here recorded for the first time. All are beautiful.

There is the wit of "Charpoy," the gentle resignation of "After All," the impish charm of "Rain Check," the turbulence of "U.M.M.G.," the flowing ease of "Boo-dah," the lyric fervor of "Day Dream," the insinuating warmth of "Snibor," the thrust of "All Day Long," and the magisterial ways with the tradition of "Rock Skippin' at the Blue Note" and "The Intimacy of the Blues."

On these, we hear the great orchestra and the great soloists at their best: Cootie Williams but twice (but with what weight), on "Snibor" and "Blue Note," taking his time in that unique way—like an elephant who is a perfectly graceful ballet dancer; visiting (and welcome) alumnus Clark Terry, who makes himself quite at home on "Boo-dah" and "U.M.M.G."; Cat Anderson, the versatile (never write him off as just a high-note man), with plunger and open on "Charpoy," and in fine form on "Intimacy"; Paul Gonsalves (but once) filling Ben Webster's triple-E shoes on "Rain Check"; Harry Carney (also but once, but always present) on "U.M.M.G.," where, at times, the whole band seems steeped in his sound; Jimmy Hamilton (the elegant one) floating gracefully over the final ensemble of "Boo-dah"; John Sanders (another visitor) impeccably impersonating Juan Tizol on "Rain Check"; and Ellington himself (the pianist in the band), with those perfect fills, stepping out gaily on "Rain Check." (Of "Lotus Blossom," more later.) Drummer Steve Little does very well indeed.

But if the album has a star, other than Strayhorn and the band, it is Johnny Hodges, for whom, in Stanley Dance's apt phrase, "Billy always wrote so felicitously." He is featured on "After All" and "Day Dream" (this new, longer version even greater than the classic 1941 interpretation), and looms large on "Snibor" and "Intimacy."

The crowning piece of work, however, is "Blood Count." This was Strayhorn's swan song, the manuscript sent down from the hospital for a special concert he could not attend. It is, even when an effort is made to disregard the circumstances of its creation, a masterpiece. Hodges, for whom it was written, plays it like an angel; a human angel. There is no milking; the taste is flawless, the sound incomparable. Words cannot adequately evoke the affect of this superb piece superbly played; it must be heard. It takes its place among the very greatest performances in the Ellington canon; a noble work, and a supremely honest one.

There is another very special piece on this album: "Lotus Blossom." A piano solo by Ellington, it was made after a session had formally ended; one hears talk and laughter in the background, but this subsides as the message comes across.

Ellington is quoted as saying that this is the piece Strayhorn best liked to hear him play. It is a piece in an almost ninteenth-century romantic vein—akin, perhaps, to Grieg or early Debussy. Some might be tempted to dismiss it as overly lush—and it is played with fervent feeling—but that would be a mistake, for what has made the modern ear suspicious of romanticism is the tendency to substitute bathos for sincere emotion. There can be no question of such substitution here: the feeling is genuine.

And this, perhaps, yields a clue to the greatness of Ellington's music (of which the work of Billy Strayhorn is an organic part): it dares the grand gesture, and with all its sophistication, it wears its heart on its sleeve. Bless it for that.

(1968)

Seventieth Birthday Concert

This double album, containing an hour and a half of mostly superb music, is one of the outstanding releases of modern times.

Recorded live in Manchester, England, in November of last year, it captures the full musical flavor of an in-person performance by the greatest band in the world. The tour during which it was taped was a grueling one, but nobody sounds tired.

Already, the album is a historic document. This particular Ellington band will never be duplicated. Johnny Hodges is gone. (By good fortune, he is well featured here.) Lawrence Brown left after the tour's end, as did Vic Gaskin. Alumnus Rolf Ericson was a temporary replacement in the trumpet section. And there were only two trombones, a shortage for which Ellington compensated by having sixth reedman Norris Turney, a most valuable addition, play trombone parts and sit in the section.

Along with such familiar fare as the medley (never before commercially recorded at such length, yet incomplete—Paul Gonsalves's "In a Sentimental Mood," one of the highlights, is missing, though the tune is hinted at in Duke's kaleidoscopic piano introduction) "Take the A Train," "El Gato," and a great "Things Ain't What They Used to Be," there are new versions of old favorites ("Satin Doll" now features organist Wild Bill Davis and a sensational Cat Anderson rideout), and several "firsts."

Among the latter: "B.P.," a jaunty vehicle for Harold Ashby's pleasant, Websterish tenor; "4:30 Blues," a fine, brooding piece with clarinets in trio and solo (Russell Procope in splendid form); "Laying on Mellow," well described by its title, and featuring Hodges at a delicious middle tempo, at length and with strength, including a startling swoop unlike anything else he ever played; "In Triplicate," a rousing tenor battle between (in this order) Gonsalves, Ashby, and Turney, with Paul the winner but Ash and Norris (who plays a booting, jump-styled tenor) holding their own; "Fife" (mislabeled "Fifi"), a charming bit of whimsy featuring Turney's tasteful, pretty, and witty flute; and "Black Swan," featuring Davis (a new color), Ellington, Gaskin, Rufus Jones, and Turney (again on flute; again very good).

Not as new but previously unrecorded is "Tootie for Cootie," its star in fine fettle. There are echoes of "Echoes of Harlem," Cootie's very special time, and a superb, Armstrong-tinged cadenza, as fine as the one on "A Train." Also not new but new to the band is Davis's "Azure Te" (mislabeled "Azure," which is a vintage Ellington piece), showcasing the composer and blessed Johnny Hodges. And a highlight of the entire program is "Black Butterfly," a 1938 masterpiece revived to feature Hodges, who caresses the lovely melody in four and a half minutes of joy and beauty. (Is the brief clarinet solo by Ash or Turney? I think the latter.)

"Perdido" spotlights Ericson, whose sly, boppish approach sometimes reminds of Clark Terry, whose feature it once was. "Rockin' in Rhythm" is a boss opener, played with fire and drive—the kind of thing most bands would save for a climax—but then, this is the band that starts where most others leave off.

Brown has only two solos: some plunger stuff on "Rockin'"—which utilizes this color, seemingly discarded by all but Duke, who after all helped to invent it, in a manner not the least "dated"—and "Do Nothin' Till You Hear from Me" in the medley. Ironic that this warhorse should be his swan song.

The piano player is amply featured in the medley, on "Rockin'," "A Train," and elsewhere. This is also a great record for ascertaining just how big a part Duke's piano (and vocal cues) plays in pacing and shaping a performance. What a master at setting the right tempo he is! And *quite* a piano player.

Nothing is perfect, and we do regret that Harry Carney is heard only on the medley ("Sophisticated Lady"—she doesn't wither) and "Rockin'" (on clarinet, which doesn't really count), and Gonsalves only on "Triplicate" (without a Gonsalves ballad, something is missing). Also, the engineering (or mastering) overbalances the rhythm section, and while Rufus Jones is his usual solid, dependable self and Gaskin sounds fine, we don't need to hear it that well.

But why carp? There haven't been enough Ellington records lately. There can never be enough. Go get this music while you can.

(1970)

Ellington at the Whitney

A nd now," Duke Ellington would announce during a concert performance with his orchestra, "the piano player!" Then, looking over his shoulder as if in search of the person he'd just introduced, he'd make his way back to the piano bench and treat his audiences to an extended solo excursion, usually on "Rockin' in Rhythm," before cueing the band back in.

Though he was a marvelous pianist, it was only late in his long career that Ellington consented to giving solo recitals. There are only three such events that we know of, and they all took place in New York. The first, in 1962, was part of the Jazz Profile series at the Museum of Modern Art, and Duke brought along his bassist, Aaron Bell, and his drummer, Sam Woodyard. The second, in 1964, was presented under the auspices of the Duke Ellington Society at Columbia University's Wollman Auditorium. Woodyard and new bassist Peck Morrison were on hand, and the maestro also called right-hand man Billy Strayhorn and mentor Willie "The Lion" Smith up from the audience to spell him at the keyboard.

The third—and last—was the event documented here: a Monday night concert at the Whitney Museum of American Art, in the Composers' Showcase series produced by Charles Schwartz. The format of these concerts included discussion by the featured composer of his music, but those who expected a concert-lecture could not have been too well acquainted with Ellington. The great composer-bandleader-pianist, while never at a loss for words, was always reluctant to verbalize about music, especially his own. So, true to form, he let the music speak for him, and, also true to form, he brought his bassist and drummer along. While he most certainly didn't need them to generate rhythm, Ellington was loath to hold the stage all by himself—perhaps the conditioning of more than a half century of bandleading.

If I remember correctly, the large and enthusiastic audience was seated on risers—the Whitney not then having an auditorium sufficiently capacious for such an occasion. It included "Flamingo" lyricist and old friend and confidant Edmund Anderson, young Ellington amanuensis Brooks Kerr, right-hand man and noted critic Stanley Dance, and other notable Ellington friends, associates, and admirers. The night before, many of us had been on hand not far from the Whitney, at St. Peter's Lutheran Church, to witness a performance of Ellington's most recent version of his *Sacred Concert*. This had taken place the day after the band's return to New York from a seven-week tour of the U.S., which had begun immediately upon their completion of a thirty-six-day odyssey that took them from Japan to Taiwan to the Philippines to Hong Kong to Thailand to Burma to India to Ceylon to Singapore to Malaysia to Indonesia, again to Singapore, then to Australia and New Zealand and finally to Hawaii! The night after the Whitney recital, Ellington was in Portland, Maine, for a joint concert with the local symphony. Eight one-nighters later, he would celebrate his seventy-third (and next-to-last) birthday one day late at Newark's Symphony Hall, greeted by two thousand schoolchildren.

Is there any other composer-performer in history who kept such a schedule? Is it any wonder that the program he presented at the Whitney was off-the-cuff rather than carefully planned? The wonder is how effective it was, how effervescently the fabled Ellington charm flowed that night, and how well he got those tired hands to work, after some warm-up motions.

Ellington structured this recital as he would have a concert with his other instrument, the orchestra. Thus, there was music old and music new, music familiar and music seldom heard, all paced with a master's touch. (It should be noted that this CD does not contain the entire concert, though the sequence of what we hear is in the order performed. Ellington's music is the best documented in the annals of jazz, yet some sources mistakenly give the date of this recital as May 5, and there is disagreement as to what was actually performed. We do know from John S. Wilson's review in the *New York Times* that "Take the A Train" and "La Plus Belle Africaine" were included.)

What first strikes the listener is the sheer sound Ellington could elicit from a piano. Here he has a fine instrument, obviously perfectly tuned, at

his disposal, but that special Ellington touch, as well as his often unorthodox voicings, no doubt developed in years of confronting pianos in varying
states of decay and neglect. The occasional hint of stride (full-fledged on
the "throwaway" "Soda Fountain Rag") reminds us of Ellington's roots in
the school of James P. Johnson, The Lion, and his somewhat younger contemporary, Fats Waller. But Ellington the pianist had long since become his
own man, with an orchestral conception and love of texture. His approach
to harmony is in the full-bodied romantic tradition, and he often makes
abundant use of chromatics. And of course he almost always keeps the
melody in view—Ellington wanted his music to sing.

Some form of medley was always a feature of Ellington concerts—it
was, among other things, a practical way to deal with requests. This one is
unusual, juxtaposing "Black and Tan Fantasy" (one of the "jungle" period
classics) with the tender ballad "Prelude to a Kiss"—both rendered out of
tempo. Then comes "Do Nothin' Till You Hear from Me" (in tempo, but
not yet swing) and the all-time hit "Caravan," most rhythmic of the four.
"Meditation," from the *Second Sacred Concert*, had become a favorite keyboard feature for Ellington, nostalgic and ruminative.

"A Mural from Two Perspectives" is something of a rarity; this may be
the only recorded version. It's a captivating little piece. In contrast, "Sophisticated Lady" and "Solitude" are two of Ellington's most famous
pieces—he could play them in his sleep, but still manages to coax beauty
from them. "Solitude" was a particular favorite of his, and he offers elaborate variations. "New World A-Coming," the longest piece here, took its
title from Roi Otley's optimistic 1943 book about the future of the American Negro. In its orchestral version, the piano played a featured role, and
thus it translates readily and completely to the keyboard. (It was premiered
at the December 1943 Carnegie Hall concert.) "Amour, Amour" and "Soul
Soothing Beach" are from the *Togo Brava Suite*, one of Ellington's last extended works. The 16-bar "Amour" is a dance pattern, and Duke reminds
of Monk here at times. "Beach" has a sunny samba flavor.

Billy Strayhorn's ultra-romantic "Lotus Blossom" became Ellington's
way of remembering his fallen comrade; it was always moving to hear.
"Flamingo," in its fine Strayhorn arrangement and with Herb Jeffries's stylish vocal, was a big hit record for Ellington. "Le Sucrier Velour," from the
Queen's Suite, is, according to the composer, "the name the French have for
a bird whose song is sweet as sugar and who feels as soft as velvet." "The
Night Shepherd," from the *Second Sacred Concert*, was a dedication to Pastor
John G. Gensel, who ministered to the New York jazz community for
decades, and hits a good groove—Ellington had marvelous time. More
good blues in "C Jam," where again there are hints of Monk (who loved
Duke's piano). "Mood Indigo," a classic, is treated to the richest Ellington hues, while "Beginning to See the Light" becomes the occasion for a

sing-along. More audience participation ensues with "Dancers in Love," from the *Perfume Suite*, in which it was a piano feature—here, it's finger snapping.

We conclude with "Kixx" (a.k.a. "The Biggest and Busiest Intersection" or "Come Off the Veldt"), a feature for Rufus Jones's crisp drumming, and also from the *Second Sacred Concert*. The encore is "Satin Doll," Ellington's last big hit tune, co-authored with Billy Strayhorn (and later equipped with a Johnny Mercer lyric). The piano player is fully warmed up by now, and this is a wonderfully loose performance.

We left the Whitney elated that night—as always after spending time with Duke Ellington, that old magician of wit, warmth, and wisdom. To have been in his presence was a special blessing, but the music contains all the magic!

(1995)

Concert of Sacred Music

Most results of that increasingly frequent ecumenical phenomenon, jazz in church, have been mixed blessings. Too often this logical wedding (is not religion a generic element of American Negro music, and has the music of the church not traditionally come from "popular" sources?) has been accompanied by extreme self-consciousness and self-congratulatory gestures. Too often the music has not been an expression of genuine religious belief.

It took Ellington to bring stature and meaning to this dimension of contemporary music and worship. With his infallible sense of propriety, he calls his offering a "concert of sacred music," not a service. Nonetheless, in spirit and content, the music is more fitting and proper to a religious context than pieces with more ambitious titles.

In typical Ellington fashion, the concert includes specially written material and reworkings of older pieces. Because he is a working musician with a need to keep his orchestra employed, Ellington cannot afford the luxury of the lengthy seclusion required for the creation of ambitious works (no foundation has ever given him a grant for this purpose; only motion-picture producers have—and their schedules are usually tightly timed).

Thus, he writes as much as he can and does wonders with the abundant existing material from a lifetime of creation. If the results are sometimes uneven, they are nevertheless remarkable; nothing touched by Ellington is without significance.

The sacred concert is a musical tapestry unified by a religious motif and the personality of Ellington. Some of the texts are traditional, literally or in terms of style; others are pure Ellington. Sometimes the music approaches the "sanctified" spirit of the root American Negro church; sometimes it is stately and grand, in the manner of Western European church music. But always it is Ellington.

"In the Beginning God," its opening six-note phrase symbolizing the first four words of the Bible, is magnificently introduced by Harry Carney's noble baritone. The voice of Brock Peters commandingly intones Ellington's catalog of what didn't exist before Creation; some of his metaphors may appear frivolous, but Ellington's seeming frivolity often is a cloak for high seriousness—the leavening of humor.

The second section of this piece involves the chorus and a driving ensemble, with leading roles for Paul Gonsalves's tenor (fluid and forceful against the orchestra and in solo cadenza), Cat Anderson's spectacular trumpet, and Louie Bellson's dramatic drums.

"Tell Me It's the Truth" opens with Lawrence Brown and Johnny Hodges in a down-home setting and features Esther Marrow's sanctified singing. This is not a polite spiritual—it's the real thing.

Marrow continues with "Come Sunday," the lovely theme from *Black, Brown and Beige*, in the setting first done for Mahalia Jackson. The beautiful melody and first-rate lyrics make this one of the most moving and meaningful artistic expressions of many American Negroes' experiences and aspirations. Later, "Come Sunday" is heard as an instrumental. After a striking introductory passage by the band, with echoes of two vintage Ellington pieces, the melody is incarnated by Hodges, whose sound here is truly holy.

"The Lord's Prayer," as done by Marrow and the band, becomes a new experience. Two spirituals from the 1963 *My People*—"Will You Be There?" and "Ain't but the One" are well sung by Jimmy McPhail, though the choral writing is rather stereotyped.

The solo-piano rhapsody "New World A-Coming," introduced in 1943 but previously only available on V Disc, is perhaps the most unexpected element in the concert. The title, taken from the late Roi Otley's book about the future of the American Negro, originally had no religious connotations, yet the mood of the piece is fitting. It is very well played by Ellington, with his wonderful orchestral touch. If the opening and concluding theme is a bit over-romantic and flamboyant, the intermittent passages are anything but, and they redeem the piece.

The concert concludes with "David Danced with All His Might" ("Come Sunday" at a fast tempo) featuring the flying feet of tap dancer Bunny Briggs, who creates marvelously melodic patterns against a gentle backdrop of swinging rhythm (piano, clarinet, and trumpet touches, plus excellent teamwork by Bellson and bassist John Lamb), building to a rousing climax.

In the context of Ellington's total output, the sacred concert is perhaps not among his greatest works (though "Come Sunday" certainly is). It is, however, a wholly convincing and impressive communication of a great musician's faith and a successful solution of the task he set himself.

(1966)

PROFILES
AND PORTRAITS

James Reese Europe

Although he is far from a household name today, James Reese Europe was New York's (and America's) most prominent dance-band leader in the early years of the century, appearing in exclusive hotels, restaurants, and cabarets, performing at social functions for the cream of society, booked for Ivy League proms. In 1913, his became the first black orchestra to make phonograph records—for Victor, then the world's foremost label. His band, playing ragtime, was a precursor of the Jazz Age, and he insisted on the importance and value of black music.

In his 1924 paean to what is now called popular culture in his book *The Seven Lively Arts*, Gilbert Seldes gives us a vivid picture of Europe at work:

> He did have contrast; it was out of the contracting stresses of a regular beat and a divergent that he created his effects. The band kept perfect time, and his right knee, with a sharp and subtle little motion, stressed the acceleration or retard of the syncope. His dynamics were beautiful because he knew the value of noise and knew how to produce it and how to make it effective; he knew how to keep perfectly a running commentary of wit over the masses of his sound; and the ease and smoothness of his own performance as a conductor had all the qualities of greatness.

A "Concert of Negro Music" held at Carnegie Hall on May 2, 1912, which will be re-created this week at Carnegie Hall, was a unique event in

American musical history. For the first time on a concert stage, prominent black instrumentalists and singers presented a program attempting to encompass the full range of their own music, formal and informal, secular and liturgical.

A church choir, a male chorus, a vaudeville quintet, solo pianists, and singers and an organist were among the participants, but the centerpiece was the Clef Club Orchestra, made up of more than one hundred members. Some performed on conventional orchestral instruments, but there was also an array of banjos, mandolins, harp guitars, drums, and grand pianos. They played marches, liturgical works, concert arias, ragtime, and virtuoso solos.

The man who presided over this ensemble, for which he also composed or arranged, was the thirty-one-year-old Europe, president and founder of the Clef Club, the first effective professional organization for black musicians. The concert, a benefit for the newly formed Music School Settlement for Colored People, was his brainchild, and it was so well received that he and his orchestra returned to Carnegie Hall in 1913 and 1914.

On its first records, the band was billed as Europe's Society Orchestra. Below, in smaller print, appeared the statement, "Recorded under the personal supervision of Mr. and Mrs. Vernon Castle." Europe's close affiliation with Irene and Vernon Castle, who had caused a revolution in American social dancing, and in fashion and mores as well, was one of the keys to his success. But Europe would doubtless have gone far even without the Castles, for he was a man of extraordinary talent, ability, and vision.

He was born on February 22, 1881, in Mobile, Alabama, into a musical family (his older brother John became a reputable ragtime pianist; his younger sister Mary enjoyed a long career as a music teacher and choral director), with whom he moved to Washington at the age of ten. He studied piano and violin and arrived in New York in 1903, preceded by his brother, who got him a job as pianist in a cabaret. He continued his studies with, among others, the composer Harry T. Burleigh, a pupil of Dvořák.

Europe soon became involved in the then thriving world of black Broadway musical shows, first as a member of a performing group, the Memphis Students (neither students nor from Memphis), who enjoyed a five-month run at the Victoria Theater. Here Europe first met the gifted drummer Buddy Gilmore, later the star of Europe's own bands.

From 1906 to 1910, Europe was active as a composer and musical director, on Broadway and on the road, for several successful musical comedies, including the Bert Williams vehicle *Mr. Lode of Koal*. The sudden decline in the visibility of black shows and performers on Broadway put an end to this stage of Europe's career. Undaunted, he turned to the dance-band field, which was generally shunned by educated black musicians like himself.

He enlisted a distinguished nucleus of composer-performers (among them Ford Dabney, Joe Jordan, William Tyers, and Will Vodery) and formed, in April of 1910, the Clef Club. According to R. Reid Badger, a professor of American Studies at the University of Alabama who is at work on a biography of Europe, his aim was to provide "a central union, clearing-house, and booking agency for the employment of black musicians anywhere in New York and to oversee their contracts and guarantee their professionalism."

Europe was elected president and appointed conductor of the club's official orchestra. One hundred members strong, it gave its first public performance at Harlem's Manhattan Casino. "Never before," reported the *New York Age*, "has such a large and efficient body of colored musicians appeared together in New York City." There were several more such events, and Europe, as skilled in this as in other areas of management, saw to it that they were well publicized, even in the white press. The Carnegie Hall concert was a direct outgrowth of these successes.

But Europe had more in mind than visibility. In an interview with the *New York Evening Post* in 1914, he explained that he did not wish to imitate white orchestras but rather wanted to develop "a kind of symphonic music that no matter what else you may think, is different and distinctive, and that lends itself to the peculiar compositions of our race."

Much had already been noted about one aspect of Europe's music. In the words of David Mannes, the violinist-educator who established the Music School Settlement for Colored People and later founded the Mannes School of Music, it had a "very imposing and seductively rhythmic quality." But in the interview, Europe put his finger on something of equal importance.

"Although we have first violins," he said, "the place of the second violins with us is taken by mandolins and banjos. This gives that peculiar strumming accompaniment . . . which is something like that of the Russian balalaika orchestra. . . . For background we employ ten pianos. That, in itself, is sufficient to amuse the average white musician who attends one of our concerts for the first time. The result, however, is a background of chords which are essentially typical of Negro harmony."

Maurice Peress, the conductor and musicologist who has painstakingly restored the music of Europe's 1912 concert (as well as the other two landmark concerts in the series), feels that this comment about harmony relates directly to jazz, and indicates that Europe had grasped a fundamental aspect of its developing nature. In his work on Europe's own compositions (some scores and parts fortunately survive), Mr. Peress said that he had encountered "unusual modulations, ragtime licks, and Sousa-like figures," and added that he perceived Europe "more as a catalyst, a great role model, than specifically a composer. The orchestral masterpiece on the program is Burleigh's 'On Bended Knee.'"

But the concert music of the huge orchestra was not Europe's main pursuit. By 1913, when a *New York Herald* reporter told him it seemed that he "has all but secured complete control of the cabaret and dance field in the city," Europe did not disagree. "Our Negro orchestras have nearly cleared the field," he said. Many bands were now operating under his name, and he had to make his nightly rounds to front each one briefly, since, a reporter noted, "Europe's band without Europe seems like *Hamlet* without Hamlet." The *Age* listed some of his current social bookings: "On Aug. 16, for debut of daughter of George I. Scott; on Aug. 18, for Mrs. Eva William Astor at the home of her son Vincent at Beechwood; on Aug. 23, for Mrs. T. Suffern Tailor, and on Sunday, Aug. 24, at Oakwood Farms for Mrs. Alfred Gwynne Vanderbilt."

During 1914, Europe and his first-string, eleven-piece band participated in the Castles' celebrated "Whirl Wind Tour" of thirty-five cities in twenty-eight days. The Castles credited Europe with having introduced them to the fox-trot, the most enduring of the many steps they popularized. Europe himself credited W. C. Handy, because it was Europe's playing, on the piano, of Handy's "Memphis Blues" that had given birth to the dance.

Vernon Castle, an enthusiastic avocational drummer, often sat in with the band. The Castles sometimes sound very up-to-date, as when Irene writes in their 1914 book *Modern Dancing* that "while we dance [we are] warring not only against unnatural lines of figures and gowns, but we are warring against fat, against sickness, and against nervous troubles." By their choice of accompanists, the Castles were also breaking down some of the "unnatural lines" of racism; according to Professor Badger, a true friendship developed between Vernon Castle and James Europe.

Europe's success had now reached such a level that the Clef Club became synonymous with his name. Not surprisingly, this caused ill feeling among some members; in any event, in mid-1914, Europe abruptly resigned and formed the rival Tempo Club. His large band now became known as the National Negro Orchestra, and as such it performed at Carnegie Hall. The new club prospered; in 1915, it handled nearly $100,000 worth of bookings, an enormous sum for the time. On October 3, the Tempo Club staged an extravaganza at the Manhattan Casino. The Castles presented Europe with a bronze statuette of themselves and warmly thanked him for all his help. They also demonstrated the fox-trot and judged a dance contest. And in an innovative "surprise," the image of James Europe, conducting, was projected on a movie screen while the band followed its disembodied leader in a live performance.

This was the climax of Europe's Castle period. In December, the British-born Vernon enlisted in the Royal Air Corps (he was killed in 1918).

When the United States entered the war, Europe enlisted in the 15th Regiment of the New York National Guard. Commissioned a first lieutenant—one of the few black officers even in this segregated unit—he was initially assigned to a machine-gun company, but the regiment's enterprising commander, Colonel William Hayward, asked Europe to put together "the best damn band in the Army." Europe explained he could not recruit good musicians for a soldier's pay, and Hayward procured a $10,000 donation from a wealthy industrialist.

Europe set about his task with characteristic energy. First, he asked to double the normal military band contingent, saying he could not make good music with a mere twenty-eight men. Hayward agreed, and also let Europe go to Puerto Rico to recruit the good clarinet players he claimed he could not find in the United States; apparently he was unaware of the New Orleans clarinet school. The unit was assigned to the American Expeditionary Force and landed in France on New Year's Day of 1918.

There were other black Army bands in France—two of them led by Europe's colleagues Dabney and Vodery—but Europe's name was magic even in the Army, and his band, dubbed the Hellfighters, was soon assigned to entertain American troops on leave at Aix-les-Bains for six weeks. In all, the band traveled more than two thousand miles, performing for Allied troops and French civilians. But Europe also saw combat and was exposed to a gas attack.

The band's resounding success is best described by Europe himself, in the last major interview he gave, published in the April 26, 1918, issue of the *Literary Digest* under the headline "A Negro Explains 'Jazz.'" Europe told how an invitation to give a single concert in Paris stretched into an eight-week stay.

"Everywhere we gave a concert it was a riot, but the supreme moment came when [we performed] in conjunction with the greatest bands in the world—the British Grenadiers' Band, the band of the Garde Republicaine, and the Royal Italian Band. My band, of course, could not compare with any of them, yet the crowd, and it was such a crowd as I never saw anywhere else in the world, deserted them for us." He goes on to tell how the French band borrowed one of his jazz arrangements, couldn't play it right, and then "felt sure that my band had used special instruments." Some of the French musicians later came to a Europe rehearsal specifically to examine the instruments.

In the interview, Europe reaffirms his thinking about the destiny of black American music. He was now, he said, "more firmly convinced than ever that Negroes should write Negro music. We have our own racial feelings and if we try to copy whites we will make bad copies. . . . We won France by playing music which was ours . . . and if we are to develop in America we must develop along our own lines. The music of our race springs from the soil, and this is true today with no other race than perhaps the Russians."

We will never know how James Reese Europe's music would have developed along its own lines. His band marched up Fifth Avenue and then through Harlem in a victory parade to the cheers of an estimated million New Yorkers on February 17, 1919. A month later, Europe presented his augmented Hellfighters in concert at the Manhattan Opera House. The *New York Sun* reported "a flood of good music" and "a gorgeous racket of syncopation and jazzing." It was the start of a projected world tour, buttressed by two dozen new recordings for the Pathe label, which advertised Europe as the "Jazz King."

But on May 9, during a Boston concert, Europe was stabbed in his dressing room by a drummer, Herbert Wright, whom he had reprimanded. The neck wound, inflicted by a penknife, seemed superficial, and Europe carefully told his concertmaster how to conclude the performance. At the hospital, doctors discovered that Europe's jugular vein had been severed. All efforts to stop the bleeding proved futile. Within hours, James Reese Europe, aged thirty-eight, was dead.

Even in death, this remarkable man made history: his was the first public funeral ever accorded a black person by the City of New York. Thousands lined the street for the cortege, and many civilian and military dignitaries attended the service, held at St. Mark's Church on May 13. A second service took place the next day in Washington, D.C., and on May 15, Europe was buried with full military honors in Arlington National Cemetery.

The *New York Times*, in an item on the editorial page on May 12, 1919, noted his success in France and his importance in "a different sort of music which may eventually possess considerable merit," and said this about him: "Europe might have done much more if he had lived. Ragtime may be Negro music, but it is American Negro music, more alive than much other American music; and Europe was one of the Americans who was contributing most to its development."

As Europe was preparing for his final tour, a young musician named Paul Whiteman had just begun his first engagement as bandleader, in San Francisco. Within a year, Whiteman was in New York, and in 1924, he presented the concert at Aeolian Hall that for so long has overshadowed Europe's Carnegie Hall presentations. Soon thereafter, Whiteman was dubbed "King of Jazz." At the very least, he would have had a rival to the title in James Reese Europe.

Europe was active at a moment when black American music was in transition from ragtime to jazz, and he did much to bring about that transition. In the words of the conductor and composer and jazz historian and analyst Gunther Schuller, he was, "along with Jelly Roll Morton, the most important figure in the prehistory of jazz." Beyond that, he "brought a new dignity to Negro musicians. . . . He was the real initiator of the Jazz Age and a mentor of countless numbers of Jazz Age musicians."

Given Europe's faith in the creative resources of music, he would likely have welcomed the appearance of a new kind of jazz, the music personified by Louis Armstrong, and by the trumpeter's only early rival as a soloist, Sidney Bechet. And perhaps it is no coincidence that Bechet's international career was launched, later in 1919, by Europe's early mentor and frequent associate, Will Marion Cook. Surely there can be no doubt that the orchestra Cook took to Europe was inspired by, and modeled on, the pioneering Carnegie Hall experiments of James Reese Europe.

(1989)

Note: In 1995, Oxford University Press published Reid Badger's A Life in Ragtime, *an authoritative biography of James Reese Europe that brought this key figure in American music fully into view.*

Paul Whiteman

Paul Whiteman, seventy-seven, died December 29, 1967, in Doylestown, Pennsylvania, of a heart attack.

In the 1920s, during the heyday of his fame, Whiteman was dubbed "King of Jazz," a title that was to haunt him in later years, and which made difficult any objective assessment of his large contribution to popular music.

The genesis of the title has often been misunderstood. It was coined at a time when the term "jazz" had a different meaning, a fact that becomes obvious when one considers that the '20s were known, contemporaneously, as "The Jazz Age," though hardly anyone at that time knew what jazz music really was. Jazz was simply a handy synonym for the peppy dance rhythms and hectic tempo of life peculiar to the period. Thus Whiteman should not be accused of usurping a title to which he had no right, for he was indeed the kingpin of the popular music world.

Paul Whiteman was born in Denver, Colorado, March 28, 1890. His father, Wilberforce Whiteman, was a music supervisor in the public schools

(Jimmie Lunceford was his student), and his mother had been a singer. The boy began on violin at seven, under the strict thumb of his father. Later, he switched to viola and became a member of the Denver Symphony, and then of the San Francisco People's Symphony.

After a hitch in the Navy, where he was a bandmaster, he formed his first dance orchestra in 1919. (This band included the New Orleans clarinetist Gus Mueller.) He was discovered by the Los Angeles movie colony, and in quick succession landed choice engagements in Atlantic City and at the Palais Royale on New York's Broadway.

In New York, Whiteman's smooth (for the period) and eminently danceable music became a sensation, and when Victor signed him to a recording contract in 1920, his popularity spread. Such records as "Whispering" and "Japanese Sandman" sold in the millions, and the band was featured in the Ziegfeld Follies, in George White's Scandals, and at the Palace Theater.

After returning from a European tour, Whiteman staged his famous (to some, notorious) concert of "Symphonic Jazz" at Aeolian Hall on February 12, 1924. For this occasion, he commissioned *Rhapsody in Blue* from George Gershwin, and four short pieces from Victor Herbert, and his invited guests included Rachmaninoff, Stravinsky, Kreisler, Stokowski, and Heifetz.

The concert was an enormous success, and later was said to have made jazz "respectable," but since no actual jazz was performed, this would seem to have been an impossible feat.

However, the concert, and Whiteman's insistence on the highest standards of musicianship in his organization, did contribute to raising performance levels in American popular music, and throughout his many years as an active bandleader, Whiteman employed many of the top instrumentalists and arrangers.

He was the first bandleader to insist on special arrangements, and many of his musicians were expert "doublers" on two or more instruments. His repertoire ranged from "symphonic" versions of light classics, and such substantial pieces as Gershwin's *Concerto in F* (which he introduced), to novelties supplied by the famous Rhythm Boys (Bing Crosby, Harry Barris, and Al Rinker).

It also included a measure of jazz, especially when one or more of his star sidemen were allowed to take a "hot" (i.e., improvised) chorus or two. In the middle and late '20s, this "hot contingent" included such players as Bix Beiderbecke, Jimmy and Tommy Dorsey, Joe Venuti, Frank Trumbauer, Red Nichols, Min Leibrook, Andy Secrest, Izzy Friedman, Ed Lang, and Bill Rank. There was also bassist Steve Brown, who had been with the New Orleans Rhythm Kings.

Whiteman's arrangers included Ferde Grofé, Roy Bargy, Matt Malneck, Lennie Hayton, Don Redman, William Grant Still, Fred Van Epps, and two men, Bill Challis and Tom Satterfield, who were especially sympathetic to Beiderbecke and often scored whole Bixian choruses for the full brass section.

In the '30s, Whiteman concentrated on film and radio work, though he still toured with the band. Jack Teagarden was with him from 1933 to 1938, and in this period, Red Norvo, Charlie Teagarden, Bunny Berigan (briefly), Trumbauer, Miff Mole, George Wettling, Rollo Laylan, and other jazzmen also passed through the ranks.

Whiteman can well be said to have created the featured band vocalist. Crosby was first and biggest. With Whiteman, Mildred Bailey became the first featured girl singer with a name band. Teagarden did vocals, and so did Red McKenzie and Johnny Mercer; in 1938, Whiteman introduced his Modernaires.

In 1943, Whiteman became music director of the Blue Network (later ABC), conducting his *Philco Radio Hall of Fame*. By the '50s, his music had gone out of style, but though he retired several times, he made comeback attempts as recently as 1960 and 1962; in the latter year, he played a month in Las Vegas. At the peak of his career, he had been the world's highest-paid bandleader, taking in as much as $10,000 for a night of providing entertainment for millionaires' parties. His income for 1925 was $680,000, and his recording of "Three O'Clock in the Morning" sold 3.4 million copies. He was famous for his generosity, paid his musicians the biggest salaries, and was considerate of their problems.

As a conductor, the 6-foot, 300-pound Whiteman was an imposing figure physically, but though his bands put on a great show, he himself was not a showman—he would merely flick his baton or wag his head: but he knew what he wanted, and how to get it from his men.

Whiteman's hobby was automobile racing, and he was a director of Daytona Speedway in Florida and several other well-known tracks. He was married four times, and is survived by his widow, a son, and three daughters.

Among Whiteman's thousands of records, a number contain fine jazz solos and good work from the band (and the arrangers) that compares well with the best of the period. It was long the fashion among jazz collectors to savor only the solos and denigrate the band as a whole, but this is an error, as such pieces as "From Monday On," "Lonely Melody," "San," "Miss Hannah," "Louisiana," "Changes," "Nobody's Sweetheart," and "Travelin' Light" will bear out.

No "King of Jazz," Paul Whiteman was by any standard one of the most important figures in the history of twentieth-century American popular and dance music, and he set the stage for many things to come.

(1968)

Hot Lips Page

In its present state, the written history of jazz is to a large degree the result of accidents. Among these accidents are the dissemination and availability of records; the personal preferences (and prejudices) of the jazz historians; the personalities, habits, and habitats of individual musicians; and that most basic and consequential of all accidents: fate. To be sure, some individuals loom so large that they couldn't be accidentally overlooked or forgotten. But others, some of equal stature, have been condemned to the shadows though their music, trapped in the grooves of obscure phonograph records, shines brightly for all time.

Oran "Hot Lips" Page is one of these forgotten giants. Or perhaps "neglected" is a better word. His name is mentioned in many of the books, his picture appears in Feather's Encyclopedia, and he is quoted (and talked about) in *Hear Me Talkin' to You*. But in death, as throughout his life, recognition is granted to Lips only halfway. Somehow, parts of the man and his music are neatly labeled and filed while the whole remains invisible. Some praise his blues, some call him a "great growl specialist"—and almost all point out his similarity to Louis Armstrong, who never growls and whose blues are New Orleans blues, not Texas and Kansas City blues. The similarity seemed to mean more than the differences. And it *was* an astonishing similarity: Lips came closer to the essence of Louis's music, in terms of feeling, projection, architecture, and force than any other jazz trumpeter. And this achievement—innate rather than acquired—was both his strength and his undoing. Fate opened many doors to Lips, but when he was set to step across the threshold, they were slammed in his face. Yet he never lost faith in the future, and his music was an exuberant affirmation of life.

Oran Page was born in Dallas, Texas, in 1908. His father died when the boy was eight. Oran started running errands and doing odd jobs to help out, but his mother, who taught general subjects in high school and gave music lessons in her spare time, saw to it that he did his homework. She wanted her son to become a doctor. But once little Oran discovered that, in his own words, "he could make more money blowing a trumpet than shining shoes," he was stuck on music. And the motivation, one can be sure, was not entirely economic. Like Louis, he got his musical start in a kids' band, organized by a bass drummer named Lux Alexander. The band played for weddings, picnics, parades, "firesales and lodge meetings." At fifteen, Lips had passed the age limit for kids' bands and spent the summer touring with a carnival and minstrel show. He soon became a regular on the famed (and infamous) TOBA circuit. One summer, he traveled as far as Atlanta, Georgia, then a Negro entertainment center in its own right. There he backed up Bessie Smith.

Another tour consisted of a series of tent shows with Ma Rainey. She took an interest in young Oran. "Ma did what she could to encourage me," he later recalled. She took him along all the way up to New York, where they played the Lincoln Theater. Around this time, Lips also took a trip on his own, up to Chicago to hear and see the band he had heard so much about: King Oliver with Louis Armstrong. "Up to then I thought I had heard everything," Lips told Kay C. Thompson in 1949. "The next time I went to hear them, I had my little old $15 Sears & Roebuck horn tucked under one arm, hoping for a chance to sit in. I'd been sitting at a table over in the corner and when I commenced to play, waiters and bouncers came running from all directions and I think they would have tossed me out then and there if Chippie Hill, who was on the floor singing, hadn't hollered at them to let me alone."

(The friendship struck up with Chippie Hill on this occasion was to last until the singer's untimely accidental death in 1950. At Jimmy Ryan's on Fifty-second Street, or at the Riviera in Greenwich Village, where Chippie worked during her fabulous comeback in the late '40s, Lips would often sit in with Chippie, following her as she took her characteristic stroll around the joint, giving all the people some direct and spicy advice. Lips would back her up, softly but *there*, with a perfect counterline to her saucy, choppy phrases. Together, making music or chatting at the bar, these two were the living presence of the past.)

As the King Oliver incident reveals, Lips heard Louis early. Like June Clark, who came to Chicago and brought the message back to New York, Lips started to spread the gospel in the South and Midwest. Almost a decade later, in 1932, Lips and Louis really got together for the first time. "While I had met him before, he had always been like God to me, and it never occurred to me that he would ever spend a whole afternoon with me, giving me pointers on this and that." There were two other trumpeters who made an impression on Lips when he was a youngster. One was Harry Smith, the other Benno Kennedy (later with Alphonso Trent), who was known for his "trick lip" and "could play the most perfect high C you ever heard." ("Of course, there is really no such thing as a 'trick' lip," Lips added.)

After finishing high school, Lips started college, but it was mainly a gesture to his mother, and soon he was a full-time musician. In 1928, he joined bassist Walter Page's Blue Devils, a territory band that already included Buster Smith on lead alto. "King Oliver, of course, was the chief influence, then Jelly Roll Morton, and then Duke Ellington, in that order," Lips recalled. Lips was the one who got a pianist from New Jersey, recently arrived in Kansas City, into the band: Bill Basie. Lips, Basie, and Jimmy Rushing joined Benny Moten's band in 1929, and Walter Page soon followed them, turning the Devils over to Buster Smith. Moten was in with Boss Pendergast, and Kansas City was jumping—perhaps like no other city has jumped before or since. In those days, Lips was known and billed as "The Trumpet King of the Midwest," and novelist Ralph Ellison recalls how the people would crowd around the bandstand when he was featured.

Lips made his first record with the Blue Devils. With Moten, he was featured on the 1932 recordings, which are the band's greatest, and his solos show that his unique and personal style had already taken shape. (Hear the difference between Lips and the other trumpet soloist on "New Orleans," for example.) When Moten died in 1934, the boys had a conference and Basie was voted leader. But Lips fronted the new band. And now fate first stepped into the life of Oran Page. Let him tell us about it:

"It was shortly after all this happened that I came to leave the band. Along with playing trumpet, I had been acting as M.C. when we put on shows, helping with radio announcements during broadcasts, and handling various promotional activities." (And that wasn't all: in a 1956 *Down Beat* interview with Jack McDaniels, Buster Smith, who was back with the band by 1935, told of the genesis of "One O'Clock Jump," the national anthem of Kansas City jazz. Basie was responsible for the piano introduction, with the modulation from F to D-flat, Buster sketched out the sax part, and Lips took care of the brass section part.) "When Decca sent out Mayo Williams to look us over, someone had given him a letter to me, and I arranged for him to meet Basie and the rest of the boys. Then John Hammond came to town. He was much impressed with what the former Moten band was doing, and, as I recall, was the one really responsible for Basie's switch East. The same night that Hammond came in, Louis Armstrong and Joe Glaser were in town, and they came to hear us, too. The next thing I knew, Glaser was urging me to come East to form a new outfit of my own. That's what brought me to New York again in 1935."

An exclusive contract with Glaser (no mass producer yet, but already a man of influence), a big band of his own, a booking at Small's Paradise in New York . . . it must have seemed ideal. And yet—had Lips remained with Basie, who can tell if it would not have been the decisive break for him? As it was, Lips's career as a leader, which spanned some eighteen years, saw him at the helm of many great bands but always just short of real success. When Basie and the boys celebrated a silver jubilee for Count at the Waldorf-Astoria a few years before Lips's death, who was asked to emcee and preside over the festivities? Why, Lips, of course, once again fronting the band for which he had done so much.

What happened in those eighteen years? Lips traveled far and wide. He was featured with Basie at Carnegie Hall in 1938, and with Fats Waller at his Carnegie Hall concert in 1942. He broke it up at the Paris Jazz Festival in 1948, triumphant in the company of such as Charlie Parker and Sidney Bechet. In 1941, he spent five months with Artie Shaw as featured instrumentalist and singer. He made a goodly number of records, many of them excellent. But he never got the "hit" he was always looking for. He "discovered" many talented musicians, featured them generously, and gave them his blessings when they left him for better-paying and more glamorous jobs. (Lips had a good ear for tenors. Among the men he helped bring to the fore are Don Byas, Lucky Thompson, Ike Quebec, Ray Abrams, Jessie Powell, Hal Singer, and Paul Quinichette; pianist Hank Jones had his first "name" job with Lips, as did drummer Herbie Lovelle.) He was a good leader—too good. Agents and managers took advantage of his good nature. Record companies signed him and gave him nothing (or inferior material) to record. Bookers cheated him. Often, especially in later years, his band would be stranded somewhere on the road. But Lips always made it back to New York and got a new band together. When he did get that million-seller record it was as Pearl Bailey's partner on "The Hucklebuck." Lips had top billing on that record, but it was Pearl who went on to the big time.

And yet—wherever Lips went the people loved him. They knew him on Fifty-second Street, at the Apollo, at Minton's, and at every other after-hours place, fancy or plain backroom, from coast to coast. They knew him at Eddie Condon's, at the Savoy in Boston, at backwoods dances and in glamorous ballrooms, at stage shows on Times Square, and deep down South. Wherever jazz went, Lips went too. And whatever the groove, he fitted. He went way back to Ma Rainey and the deep Texas blues, and far ahead with the boys at Minton's before bop was a concept.

In the early '40s, pianist Marty Napoleon once told me, a band of which he was a member played at the Grand Terrace in Chicago. The leader of the relief band was Lips Page, and in the middle of the engagement, his tenorman, Cecil Scott, suddenly took ill and had to be sent home to New York. Lips wasn't worried. He said he knew a good tenorman in Chicago. "The next night," Marty remembered, "we were gabbing during intermission when I hear this saxophone. I moved a little closer to the bandstand, and I never missed a set after that one." The tenorman that Lips had had up his sleeve was one Charlie Parker.

Lips and Bird were a double bill at Birdland in the very early days of that club. Lips had a wild little band with the great Rudy Williams on alto, Joe Buxton on trombone, and Jack "The Bear" Parker, an unsung hero, on

drums. Their whirlwind version of "Sweet Georgia Brown" knocked Charlie out every time. And around the same time, Lips would drop by at Jimmy
Ryan's or the Stuyvesant Casino and teach the kiddies a thing or two about
traditional jazz.

But though Lips knew the traditional repertory backward and forward
and could hold his own with the boppers, he was really at home in a swinging, jumping mainstream setting. Lips had many big bands during his career,
and they were good ones. (His 1938 band is at its best on "Skulduggery"
[Bluebird], arranged by Harry "Father" White, and his powerful 1945
band, with Ben Webster, Don Byas, Earl Bostic, Benny Morton, and Sandy
Williams can be heard on "Corsicana," one of the best big-band records of
its kind, Basie and the somewhat shallow recorded sound notwithstanding.)
But frequently, circumstances did not allow for a big outfit, and Lips would
put together jumping little crews, mostly consisting of trombone, alto,
tenor, and a full rhythm section—the kind of band that could wash away
any competition, no matter what the size. Lips was full of ideas, and he
could take a seemingly simple riff pattern and dress it up in style.

These little bands provided a kind of jazz that is rarely heard today. It
was a combination of Kansas City and Harlem; a shouting, pulsating music,
freewheeling and yet precise, and solidly steeped in the blues. Sometimes,
when Buddy Tate's or Buck Clayton's small bands really get loose, there is
an inkling of what Lips's jazz was like—but without Lips it isn't quite the
same.

The blues have been granted Lips, but not emphatically enough. Lips
was a master of the blues: vocal or instrumental, happy or sad, fast, medium,
or slow. His blues came straight from the roots, and were distilled by city
life and city experience. In most cases, Lips followed the classic blues pattern. His vocal blues are mostly love blues—all shades of love. And love, the
universal denominator of the blues, is transmuted into all facets of experience: joy, scorn, hunger, thirst, laughter, ballin' it up. Lips's voice, a jazz instrument beyond compare, was rich in shadings and inflections that could
transform the simplest blues lines into a fresh discovery. The words were
his own, and like all great bluesmen, he drew freely on the tradition. And
when he took up the trumpet after the vocal, there would ensue a demonstration of why the blues are the eternal wellspring of jazz—and of jazz
melody. Lips could growl out the blues with a plunger mute, or sing them
on open horn, with that powerhouse trumpet sound that could soar above
the most shouting big band, or drive an unorganized jam ensemble right
home together.

The jam session was Lips's element. Only Roy Eldridge, who in recent
years has become the carrier of Lips's message (they were always close, but
nowadays Roy seems to get into things that spontaneously bring Lips to

mind as never before), has a comparable love and affinity for the free exchange and unfettered blowing that a jam session in its real sense can offer. Lips could vitalize the dullest session and inspire men who had seemed mediocre musicians before to blow their hearts out. He was never too big to play with the beginners, or the has-beens or never-weres, and he was always ready to take on all high-powered comers. At the Central Plaza or Stuyvesant Casino, he could take the tired old "Saints" out of their pseudo-Dixieland setting and rock the house with Louis-like flights. He even took the "Saints" uptown.

In the heart of Harlem, there used to be a spot called the Lotus Club. It was what is known as a "bucket of blood," an awesome-sounding term somewhat synonymous with "barrelhouse." The Lotus had Wild West–type swinging doors, paint peeling from the walls, a stand-up bar, a few wooden, clothless tables separated from the bar area by a fence with a gate, and a small bandstand tucked away in a far corner. Bottled beer was twenty-five cents (who needs a glass?), and there was plenty of whiskey and conversation. The Lotus was jammed to the rafters any night. The resident trio was led by a tenorman nicknamed "Sleepy" (Charlie Brown), who invariably took off for the land of nod between sets (and sometimes during piano solos on slow numbers); there was an out-of-tune upright piano and a battered set of drums. Sitting in was frequent, and Lips's protegé, Nat Lorber, often played here, as did Shad Collins and Lips himself.

Lips would sing some blues here that never got on record, and the people knew what he was singing about. He would growl a few choruses, with a plunger, or a water glass, or just with hand and throat. No other jazz growl came as close to an utterly human vocal sound, reaching back into the primeval sources of jazz sound. Tricky Sam was contender No. 1, Bubber and Cootie in the race. (If you can lay your hands on it, or if it is ever reissued, try "I Won't Be Here Long" [Decca] for a sample.) Sometimes, Lips would take just the mouthpiece of his horn and a glass, and growl away—as he does on "Sweet Sue," first solo, on the LP *Jammin' at Rudi's.*

When the Lotus crowd got a little rowdy, Lips would unleash some fast stuff, and pretty soon everybody was too busy listening and foot-tapping to worry about playing the dozens. Once, when the place was at its loudest, Lips intoned the "Saints," and took them for a little ride. At the end, you could have heard that metaphorical pin drop. Not even Lips, with his huge capacity, could have accepted all the proffered drinks—for how else can you show your appreciation under the circumstances?

Lips was a regular at Monroe's and Minton's whenever he was in town. At that time, around 1941–42, Lips had done his stint with Artie Shaw, who broke up his band to join the Navy, and was a big name in Harlem. Harlem had become Lips's hometown, perhaps more than Dallas or Kansas City ever had been. If Dizzy ever outblew Roy at Minton's . . . well, was you there? Charlie Christian, who was, can no longer tell. As for Lips, Dizzy had this to say about him not too long ago: "When Lips gets on the blues, don't mess with him; not me, not Roy, not Louis—nobody!" And Diz went on to comment on Lips's "false fingering" (i.e., the unorthodox use of the trumpet valves). On that subject, Howard McGhee, who once played a "battle of the trumpets" with Lips at Birdland, has the classic statement: "He was some trumpet player. He'd push down the wrongest valve, and man, out came the rightest note . . . don't ask me how." Diz and Howard, of course, are "schooled" trumpet players—Lips's technique was strictly jazz. Other false-fingerers are Roy—and Bix Beiderbecke. For a sample of Lips's false fingering (and his share in the shaping of modern jazz), try *Lips Flips* on the Esoteric/Counterpoint album of Minton's jazz. (Ironically, Lips is not mentioned anywhere in Leonard Feather's liner notes or in the lineup of participating musicians. And none of the reviewers caught on to the significance of the title. Was it a matter of posthumous royalties, or someone's idea of a clever joke? Or did Leonard think it was Joe Guy?) The tune is "Stomping at the Savoy," and is a classic sample of Lips at that time, and in his element, the jam session. An interesting sidelight is the ending. After an unknown tenorman has rudely interrupted Charlie Christian's solo, Lips castigates the offender by taking the number out in no uncertain fashion.

Lips knew the etiquette of the jam session better than anyone. Unmusical behavior, on or off the stand, always pained him. He was a great teacher of manners. If a musician indulged in showing off, Lips would gaze at him with a bemused expression, and give him all the time he wanted. Then he would proceed to produce some music that made everyone forget that the other man had even picked up his horn. If someone came up with a serious challenge, Lips would be ready. He once took care of Red Allen so that Red, God bless him, really turned the color of his name. But Red Allen had started it. There was no meanness in Lips.

Lips was all music. He couldn't help himself: juiced, tired, beat to the socks—if he felt the urge, he would play. Early one morning, after a strenuous night at the Central Plaza followed by some impromptu blowing at the Riviera in the Village, Lips dropped in at Lou Terassi's, a short-lived jazz club on West Forty-seventh Street. Charlie Shavers was working there, and when Lips asked to sit in, Charlie, who was knocked out, turned the bandstand over to him and withdrew to the bar. The band—Slam Stewart, Kenny Kersey, and drummer Jackie Mills—backed Lips on a whirlwind version of "Royal Garden Blues," Lips leaning against the back wall, blowing with his eyes closed. At the end of a chorus, after glissing to a high note, Lips suddenly slid down the wall and folded up in a sitting position with his legs outstretched. Out cold. Helpful hands brought him to, got him on his feet (the horn was safe in his grip throughout), and tried to guide him off the stand. "Where you going?" Lips asked. He shook the cobwebs from his eyes, and after the bass solo, he commenced to blow. A little rocky at first, he soon found himself, and the four choruses that followed had all the ears and eyes of the place. Charlie's mouth was open. It wasn't showing off; it was his powerful urge to overcome circumstances that made Lips do such things. Big Sid Catlett, who was there that night, took Lips aside and begged him to take it easy. A few months later, Big Sid was dead. Lips wept when he recalled his advice.

Those days were hard times for musicians like Lips. The modern scene was *it*; the men whose kind of jazz was neither "far out" nor Dixieland had to scuffle. Lips (or his managers and advisers) tried a rhythm-and-blues groove—he was wonderful at it, even with silly material like "Open the Door, Richard," and had things of his own, like "Miss Larceny Blues" (Columbia), the story of a sap in the claws of a scheming gal, or "Dolla a Swalla," the tale of an after-hours clip joint. There were the kind of things that later made Ray Charles famous, and had the time been right, Lips would have made the climb, too. Today, he would have had that "hit" he was always looking for.

"Luck's in my corner, and I keep rollin' on," Lips sang on a record in 1944. In 1949, it was "Walkin' in a Daze." "I'm tired of fattening frogs for snakes, and let no one use me for a tool," he sang in a bitter mood. But his great good nature always won out. His first wife, whom he loved dearly, died in 1946. The critics were often unkind. In the late *Record Changer*, a brief review of a good record ("Walkin' in a Daze") had this to say: "Hot Lips Page may not be the best trumpet in the business, but he sure as hell is the loudest." But Lips kept rolling on.

The last real good time he had was spent in the company of his friend and favorite drummer, Zutty Singleton. They spent a summer at Knokke, a shore resort in Belgium, working with André Reweliotty's band. Lips, who was quite a cook, had a ball teaching the chef how to fix real Texas chili con carne, and the dish soon became the favorite of the entire staff. There was real recognition of his talent—as always, in Europe and not at home. Zutty tells a funny story about those days: For some reason, the rumor had spread that Lips was from the Congo. A well-meaning lady, who had an early-morning radio show, had invited Lips to come by for a chat on the air. The first question she sprung on him was: "Well, Monsieur Lips, when did you leave the Congo?" Lips, who had been up all night, was somewhat taken aback. "What old m—f— Congo?" was his response. Zutty, who was listening to the radio, fell out. It is probably the only time that notorious word has been spoken on the air. The nice lady, however, didn't know what it meant.

I saw Lips right after he returned from Knokke. He was happy and full of confidence, and looked wonderfully well. But the old New York grind soon had him going again. In the fall of 1952, he made another, briefer, tour of Europe, playing in Scandinavia. In 1953, he suffered his first heart attack. Lips was a strong man, full of zest for life, and though he was shaken by the attack and promised himself and his friends to take care, he soon felt well again and went back to work, back to looking for work, back to the tough old grind. And a man needed a couple of drinks and good company to forget. The fall of 1954 was cold and wet, and Lips caught pneumonia. His heart, the heart that, as Budd Johnson once said, "was as big as a house," could not pull him through. On November 5, 1954, Oran "Hot Lips" Page died in Harlem Hospital. His body was laid out at a funeral parlor, and Jackie McLean tells that Charlie Parker took him there to see Lips. "Bird stood a long time before the body, finally saying, 'Damn, his big wig sure looks good.'"

Lips had a beautiful funeral, for he had many friends. There was a benefit for his wife and son at the Stuyvesant Casino, and there was another at the Central Plaza. Everybody from B.G. and Dizzy to Willie "The Lion" Smith was there. It made *Life* magazine, but the publicity came too late to help Lips.

There is enough of Lips Page on record to trace his stature for posterity. From the Blue Devils in 1929 to the last date, with the Marian McPartland Trio, in May 1953, there is much beautiful music captured in the grooves of both commercial and private recordings. To cite some of the greatest, aside from those mentioned in the text, one might start with the 1940 "Anything for You" and "Gone with the Gin," from the same Decca date as "I Won't Be Here Long." Also on Decca, made some eleven months later, is the exciting "Harlem Rhumbain' the Blues," showing that "experiments" with time signatures other than 4/4 didn't start with bop. Lips and Chu Berry get together on "Monday at Minton's" and "Blowing Up a Breeze," on Commodore. (There is rarely enough of Lips on his records; he was generous in assigning solo space to his sidemen, and sometimes he "pulls a Louis," just singing and not picking up the horn. But even very short solos can be gems, and are well worth looking up.) A great record is "Paging Mr. Page" (Savoy, 1944), a jumping blues with Clyde Hart's piano, Lips on mellophone (which he often played), Don Byas and George Johnson on saxophones, Big Sid Catlett's marvelous drumming and a brilliant closing ride by Lips on trumpet. "Double Trouble Blues" (Savoy, 1944) has a wonderful vocal and fine, if brief, trumpet. (This has also been released as "Lips' Blues"). "I Got What It Takes," from the same session, shows that Lips could write and sing a tender ballad with the best. "You Need Coachin'" (Commodore,

1944) is a great medium blues, with fine work by the band. "Birmingham Boogie" (Apollo, 1947) leaps and has a soaring flight by Lips in a vein only mined by himself and Louis. The 10-inch Circle LP, *Jammin' at Rudi's*, is a somewhat raggedy session, but Lips gets things together on "Skiffle Jam" and "Sweet Sue." "Last Call for Alcohol" (King, 1952) gets André Reweliotty's boys in the groove. And "The Devil's Kiss" (King, 1952), made with a crack white studio band in New York, beautifully captures the true sound of Lips's horn and has a vehement, moving vocal.

These are all collector's items that have never been reissued. Available on LP are Lips with Count Basie in *Spirituals to Swing*, good but not representative of the man at his best, and the fine two-part *St. James Infirmary* with Artie Shaw's excellent 1941 band, including Dave Tough. Lips is briefly featured on Shaw's "Solid Sam," "Two in One Blues," "Carnival," "Needlenose," "Just Kiddin' Around," "Dusk," "Blues in the Night" (trumpet and vocal), "Motherless Child" (vocal only), "Take Your Shoes Off, Baby" (vocal), and possibly others. There is a Lips solo on Billie Holiday's "Long Gone Blues," in the Columbia *Story*. There is a European EP of a 1940 session, with Teddy Bunn and some of Leonard Feather's blues; best of these is the all-instrumental "Do It if You Wanna." The last session, a happy public appearance before GIs at Fort Monmouth with Marian McPartland on piano, has a fine "Sheik of Araby," which was a Lips speciality. He treats the lyrics in the tradition of Fats Waller and Louis, with his own touch. This is on an LP called *Jazztime, USA, Vol. II* (Brunswick/Coral). In 1962, a new company, Continental, drawing on masters from the long-defunct 78 label of the same name, issued an LP called *Hot & Cozy*. This is the closest thing to a Lips LP so far, but has Cozy Cole on the cover and devotes only one side to Lips. The marvelous "Corsicana" is included, and the other tracks, both big band and small groups, are very fine if not among Lips's all-time best.

There is still no real Lips memorial LP. Decca has enough for one, including some unissued masters from 1940. Savoy has plenty, also some unissued stuff. Commodore has enough. Jerry Newman (Esoteric) has enough Lips from Harlem jam sessions for three LPs. Columbia has enough, plus unissued material. If these companies could be convinced that there is a market for Lips Page, they might be aroused into action.

Some day, Oran "Hot Lips" Page will be accorded his rightful place in the Jazz Hall of Fame, while many reputations now outshining his will be relegated to footnotes in the history of jazz. He was one of those happy few who seem to be the spirit of jazz incarnate. He gave freely, and the world took. Many lived longer, but few lived more.

(1962)

Note: Almost all of Page's recordings have since become available on CD.

Eddie Condon

When Eddie Condon played a concert in Japan last spring, leading a band of star mainstream jazzmen, the local emcee introduced him to the audience as "the King of Bop and the Mayor of Greenwich Village."

This gaffe was as amusing to Condon as it will be to those who recall the guitarist's celebrated definition of the difference between bebop and the brand of freewheeling, tradition-grounded jazz that has been synonymous with his name for more than forty years: "The boppers flat their fifths—we drink ours."

The second half of the Japanese accolade, however, was more to the point. Though he never has held that honorary title, Condon has been a resident of the Village for many years, and he has played an important role in the jazz history of the area, from the time he went to work at Nick's in 1937 until early 1958, when the nightclub that bears his name moved uptown.

When his club first opened in 1946, it was located on West Third Street, off Washington Square, where Condon occupies a spacious, high-ceilinged apartment in a house that is part of the last remaining row of the fine nineteenth-century buildings that once graced the square on all sides.

"I used to say," Condon recently reminisced, "that I could walk to work in two and a half minutes and reel back in two and a half hours."

The remark is characteristic of Condon. Guitarist, former club owner, bandleader, A&R man, promoter, author, erstwhile columnist, and celebrated raconteur, Eddie Condon is a man of so many parts it may be hard to realize that all his energies and talents have been dedicated to lifelong service in the cause of the music he loves. A tireless fighter and missionary, Condon has drawn thousands of listeners into the jazz orbit, and even those who may have forsaken his particular kind of music in favor of other styles will acknowledge their debt to the man who lit the spark.

Last year began as a good one for Condon, who left March 6 for a six-week tour of Australia, New Zealand, and Japan with a typical assembly of jazz individualists. They were trumpeter Buck Clayton, trombonist Vic Dickenson, tenor saxophonist Bud Freeman, clarinetist Pee Wee Russell, pianist Dick Cary, bassist Jack Lesberg, drummer Cliff Leeman, and singer Jimmy Rushing, and the trip, though tiring, was a success.

"It was sensational," said Condon, who uses superlatives sparingly. "I'd never seen such hospitality as we encountered, particularly in New Zealand. You couldn't light your own cigarette, and if you wanted to cross the street, there'd be a chauffeured limousine to take you. A drink was never less than a triple shot, and the steaks—they are very proud of their beef— big enough for three people. . . ."

Prior to its departure, the band played for a few nights at Earthquake McGoon's, trombonist Turk Murphy's San Francisco club. "I never had much use for California," Condon remarked. "In fact, it always made me think of Fred Allen's reply to the question of what he thought of the state: 'It's all right if you are an orange' . . . but the audiences we had in San Francisco were the best behaved I've seen in this country."

But not long after the tour, Condon, who turned fifty-nine on November 11, was taken ill and went under the surgeon's knife for a delicate and painful operation. His friends were worried, and in August, a "Salute to Eddie Condon" was presented at Carnegie Hall, which resulted in some rather doleful publicity. More accustomed to donating his services to others than to being on the receiving end, Condon was annoyed with the way the event was handled.

"They practically had me in an iron lung," he stated.

Since then, Condon has put together several bands for weekend gigs in the New York–New England area, including a stint at a West Point homecoming, and seems well on the road to recovery. The recuperative powers of the compact, wiry guitarist are legendary. Twice within fifteen years he was stricken with acute peritonitis, and each time his doctors were doubtful of his survival.

"The first time, they had me in the death room—a little windowless alcove in the ward where the other patients wouldn't be frightened out of their wits by looking at you," Condon recalled. "When they realized I was going to be all right, I became a prize exhibit."

Condon attributes his resiliency to the regular intake of large quantities of milk, though he is probably more closely associated with the consumption of stronger stuff. He makes no bones about his drinking, but exaggeration annoys him.

"In England some years ago," he said, "an interviewer asked me, in all seriousness, 'Mr. Condon, how many quarts of Scotch a day do you drink?' I told him that even a single quart of whiskey a day would be enough to do away with a man in a very short time."

Condon was asked if he had seen the recent Columbia records reissue set devoted to jazz in Chicago, in which the personnel listing of his first recordings (the famous McKenzie-Condon Chicagoans dates of late 1927) had been newly revised to include Mezz Mezzrow on tenor saxophone in place of Bud Freeman on two performances, including the famous "China Boy."

This was news to Condon. "Mezz wasn't on those records," the guitarist said. "He did make the next session we did [for Brunswick in April 1928], but that was Bud. I thought everybody knew that by now. Those things still stand up pretty well today, I think. If I walked into a barroom, and they were playing them on the jukebox, it wouldn't embarrass me a damn bit. It was fair for a bunch of kids. . . ."

Considering the fact that these recordings, and others in which Condon participated in the late '20s, are the cornerstones of the so-called Chicago style of jazz, the guitarist's reaction to the term is interesting:

"The critics invented that. We were just a group of musicians who happened to be in Chicago at the time. When I was being interviewed on the Mike Wallace show some years ago, he asked me what the difference was between New Orleans and Chicago style. I told him: 'About one thousand miles.'"

Like most jazz musicians, Condon is not a record collector, though "we keep a player in the house for the girls when they come home from school [the girls are Condon's two pretty daughters, Liza and Maggie]. But I never use it myself. I had some records once—things that I liked by Louis Armstrong, some Bessie Smith, a few others—but I lost them. It was right after prohibition had been repealed. Max Kaminsky and I were rooming together at a hotel in midtown Manhattan. Things were pretty bad then. One bitter cold morning at four (it was fourteen below zero) we came home—peacefully drunk—to find that we had been locked out. I told the desk clerk: 'It's cold out there.' He said he was sorry, but he had his orders. We could see that he wasn't a bad guy and couldn't help it.

"Still, we couldn't face that cold, and we were very tired. Who could put us up? Our first thought was a clarinet player who had a cozy bachelor apartment on Fifty-seventh Street—we'd been up there a few days before. All we wanted was some floor space to sleep on. Maxie called him up, found out that he was alone, and told him of our sad plight. I could tell from Maxie's reactions that he was hemming and hawing, so I grabbed the receiver and hung up. What now?

"Then I remembered that Gene Krupa was in town, with Buddy Rogers's band, and that we knew where he was staying. There was just one small problem—Gene was on his honeymoon. But it was getting cold even in the hotel lobby.

"I called Gene. 'Sure,' he said, without a moment's hesitation. 'Come right over.' I would like to say here that Gene Krupa is one of the nicest guys I've ever known in my life. Well, Maxie got a job with Joe Venuti, and I managed to get some work (Gene and I wore the same size clothes), but by the time I made it back to the hotel to bail out my stuff, the records were gone. And that's how I stopped collecting records. . . ."

(Thus related, the story lacks the personality and presence of Condon at first hand, for he is a great storyteller. In action, Condon's stance and expressions are reminiscent of James Cagney, to whom he also bears a distinct resemblance.)

Though he is a modest man, Condon takes just pride in some of the achievements of his career. Among them is the organization of the first real integrated jazz record date.

It took place in New York in February 1929, for Victor records.

"The Victor people didn't like the idea," he remembered. "'What do you want those guys for?' they complained."

But Condon was persistent.

"'Because they can do something, that's why,' I told them. Finally, they let me have my way." The two sides, originally issued under the name Eddie's Hot Shots, featured Harlemites Leonard Davis, Happy Cauldwell, and George Stafford on trumpet, tenor saxophone, and drums, in the company of Jack Teagarden, Mezz Mezzrow, Joe Sullivan, and Condon.

Once the ice was broken, a number of integrated recording dates were held, though the practice continued to be an exception rather than a rule for some years to come. Condon himself was present on many of these, including a date with Louis Armstrong, and several with his good friend Fats Waller.

Condon also looks back with satisfaction on his pioneering efforts to bring jazz to the concert stage. In collaboration with his friend Ernie Anderson, Condon organized Waller's 1942 Carnegie Hall concert, which turned out to be more remarkable as a social than as a musical event, as Condon recalls it:

"Fats was a gin man, but this was a gala occasion, so champagne was called for. You couldn't even move backstage, and the champagne kept flowing. After the intermission, Fats played what sounded to me like 'Summertime' all the way through the second half of the concert. . . ."

Shortly after this memorable occasion, Condon initiated a series of jazz concerts at New York's Town Hall, using a format similar to the club jam sessions he had been organizing since the late '30s. The concerts were successful, and the series continued for several years, setting a precedent and making jazz history. During World War II, Condon also was in charge of a series of jazz broadcasts on the Blue Network (now the American Broadcasting Company) and made numerous transcriptions for the Armed Forces Radio Service.

In 1948 Condon had the first regularly scheduled jazz show in television, *The Eddie Condon Floorshow*. Well directed and produced, the show reflected the informality-plus-organization that had become a hallmark of the Condon approach to jazz. Though this was at the time when the jazz world was deeply embroiled in wordy debates about moldy figs vs. boppers, during which Condon was often depicted by well-meaning press agents as a kind of symbol for the traditionalist faction, it is characteristic of Condon's integrity that the show had an open and broad musical policy.

Like Freddie Green, the great rhythm guitarist, Condon never takes a solo (the closest he ever came was a two-bar break on the record of "We Called It Music"). But he makes his presence felt whenever he picks up his guitar—which still is a four-string model. And he is the only man who can stand in front of a group of jamming musicians and "conduct" without appearing absurd. With a flick of the wrist, a casually pointed finger, or *sotto voce* humming of a riff, Condon can set the pace and pattern for solo order, background support, breaks in rhythm, organized unison ensembles, chase choruses, or whatever may be appropriate, causing a seemingly ill-assorted collection of individualists to perform like a well-rehearsed group making swinging musical sense. He is the picture, at times like these, of a man who knows what he is doing.

Today, Eddie Condon looks back on his more than four decades in music with serenity. He knows, as he always did, what he likes in jazz and what he doesn't like, and his wit can still be barbed. But he is not much concerned about the "new thing" and prognostications about jazz. He is more interested in his good old friends and musical comrades-in-arms, "the guys who can play," and in the man whose work has always been an inspiration to them and himself.

"As far as trumpet playing is concerned, there's Louis Armstrong," he said. "And if Louis ever gives up playing trumpet, he can sing better than anybody thinks they can. If there's any doubt in your mind, ask anybody who thinks they can sing. Louis Armstrong accomplished more in his sleep than any dozen bums who think they're wide awake."

Condon is happily married ("marrying Phyllis was the best move I ever made") and proud of his two talented daughters—Liza plays guitar ("she studied with a pupil of Segovia"), sings folk music ("there was a contest at a folk festival this summer, and from a field of 2,300, they picked nine guys and Liza Condon"), and has worked at the Belgian Village at the New York World's Fair; Maggie attended the Rhode Island School of Design and is a gifted photographer.

He is a man at peace with himself and the world, a man who can say about himself "Look, I've never 'put on' anything . . ." and make it ring true.

(1965)

Earl Hines

The musical career of Earl Hines—pianist, bandleader, singer, and master showman—has spanned five decades. In 1928 Hines made a revolutionizing impact on jazz history with a series of astonishing piano solos recorded for QRS and OKeh records, and his no less amazing contributions to the small-band recordings made by Louis Armstrong in that same year provided incalculable inspiration for jazz pianists at the time and in the years following.

Paradoxically, 1928 was also the year in which Hines took a crucial step in a direction that de-emphasized his stature as a virtuoso pianist but brought into play his abilities as an organizer, teacher, and talent spotter. On his twenty-fifth birthday—December 28, 1928—Hines took his first big band into Chicago's Grand Terrace Ballroom.

For the next twenty years, Hines nursed and nurtured his band. It became one of the best large jazz groups in the business (and make no mistake, bands were a business in those years), one of the first to broadcast on a regular basis, and one of the great talent incubators in jazz history.

A legion of brilliant instrumentalists, arrangers, and singers came up through the ranks of Fatha Hines's school. Among them were trumpeters Walter Fuller, Ray Nance, Freddie Webster, Benny Harris, Dizzy Gillespie, and Willie Cook; trombonists Trummy Young and Bennie Green; saxophonists Charlie Parker, Budd Johnson, Bob Crowder, Franz Jackson, and Wardell Gray; clarinetists Omer Simeon and Darnell Howard; drummer Alvin Burroughs; arrangers Cecil Irwin (an unsung early talent) and Jimmy Mundy—and last but not least, singers Ivie Anderson, Herb Jeffries, Billy Eckstine, and Sarah Vaughan.

In 1943, when Parker, Gillespie, Green, Eckstine, and Harris were in the band, it became the first reasonably stable laboratory for bebop. A bit later, it was a veritable traveling revue, complete with strings, exotic instrumental doubles like oboe and French horn, and dancers and singers galore.

Throughout these two decades, Hines gave only occasional glimpses of his own instrumental brilliance. For while his unmistakable keyboard accents gave the band its pace and stamp, an occasional chorus or two of piano was the general limit the leader set himself. There was, of course, the famous 1941 "Boogie Woogie on St. Louis Blues"—the band's biggest pre-Eckstine hit—or the scintillating "Piano Man"; both piano features supreme. And there was the occasional solo or trio record (but not one between 1932 and 1939) to remind the jazz world that there was no decline in brilliance. But to Hines in those years, the band came first.

Today, Hines can still say: "Big bands are my first love. . . . I just love to have a big band around me." It was the decline of the band business that caused him to break up his organization and to join his old comrade-in-arms, Armstrong, in the trumpeter's first (and greatest) all-star sextet.

Three years later—in 1951—Hines again became his own man, leading a series of often excellent small bands. He settled in San Francisco. As was then the lot of so many mainstream jazzmen, Hines had to turn to Dix-ieland for sustenance. For several years, his band at the Hangover featured cornetist Muggsy Spanier, trombonist Jimmy Archey, old alumnus Howard on clarinet, and bassist Pops Foster—and an occasional piano display in a musical orbit far removed from the norm of the band.

Every now and then, Hines would break away from the confining mold for a while. In 1958 he went to New York with a quartet featuring a modern rhythm section that included guitarist Calvin Newborn. And in that same year, he made a record (at a session organized by his staunch supporter and longtime friend, critic Stanley Dance) that once again astonished those who had forgotten what a pianist Hines was—"Brussels Hustle."

But critical hosannas notwithstanding, the record soon disappeared, and Hines was back at the Hangover. In 1963 he was rehearsing a big band in his spare time and working with a group of young non-traditionalists. He also realized an ambition of long standing when he opened his own night-club in Oakland, across the bay from San Francisco. Characteristically, it featured an international floor show starring a Japanese singer; the house band included a tenor saxophonist, an organist, a drummer, and an occa-sional piano solo from the boss.

The club was still in existence in early 1964, when David Himmelstein and I produced a series of jazz concerts at the Little Theater on Broadway in New York City. The first thing we agreed upon was that we wanted Earl Hines—and we wanted him to play the piano, sans international floor show, organ, et al. To our incredulous disbelief, we discovered that Hines never had played a concert as a featured pianist.

"Are you sure you just want me to play the piano?" he asked. "I've done concerts with my bands, but do you think the people want to hear just me?" We assured him they would, and a compromise was worked out—Budd Johnson would be a guest soloist.

There are few undiluted moments of joy and pride in anyone's life, but I will never forget Hines's first Little Theater concert on that March night of last year.

"A triumph," proclaimed *The New Yorker*'s Whitney Balliett, a critic not given to hyperbole. And a triumph it was. From the first moment, when he invited the audience to think of themselves as guests in his "living room," to the final note, Hines held his listeners spellbound. During intermission, the conversation was studded with superlatives. At the end of the concert, he received a standing ovation.

This pace was maintained through three concerts (one of which was recorded), and for good measure, Hines also found the time to go to a studio and set down an album of superb solo piano. It was apparent that a giant of jazz, a talent too large to remain mostly unsung, had returned to its rightful place in the spotlight.

Since those first concerts, Hines has mesmerized audiences in the United States and Europe with his virtuosity—at festivals, concerts, and in clubs. French critics, forgetting their notorious infighting and overlooking the fact that Hines's Continental tour was booked and organized by Hugues Panassié, standard-bearer of antimodernism, had nothing but praise for the pianist. Hines, wrote Demetre Ioakimidis in reviewing the San Remo Jazz Festival in the French magazine *Jazz Hot*, "was not content to rest on his past glory, but on the contrary showed a vitality, inventiveness, and joy in playing that was truly youthful. ... Hines' place of honor on the program ... was irrefutably confirmed by the ovation of the public."

In Rome, the *Daily American* proclaimed in a banner headline: "Father of Jazz Enlightens Rome."

And so it went everywhere.

Back in the United States, the pattern was repeated. He stole the show at the Pittsburgh Jazz Festival, topping off his performances with a piano duet with Duke Ellington. And not one review of the Newport Jazz Festival failed to point to Hines's twenty-minute set as one of the event's highlights.

Yet Hines himself, having won the *Down Beat* Hall of Fame as well as second place among pianists in the 1965 International Jazz Critics Poll and having been profiled in *The New Yorker*, looking forward to appearances at the *Down Beat* and Berlin jazz festivals this year, and an extended European tour in early 1966, besieged by requests for return engagements at all the clubs he has played, with three recent LPs on the market—two to be released this month, two more in the can, and one just issued in France—Hines himself remains oddly unimpressed.

"I never aspired to be a soloist; I didn't think I had that much to offer," he said. And he was not being coy—that is not his way.

"It seemed that every time I played with the bands," he said, "or had a record come out, the people and the writers would say they didn't hear enough of me. So I decided to feature the piano. But as far as I'm concerned, I can work solo or with three men or twelve men or thirty men—I've tried it all, I've had the experience, and whatever the public wants, I can do."

He seems a bit wistful about having had to close his club—though this might be due as much to his desire to stay home with his family as to artistic considerations. Not that he isn't delighted with the reaction to his current format. "I had a wonderful trip," he said. "I'd been planning to go to Europe for a long time, and it was a beautiful experience." He is grateful to Panassié, "an old friend," and full of praise for the Alex Welch band, with whom he worked in England. "I'd like to bring them over here, if it is possible. They are fine musicians."

Hines plans to form his own trio (or perhaps quartet: "people do like to hear a horn") in the fall. Of the many rhythm players he has worked with in the past eighteen months, he was particularly pleased with drummers Alan Dawson and Oliver Jackson and bassist George Tucker. "But I can work with anybody, as long as they know the music," he said. "We'll get it together." And they usually do, indeed. Hines takes command of a situation.

Some thirty-seven years after his historic recording of "Caution Blues," Hines is still as timelessly modern as ever. "Earl can go on for ninety years and never be out of date," said one of Hines's greatest fans, Count Basie. "It's Time Again to Cry 'Fatha Hines'" proclaimed a headline in the *New York Times*, alluding to the days at the Grand Terrace when the strains of "Deep Forest," the band's theme, would rise to the accompaniment of shouts of the leader's nickname.

As he enters his sixties, Earl Hines is writing a new and brilliant chapter of his musical autobiography. Indeed it is time again to cry "Fatha Hines." But, then, it always was.

(1965)

Roy Eldridge: "Little Jazz"

*J*immy Ryan's is a small jazz club in mid-Manhattan. Though now located two blocks north and one block west of what used to be "Swing Street," it was the last bastion of jazz on that fabled thoroughfare, and is today, if not geographically then at least spiritually, the sole physical remnant of Fifty-second Street.

Especially so since Roy Eldridge took over the house band a few months ago. Prior to that, the music at Ryan's was often a rather tired brand of Dixieland, sparked mainly by the presence of Zutty Singleton, and after Zutty left, rarely sparked at all. But Little Jazz has changed all that with his sparkling horn and vibrant personality. There is nothing tired about the music now, not with Roy in charge, and business has never been better. It's hard to realize that Roy will be sixty

come January 30 and has been blowing his horn professionally for nearly forty-four
years, his love of playing still burns so brightly.

Roy David Eldridge was born in Pittsburgh, Pennsylvania, in 1911. At six, he began to play drums, then picked up a bugle, and soon graduated to trumpet, receiving early tutoring from his brother Joe, three years his senior and later to become a fine alto saxophonist and arranger.

Characteristically, Roy's first big job was as a leader. He left home in 1927 (ran away, in fact) at the helm of a juvenile band (including the brilliant drummer Alvin Burroughs) that provided the music for a small touring company called *Rock Dinah*. It folded in Sharon, Pennsylvania, and Roy quickly received the graduate diploma of the working musician—he was stranded.

Not for long, however. He left town with another traveling show, the Greater Sheesley Carnival, tripling on trumpet, tuba, and drums. This group, too, ran into bad luck, and young Roy was soon stranded for the second time—in Little Rock, Arkansas, where he found a job with Oliver Muldoon's band.

Back home in Pittsburgh, Roy formed his own band, changing his name for the first and only time in his career. "Roy Elliott and his Palais Royal Orchestra" gigged for a couple of months, and then, Roy Eldridge once again, the young trumpeter began several years of barnstorming with some of the best territory bands in the Midwest. Among them: Horace Henderson, Zach Whyte, Speed Webb, and Johnny Neal's Midnight Ramblers. All provided valuable seasoning, and the latter job—in Milwaukee—also offered a radio wire and firsthand experience with the peculiar codes and mores of the underworld: the club was a cooling-off spot for "hot" Chicago gangland figures.

Roy hit New York for the first time in late 1930, soon finding berths with the best Harlem bands of the day—Cecil Scott, Charlie Johnson, Teddy Hill, and Elmer Snowden. The latter's band included Dickie Wells, Al Sears, and Otto Hardwick, and made a short film, *Smash Your Baggage*, which offers the first glimpse of early Roy, soloing in "Bugle Call Rag."

It was around this period that Roy met Hot Lips Page, the trumpet star of Benny Moten's Kansas City band. Up to then, Roy's main influences had been Red Nichols, Jabbo Smith, and maybe Rex Stewart—he admired speed and precision. And he'd very early taught himself, off the Fletcher Henderson record, Coleman Hawkins's famous solo on "Stampede," already fascinated by the mobility of saxophone lines. But he was sacrificing sound and soul, apparently, for Lips, in a friendly manner, told him that he "sounded white," and urged him to listen more to Louis Armstrong.

Though skeptical, Roy took the advice. Louis was playing at the Lincoln, and Roy "sat through three shows with my mouth open—especially when he got going on 'Chinatown.'" The rest is history.

At Ryan's, with a small band including trombone and clarinet, a traditional flavor is at least an occasional must. Like most swing players, Roy had to learn the Dixieland repertoire when bop came in and his kind of jazz went underground. It presented no great problems, but while he plays it better than many a lifetime Dixielander, it's still not where his heart is. So while you'll hear "That's a Plenty" and "Muskrat Ramble" and a very occasional "Saints," you'll also hear "Somebody Loves Me," "Blue Lou," "In a Mellotone," ballads like "The Man I Love" and "I Can't Get Started." And such Eldridge specialties as "No Rollin' Blues," "School Days," "Let Me Off Uptown," "Knock Me a Kiss," and "After You've Gone"—all but the last featuring Roy's vocals. He is a wonderfully warm, natural jazz singer.

He also sings on "Saturday Night Fish Fry," Louis Jordan's tale of a New Orleans party, which is a portion of Roy's nightly "Tour of New Orleans" set—typical of his inventiveness within what some musicians would consider a restricting setting. It starts with "South Rampart Street Parade," features Joe Muranyi's liquid clarinet on "Closer Walk with Thee," Bobby Pratt's fine trombone on "New Orleans," a Muranyi vocal an "Bourbon Street Parade," Claude Hopkins's piano in a number of his choice, and an Oliver Jackson drum spectacular.

Roy also honors any reasonable request with grace and good nature. Also rather unreasonable ones, such as "Sugar Blues," from an elderly couple. "He's not as good as Clyde McCoy, but he plays it very well," opined the lady while Roy dished out the real McCoy. (When the remark was conveyed to him, Roy cracked up. "But they'll be back, you'll see," he added.)

A visit home to Pittsburgh in 1933 led to the formation of a band with Brother Joe and a youngster named Kenny Clarke on drums. (An excellent drummer himself, Roy always picked good ones.) Roy left town again with McKinney's Cotton Pickers, a once famous band in its final stages. A never-to-be-heard-from-again trumpeter named Buddy Lee was featured and impressed Roy. In 1935, he was back in New York, playing with Teddy Hill's band at the Savoy Ballroom. Such fine musicians as Dickie Wells, trumpeter Bill Coleman, and Coleman Hawkins's first serious rival, Chu Berry, were in the band. Chu and Roy struck up a friendship that was to produce some of the decade's greatest music and ended only with Chu's untimely death in a car crash in 1941.

Hill's band had a national radio wire, and now Roy's crackling, surging and boldly inventive horn could be heard by musicians and fans throughout the land. Among those who made sure not to miss a single broadcast was eighteen-year-old Dizzy Gillespie in Philadelphia, who came to idolize Roy and tried his best to play like him. Hill also recorded, albeit the material was very commercial, but Roy constructed some remarkable pithy statements in his long overdue recording debut. Later that year, Roy led a small band at the Famous Door on Fifty-second Street, which made two sides for Decca as the Delta Four. Roy recalls that the A&R man, fellow trumpeter Wingy Manone, cut the date short after he heard a sample of what Roy could do. Mysteriously, a tune by Roy was credited on the label to "Leather Lip," one of his early nicknames. The one that stuck, though, was "Little Jazz," laid on him by Otto Hardwick.

Little Jazz, among other things, extended the operative range of the jazz trumpet. Louis, who certainly could hit them high, mostly saved the uppermost register for fanciful cadenzas or climactic solo passages, and after 1935 his style became increasingly sober. Roy, on the other hand, might start off a piece or a solo way up high, and stay there, climbing even higher for the climax. Or he might work in the middle range, then suddenly detonate an F or a G with great dramatic effect. To a few, this was "showing off," and some critics have accused him of being "exhibitionistic." But if you understand Roy's music at all, you know that far from being theatrical or pretentious, his high notes are a reflection of his natural exuberance and joy in making music. He never does it unless he feels it (except, perhaps, when he has a special feature in a staged setting), and it can be one of the most exhilarating experiences in jazz.

At Ryan's, Roy will get up his "whistling chops" toward the middle of the night, startling some unprepared listeners and brightening his sidemen's faces. He is among those players who rarely are satisfied with their own performance. He claims that on only two or three nights a year things really come off to his liking. Yet he never fights the horn as some perfectionists do. What he plays may not be up to his own high standards, but is liable to surpass anyone else's. Still, the significance of inspiration to his playing is one of the things that make Little Jazz all jazz.

From Teddy Hill to Fletcher Henderson—graduate school. It's Fletcher's last great band, with Chu in it, plus Big Sid Catlett, Buster Bailey, Joe Thomas, and other heavyweights. It's still a big-band setting, but Roy is well featured, and on records gets off such classic statements as on "Stealin' Apples," "Christopher Columbus," "Jangled Nerves," "You Can Depend on Me." He also breaks through on small-group dates with Teddy Wilson, with or without Billie Holiday: "Blues in C-sharp Minor," "Mary Had a Little Lamb" (his first recorded vocal), and "What a Little Moonlight Can Do," with its thrilling, Roy-led climax. Young (and older) trumpeters all over the land are picking up on Roy's innovations, speed, range, and fire as best they can.

By late 1936, Roy knows it's time for him to go out on his own in earnest. Chicago's Three Deuces, where Art Tatum is on intermission piano (!) is the launching pad and stomping grounds for a band of two altos

(Scoops Carry and Brother Joe), tenor (Dave Young), Cozy Cole's brother Ted on piano, John Collins's guitar, Truck Parham's bass, and Zutty Single-ton's drums.

With a powerful rhythm section, Joe's good arrangements, and Roy's composing talent (given exposure for the first time), the band's 1937 recordings are the first to *really* show what he can do. The superfast "Heck-ler's Hop" has two brilliant choruses that are among the things that gave birth to bebop. "Wabash Stomp" (real title: "Dismal Days") is almost all Roy at medium tempo, flowing, passionate, and beautiful, and "After You've Gone" is the first version of an Eldridge standby—great new py-rotechnics in the Armstrong mold. This is classic swing music at its best: Roy has become fully himself. (Four slightly earlier sides with an all-star band joining, under Gene Krupa's leadership, Benny Goodman, Jess Stacy, and Allan Reuss from B.G.'s band and Roy, Chu Berry, and Israel Crosby from Fletcher's also have top-drawer Roy. Among them is the prophetically titled "Swing Is Here.")

Roy takes the band on the road, hitting the Savoy in New York in 1938, records "Body and Soul" with Chu, double-timing his chorus; disbands, takes time off to study radio engineering (a lifelong hobby), forms a new, bigger band (with Joe, Scoops, Franz Jackson, Prince Robinson, Kenny Kersey, and Panama Francis aboard), and now casts himself in a Louis-inspired mold, doing streamlined takeoffs on Satchmo hits like "St. Louis Blues" in a way that spells a direct challenge. (No commercial recordings at this stage, but some fantastic airshots from the Arcadia Ballroom in New York exist.) A confrontation never comes about, for Joe Glaser, Louis's manager, signs both Roy and the other top Louis man, Hot Lips Page.

Today, Roy doesn't think about battling Louis. Those were youthful impulses. At last summer's Antibes Jazz Festival, he plays a much-acclaimed set dedicated to Satchmo, and at Ryan's, he may deliver a sincere tribute in the form of "Sleepy Time Down South" (no vocal, though) or a rousing "Struttin' with Some Barbe-cue." (They did get together once, at Esquire's All-American Jazz Concert in 1943, but no swords were crossed.)

Like all true and great jazzmen, Roy is intensely competitive. He loves, to this day, to lock horns with a fit adversary, and sparks will fly. Beyond that, Roy loves to just jam. The days of real jam sessions are past, but Roy is always ready when the rare occasion arises. And if there is a place where spontaneous music can be made, he'll know about it. If there's no piano player, he may sit down at the keyboard himself—and while he's no master technician, he plays with the same tremendous drive that inhabits his trumpet. (He recorded a few piano solos in France, one a barrelhouse blues, the other a free improvisation with some astonishing runs.)

In April 1941, after disbanding his large orchestra and leading a small group in Chicago, Roy joins Gene Krupa's popular big band. He is featured on trumpet and vocals, but at his own insistence (and with Gene's blessings) also sits in the brass section as a regular member of the band. Thus he becomes the first black jazz artist to join a white band as a regular bandsman. Occasionally, when Krupa conducts or isn't feeling well, Roy takes over at the drums.

Though he quickly becomes a favorite with the public and is extremely popular among his fellow sidemen, it isn't a picnic. Indignities and abuses large and small are almost daily occurrences, and Roy is a proud man. But his awareness of being a pioneer carries him through, and he stays on until Krupa disbands in the spring of 1943.

Musically, he not only inspires the band, and charms audiences with his vocal duets with Anita O'Day, but also rises to new heights on feature pieces, above all the classic "Rockin' Chair," in its recorded version one of the greatest jazz trumpet performances ever put on wax.

Back on his own, Roy leads small bands, briefly joins Paul Baron's CBS staff radio band in New York (another pioneering effort), then goes with Artie Shaw in late '44 in the same capacity as with Krupa, remaining for eleven months. (Shaw had hired Hot Lips Page not long after Roy joined Gene.) It's a good band, and Roy has such features as "Little Jazz" and also stars with the small group, the Gramercy Five. But when he quits, he states he'll never go on the road with a white band again.

However, after another attempt, quite successful, at leading his own big band for a couple of years, he rejoins Krupa for seven months in 1949, leaving to star in the first national tour of Jazz at the Philharmonic. Bop is king now, and while Roy works and gets along fine with Charlie Parker, and of course continues to enjoy the respect and friendship of Dizzy Gillespie, some of the younger boppers taunt him, call him old-fashioned, and cause him grief.

So, when a trip to Europe with a Benny Goodman combo including Zoot Sims gives him the opportunity to remain, he settles in Paris for a year, winning new friends, working steadily, recording, and even writing a column for a Paris newspaper. His confidence fully restored, he comes home and opens in the lion's den, Birdland, with a swinging combo including Zoot and Billy Taylor.

That was April 1951. From then on, Roy toured annually for years with JATP (also recording for Norman Granz's Verve label throughout the '50s, producing such masterpieces as "Dale's Wail" and many others); also led his own small groups at such venues as The Embers, played all the major jazz festivals, and often teamed up with his good friend and early idol Coleman Hawkins, including for JATP and a long residency at the Metropole in New York.

After the demise of JATP, Roy leads Ella Fitzgerald's accompanying group from late 1963 to March 1965, but while the bread is good, this is no fit role for a still very vital and creative musician—especially since Ella, never the most secure performer, seems to resent any applause going to Roy and gives him progressively less to play.

After forming a quintet with Richie Kamuca as co-leader that regularly works at the Half Note, Roy tries another experiment. In July 1966, he accepts an invitation to join Count Basie. But for unfathomable reasons, Basie features Roy only sparingly. So, on September 17, Roy tells Count he's being paid too much to just sit in the section, and resumes his independence. (Among the things that irk him most during the Basie stint are the people who comment that he's taking it easy now and has tired of carrying the ball.)

In the last few years, there have been tours of Europe, festivals (New Orleans, Antibes), many club dates, and now Ryan's, which is near home (Hollis, Long Island), steady, keeps the chops in shape, and, by his own doing, congenial. There has been far too little recording in the last decade or so, but a recent date, albeit for a small label (Master Jazz Recordings), offered an opportunity to do what he wanted.

It was a happy date, with Budd Johnson, tenor and soprano; Benny Morton, trombone; Nat Pierce, piano; Tommy Bryant, bass; and Oliver Jackson, drums. No tired standards or remakes of past hits, but four brand-new Eldridge originals and a straight-ahead slow blues, with a vocal.

Everyone is surprised when Roy keeps pulling new pieces from his sleeve—the sketches quickly turned into functional parts by Budd, a gifted and perceptive arranger. One, called "Cotton," is a haunting minor mood piece featuring Roy's muted horn (he's a past master with Harmon or cup). The others are worthy additions to such previous Eldridgeiana as "The Heat's On," "Fish Market," "Yard Dog," "Feelin' a Draft," and the lovely "I Remember Harlem."

After the session, Roy is delighted. "I can't believe it," he says. "They let me play my own music. It was like recording in Europe." By his own music, Roy means not just his own tunes, but the kind of mature, solid, contemporary mainstream jazz he loves to play. And that, friends, is the real underground music of today.

At Ryan's, the music is not Roy's real thing. But whatever he touches comes alive. The ranks of the giants dwindle with the passing of each year, but we are blessed to have Roy Eldridge among us, still making music that is no pale echo of past glories but rich and vital and full of the sap of life. The horn that made so much history is still a horn of plenty. Blow, Roy, Blow!

(1971)

Roy Eldridge: "Little Jazz" for the Ages

I t all happened so suddenly—as if the sense of drama that imbued Roy Eldridge's music had been transmuted into the last act of his life.

On January 24, Roy and his devoted wife, Viola, celebrated their fifty-third wedding anniversary. On January 29, the day before Roy's seventy-eighth birthday, his great friend and champion Phil Schaap hosted a birthday party at St. Peter's Lutheran Church, New York's jazz church, and the vespers service that followed was dedicated to a celebration of Roy by the Rev. John Garcia Gensel, another great friend. It was a joyous occasion, especially so since Vi Eldridge, long in ill health, was there.

Within forty-eight hours, Vi died. Roy was devastated, but bore up well during and immediately after the funeral. His daughter, Carole (their only child), and his many friends looked after him as best they could, but the inevitable depression set in. When it reached a point where her father stopped eating, Carole took him to the hospital, where he was placed in intensive care and fed intravenously.

He seemed to make good progress and had been taking solid food again, but he died on February 26. On March 1, a funeral service was held at St. Peter's. Many of the hundreds in attendance had been there for the birthday celebration three weeks before. It had been a stunning sequence of events.

But the drama was not yet over. Not long after his interment at Pinelawn Memorial Park in Farmingdale, the owner of the cemetery contacted Carole. He had been a fan of Roy, it seems, and asked if she would permit the body to be exhumed and reburied in a larger plot, prominently located in one of the most scenic spots at Pinelawn. Permission was granted.

For me, there was yet another chapter to the drama. I had invited Roy and Vi to my oldest son Adam's bar mitzvah on January 28. When I hadn't heard from Roy a few days before, I called him. Though his voice had its customary (and unique) vibrant intensity, he told me that he'd just recently recuperated from a bout with the flu. "Around the holidays, there was a fire across the street one night, and I ran out to look without a coat on . . . I guess that's what did it. It was rough—please believe me, baby! I've lost so much weight I can't fit into any of my clothes, and I had such a stack of mail to go through when I got better. I thought I'd missed Adam's party, but I'll be there somehow, though I'll be looking like Old Man Mose! But Vi won't be able to make it . . . she's not up to it with the birthday party coming up."

He did come, and while the loss of weight was apparent, he was his old lively self. He enjoyed himself, and after lunch, the music of our little trio (Loren Schoenberg, tenor sax; Keith Ingham, piano; and close friend and longtime compatriot Eddie Locke, drums) got to him. "Don't you think it would be all right to do a little vocal?" he asked me. Would it be all right? It was what we'd secretly hoped for but never would have asked. "I think 'School Days' would be just right, don't you?" was the next question, and before you could say Jack Robinson, Roy was in front of the band, doing his thing as only he could.

After the standing ovation, he told me that he loved bar mitzvahs. "I've done so many of them in the neighborhood, you know, but this is the first one in a long time. I just wish I had my horn . . ."

There must have been few waking moments in Roy's life after the heart attack he suffered in October 1980 put a stop to his playing when he didn't wish for that horn at his side. When, after recuperating, he first gave in to the urging of such friends as Eddie Locke and Phil Schaap, and started singing (and on rare occasions, playing the drums, which he found too exhausting) in public, he said that he "felt naked" without his beloved trumpet. "But I talked it over with my doctor," he said, "and we agreed that if I were to play again, I'd start reaching for those high ones, and that would be it."

As it was, his singing, always great, took on a new level of inspiration in those final years, and those of us who were privileged to hear it kept talking about a record, including his most stalwart champion, Norman Granz, who stood by him all the way. ("I know of no other musician whose playing better depicts and typifies the spirit of jazz," Granz once wrote.) But it was not to be. Along with the singing, however, there were occasional lectures in schools, though "lecture" is much too dry a word to describe the way in which Roy communicated with children—he was indeed the spirit of jazz incarnate, horn or not. And there were many tributes, if not enough. So Roy endured, from time to time working on his autobiography (of which there might just be enough for publication—that remains to be seen), woodshedding at home on piano and bass, and, in very recent years, on a synthesizer he'd received as a Christmas present, and which he greatly enjoyed. The spark was still there, and when I last spoke with him, he was explaining how his experiments with multitracking on the synthesizer were coming along, with horn-like lines.

We'll never get to hear those multiple lines, yet we are blessed that Roy left behind a monumental legacy. We can hear him on hundreds of records and tapes and see him on film and video—like that remarkable sequence in "Fine and Mellow" from *The Sound of Jazz* where all the instrumentalists in the stellar cast surrounding Billie Holiday take one chorus, but Roy, up last before Billie resumes, takes two. There is no grandstanding or ego-tripping involved; Roy simply could not contain himself and his second chorus begins with one of those unique "whistling" high notes (on fluegelhorn, yet) that Roy could hit when the spirit was upon him.

"It happens maybe three or four times a year," Roy told me in 1958, during the first interview I ever did with him. (It was a sign that he'd accepted me and trusted me, and that was a milestone in my life—professionally and personally.) "You pick up the horn and everything comes out just right—feeling, range, speed—you know just what you want and you can get it. It's a mysterious thing."

"Mysterious" was one of Roy's favorite words, applied both to matters musical and thoughts about the ways of the world. The latter were sometimes hurtful or puzzling—indeed mysterious—to this most open and honest of men and artists. His legendary combativeness on the horn, for instance, had not even a smidgen of meanness. To lock horns with all comers was second nature to Roy. "I was just trying to outblow anybody," he explained, "and to outplay them my way." No one loved making music more than he, and in the process, he created an electric, visceral excitement that none could match. And when there were no challengers, he challenged himself.

At the funeral service, George Wein pointed out that Roy was the only jazz musician whose nickname was synonymous with the music itself. "To the public, he was 'Little Jazz,' but among musicians, it became just 'Jazz,'" he pointed out. That service was at ten in the morning, an early hour for the jazz world, but the church was filled to overflowing. Dizzy Gillespie was there, explaining that he almost hadn't come because "I didn't want so many people to see me cry." Master and erstwhile disciple himself become master, they were the best of friends. Without Roy, there would have been no Dizzy, but Roy was far more than that tired cliché of jazz history describing him as "the link between Armstrong and Gillespie" would have it. Long after Diz had become fully formed, Roy continued to blow and grow, never standing still. And at all times, he was himself, a man and artist.

"He had a way of looking at you," said pianist Dick Katz at the service, "that said: 'I know who I am—who are you?' Roy changed my life."

In many and mysterious ways, Roy Eldridge changed every life he touched. He knew who he was. The world didn't always know, and didn't do him justice in exchange for the gifts he bestowed on it, giving us everything he had. But as long as there is a music called jazz, Roy Eldridge will be synonymous with its spirit and soul. Little Jazz was *all* jazz, for all the ages.

(1989)

Bunny Berigan

The best of them? That's easy. It was Bunny," said Louis Armstrong when asked about the trumpeters who followed in his musical footsteps.

That was in 1948. Bunny Berigan had been dead six years, and Louis was feeling the sting of what he called "that modern malice": downgrading and belittling by younger musicians. Maybe that's why he picked Bunny, who had adored him openly. (Once, asked what a traveling musician needed to carry with him on the road, Bunny answered, "A toothbrush and a photo of Louis Armstrong.")

But maybe not. Louis consistently spoke highly of Bunny and steadfastly refused requests for the tune synonymous with Berigan's name—his one and only big hit, "I Can't Get Started." I heard Satchmo play it just once in response to an intermission plea by a Berigan fan. He dedicated it to Bunny and played the hell out of it.

"I Can't Get Started" was Bunny Berigan's theme song, and it has been said that the title was appropriate. But that is a facile gimmick—if anything, Bunny got started too fast, and during his meteoric career, he never stopped. His immortal recording of his theme, still heard on jukeboxes and airwaves today, is all some people remember him for. Thus, it is high time for an album reintroducing some of the best work of one of the truly great trumpeters of the golden age of jazz—a man who lived his short life not wisely but fully, and who gave to music everything he had.

Bunny was born Rowland Bernard Berigan in Hilbert, Calumet, Wisconsin, on November 2, 1908 (not 1909, as some sources have it). His family was musical. His mother played piano, his brother Don played drums, and his grandfather was a local bandleader. Bunny started violin at a tender age, the instrument played by his grandfather—and did well. (He continued to double on it until 1927.) But—it is told—one day the grandfather brought him a trumpet, saying, "Here, this is you. Play you!"

If true, the anecdote speaks well for the old man. The trumpet was indeed the perfect vehicle for Bunny's volatile, dramatic musical persona. Soon he was playing dance dates with his granddad's band, and at thirteen he worked locally with Merrill Owen and his Pennsy Jazz Band. That would have been in 1921, a time when the word "jazz" was used quite broadly. But we know that the first jazz records young Bunny listened to were by the Original Dixieland Jazz Band, and we also know that a few years later he sat in with another pioneering band, the New Orleans Rhythm Kings. (Wisconsin isn't far from Chicago, the NORK's home base.)

Madison and the University of Wisconsin were also close to Bunny's home. Though never a student there (as has been erroneously reported), Bunny often played with dance bands from the university. Those were Prohibition days, and the college boys, older than Bunny, surely experimented with liquor. It seems likely that this association was the source of the fondness for the bottle that became Bunny's nemesis.

By the time he was seventeen, Bunny was working steadily in Madison with the bands of Jesse Cohen (U. of Wisconsin paraprofessionals who recorded for Paramount, but without Bunny, discographies to the contrary notwithstanding), Cy Mahlberg, and the various leaders who "fronted" at the Chanticleer Ballroom.

Hal Kemp, who had a "hot" band then, heard Bunny there around 1926 or 1927 and later said he was impressed with the youngster's fire and ideas, but not with his "peashooter" tone. Perhaps that was the reason the young man returned home soon after having ventured to Philadelphia and New York in 1928. But when he went to the big town again in early 1929 and played with violinist Frank Cornwell's band, he had heard Louis Armstrong. Perhaps turned on by the young Chicagoans who were the first white musicians to consciously emulate Negro jazz and with whom we know he jammed, and by Bix Beiderbecke, the Chicagoans' white idol, he had developed that fat, beautiful sound we know him by.

In any case, Kemp was impressed enough to send to Wisconsin (Bunny had returned home again) for the young trumpeter, who joined the band at the Hotel Taft in the spring of 1930. Bunny soon found himself on the way to Europe. He toured with Kemp in England and on the Continent from May to September and also recorded his first authenticated solos with the band that year. From then on, Bunny never looked back. After his return to the U.S., he began to freelance in the New York recording and radio studios, soon finding a regular berth with Fred Rich and another leading contractor of the day, Ben Selvin.

The Depression was on, and the record market hit bottom in 1931, but even when there was less work, Bunny got the calls. And no wonder: the combination of solid professional musicianship and jazz soul that Bunny could offer was matched by no other white trumpeter of the day.

There were few jazz kicks in the studios, but opportunities availed themselves. He often gigged with the Dorsey brothers, Benny Goodman, and other jazz-minded studio colleagues. (Benny recalls a college date on which he used both Bix and Bunny, the only known instance of the two legendary B.B.s playing together.) And there were jam sessions; we know that Bunny often made it up to Harlem in those days.

In 1931 he worked in a Broadway pit band led by the Dorseys (*Everybody Welcome*) and spent the summer with singer Smith Ballew, who always had good jazzmen in his bands. The next year, he followed in Bix's footsteps, joining Paul Whiteman's huge, showy band in which Frank Trumbauer was still a member. Bunny got less of a jazz break than Bix with Whiteman, then in one of his least interesting periods.

A month with Abe Lyman in late 1933 was followed by a CBS studio contract and more freelance recording work. The Berigan collector has his work cut out for himself: Bunny is present on hundreds of records made between 1931 and 1937 with all manner of bands and singers. Many of them contain no jazz, but even the most unlikely can't be dismissed. There are good recordings with Jane Froman, for instance, Richard Himber, Dick Stabile, great things with the Boswell Sisters, the Dorsey brothers, Mildred Bailey, Trumbauer, Red McKenzie, Red Norvo, Ethel Waters, Billie Holiday, Bing Crosby, the Mills brothers, Gene Gifford, etc.

The breakthrough year for Bunny was 1935. He'd already made a name among musicians and the few knowledgeable jazz fans. But 1935 was the dawn of the swing era—and Bunny was born to swing.

In June he joined Benny Goodman's band, still in its infancy. This was when Fletcher Henderson had just begun to write for Goodman, and it was Bunny who infused his heart and fire in the band's first great record, "King Porter Stomp" and "Sometimes I'm Happy." He made the cross-country tour that ended with the band's triumph at the Palomar in Los Angeles. Always restless, he then quit B.G. and went home for a visit before returning to New York and CBS.

The network had become aware of Bunny's true worth, and for a while he was featured with his Blue Boys on a regular program, *Saturday Night Swing Session*—still remembered as one of radio's best jazz shows. By this time Fifty-second Street had discovered jazz, and Bunny soon became a fixture there. He backed Bessie Smith in her legendary appearance at the Onyx. He also worked with two good friends and drinking companions, Eddie Condon and Red McKenzie, at the short-lived club fronted by the former and galvanized Red Norvo's innovative Swing Octet. Occasionally, he'd lead a pickup group of his own on records or in person.

In early 1937, Bunny did for Tommy Dorsey what he had done for Goodman. For five weeks he played and recorded with the then lagging band—and promptly raised it to a new plateau, musically and commercially. Inspired by Dave Tough's drumming and Bud Freeman's tenor sax, Bunny put his indelible stamp on "Marie" and "Song of India." Nearly twenty years later, both solos were still being played by the entire Dorsey trumpet section. And then there was "Liebestraum" and "Who'll Buy My Violets" and "Melody in F" . . .

The boost Bunny gave T.D. became the impetus for a big band of his own. Swing was king, and the fiery trumpeter's name was now known far beyond the inner circle of jazzdom. It seemed only natural that the man who'd sparked two of the best big bands should have his own outfit. He was in his prime, and success beckoned.

Tommy Dorsey, always a shrewd businessman, knew he couldn't keep Bunny long and decided to help him go for himself. Arthur Michaud, Tommy's business manager, took on Bunny, and the new band was patterned on the Dorsey model—or at least the hot half of it.

Bunny's band began promisingly, making its debut in March. He found good sidemen: eighteen-year-old tenorist George Auld; drummer George Wettling; bassist Arnold Fishkind; clarinetist Joe Dixon; trombonist Sonny Lee; pianist-arranger Joe Lippman from Artie Shaw's first band; and later discoveries such as Joe Bushkin, Ray Conniff, and Buddy Rich. Somehow this fine talent never added up to a great band—though it could rise to the occasion when Bunny was inspired.

By August the band had its first hit, but for some unfathomable reason the formula of "I Can't Get Started" was never repeated. Perhaps Bunny didn't want to feature himself that much. In any case, few of his own records show enough of him, and the band never found a style of its own, though the leader's horn, in section as well as solo work, was always unmistakable.

Judging from contemporary accounts in the music press and statements by former sidemen, it seems that Bunny simply wasn't cut out to be a leader. He was no disciplinarian, to say the least. In fact, when there was fun to be had, he was the first to have it, and he liked company.

Most successful leaders, especially of bands containing jazz musicians, had to divorce themselves from the comraderie that is so much a part of the music. In a sense, leaders such as Goodman and Tommy Dorsey were not dyed-in-the-wool jazzmen, jazz talent notwithstanding. Bunny was *all* jazz. His playing proved it: no set routines for him; no mechanics to fall back on when the muses failed. Each solo was a gamble with fate: he either made it or he didn't—but he always tried.

The miracle was that he made it so often. The tragedy came with his dependence on alcohol to drown out troubles with agents, ballroom operators, hotel managers, accountants, song pluggers, record executives . . . all the middlemen a bandleader had to deal with.

Bunny had always been a heavy drinker. Tales of his huge capacity would be judged exaggerated if they didn't come from such unimpeachable sources. Playing a trumpet the way Bunny did is physically taxing under the best of circumstances; therefore, it seems incredible that he could stand up as long as he did under the grind of leading a relatively unsuccessful band.

The stories would be funny if the ending had been different: a hurricane

blew the roof off the Ritz-Carlton in Boston just when the band was beginning to click via a national radio wire (the ballroom was a roof-garden affair); the band hit Bristol, Connecticut, just in time for a one-nighter, only
to find Gene Krupa's crew setting up . . . the Berigan gig was scheduled for
Bridgeport; Bunny, feeling no pain, strode out from behind the curtain on a
movie-theater stage blowing his theme, took one step too many and
crashed into the pit; he continued to blow, still feeling no pain, even though
his ankle was broken. . . .

For three years Bunny held on, surviving several complete turnovers in
personnel and a change in management. In the spring of 1940 he disbanded
and declared bankruptcy. Tommy Dorsey, again in need of a spark plug,
hired Bunny immediately, and once more his horn raised the level of another man's band. (Hear "East of the Sun," "I'm Nobody's Baby," and
"Whispering.")

But Bunny had been his own boss for too long; besides, both he and
Tommy tended to get their Irish up quickly. After five months Bunny quit
in a huff, claiming he wasn't getting enough to play. Records and broadcasts
from the period bear him out.

For a while Bunny led a combo at the 47 Club in New York, and all
seemed well. But the success image of the day still called for a big band, and
within Bunny's complex personality, there must have been a drive to prove
that he could make it. Or could it be that others drove him?

Whatever the reasons, Bunny soon took a new big band on the road. An
offer from Hollywood to do a soundtrack for a so-called jazz film, *Syncopation*, caused him to disband again in late 1941. The film was nonsense, but
his music was beautiful.

A new band followed: it was to be his last. Young and green, it put
Bunny's failing health to a test he could no longer pass. In April 1942 he was
hospitalized with pneumonia. Loyalty to the band or some unknown
demon wouldn't let him take a much-needed rest. On May 8 he left the hospital and rejoined his band on the road, determined to make an important
date at New York's Manhattan Center.

He got to New York but never made the date. On May 30 he suffered a
severe hemorrhage and was rushed to Polyclinic Hospital. The diagnosis
was cirrhosis of the liver and complications.

His old friend Benny Goodman brought his sextet to Manhattan Center
to help out the leaderless band. Bassist Sid Weiss, a small, frail man, visited
Bunny. "And they tell me I'm sick," the dying man joked. "It looks like you
should be here instead of me."

On June 2, 1942, with Tommy Dorsey at his bedside, Bunny Berigan
died, just five months before his thirty-fourth birthday.

(1972)

Lionel Hampton

There can be little doubt that Lionel Hampton's name is one of the most important in jazz. It is almost impossible to mention the vibraharp without instantly thinking of the man who "invented" it as an instrument worthy of jazz consideration, the man whose playing remains the mark against which others' efforts must be measured.

But Hampton is also a bandleader. For nearly twenty-five years—since September 1940—he has led one of the most popular and hardest-working big jazz bands of all.

Nevertheless, the Hampton band is often omitted from those recurrent discussions about the decline of the big-band field, and one would have to search diligently in the pages of current jazz magazines to find it mentioned. With the exception of Hugues Panassié and Stanley Dance, few critics have given the band due credit.

Sad to say, even Hampton's own impassioned outburst concerning the unfairness of this attitude (*Down Beat*, May 10, 1962) has had little effect on the consensus of printed opinion. The tendency to dismiss the band as "show business" remains dominant.

Admittedly, showmanship plays a large role in Hampton's approach to bandleading. "Trying to get to the people" has always been the number-one rule in Hampton's book. And that, of course, conflicts with the art syndrome that characterizes contemporary jazz criticism.

To be sure, no jazz listener who has witnessed the Hampton band at its most orgiastic could be expected to issue a blanket endorsement of its work on purely musical grounds. But even if the listener can't bring himself to accept a twenty-minute whirlwind of "Flyin' Home" as sheer Dionysiac fun and games, the band always has had much more to offer than just that. In a club, hardly a set goes by without a lovely ballad featuring the leader's peerless vibe work, and if the time is right, the band may relax and stretch out on one of the many fine instrumentals in its book.

In that mood (and at a dance, there are more changes in moods than in a club or at a festival), the Hampton band has few peers. There has never been a time during the band's existence when it hasn't been a band that could swing and one that had more than a few outstanding players in its ranks.

Look at the record and sift through just some of the talent that has passed through the Hampton ranks since 1940.

First, the trumpet players. Karl George, Ernie Royal, Snooky Young, and Joe Newman—that was the section on the band's first record date, in

1941. Among those to follow were Cat Anderson, Lamar Wright, Wendell Culley, Jimmy Nottingham, and Richard (Duke) Garrette; three fine players who are no longer living—Al Killian, Joe Morris, and Dave Page; then Teddy Buckner, Joe Wilder, Kenny Dorham, Benny Bailey, Eddie Mullins, Idrees Sulieman, and Walter Williams. The last named was in the band when it boasted a trumpet section that also included Art Farmer, Quincy Jones, and the late Clifford Brown. More recently, there have been Virgil Jones, Floyd Jones, Richard Williams, and a man still with the band and who is probably one of the most underrated trumpeters around, Eddie Williams.

Consider the trombonists. The late Fred Beckett, J. J. Johnson's inspiration, was in that first band. Then came Michael (Booty) Wood, Al Hayes, Britt Woodman, James Wormick, and Paul Higaki, who was on board when his teammates were Jimmy Cleveland, Al Grey, and Benny Powell (and how's that for a trombone section?). Later, there were other good men, including Lester Robertson.

Now the reeds. Among the alto saxophonists were Marshall Royal, Earl Bostic, the late Ray Perry (a great violinist, too), George Dorsey, the late Herbie Fields, twenty-year lead man Bobby Plater, Pony Poindexter, Jerome Richardson, and Gigi Gryce.

When it comes to tenor saxophonists, a good case could be made for the Hampton band's being responsible for initiating the tenor vogue. That started with "Flyin' Home, No. 1," which featured Illinois Jacquet in the solo he still plays today and which he bequeathed to several other tenorists and Hampton's full reed section. Then came Arnette Cobb, with "Flyin' Home, No. 2." By that time, Dexter Gordon had passed through the ranks. Then there were Al Sears, Jay Peters, Johnny Griffin, the late Morris Lane, John Sparrow, Curtis Lowe, Johnny Board, and another long-timer, Andy McGhee (now with Woody Herman), whose place was taken by George Coleman.

There were baritone sax men, too. Jack McVea, better known for his tenor work, was among the first. Basie's Charlie Fowlkes was around for quite some time. And then there were Ben Kynard, Pepper Adams, and Tate Houston.

Hampton's rhythm sections always had their work cut out for them. In this band, it's keep the rhythm going, no matter what else is happening. Hampton has never dropped guitar (excepting brief interludes), and he has had such stellar players as Irving Ashby and Wes Montgomery. But the man who, with a few interruptions, has been in the band since 1944, is without doubt one of the greatest jazz guitarists around, then and now—Billy Mackel, a modest man, one who doesn't hog the spotlight.

Currently on bass is another Hampton veteran, Lawrence (Skinny) Burgin, a fine player. Among his predecessors have been such men as Vernon

Alley, Vernon King, Charles Harris, Ted Sinclair, Joe Comfort, Monk Montgomery, and Charles Mingus, whose feature, "Mingus Fingus," remains one of the band's outstanding records.

The piano, next to tenors and trumpets, got a large share of the spotlight in Hampton's earlier bands. Milt Buckner, the man credited with developing the locked-hands or block-chord style (though Hampton himself can be heard playing this kind of piano on his April 1939 recording of "Denison Swing"), took care of business for some time. Douglas Duke, a superior organist, held the piano chair for a time, as did two other men better known today for their organ work, Bill Davis and Bill Doggett. And Hampton had a wonderful, unsung pianist in the late Oscar Dennard, who never was sufficiently featured.

Drummers must work hard for Hampton, himself a drummer of considerable accomplishment. Among the men on the spot have been George Jenkins, Fred Radcliffe, Curley Hamner (a master showman), Ellis Bartee, and, more recently, Oliver Jackson, who also is among those Hampton alumni who must be singled out for special mention—a marvelous musician.

There were singers, too. Dinah Washington got her first big break with Hampton. Sonny Parker, not as well known as he should be, also had a way with the blues. And Annie Ross briefly sang with the band. For quite a while, the main vocalist has been Pinochio James, who, if he would be himself rather than try to decide if he is Joe Turner or Joe Williams, might accomplish more than giving the audience a good time.

All told, a roster of alumni second to few.

On records, the band often rose to the occasion. There were "Loose Wig," "Tempo's Birthday," "Goldwyn Stomp," "Cool Train," "Pigs' Ears and Rice," and, if one likes jazz wild and woolly, "Air Mail Special, Pts. 1 & 2."

Yet Hampton's own best recorded work has most often been done without the band, and that, perhaps, is the root of the Hampton band's problem. The leader, a musician of stature and a performer of vast and sometimes almost frightening energy, tends to overshadow the band. And he demands as much from his men as he does of himself, perhaps without realizing that his work is more fulfilling than theirs.

Yet Hampton's ferocious vitality and endurance is also the band's source of strength, and when everyone is right, it's something to hear. As a school for musicians, a talent incubator, a showcase for a great performer, a source of vital and exuberant rhythmic release, and often also as a source of first-rate, swinging orchestral jazz, the Hampton band's rightful place in the musical scheme of things could be denied only by snobbery or ignorance of fact.

(1965)

Jo Jones

There isn't one drummer in the world—whether he knows it or not—who doesn't owe a debt of gratitude to Jo Jones," said Chuck Lampkin, the gifted young percussionist with Ahmad Jamal's trio, recently. His sentiments are consistently echoed by the young players whom Jones affectionately refers to as his "kiddies." He, in turn, is often identified as "old man Jo Jones," to avoid confusion with another famous drummer, Philly Joe Jones.

There is nothing old, however, about Jo Jones's appearance or out-look—nor is anyone who has ever seen him in action likely to confuse him with any other drummer.

The effortless grace of his movements, on or off the stand, bespeaks his early days as a dancer, just as his solo work may sometimes remind of the fascinating rhythmic patterns created by the masters of the vanishing art of jazz tap dance. His superb coordination, erect posture, and flashing smile make Jones one of the visually most exciting of jazz drummers, though he never indulges in musically superfluous displays. Behind the drums, Jones is the image of the professional—a man with pride in his art. With this pride goes a deep concern for the welfare—spiritual and material—of those who hold the future of jazz in their hands: the kiddies.

"I live, sleep, eat, and think music and the people who make it," Jones said, adding, with a touch of humor, "I have five radios and three TV sets, a tape recorder, three record players that don't work, and two phones.

"So many mechanical improvements have been thrust upon us that we don't even have time to read the instructions. There are more musicians out here now, and fewer places to play. But it has happened before, and we managed to cope with it. First radio came in, then the talkies—thousands of musicians who worked in silent movie theaters were thrown out of work—and then television. But it's not a Frankenstein—you don't have to combat what man has created. Nothing mechanical can take the place of what is natural. And the population is growing."

Jones is a quick, fluent conversationalist, and while his talk is sometimes elliptical, he always gets to the point.

"Musicians have lost perspective on how to play *with* people before they play *for* people," he said. "The emphasis on records, publicity, and propaganda doesn't help. Yet we have a better grade of musicians in jazz today than ever before. One thing that is wrong with the music business today—

the shortage of available experience—the musicians can't cure. But fundamentally, academically, they are better equipped to perform now."

What, then, is the trouble? "Attitude," Jones said. "I hear ne'er-do-wells browbeat the successful: 'I can play better than so-and-so, and he's got all the gigs.' Sure, I say. But can you be there on time, sober, and ready to play?"

A reasonable answer to this reasonable question is rarely forthcoming, Jones indicated.

"Everybody wants to find an excuse," he continued. "Nobody wants to work. They want to pick and choose. They ask questions: 'Who else is playing on the gig? Do I have to wear a tuxedo?' They ask for the money before they do the job; they say yes, but don't show if a better offer comes up."

Such criticism might sound overly stern if it did not come from a man who has set—and kept—the highest standards of professional conduct for himself. Anyone who has observed Jones in different working situations can attest to the fact that he shows up neat, clean, ahead of time, and ready to play his best, whether the job is at Carnegie Hall or at a decidedly unglamorous neighborhood bar.

"In music," he said, "if you accept a responsible position, you have a responsibility to yourself. Musicians tell me they are not respected. You should command respect, not request or demand it. In forty-three years as a professional, I have never done anything wrong on the bandstand." And he amplifies this: "If it seemed wrong, it was right," implying that there sometimes may be more to a musical situation than meets the eye of the outsider.

"People wouldn't hire me years ago because, they said, I was eccentric. I'll stay eccentric, in their terms. Youngsters today have everything but self-respect."

Jones is aware of the factors that have caused the attitudes he considers reprehensible.

"In jazz," he stated, "we don't have the minor leagues anymore, where one could prove himself before going out into the big time. We despoiled our potential geniuses by bringing them out too soon. Your emotions aren't stable enough at nineteen or twenty-three to know the whys and wherefores of life."

And he is aware of other complicating circumstances:

"There are all kinds of overworked terms, like 'free form,' 'freedom,' 'modern.' . . . Modern was an old phrase a hundred years ago. I've just read a book published in 1856, which was full of references to 'modern' philosophy. I've played through ragtime, gutbucket, hokum, get-off music, swing, bebop, cool, rhythm-and-blues, rock-and-roll. Every two years someone comes up with a new descriptive adjective. You must be flexible. If you run a liquor store and don't stock gin because you dislike it yourself, you're bound to lose sales. The musician has a commodity to sell. And it wasn't so different in the 'old days.' The jazzmen wanted to do just 'hot tunes,' not the waltzes and rhumbas they also had to play."

Jones also resents musical intolerance and the tendency among some younger players to put down musicians who ask them to play in ways that may not be of their own choice. He's had to play accompaniment to all kinds of different players, he said, trumpeters, clarinetists, pianists. These men were stylists, and since it takes time to become one, the stylist, in Jones's estimation, has the right to demand certain things from his accompanist that fit his style.

"You play for the leader," he said. "But it's very hard to convey this to young musicians."

The drummer is quick to point out, however, that the blame for this state of affairs must be shared by the leaders themselves.

"To establish leadership is a problem," he said. "It has always been like that; to be a leader takes special talent. Bennie Moten was the greatest bandleader who ever lived, but though he was a pianist, he didn't play with the band. Today's leaders are all playing leaders, but there never were too many men who could be both great leaders and great players. Tommy Dorsey was one of the few. Chick Webb was another. Cab Calloway was a master showman, not a player. And Jimmie Lunceford didn't play; he just had his baton. Since World War II, the only real leaders have been the established leaders."

Among these, of course, Jones counts Duke Ellington, "who is something all unto himself," and his own former boss, Count Basie.

"I traveled for fourteen years with a bunch of *men*, and there was not one fight," he said of his Basie days. "I came out of the band thinking that everybody was like that, and I soon found differently. But to this day, I can't play with anybody who has hate in his heart."

It was with Basie, of course, that Jones established himself as "the man who plays like the wind" (a phrase coined by an admiring colleague), laying the foundation for perhaps the swingingest big band in jazz history, and, with his pioneering use of the ride cymbal, the hi-hat cymbals, and bass-drum "bombs," becoming one of the founding fathers of so-called modern jazz drumming. (In this context, Jones would like to correct the history books, pointing out that he joined Basie in 1934, not 1935, "and my birthday is October 7, not July 10.")

Looking back on his Basie days, Jones, who has no current plans for organizing a group of his own, said he would like to record some of the feature things he did with Basie, inasmuch as the band never got around to them in the studio.

. . .

Jones has traveled to Europe a number of times—most recently with the mammoth tour conducted by George Wein last summer ("musically, it was very good, but there was a certain lack of experience in logistics")—but has little regard for the often-encountered view of Europe as a utopia for U.S. jazzmen:

"The kiddies say, 'Get out of the U.S.A.; they treat you like a man in Europe.' But is the treatment of the Negro really better there? In America, you have all kinds of outlets. If you don't like one place, you can go somewhere else. But in Europe, you have to accept what they have to offer. If you can play, you can play anywhere."

He has no patience with people who claim that there is no future in music.

"Casals, Toscanini, Kreisler—they never rested on their laurels." he said. "And look at all the men in jazz who are still playing: Ellington, Armstrong, Hawkins—what if they had said forty years ago, 'There's no future in it; people don't know who I am'?"

Jones has some advice for aspiring players on a level different from the practical and materialistic: "To become a good jazz musician, you must try to hear and see things that are beautiful. Be like a sponge; absorb experience and play it. Music is therapy for people, and the most stimulating music there is is jazz. It is also the most spiritual of all musics—a delicate thing. You can't play it unless you have found yourself, and it takes time to find ourselves. An individual who plays music and a musician—those are two different things."

There's little doubt which of the two Jones is.

(1965)

Milt Hinton

The undisputed dean of bassists and long one of the most beloved and respected members of the jazz community, Milt Hinton is jazz history personified. As he approaches ninety (he was born on June 23, 1910), the man known to myriad friends and fans as "Judge" (he once joked that he earned his nickname because he "sentences everyone to thirty days of listening to good music") stopped playing his demanding instrument a while ago, but he is still a vibrant presence on the jazz scene. You might encounter him as an honored guest at a concert, a festival, a jazz party or a cruise, where he may consent to take a solo chorus, or sing what became his theme song late in life, "Old Man Time." Or you'll find him as an invaluable participant in a seminar or panel discussion. Just this past December, he shared his keen insights with those present at a Local 802 Jazz Advisory Council meeting billed as "A Conversation Between Generations" on the theme of "Building a Jazz Career in New York." No one, it's safe to say, knows more about that subject than Milt Hinton, whose truly astonishing career spans most of the twentieth century.

His encounter with jazz began in Chicago, where his family had moved in 1919 from his native Vicksburg, Mississippi. He started on violin at thirteen, but by then he'd already heard and seen most of the great bands and musicians active in his South Side neighborhood. He was good at the fiddle, but as a sophomore in high school he decided to join the marching band, noting that it "gave a boy with a name like Milton who was really skinny and carried a violin around all day" more and better visibility with the girls. He wound up on tuba, the instrument on which he made his recording debut on November 4, 1930, with the band of pianist Tiny Parham (so named because he weighed about 350 pounds). By then, however, Milt had been playing string bass for a couple of years. He'd turned pro during his final year of high school and then went on to study music at Crane Junior College, and briefly at Northwestern University. (He continued his bass studies intermittently for another fifteen years with private teachers.) Milt wasn't very pleased when the rare Parham 78s were reissued on LP in the 1960s. "I was never much of a tuba player," he said, "and you can hear me running low on wind before the records are over."

On his next record date, with a group led by one of the two musicians Milt has said were his greatest influences, the wonderful violinist Eddie South (the other was drummer Zutty Singleton), Milt was not only playing bass but also took one of his rare vocals, on "Old Man Harlem." This was in the spring of 1933, and the young bassist already had under his belt experience with the legendary trumpeters Freddie Keppard and Jabbo Smith, the brilliant but troubled pianist Cassino Simpson, and with Erskine Tate's big theater orchestra. Milt had already acquired the habit of listening intently to the conversations among elder musicians, and even asking questions when that seemed appropriate. And he remembered, years later when his nascent interest in jazz history had ripened, much of what he had heard.

After several years with South, Milt went to work with Zutty Singleton's band at the Three Deuces, then one of Chicago's hottest jazz spots. The intermission pianist was Art Tatum, and Milt listened, and sometimes sat in with the great man. One night in 1936, Cab Calloway, already one of the most successful swing-band leaders, heard and saw Milt, and (with Zutty's kind permission) hired him on the spot.

The association would last for some fifteen years, during which a host of fine players passed through the Calloway ranks. Among them were some of the greatest tenor saxophonists in jazz: Ben Webster, Chu Berry, Illinois Jacquet, and Ike Quebec. The trumpeters included a young firebrand named Dizzy Gillespie (and another survivor from Milt's generation, Jonah Jones, who recently turned ninety-one). And for a long time, Milt, guitarist Danny Barker, drummer Cozy Cole, and the unsung pianist Benny Payne made up one of the swing era's great rhythm sections.

Gillespie and Milt struck up a lifelong friendship. "Milt Hinton—that guy is a real musician," the trumpeter told the *New York Times*' Peter Watrous on the occasion of the bassist's eightieth birthday. "I'll tell you something. In 1939, I was a modern guy, and he was from the Art Tatum school. I was showing him what we were doing, and he went for it . . . he's incredible." Sometimes, Milt recalled, these informal seminars would take place between sets on the roofs of hotels where the band was playing. It was with Calloway that Milt recorded one of the very first (maybe the first) bass features, "Pluckin' the Bass," in August 1939—some two months before Jimmy Blanton came on the scene with Duke Ellington. (It may or may not be a coincidence that Blanton's first recorded duet with Ellington, made in November 1939, is called "Plucked Again." According to Gillespie, "Jimmy Blanton was crazy about Milt.")

In 1941, Milt cut a splendid bass showcase created for him by arranger Andy Gibson, "Ebony Silhouette," and a bit later on came his third Calloway feature, "Bassically Blue," not recorded commercially with the band (though airchecks exist), but done in 1946 with his friend Ike Quebec for Blue Note.

During his Calloway years, Milt had many opportunities to record in other settings when the band was on location in New York, Chicago, or Los Angeles. Thus he appears on some classic Billie Holiday–Teddy Wilson dates; with Billie's early influence, Ethel Waters; with Coleman Hawkins; with Benny Carter; and notably with Lionel Hampton (these two great survivors first met when both were members of the *Chicago Defender*'s Newsboys marching band). Check out "Shufflin' at the Hollywood," with the great Chu Berry (whose pipe and tobacco pouch Milt retrieved when the tenorman was fatally injured in a car accident, hoping to return it to him; it occupies a place of pride among Milt's memorabilia). And then there was the truly all-star Hampton date, with a saxophone quartet of Carter, Berry, Hawkins, and Webster; Gillespie; Charlie Christian on guitar; pianist Clyde Hart; and Cozy Cole. That was in 1939, a banner year for Milt because he met and quickly married Mona Clayton, a pretty schoolteacher.

Milt and Mona have been together ever since, and if there is a closer couple, I'd be surprised.

When their daughter, Charlotte, was born in 1947, they found a house in Queens, New York. Milt's qualms about being away on the road too much ceased when Calloway was forced by economics to break up his band in 1951. Then came the only brief period of scuffling in Milt's long career. As he tells us in the second of his two marvelous books, *Over Time*, "there were nights when Danny Barker and I would take the ferry to New Jersey and go from bar to bar playing for tips." But before long, another Calloway friend, Cozy Cole, recommended Milt to Louis Armstrong, and after driving a hard salary bargain with Joe Glaser (wonderfully described by Milt in his first book, *Bass Line*, and settled by Louis in his inimitable way), Milt joined the hard-working Armstrong All Stars for several months that included his first visit to Japan. He left when he was offered a steady job with the band on a CBS radio show.

Milt had already begun to break into the charmed circle of New York studio players a bit earlier on, and he credits Jackie Gleason, a jazz fan whom he'd first met in the comedian's struggling days, with helping to open that door (closed to all but a very few African-American musicians) for him. Once at CBS, Milt's musical flexibility, reading skill, and dependability led to more and more broadcasting and recording calls. Milt estimates that he spent some fifteen years in the studios, during which he became the most recorded bassist in history, appearing in every imaginable musical setting on almost every label. "I might be on a date for Andre Kostelanetz in the morning, do one with Brook Benton or Johnny Mathis in the afternoon, and then finish up the day with Paul Anka or Bobby Rydell. At one time or another, I probably played for just about every popular artist around in those days," Milt wrote. After a while, he had to keep two instruments in daily circulation, and hire a reliable man to make sure that one would always be on hand in time for his arrival at the next studio— often a close call.

In addition to the commercial and broadcast work, there was no shortage of jazz record dates. For quite a while, the team of Milt, pianist Hank Jones, guitarist Barry Galbraith, and drummer Osie Johnson was known as "The New York Rhythm Section," a quartet of stellar pros that could adapt to many different artists and even contribute on-the-spot arranging touches. They even made an album, *The Rhythm Section* (on Epic), from which my favorite is Milt's "Mona's Feeling Lonely." Milt's recorded jazz work covers the entire spectrum of the music, ranging from traditional New Orleans style with Pee Wee Erwin to cutting-edge music with George Russell. And Milt's live work, which he by no means neglected during his studio period but which picked up when the recording business and the use of live music in broadcasting started to decline, is just as multifaceted. He toured with Paul Anka, went to Russia and the Middle East with Pearl Bailey, and participated in Bing Crosby's very last go-round in Europe and on Broadway.

At this point in time, the jazz party phenomenon was starting up, and Milt was in on the ground floor, at Odessa, Texas, and then at Dick Gibson's Colorado affairs, always helping to broaden the musical horizons of these events by recommending younger players. For a lengthy stretch in the mid-'70s, he was the bassist-in-residence at Michael's Pub, backing such luminaries as Red Norvo, Teddy Wilson, Bobby Hackett, and an old acquaintance from the Eddie South days, the irrepressible Joe Venuti. Here he also encouraged and nurtured young talent. The singer and pianist Daryl Sherman recalls that when she first arrived in New York and began to hang out at Michael's Pub, "Milt introduced me to lots of musicians, sometimes let me sit in, and would give me a ride home. A bit later, he invited me to play for and talk to the jazz class he was teaching at Hunter College."

Always aware of and concerned about the welfare of musicians and the future of jazz, Milt not only taught at various colleges and music camps, but also became active in the International Association of Jazz Educators and the International Society of Bassists. And for several years, he served first as panelist and then as co-chairman (with me) of the National Endowment for the Arts' jazz panel. Though I had known Milt for some time, it was through our work together at NEA that I became fully aware of his true stature as one of the most righteous of men and of his profound knowledge of jazz history and human nature.

Milt also played a central role in NEA's Jazz Oral History Project, for which he became a peerless interviewer, but this was nothing new for Milt. For years he'd been conducting a jazz oral history project of his own, inviting musicians to his home and interviewing them in the comfort of his den, surrounded by Milt's memorabilia, and his marvelous photographs—yet another way in which he had long been documenting jazz history from a unique perspective.

Milt got his first camera—a 35mm Argus C-3—as a present for his twenty-fifth birthday. From the start, he wrote, "I was never much for taking formal pictures. I always tried to capture something different. I'd sneak up on people and capture them when they were off guard." Hamstrung in the early days by the lack of a flash feature and the slow film speed, he graduated to a Leica, inspired by his friend and Calloway colleague, trombonist Keg Johnson. For a while, the two would process their own film while on the road—no easy task. Once settled in Queens, Milt set up his own darkroom. By the early '60s, his camera of choice had become a single-reflex Nikon F; he's always preferred black-and-white photography. With charac-

teristic modesty, he downplays his technical acumen and formal knowledge
of photo history, but he takes just pride in many of his pictures, which grace
his two books, were the subject of a calendar, have frequently been exhibited, and have appeared in many publications.

In 1959, Milt and Mona, the latter armed with a recently acquired 8mm
movie camera, copiously documented the now famous gathering of jazz
greats for a centerfold in a jazz issue of *Esquire* magazine. While the formal
shot was being set up, Milt and Mona captured the informal interaction between the musicians, and this treasure trove eventually became the cornerstone of Jean Bach's terrific 1994 documentary film *A Great Day in Harlem*.
Just as Milt's keen eye captured the essence of his photographic subjects, so
his oral history interviews often focused on the everyday aspects of musicians' lives, yielding priceless vignettes, some funny, some tragic. And his
Bass Line is one of the essential jazz books, required reading for young musicians for what it can teach them about music and life. It is history as observed by a participant and worth a bushel of academic product.

One of the friends and colleagues Milt interviewed for NEA and wrote
about in *Bass Line* was trombonist Quentin "Butter" Jackson. In the foreword I had the honor of writing for that book, I quoted Milt on Butter because I felt that the words applied equally to him. I do so again:

> Musically, his mind was always working. He could hear everything
> that was happening when the band played . . . I don't know of any
> better sideman. [He] played with just about everybody . . . and when
> you look back on his career you realize that his greatness came from
> an ability to adapt to the changes happening in music throughout his
> lifetime.

Amen. In what may well be the earliest magazine piece about him (in
Music and Rhythm, August 1941), Milt advised his fellow bassists: "Be in
tune at all times." Milt Hinton has been in tune with the world throughout
his long and rich life, and we are lucky to have shared time with him. Walk
on, Judge!

(2000)

Vic Dickenson

The mystery of heredity assures each living thing of uniqueness, but some are blessed with more of it. Vic Dickenson was special, even among that first generation of fully realized jazz musicians to which he belonged—a breed the like of which we shall not see again.

Vic was a master of timing. He never wasted a note or a word or a motion. The trombone is a clumsy instrument, but he handled it with casual elegance. He said more with a flawlessly placed and executed pedal tone than verbose virtuosi could express in a string of choruses. Everything he did was perfectly poised and paced. In his spanking-clean kitchen, everything was in easy reach, and to watch him prepare a meal was a lesson in time-and-motion efficiency. Each component, done to perfection, was ready at the right time. Fancy cuisine was not his thing, but the food was fit for a king. No five-star restaurant could equal his roast beef or stuffed pork chops.

Vic did everything in style, without ostentation. It was a pleasure to drive with him—not too fast, not too slow, no foolishness, and that infallible sense of direction and place. You were safe with him, even when he'd had a few. And a few it was; Vic indulged, but he knew exactly when to start and when to stop. Having a taste with Vic was a ritual. In music, he was a stylist; in life, he had style.

In his youth, while working for his father, a building contractor, Vic was severely injured in a fall from a ladder. The bones never mended properly, and he was often in considerable discomfort, even pain. But he kept it to himself. Unlike most of his colleagues, he never complained about musical situations or the unjust ways of the world. If you asked, you'd get an honest opinion, tempered with Vic's innate compassion. It's a pity he wasn't called upon more often to be a leader; he was good at it, and had ideas about music and bands. But he waited to be asked; he wasn't pushy. In a way, of course, Vic led every band he played in. He was the one who knew the right changes, the proper tempo, the best key. And he knew how to signify. A young trumpeter of whom Vic was fond would sometimes find the bell of Vic's horn in close proximity to his ear, delineating the melody he'd strayed from. In hopeless settings, Vic would simply dig in, do his fine thing as well as circumstances allowed, and growl a lot in the ensembles. The final note in a messed-up, out-of-tune ending might be one of those singular pedal tones from Vic, on perfect pitch.

The happiest musical association of Vic's life was with Bobby Hackett. They were men without guile, and their friendship was a joy to behold.

Once, in Chicago, they opened at a new club to an audience of ten, half of it musicians. They played a perfect set and called it quits, agreeing with the boss that their scheduled week's run would end at half pay the next night if there was no improvement in attendance. Then they went off with friends to have a bite, a taste, some laughs about unfortunate gigs of the past, and a listen to Bobby's Louis tapes. When the job folded the following night, Bobby wrote TILT! with a red marker on a poster announcing the engagement. (I still have it.)

Vic never quite got over Bobby's death. Essentially, he was a loner, and not that many had gotten close. (Lester Young had been another.) At the services for Vic, there was beautiful music and moving talk. Doc Cheatham played and sang "My Buddy" and told us what Vic had meant to him. Ruby Braff and Dick Hyman (Dick on the church's fine organ) played "Memories of You"; Vic would have approved of the way they treated the melody. Phil Wilson came down from Boston to play "Thanks for the Memory," *a cappella*. George Wein's eulogy was a tribute to a fellow musician and a salute to a friend and mentor. There were other offerings, but nothing could follow Ed Polcer's Thanksgiving Prayer.

The presence of Vic Dickenson among us was something to be thankful for. I hope he knew how much he was loved.

(1985)

Dizzy Gillespie

There is nothing like steady work to keep a band together." That is trumpeter Dizzy Gillespie's succinct reply to a question about his formula for successful bandleading.

Few on the jazz scene are better equipped than Gillespie to answer such a question. He has been a leader of his own groups—big and small—for more than twenty years. His current quintet had its last change in personnel thirty-one months ago (when pianist Kenny Barron joined), and none of his sidemen has plans to leave what certainly is one of the most consistently employed jazz groups.

To a fairly constant observer, one of the most striking aspects of the Gillespie quintet is its air of togetherness—on and off the stand. When the group is on, there is no coasting. A master showman and an extraordinary musician, Gillespie heads a unit that must be not only musically alert and prepared to do its best at all times but also must be able to function as an integral adjunct to the leader's volatile and effervescent personality.

For when Gillespie and his group are at work, there is, in addition to jazz of the highest caliber, a constant flow of entertainment: jokes, comedy routines, dancing, byplay among the musicians, mock arguments, and all manner of humor. Yet the comedy never becomes strained, the jokes never sound stale, and the musicians seem to be enjoying themselves as much as the audience.

Drummer Rudy Collins, who has been with Gillespie for more than three and a half years, provided a clue to the spontaneous quality of the band's comedy: "We don't rehearse those things. Dizzy comes up with something; we react; and if it goes over well, we keep it in."

Bassist Chris White, in his fourth year with the group, and the most frequent foil for the leader's humor, commented, "I'm a born ham. I'd like to try legit comedy if I had the chance. I was on stage at the age of four, in a community theater group in Brooklyn, so you might say I lean toward that kind of thing."

But it isn't just a question of doing what comes naturally. Even the previously taciturn James Moody, the group's triple-threat man, on alto and tenor saxophones and flute, has become an accomplished humorist during his "going on three years" with Gillespie, displaying the same beautiful sense of timing in his comedy as in his music.

The music, of course, is the main thing. And it is demanding music, of a variety in tempos, textures, and moods that few small groups can equal.

"Nowhere else could I get this kind of experience," White said. "There's no one like Dizzy to demand from you what is right at all times. And the discipline gives you the freedom to do anything you can do, in every situation. Some young players may think of discipline as something negative, but it's really constructive. It took me a year and a half just to play the book the way Dizzy wants it. I couldn't repay anybody for playing in this band. My only problem is—what next?"

White, who was discovered by Gillespie while the bassist was playing with Michael Olatunji and his African entourage, also points to one of the reasons for the band's relaxed and easygoing camaraderie.

"We all respect each other," he said. "Differences of opinion are rare; if there are any, we talk them out. And what's great is that if you want to be alone, they don't bug you. When you split, you don't feel a draft."

This is echoed by Collins, who remarked: "We stick together. There's no friction. We know each other and are used to each other. And Dizzy is a good cat."

"And a gentleman," added Barron, the youngest and quietest member of the group. "I was in Moody's last band, and he recommended me to Dizzy. I'm very lucky to be here."

To Moody himself, the fact of having been a leader of his own groups constitutes no problem in his work with Gillespie. "Dizzy is a different type of leader, you know," he stated. "I had a blues band." And he added, "I've been with Dizzy before, in the big band. We get into something. I'll be here till Dizzy fires me."

That is not likely to happen.

"Moody is one of the most complete men I know," Gillespie said. "He has his own philosophy of treating the leader and of getting along with the sidemen and the fans. When Moody first joined the band, somebody said, to me, 'Oh, you've got Moody with you now; you'll have to straighten him out.' And I answered, 'If I don't watch myself, he'll straighten *me* out.' Moody is the most underrated musician I know of, perhaps with the exception of Dud Bascomb." (Bascomb, with the Erskine Hawkins band from 1935 to 1944, is a trumpeter of whom Gillespie said, "He's beautiful. A lot of the harmonies that Clifford Brown used to play reminded me of Bascomb.")

Moody, whose credo is "I'm trying to become a better musician," is currently engaged in improving his sight-reading technique. For this purpose, he carries with him books of fiendishly difficult exercises, from which he and Gillespie sometimes practice together between sets. "Oooh, Moody—dig this one!" the trumpeter will say, and off they go. "It makes no sense musically, but it sure is hard as hell to play," Gillespie remarked after one of these excursions.

Moody's presence in the band has given Gillespie the inspiration of the constant company of a peer. "He just thrills me," the trumpeter said.

White commented: "There is Dizzy, and there is Moody. Each demands something different. We rhythm players are players in mufti; we must adapt ourselves. It all jells because Dizzy is Dizzy. . . ."

The band's arrangements—and they are excellent ones—are in the main by Gillespie himself. Some were put in the book by pianist Lalo Schifrin, and others are by his successor, Barron.

"Kenny is a gas," Gillespie said. "He's a marvelous musician. He was very quiet at first; it took him a little time to get acclimated. He plays good bass, too—all the right notes. Chris is a fine, strong player, and he really works with me; musically and otherwise. When I hired Rudy Collins, I had my choice of two or three drummers. I picked Rudy because I noticed that he played on his bass drum, too. So few drummers do, nowadays. There was a guy with King Curtis I heard at Birdland; he really knocked me out. I'm a rhythm man, you know. I used to play for dancers. . . .

"There's no underhanded stuff in this band," Gillespie continued. "Young guys don't understand a lot of things, but they learn if they stay around. You can't get your experience in two or three years. I got mine in all those bands I worked with, and I was no angel. When Teddy Hill's band [Gillespie's first major job was with Hill, with whom he took Frankie Newton's chair in 1937] was going to Europe, several of the guys in the brass section told Hill they wouldn't go if I made the trip. I made it, though—and they did, too. Bill Dillard, who was the lead trumpet, really taught me a lot. He was so nice—I'll never forget him. If there's ever anything I can do for him, I will."

Today, Gillespie listens to the advice of his wife, Lorraine. (The Gillespies celebrated their silver anniversary May 10.) "My wife gives me the proper perspective." the trumpeter said. "She gives me the anchor I need. She has real mother wit, and besides, she knows all there is to know about show business. She used to be a dancer, you know, and I still try to phrase like that. I loved to play for that chorus line at the Cotton Club! One night—I had just joined Teddy Hill—I was playing something that really made that line step, and Bill Robinson was watching in the wings. He turned around to somebody and asked: 'Where did that little bastard come from?' I'm still a rhythm man. . . ."

Gillespie led some of the most brilliant big bands in jazz history, so one might wonder if he still yearns for a larger group. "Big band or small group, it doesn't matter," he answered. "I can play with any size of band; me and a drummer, or me and a bass player. Charlie Mingus and I want to record some improvisations together, just the two of us."

But he would like to do something special with a big band. "I'd like to rehearse one for a couple of months, all new music by good arrangers, and go on a tour, using the small group as well, plus the Double Six, and play with all three of them. It would be rough on the chops but a ball."

On the basis of current performance, however, he would not have to worry about his chops.

"You have to stay in shape to play the trumpet," he said. And he is the best evidence of this dictum. After a recent diet, twenty-five pounds lighter and watching his eating and drinking (though still capable of consuming both victuals and beverages with undiminished relish), Gillespie is in prime condition. And he has to be, considering the kind of schedule the band keeps, and the share of the blowing he always does.

"We play clubs, big and small, concerts, and college tours," Gillespie said. "I like the college things; we can play a couple of dates a week, have some time off, and I can still give the guys full salary for the week. And then there are the 'jelly gigs,' like the frosting on a cake, which really give everybody a nice taste."

Gillespie knows about the payroll, too. Unlike most famous leaders, he makes it up himself, computing everything meticulously ("you have to be a CPA for this job").

Recording is important to a permanent group like Gillespie's. "I try to make records so that people will be buying them for some time to come, not just here today and gone tomorrow," he remarked. "But I would like to get a nice single—when you have a hit, people become more amenable to listen to all that you do."

Not that this group has problems in communicating amenably with an audience. Gillespie's standard opening line, "Thank you, ladies and gentlemen, for your marvelous indifference," is an example of true irony, since warm and generous applause is never lacking where Gillespie & Co. are at work. "Our audiences are jazz-minded," Gillespie said, "so mostly, we play in jazz-minded places. Louis Armstrong can play in all kinds of places; maybe, when I've been around as long as he, I'll be able to do that, too."

That prospect is not so unlikely when one considers the parallels between these two remarkable trumpeters: consistency of unstinting performance (no matter the circumstances), capacity for hard work, genuine gifts for entertainment, concern for the welfare of those who work with them, and ability to inspire loyalty and devotion in generations of musicians, fans, and listeners.

One thing is certain: after thirty years of professional music-making, the trumpet and personality of John Birks Gillespie still sparkle with undiminished luster.

(1965)

Clark Terry

Clark Terry is a man of many parts. He is a staff musician at NBC in New York; he is one of the city's most sought-after trumpeters for record dates of every description, from jazz to jingles; he leads his own quartet and has recently formed a big band; he does college and high school band clinics; he tours with Jazz at the Philharmonic; he is president of a new music production company—and he is, of course, one of the most original and personal trumpet stylists in jazz.

The man behind these varied activities is warm, relaxed, and outgoing, never harried in spite of his busy schedule. To say that he is well liked would be an understatement—even those who are envious of his success can find nothing bad to say about him and have to content themselves with sneering at his commercial activities.

To Terry, there is no conflict between his commitment to jazz and his more worldly musical involvements.

"I made up my mind when I came into town that I would answer as many calls as I could," he said recently. "I like to do a variety of playing. I never did feel that an instrumentalist should settle too much in one groove—you should be able to do anything on the horn. Some ultramodernists look down their noses at studio work and say it's not creative. On the contrary, I find that it is . . . it keeps you ready."

It was in late 1959 that Terry, then thirty-nine, decided to come off the road and settle in New York. His last job had been with the Quincy Jones band in the ill-fated *Free and Easy* touring company that traveled in Europe. Before that, he had put in eight years with Duke Ellington, three with Count Basie, and shorter time with Charlie Barnet, Lionel Hampton, Eddie Vinson, and various other bands, beginning with George Hudson in Terry's hometown of St. Louis, Missouri.

Thus, he brings considerable first-class experience to his new avocation of big-band leadership. The Terry band was formed early this year.

"People had been saying to me, 'Why don't you get a big band?' and it looked like it might be a good idea," he said. "It seems like big bands are coming back. Thad Jones and Mel Lewis have been pretty successful, and New York should be big enough for two jazz bands.

"With the personnel we have, the main problem is getting everyone together at the same time. They're all pretty busy people. But we've had beautiful results in this short period."

The busy people in the band include trumpeters Ernie Royal, Marvin Stamm, Jimmy Owens, and Randy Brecker; trombonists Melba Liston, James Cleveland, Tony Studd, and Wayne Andre; reedmen Phil Woods, Bobby Donovan, Zoot Sims, Frank Wess, and Danny Bank; pianist Don Friedman; bassist Ron Carter; and drummer Grady Tate.

Arrangements are by Miss Liston, Woods, Allan Faust, and Rick Henderson, a former Ellington colleague of Terry's and the band's "utility reedman—we always seem to be short one man."

"The music is very fresh," Terry continued. "Phil's approach to writing is especially exciting."

At rehearsals, Terry's lively sense of humor keeps the atmosphere happy and relaxed, and his complete musicianship is fully evident. He has a unique, extremely effective way of counting off: "One, two, you-know-what-to-do." It's funny, it works, and one wonders why nobody thought of it before.

"The enthusiasm in the band is tremendous," Terry said with pride. "And we have good subs—we're developing a bench like a baseball team."

The band's first official booking is at the Greenwood Lake, New York, Jazz Festival, July 20–22, but Terry hopes to have the band ready to perform in public some weeks before then:

"We'll probably do some Monday nights at the Half Note; they've enlarged the bandstand. We had some rehearsals there, but now we start them so late that it isn't practical. We've been approached for some social-club dances in the fall, and we intend to play for dancers. If you hope to bring back big bands, that's one sure way of getting to the kids."

Terry described his music company, Etoile Music, Inc., which he operates in partnership with Miss Liston and Woods, as "the backbone of the band." In its offices in the Times Square area, the writing and copying of the arrangements are done.

"We're also set up to record, manage, produce, provide any kind of service in the line of music," he added. "We've even done a couple of rock-and-roll things that will hit the market soon. And we booked our first date recently—a thing in Pennsylvania for Phil, with my rhythm section."

Currently, Terry is commuting to Jazz at the Philharmonic dates, mostly on weekends. He gets back in time to do the *Tonight Show* taping on Mondays.

"It's a ball to go back on the road," he said. "It gives me a few more hours for sleeping than I'm used to. I get a chance to rest up; with only two concerts a night, you can sleep in the daytime. Traveling conditions are much better than they used to be—when we got to where we were staying, they used to have to carry the iron lung from door to door!"

Terry's chronic lack of sleep arises from his busy schedule when he stays in town. He knows that when a musician is called for a record or jingle date, "you can't say no—if you do, you get scratched off a number of lists. Going out of town, of course, is a good excuse—provided you don't stay out too long."

He also does quite a bit of nightclub and concert work with his quartet and, occasionally, with his old partner, trombonist Bob Brookmeyer ("in fact, we're going to the London House in Chicago in August for two weeks"). He was a judge at the Villanova Intercollegiate Jazz Festival in March. He has done a few clinics this year and has a few more coming up in Illinois and Iowa.

"They're fun to do," he said of the clinics. "Most of them include a concert as well. I get on well with the kids, and there is lots of interest in big bands. I get requests from all sorts of places, but to accept them all would be a physical impossibility."

As an indication of the kind of talent that can come out of the collegiate music scene, Terry cites trumpeters Brecker and Stamm, both in his band, and "both fantastic players."

Terry is, naturally, pleased that his services are in demand:

"To see this acceptance by the public is heartening. It's very gratifying, and it makes me work harder and try harder."

A contributing factor to Terry's popularity has been his singing—particularly the humor-filled wordless blues patter he calls "mumbles." He'd never expected this joking to take hold. He explained how the original recording came about:

"I was doing the *Oscar Peterson Plus One* date, and it went down so smoothly—we finished all the numbers in one take—that we were just sitting around gassing, with plenty of time on our hands. I wanted to make a party tape; just put it on and see people's reactions, and Oscar was for it. So we worked out a routine, and when we did it, Oscar fell on the floor. 'This has got to go on the album,' he said. So we worked out two numbers. . . .

"It was really my version of a put-on of old blues singers—St. Louis had lots of what you might call blues festivals, get-togethers where one singer after the other would come up and do his blues. Feeling mattered more than what was being sung about. Some guy would start singing about a chick in the audience, and it didn't matter what the words were, as long as the groove kept going.

"I've always loved to listen to blues singers, from way back, but even on my records at home, there'd always be one or two lines you couldn't make out. The feeling is what counts. From just fooling around like that, I decided to do some straight-life singing, on tunes that don't require a balladeer's voice, like "Gee, Baby" or "I Want a Little Girl," and I found that there was a little market for that, too. We have some arrangements in the big band for that."

Terry's singing, like that of other fine jazz instrumentalists, is a happy and engaging reflection of his personality, and "Mumbles," when done in person, comes out just a little differently each time. At benefits or festivals, after lengthy sets of "serious" jazz, the singing is a delightful change of pace.

In addition to playing trumpet and singing, Terry doubles on fluegelhorn. He has used it since his Ellington days and even does a specialty, alternating phrases on trumpet and fluegel. But he does a lot of serious playing on the large-bored horn, too.

"I found it to have a more intimate feeling and sound," he explained. "You don't have to use the same vicious attack as on the trumpet. I use it for a change of pace, like a pitcher with a fast ball and a curve. It's really an extension for one's expression."

The big horn is becoming increasingly popular, Terry noted with pleasure, adding:

"They allow it on staff as a double now; before, it wasn't quite recognized as a legitimate instrument. Many of the new sounds in jingle music are geared to the fluegelhorn sound. It can be used in many combinations: with winds, with trombones; there are so many ways to use it effectively."

The use of fluegelhorns is not the only positive factor Terry finds in today's commercial jingles. "They seem to be writing better music for jingles now than you hear on a lot of the jazz programs," he said. "You can turn on your radio and hear some good jazz on the commercials. Jazz seems to be a good medium for selling—it doesn't have to be corny."

Terry said he also enjoys some of the challenges involved in the careful timing required for this kind of functional music:

"It has to be worked out to the precise second. You may have to make a 5/4 bar out of a 4/4 bar, cut bars, put in irregularities. And when you get the chance, it's good to get that little bit of your own in. . . ."

As a network staff musician, Terry is a member of the still far too small minority of Negro musicians in such jobs—roughly a dozen among the 195 men employed by the three major networks in New York. To Terry, the job means more than mere security.

"I like to think," he explained, "that I'm supposed to prove to nonbelievers that they *can* believe—that we can do what's required, and that proving this has made things just a little more comfortable. . . .

"I have to think of more than just my gig. I'm representing all the people who'd like to do the kind of work I'm doing. I have to think ahead— I feel that I'm not doing it just for myself, but that I'm representing the Negro in my field. . . ."

Asked his opinion of the current state of jazz, Terry replied that he finds it difficult to evaluate. "It seems great for some, bad for others," he said. "I guess it's always been that way. But in some cities, there are no places now to hear jazz. It's terrible if a town can't support at least one or two places, even just for the local musicians."

But on the whole, Terry is optimistic:

"I don't think that jazz will ever die. There'll always be somebody playing some kind of jazz somewhere, and somebody will come and listen to it. The kids have been smothered with rock-and-roll, but it looks as if they're getting tired of that and want to hear good melodies with a good swinging feeling—it may be old hat to us, but it's new to them."

In Terry's opinion, "jazz goes through a lot of phases, but it always comes back to foot-patting music. I like to hear some of the new things that are being tried—I don't mind a cat going way out, as long as he comes back. Some of it is successful, some not.

"I just like to stay abreast of everything that's going on. A house doesn't have to be a home. A lot of times it means that I have to subsidize my own yen for jazz. I do benefits and small-paying gigs or take a sideman's fee for the sake of someone who needs it more. I think of those things primarily because nobody was thinking of them in my behalf when I was coming up."

Terry is aware of the danger of becoming stale and stagnant:

"Being satisfied and just grooving is an unwise thing to do. As the old saying goes, the only difference between a groove and a grave is the dimensions. You can't let the world go by.

"I learned many things from the older guys, like Duke and Coleman Hawkins. They always managed to keep themselves surrounded with youth and to keep their minds open. Not necessarily in the sense of accepting everything that comes along but in keeping open to it. You shouldn't close your mind and your ears to everything that's going on; you should at least hear it out. Bean or Maestro wouldn't be as fresh and interesting in their ideas as they are if they had closed their minds to youth."

It is clear that success has not spoiled Clark Terry.

(1967)

Billy Taylor

Out of the hotly contested race for ratings between the big three of television talk shows but certainly not out of the running is the increasingly popular *David Frost Show*, always relaxed, often sophisticated, and presided over by its genial and civilized British host.

When it comes to bands (an important ingredient in all talk shows), Frost's show certainly is in a class by itself. While the big three boast large, smooth, well-oiled orchestras mainly made up of studio veterans, the Frost band is smaller (eleven pieces), younger, hipper, and admirably well balanced, musically and racially.

By any standard it is a jazz organization, and its leader is Billy Taylor, a man with impeccable jazz credentials. He will celebrate his second anniversary with Frost come July.

"The band is just the right size," says Taylor. "It can sound big but can also get a small-combo feeling. The guys can blast, but they can also play softly." (All three reedmen double flute, and the two trumpets double fluegelhorn.)

The personnel is impressive: trumpeters Jimmy Owens (one of the most brilliant young brassmen of his generation) and Dick Hurwitz (who is well remembered as the principal soloist on Dick Grove's *Little Bird Suite* LP of some years ago); trombonist Morty Bullman (a big-band veteran who earned early jazz spurs on a V Disc date with Roy Eldridge), reedmen Frank Wess (one of jazzdom's premier flutists and spark plug of one of the greatest Basie bands), Seldon Powell (a stellar tenorman whose jazz credentials would fill this page), and George Berg (Red Norvo, Benny Goodman, and featured tenor in Buddy Rich's 1947 big band); guitarist Richie Resnicoff (the band's baby, a graduate of Berklee and Buddy Rich); bassist Bob Cranshaw (Eddie Harris, Sonny Rollins, Junior Mance, and Lord knows who else); drummer Bob Thomas (the Montgomery Brothers, Billy Taylor trio), and percussionist Marty Grupp (heir to a famous musical name).

Except for Powell, who was preceded by Hubert Laws and Al Gibbons, and Resnicoff, who took over from Barry Galbraith, the men have been on hand since the band's inception, and the band has a family aura.

"I have to like the people I work with," Taylor explains. "You wind up married to the guys in your musical organization. When I like the guys, I relate to what grooves them, and it winds up grooving me. I enjoy the soloists so much that I wind up often not even taking a solo myself. . . ."

Grooving, of course, is only a fringe benefit when working in a TV show band. The job is exacting, and there isn't much room to stretch out— two minutes and twenty seconds of music is about the maximum time a commercial break with segues front and back allows for. Those breaks are the basic work, but more important is providing appropriate backing for singing and/or playing guests, always with a minimum of rehearsal time.

"We usually don't have any idea of what's happening until we get out there," Taylor says. "Frost works like a jazz musician—he states the melody and goes from there. He doesn't plan his interviews; he has a general idea and then he'll see what happens. He does his homework, though. It's his show. He calls the turns."

The musical guests, however, call the tunes, and it's up to the band to take it from there. "Frequently," Taylor explains, "we get people who bring in arrangements that call for strings or other instruments not in the band. But the beauty of having jazz musicians is that they can take these parts and fill them out. The individual can add much more to what we do than in the usual show band."

High praise from guests like Louis Armstrong, Mel Tormé, Peggy Lee, and Sammy Davis, Jr., bear out what Taylor says.

"The main ingredient," the leader continues, "is musicianship. Man for man, the band is as good as you can get. Nobody can come in and bring us something that *somebody* hasn't been into. Even when someone tries to throw the band a curve, it works out fine. Their jazz background gives the guys the ability to have a complete conception of something very quickly. You don't have to spell it out, and that's what TV is all about. I can say,

'Give me an ending in B-flat,' and it comes out sounding like an arrangement. The things we're able to do come from playing together—being together."

Taylor's remarks yield a significant clue to why the most important roles in almost all TV and studio bands are filled by musicians with a jazz background, and should give pause to those who toss around concepts like "jazz is playing what you feel" and "technique is not important."

The Frost show's studios and facilities are compactly housed in what once was The Little Theater, in the heart of Manhattan's theatrical district. Taking a look behind the scenes was a nostalgic trip for this reporter, who in 1963 co-produced a financially disastrous but otherwise successful jazz concert series on these selfsame premises.

Backstage, things look different now. The band is accommodated on platform risers at stage right, hidden from audience view behind a system of movable screens during interview portions. The proscenium has been enlarged, and the musicians can neither see nor hear a performer doing his or her thing on the stage apron. Headphones and monitor screens compensate.

A cozy little room backstage allows the visitor to view the proceedings in color in a screening-room atmosphere. Set off from this is an area reserved for last-minute warm-up and makeup touches by guest performers. Here, on the day in question, one could see and hear special guest Louis Armstrong playing along softly with the band's musical breaks while main guest Bing Crosby was out front with Frost—and to hear Pops doing "More Than You Know" and "Pennies from Heaven" with a practice mute was worth the trip in itself.

Earlier, in the downstairs dressing rooms, Pops and Bing had rehearsed their "surprise" duet. It took them just a few minutes to decide on the tune ("Blueberry Hill"—Louis reminding Bing that they'd done it together on a radio show years ago), the best key, and the routine (arrangement by Mr. Armstrong). They ran through a chorus, gave each other some skin, and nothing further was needed.

Earlier, Louis, Billy Taylor, and trombonist Tyree Glenn (Louis's musical director) had just as quickly established that "Blueberry Hill" would be no problem to the band (Glenn was to play obbligato), and that Louis's two other numbers would be "That's My Desire" (with Glenn as "Madame Butterfly," re-creating the late Velma Middleton's role in the piece) and "The Boy from New Orleans," a song with autobiographical lyrics set to the tune of "The Saints." Deciding on keys and humming a few bars of melody was all the "rehearsing" required.

The actual performance went down just as smoothly, with no mishaps. The band's small-combo feeling was to the fore, Wess creating clarinet parts appropriate to the Armstrong context, and Glenn giving simple but effective cues.

Having been involved in other television scenes, this writer can say without hesitation that it was the most relaxed, effortless, and non-uptight taping he has ever attended—and it would have been even faster and simpler if Frost's plane had not been delayed, requiring a few hours of waiting around. (Considering the company, that was a bonus.)

When it was over, Owens (a great Louis fan) and other members of the band visited with Pops and were promptly promised copies of his latest album. The feeling was warm. A bit later, Louis opined that it was always a ball to do the Frost show and "work with all those fine musicians."

Glenn, too, had a good time. In his honor, the band jammed on his own "How Could You Do a Thing Like That to Me" (alias "Sultry Serenade") during one of the commercial breaks. Bullman seemed pleased rather than miffed that another trombonist was sitting in—a simple little thing, but indicative of the band's loose spirit and freedom from star eyes. (It is not always thus in televisionland.)

The band has its own recently released LP on Bell Records. Called *O.K., Billy!* it includes excellent arrangements by Johnny Carisi, Garnett Brown, and Wess, with plenty of blowing room for the soloists. Taylor, who says that concert material is being written for the band, would like to see it "become a working unit as well as a show band" and trusts that opportunities to realize this will arise. Meanwhile, the band was set to perform live for the annual Television Academy banquet on February 21.

Though a schedule of a minimum of five weekly tapings takes much of his time, Taylor has other irons in the fire. "I have to do outside things to keep on an even keel," he explains, and among these are appearances with his trio—he opens at the Top of the Gate in March.

Then there is his favorite project, the Jazzmobile, of which he is a director. "In six years, we've gone from a budget of five thousand dollars to one of a quarter million dollars, and from a single summer concert program to three year-round projects. There's nothing like it anywhere in the country. The outdoor concerts are unique; they take the music to people who can't afford to go out, and here they can literally touch the artists. It does so much for young people, especially—it gives them something to aim for other than the pimps and neighborhood hustlers when they see that somebody cares enough about them to come out and play for them. . . .

"Then there are the school lecture-concerts; we had seventy of them last year. And our workshop program: two hundred kids, including fifteen guitarists! It's something to have musicians of the caliber of Joe Newman, Max Roach, or Lee Morgan sit in and do a class with the kids."

This doesn't exhaust Taylor's outside activities. He is currently serving on the Temporary Commission on Cultural Resources of New York State, and has found that there is "a far greater demand for 'culture' in all its forms than most people realize. The demand for neighborhood-oriented cultural projects is phenomenal; people want to get into their own things and are making it happen."

The commission, Taylor explains, is "looking into the short- and long-range problems of artists and cultural organizations. So many things can be done under the existing system—people just don't realize it."

The New York State Council on the Arts, Taylor points out, "predates the National Endowment for the Arts and has given more money to jazz. It takes a broader view."

In addition, Taylor is much in demand for lectures, commencement addresses (he gave the one at Berklee last year), discussion panels, etc. He tries hard to give of his time to any worthy cause, but admits that it is sometimes difficult to be cast in the role of articulate spokesman for jazz.

Closest to his heart, aside from playing, is composing. "Essentially," he confesses, "I'm a songwriter. I like to write melodies and lyrics."

His biggest success in this field has been "I Wish I Knew How It Would Feel to Be Free," which was included, he proudly notes, in the recently published anthology *Great Songs of the '60s:* "That tune has been everything I wanted to do with a tune, from Operation Breadbasket to Nina Simone and pop recordings to the sixth graders who sang it for me when I visited their school. I'd like to have more time for writing. . . ."

Apparently, Taylor is able to find some of that time, since he recently completed scoring the film *Hitch*, for which he also wrote three songs.

He also misses one area of activity that took up much of his time before he joined the Frost show.

"The one thing I really miss is being on the radio. It took me time to realize that. There were things I was able to do in the community [Taylor was program director of Harlem-based station WLIB and conducted his own jazz show]—I hope to be able to get back into radio when possible," he says.

While he was at WLIB, Taylor at his own expense conducted a series of seminars for jazz musicians dealing mainly with economics and business problems, and it makes him happy that some participants, at least, "got information that put some money in their pockets."

In general, he feels that young musicians today are "much better trained and prepared and are looking into business aspects of jazz. They're joining AGAC, ASCAP, and BMI and learning to protect their music. It's a far cry from the days when I used to sell songs for twenty-five to thirty dollars outright."

But then, Billy Taylor today is a far cry from the gifted young pianist struggling to be recognized. "It took me years to live down my reputation as a good accompanist," he recalls. "On Fifty-second Street, on the Birdland scene, almost every job I was offered was tied to a singer. I even had a row with George Wein at Newport one year about that. I really like to play for singers, but that wasn't all I wanted to do. That was one reason I never made a big effort to get into the studio thing."

If he's in it today, and in a big way, it's because his reputation has grown to the point where the Frost people called him—not he them. Success has not spoiled Billy Taylor.

(1971)

Miles Davis

D aring and style, or if you prefer, guts and grace, are two essential characteristics of the extraordinary trumpeter, leader, composer, and perpetual catalyst born Miles Dewey Davis, Jr., in Alton, Illinois, on May 26, 1926.

Alton lies about twenty-five miles upstream from St. Louis on the Mississippi, and Miles actually grew up even closer to that venerable ragtime and jazz center—in East St. Louis, right across the river. The town is notorious as the site of the First World War's ugliest race riot, on July 2, 1917. The trigger was employment of blacks in a factory holding government contracts. Six thousand blacks were driven from their homes; forty of them and eight whites were killed. The riot was followed by the NAACP's famous "silent parade" down New York's Fifth Avenue on July 28, an event that in its dignity and moral force was a direct precursor of civil-rights actions to come.

By 1927, when the Davis family moved there, East St. Louis was once again a relatively peaceful industrial town of no particular distinction, with a sizable black population. The family was a solid and highly respectable one. Miles's father was a successful dentist and oral surgeon. A grandfather had held a large parcel of land in Arkansas, and Dr. Davis owned a two-hundred-acre farm in nearby Millstadt, Illinois, where he raised prize hogs and cattle. Mrs. Davis was socially active and later became a prominent Urban Leaguer in Chicago.

Miles's course in life was set on his thirteenth birthday, when his father presented him with a trumpet. Mrs. Davis had wanted the instrument to be a violin, but, as Miles quipped years later, "my father gave me the trumpet because he loved my mother so much." Actually, there was a less indirect reason for the choice. Dr. Davis had a patient, Elwood Buchanan, who taught trumpet in the St. Louis high school system and also came to the East St. Louis grade schools once a week. He strongly recommended that the dentist's son be given a trumpet.

St. Louis was a trumpet city, close enough to New Orleans to have heard Louis Armstrong early, when he played on the riverboats and made forays inland to jam. Charlie Creath, Ed Allen, Dewey Jackson, and Louis Metcalfe were among the native sons who'd made musical names for themselves, locally and far afield, during the 1920s. During the next decade, it was the turn of Harold "Shorty" Baker, Irving "Mouse" Randolph, and golden-toned Joe Thomas from nearby Webster Groves. Baker, after playing with Andy Kirk, became a star in the Ellington firmament and later joined Johnny Hodges's little band when John Coltrane was a member; he was an early and lasting Davis favorite. Randolph played with Fletcher Henderson and Cab Calloway; Thomas was in the lead chair of Fletcher's great 1936 band. There were also such local favorites as Walter "Crack" Stanley, with the Jeter-Pillars orchestra at the Coronado Hotel; George Hudson; and the up-and-coming Clark Terry. Many of these trumpeters were notable for their purity of sound and sparing use of vibrato.

Vibrato was Mr. Buchanan's *bête noire*. He told his students, of whom Miles soon became one, to avoid a wide vibrato at all costs. He pointed to players like Baker and Bobby Hackett (another lasting Davis favorite) as models, and told the kids: "You're going to get old and start shaking anyway, so play without vibrato." Buchanan, who taught Miles for the remainder of his school days, was a strong influence. But Miles also made his own discoveries. A friend of his father's brought him a book about chromatic scales and showed him how to use it, and he stole a march on his schoolmates.

Competition was fierce, and there were all sorts of lessons to be learned. "In high school, I was the best in the music class on trumpet and all the rest knew it," Miles told a *Playboy* interviewer in 1962, "but all the contest prizes went to the boys with blue eyes. It made me so mad I made up my mind to outdo anybody white on my horn. If I hadn't met that prejudice, I probably wouldn't have had as much drive in my work. I have thought about that a lot. I have thought that prejudice and curiosity have been responsible for what I've done in music."

At age fifteen, still in high school, Miles got his first union card. Soon he was playing with Eddie Randall's Blues Devils (who patterned themselves on Harlem's noted Savoy Sultans, the swinging nine-piece outfit that was the house band at the Savoy Ballroom and took on all comers). Clark Terry, who is about five years older than Miles, heard him with this band, but it was not his first encounter with the youngster. As he told Stanley Dance (in an issue of *Metronome* magazine that has Miles's picture on its cover), Clark was with a band that had been hired for a picnic in Carbondale, Illinois. The day included high school sports events, and there were several school bands playing in support of their teams. As Terry recalled, "One of the bandleaders was an old friend of mine. He wanted me to meet a little trumpet player he admired very much and brought the kid over to introduce us. The kid started right in asking questions—how did I do this, or that? We talked, but my mind was really on some girls dancing around a Maypole and I kind of fluffed the kid off."

About a year later, Terry went to the Elks Club in St. Louis, where he liked to jam. "As I was climbing the long flight of stairs, I heard a trumpet player flying about on his horn in a way I couldn't recognize. Eddie Randall had the band, and I knew everyone in it but this little trumpet player. After I got over by the stand, it dawned on me I'd seen the fellow before. As I said 'Aren't you . . .' he broke in with, 'Yeah, I'm the kid you fluffed off in Carbondale.' We've often laughed about that since."

The kid obviously already had something. At about the same time, in 1942, Sonny Stitt came through St. Louis with Tiny Bradshaw's big band and dropped by the Rhumboogie, where the Randall band was playing for the floor show. Stitt told Miles: "You look like a man named Charlie Parker and you play like him, too. C'mon with us." Stitt was serious, and Bradshaw offered Miles a job. As Miles recalled, "The fellows in the band had their hair slicked down, they wore tuxedos, and they offered me sixty whole dollars a week to play with them. I went home and asked my mother could I go, but she said no, I had to finish high school. I didn't talk to her for two weeks." Later, Illinois Jacquet also tried to take the young trumpeter on the road with him.

Miles graduated in June 1944. His first job as a full-fledged pro was with a band from New Orleans, fresh from a long run in Chicago, where a then unknown singer named Joe Williams had worked with them. They were Adam Lambert's Brown Cats, and when they were booked for a date at the Club Belvedere in Springfield, Illinois, their trumpeter, Thomas Jefferson, returned to New Orleans. Miles was contacted and joined guitarist Lambert, pianist Phamous Lambert, bassist Duke Saunders, and drummer Stanley Williams for two weeks at no less than a hundred dollars per week. (The band, lest anyone should be misled, didn't play New Orleans style, but contemporary small-band swing.)

In July, Billy Eckstine's sensational band came to St. Louis. Miles and a friend were among the first to arrive at the Club Plantation on opening night. Miles had come from a rehearsal and had his trumpet case under his arm. A man he did not immediately recognize rushed over and asked, "Have you got a union card, kid?" It was the Eckstine band's musical director, Dizzy Gillespie. The band's third trumpet, Buddy Anderson, was ailing, and Miles was asked to take his chair. "I couldn't read a thing from listening to Diz and Bird," Miles recalled. He stayed in that chair for the band's two weeks in town. After this experience, no doubt whatsoever remained about wanting to be a musician.

His mother was insisting he go to Fisk University. But Miles had acquired a copy of the newly published *Esquire Jazz Book*, full of pictures of the jazz scene in New York. Mrs. Davis wasn't impressed, but Dr. Davis said the young man could go to New York, where he had a friend who was studying at Juilliard. He got his fare, his tuition, and a generous allowance. (Much later, as an adult, Miles discovered that his mother played the piano quite well and also knew the violin; things she'd never owned up to when she was trying to save her oldest son from becoming a jazz musician.)

Before taking leave of Miles's journeyman period, it is worth noting that his sister once told an interviewer that he had made a record in St. Louis with "some rhythm-and-blues outfit," adding that he sounded "terrible" on it and that it was still in some closet at home at the time. Discographers take heed!

Charlie Parker had left the Eckstine band not long after the St. Louis engagement, and Miles spent his first week in New York and his first month's allowance looking for the elusive genius of the new music. He did find Bird a bit later, at a jam session at the Heatwave in Harlem, and renewed the acquaintance. Meanwhile, he had been attending Juilliard in the daytime and hanging out in Harlem and on Fifty-second Street at night.

At Juilliard, in addition to theory and harmony, Miles studied piano. Dizzy, always the proselytizer, had told him that he had to know the keyboard in order to understand chords and learn how to build a solo. He also befriended Freddie Webster, a trumpeter with a beautiful tone and advanced conception. Webster wanted to know about some of the theoretical things Davis was learning at Juilliard, and in return he gave pointers about tone production.

As any reader of Dizzy Gillespie's autobiography, *To Be or Not to Bop*, will know, the new music that was then taking shape had at least one important thing in common with the older jazz: a tradition of freely shared knowledge among musicians. If anything, that tradition became intensified. The newcomer got help from Tadd Dameron and Thelonious Monk, among others—and of course from Gillespie, who showed him how to shorten the trumpet mouthpiece shank ("to make a note faster") and who told him, when Miles wondered why he couldn't play as high as Dizzy: "You don't think up there; you think in the middle register."

And from Parker. "I roomed with Bird for a year and followed him around down to Fifty-second Street. Every night I'd write chords I heard on matchbook covers. Next day, I'd play those chords all day in the practice room at Juilliard instead of going to classes. Because everything at Juilliard, I knew." Parker kept trying to persuade his young friend (and no doubt benefactor; Miles hasn't said so, but it is likely he paid the rent) to get up and play, saying, "Go ahead. Don't be afraid." But Miles wasn't ready to sit in with the masters yet. In early May of 1945, he made a record date (officially his first) with Herbie Fields, a tenor saxophonist and clarinetist then featured with Lionel Hampton. But as he confessed later, he was too nervous to take a solo on any of the four sides, just playing "in a mute" in the ensembles.

In that month, Coleman Hawkins, already a staunch supporter of the new sounds, opened at the Down Beat on Fifty-second Street with Joe Guy as the trumpeter in his group. Also on the bill was Billie Holiday, who had just married Guy. The trumpeter showed up for work only about half the time, and whenever he didn't, Miles would sit in. Otherwise, Miles would cross the street to the Spotlite and sit in with Eddie "Lockjaw" Davis and altoist Rudy Williams, and eventually Lockjaw hired him.

In the fall, Miles joined Charlie Parker at the Three Deuces. Parker was overpowering, but the young trumpeter found a solution of sorts. "I'd play under him all the time. When Bird would play a melody, I'd play just under him and let him lead the note, swing the note. The only thing I'd add would be a larger sound. I used to quit every night. I'd say, 'What do you need me for?'"

But Parker insisted. Another job, with Bird leading a different lineup including Dexter Gordon on tenor, followed. Then came another stint with Hawkins, this time for pay. In late November, Miles took part in Parker's first record date as a leader, for Savoy. This time he played solos, though Dizzy, who came by to listen, wound up handling the taxing ensemble passages on "Ko Ko," Parker's masterpiece of the date. A most insensitive *Down Beat* review of the two tunes on which Miles soloed, "Now's the Time" and "Billie's Bounce," might be one reason for his long-standing low opinion of jazz critics. (He always spoke well of Ralph Gleason, however, and also likes Nat Hentoff.) In retrospect, the solos reveal a more-than-budding originality, a personal sound, and that rare thing, musical intelligence. And he sounds even better on the then unissued earlier takes.

When Parker left New York for his ill-starred journey to Los Angeles with Dizzy's group, Miles quit school and went home. In St. Louis, he found Benny Carter's band in residence at the Riviera. He joined the trumpet section and went west with Carter, winding up in L.A. and soon doubling into the Finale Club with Parker's group. When the union found out about the two gigs, Davis was severely fined; the choice of which job to keep could not have been a difficult one.

The Finale soon collapsed; California was not ready for bebop. But there was a date with Parker for Ross Russell's Dial label, and this time the reviews were better. Parker's breakdown came in July, and he was hospitalized at Camarillo for treatment. Miles found work with Lucky Thompson in a short-lived band also including a young bassist named Charles Mingus. In September, the Eckstine band, on its last legs as it turned out, hit town, and Miles rejoined, staying until the singer dissolved his noble experiment in the spring of 1947. Miles then gigged around Chicago for a while, appearing at Jumptown with Gene Ammons and Sonny Stitt.

In April, Parker returned to New York to form the best regular group of his career: Miles; Duke Jordan, piano; Tommy Potter, bass; Max Roach, drums. As the records show, Miles had by now developed his own voice. Unlike most modern jazz trumpeters, he eschewed Gillespian runs and pyrotechnics. There was no need for flamboyance when playing with Parker. Instead, Davis offered contrast. It was an indication of the barely twenty-one-year-old's sensibility and musicality that he could follow Parker's staggering solos on "Embraceable You" (both takes) with personal inventions of his own without, in the words of Martin Williams, "sounding a hopeless anti-climax." (It is well to bear in mind that these Parker solos easily rank among the greatest jazz works extant.)

To what extent Miles had become his own man was made even clearer by his first recording session as a leader, in August 1947. The group was actually Parker's, although, probably in deference, Bird played tenor. John Lewis had replaced Duke Jordan, and Nelson Boyd was the bassist. It's not just the sound of Parker's tenor that makes these sides different. The themes, all by Miles, are more structured than most of Bird's, the harmonic schemes more complex, and the general atmosphere more relaxed. The kid was no longer in awe of the master, in part perhaps because he had discovered the master's too-human weaknesses. (During his tenure with Bird, Miles often had to take charge when the leader was unwilling or unable.) But it goes almost without saying that Parker was the prime source of Davis's confidence. Some of his later comments on Bird have a tinge of ambiguity, but this one (quoted in Dizzy's autobiography) surely doesn't: "He used to do some shit, boy, you couldn't believe!"

In 1948, in his celebrated series of articles on bebop for the *Record Changer* magazine, Ross Russell could state: "Miles Davis may be said to belong to the new generation of musicians. There is now a mounting body of evidence that Davis is leading the way to, or even founding, the next school of trumpet playing."

As it turned out, it was not so much a new school of trumpet playing as a new school of *jazz* that Davis was about to found, with help from some new friends. During 1948, the last year in which he played regularly with

Parker, Miles led his own groups at the Royal Roost on two occasions. One was with Parker, Allen Eager, and Kai Winding. The other made history, though it only worked two weeks.

This was the celebrated *Birth of the Cool* nonet; a group with an unprecedented instrumentation of trumpet, trombone, French horn, tuba, alto and baritone saxophones, piano, bass, and drums. The concept began in an unlikely place: pianist Claude Thornhill's big band. Since the early '40s, Thornhill, himself an arranger, had been refining a conception quite unlike that of the mainstream swing bands. Using a section of French horns, clarinets, and tuba (the latter as a melody rather than rhythm voice), he sought a lush, almost static climate of sound. But it was only when the brilliant Gil Evans joined the Thornhill arranging staff that the band's music began to acquire jazz content. "At first," Evans has said, "the sound of the band was almost a reduction to an inactivity of music, a stillness. . . . The sound hung like a cloud." Then the band acquired such gifted young soloists as altoist Lee Konitz and trumpeter Red Rodney. And when Evans, inspired by the discoveries of Parker and Gillespie, began to adapt such pieces as "Anthropology," "Yardbird Suite," and "Robbins' Nest" to the band's sound, musicians took notice.

Among them was Miles Davis, who told a *Down Beat* staffer in 1950: "Thornhill had the greatest band, the one with Lee Konitz, during these modern times. The one exception was the Eckstine band with Bird." His friendship with Evans, a deep and lasting one ("We couldn't be much closer if he was my brother," said Miles in his famous September 1962 *Playboy* interview), began when the arranger approached Davis for permission to use his "Donna Lee" for the Thornhill band. The trumpeter agreed, but in return asked Evans to show him some things about chord structure and to let him study some of the Thornhill scores.

By mid-1948, the second recording ban called by the musicians' union (the first had stretched from mid-1942 to late 1944) was in effect, and musicians had time on their hands. Evans's one-room cellar apartment on West Fifty-fifth Street became a hangout for a host of enterprising musical minds, including Parker, Gerry Mulligan, John Lewis, George Russell, John Benson Brooks, and Johnny Carisi. "We all gravitated around Evans," Mulligan said years later.

The Thornhill band had temporarily disbanded, and Miles had done well enough during his first Royal Roost engagement to be offered another. It was decided to reduce the Thornhill sound to what Evans has called "the smallest number of instruments that could get that sound and still express all the harmonies [the band] used. Miles wanted to play his idiom with that kind of sound."

The two-week booking was as relief band opposite Count Basie. Miles broke precedent by insisting that the sign in front of the club (a forerunner of Birdland, a bit further down Broadway) read: "Miles Davis Band—Arrangements by Gerry Mulligan, Gil Evans, and John Lewis." Never before had arrangers been so prominently credited. Basie was impressed: "Those slow things sounded strange and good. I didn't always know what they were doing, but I listened and liked it."

The band's personnel included Konitz, Mulligan, Lewis, and Roach, plus Junior Collins on French horn, Bill Barber on tuba, and bassist Al McKibbon, with Ted Kelly and Mike Zwerin alternating on trombone. There was even a singer, Kenny "Pancho" Hagood. When the recording ban was lifted in late 1948, Miles signed with Capitol Records, then on a bebop spree. The nonet's first session took place in January 1949, with Kai Winding on trombone, and Al Haig and Joe Shulman replacing Lewis and McKibbon, who were out of town with Dizzy's big band. Four sides were cut. A second session, with some changes in personnel (notably J. J. Johnson and Kenny Clarke), was held in April, and this produced the band's acknowledged masterpieces, Carisi's "Israel" and Davis and Evans's "Boplicity." The third and final session did not take place until March 1950, at which time the band also did a week at the Clique Club, a short-lived predecessor to Birdland. Roach and McKibbon were back for this, and the French horn player was Gunther Schuller. Some of the dozen sides by the nonet were not issued until considerably later, but those that appeared at the time made a deep and lasting impression on musicians. And contrary to generally held opinion, they were also quite well received in the leading jazz publications, *Down Beat* and *Metronome*, if not as enthusiastically as hindsight might demand. (During 1950–51, Bill Russo and Lloyd Lifton devoted four of their *Down Beat* columns, "Jazz on Record," to analysis of solos from the sessions: Miles's "Israel," "Move," and "God-child," and Konitz's "Move.")

There can be little doubt that these records (which were reissued in 1957 on a Capitol LP that was titled *Birth of the Cool*) triggered the advent of a successor style to bebop (though bop, of course, did not fold up and steal away, but returned with a vengeance under the new guise of "hard bop" in the mid-'50s). But they also remain classics—regardless of their influence—as *music* pure and simple. And while the arrangers' contributions to the success of the venture (artistic success; initially, the records did not sell very well) have rightly been stressed, it was Miles who was the catalyst and primary soloist. As Gerry Mulligan has written: "He took the initiative and put the theories to work. He called the rehearsals, hired the halls, called the players, and generally cracked the whip."

Thus, the leadership capabilities of Miles Davis became apparent while he was still in his early twenties. In May 1949, in the midst of the *Birth of the Cool* period, came an invitation to the Paris Jazz Festival, the first international event of its kind. Parker and Sidney Bechet were the stars but Davis was among the headliners: he and Tadd Dameron (the great arranger-composer-pianist who had helped Miles when he first came to New York) co-led a quintet that included James Moody and Kenny Clarke. Broadcast recordings from the concert, legitimately issued for the first time in 1977, reveal an interesting aspect of Miles, who plays as close to Gillespie's conception as on any records he ever made, including some uncharacteristic high-note forays, brilliantly adapting himself to the strict bebop format of the group. Presumably, appearing on the same bill as Parker but separately from him, plus the presence at the festival of Kenny Dorham as his replacement in the Parker quintet, represented both liberation and challenge to Miles, and he rose to the occasion—as he almost always would do throughout his career.

Ironically, however, this period of his first important impacts on the jazz scene coincided with perhaps the most difficult time in the young musician's life. As he told Marc Crawford in a candid interview for *Ebony* years later: "I got hooked. . . . I got bored and was around cats that were hung. So I wound up with a habit that took me over four years to break."

Those were listless years. During the year between the second and third nonet dates, there was no other commercial recording. And after that March 1950 date, Miles did not get back to the studios as a leader until his first session for Prestige, on January 17, 1951.

A year earlier, he was interviewed by *Down Beat*'s Pat Harris during a Chicago gig. He attacked those who "say there's no music but bop," praised Sidney Bechet, had kind words for Dixieland jazz, cited Roy Eldridge and Harry James among his early influences ("You've got to have a foundation . . . before you can play bop") and took pride in his three-year-old son, Gregory, who already was playing a horn. But he ruefully described his current life as months of no work. "I've worked so little," he said, "I could probably tell you where I was playing any night in the last three years." And he attacked promoters and club owners for not treating musicians with respect, and said he would like to spend "eight months [of each year] in Paris and four months here. Eight months where you're accepted for what you can do, and four months here because—well, it's hard to leave all this."

The piece concludes: "During the last year, he worked a couple of weeks at Soldier Meyer's in Brooklyn, played the Paris Jazz Festival, four one-nighters around New York, and a month at the Hi-Note. When he closed here, nothing substantial was in sight."

And nothing much of substance did turn up while Miles was struggling with his demons. Having fallen into the same trap as so many (too many of them dead) of his contemporaries must have gone against Miles's basic nature. Handsome, proud, intelligent, competitive, and already fiercely individualistic, Miles was not psychologically predestined for the draining curse of addiction. We needn't dwell on this long-ago episode in the life of a man who went on to make so much of himself, but it does help to put into focus some of the music on these discs.

What is significant is that Miles came back, with relative speed, and that he did so without breast-beating, and by himself. As he told Marc Crawford: "I made up my mind . . . I was sick and tired of it. You know you can get tired of anything. You can even get tired of being scared. I laid down and stared at the ceiling for twelve days and I cursed everybody I didn't like. I was kicking it the hard way. . . . Then it was over."

During those days before it was over, Miles was sought out by Bob Weinstock, a bear of a man and a contemporary of Miles, who had begun his jazz involvement as a record collector. He had gone from collecting to selling, first through the pages of the *Record Changer* (we have mentioned this estimable magazine before; it was edited by one Orrin Keepnews), then in space rented at a jazz record shop, and finally in his own store, just a block west of the Royal Roost. Called The Jazz Record Corner, it began to issue records under that label name in 1948. (They were leased Australian masters featuring the revivalist Graeme Bell band. Weinstock's tastes were mainly in that direction then, but under the tutelage of Ross Russell, he began to veer toward bebop, aided by the proximity of the Roost, then billing itself as "The Metropolitan Bopera House.")

By early 1949 Weinstock had issued his first modern jazz record, by Lee Konitz, on a label he called New Jazz. Subsequently, it became Prestige. He knew and liked Miles, personally and musically. As he told Joe Goldberg for *Jazz Masters of the Fifties*: "Miles sort of disappeared from the scene, and I was on a business trip to St. Louis. . . . I made some calls (and reached his home). They told me he was in Chicago. . . . Finally, he got in touch with me, and he came back East. . . . At that time, though he still dug the cool music of Mulligan and Evans, some of the primitiveness in him started to come out. . . . On his first date, you can hear a very different Miles Davis than on the Capitols."

Sonny Rollins was present on that first date. He'd met Miles when he was eighteen and just about to graduate from high school; they jammed together in the Bronx. "Miles was only four years older than I was," Sonny told Conrad Silvert, "but at that time, four years could be pretty big. . . . Miles was the first major player to hire me. I went on the road with him, I think in '49—to Boston, Philadelphia, Baltimore. That's when I first met Coltrane. We played with Miles at the same time, both on tenor." (And who wouldn't like to have heard that band?)

Record dates (there were six for Prestige and two for Blue Note during the gray period, 1951 through '53) must have meant sustenance for Miles, though nobody got rich making jazz dates for independent labels. In any case, he tried to get what money he could from Weinstock (and from Blue

Note's Alfred Lion and Frank Wolff as well). The well-authenticated legend is that he and Weinstock would sometimes sit and stare at each other for as much as twenty minutes without exchanging a word after Miles had made a forceful request for more. Basically, more money meant more sides would be recorded, and most of these sessions did turn out to be quite productive.

But what a difference when 1954 came along! Five dates for Prestige and one for Blue Note, and what dates! This was the real comeback year for Miles—not the following one, when he appeared at the Newport Jazz Festival and the jazz press officially rediscovered him. Miles scorned the comeback talk. "You'd think I'd been on the moon," he quipped. "What are they talking about? I just played the way I always play."

Yet there was some truth to the resurgence theory, for reasons obvious and not so obvious. Clearly, the weight off his back was an enormous relief. But also, there were changes in approach. Tone had always been an essential aspect of Miles, but by 1954 he had found his own true sound. Musical logic and a splendid sense of balance and structure had also been evident, but now they all came together, as in that wonderful solo on "Bags' Groove." Miles was telling a story now, and the world was ready to listen.

The mid-'50s was among those recurring periods when the public (which is to say the media) rediscovers jazz. It was also the time when the long-playing record came fully into its own, both in terms of salability and creative use. As Weinstock well knew, it was only a matter of time until a major label would become interested in Davis and make a contract offer he could not hope to match. It turned out to be Columbia, and a deal was struck: Miles, by now at the helm of his greatest band, would do a sufficient amount of recording to allow Prestige to release "new" material for the next few years. Immediately after recording he would be free to begin work for Columbia. Thus the marathon 1956 sessions that conclude this package.

What had transpired in the interim was that Miles had further refined his ability as a talent spotter, and his knowledge of what he wanted to do in music. The great quintet, which begins to take shape with the *quartet* session of June 7, 1955, had been fully formed by year's end, with a personnel of Red Garland, piano; Paul Chambers, bass; Philly Joe Jones, drums; and John Coltrane, tenor saxophone.

It is easy to forget that none of these players were at all well known at this stage of the game. Chambers, just twenty, had come to New York that same year, played just a few gigs, and been hired on the spot when Miles heard him with George Wallington's group. Garland, three years Miles's senior, had kicked around on the periphery of jazz for years until he came to Davis's attention. (The fact that Garland had been a professional boxer, and that boxing had become Miles's favorite sport and pastime, would not have had any bearing on the matter if Miles hadn't liked his playing.) The remarkable Jones had first worked with Miles in 1952, not long after the drummer had settled in New York. Although known and appreciated among musicians, his was hardly a household name, and fans still got him mixed up with Jo Jones of Basie fame. And Coltrane, though he'd played with Dizzy's last big band and subsequent combo (as well as with Earl Bostic and Johnny Hodges), was a near-unknown quantity.

But Davis knew what he was doing. He paid no attention to criticisms of Coltrane for his "harsh" (even "ugly") sound or "strained" style. In Coltrane's dense, vertical style, gritty sound, and emotional ferocity, Miles had found the perfect foil for his own sound and style. It was a bit like the contrast between himself and Parker—only this time, it was the trumpeter who played lead. And the rhythm section was perfectly suited to his aim: it could swing hard, it could listen, and it could leave the space he wanted without dropping a beat. It could simmer smoothly and also provide the accents and polyrhythms Miles loved.

At the time, Miles was profoundly influenced by an unlikely source, pianist Ahmad Jamal, who, whatever his other virtues or flaws, had a unique feeling for space and openness in his music. Miles instructed Garland to play as much like Jamal as he could, and it is not insignificant that the pianist's features with the quintet included "Ahmad's Blues." (It should go without saying that there were decided stylistic affinities between the two pianists to begin with; Garland didn't just copy Jamal.)

As for Chambers, he was a marvel who had everything—tone, time, taste, technique—and also was an outstanding soloist and shaper of swinging countermelodies in the ensemble. No wonder that within a year or so the trio was affectionately known in jazz circles as simply "The Rhythm Section"—the first since the glorious "All American" rhythm quartet of the Count Basie band of the '30s to earn a sobriquet of its own.

Certainly the quintet, which stayed together until the spring of 1957 and was basically reconstituted as a sextet (with the addition of Cannonball Adderley's alto sax and the substitution of Bill Evans on piano) early in 1958, was the most influential jazz group of its time, and one of the most memorable of all time. It marked, for Miles Davis, the distillation of the essence of his musical ideas up to that time—ideas related to yet different from those that had fueled the nonet. And it established him for the second time within a decade as one of the most influential figures in jazz.

What happened subsequently is part of basic contemporary jazz history. How Miles, with a single album (*Kind of Blue*), set in motion some of the major trends of the 1960s and his own third phase as a key influence. How these ideas and approaches were refined by the second great quintet, the one with Wayne Shorter, Herbie Hancock, Ron Carter, and Tony Williams (the latter only seventeen when he joined the band and possibly the trumpeter's single greatest outright discovery). How, intermittently, he resumed his collaborations with Gil Evans, yielding a series of masterful meldings of soloist's and arranger's arts. How, to the consternation of many dedicated fans (some musicians among them), he turned to so-called, mislabeled "jazz-rock fusion" with *Bitches Brew*, the best-selling jazz album of its time. How he continued to bring to the fore new talent (Chick Corea, Keith Jarrett, Jack DeJohnette, Dave Liebman, Mtume, Airto, and others), while continuing to play a new kind of music that reached a new generation of listeners while alienating more than a few older ones. Then, basically due to illness and exhaustion, he disappeared from the active list, amid rumors of all sorts, in mid-1975. Since then, instant scuttlebutt news could be made by the merest whisper of his impending return to concert stage or recording studio.

Behind all that, the legend of Miles Davis, Prince of Darkness, Man Walking on Eggshells, Evil Genius of Jazz, etc., etc., began and kept building. At first, one might have theorized that the Davis mystique was the creation of the more-than-enterprising and imaginative Columbia Records publicity department, pouring forth pictures (excepting only Louis Armstrong, Miles must be the most photographed of jazz musicians), adjectives, and fancies. But the real story was the tension set up between the publicity drive and the actual character of its object.

So much that has been written and said about the man's personality and its seeming mysteries points up the wisdom of a choice once made by the late Ralph Gleason. When assigned yet another set of Miles Davis album-liner notes, Gleason (who had certainly written a great deal about Miles—and was credited by his subject as being the *only* jazz writer who knew what he was talking about) chose to turn out impressionistic prose-poems based on Davis album titles or to ring poetic-phonetic variations on the man's name (*Ma-ulz, My-ulz, My-ills*)! It was at least as good a solution as any, for the torrent of words—in the jazz press and the daily press, and then in magazines like *Playboy, Esquire, Nugget*, and *Cavalier*, and later in *Rolling Stone* and the *Real Paper* and *The Village Voice*—had rolled well past the saturation point. Every journalist within earshot of the artist seemed to have become a qualified psychologist and self-anointed mythmaker.

What chiefly fascinated writers, and obviously readers as well, was his seeming flamboyance—elegant and style-setting clothes, fast cars, exotic house and equally exotic paramours—and his contrasting surliness, profanity, and (or so it was assumed) outright rudeness.

It all started with the story of Miles turning his back on audiences and refusing to acknowledge applause. It mattered little that from the start he attempted, with impeccable logic, to explain these actions. He was—he pointed out—in a nightclub or concert hall only to play music; he didn't believe in distracting, or taking attention away from, the other performers when they were soloing and he had nothing to do. He saw no need to introduce players or compositions: the former were surely well known to audiences; the latter were often decided only on the spur of the moment and should be recognizable from recordings to those who really cared. He believed that his music was not an entertainment. But few cared to read between the lines of such statements to arrive at the realization that their hero was basically a shy man who didn't (indeed *couldn't*) go through the show-business routines expected of popular performers.

Musicians and writers who knew him well often said so, but the mystique prevailed. It prevailed even though most of the articles, even those that made the most noise about the controversial aspects of the Davis image, wound up stating that there was a nice guy "behind the mask."

Dizzy Gillespie told me: "Miles talks rough—you hear him use all kinds of rough words. But when you hear the pathos in his music, that's a different story. His music reflects his true character. I once had a long conversation with his daughter, Cheryl. We talked about him—oh, did we talk about him! Seriously, I made a statement during that conversation. I said: 'Miles is shy. He is super shy.' A lot of people don't believe that, but I have known him for a long, long time."

And Sonny Rollins told Conrad Silvert: "I hate to use that word 'shy,' but he is a shy guy. Which is why he turned his back sometimes, and then people would say, 'Oh, gee, he's arrogant.' Miles wanted to hear the music, and he'd play something soft for us that he didn't want the public to hear because we were getting the music together. It was more the feeling of a workshop. . . . We were all experimenting, and Miles encouraged it. It was music, music, music."

Indeed, it is because he takes the music so seriously that Miles refuses to dress it up with stage business, which is not to say that he, with the help of the aforementioned publicity, was not clever enough to turn his shyness to an advantage, to make a new kind of show business out of his anti-showbiz attitude. And there's no reason to be so naive as to ignore his studied sartorial flair, though it must be noted that he is as original and spectacular a dresser off stage as on.

In part, Miles's shyness is due to a handicap. In the mid-'50s, he had a routine operation to remove some benign nodules on his vocal cords. While still recovering, he was infuriated by a club manager, raised his voice against doctor's orders, and suffered permanent damage, so that he speaks in a hoarse semi-whisper, not at all unappealing, but difficult to project. If he had chosen to make a practice of casual conversation with the customers in a noisy club, the resulting "what did you say" would quickly have driven him up the wall. (I've actually seen this happen, for, contrary to legend, Miles is basically friendly and on occasion has tried to oblige his fans.) Public-address announcements obviously also became a problem under these circumstances.

Another contributing factor to the myth is his unsparing honesty in musical matters. His famous *Down Beat* "Blindfold Tests" bear witness to this, as do many of his quoted remarks. The fact is that Miles never curries favor or goes easy on his friends. If he doesn't like something, he says so, and *why*, usually with profanities added for emphasis. But actually the bulk of his publicly expressed opinions on music have been positive. When they're not, it's usually with good reason. Tastes may differ, but Miles has a broad and deep appreciation for all good music, and his critical opinions are based on a sharp and discerning—and certainly highly experienced—ear.

In any event, it seems impossible to dislike Miles Davis if one knows him at all, though, like all of us, he may have done some not-so-nice things during his lifetime. I cannot claim to know Miles well, but whenever I've had personal contact with him, I've come away with warm feelings. He is a kind, generous, witty, even considerate man. And for the past five years, and probably well before that, too, he has suffered some degree of physical discomfort and pain for most of his waking hours. First operated on for a hipbone problem in 1965, he underwent surgery again ten years later. A few years before that, he broke both ankles in a car accident. His preoccupation with physical fitness is in part due to these problems, and otherwise motivated by his firm belief that a black man in America, no matter how famous or well-off, has to be ready to defend himself at any time.

Among the mass of interviews with Miles, the most personally revealing and touching was the one in *Playboy* in 1962. It ought to be required reading for all who carry with them a distorted image of the man, for it clearly shows his innate decency, as well as his just pride. At times, Miles has indulged himself in putting on (or putting off) interviewers. But in this instance, he clearly spoke straight from the shoulder and from the heart about what motivates him as a man and an artist. And of the racism that gnaws "like a big sore inside your belly" at every black American—advances to the contrary notwithstanding, as surely in 1980 as in 1962.

What he said about trumpet players bears quoting. The interviewer, taking note of Miles's many poll victories, asks: "After yourself, how would you rate others?" and Miles explodes.

"*After* me! Hell, it's plenty great trumpet players don't come *after* me, or *after* nobody else! That's what I hate so about critics—how they are always *comparing* artists . . . always writing that one's better than another one. . . . That bugs the hell out of musicians. It's made some damn near mad enough to want to hang up their horns. . . . The thing to judge in any jazz artist is does the man project, and does he have ideas. You take Dizzy—he does, all the time, every time he picks up his horn. Some more cats—Clark Terry, Ray Nance, Kenny Dorham, Roy Eldridge, Harold Baker, Freddie Hubbard, Lee Morgan, Bobby Hackett—a lot of them. Hell, that cat down in New Orleans, Al Hirt, he blows his ass off, too!"

And then about Louis Armstrong: "I love Pops, I love the way he sings, the way he plays—everything he does, except when he says something against modern jazz music. . . . A long time ago, I was at Bop City, and he came in and told me he liked my playing. I don't know if he would even remember it, but I remember how good I felt to have him say it."

(A fond personal memory of Miles and Louis: some years back, I found myself seated next to Miles at Basin Street East when Louis was appearing there. Davis was accompanied by his then lawyer Harold Lovette, a loquacious man. Louis's set had begun, but Lovette was still talking. Without taking his eyes off Louis, Miles said: "Shut *up*, man! I want to hear Pops!" And from the way Miles reacted to that set, one confirmed Armstrong fan could tell he was in the company of another.)

While Miles has disavowed any direct influence from Louis, he has also said: "Nobody can play anything on a horn that Louis hasn't played already." And I agree with Martin Williams when he concludes his chapter on Miles in *The Jazz Tradition* with these words:

"More than any other player, Miles Davis echoes Louis Armstrong; one can hear it, I think, in his reading of almost any standard theme. And behind the jaded stance, behind the complaints, and behind the sometimes blasé sophistication, Miles Davis's horn also echoes something of Armstrong's exuberantly humorous, forcefully committed and self-determined joy."

If he should never pick up his horn again—an eventuality that anyone at all concerned about jazz abhors but nevertheless must (as of this writing in mid-1980) contemplate—Miles Davis will have left his indelible mark on jazz. The best of the music contained herein is among the reasons why.

(1980)

Miles in Motion

I approach the prospect of interviewing Miles Davis with some trepidation. We've had a nodding acquaintance for years—since the time, way back in '48, when a little trumpet player named Nat Lorber (they call him "Face") introduced us on Broadway. I remember that Miles was wearing a beautiful dark-blue double-breasted pinstripe suit. (He's always been sharp.)

Since then, many brief encounters, in clubs, backstage at concerts, etc., Miles sometimes friendly, sometimes not. And nine years ago, an evening at his house, with a whole bunch of writers and players in a "confrontation," as they call it now, between critics and musicians arranged by a press agent. Miles was a beautiful host. So why am I uptight?

I remember the house, in the West Seventies, but as the cab pulls up and I spot Miles lounging near the entrance, it looks different. Above the front door, there is now a Moorish turret. Miles greets me, and we enter. There are men at work inside. The place is being completely redecorated. An Egyptian mural graces the patio walls. A tempting honeydew melon rests on the kitchen table.

"Want a piece?" Miles asks. It's a hot day. He cuts two slices expertly. The melon is delicious, tasting just right at room temperature. "It's best when it's not too cold," Miles comments. "Come in here—I want to show you something," he adds, moving toward the front room.

There stands a new Innovex unit. "They sent me this," says Miles, turning on the power and picking up his trumpet. "Dig this."

A foot pedal has been connected to the unit, and Miles works it while he blows. The sound is not unlike that achieved by moving the hand in front of the bell, in this case Harmon-muted. Miles obviously likes the sound; he's never played wah-wah style, and this way, he can also bend the notes subtly. He turns up the volume to show the power of the speaker system. Then he puts the horn away.

Glancing at the multiple controls atop the unit, I ask if he uses any of the other devices. "Naaah," he shrugs disdainfully. Like any musician with his own good and distinctive sound, he has no desire to distort it. He likes the pedal effects and the amplification, but that's all.

"Let's go upstairs," he says. It's a duplex apartment, and the redecorating upstairs is finished. The living room is like a cool oasis. Everything is built in—aside from a low, round table, there is no standing furniture. (A recent article about the house in the *New York Times* quotes Miles to the effect that he doesn't like corners. Everything is rounded off.) The soft, blue carpeting looks inviting, and when Miles answers the phone, he reclines on the floor. You can move freely in this place. The bedroom is so groovy that if it were mine, I might never leave it.

"You want to hear something?" Miles asks, approaching the wall that holds his music system—tape decks, amplifiers, turntable, some records, lots of tapes. He finds the reel he wants, unravels it, and puts it on. The speakers, invisible, built into the ceiling somewhere, are a gas, and so is the music, by Miles's new band, obviously recorded live. It's quite a change from *Bitches Brew*—this man doesn't stay in one place too long. I listen, and let the music carry me away.

What I've heard, I learn, is from a forthcoming Columbia album, recorded live on three consecutive nights at the Fillmore East. It will be released in September and is the first live Miles LP in many years. Keith Jarrett is on the band (as well as Chick Corea—Chick on electric piano, Keith on Fender Rhodes combo organ), and he is a significant addition. Miles is obviously pleased with him.

"Did you hear what Keith was playing behind me there?" he asks, rolling back the tape. "He's a bitch. Chick, too." After the passage has been replayed, he demonstrates at the piano, built into one side of the seating unit, and within easy reach from the hi-fi system.

"With a C going on in the bass, you can play anything against it," he explains. I ask if he does most of the writing for the group now, since Wayne Shorter's departure, and he says yes.

When he has to write something for a record date, he adds later, he usually does it at the last moment, so it will be completely fresh.

"You write to establish the mood," he points out. "That's all you need. Then we can go on for hours. If you complete something, you play it, and it's finished. Once you resolve it, there's nothing more to do. But when it's open, you can suspend it. . . ."

"Suspension" is a word Miles uses frequently when talking about his music. It is a music very much of today, in sound and feeling. Once again, Miles is setting the pace, as he has been doing at frequent intervals since 1948 and the Capitol nonet. There was the pioneering quintet with Coltrane, Red Garland, Paul Chambers, and Philly Joe Jones; *Miles Ahead* and the other memorable collaborations with Gil Evans; the great sextet with Trane, Cannonball Adderley, and Bill Evans, which in *Kind of Blue* established a whole new syntax for jazz improvisation; and then the series of surprises beginning with *E.S.P.* and running on through *Bitches Brew*.

When the Fillmore album comes out, there'll be new surprises. In a sense, Miles is a perfectionist, but not the polishing kind. Once he has perfected a thing, he needs to move on to something new. His music today is in constant motion, ideas bouncing off each other, interacting; many things going on at once; cyclical, unresolved, suspended and full of suspense, electrified and electrifying.

Miles has some private business to attend to. He invites me to come back the following afternoon. "We'll go up to the gym. You can watch me work out. . . ."

Another sultry New York day. Inside, it's cool and dark. We join our host in a cup of refreshing mint tea, then take a stroll to a nearby garage.

Again a surprise—no more red Ferrari, but a new battleship gray Lamborghini; a magnificent machine, low and trim, built like a racer. We shoot out onto the West Side Highway, heading north.

Miles drives with the superlative reflexes of a pro, fast but not taking any dumb chances; not showing off, always in complete control. We learn that the Ferrari was "full of bullet holes," unwanted souvenirs of the stupid attempt on Miles's life by obviously amateur gangsters earlier this year.

What happened to them? "They're all dead," Miles answers matter-of-factly, not gloating. "I don't know how or where, but that's what I heard."

On our way to pick up Miles's trainer, we stop for a red light in Harlem. A young black man on a monumental yellow Honda pulls up next to us, eyeing the car with open admiration. "What kind is that?" he asks. "Tell him a Lamborghini," Miles instructs. The motorcyclist is on my side of the car, and Miles can't shout. I convey the information, repeating the unfamiliar name, and adding that it's an Italian make.

"Ask him how much is that Honda," Miles requests. "It's sixteen hundred dollars," the cyclist responds proudly, obviously pleased at the question. The car is more than ten times the price of the Honda, but in asking, Miles has equalized them—two men admiring each other's strong machines.

At Bobby Gleason's Gym in the Bronx, a comfortable, old-fashioned place where some of the city's best fighters work out, Miles, in bright blue trunks, is shadowboxing under the watchful eye of his trainer, a slim, trim, soft-spoken man who looks and acts not at all like the stereotype of the ex-boxer. He's been with Miles for years.

Afterward, while Miles does exercises in a corner, the trainer tells me: "He's really coming along. His reflexes are getting better all the time. And he's in top shape."

As I have noticed. Not an ounce of excess fat. All solid muscle, but not of the bulging kind displayed by some of the men in the gym. Sleek and compact like a panther. It's obvious that everyone around the gym and on the street outside knows and likes Miles Davis.

"Boxing is like music," Miles says later, as we drive downtown. "You keep adding to it." He works out four times a week, he says, and does forty push-ups and forty sit-ups each day.

He talks some more about music. "We're not a rock band. Some people get that idea because we're amplified, but with amplification, we can be heard, and we can hear each other. This is a new day, and we can do what we want. With a good system, you can play soft or loud, and people can hear.

"For years," he goes on, "I've been going to clubs to listen to something—like Ahmad Jamal playing piano—and once I'm there, I can't hear anything." And there are other things he dislikes about most clubs: "You have to give people something, not just take from them."

But he doesn't mind playing clubs, he says, provided things are right and the music can be heard. "For a while, I thought we had something good at the Village Gate [where, earlier this year, Miles had worked out an arrangement with owner Art D'Lugoff enabling him to book acts of his own choice to work opposite his band, getting the admission gate while the club took in the proceeds from drink and food sales], but Art didn't seem to want to keep it going."

We're nearing our destination, and Miles gives me fair warning to hold on before he negotiates a hairpin turn that takes us off the East River Drive.

"Our music changes every month," he says. "We extend each other's ideas. I may start a phrase and not complete it because I hear something else behind me that takes me to a different place. It keeps going further. Our Latin drummer [Airto Moreira] gives us something else to play off. Most of the guys in the band can play other instruments, and that expands their conception. Jack [DeJohnette] can really play the piano, and Chick plays the shit out of the drums. Keith plays clarinet. So when they ad lib, you know it's going to be something you like to hear."

In jazz today, there are many seekers of new ways. Often, the searching seems forced, and the results not natural. Miles Davis, however, has that rare gift of being able to give birth and life to new things that, no matter how startling, always seem natural and logical, and open up new roads for others to travel after he has moved on.

The sole photograph in Miles's living room, unobtrusively displayed, is a color shot of a pensive John Coltrane, dating from his days with the trumpeter. It's pure speculation, of course, but if he were still among us, I have a feeling that Coltrane, that restless seeker, might well once again feel very much at home with Miles.

(1970)

Charles Mingus

Charles Mingus had three musical gods: Art Tatum, Duke Ellington, and Charlie Parker. That is the order in which they revealed themselves to him, and to attempt other rankings is to invite trouble. Each bestowed upon him unique gifts.

From Tatum, Mingus learned that the jazz tradition had room for virtuosos, and through Tatum, he was initiated into the mysterious rites of interpretative transformation through harmony and rhythm. From Ellington, he first of all received the revelation that jazz could be a composer's music, that ideas which couldn't be played on one's own instrument could be fully realized in concert with other carriers of the message—and then many other things. And through Bird, he came to understand that the music could take new wing on flight patterns that had seemed near exhaustion as paths for soaring—that the jazz tradition still could encompass innovation without genuflections to alien idols.

From such revelations he forged his own music and ascended to the pantheon of jazz. Getting there was a hard task, and Mingus was often a hard taskmaster. He had to make what some considered a nuisance of himself, for he needed others in order to fully express himself. But he made that need as much theirs as his own, guiding them, prodding them toward the unfolding of the creative essence, the flowering of self within a sustaining musical community. Thus, he had to bring out the self (and that includes the ego) in other players to make them confident and strong, but also take care that they did not in the process lose sight of the message he had entrusted to them.

It has been said that Mingus was a violent man. It would be truer to say that he was a passionate man, a man of great imagination and with desires to match—not least among them the urge to experience life to the fullest. It is a truism that great artists are self-centered, but to say that means nothing. Mingus's center was not a vortex of self-contemplation that sucked in, absorbed, or stifled otherness, bur a volcanic center from which flowed a pro-creative lava, interacting with everything it touched. Not a black hole, but a bursting sun, with rays that could scorch.

Mingus called himself a "spontaneous composer," and spontaneity was of the essence to him, as it must be to any musician truly in touch with the jazz tradition. As artist and as man, Mingus often acted on impulse. One of the many unique aspects of his music is its ever-shifting pulse—a result of his impulsiveness, his will to chance it, his willingness to take risks. If emotion came into conflict with discipline and chaos threatened, so be it. And when chaos did take hold, it was only momentarily, as Mingus knew it would be, and beneficially, too, for in going to the brink, he learned just how far he could stretch the boundaries of control.

Mingus was a juggler. He had to balance his needs as a player with his needs as a composer-leader, his needs as an artist with the necessities of life. Like every jazz musician born, he had to take care of business, and business was not among the many things in life he loved. His head for business made every business encounter a matter of principle—moral, ethical, artistic—and thus by inevitable implication, a scene from a morality play. Such plays can be tragic or comic, and touch on every dramatic nuance in between, and they always test the players. The world of jazz is full of people who made jazz their business from an initial impulse of love for the music, and such businesspeople were severely tested in encounters with Mingus. He wanted to keep them honest, and if he could not, there could be no further relationship.

Mingus wore his heart on his raveled sleeve. When he trusted someone, he trusted all the way, and thus the slightest slight, imagined or real, became cause for wounds and recriminations. You were with him or against him; there could be no middle ground. Mingus, like every artist with much to say, was fighting time, and you'd better be ready to give him yours. (It should be unnecessary to add that it was time well spent.)

Mingus's career was filled with notorious incidents, but there was good reason behind most of them. The famous 1963 Town Hall concert was a case of ideas in conflict with time and space. Those who found the sight of music copyists working away on stage absurd or affronting missed the pathos of the occasion: a great artist with so few opportunities to realize works on a large scale that he found it impossible to contain himself. They also missed the moving central spectacle of just how much music Mingus was able to salvage from the shambles of a dream.

The famous Newport Rebellion, of which he was the catalyst, was perceived by some as an act of hubris or a tantrum, by others as an act of profound esthetic or social implications. But it was simply an act of artistic necessity. Newport, of which he justly considered himself a godfather, had become swollen with serendipity and no longer had room for singular artists. Mingus would not have his sets cut short. He was a main event, not a sideshow. So he did what he had to do, carrying with him others who might never have taken a decisive step on their own. It was his finest hour as a leader of a general cause within jazz, but in the brief and bizarre alliance of artists formed after the end of the great counter-festival, he played no leading part. He had no patience for games.

Of course Mingus did come back to Newport, and for great moments, such as his unforgettable appearance at Radio City Music Hall in 1971, when he sparked a jam session set and then held six thousand people spellbound, playing the blues on his bass, one man with one instrument on that huge stage. Those who thought he had wanted to destroy Newport with his "rebellion"—whether they approved or disapproved of such intentions—had little understanding of Mingus, or of Newport. He wanted to keep the festival honest. And just so, most of the musicians with whom Mingus had confrontations (even violent ones, though Mingus's use of violence was far more often verbal than physical) came back to him. Or were asked to return, for Mingus was not afraid to admit, albeit in roundabout ways, that he had been at fault. And those who knew him well enough understood that his excesses were self-lacerations as much as lashings out at the world.

Mingus forgave Ellington for having cast him out of his Ducal paradise. In his astonishing book *Beneath the Underdog*, flawed by over-editing but full of Mingus nonetheless, there is a masterly description of this expulsion. It is full of humor, as Mingus often was. (What made his protest pieces the only esthetically successful music of this genre in jazz was that their anger is leavened with humor.) It is said that Ellington never fired anyone. Indeed, this is asserted by Ellington himself in Mingus's story. Mingus fired everyone, often on the bandstand. Where Ellington was private, working behind the scenes or through emissaries, Mingus was public, willing to risk his dignity. Decorum was a word without meaning to him. When he performed his music, he bared his innermost feelings, and if they were bruised, intentionally or unintentionally, he retaliated instantly. This happened when his players let him down, and when his audiences did. Full involvement was mandatory with Mingus, at all times.

Mingus was often let down by his body and, I'd wager, by some of those he entrusted it to. At one such time, when he was vast in girth and full of whatever it is that physicians of the psyche or soma feed us when they know not what else to do, he did not have the energy to shore up a flagging performance with his customary words and gestures of exhortation. And so he did it with his bass, forcing the issue by musical means alone, getting from his players what the music needed. It was a show of great strength.

Whatever Mingus did, he did with conviction and courage. In a world of codes, charades, and compromises, he refused to play by rules for which he had contempt. Always ready to strike the first blow, he left himself wide open in the process. It was this openness—to experience, to emotion, to action, to risk—that made Mingus and his music such intense and involving forces. Unafraid to scream, to holler, and to cry, he was equally unafraid to sing, laugh, and rejoice. Once he had found his own voice, he used it to the fullest, and if his mountaintop had to be a nightclub stage, he made it serve just as well for his sermons.

The spirit of those sermons will long be heard in the land, both through Mingus's own rich musical legacy (he got things *done*) and in the work of his heirs. Mingus never bowed to fashion, and thus his music will never be out of style.

(1979)

Gene Ammons

Gene Ammons was a big, gentle bear of a man who played the tenor saxophone with a sound and feeling synonymous with soul. His musical life spanned four decades, and he had hits in each of them—a record matched by few (if any) jazzmen. His music was direct and honest, and it reached and touched people. But forces of evil and ignorance in society made him pay dearly for the very human mistakes he made. And so the life of this man, who made so many people happy with his music, was scarred by injustice and misfortune. Yet he and his music remained whole to the very end, even through the ordeal of bone cancer, which finally struck him down in his fiftieth year, on August 6, 1974.

An important part of his legacy is illuminated by this album. It brings together for the first time Gene Ammons's entire output for Mercury, the label for which he first recorded under his own name. It's all here, including two excellent numbers never before released and the only date he made with his famous father, pianist Albert Ammons.

If, as Peter Keepnews, one of the brightest and best of the new crop of jazz writers, has pointed out, "few musicians put so much real, unaffected emotion into everything they played [as Gene Ammons]," it might well have been because he was born into music. His father, who became famous for his rolling, stomping boogie-woogie style in the 1940s, was an all-around jazz pianist and musician who led little bands at various Chicago clubs in the '30s. The boy started on clarinet and received excellent musical instruction at Du Sable High School under Walter Dyett, whose illustrious pupils included Nat Cole, Ray Nance, Benny Green, Dorothy Donegan, Ahmad Jamal, Johnny Griffin, and Richard Davis.

At seventeen, Gene joined the big band of trumpeter King Kolax, an important man in Chicago jazz. It was by all accounts an excellent band, and the teenaged tenorman became its featured soloist. When the band went on tour in 1943, the youngster had his first taste of the road. In 1944 he was

heard by Billy Eckstine, who tagged him for his newly organized big band—
the chief incubator of budding bebop talent. Gene stayed three years, during which his fellow tenorists included Dexter Gordon, Wardell Gray,
Lucky Thompson, and Budd Johnson. It says a lot for the young man's abilities that he remained the band's star tenor voice throughout his tenure.

Gene formed his own quintet (soon expanded to six pieces) in 1947, and
the group's first visit to a recording studio, on September 2, produced a
durable hit in "Red Top." Gene's idol, obviously, was Lester Young, but he
had also heard Charlie Parker and other voices. As he developed his own
style, other influences came into the picture. Interestingly, the warm ballad
style that was to become a key ingredient in his success does not emerge
until the final session of October 4, 1949. Other such aspects of his art as
the fluent blending of swing and bop elements, the strong feeling for the
blues, the unflagging commitment to a swinging pulse, and the ability to
construct succinct, coherent solo statements are evident from the start.

By the time Gene made his final Mercury session, he had spent five
months as featured tenorman in Woody Herman's Herd, replacing Stan
Getz in May 1949. This was Gene's last stint as a sideman.

In 1950 he joined forces with his former Eckstine colleague Sonny Stitt.
Co-leading a robust septet, these two formalized and greatly popularized
the tradition of the tenor battle, which had its roots in the juxtaposition of
the contrasting styles of Lester Young and Herschel Evans (in the classic
Count Basie band) and with duelists Illinois Jacquet and Dexter Gordon (in
the first Lionel Hampton big band). Ammons himself was involved with
Gordon in the first famous recorded tenor battle, "Blowin' the Blues Away"
by the 1944 Eckstine band.

The partnership with Stitt dissolved in 1952, though they periodically
renewed it throughout Gene's career. These encounters invariably pleased
the public, particularly at in-person performances, though critics were
wont to dismiss them as fabricated excitement. They also routinely put
down Ammons's readings of popular ballads, which found great favor with
record buyers. Gene's first great hit in this genre was "My Foolish Heart,"
which no less than Billie Holiday chose as one of her ten favorite records in
a *Metronome* poll of the early '50s.

When Ammons approached such material, he played close to the
melody (critics notwithstanding, he was following in the honorable footsteps of, among others, Louis Armstrong, Jack Teagarden, and a considerable tenor influence, Don Byas), imbuing it with his big, warm sound,
impeccable time, and personal turns of phrase. He also included in his
repertoire such novelties as "Who Put the Sleeping Pills in Rip Van
Winkle's Coffee" and even "When the Saints Go Marching In," as well as
many a vocal blues. And while the term was not in vogue at the time, he became a "crossover" artist between jazz and R&B.

It must be understood that Ammons's chief appeal, throughout his career, was to black audiences, and that the artificial dichotomy between popular and serious art is never more pointless than when applied to black music in America. Critics, influenced by traditional Western concepts, have had a hard time with this bugaboo, and Gene Ammons is a prime example of the jazz artists who suffered unfair critical neglect because of it. There were some writers, particularly Ira Gitler, who understood and appreciated Gene's artistry, but generally speaking, it was not until the early '70s that Gene was given just critical recognition as one of the major tenor voices in jazz.

By then he had more than paid his dues. The heroin habit, the scourge of post–World War II jazz, caused many tragedies. Gene's involvement with it did not cost him his life, but it deprived him of his freedom twice— the second time for a full seven years behind bars.

It speaks well for Gene's integrity and essential straightness as a man that he never fell back on the easy, conventional excuses for having become an addict. He discussed the question in depth with Leonard Feather in *Down Beat* in 1970, some six months after he had regained his freedom.

Gene noted that ". . . some say it's partly due to the environment, partly due to conditions they're living under, or the fact that they're trying to get away from something. . . . The only thing I can say about that is the way I got in was through curiosity. . . . It's just how far a man wants to go, and in my case, I just didn't have forethought enough to stop when I should have. . . . When I looked up, I was so deep in it that I couldn't get out."

Ironically, Gene had remained clean throughout his stay in the Eckstine band and with Woody Herman's notorious Second Herd. It was in early 1950 that he became hooked, by association with someone he describes, with characteristic charity and discretion, only as "another musician" he was touring with. There were no drastic consequences until 1958, when Gene was convicted of narcotics possession and sentenced to a two- to three-year term. He was paroled in June 1960, but was refused permission to re-enter the music field. After a few months (during which he kept asking how soon consent would be granted and repeatedly was told he would be notified "in a few weeks"), he took matters into his own hands and went back to work.

"Then they said I had violated my parole and sent me back to the penitentiary. Luckily I didn't have but five months left to serve, so I went back and did that and came home on a discharge in January '61." The logic of a system of "justice" that first penalizes an illness with a harsh prison term and then offers parole but refuses a man the right to earn his bread seems topsy-turvy, but there was worse in store.

Gene resumed his career and soon recorded one of his biggest hits, "Canadian Sunset." He was at the peak of his popularity when he was busted, again in Chicago, in September 1962. It was a clear case of entrapment, including extortion of a bribe ($5,000, according to Gene), but there was no mercy. "What it boiled down to, it seemed to me," Gene told Feather, "was they were going to make an example of me, due to the fact that I had a fairly big name in the music business."

Illinois had tough narcotics laws. Gene was first sentenced to fifteen years to life, but the judge relented after his lawyer had gotten the right to a new trial. "The judge told me personally that he thought the sentence was a little excessive . . . so he broke it down and wound up giving me ten to twelve years, out of which I did seven calendar years, from September 1962 to October 1969."

Gene kept his sanity and health, and, thank God, his horn. "By me being who I was they more or less put me in charge of everything in the music department. I directed the band, played in the band, wrote music for the band, I taught some of the students, I was in charge of the variety show they put on once a year and also participated in some of the church services." And during his last eighteen months in prison, he was also put in charge of the radio system, which entitled him to a radio, personal TV set, phonograph, and tape recorder and enabled him to catch up with what was going on outside in the music world.

Thus Gene was ready when he got out, and just twelve days after his release, he opened at Chicago's Plugged Nickel. I was there that night, and the standing ovation that greeted Gene as he made his way to the stand was just the first of many. He was relaxed, happy, and in full command of his horn and music.

"Dudes are trying new directions, and I dig it," he told me between two sets, "but the avant-garde wouldn't fit my bag. I might try a free lick here and there, but I'll stick mostly to the Gene Ammons I know." And that's what he did in the remaining years granted him. He experimented with the Varitone amplification system but soon realized that a player with his big, natural sound didn't need it. Beyond that, he applied his skill and soul to what suited him best of the new crop of songs, put together some excellent blues and jazz pieces of his own, and rounded out his repertoire with evergreens and time-tested Ammons staples. He played in Europe for the first time in his life and was well received. He made new hits and new friends, and then the fatal illness took hold.

The last time I saw Gene Ammons, at Joe Segal's Jazz Showcase in Chicago in the spring of 1974, he looked thin and gray, but he played with the old warmth and swing. As always, he had no time to feel sorry for himself; there was music to be played. And in spite of everything, the music came out strong, clear, and affirmative—a message of life and hope.

(1976)

Dinah Washington

D inah Washington was one of a kind.
Her range as an artist was as wide as the range of her voice. Nurtured on gospel and raised on the blues, she ripened in jazz and then surmounted all categories, becoming one of the greatest popular music stars of her time. But even when she had reached the top, she remained true to herself and her art.

That's why she has survived. Though nearly thirteen years have passed since her untimely death, her music is still very much with us. It speaks as plainly and directly to the listener as it ever did.

It is our good fortune that Dinah (or "Miss D" or "The Queen," as those who loved her used to call her) recorded prolifically, making nearly four hundred sides in her eighteen-year association with Mercury Records. She made her recording debut in December 1943 with a session organized by Leonard Feather that included the famous "Evil Gal Blues." Her final album for the label was made in December 1961.

From this embarrassment of riches, we have culled, for the first Dinah Washington collection in this new series, some of her finest work in a jazz context. Included are two complete studio sessions from the mid-'50s with all-star jazz groups and a jam atmosphere, and her only live recording (aside from a brief appearance at a 1945 Carnegie Hall concert with Lionel Hampton's band), from the 1958 Newport Jazz Festival.

These performances capture Dinah at the zenith of her jazz stage. She functions as a horn among horns, trading improvisatory skills with some of the best players in the field. Clearly she was having a great time, and when "The Queen" was enjoying herself, she made everyone within hearing range feel good.

There are all kinds of singers. Somehow, Dinah made most of the others sound like little girls. She was a woman to the core, singing of a woman's pleasures and pains. When she turned it on, she hit home. She sang what she felt and did what she pleased. She was the real thing.

Dinah Washington was born Ruth Jones in Tuscaloosa, Alabama, August 29, 1924. (Her professional name was bestowed upon her, according to what sources you consult, by talent manager Joe Glaser or Chicago nightclub owner Joe Sherman.) She was raised in Chicago, where she became a gospel singer as a child, playing piano and singing in religious groups. Commenting on one of the sessions on this album, Quincy Jones pointed

out: "The fact that Dinah is a musician herself made things that much easier. We had asked her only for keys on these tunes, and when she ran down
the arrangements, she read the music almost at sight."

The gospel background left its mark on Dinah's style, but she did not
mix the secular and religious in her music, as Ray Charles would do later.
When she won an amateur contest at fifteen at Chicago's Regal theater
(that city's counterpart to Harlem's famous Apollo), she was singing blues,
and it was pure blues. To be sure, her way of projecting her voice had much
in common with the gospel "shout," and those roots also bore fruit in her
exceptionally free phrasing, marvelously clear and unaffected diction (no
matter how much she invented and improvised, Dinah never lost a single
word of a lyric), and superb use of melisma, that bending and sliding
and blueing and "worrying" of a single held note that is part and parcel of
the gospel singer's art. But she transformed rather than transplanted these
elements.

The contest victory led to a job at the Flame Show Bar. She was still
Ruth Jones when she was singing at the Garrick Grill in Chicago. The great
jazz trumpeter and showman Henry "Red" Allen got the message, told Joe
Glaser, and by the fall of 1943, Lionel Hampton's band had a new vocalist
named Dinah Washington.

Leonard Feather, whose career as a critic has obscured his success as a
songwriter, particularly in the realm of blues, took the nineteen-year-old
singer into a New York studio with a small group culled from Hampton's
ranks. Four of Leonard's blues were waxed, one of them a sex-change revision of "Evil Man Blues," originally written for the great Hot Lips Page,
and Dinah had herself a rhythm-and-blues hit. (It should be noted that the
session was done for the small Keynote label; it wasn't until Mercury took
over the masters that the record really made its mark.)

Dinah stayed with Lionel for three years, no doubt learning a lot about
her craft but getting little exposure on records. (An exception was yet another Feather opus, "Blow Top Blues.") Then she went out on her own and
things started to happen. Hardly a year went by without a hit or two. Between 1955 and 1962, no less than nineteen of her records made the charts.

But even after Dinah had become a star, she didn't forget where she had
come from. To hear her at her very best, you had to catch her at Birdland,
where the instant and total communication with the cream of show business and the ladies and gentlemen of the night was something to behold, or
at the Apollo, where she went all the way down home, eliciting those
unique responses from the audience that have so much in common with
what goes on in black sanctified churches.

In her personal life, things didn't go as well. Dinah had a powerful ego
and a consuming appetite for living. Her temperament was tempestuous,
and she often made public scenes that could be painful.

Of course she was hardest on herself. Married for the first time at seventeen (to a fellow high school student), she went through a succession of husbands that numbered seven, eight, or nine, according to various obituaries. Three of these were musicians who also acted as her musical directors. They were drummers George Jenkins and Jimmy Cobb and tenor saxophonist Eddie Chamblee. She put them through their paces. "I change husbands before they change me," she once said. Her extracurricular affairs were legendary. Ironically, her final union, with Detroit Lions cornerback Dick "Night Train" Lane, promised to be her most rewarding.

However, it was another obsession, her constant concern for her appearance, that snuffed out her candle at thirty-nine on December 14, 1963. Dinah was on the plump side by nature, and pleasingly so, but she would go on periodic crash diets without regard for her health. She would suddenly appear quite unnaturally thin, and then she'd let herself go again.

At the time of her death, she was once again on a diet, taking pills to curb her appetite. She was reportedly in excellent spirits, anticipating the Christmas holiday homecoming of her two teenaged sons. She had been happily married since July and was taking time off from work. So it certainly wasn't depression that caused her to indulge in the fatal, synergistic mixing of diet pills and alcohol that caused her to suffer an apparent heart attack.

Though Dinah was five years younger than Billie Holiday and Bessie Smith when death took her, we do not tend to think of her life as tragic. She was so full of life and affirmation in her art and person that the sense of loss is tempered by a feeling that, though far from exhausted, her potential was fulfilled. Although there were self-destructive elements in her personality, they were balanced by her vitality and exuberance. She left us in the midst of life. While it is more than sad that she was not allowed to go on, her legacy is whole—all of a piece, as indeed was Dinah Washington, the woman.

"I like to get inside of a tune and make it mean something to the people that listen, something more than just a set of lyrics and a familiar tune," she once said. "And I can sing anything—anything at all."

Dinah Washington was one of a kind.

(1976)

Bill Evans

There can be little doubt that Bill Evans is one of the most influential pianists—if not to say one of the most influential musicians—in jazz today. His strikingly personal conception has not only touched younger players whose styles were formed after Evans became widely known through his tenure with the Miles Davis sextet in 1958, but it also has affected many pianists with longer roots.

At another stage in the development of jazz, there might be nothing very surprising about this, for Evans's music—lucid, lyrical, melodic, and infused with a sense of, and search for, beauty and balance—is firmly grounded in an astonishing command and organization of the musical materials in the mainstream of the jazz tradition. And his approach to his instrument reflects a firm commitment to the heritage of Western keyboard music that began with Bach and perhaps reached its final splendor in Debussy.

Such an orientation is not exactly typical of the trend in contemporary jazz, sometimes called the "new thing," sometimes "avant-garde," and which seems more concerned with discarding tradition than with building on its foundations. The watchword of this school is "freedom"—a word open to many definitions.

Evans, too, is concerned with freedom in music. But he said recently, "The only way I can work is to have some kind of restraint involved—the challenge of a certain craft or form—and then to find the freedom in that, which is one hell of a job. I think a lot of guys either want to circumvent that kind of labor, or else they don't realize the rewards that exist in one single area if you use enough restraint and do enough searching.

"I have allowed myself the other kind of freedom occasionally. Paul Bley and I did a two-piano improvisation on a George Russell record [*Music for the Space Age*] which was completely unpremeditated. It was fun to do, but there was no direction involved. To do something that hadn't been rehearsed successfully, just like that, almost shows the lack of challenge involved in that type of freedom."

Just turned thirty-five, spiritually and physically refreshed after a troubled interlude in his life, Evans spoke softly but firmly, the even flow of his words reflecting not glibness but long and careful thought about his art and craft. The pianist recently returned from a rewarding European tour at the helm of a revitalized trio and seems poised on a new peak in his career.

"I'm extremely happy with the group," he said. "Larry Bunker is a marvelous musician. [Drummer Bunker recently gave up a lucrative studio practice in Los Angeles to go with Evans.] He plays excellent vibes as well as being an all-round percussionist, and being so musical he just does the right thing because he's listening. He really knows music, feels music—and he is a superlative drummer. . . . I hope you can get to hear him at his better moments, which depend, I guess, a lot on me, because if I'm in the least falling apart, they're always so sympathetic to what I'm doing that it's hard for them to come out if I'm not. [Bassist Chuck Israels is the third member of the group.]

"We probably make a stronger emotional projection than at almost any time in the past. Maybe one criticism of the group that could have been valid is that we didn't reach out to the people who weren't interested enough to come in, and I would like to get out to people and grab them a little. That's something that has to happen or not happen, but I think it's happening more and more."

Evans's desire to reach out to his audience may come as a surprise to those who have overemphasized the introspective qualities of his work. His music also has been characterized as intellectual, and critic Whitney Balliett once wrote that "no musician relies less on intuition than Bill Evans." The pianist said he was aware of Balliett's statement.

"I was very surprised at that," Evans said. "I don't consider that I rely any less or more on something like intuition than any other jazz player, because the plain process of playing jazz is as universal among the people who play jazz correctly—that is, those who approach the art with certain restrictions and certain freedoms—as, for instance, the thought processes involved in ordinary, everyday conversation.

"Everybody has to learn certain things, but when you play, the intellectual process no longer has anything to do with it. It shouldn't, anyhow. You have your craft behind you then, and you try to think within the area that you have mastered to a certain extent. In that way, I am relying entirely on intuition then. I have no idea of what's coming next, and if I did, I would be a nervous wreck. Who could keep up with it?

"Naturally, there are certain things that we play, like opening choruses, that become expected. But even there, changes occur all the time, and after that, when you're just playing, everything is up for grabs. We never know what's coming next. Nobody could think that fast . . . not even a computer. What Balliett hears, I think, is the result of a lot of work, which means that it is pretty clear. I know this: everything that I play I know about, in a theoretical way, according to my own organization of certain musical facts. And it's a very elementary, basic-type thing. I don't profess to be advanced in theory, but within this area, I do try to work very clearly, because that is the only way I can work.

"When I started out, I worked very simply, but I always knew what I was doing, as related to my own theory. Therefore, what Balliett hears is probably the long-term result of the intellectual process of developing my own vocabulary—or the vocabulary that I use—and he may relate that to being intellectual, or not relying on intuition. But that's not true."

Another critic, Andre Hodeir, has stated that the musical materials used by most jazz players, such as the popular song and the blues, have been exhausted and that the greatest need for jazz is to develop new materials for improvisation. Evans said he is well acquainted with these views but does not share them.

"The need is not so much for a new form or new material but rather that we allow the song form as such to expand itself," he explained. "And this can happen. I have experienced many times, in playing alone, that perhaps a phrase will extend itself for a couple of moments so that all of a sudden, after a bridge or something, there will be a little interlude. But it has to be a natural thing. I never attempt to do this in an intellectual way.

"In this way, I think the forms can change and can still basically come from the song form and be a true form—and offer everything that the song form offers. Possibly, this will not satisfy the intellectual needs of somebody like Hodeir, but as far as the materials involved in a song are concerned, I don't think they are restricting at all, if you really get into them. Just learning how to manipulate a line, the science of building a line, if you can call it a science, is enough to occupy somebody for twelve lifetimes. I don't find any lack of challenge there."

Along with this regard for the song form goes a commitment to tonality, Evans pointed out. It is not an abstract idea, he said, or one to which he is unyieldingly bound, but it is the result of playing experience and a concern for coherence.

"If you are a composer or are trying to improvise, and you make a form that is atonal, or some plan which has atonality as a base, you present a lot of problems of coherence," he said. "Most people who listen to music do listen tonally, and the things that give certain elements meaning are their relationships to a tonality—either of the phrase, or of the phrase to the larger period, or of that to the whole chorus or form, or perhaps even of that to the entire statement. So if you don't have that kind of reference for a listener, you have to have some other kind of plan or syntax for coherent musical thinking.

"It's a problem, and one that I have in a way solved for myself theoretically by studying melody and the construction of melody through all musics. I found that there is a limited amount of things that can happen to an idea, but in developing it, there are many, many ways that you can handle it. And if you master these, then you can begin to think just emotionally and let something grow. A musical idea could grow outside the realm of tonality. Now, if I could master that, then maybe I could make something coherent happen in an atonal area.

"But the problem of group performance is another thing. When I'm playing with a group, I can't do a lot of things that I can do when playing by myself, because I can't expect the other person to know just when I'm going to all of a sudden maybe change the key or the tempo or do this or that. So there has to be some kind of common reference so that we can make a coherent thing."

Evans became emphatic.

"This doesn't lessen the freedom," he continued. "It *increases* it. That's the thing that everybody seems to miss. By giving ourselves a solid base on which to work, and by saying that this is accepted but our craft is such that we can manipulate this framework—which is only like, say, the steel girders in a building—then we can make any shapes we want, any lines we want. We can make any rhythms we want, that we can feel against this natural thing. And if we have the skill, we can just about do anything. Then we are really free.

"But if we were not to have any framework at all, we would be much more limited because we would be accommodating ourselves so much to the nothingness of each other's reference that we would not have room to breathe and to make music and to feel. So that's the problem. Maybe, as a solo pianist, I could make atonal things or whatever. But group improvisation is another type of challenge, and until there is a development of a craft which covers that area, so that a group can say: 'Okay, now we improvise, now we are going to take this mode for so long, and then we take that mode with a different feeling for so long, and then we go over here' . . . and if I were to construct this plan so that it had no real tonal reference, only then could it be said that we were improvising atonally.

"What many people mean when they say 'atonal,' I think, is more a weird kind of dissonance or strange intervals and things like that. I don't know . . . I don't feel it. That isn't me. I can listen to master musicians like Bartók or Berg when they do things that people would consider atonal—although often they're not—and love and enjoy it, but here's someone just making an approximation of this music. It really shows just how little they appreciate the craft involved, because there's just so much to it. You can't just go and play by what I call 'the inch system.' You know, I could go up eight inches on the keyboard and then play a sound down six inches, and then go up a foot and a half and play a cluster and go down nine and a half and play something else. And that's atonality, the way some guys think of it. I don't know why people need it. If I could find something that satisfied me more there, I'd certainly be there, and I guess that's why there are people there. They must find something in it."

It was suggested to Evans that this was a charitable view, that, in fact, much of this kind of music reflects only frustration, and that the occasional moment of value was no adequate reward for the concentration and patience required to wade through all the noodling.

"Yes, it's more of an aid to a composer than a total musical product," he answered. "If you could take one of these gems and say, 'Ah, now I can sit down and make a piece. . . .' But it's the emotional content that is all one way. Naturally, frustration has a place in music at times, especially in dramatic music, but I think that other feelings are more important and that there is an obligation—or at least a responsibility—to present mostly the feelings which are my best feelings, which are not everyday feelings. Just to say that something is true because it is everyday and that, therefore, it is valid seems, to me, a poor basis for an artist to work on. I have no desire to listen to the bathroom noises of the artist. I want to hear something better, something that he has dedicated his life to preserve and to present to me. And if I hear somebody who can really move me, so that I can say, 'Ah, there's a real song'—I don't care if it's an atonal song or a dissonant song or whatever kind of song—that's still the basis of music to me. . . ."

What did Evans mean by "song"? Was it melody? "Essentially, what you might consider melody or a lyric feeling," he replied. "But more, an utterance in music of the human spirit, which has to do with the finer feelings of the person and which is a necessary utterance and something that must find its voice because there is a need for it and because it is worthwhile. It doesn't matter about the idiom or the style or anything else; as long as the feeling is behind it, it's going to move people."

But style can get in the way of hearing, it was pointed out.

"I remember discussing Brahms with Miles Davis once," the pianist commented. "He said that he couldn't enjoy it. And I said, 'If you can just get past the stylistic thing that puts you off, you'd find such a great treasure there.' I don't know if it had any effect or not; we never talked about it again. But I think it's the same problem in jazz; if you can get past the style, the rhythm, the thing that puts you off—then it's all pretty much the same. Things don't change that much.

"That's why I feel that I don't really have to be avant-garde or anything like that. It has no appeal for me, other than the fact that I always want to do something that is better than what I've been doing. If it leads in that direction, fine. And if it doesn't, it won't make a bit of difference to me, because quality has much more to do with it, as far as I'm concerned. If it stays right where it is at, and that's the best I can find, that's where it's going to have to be."

Evans paused and then added wistfully: "I hope it doesn't, though . . . I'd like it to change. I never forced it in the least, and so far I do think there have been some changes. Still, essentially, the thing is the same. It has followed a definite thread from the beginning: learning how to feel a form, a harmonic flow, and learning how to handle it and making certain refinements on the form and mastering more and more the ability to get inside the material and to handle it with more and more freedom. That's the way it has been going with me, and there's no end to that . . . no end to it.

"Whatever I move to, I want to be more firmly based in and better in than what I leave. What I want to do most is to be fresh and to find new things, and I'd like to discard everything that I use, if I could find something to replace it. But until I do, I can't. I'm really planning now how to set up my life so that I can have about half of it in privacy and seclusion and find new areas that are really valid. After the Au Go Go [the Greenwich Village club where Evans is currently playing] and maybe a week somewhere else, I hope to take off about a month. It will be the first time in two or three years that I will have devoted time to that."

In this quest, Evans will be aided by what he describes as "one of the most thrilling things that have happened in my career"—a very special gift. At the Golden Circle in Stockholm, Evans performed on a piano built on new structural principles: a ten-foot concert grand designed and built by George Bolin, master cabinetmaker to the Royal Swedish Court.

"It was the first public performance on the new piano," Evans said. "One night, Mr. Bolin came in to hear me and expressed respect for my work, and before I knew it, my wife had negotiated with his representatives for me to be able to use the only such piano in the United States—it was on exhibit at the Swedish Embassy—for my engagement at the Au Go Go. It is one of only three, I think, in existence in the world right now. And after the engagement, the piano will be mine as a gift. Mr. Bolin dedicated it to me.

"It came at a perfect time, because I didn't have a piano of my own just then. It is a marvelous instrument—probably the first basic advance in piano building in some hundred and fifty years. The metal frame and strings are suspended and attached to the wooden frame by inverted screws, and the sound gets a kind of airy, free feeling that I haven't found in any other piano. Before this, Bolin was famous as a guitar maker—he made instruments for Segovia and people like that. To build an instrument like this, a man has to be as much of a genius as a great musician."

Such gifts are not given lightly and are an indication of the stature of the recipient as well as of the giver. Whatever music Bill Evans will make on his new piano, one can be certain that it will do honor to the highest standards of the art and craft of music.

(1964)

Paul Desmond

Paul Desmond is perhaps the most famous sideman on today's jazz scene. For fourteen years, he has been the alto saxophonist with the Dave Brubeck Quartet, from the group's early days of struggle to the notably successful present. Over the years, the quartet has often been the target of hostile criticism, but Desmond usually has been singled out for praise, even by the group's strongest detractors.

Considering these circumstances, and the common urge of jazz sidemen to become leaders, Desmond's reluctance to step out on his own is indeed an exception to the rule. But then, the tall, slender, soft-spoken altoist is an exceptional person in many ways.

He is indifferent to publicity. "I still think you should save this whole story for some significant event," he said during the course of this interview, "like when I die—you could have a picture of an alto and an empty chair and a bottle of J & B. . . . I always wanted to be a romantic jazz player."

His sense of humor—or, rather, his wit—notwithstanding, Desmond *is* a romantic player. This is evident both in the graceful, warm lyricism of his playing and in his stage personality: somewhat diffident, introspective, and slightly withdrawn. This image has given rise to frequent speculation that Desmond is detached from the rest of the quartet—though both his playing and his words belie that interpretation.

"It's weird," he said; "so few people really know or care what we are trying to do—which isn't really that complicated. The questions people come up and ask after we play run like this: 'How do you know when to come in and when to stop?,' or 'Who writes the choruses?,' or 'How many of you are there in the quartet?' . . . It gives you a feeling of futility. Only very rarely—monumentally rarely—does a person come by who realizes what we are trying to do, and when we did it and when we didn't.

"Everybody else takes from it a number of things; there are a lot of levels on which the quartet can be enjoyed, so they go away perfectly happy, but that doesn't necessarily have any relation to what we are trying to do."

The quartet is in a position now to pick and choose jobs, and as befits its role as one of the pioneers in the jazz-concert field, it now plays concerts exclusively.

"We don't play clubs anymore—for at least three years, maybe longer," Desmond said. "The last club we played was Basin Street East, which almost doesn't count. We were playing two sets a night, which equals one concert, and we just ended up with the difficulties of both situations. The club was always pretty full, so there was none of that last-set loose experimenting which is one of the fun things about working clubs, and still we had the club atmosphere. Do I miss the clubs? Musically, yes . . . but we did so much of that, for ten years or more, and if we had continued, we probably would be disbanded by now."

The Brubecks average about two concerts a week, "and if we do go out on a week of one-nighters, we have a week or two off afterwards—it's a lot more civilized."

Among the group's concert appearances have been special events featuring Brubeck's writing for symphony orchestra and combo. The most recent was *Elementals*.

"I kind of hope it stays the last," Desmond said. "That sort of thing is more gratifying to the composer; to perform it is a kind of struggle. It's a little frustrating when you are on stage with eighty symphony musicians and succeed in functioning just about as well as you ordinarily do, and it's considered a great accomplishment—like tap-dancing under water."

Not that he rejects this kind of musical experimentation, he pointed out: "The challenge will always be there to make an alliance between the two forms, and it certainly makes more sense than a lot of current classical music—or jazz, for that matter."

Reflecting on the current jazz scene, Desmond grew wistful.

"In the jazz world at the present moment, I get a funny listless feeling, like a graduate of a school that's about to fold wandering around the halls," he said. "Between the discotheques and the avant-garde and the folk scene, there isn't much left. If jazz is really going to become increasingly a form of personal protest—which will make it difficult to listen to even for people who love jazz—then it's hard to see how it's going to be supported, besides as a spare-time hobby."

But, he said, he is not at odds with all the goals of the avant-garde: "I don't see any reason why jazz shouldn't have a wider range of emotional expression. Charlie Mingus, for instance, covers a wide range. He can be fascinating and very moving to listen to, as well as really hitting you with something very difficult. But you can't just do one thing and expect people to come out and pay to listen to it."

. . .

Desmond's own listening preferences lean toward what must in the current spectrum be considered mainstream jazz. "I find myself listening to Al Cohn and Zoot Sims, Bill Evans, Miles Davis, Jim Hall," he said. "A couple of more years of this, and I'll have become an archconservative, the way things keep moving in jazz. But I don't know what the alternatives are; you have to either reprogram yourself every six weeks, like Jimmy Giuffre (which I admire the spirit behind but certainly couldn't do myself), or maybe John Lewis has the best solution—he's always terribly involved in the avant-garde music, but it doesn't change his own musical approach at all—he has the best of both worlds."

The freewheeling and always swinging tenor-sax tandem of Cohn and Sims, Desmond said, "are still my favorite band to listen to. So many things you hear are like working—you feel dutifully that you should go and hear what the guys are doing, and you do, and you may enjoy parts of it or aspects of it. But after that, to go and hear Al and Zoot is like having your back rubbed. It's pure self-indulgence, but I don't see anything wrong with that at all. If somebody feels that way musically, that's the way the music should be. They're not sacrificing their integrity or doing anything they don't want to do. . . . They enjoy it and you enjoy it, and that's where I think it should be at."

Desmond, however, said he sympathizes with the young players.

"It's really incredibly difficult for anybody starting out today," he commented. "I'm glad it's not me. To become acceptable to the contemporary musicians—if you are a kid—you have to more or less do what they're doing, so it's almost compulsory that you have to be a 'new thing' player, or else go to Eddie Condon's, which is practically no choice. That's not really a good state of affairs, but I have no idea what can be done about it."

Such matters evidently are a genuine concern to Desmond, but there are aspects of the "new thing" that his sense of the absurd responds to:

"I remember seeing a TV 'happening' with Don Ellis—guys on ladders and guys waving sheets and hitting the piano, and I took a look and there was Eddie Shaughnessy, and there was Lalo Schifrin, and I said to myself: 'My God . . . they can't be serious, running around waving sheets and climbing ladders. I'd like to do something like that with Al and Zoot and Bobby Brookmeyer, three or four guys like that, but everybody would get totally drunk first. That way there would be some justification. But if you don't have that kind of rationale for a thing like that, you're in terrible trouble."

The spectacle of discotheques also stirs the sardonic side of the Desmond wit.

"It's almost compulsory; every party in New York for the past four years has been a gradual progression from *The Dick Clark Show* to the discotheque," he said. "It's one of the smaller steps of the century. There are all kinds of enforced techniques of communication, when conversation is required. It's like one-way radio communication with Mars. You get some-body's ear in your mouth and you give your signal, and then over and out and change position.

"It discourages small talk, because few things are worth such a mas-sive effort to communicate—except 'Will you come home with me?,' or something like that, but not 'It's certainly hot in here.' If it edits Amer-ican social conversation, the discotheque may have performed some small function.

"I still think it might be possible to have a discotheque with all the fever-ish animation and social mystique and yet with some kind of music that wouldn't be all that painful: Muddy Waters, Count Basie, Mose Allison—all kinds of straight-ahead, no-problem-to-dance-to funky music. In a way, the current idiocy is part of it, but it can't last—that quality of having your mind obliterated—because it doesn't work like that if you have any reaction to music . . . it doesn't banish thought; it's more like constant fingernails on the blackboard. If anything, it makes you think too much. There must be a large number of people who just put up with it because it's the only game in town."

The dancing, too, leaves much to be desired, according to Desmond:

"It really seems nostalgic now to think about the days when bands were playing really beautiful arrangements, and kids were doing very fantastic and intricate dances and were totally happy with their dancing, which, God knows, was a different thing from the frug and all that. And they were en-joying the music at the same time. We didn't realize it then, but I guess that was one of the last outposts of the vanishing elegance of this world."

Desmond, who himself could be described as one of the outposts of vanish-ing elegance in the jazz world, still has no plans to form his own group, though he said he feels that changes are forthcoming.

"Sometimes I get the urge," he said about forming a group, "but in ex-change for the few minor problems I have with the quartet now, I would probably inherit some very comparable ones, plus a whole raft of others I don't have to worry about now. With the jazz scene the way it is, to start out all over again, playing clubs and going through that whole in-between pe-riod, seems pointless—though it would be fun in some ways.

"I would imagine, though, that the quartet will grind to a majestic halt in about one and a half years. . . . I'm not sure; I've been saying things like that since 1954, so you can't really put too much faith in it. But it's getting along toward that time. I could be wrong; it might go on for centuries, but I think Dave will probably want to stay home and write and do other things.

I'll pretty definitely be leaving, whether the quartet continues or not, unless some horrible disaster takes place between now and then."

Desmond, too, wants to do other things:

"I'm working on a play (it's too formless yet to say anything about it much) and a couple of magazine pieces, things like that. I have this great reputation as a writer, primarily because I haven't written anything, and it almost seems a shame to spoil it, but sooner or later I'll have to make a move. I'm interested in making people laugh, which seems like a worthy cause. Not that I'm looking for worthy causes. . . ."

In addition to the writing, Desmond plans to "go back and look at some of the places I ran through with the group, make some records, possibly even work some with a group similar to the one I've been recording with."

Desmond's own recording groups have unfailingly included guitarist Jim Hall, a musician for whom he is full of praise: "Jim, in addition to his other incredible accomplishments, is the world's most perfect accompanist on guitar. His playing on my next album—all ballads—is among my favorite things I've heard him do. Jim is very success-resistant. He is very reluctant to do anything that even remotely approaches being considered crafty or being an operator. He knew all about bossa nova long before anyone here did anything with it, and he plays it so much better than anyone else has done it."

The new album, Desmond said, will not be like an older one, *Desmond Blue*, which had a picture of a pretty girl on the cover. "Then I spent about a month or so locating her after the album had come out," he said. "This time I found the girl first. It's a beautiful cover. No matter what you may say about my records, the covers are great. My notes to the last two albums have been getting better reviews than the music. . . ."

For all his sometimes self-deprecating irony, Desmond is serious about his own playing, and his modesty shields a constant search for self-improvement.

"I don't really know what I'll be doing musically," he said, reflecting on the future. "I still haven't quite gotten myself together on the horn the way I would have liked. I don't know if I ever will, and I don't know if it will make any difference to anybody if I did.

"With our audience today, I could finally put together the perfect chorus, and the only reaction would probably be that someone would come backstage and say, 'Reed went sour on you, eh?,' which they usually do when I think I'm playing well. When I think it's terrible, they say, 'Magnificent! I've never been so moved in my life!' I may be totally wrong about what I think I should do; there's always that possibility.

"But nobody else, I think, will bother with it. Everybody else is headed at top speed in the opposite direction, so my little corner of the garden is not going to be trampled down."

And what is Desmond cultivating in that corner?

"There is so much interior room within the limitations of harmonic and melodic playing," he answered, "you don't have to cancel out all the rules to make progress. In some ways, it's more of a challenge to refine one thing and find something in it that hasn't been done."

Chances are that Desmond won't find himself alone in that corner, though the things he will grow will all be his. The company he will have, though, will not be the trampling kind.

(1965)

Bob Brookmeyer

Bob Brookmeyer is a big, solidly built man who looks like anything but a jazz musician. Behind his often somber mien lurks a dry, caustic wit (his humorous barbs are frequently delivered with a deadpan expression that catches the listener off guard) and a keen, lively intelligence that encompasses considerably more than the world of music.

For the last eighteen months or so, watchers of late-evening television have heard (but rarely seen) Brookmeyer in his role as a member of the *Merv Griffin Show* orchestra, an excellent ensemble unfortunately not featured as much as its counterpart on Johnny Carson's *Tonight Show*.

The job keeps Brookmeyer busy each weekday from 3:30 to 8 p.m. with rehearsals, run-throughs for blocking, and the actual taping of the program.

"It's a fairly relaxed job," he said recently. "The conductor, Mort Lindsay, is a very nice man and respectful of musicians—not like some other show conductors I have known. And it's a very hip band. . . ."

A glance at the personnel, which currently includes trumpeter Bill Berry, saxophonist Richie Kamuca, guitarist Jim Hall, bassist Art Davis, and drummer Jake Hanna, bears out Brookmeyer's contention, but these talents are employed mainly to back visiting singers and to entertain the studio audience during commercials.

More satisfying from a creative standpoint is Brookmeyer's association with the Thad Jones–Mel Lewis big band.

"The band is a joy," Brookmeyer said without hesitation. "We've prayed for a band like this in New York for years. Some time ago, I went to extraordinary lengths to arrange for something like it to happen—George Russell and I recruited for a band which never had a rehearsal, but we lined up an amazing lot of people. This time, we have a band first, and it took Thad and Mel to do it.

"The band includes diverse musical attitudes, people from different eras, but the result is homogeneous and happy. There's a great spirit in the band."

Brookmeyer has contributed several excellent arrangements to the growing book, notably a lovely setting of "Willow, Weep for Me," but he doesn't have time to write as much as he would like.

"I deeply regret it," he reflected. "I'd love to do more writing. When I finished the *Gloomy Sunday* album [a 1962 Verve release highly praised by reviewers and musicians and characteristically titled, in full, *Gloomy Sunday and Other Bright Moments*], I was just getting on to some ease and facility and knowledge. But I had to go back to playing."

Not that playing is a chore to Brookmeyer—except when it is pure routine. This is evidenced not only by his sparkling work with the Jones-Lewis band but also in infrequent small-group settings, as with a recent quintet led by Griffin teammate Kamuca at New York City's Half Note, or with the splendid little band he has co-led for some years with his friend, trumpeter-fluegelhornist-singer Clark Terry.

The Terry-Brookmeyer quintet has not been very active during the last year, but the group has not disbanded.

"It's just that we've both been busy," Brookmeyer said, "and Clark has been working a lot on his own recently. Things have broken for him, as they say in the trade, and he's getting some long overdue recognition.

"So we haven't been able to work together as much as we'd like. But the group is getting better and better; last time we played, the musical and personal elements really seemed to fuse—we could tell from the audience reaction."

With all these groups, Brookmeyer plays an instrument that, mainly through his efforts, has begun to gain some recognition but is still often regarded as something of a hybrid—the valve trombone.

Brookmeyer started out in music on clarinet. He also is an accomplished pianist; during most of his early big-band career, which included service with Ray McKinley, Louis Prima, Jerry Wald, Woody Herman, and Claude Thornhill, he held down the piano chair. Before taking up the valve horn, Brookmeyer played a conventional slide trombone. "I was really a frustrated trumpet player," he said jokingly. "I didn't make the complete switch to valve until 1952, when I was with Thornhill. The other trombone player had a 78 H Conn—a monster—much too big and loud for the band. So I sold him my slide.

"I was a pretty bad slide trombonist. I sounded like Bill Harris and Earl Swope under the weather, not at all fashionable. I last heard Bill a couple of years ago at the Silver Slipper in Las Vegas. He was working with Charlie Teagarden, and I was there every night. He can still make your heart leap. . . . It's a shame that he was so rarely recorded like he deserves. And Earl, too, was never heard enough."

Do parts written for slide trombone present any problems to a valve player?

"It depends on what kind of part it is," he replied. "If there is a long glissando, you're in trouble. But I have learned to fake glisses with half-valve effects. Manny Albam is really responsible for the acceptance of the instrument in the section. He was always insisting that you can't tell the difference.

"I play lead trombone with Mel and Thad and also did it with the Gerry Mulligan band. It's good for lead—remember Juan Tizol with Ellington? You're just an octave under the lead trumpet, and the fact that you have identical execution makes things sound more crisp . . . at least I think so, but I'm prejudiced."

One of the reasons why musicians, by and large, are "still suspicious" of the valve trombone, Brookmeyer said, is "that most people play it rotten. Even excellent slide men play it in pedestrian fashion. It takes an awful lot of woodshedding to get what you want from the instrument. But to me, the valve trombone is the most satisfying medium for what I like to express."

Brookmeyer suggests a reason for his loyalty to the valve when he said that "the trombone became a victim of the system. Until the new wave came along, all trombone players were sounding like J. J. Johnson—which is a fine way for J.J. to sound. But the new-wave trombonists seem to have more personalization and variety."

Brookmeyer, however, disclaimed any expertise on what he refers to as the new wave.

"Coltrane, Rollins, and Ornette Coleman are the last part of the new wave I knew intimately," he said. "The new fellows around remind me uncomfortably of the Charlie Parker wave when I was very young: there was just one way to play and one way to live. That's okay with me, but I can't do it that way."

But Brookmeyer's mind is far from being closed to what young musicians are doing. Quite to the contrary, he is concerned about the lack of real contact between musical generations:

"It is very satisfying for a man of years—I may not seem that old [he has just turned thirty-seven], but believe me, I feel it—to be able to bridge the gap of age, especially with young musicians who are in another bag. To make contact, personal and musical, with young musicians is rewarding.

"The young people often seem withdrawn and have only hostile words for the older chaps, which is a frightful mistake on their part. When I first worked with Coleman Hawkins or Ben Webster, it was an honor to me, and that still goes for anyone in that age group. It's a pity that musicians have to shut themselves off from others. They could profit by the association, become a little hipper and a little wiser in their lives. A fascist attitude in music is as absurd as any fascist attitude."

It is natural, Brookmeyer said, for young people to strive to overthrow the old, "but when you get older and wiser, you learn that things don't change one hundred percent for the better through revolution. There's no good will or approbation—Southerners and Nazis live that way.

"Anger and protest movements are fine; people overthrowing outmoded ideas is marvelous—but . . . I don't know the new wave personally, but all the pronouncements and manifestos I have read reflect this abrogation of contact between generations. It seems silly. People can differ widely and still make contact and talk. Music is still part of life."

Brookmeyer's own musical youth, spent in his native Kansas City, Missouri, was not marked by hostility between old and young. He recalled:

"I grew up with those Kansas City bands: trumpet, alto, tenor, and an excellent rhythm section. The great jazz scene was fading, but at fourteen and fifteen, I was sitting in at clubs, Negro and white, with people twenty or thirty years my senior, and there was no thought of protesting the music.

"The racial scene was terribly formal, but we went to each other's outings and functions, et cetera—it was not like the big-city situation today. I didn't even think about it until much later; we thought about music, and playing well, and having a good time. It was a very relaxed scene."

Brookmeyer went to the Kansas City Conservatory of Music with players who had gone to school with Charlie Parker, and he heard many stories about how Parker grew up.

"There was a drummer in town, Edward Phillips (we called him 'Little Phil'), who'd come to sessions with just a snare drum, a sock cymbal, and brushes and play all the drums you'd want to hear," Brookmeyer recalled. "Bird used to write to him about coming to New York. 'Those bebop drummers are driving me crazy,' he said in one letter. But Phil never left town."

Brookmeyer gets angry when he hears people "put down Charlie Parker for the way he lived. They don't know what he had to go through. If they did, they wouldn't criticize, but be amazed that he accomplished what he did."

By 1950, according to Brookmeyer, the Kansas City jazz scene was dead.

"The populace and the boppers helped to kill it," he said. "But when I was growing up, the guys I played with were still telling stories of those fourteen-hour jam sessions."

. . .

The trombonist is outspoken about the state of popular music today:

"I thoroughly deplore the worship of amateurism that has crept into the arranging field. In the past five years, I have witnessed a change from seeing talented, knowledgeable arrangers working for pop record dates to the present morass of ignorance. Now the question of talent doesn't enter into it; pop music, like pop art, is the supreme effort of people who don't know anything, can't do anything, and assert their right to artistic expression."

Warming to his subject, Brookmeyer continued, "No talent or experience is required. It's all part of the cult of adolescence—selling Brillo pads and fried eggs. In all the arts, we have the cult of the ignorant. If you can't do something, you're a success."

This is not a total condemnation of the current pop scene ("John Lennon writes some good tunes"). Nor is it an expression of bitterness. Rather, it is a matter of personal choice: "You either accept the world you live in, or you don't. When you're sold a bad bill of goods, you don't have to say 'thank you.'"

For relaxation, Brookmeyer indulges in a pastime for which his enthusiasm is shared by such notables as Senator Robert F. Kennedy and Mayor John V. Lindsay of New York City.

"I'm a complete addict to touch football," he confessed. "Last year, I had five footballs and about twenty-five books on the subject; today, I have a few more books, but I've lost two footballs. It's a marvelous release when you have to sit and read music all week."

The clock at Jim Downey's, where this interview took place, indicated that it was time for Brookmeyer to return to the studio for the taping of the Griffin show. Polishing off his last Scotch sour, the trombonist fired a parting shot: "You said this interview was for the brass issue? I have a pertinent comment about the trombone: it's cold in the morning and it hurts at night!"

But when Brookmeyer plays his big brass horn, the music comes out warm and doesn't hurt one bit.

(1967)

Dick Wellstood

There aren't many jazz pianists equally at home with a Scott Joplin rag and a Thelonious Monk piece, whose taste and understanding encompass jazz from Bunk Johnson to Albert Ayler and "serious" music from baroque through the romantics to the moderns, and who love to indulge themselves in Viennese operetta and the Weill-Brecht musical canon.

There are probably even fewer jazz musicians who are graduate lawyers admitted to the bar, and certainly none who accomplished this feat, including college and pre-law studies, in four years, becoming president of the Student Bar Association in the process, all the while supporting a family by working in music.

Add to this a talent for writing, particularly humor and satire; an avocation for Latin (actually reading the Roman classics for pleasure and conducting an extensive correspondence with a friend in this ostensibly dead language); an expert knowledge of chess, practical and theoretical; a sharply honed skill with a pool cue; a passion for bicycle riding (to the extent of qualifying for the Olympics); and a nice way in the kitchen (specialty: lentil salad), and one has the outline of a portrait of Richard McQueen Wellstood.

Dick, as he is known in jazz circles, was born in November 1927, in Greenwich, Connecticut. (He points out that he has "almost the exact chronological and geographic background" as Horace Silver.) He has been a professional musician since 1946, has made quite a few records, and is listed in all editions of Leonard Feather's *Encyclopedia of Jazz*, but chances are that many jazz enthusiasts have never heard him play.

The loss is theirs, for hearing Wellstood at the piano is one of the great pleasures in jazz. He is, of course, at his best in congenial musical company, but circumstances of the working jazz life sometimes lead him to rather bleak (or bleary) surroundings on the bandstand.

But no matter how adverse the conditions, Wellstood shines through: in solo (even when he has to fight his accompanists), in apt ensemble work, or in a witty aside or fill sneaked in with perfect timing. He never lets himself be trapped; when all else fails, his humor prevails.

Wellstood is a two-fisted piano player. He has the true pianist's touch. He knows and loves his instrument. And he can play with almost anybody and fit. He came up with the revivalist jazz movement that ran counter to bebop in the mid-'40s, which has caused critics, those lovers of categorization, to classify him as a traditional player, but this is a manifest injustice.

His many associates have included Bunk Johnson, Sidney Bechet, Jack Teagarden, Roy Eldridge, Charlie Shavers, Rex Stewart, Lips Page, Gene Sedric, Clark Terry, Steve Lacy, and Gene Krupa, to name only a handful— a complete listing would take a page. To an article about Fats Waller in the now defunct *Jazz Review*, Wellstood appended a funny biographical note that included a list—in alphabetical order, from Ahmed Abdul-Malik to Abdullah Zuh'ri—of 189 musicians he had played with, followed by "and many others." The list included such diverse figures as George Lewis, Illinois Jacquet, Django Reinhardt, Mutt Carey, Coleman Hawkins, Baby Dodds, Wellman Braud, and Buell Neidlinger. It was a surrealistic indication of the scope of the pianist's musical experience.

The main facts of Wellstood's career, in chronological order, begin with a performance of boogie-woogie (Mary Lou Williams's "Little Joe") at Wooster Prep School in Danbury, Connecticut, followed by early professional experience with clarinetist Bob Wilber's Wildcats, one of the best of the revivalist groups (most of the players involved have become well-rounded pros, among them trumpeter Johnny Glasel, trombonist Ed Hubble, bassist Charlie Traeger, drummer Eddie Phyfe, and of course Wilber himself); subsequent association with Wilber in a more mature band that had veterans Henry Goodwin, Jimmy Archey, Pops Foster, and Tommy Benford, followed by two years with Archey's band, which toured Europe in 1952; long stints with Roy Eldridge and Charlie Shavers at Lou Terrassi's club in Manhattan, one of the best jazz spots of its day; then a seven-year on-and-off association with trombonist–actor–art gallery manager Conrad Janis, whose bands often included such men as Herman Autrey, Gene Sedric, Eddie Barefield, Danny Barker, and Panama Francis (during this period, Wellstood also freelanced around New York and did a solo piano stint at Eddie Condon's club); two years as house pianist at the Metropole with, among others, clarinetists Tony Parenti and Sol Yaged and trumpeter Johnny Letman; a two-year stretch at Nick's, most of it with an all-star band led by Wild Bill Davison (with Buster Bailey and Vic Dickenson); a USO tour of Army bases in Greenland with trumpeter Carl "Bama" Warwick; a stint as house pianist at the short-lived Bourbon Street in New York, where the tradition of jam sessions was briefly revived; eighteen months with Gene Krupa's quartet, including tours of South America and Israel; and, for the last year or so, charter membership in the band at the Ferry in Brielle, New Jersey.

Wellstood once summed up his career with characteristic wit: "I played my first gig at the American Newspaper Guild Award Ball at the Waldorf-Astoria, and it's been downhill ever since." He says that he "came up playing Dixieland, and everybody putting you down" (example: a radio-studio confrontation between the Wildcats and a bop band including Monk, trumpeter Idrees Suliman, saxophonist Sahib Shihab, and bassist Tommy Potter—"I loved it, and Monk hated us; 'at least we are musicians,' he muttered, and he was right, except for Wilber, who was then, too"), but he appreciates his early training.

"I was lucky in starting out playing rags and blues," he said recently. "It meant something to me, and I've never lost respect for it. It helped me not to become a prisoner of style. . . . I guess I've been getting my own style lately, for I have been getting so many complaints from other musicians."

Becoming serious again, Wellstood said, "My playing is such that musicians seem to like it and critics don't [not quite so: critical praise has come from John S. Wilson, Martin Williams, Nat Hentoff, and others], because my gifts seem to lie in the way I respond to practical music-making situations which have already been defined and not in any startlingly new areas I open up.

"In other words, I'm talented, but not original.

"In my playing, I try to be sensitive rhythmically and pianistically and economical melodically. Harmonies don't concern me so much as voicings and phrasing. For the past few years, I've been trying to develop the pianistic side of my playing, to utilize some of the Chopin–Liszt–Tatum–et cetera tricks which I now have the technique to do. This sort of thing, when it doesn't come off, is pretty terrible, and as accompaniment it drives other musicians crazy—especially Ruby Braff."

When Wellstood mentions the classical piano tradition, he knows whereof he speaks. His extensive formal studies have been with two outstanding teachers, Albion Metcalfe and Richard McClanahan. (Two other McClanahan students were Teddy Wilson and Billy Taylor.)

Wellstood has also studied composition with Ludmilla Ulehla at the Manhattan School of Music, but he did *not* study with Willie "The Lion" Smith, though Smith, in his autobiography, claimed him as a pupil. ("I listened enrapturedly, though," Wellstood said. "I *dig* Lion.")

Continuing his discussion of his pianistic side, Wellstood said, "I don't mean that I'm trying to play lots of stupid scales in thirds or anything, but that I would like to develop a contemporary piano style which is enjoyable to *play*. Jazz and classical music are in the same boat—except for Tatum, there hasn't been a pianistic pianist since Fats Waller, just as there is very little piano music in the classics since Ravel. Ever since somebody invented the rhythm section, jazz pianists have been in trouble."

To Wellstood, "music is expression. The method is mathematical, but if you don't express something, to hell with it. Different times express it in different ways."

His understanding of all periods of music causes the pianist to be impatient with historical generalizations and inspires his hatred of "style playing." On this subject, he is fond of quoting from a book by British composer, critic, and music scholar Sir Donald Tovey: "The first step toward understanding the integrity of art is to recognize that it consists in the integrity of each individual work of art, that . . . there is no such thing as art with a capital A. Progress . . . is a word certainly applicable to science, but almost invariably misleading when applied to art."

Wellstood's soundly grounded outlook enables him to thoroughly enjoy and appreciate, for instance, the music of Jimmy Yancey as well as that of Cecil Taylor. Taylor, in fact, has long been a special favorite of his ("I think he is the greatest thing going"). Recently, he has discovered Albert Ayler, and would like to play with the saxophonist, though he realizes that Ayler's music presents special problems to a pianist, particularly in terms of pitch.

He also greatly enjoys "good rock-and-roll" and is in the process of wearing out his copy of *Revolver*, a recent Beatles album ("I'd like to join a good rock group on electric piano").

His attitude toward style playing is reflected in his statement that "the difference between an oompah and a block chord is mechanical." He has found that Dixieland and mainstream playing situations offer more freedom of expression than modern jobs: "Playing Dixieland or mainstream, you can play anything you want, but when you play a modern gig, you've got to play modern."

Wellstood prefers the challenge of impromptu musical "happenings" of the kind that often arose when he was working at Bourbon Street, where there was much sitting in, both professional and amateur. A lot of what he affectionately calls "dopey things" would happen.

One night, for example, there were Wellstood; bassist Ahmed Abdul-Malik; a would-be "new thing" tenor player; and Lew Black, who in the '20s was banjoist with the New Orleans Rhythm Kings. In situations like this, Wellstood's prescription is "just do it and see what happens." And what did happen, amazingly enough, was more rewarding to hear than much organized jazz. (For the next set, Gerry Mulligan, playing clarinet, replaced the tenorman.)

But Wellstood is concerned about "the vanishing function" of jazz.

"There used to be dancing," he said, "but hardly anymore. This has led to troubles with tempos—everything is either fast or slow. The middle is what's missing."

How does a musician who began as a New Orleans revivalist arrive at so comprehensive a view of the spectrum of jazz?

"What saved the Wildcats," he recalled, "was Fifty-second Street." The band played at Jimmy Ryan's on the street in 1947, opposite a group led by alto saxophonist–arranger Joe Eldridge, elder brother of trumpeter Roy, which also included drummer Big Sid Catlett.

"Joe was a very big influence on me," Wellstood said. "He was worried about us playing the way we did. He thought we should at least *want* to become musicians. He took me aside and showed me chords. He was fatherly—and strict."

Another important formative experience was Wellstood's involvement in the final glories of a vanishing chapter in jazz history:

"I used to go to Tom Tillman's, in Harlem, at a Hundred and Thirty-seventh Street and Seventh Avenue. Monday night was piano night. You'd find Marlow Morris, Billy Taylor, Willie Gant, The Beetle, Tatum. . . . I had to follow Tatum one night, but it was not as bad as having to follow Erroll Garner one night at Terrassi's with Charlie Shavers."

Tatum and Garner are among Wellstood's favorite pianists, whose number also includes Cecil Taylor, James P. Johnson, Willie the Lion, Don Ewell, Duke Ellington, Monk, Phineas Newborn, Horace Silver, Dave Frishberg, Pete Johnson, Joe Sullivan, "recent" Roland Hanna, and—Charlie Shavers.

After more than twenty years of playing music for a living, Wellstood is not bitter. (His involvement with the law was brief: he hung out his shingle after passing the New York bar at first try, handled a Mexican divorce, found he didn't care for the field, went back to playing, and made a final, abortive attempt to practice some five years ago, handling some domestic-relations and real-estate work.)

He has, he points out, been working steadily (with a total of only a few months off) since early 1959.

"I don't know any other pianist who works as much as I for so little money," he said jokingly. His current job, six nights a week on the upper deck of a well-appointed converted ferryboat owned and operated by the leader of the band, trumpeter George Mauro, has musical and personal compensations, though the going gets a bit heavy at times.

One of the band's most popular numbers is a zany rendition of "Battle Hymn of the Republic," replete with such comedy routines as clanging a ship's bell, wearing funny hats, and throwing a blanket over the drummer. But it also leaves an opening for completely "free" playing by Wellstood and his cohorts, who include clarinetist Kenny Davern, a close friend whose playing the pianist much admires ("a very original successor to Pee Wee Russell") and who has much in common with him in musical orientation; bassist Jack Six and drummer Al McManus, solid musicians both; and trombonist Ed Hubble, a friend from the earliest days of the Wilber Wildcats.

Wellstood realizes that in order to be successful in big-time terms, a musician has to be "very facile, very lucky, or extremely talented." While many would hold that he fulfills the latter of these prerequisites, he has learned to be patient and has sufficient inner resources to sustain him.

He would like, though, to have the opportunity to record again, for once under conditions of his own choosing. Wellstood's disc career began in 1946 with the Wildcats and has included several early solo sessions for minor labels, a 10-inch piano LP (with drummer Tommy Benford) for Riverside in 1954, two sessions with Bechet, a Chicago date with guitarist Marty Grosz, several later dates with Wilber (an all-blues album, with trumpeter Clark Terry also on hand, contains fine examples of Wellstood's completely authentic playing in this idiom), a big-band date with drummer Panama Francis, a semi-Dixieland session led by arranger and multi-instrumentalist Dick Carey, albums with singers Nancy Harrow, Meg Welles, and Odetta (for the latter, Wellstood made excellent, functional small-band arrangements), a quintet date with trumpeter Johnny Letman and guitarist Kenny Burrell, albums with clarinetist Leroy Parkins and Wild Bill Davison, an all-star Dixieland session for Prestige, and half his own album for that label, using ex-Wallerites Autrey and Sedric, bassist Milt Hinton, and drummer Zutty Singleton.

Most of these are collector's items, a euphemism for out-of-print records. Today, Wellstood would like to make a piano album, a small-group date with Davern and other congenial souls, or a combination of both. "I always wanted to make a record of 'Trouble in Mind,'" he said with a smile, "but then Red Garland went and did it . . . but there are some numbers they haven't caught up with."

Wellstood has a vast repertoire (his Monk interpretations are something to hear, and when he plays a rag, there is none of that antiquarian aura that customarily surrounds attempts to bring this music to life). In addition, he has shown considerable talent as a composer.

"One thing you learn from twenty years of playing music is playing music," Wellstood once said.

After such knowledge, it seems a shame that this fine musician's talent and experience should not be heard by a wider audience, for Dick Wellstood is his own man, and jazz needs his kind, today more than ever.

(1967)

Ornette Coleman

When Ornette Coleman came to New York City in the fall of 1959, his decidedly unorthodox approach to music immediately became the center of stormy controversy. Some hailed him as an innovator of profound importance, one whose music signaled a new and liberated era in jazz; others dismissed him as a musical charlatan or an unformed primitive.

More than five years later, the controversy remains unresolved but the voices of derision are no longer as sharply abrasive. After all, it has become obvious that the thirty-five-year-old Texas-born alto saxophonist was not just a flash in the pan or the creation of critical press agentry. A whole new music, referred to as either the "new thing" or simply avant-garde jazz, has sprung up in his wake, unquestionably influenced by his conception, though often quite unlike his own music in terms of content or execution. Though the merit of his music might still be disputed, the fact of its impact cannot.

When Coleman ended a two-year period of self-imposed exile from public performance with a three-week January engagement at the Village Vanguard in New York City, his reception indicated that his prolonged absence had not dulled public interest in him and his music. *Time*, *Newsweek*, *The New Yorker*, and the *New York Times* covered his opening, and he drew good crowds despite freezing weather.

Once again Coleman was making news, and the fact that he was now playing violin and trumpet in addition to alto did not lessen the effect of his return. Yet at the conclusion of his engagement, he had no definite plans for future appearances.

If it seems odd that such a well-known performer should not be scheduling a string of appearances in the wake of such publicity and established drawing power, it is in keeping with the rather baffling aspects of the business side of Coleman's career—aspects that are in character with the complexity of the man himself.

Superficially, Ornette Coleman has changed remarkably little during the time span that brought him from near-obscurity. (Many years of his professional playing took place within the confines of rhythm-and-blues bands, and little jazz notice was taken of him until his first album appeared in 1958.) He is still the soft-spoken, somehow self-contained, and youthful man who shook up jazz with his New York debut at the Five Spot five years ago. Now as then, he is reserved but readily approachable, warm and friendly when approached, and remarkably candid and unaffected in speech and manner.

Coleman has become a New Yorker—a Villager, to be exact. People who judge by appearances may consider that the unusual old fur coat he has been wearing this winter, the soft felt hat similar to those worn by painters at the turn of the century, and, of course, the beard are manifestations of calculated eccentricity. Yet, he somehow looks right—and at the Vanguard, his working attire was immaculate and tastefully conservative. He is not a man to be hastily judged in any of his ways.

As soon as the following interview began, Coleman settled into an easy chair and began to talk. Excepting a few brief interpolations, he talked for an hour and a half. The focal point was music, but he touched on many things. Some of these are perhaps not customarily discussed in a jazz magazine, but they are pertinent to the subject at hand.

(Since Coleman's thoughts move with a flow and continuity that are his own, his statement formed a whole, and excerpts may not do full justice to his words, but, though the cadences may have been changed, the meanings are retained.)

He said he wanted to begin with the problem of being a performer-composer.

"In America, especially," Coleman said, "people seem to confuse the composer with the player because most jazz players today write their own music. In my own playing and writing, I'm at a loss for a category, as far as the relative positions of player and composer are concerned. I'm classified as a jazzman . . . many people have it in their minds that if you improvise, you are automatically playing jazz."

This is an error, Coleman said. "Composers were improvising in the seventeenth and eighteenth centuries," he explained. "But there is something about the word 'jazz' that identifies you more as a player than as a composer, and that's the roots of it."

Burdened with history, the music of white society, he continued, "is basically involved in challenging written music," while in a society "which allows you to express your own feelings, jazz seemed the most acceptable music. Regardless of race or nationality, if you are not trying to compare your values with those of other people, but are interested in expressing musically something that you have in your mind and not trying to get anyone's approval—then jazz seems to be the most honest and freest form of taking the opportunity to see if you can express something that has nothing to do with keeping history going or creating a new history."

History, and its effect on the present, was a subject to which Coleman often returned. Perhaps he came closest to defining the essence of his conception when he said, "It is not easy to find ways to become involved with existence in its relation to the history that one has been exposed to, to use that history to become better, and not to let it fence you in from anything else that could possibly exist. The menace in America is that everyone— black or white—is enslaved in history. This enslavement tends to make you remember history more than to think of what you could do if it were nothing *but* history.

"In music, especially, I have yet to hear a composer or performer or player who doesn't give me the feeling that he is trying to eliminate some of history or to dominate the present—as a reason for doing it, *not* because that's where he was going. For myself, I find that playing allows me to be more concerned with avoiding history than writing does."

Part of the history of American music, of course, is the popular song. "Song-form composition is the hottest form of composing in America," Coleman stated. "Whether it's Stravinsky or Mancini or the Drifters—it doesn't matter, as long as the composition can be put into song form, words can be put to that song, the song can be translated with words, and everybody can hear the melody. The composer of instrumental music sneers at this, as related to his idea of what composition should be. But somehow I never made a value distinction between writing a song to make lots of money and writing a song to have something to play. I've written lots of music and thought about it as writing to have something to play.

"Lately, I've tried writing songs, and there is one that I've written lyrics to. When we were playing it in the club, somebody would always come up and ask me what it was. That made me realize that the composer who writes a pop song has a musical outlet in which both composer and listener are striving for the same goal.

"In jazz, people seem to think that's not the thing to do—to be interested in the composition as well as the playing. But that seems to me a grave mistake. I've never heard composers of hit tunes complaining about somebody else playing their tunes. . . ."

But how does this relate to the music of a composer-player-performer in which improvisation plays such a basic role?

"If I could learn to create instant compositions without having to worry about when I'm going to play each of them when I perform," Coleman answered, "that would be a challenge to develop. I've tried it. You really have to have players with you who will allow your instincts to flourish in such a way that they will make the same order as if you had sat down and written a piece of music. To me, that is the most glorified goal of the improvising quality of playing—to be able to do that.

"But you begin to do that before you learn about the rudiments and the laws of music. If you can learn those laws and rudiments and still do that, then you have begun to be free—if that's a good word. You've begun to learn how to give a performance without trying to satisfy your own ego, and your image of what you think your possibilities are. You don't have to worry about how good or bad you are, if the goal you are trying to achieve is to create instantaneously a piece of music as concentrated as if you were to sit down and write it."

Coleman said he feels that such a music would have no financial value in the pop-tune sense of capital gains, unless the composer-player "could find out how to emerge into the song form and make his ability fit in that same sense."

This is not the easy way. The easy way would be to play a song everybody knows.

"But the song-form music, in the last ten or fifteen years," he explained, "has caused myself and many like myself to feel like avoiding help when that help is only to make your public acceptance more easy for you.

"Yet the public can be reached. I never think about writing a piece in terms of who can remember it and who can play it, because if you were performing in a place where nobody had ever heard you, and they loved your music, it would be the same as if you heard a song you had never heard before and liked it.

"I'd rather take my chances and truly play—and see if a person really liked it—than try to figure out something that people are likely to like, play that, and believe that that's what they really like."

This is the outlook of a man to whom music is more than a craft or means of subsistence.

"I have always wanted to do as many things as I could learn to do," Coleman said. "The reason why I am mostly concerned with music is because music has a tendency to let everybody see your own convictions; music tends to reveal more of the kind of person you are than any other medium of expression. It's not like painting, where all of a sudden it's there. It's unlike any other activity, and I love it because of that.

"Music has the greatest social integrity. Performer, listener, composer—music allows everyone to accept or reject according to their own likes or dislikes. No other medium, to me, is that honest.

"Music has these qualities. But sometimes it isn't music; it may become all psychic ego, or personality may dominate. One of the most important things about playing or writing or doing any service that people get pleasure from is your own reason for doing it. I don't feel compelled to write or play music simply to have people remember me or to satisfy myself."

This concern for artistic integrity is, of course, considered a luxury in the marketplace of music where, regardless of his personal concerns, the player-performer must make his stand.

"The one thing performers in jazz have never been able to do," Coleman said, "is to exercise a choice of audience and their means of existence as related to the audience, because the player is more of a public image than the composer. You don't see composers in nightclubs every night; they're at home composing. But the player is the man on the market. He is the one constantly trying to find something that will keep him on the market.

"Any time music is being performed for anything less than the fact of the interest of the audience in it, such as the fee that you are getting, it is looked upon as a business. Music as a business means performing for an audience and yet working for the person who is giving you the opportunity to perform."

Coleman has had his share of problems with this system.

"As a Negro," he explained, "I have a tendency to want to know how certain principles and rights are arrived at. When this concern dominates my business relationships, I'm cast into schizophrenic or paranoid thinking. People tell me that all I should be interested in is playing and making money, not the principles of how it's being done. I could accept that, but when I see that a booking agent books a major artist, and then books me into the same place, and I go in behind these people and see that they are not trying to reach the same goal with me as with them, then it seems to me that they are not as much for me as they are for them."

Coleman, in other words, has no desire to be sold short. If his refusal to accept any terms not equal to the best may appear to some to be misguided, some reflection upon the careers wrecked or thwarted by inept or corrupt agents and managers, wrong bookings, and under- as well as overexposure of talent might give them pause.

"The things that are important," he said, "are the chances the individual can find of being used in such a way that his own growth, and his own reasons for wanting to get ahead, and his own purpose of existence are involved." Coleman said he does not wish "to be exploited for not having the knowledge or know-how" required for survival in today's America.

"It has gotten so that in your relationships to every system that has some sort of power, you have to pay to become part of that power, just in order to do what you want to do," he continued. "This doesn't build a better world, but it does build more security for the power. Power makes purpose secondary. But it is not important to want to be part of an organization just to have power; it is much more important to be able to be beneficial to whatever organization may exist for the simple reason of your own existence as a person with a purpose in your own life."

This dilemma, he said, is a product of our age, "the machine age, which is the greatest concentration of power. The electronic machine age doesn't allow a person to be an individual unless his intelligence is attached in a relationship to machines. The only way people have been able to exist without being part of organized machinery has been to find ways of writing or playing or doing any service which really includes the human being in a dominant role. In America, the human person as a dominant factor is left in just a handful of these things."

Such a state of affairs drives some artists to anarchy.

"I hear about people trying to destroy art," Coleman stated, "trying to destroy the melody line, trying to destroy anything that might make them become a machine. Yet I wouldn't change my attitude towards what I want to do simply because I felt unable to understand the function of the machine in relationship to my own talent. I wouldn't try to destroy my own talent just to make it seem as if I was trying to get further out than the machine. I'd rather be able to accept whatever man can create that will allow him to become more human . . . you just have to be able to accept what is affecting you and try to develop enough sensitivity to accept it without feeling that it is trying to deteriorate your existence."

Yet there are things that are unacceptable, he said: "Since man has created hostility and corruption, you have to take a certain responsibility upon yourself to reject the things you would want to see eliminated from life. I would like very much to find a principle that I could believe in, that I knew was working for the purpose of human betterment. I have nothing against being useful in a group—political or whatever—but if they were looking for the same thing I am, there wouldn't have to be a group.

"It seems to me that the conception of a possible change in human existence is still embedded in religion rather than in the making of human scales of values. It's just too bad that the religious conception is based on organization rather than principle. Organized religion has created special positions—priests, rabbis, deacons—to make others believe. It is hard to accept a power to make decisions for you. It is more beautiful to me if a person, whoever he is, is out there doing and fighting for his principles, if a person representing God is taking his chances with changing the world rather than holding a position.

"When I hear a really beautiful Negro spiritual, I feel much closer to God, hearing the beauty of someone really wanting to believe in something and to worship something, though not even in a position to be accepted in an ordinary man's life. It makes me realize that, regardless of who represents Him, God has been made known to everyone.

"That's why music is such an outlet for people's emotional problems and social anxieties. Everyone seems to want to be loved and to give love through something that eliminates fear. Fear means that people can't be what they want to be to you."

Fear—and its handmaidens, ignorance and prejudice.

"I haven't as yet spoken of anger," Coleman said, "the anger I feel as a Negro, the true anger I have to confront every day just in order to survive. When a person is exempted from having principles simply because of his origins being mixed with this or that, you tend to let anger develop within your mental framework. The greatest anger I'm constantly threatened with is caused by the values of people who accept your abilities and yet disillusion you by not accepting you as a person."

That, too, is a result of history. Earlier, Coleman had said: "Americans are so wary in giving you any sort of human respect in relationship to what you are trying to do that they would rather make you feel guilty of history than accept any pleasure they are receiving from you."

One hopes that this singularly uncompromising and impractical man will find a way for himself and his art in a world dedicated to compromise and practical know-how.

(1965)

Charlie Haden

When Ornette Coleman arrived in New York City in 1959 with his quartet, reactions to the music of the leader and trumpeter Don Cherry ran from ecstatic approval to surly ridicule. But almost all listeners were full of praise for the group's drummer, Billy Higgins, and bassist, Charlie Haden.

Haden, then twenty-two, was practically unknown. He had met Coleman while working with pianist Paul Bley at the Hillcrest (now the It Club) in Los Angeles. Vibraharpist Dave Pike and drummer Lennie McBrowne were also in the group.

"One night," said Haden, a soft-spoken young man with an open and friendly manner, who gives the impression that he really means what he says, "Lennie brought a gentleman into the club and introduced me to him. It was Ornette, and he invited me to come over to his house and play some. I did, and he started playing music that I'd never heard in my life.

"It was very exciting to me. There was a feeling there that I was sure was very, very valid. I was startled by his music because he wasn't playing on the chord changes—and in 1958, everyone was still doing that. To play with Ornette, you really had to listen to everything he did because he was playing off the *feeling.*"

After several weekly get-togethers, Bley hired Coleman, Cherry, and Higgins for the job at the Hillcrest.

"Ornette hadn't had a chance to work playing his music before because of the way people reacted to it," Haden recalled. "And it was the same kind of situation there. The owner got bugged at the music, and in a couple of months, it was all over."

Yet, the experiment was fruitful, for when the time came for Coleman to go to New York, Haden was with him.

When that first encounter took place, Haden had not been playing jazz for very long. But he had been surrounded by music since birth. Born in August 1937, in the small Iowa town of Shenandoah into a family of professional singers and musicians, Haden spent his childhood years performing on the circuit where hillbilly music was the thing. He and his parents, brothers, and sisters were known as the Haden Family. Charlie was the youngest. In addition to singing, his two older brothers played guitar and bass, respectively; one of two sisters was also a guitarist; his mother sang; his father acted as emcee and manager.

"We were all self-taught," Haden said, "singing harmony parts by ear. When I was two years old, I was singing hillbilly music on the radio. We were like the Carter Family. My mother sang old folk tunes, like 'Barbara Allen' and 'The Great Speckled Bird'—all those numbers now being recorded by college students."

When Haden had reached his teens, his bass-playing brother became interested in jazz and in the kind of modern, four-part harmony featured by the Four Freshmen. ("He had us learn the records, and we started rehearsing things of our own, but then my father decided to retire.")

Haden listened to his brother's records, but the greatest impression was made by his first contact with live jazz. It was a Jazz at the Philharmonic concert in Nebraska. Lester Young and Charlie Parker were in the JATP troupe.

"I didn't know what jazz was, but I knew I liked it," Haden said, smiling. Nor did he know who Parker and Young were, "but it was a fantastic experience." He wanted to learn to play an instrument, but there was no opportunity.

"I always had a feeling for my brother's bass fiddle," he recalled, "but he had no time to show me and was afraid I'd drop the instrument." But after Charlie was graduated from high school in Forsythe, Missouri ("population four hundred, with thirty-four kids in the class, mostly farmers' children from the Ozarks"), he got a bass of his own and began to take music lessons.

"My teacher told me about Oberlin College," he said. "And though I couldn't read, he made an audition tape—bass and piano—with me. He showed me the notes on the bass, how to hold the bow, et cetera." The young man must have shown an indication of things to come, for the tape resulted in acceptance, with a scholarship, at the music college in Ohio.

But Haden turned it down; he wanted to be around jazz. He decided to go to Westlake College of Music in California.

"I sold shoes for one year and went out there," he said, "but I found it wasn't what I wanted. I stayed for a half semester."

At Westlake, Haden played club dates with other students, but his first real break came through a chance meeting with an early idol.

"I always did my homework in a drive-in, and one night, Red Mitchell was there," Haden remembered. "I walked up to him, introduced myself, and asked if he had some advice. He invited me to come over to his house. He didn't want to teach me bass, but he played piano, with me on bass, and told me to come whenever I could."

Not too long after, Mitchell, who had been working with altoist Art Pepper at a local club, found that he couldn't stay on the gig and asked Haden to come by and sit in.

"I was very scared," Haden said, "but I did it. I can't remember what we played, but as soon as the tune was finished, Art asked me if I wanted to work with him for the rest of the gig."

The answer, of course, was yes. After four weeks with Pepper came the job with Bley at the Hillcrest ("on and off for about two years"), the meeting with Coleman, and, before the trip to New York, some work with pianist Hampton Hawes.

There was also, before New York, a significant friendship with another brilliant young bassist—the late Scott LaFaro. "Scotty was in Los Angeles, and we met and became very close," Haden said. "We shared an apartment for a while, and he went to New York about the time Ornette's group did." Later, of course, LaFaro was to play with Coleman's group, and he and Haden would record together on Coleman's famous *Free Jazz* double-quartet album.

When Coleman had told Haden that they were going to New York, the bassist's response had been "beautiful." But what followed was anything but.

"I was already pretty mixed up personally," Haden said, "and after coming to New York, it got worse and worse. It finally reached the point where

I was coming late on the gig every night. Ornette was upset, told me please to try and straighten out, but then one night I was two hours late, the second set was already on, and I told Ornette, 'You don't have to say it—I'm going to a hospital.'"

After unsuccessful attempts to be admitted to a New York hospital for narcotics addiction ("they had no addiction programs then"), Haden went to Lexington, Kentucky, and entered the U.S. Public Health Service hospital there.

"After a couple of months, I was back in the city, started working again, and made the double-quartet album," he said. "Right after we'd finished, Ornette told me that George Russell was looking for me for a Birdland gig. But the day before the opening, I was arrested and had my cabaret card taken away."

Unable to work in clubs, Haden played concerts and coffeehouses while on probation, which he evidently broke by going back to Los Angeles, where he worked with, among others, Buddy DeFranco and Charlie Barnet, "trying to stay clean by drinking."

Ironically, that was the year Haden won the *Down Beat* International Jazz Critics Poll New Star Award. ("I had no address to which they could send my plaque.")

Things got worse. Finally Haden—"like a walking dead person, doing nothing constructive, not playing any more," scuffling back in New York, resting up at home in Missouri, trying the cure in the federal hospital in Fort Worth, Texas (where he had the chance to play daily with Hampton Hawes), and sliding back again—decided to go to Synanon House, the independent, unorthodox narcotics rehabilitation community in Santa Monica, California.

"It was a last resort," Haden said. "I went in September 1963, and I didn't plan on staying. It was just like any other hospital, I thought. But soon I found out it wasn't. I saw people I'd known completely changed, grown-up, matured. And some, like Joe Pass, were instrumental in getting me to stay."

Gradually, he began to make progress, discharging various communal responsibilities. First, there were such chores as being breakfast cook for 150 people; later, he became a public-relations man for Synanon.

For a year, Haden stopped playing entirely, but when he was transferred to the Synanon chapter in San Francisco, alto saxophonist John Handy, who'd heard that he was staying there, asked the bassist to join his group.

"We discussed it," Haden said (discussion plays a large part in Synanon therapy), "and decided I should play one night a week to start."

That was the beginning of a new career. Haden next joined the trio of pianist-psychiatrist Denny Zeitlin, who was interning at a San Francisco hospital and working Mondays at the Trident in Sausalito, California, as well as playing concerts and jazz festivals.

In May 1966, Haden went to New York City to help establish a Synanon House. When the job was successfully completed, Haden moved into his own apartment, and, though he no longer lives at Synanon, he keeps in close touch and helps whenever he is needed.

Haden is convinced that the Synanon approach to the problem of addiction is the only right one.

"I tried every kind of hospital and psychiatric care," he said, "but Synanon was the only solution. Their work should be recognized much more. They are doing something that the government has never been able to accomplish . . . millions are being wasted, while right under their noses, Synanon is doing the job. But the Establishment bureaucracy has a vested interest in the drug problem; so nothing happens."

Before returning to New York, Haden had worked with Archie Shepp in California, and being able to play with the tenor saxophonist again was an additional reason for coming back, he said. Last year, Haden made his first visit to Europe, with the Shepp quartet, which he described as "one of the most exciting musical groups I've ever worked with."

But the bassist's recent musical activity has not been confined to this association. He has been working clubs with guitarist Attila Zoller and pianist Bobby Timmons and with clarinetist Tony Scott. He has subbed for Richard Davis in the Thad Jones–Mel Lewis big band, played a concert with veterans Henry ("Red") Allen and Pee Wee Russell, and made a number of record dates (with Shepp, with pianist Keith Jarrett, and with trombonist Roswell Rudd). He was also reunited with Coleman, for the first time since 1962, on a trio date for Blue Note (Coleman's ten-year-old son, Denardo, played drums).

About the Coleman session, Haden said: "The music was completely fresh and brand-new. Denardo is going to startle every drummer who hears him."

Such diverse musical associations indicate Haden has the open mind of the truly creative musician. "When music is played from a person's heart," he said, "it's true. Wisdom includes both the old and the new, merged. I play the way I play no matter who I'm with.

"People want to put music in categories. But with Ornette, we didn't say we were playing any brand of music. We just wanted to *play*; we had a need inside. To talk about music in terms of categories is catering to the public. I get the same good feeling from listening to all sorts of music, from Bach to Bird, from seeing a painting by a beautiful painter. . . . It all comes from the same place—the place where all creation comes from.

"In a categorical sense, perhaps things have to be labeled, studied, analyzed. . . . But in the end, as a poet has said, 'Word knowledge is but a shadow of wordless knowledge'—feeling came first, words later."

But while in his approach to music Haden prefers intuition and feeling to analysis, he is by no means otherworldly. He is deeply concerned about social and political issues.

"So many things have been written and said about the political, economic, and cultural state of our country," he remarked, "that one would almost feel inclined to avoid the issues completely, giving in to a sense of futility. But I'm unable to do this. Because, after all, it is my country, too, and I feel very concerned.

"It's tragic to think that $5,479,452 a day is being spent on the killing of innocent people and the burning and crippling of children in Vietnam, while major problems in our own country are being neglected—poverty, civil rights, mental illness, drug addiction, unemployment. And in this, the richest country in the world, we have a situation where most creative artists can't live on what they earn from their art.

"Gifted musicians have to take day jobs or play commercial music seven nights a week in order to make a living for their families. I know this has all been said before, but no change can begin to take place if everyone remains silent. The truth that came from Charlie Parker and Billie Holiday, and that which comes from the creative musicians today, is equal in truth to that of the poet, painter, sculptor, and composer of the past and present. Both truths are spelled as one and come from the same place."

Haden said he is trying to find some way to be creative in his art and "make a living as a side effect from that." He is painfully aware of lost time. ("I have to make up for eight years, and there aren't enough seconds in each day to do the things that have to be done.")

He wants to study his instrument, study history and government, "know the society I live in," do all the things that "are included in becoming a more fully aware human being, and developing oneself to the greatest potential, becoming a productive person."

His ideas in this respect, he said, have been influenced by psychologist Abraham Maslow's theories of the self-actualizing personality.

"So much time is wasted in every person's life," he said. "People think only of themselves. I'm trying to open myself up to interaction with others, to asking and thinking and giving—not only with musicians, but with everyone."

The theory that musicians are playing only for themselves is not true, according to Haden—"you only have to open yourself up to the feeling of the musician."

Haden is aware that these feelings are sometimes difficult to communicate, especially because "musicians have to play in such depressing environments to make a living. In Stockholm we played in such a beautiful club—clean and healthy, nobody getting drunk." Jazz musicians, he said, should be playing mainly concerts, doing "two sets a night and making about eight hundred dollars per week."

As a bass player, Haden had a communication problem to which he found an immediate, practical solution: he recently purchased an amplifier for his bass.

"I tried it out for the first time on a Monday night gig at the Five Spot with Don Cherry," he said. "I'd found that the amplification systems in most clubs were very inadequate, as far as picking up the bass goes, and it struck me that I could never hear the bass player, and when playing, I had acoustical and volume problems. But I was determined to be an equal voice with the rest of the music.

"My amplifier has inside and outside mike pickup and has the closest thing to a natural bass sound. There are situations where I don't have to use it, but when I do, it has worked out very well."

Speaking of his instrument, Haden wanted to mention "those bassists whom I have a very strong feeling for and identify with." His choices include Wilbur Ware ("one of the most underrated, fantastic musicians of all time"), Walter Page, Israel Crosby, Jimmy Blanton, Oscar Pettiford, and Henry Grimes.

Haden has been approached to give bass lessons, and he thinks that he might teach someday, "but first I have a lot of playing to get out of my system—a lot of music inside of me to be played. Right now, it's like beginning all over again for me. Every experience is a new one, and every day something new happens to me."

(1967)

Freddie Hubbard

When the talk turns to trumpet players these days, it doesn't take long before the name Freddie Hubbard is mentioned. With his bold attack, bright and brassy tone, and adventurous ideas, this young man with a horn from Indianapolis is most decidedly a trumpet player in the grand, expressive tradition of his instrument.

"A trumpet is a trumpet," Hubbard said recently. "If you're going to play a bugle, that's one thing, or if you're going to play a cornet, that's another approach, but the trumpet—well, there's a certain thing that you have to get. It's brass, and you have a brass mouthpiece against the flesh, and if you just try to hum a note and then play it, that's not tone quality. There's a certain amount of control involved.

"Some of the trumpet players," he continued, "who are playing so-called avant-garde or whatever-you-call-it music fail to realize that it's still a trumpet. It's not that you have to play with a straight 'legit' tone, but you still try to get the body out of the horn."

It would be a mistake, however, to conclude from this attitude that Hubbard is a musical conservative. To the contrary, he is intent upon widening the effective scope of the trumpet, to do "some things that I know are not the normal kind of trumpet playing, technically speaking.

"A lot of the things I play are not 'normal' for the trumpet . . . they might be more like a violin or a piano. I'll try something, and people will say, 'Man, you sound like a tenor sax; what are you trying to do?'"

But Hubbard, who at twenty-eight has behind him considerable playing experience in a variety of musical settings, does not allow such occasional resistance to frustrate him unduly. "When you're young and playing your own ideas," he said, "they are not always taken for granted. People seem to say they're going to listen to this for a period of time before they accept it." Nor is he unaware of the musical trap of "getting hung up in your own thing." He wants, he said, "to be a musician," and this means "to be able to do anything I'm capable of and have it accepted."

He explained: "If Count Basie called me for a gig, I'd want to be able to fit and project my own things, and if I'm playing with Friedrich Gulda, I'd want to be able to do that, or with Elvin Jones or with Art Blakey or Manny Albam—and still, it would be me. It can be done."

Currently, Hubbard is a member of drummer Max Roach's quintet but works and records with his own group when Roach lays off. In his own quintet he often uses men from Roach's group, such as pianist Ronnie Mathews and alto saxophonist–flutist James Spaulding, a boyhood friend and longtime musical associate from Indianapolis. Prior to joining Roach, the trumpeter spent considerable time with Blakey's Jazz Messengers.

"I'm having quite an experience playing with Max," Hubbard said. "He knows such a wide area of music—dynamically, musically, and in terms of drums. He doesn't drown you out, like most drummers do; they tend to overplay, because they don't know the timbre of the instrument.

"Max has all this in his head. I'm a spoiled trumpet player in terms of drummers, because, after working with Max, Art, Philly Joe Jones, Elvin Jones, Tony Williams, Clifford Jarvis . . . you get to playing with some of the young cats, and you don't feel there's any bottom with them."

Finding the right drummer for his group has been a problem. "It's almost like asking too much," the trumpeter said, "because it's age and experience that's involved, and I've always been looking for a young drummer with the maturity of the masters." At the time of this interview, however, Hubbard had just finished rehearsing for a record date with a young drummer from Indianapolis, Ray Appleton, and was enthusiastic about his work: "I think he's what I've been looking for—not because he's from my hometown, but because he seems to take all the important things into consideration: bottom, beat, pulse. We grew up together; he's younger than Spaulding and myself and used to come to sessions and listen. He always wanted to play, but he didn't know too much then. Later he went with Buddy Montgomery to San Francisco, and I heard him out there recently. He sat in, and I hired him."

Coincidentally, Hubbard made his first record with vibraharpist-pianist Buddy Montgomery and his brothers, guitarist Wes and bassist Monk. "I was eighteen and thrilled to death," he recalled, "but I think the date that really got me started was the one I made with Paul Chambers, Cannonball Adderley, Wynton Kelly, and Jimmy Cobb [*Go!*, a 1959 Vee Jay LP issued under bassist Chambers's name]."

By that time, Hubbard had left Indianapolis, and today he looks back on his early years in that Midwestern city with mixed emotions.

There are good memories: "I'll never forget the club called George's Bar on Indiana Avenue, a street where everybody would come out on weekends in their best attire and go from club to club. That was the thing. A few of the guys and Spaulding and myself formed a group called the Jazz Contemporaries. We'd rehearse and rehearse, and finally we got the job at George's Bar, and all the musicians, like James Moody and Kenny Dorham and many others, would come by and listen when they were in town. That was an inspiration."

But other recollections are less happy: "I went to a mixed high school outside my own neighborhood. You might say I was almost transplanted. I was integrating a high school for the first time and growing up with Caucasians . . . which was quite a different experience. A lot of times, I would be the only Negro kid in a class, and the vibrations I felt, I think, made me sort of rebel . . . so I didn't dig a lot of subjects, like American history and math—mainly because of the teachers and the kids."

But one subject was not affected. "Music always held out, no matter what I was in," he said. "Music was it." He studied French horn and played in the marching band, doubling on trumpet. At times he "wanted to do something else with the music, because I felt it wasn't me," but the band director would tell him, "Play it like it is on the paper, Freddie." He tried for a scholarship to Indiana Central College, but though he had an A average in music, his major, his overall academic average was too low to qualify him. "I wasn't interested in anything except music until I got into the twelfth grade," he explained, "and by then I tried to cram, but I didn't get the scholarship."

Instead, he enrolled at Jordan Conservatory, a branch of Butler University in Indianapolis. "Everything was good, I was taking harmony, theory, private instruction on trumpet," he said. "But then, after the first semester, the dean tells me I have to take a test in other subjects. So I get all my books out, my electricity books, my algebra books, and go through them in a couple of days, which was a heavy thing. . . ."

Hubbard was told that he had failed the test.

"Even my teachers tried to keep me in," he recalled. "They knew I didn't have any money, that my mother was poor, and that I was gigging trying to get some money for her. But they put me out because my point average wasn't high enough academically. But I was doing fine in music, which is what I was there for—the real reason was that they didn't want you to mix with the white ladies."

The young man accepted this turn of events, fortified by a maxim taught him by his father, which, he said, he often recalls when confronted with the lack of acceptance for the music he plays, a music that he, like so many musicians of his generation, doesn't like to call jazz. "I am what I am; otherwise, I place myself as nothing—that was one good thing my father taught me," Hubbard said.

His thoughts on jazz are centered on the stigma that, he feels, is still attached to the word, at least in the United States. "It's American music," he said, "because you have different ethnic groups involved in it, but the word 'jazz' seems to be a dirty word. I think the hang-up is what Americans associate with the word, and I don't know why they're trying to oppress this music. The word doesn't mean a thing. I play all sorts of music. Louis Armstrong doesn't play 'jazz,' he plays music that makes you grin and feel happy."

Hubbard is distressed, also, at the lack of acceptance for jazz among Negro audiences: "They'd better wake up, and I'm saying this in all sincerity, because we created this thing, and they can't even accept it. Colored people can't dig Charlie Parker; they're so busy listening to cornball crap. Real music swings, you can dance to it—if you can dance. . . ."

He is not, however, putting down other types of music. "I like classical music, I like commercial jazz, I like television music. It's all part of what's happening, and I'm going to get with everything I can get with. I want to check out everything. I'm not going to be limited."

To prove his point, his next recording venture is going to be different from what he has attempted before. "I'm doing mostly short things," he said, "and the majority of them will be of a commercial type—just to see what I can do with it. It's the most popular thing today. . . . Little Anthony and the Imperials used to do it a long time ago; all of a sudden, the name put to it has changed, and it's accepted."

Hubbard said he was strongly influenced by Sonny Rollins, with whom he worked shortly after coming to New York City. "He has been my greatest inspiration," Hubbard said. "When I worked with him, I learned more than I ever learned, because I never knew what he was going to do next. And he's *rooted*—I've heard him sound like Coleman Hawkins, which is pretty hard to do."

Another musician Hubbard greatly admires is Thelonious Monk. "I'd like to study with Monk," he said, breaking into his characteristic, infectious laugh. "Study trumpet with Monk—hah! If he could take the time . . . Monk told me something once at the Five Spot; he said that everybody's playing chords, but Sonny Rollins is playing *ideas*. 'That's all you've got to do,' he said. 'Don't just play chords, you've got to play some ideas.'"

The remark stayed on his mind for quite a while, Hubbard said, because "you can play on chords, and just run up and down, but there is a way of playing ideas on the chord that really makes it—you can't play all the notes in a chord, anyway."

Since much avant-garde jazz is based on playing without chord progressions, and since Hubbard was involved in two of the key record dates of the "new music"—Ornette Coleman's *Free Jazz* and John Coltrane's *Ascension* (he pointed out that solo credits for himself and trumpeter Dewey Johnson were erroneously reversed on the Coltrane record's liner notes)—his ideas about musical "freedom" are of interest.

"*Ascension* was still based on scales," he said. "At least, it wasn't based just on playing without any vibrations from the other musicians. In other words, we knew when we had to build something off a certain scale or something. It wasn't just playing—at least, that's what I got out of it."

Hubbard said he believes that this kind of music doesn't work unless one is working with musicians "who feel the same vibrations." In his own recorded work, both with pianist Herbie Hancock and on his own album *Breaking Point*, this was the case, he said, and there were certain basic guidelines as well.

"I had a certain mode that I was playing off," he explained, "and we built on that mode. We would take the notes in that scale and expand on it. For example, if it was an A major-7th chord with a raised 5th, we might play in the key of A, which is an extension of the chord, and then, from there, we might go F/G/A/D/D/E and then go off into another chord, but still, it made sense, because the piano player was listening.

"It's not like just playing anything that comes into your mind, and that's where the mistake is made, I think. A lot of guys are talking about 'freedom,' and it's not really freedom. Freedom of what? Speech? Is it free because you embarrass someone with what you say—is that being free? Or is it telling someone what you feel? Freedom is just a word; it's what you make it, and a lot of the things guys are playing just don't make musical sense to me, when they're just *playing*."

Hubbard also said he feels that there is a certain danger in pursuing music without any rules or standards: "If they don't watch out, this so-called freedom music will be overrun by people who know nothing about chord progressions, melody, tone quality, and basic musical background. It's like opening the doors for people who know nothing about music. . . . Anybody might have a love for musical sounds, but if it's not a good sound, it's no good."

As for himself, Hubbard said, "I make dates with certain people who know something about music, but I'm not going to make it with anybody who I feel doesn't know anything about the background of music. You have to know something about what you're doing. It's beautiful to express your emotions, but I think they should be expressed in terms of unity. It's like playing and listening and contributing at the same time, which is hard, and if you don't have the right guys together, it's not going to happen."

But Hubbard is no dogmatist and wants it understood that this "is a very touchy subject, because everybody has their own ideas about what type of music they want to hear." It is his own musical standards he is concerned with.

Among the things Hubbard would like to do in the future is to bring his brother, Herman Hubbard, Jr., to New York to record with him. ("He plays good piano, but he's hung up because he doesn't read.") The trumpeter credits his brother with first opening his ears to a kind of jazz other than the then popular West Coast sound he was exposed to on the radio as a youth: "I'd be listening to Shorty Rogers, and he would be playing this weird music all day, so I'd say, 'Man, what are you doing, I don't hear this stuff on the radio—what is it?' and he'd say, 'Man, this is patting music!'—he was a stone bebopper."

Clifford Brown was Hubbard's first idol. "He amazed me—he had such depth," he recalled. "His sound was brilliant and at the same time, it was large; he had a broad tone, and he was warm. For a long time, I tried to play like Clifford, but I couldn't get the tone going—his attack was so pronounced, almost like a legitimate trumpet player's."

Before Brown, there was an Indianapolis musician, Charles Hummel, who called himself Diz and "lived like a hermit. He played very well and was my first big influence on learning jazz trumpet. There was one thing he always tried to show me about the attack of a note—I haven't got it yet, but I'm working on it. He taught me a lot."

Hubbard is also grateful to the teacher with whom he studied for three years after leaving Jordan Conservatory—Max Woodbury, first trumpeter of the Indianapolis Symphony. ("He really helped me on my breathing, because I was losing air out of the side of my mouth, trying to get a big sound.")

About the future course of music, Hubbard says that "nowadays you have to be able to do almost anything, because anything might happen—it's in the air." Whatever it might be, Hubbard aims to be ready to play "with just about everybody and still be able to sound like me."

(1966)

Warren Vaché

Some eight years ago I was about to complete a long interview for the National Endowment for the Arts' Jazz Oral History Project with the eminent trombonist Vic Dickenson. As an afterthought, I asked Vic if he could think of a young musician of particular promise who could carry on in the classic jazz tradition. The answer came without the slightest hesitation. "Warren Vaché," said Vic. "He's a fine player already, but he's going to be someone special; you'll see."

At twenty-three years old, Vaché was then just beginning to make his presence felt on the jazz scene. He had joined the house band at Eddie Condon's in New York City, where his frontline partners were Vic and clarinetist Herb Hall; he'd been working in an ill-fated Broadway show, *Doctor Jazz* (it previewed for three months, then closed within four days); he was soon to get a call from Benny Goodman, with whom he worked on and off until last summer; and in 1975, he was chosen to play the demanding role of Bix Beiderbecke in the New York Jazz Repertory Company presentation of the legendary cornetist's music.

Today, with some twenty LPs to his credit (including six as a leader), Vaché is perhaps best known for his long partnership with tenorist Scott Hamilton and his tours and albums with the Concord Super Band named for the label for which he's done most of his recording. Few who've heard Vaché at his best would deny that Vic Dickenson's prediction has come true.

Among those few, on occasion at least, might be Vaché himself. Though a confident and often adventurous player, he is also a perfectionist and his own severest critic. He admits to being "just too painfully aware of where I am when I'm recording. I feel that so intensely when I'm listening to myself on records. I start analyzing myself into a knot. Bobby Hackett was right—listening to your own records is like talking to yourself. I hope to get by that one; it's been a long one for me."

When pressed, however, he'll admit that he's pleased with *Iridescence*, a quartet album that finds him in the company of Hank Jones, George Duvivier, and Alan Dawson. And he was looking forward to the impending release of his first LP with the trio that is his favorite working format—John Bunch on piano and Phil Flanigan on bass. "I really prefer that. I feel the loosest there, and with guys like these I can call pretty near anything. If I want to play 'I Want a Little Girl' one minute and 'Donna Lee' the next, they don't find anything wrong with it. I can have fun with 'The Man I Love' and turn around and play 'Apex Blues' [the Jimmie Noone classic]. It doesn't bother me, but I've been getting the feeling that something is wrong with me because it doesn't."

These remarks, of course, relate to the passion for categorizing music and musicians that has been the bane of jazz for many decades. The climate may be a bit more ecumenical now than in the days of boppers versus moldy figs, or in the turbulent '60s, but the malady lingers on. And it especially affects young jazz players like Vaché who don't fit any preconceived stylistic mold.

"I've been accused of being eclectic and noncommitted," he said, "and maybe I am. But I just have to play what fits—or what *I* think fits. I started to play club dates with a dance band when I was fifteen, reading stock charts. The first jazz band I played with was a bunch of guys who went to a summer band school in New Jersey—trumpet, alto, and a rhythm section. The pianist was Alan Pasqua, who later went to Indiana University, and then with Kenton. We were the Atlantic Jazz Quintet.

"Then I worked everything from Your Father's Mustache to Polish weddings and Easter sunrise services . . . I just always figured it was better to be playing and making money than to be doing something else and making money. I always wanted to be a jazz musician, but I didn't always get to play jazz. And when I started to play jazz, it was with Dixieland bands like those led by Chuck Slate and Red Balaban. And when you do that—it always amazes me—everyone automatically says, 'Oh, *that's* what he does.' Then, when you do something else, the ones who said that turn their backs on you and get very affronted because you've departed from their particular cross-bearing session, and the people at the other end of the spectrum all look at you and say, 'Hell, in another couple of years, maybe.' Look, I'm right here now, and this is what I can do, and it doesn't fit here and doesn't fit there, but this is what I do."

. . .

Rahway, New Jersey, where Vaché was born and raised and still makes his home with his wife, Jill, and infant son, Christopher, may not be everyone's idea of a jazz mecca. But Warren grew up with jazz all around him. "I never remember thinking about being anything else but a musician—maybe a cowboy," he said with a smile. His father, Warren Sr., is a sales representative for a musical instrument company and a self-taught jazz bassist. (He is also one of the prime movers in the New Jersey Jazz Society and editor of its monthly magazine.)

"Dad had a marvelous record collection, and when I was a kid, he used to take a tape recorder with him on gigs, so on Saturday mornings I'd wake up to the sounds of the date he'd played the night before. The grown-ups who came to our house were musicians or interested in music, and like all kids, my brother and I wanted to be part of their conversation." [Warren's youngest brother, Alan, a clarinetist, makes his home in San Antonio, Texas, as a key member of the successful Happy Jazz Band.]

"Sometime around third grade, Dad started me on piano lessons. That went well until a year or so later, when they started a band in school and I came home and said I wanted to be in it—on the bass, I thought, since there was one in the house. But Dad said no, be a trumpet player. There's more work, and you don't want to be in the rhythm section—nobody ever tells you what key the song is in. He got me a horn and a teacher."

That teacher was Jim Fitzpatrick, who'd been with Hal Kemp and other name bands of the '30s, and was a tough taskmaster. Others followed, but the man whom Warren credits with keeping him in college, and much more than that, is the late trumpeter Pee Wee Erwin. "I was going to Montclair State College, and while the instruction was fine, it wasn't always my cup of tea. I expressed a great deal of dissatisfaction to Dad, who had just discovered the Erwin-Griffin School of Music in Teaneck, New Jersey [Griffin is Chris Griffin, like Erwin a veteran of the big bands and New York studios]. He mentioned he had a kid who played trumpet, and Pee Wee, being Pee Wee, said he'd like to meet me, and it blossomed from there. He was exactly the right guy, and it was just the way to get me out of feeling the pressure from school. Pee Wee showed me a hell of a lot and kept me involved and interested in the music and kept me in school. I thank him for it—not that I think I'll ever have to use that degree, but it's nice to know that it's there.

"I'd go to see Pee Wee about three or four times a week. I'd mind the store for him, and then we'd play, and he started me on some French etudes that were real ballbusters. I'd fumble all over the damn things, and he'd be very kind and say, 'No, no, no . . . you've got to do this and that, let me give you the idea.' So he'd put his cigarette down and cough about nine times— he had emphysema, and much worse than we thought then—and tell me that he hadn't got his reading glasses fixed yet and how he'd have to try to play from memory. And then he'd rattle the S.O.B. off as pretty as you'd ever want to hear it played.

"He was one hell of a trumpet player—very underrated. There was nothing about the horn he didn't know or couldn't do. Even with that emphysema, he could play sixteen bars without breathing, and had tremendous flexibility and control. And he had an ancient Besson horn with patches all over it! I lent him my new Benge cornet, and after that, every time I'd walk in on a gig of his, he'd say, 'Oh, you want your horn back!' He was a beautiful guy. I hope I can get through life and take everything I get and come out of it as positive an influence on people as he was. He had a lot of tragedy in his life, but came out without the slightest edge of bitterness."

Once Warren had started on the trumpet, he began to listen to his father's records in a new way. "I got to love Louis [Armstrong] and Bobby [Hackett] and Roy [Eldridge]—of all the records, theirs intrigued me the most. There was a Bobby Hackett quartet record, with Dave McKenna [the pianist was to become Warren's teammate in the Concord Super Band], that had a thing on it called 'Stereoso,' and I'd play along with that. A bit later I got to like Cootie Williams, and the Condon stuff—I loved Wild Bill Davison and Billy Butterfield. I didn't go much to live jazz things until later, when Dad had started to work with Chuck Slate's band and I'd go up on weekends and sit in for a tune or two."

Then came the club-date bands and the jazz quintet, and the first musical disputes with his father. "I started to bring home Miles Davis records—at fifteen and sixteen I was very into Miles—and Art Blakey, Stan Getz, things like that, and we had arguments. He just didn't want to hear any kind of modern jazz at all. I also liked Clifford Brown and Fats Navarro. Clifford's sound was marvelous; he was so damn *clean.* But for me, Fats was a little more exciting. They're both monster musicians. I had a lot of respect for Dizzy, but he never landed on me."

Despite the disputes with his father, Warren feels he was fortunate to be far removed from the jazz battles of the time, which in retrospect make no sense to him at all. "I don't think I could have handled it," he said. "What vestiges are left of it make me nervous. For Christ's sake, it's music! So a man plays differently from the way you do—what's the difference? What is it you've got to defend? Why all the defensiveness?"

His first experience in the "big time," the *Doctor Jazz* show, did nothing to change his outlook. "It was a beautiful job—one hell of a good band. Luther Henderson and Dick Hyman wrote the charts; Sy Oliver was involved, Bob Stewart, Danny Moore—fine player—and there was a warm feeling in that orchestra pit. We all liked each other."

What he calls his "Bix for a day" experience was also memorable. "I got to meet and play with Joe Venuti, Bill Rank, Chauncey Moorehouse, Spiegel Wilcox . . . all gone now except Spiegel, who's still going like a house on fire. Being involved with all that living history was a real thrill." He also learned that not all involved agreed with the concept of re-creating fifty-year-old solos, especially their own. Trombonist Rank requested not to play a solo that he claimed never to have liked.

Next among living legends in Warren's working life came the King of Swing, Benny Goodman. "I was awed in the beginning, and I'm not blasé about it yet," he said. "I don't agree with lots of things he does, and I certainly don't ever want to act that way, but nobody's ever played like that, and he can still play his ass off. He can also be very funny.

"He has a sense of humor about everything but money. Through the years I worked with him, there were some fantastically good nights, but most of the time it was just a waste of a damn good band. You learn to think on your feet with him, though. He may start to noodle between tunes and come out playing some song you've played all your life, like 'Runnin' Wild,' except that where he's been noodling is not where you're used to it on that tune. He'll come out playing 'Runnin' Wild' in E. Wherever he happens to be at the time, that's where you'll play it."

Warren recalled that on his first job with Goodman he was "so nervous I could hardly talk. But Hank Jones was the nicest cat in the world and took the time to show me things." Finding support from older musicians has, with a very few exceptions, been Warren's experience, and he can't comprehend "the attitude that some young guys have—that here's an old guy, and I'm what's happening now. When I'm going to work with Vic Dickenson, well, here's a man who's been playing the trombone much longer than I've been alive—he's seen more situations and gotten himself successfully out of more stuff than I'll ever see in my life—and I'm going to tell *him* what's right and what's wrong?

"Vic is terrible for busting trumpet players, you know, because he's got an idea that everybody should phrase the same way, and Vic's idea of phrasing is flawless, and if you start to get too fancy with the melody and too pyrotechnical, Vic will turn around and point the trombone at your ear and play the melody to you. There are guys who get very upset by that, and I'll admit that it sort of affronted me the first couple of times. But then it occurred to me: hey, dummy, when it's your turn to solo, he leaves you alone—you can stand on your head if you want to, he doesn't mind—but you're playing with a *band*, so let's all get together.

"So I learned a hell of a lot about how to pace yourself through an evening, how to make music without trying too hard, how to let the music happen. And yes, let's find out how to make a melody say what it's supposed to! It's incredibly difficult for me just to play a melody. It's hard for most people, I think. I always get involved in something that takes me away from it. Vic, or Benny, can play just straight melody for a chorus and make it swing, make it sing, and make it mean something. Just play the melody—that's taste, that's intelligence, and that's art—a hard thing to do.

"And Vic knows such great songs, from all over. He'll play 'Gigi,' or he'll play the theme from *Spiderman*. And he has fun on the job. Guys like that are worth admiring. Hackett and Vic and McKenna—those are guys who've figured out how to put their personality and their musicality together, and get comfortable with it. That's the trick."

Sound also has a great deal to do with putting this kind of personal message across, and Warren is very conscious of sound. He has not played trumpet for some years now, preferring the cornet and the fluegelhorn. "The cornet, for the stuff I do, is a much more comfortable instrument. When you try to play soft on the trumpet, it always tends to get very brittle and airy. Soften down on cornet, and you still get a sound with some kind of fatness to it. It's just friendlier for a small-band kind of thing, and if I cheat a little and pull out the tuning slide, I can always make it a bit brighter if needed. The idea is to sound like yourself all the time, and I prefer the feeling of the cornet.

"The fluegelhorn is a marvelous instrument, but it's so frail. It takes a lot of care to get the sound I want. I might be playing it exclusively if I could figure out how Freddie Hubbard or Clark Terry get it to sound just right all the time. It's a little like walking on eggshells when you play it. But on the cornet, I can try something and be ninety-nine percent positive that it'll come out. Those are the pitfalls of doubling. . . ."

Whatever musical situation Warren may find himself in, he said, he "always just tries to play *with* the band. I have the greatest admiration for players who intuitively know not what *should* happen next, but can think on their feet enough to *make* something happen next. Ruby Braff—there's another underrated musician—is one guy who can really do that, and make everybody on the stand with him play their best. But I'm afraid that's going out. I find very few guys my age who really know how to work with the band. They may be great soloists and may be able to play a thousand notes a minute, and they know every chord change to 'Donna Lee' and every permutation thereof, and they can play in fourteen modes, but when it comes to playing with a band, they either don't know or don't care about making the band sound like a unit."

One reason, Warren suspects, is that "today, instead of bands, we've got schools." He has nothing against jazz education per se, but feels that it is often lacking in the emotional perspective that he himself has found to be supremely important.

"Charlie Parker was a genius, I agree. I love the way he played. So was Louis Armstrong. I guess from the intellectual aspect, you can focus on Parker because he came out of Louis and you should be able to get Louis's harmonic theory through Parker. But all of that just doesn't compute by looking at chord changes. There's another flavor and emotionalism that is present in the one and not present in the other. It works both ways. There's a different aspect of the human personality in each essence, and for me the idea would be to assimilate both of them. Each strikes some sort of emotional chord in my ears. So the idea for me would be to study and go through life and come out with some sort of synthesis.

"It's not going to happen overnight. God knows I wasn't born with the gift of doing it. I've got to work at it—that's what it is about."

Warren said his friend Scott Hamilton often chides him for being overly analytical and "looking over his own shoulder." He admits to all of that, but points out that he is also a firm believer in spontaneity, in taking risks even "if it doesn't always come off great. Looseness and blind faith that something will happen—you don't have to be worrying the music to death every day. That's one part of the music I fell in love with, and one of the reasons why I love to play jazz."

It speaks well for jazz, that music of continuing surprises, that it is still capable of producing unclassifiable players like Warren Vaché, who find new and personal ways of using aspects of the jazz tradition that others may have overlooked or neglected, or never been exposed to. Eclectic he may be (and that's no sin, by the way), but uncommitted he most certainly is not. He's got his own story to tell, and one looks forward to its further unfolding. Thus far, it's been getting better with each new chapter.

(1983)

LINER NOTES

Ma Rainey

The origins of the blues are shrouded in obscurity, and we know nothing of the men and women whose transmutation of life experience into words and music gradually took the particular shape and form we call blues.

But we know that Ma Rainey's right to the title "Mother of the Blues," under which she was billed on stage and records, was not challenged, though hers was a time when others who might have laid claim to it were still around. The very least it might be modified to is "Mother of the Professional Blues Singers." There can be no doubt that she was that.

Gertrude Malissa Pridgett was born in Columbus, Georgia, on April 26, 1886. Her parents had been in show business. According to her brother, Thomas Pridgett, Jr., in a 1940 letter to *Jazz Information*, America's first serious jazz magazine (it had a youngster named Ralph J. Gleason on its masthead), her talent as a singer was "very noticeable at an early age." She made her first public appearance at age twelve, in what Pridgett describes as "a school show that was gotten up among the local talent."

Six years later, Gertrude Pridgett married William "Pa" Rainey, a dancer, comedian, and sometime singer some years her senior. He was prominently featured with the Rabbit Foot Minstrels, one of the most popular traveling shows in the South. The newlyweds became an act, and since he was Pa, Gertrude, at eighteen, became Ma Rainey. (The sobriquet, premature though it may seem, apparently did not strike the public as incongruous. Gertrude was no glamour girl.)

Today, the term "minstrel show" conjures up all sorts of negative imagery, but it must be understood that black minstrelsy was something on a quite different order from Mr. Bones routines and a black-faced Al Jolson singing "Mammy." In the words of the pioneering and perceptive jazz historian Charles Edward Smith, "Negro minstrels not only preceded their white imitators, but outlasted them." Traveling shows such as the Rabbit Foot troupe included dance, song, and comedy *by* and *for* black audiences in the Deep South. The entertainment was direct and basic but certainly not without professionalism and polish, and the relationship between performers and audience was of a very special nature.

When Ma Rainey got her professional start, the blues were not as yet part of minstrelsy, but a rural folk music. When she was interviewed near the end of her career by the noted musicologist John Wesley Work, Jr. (who was following in his father's footsteps as collector and annotator of black American song; both Works taught at Fisk University), she told him that she first heard the blues in a small town in Missouri, where she was appearing with a tent show.

"She tells of a girl from the town," Work writes in his *American Negro Songs* (published in 1940), "who came to the tent one morning and began to sing about the 'man' who had left her. The song was so strange and poignant that it attracted much attention. Ma Rainey became so interested that she learned the song from the visitor and used it soon afterward as an encore in her act. The song elicited such response from the audience that it found a special place in her act. Many times she was asked what kind of song it was, and one day she replied, in a moment of inspiration, 'It's the blues.'"

The singer told Work that a fire had destroyed some 1905 newspaper clippings that mentioned her singing of these strange songs. She added, however, "that after she began to sing the blues, although they were not so named then, she frequently heard similar songs in the course of her travels."

Work, who spoke with Ma at the Douglass Hotel in Nashville after having attended her performance, describes her as "an interesting woman, with a picturesque stage appearance, a deep contralto voice, and an authentic manner of singing the blues." He does not mention, in his serious and scholarly work, that he was accompanied by a friend, the poet and literary scholar Sterling Brown, then also on the Fisk faculty.

Brown, interviewed years later by the British blues expert Paul Oliver, brought out different details. He had heard both Bessie Smith and Ma perform, and felt that, while "Bessie was the greater blues singer . . . Ma really *knew* her people. She was a person of the folk; she was very simple and direct. The night we saw her she was having boy trouble. You see, she liked these young musicians, and in come John Work and I—we were young to her." (Both men were born in 1901; the encounter probably took place in the early '30s.)

"We were something sent down, and she didn't know which one to choose. Each of us knew we were not choosing her; we just wanted to talk. But she was interested in other things. She was that direct. . . . She was the tops for my money. She would moan, and the audience would moan with her. She had them in the palm of her hand."

Brown commemorated Rainey in a moving poem included in his first collection, *Southern Road*, published in 1932. It tells of the special way in which she reached and ruled her audience. There are only two references to her physical appearance: "gold-toothed smiles" and "little and low."

Champion Jack Dupree, the blues singer and pianist, is blunt in his description of Ma: "She was really an ugly woman . . . but when she opened her mouth, that was it. You forgot everything. She knew how to sing those blues and she got right into your heart. What a personality she had!"

Jazz and blues history, fixed on theories of succession (Buddy Bolden begat King Oliver who begat Louis who begat Roy Eldridge who begat Dizzy who begat Miles, and so forth), would have it that Bessie Smith, greatest of all blues singers and nine years younger, was discovered and tutored by Ma Rainey. Long accepted as gospel, this claim was eventually questioned by serious researchers and found impossible to substantiate. Bessie biographer Chris Albertson found no proof that the two ever worked together but, on evidence given by his primary source, Ruby Walker (alias Ruby Smith, Bessie's adopted niece), writes that they knew each other well and were friends.

Others who've investigated the matter think the two great ladies did work in the same show somewhere early along the line. Paul Oliver votes for the Rabbit Foot Minstrels; Charles Edward Smith for Tolliver's Circus and Musical Extravaganza, with which the Raineys appeared from 1914 to 1916, billed as "Rainey and Rainey, Assassinators of the Blues." Whatever the historical truth, the artistic truth is that Bessie (and all others who followed in time) learned her art and craft from Ma, directly or indirectly. What today is called "classic" blues style came into being when young Gertrude Rainey, impressed and moved by her first encounter with country blues, made this "folk" music part of her more sophisticated, professional performance routine. It takes no more than objective listening to their recordings to verify that Ma Rainey influenced—even shaped—the art of Bessie Smith. (There is some evidence that they did work together briefly near the end of Ma's career, in an early '30s stock show in Fort Worth.)

Almost all who heard and saw both the Mother and the Empress of the Blues concur with Sterling Brown: Bessie was the greater singer, Ma the greater performer. Perhaps she had to be: photographs show a kind, even a sweet, face—far from Jack Dupree's "ugly" but certainly not pretty. With her gold-lined teeth, unruly hair, and short, squat body, she was no match for Bessie's ripe beauty.

But she used what she had with a sure sense for the theatrically effective. Her gowns were of extravagant material; she wore necklaces made of gold pieces and genuine diamonds. An inevitable headband, feather boas and plumes, long earrings, tiaras, etc., rounded out an extraordinary getup.

This, of course, was at a stage in Ma's career when she had long left Pa behind and had become a single attraction, heading her own show if not starring in someone else's, but always at the top of the bill. In her publicity, she was now "Madame" Rainey, not Ma—the only blues "artiste" to be granted this honorific title, according to an advertisement by the company for which she made all her ninety-odd recorded sides, Paramount Records of Grafton, Wisconsin.

She made her first record in December 1923, when she was thirty-seven, and her last exactly five years later. Paramount was a subsidiary of a furniture company that had discovered that its phonographs sold better when records were given away with a purchase, and thus decided to manufacture the discs. Its chief talent scout and recording director was an aggressive young black man named J. Mayo Williams; his nickname among performers soon became "Ink," because he was always ready to sign any promising talent he encountered. Williams was responsible for making Paramount the leading "race" label, until the big companies got into the act, and brought to it such artists as Blind Lemon Jefferson, Ida Cox, Lovie Austin, Blind Blake, and many others.

Through recordings, widely sold through mail-order catalogs, the voices and personas of Ma Rainey and other great performers of the '20s penetrated to the farthest corners of the rural South, and when the artists played in one of the cities, big or small, on the TOBA circuit (the initials stood for Theater Owners Booking Association but were transformed by the performers into Tough On Black Asses), people came from miles and miles around. Ma, because of her country roots, had perhaps the broadest appeal of them all.

What could happen, even in a big northern city, when she was really "on" has been described by her longtime accompanist and musical director, Thomas A. Dorsey. Composer of "Precious Lord, Take My Hand" and some four hundred other religious songs, he also wrote "It's Tight Like That" (and scores of other blues and good-time songs) and recorded as "Georgia Tom." He was introduced to Ma by Ink Williams. "[He] took me over to her apartment in the old Angelus Building at the corner of Thirty-fifth and Wabash. . . . She was grand, gracious, and easy to talk with."

The first performance Dorsey directed was at a Chicago theater. "Ma had the audience in the palm of her hand. Her diamonds flashed like sparks of fire falling from her fingers. The gold-piece necklace lay like a golden armor covering her chest." Dorsey noted that, at Ma's entrance at the end of a long evening, it was as if the show had started all over again. "When Ma had sung her last number and the grand finale, we took seven calls. . . ."

Though Ma apparently maintained a well-appointed apartment in Chicago, and could elicit seven curtain calls from a demanding audience there, historians tell us that her reception in the North was less enthusiastic than down South. Some sources claim she never played New York, but trumpeter Hot Lips Page recalled in an interview that he first visited New York with Ma, playing the Lincoln Theater.

Up North Ma's act could perhaps seem a bit strange, as it did to teenaged Mary Lou Williams in Pittsburgh: "The fabulous Ma Rainey came into a little theater on Wiley Avenue. Some of the older kids and I slipped downtown to hear the woman who'd made blues history. Ma was loaded with real diamonds; . . . her hair was wild and she had gold teeth. What a sight! To me, as a kid, the whole thing looked and sounded weird."

Such gaps might have been regional as well as generational. In any event, Ma Rainey (whose act at one time opened with her emerging from a giant Victrola) stopped recording well before the Depression put a halt to the "race" record business. Paramount, which in the spring of 1924 had run a promotion featuring the famous Ma Rainey "Mystery Record" with her picture on the label and $14,000 in prizes for naming the song, dropped her from its roster less than five years later. A Paramount executive, when questioned about this by Charles Edward Smith in the '50s, simply said that "her down-home material had gone out of fashion."

She continued to draw in theaters and tents, though, until the Depression caught up with this form of entertainment as well. In 1930, her own show, *Arkansas Swift Foot*, collapsed on the road, and she joined Boise DeLegge's *Bandana Babies*. She carried on, undaunted, for three more years. But in 1933, her mother and sister died in quick succession. (The married name of that sister—Nix—is, incidentally, still given as one of Ma's middle names in many reference sources, though the error was pointed out by C. E. Smith some years ago.) She then decided to come home to keep house for her brother. Like Bessie, she was family-minded. Years before, according to the brother, she had "purchased a beautiful home for her family in Columbus." Unlike Bessie, she was a good businesswoman. She owned, and after her retirement from the road also operated, two theaters in Rome, Georgia: the Lyric and the Airdome. Her final years were spent quietly in Columbus, a town which, when I was stationed at nearby Fort Benning, called itself "the South's most progressive city." She joined the Congregation of Friendship Baptist Church, where her brother was a deacon. Ma died on December 22, 1939, in her fifty-fourth year, and is buried in Portersdale Cemetery in Columbus.

The thirty-two songs by Ma Rainey collated here include her finest work on record. Some commentators have emphasized the heavy, "tragic" quality of her voice, but she had humor and vitality, too—and not just the broad kind exemplified by "Ma Rainey's Black Bottom."

The accompaniments often, if not always, do her justice. There is young Louis Armstrong, the incomparable. There are the sweet-toned cornet of Joe Smith and the gruff trombone of Charlie Green—two of Bessie's favorite accompanists. There is the Chicago piano of Jimmy Blythe. These are jazzmen of note. But some of the most striking and apt backing comes from what was billed as her Tub Jug Washboard Band, and from just Georgia Tom's piano and Tampa Red's guitar—blues and "hokum" stuff. And fittingly so, for of all the great classic blues singers, Ma Rainey was closest to country roots. In 1929, perhaps, "her down-home material had gone out of fashion" for the moment, but it can never really go out of style.

There are many lovely things on this album—the stately time and tempo on "See See Rider," with Louis's beautiful responses; the very Bessie-like belting on "Prove It on Me"; the country atmosphere of "Sleep Talking"; the really *down* feeling of "Blame It on the Blues"; the message of "Sweet Rough Man" that Billie Holiday would have dug. But she comes through most clearly to me on "New Boweavil Blues" (an electric remake of her very first recording), especially in the stop-time passage that says:

> Lord I went downtown
> And bought me a hat
> I brought it back home
> And laid it on the shelf
> Looked at my bed
> I'm tired of sleepin' by myself. . . .

Ma Rainey, you're *beautiful*, no matter what they say!

(1974)

Benny Goodman and Jack Teagarden

The first thing that strikes a listener about this music is how grace-fully it carries its age. It is fresh and joyful; a pleasure to hear. And why shouldn't it be? After all, it was made by young musicians (on the earliest of these sessions, Benny Goodman is only nineteen, tenorist Babe Russin a mere seventeen, Gene Krupa just twenty, leader Red Nichols all of twenty-three, and none of the bandsmen yet thirty) filled with a spirit of discovery.

A handful of these youngsters (the Rollini brothers, Russin, Manny Klein) were native New Yorkers, but most of them had come to the big town from all corners of the United States. Then, as now, New York was where you came to test yourself against the best in the performing arts, and these kids were making it.

In fact, a record date such as one of these was a kind of busman's holiday. The bread-and-butter musical fare was dance music (including waltzes and tangos as well as snappy fox-trots and Charlestons) and accompaniment to singers (a breed that included many who knew nothing of jazz phrasing and some who had trouble carrying a tune); live, on the still new but already powerful radio, and in the recording studios. If you were in a successful or-chestra such as Ben Pollack's, you might also be sitting in a Broadway pit band, as indeed our two main protagonists were in the spring of 1929. The show was *Hello Daddy*, with a score by Jimmy McHugh and Dorothy Fields; after the final curtain, Benny and Jack and their colleagues would hustle over to the Park Central Hotel to play for the late-into-the-night dancers of that prosperous pre-Depression era.

Benny Goodman and Jack Teagarden stood out. Extraordinarily gifted instrumentalists fully in touch with the developing language of jazz, they'd come to New York somewhat earlier—Jack in the winter of 1927, Benny some four months later. The trombonist, who'd been barnstorming in the Southwest, came from his native Texas; Benny arrived from his native Chicago as a member of Pollack's fine crew, which Jack joined in the sum-mer of '28.

Both had been early starters. The Teagardens were a musical family, and Leo Weldon (the "Jack" came later) started on piano at five, took up bari-tone horn at eight, and settled on trombone at ten. He played his first pro-fessional engagement when he was thirteen, duetting with his pianist mother at a local movie theater. Born in 1905, he was on the road by 1921;

his brothers Charlie and Clois and his sister Norma all became professional musicians.

David Benjamin Goodman had to wait until he was ten for his first musical instruction, but he caught on quickly. At thirteen, he got his first union card; in 1925, just a few months past his sixteenth birthday, he headed west to California to join Pollack. Benny also had musical siblings; his older brother Harry joined Pollack on bass and tuba, and Irving and Freddie became competent big-band trumpeters in the swing era.

In 1926, a twenty-two-year-old trombonist and budding arranger from Iowa, Glenn Miller, joined Pollack. And in 1928, a bunch of Chicagoans who'd often shared bandstands with Benny came to New York, among them Gene Krupa and Joe Sullivan. Both sets of parents were loath to see them go; they wanted their sons to study for the priesthood. Instead, they helped spread a new musical gospel to the land.

When Krupa and Sullivan (along with the brilliant clarinetist Frank Teschemacher, the already original tenor man Bud Freeman, the erratic but messianic reedman Mezz Mezzrow, and the charismatic banjoist-guitarist Eddie Condon) hit the Big Apple, they shook up the jazz establishment. Led by the brass team of Red Nichols, cornet (from Utah), and Miff Mole, trombone (from Long Island); subsequently joined by a brilliant Italian-American string duo from Philadelphia, Joe Venuti (violin) and Eddie Lang (guitar), the clarinetist Pee Wee Russell (from Missouri), and the brother team of Jimmy and Tommy Dorsey (the sons of an Irish-American coal miner from Scranton, Pennsylvania) and including an earlier Chicago import, the inventive Jewish-American percussionist Vic Berton, they'd been making records—as Red Nichols and his Five Pennies and under other group names—that featured highly sophisticated ensemble playing, intricate harmonic schemes, and brilliant instrumental displays. Why did the young Chicago contingent shake them up?

Because it had a rhythmic drive, swing, that took its cues from the jazz of Chicago's South Side—a much hotter brand of black music than what was then heard in Harlem, or downtown Manhattan, where Fletcher Henderson's "dicty" dance band held forth. To be sure, the King of Jazz himself, Louis Armstrong, had spent a year with Henderson starting in the late fall of 1924, but in part because Henderson kept him under relative wraps, he had no major impact on the city's white musicians. (When Pops came back in 1929, it was quite a different story, but by then he had the Hot Five records behind him.)

It was another trumpeter (or to be exact, cornetist) who had the biggest influence on the New York jazzmen, and of course on the Chicagoans as well: Bix Beiderbecke, born in 1903 in Iowa. Jazz in the '20s was a two-way street: Many black musicians have testified to considerable influence from Bix, his sometime sidekick Frank Trumbauer, and such instrumental virtuosos as Mole, the Dorseys, and Venuti-and-Lang. The Bix we hear on this disc was in the twilight of his career, with just fourteen months left to live, but his lyrical spirit could still dominate a performance.

Red Nichols idolized Bix, but his highly syncopated rhythm and slightly "militaristic" attack (his father was a brass-band leader) could never approximate Bix's cornet poetry. However, we hear on "Indiana" that he could fashion a lively solo statement and that he was a superb executant. Glenn Miller's excellent arrangement propels this performance with riffs and other background devices that presage the big-band vocabulary to come; this holds true for all of Miller's charts heard herein, which means all the Nichols cuts save "On the Alamo." That one, also very good, is by Fred Van Eps, who also wrote for the 1934 Rollini date. Nichols had the good grace to occasionally feature other trumpeters, and it is sixteen-year-old Charlie Teagarden who is heard on "Sheik of Araby" and on "Peg o' My Heart" (opening solo only; Nichols leads the closing ensembles, contrasting his clipped phrasing with young Teagarden's clearly Louis/Bix-inspired relaxation).

Another kid, Babe Russin, acquits himself impressively on these Nichols sides, influenced in seemingly equal parts by Freeman (fast) and Coleman Hawkins (ballads). Russin went on to featured roles in Goodman's and Tommy Dorsey's big bands and a successful Hollywood studio career. Joe Sullivan is marvelous in solo and accompaniment; sadly forgotten today, this was one of the *great* jazz pianists of his generation. Next time you hear Billie Holiday's records of "The Man I Love" or "Night and Day," listen for Joe behind Lady. Krupa (the 1929 Nichols session was his first encounter with Benny on records) has been accused of bashing too much on some of these performances, but to these ears, he's always an uplifting rhythmic presence; like all great jazz drummers, he plays differently behind different soloists. The guitar of Carl Kress (from Newark, New Jersey) is a rhythmic boon on the first session (hear his shuffle beat behind Benny on "Dinah"); he too would go on to many fine things, including a late-in-life partnership with George Barnes. His mentor, Eddie Lang, shines on the date he coleads with Venuti. This guitarist's death at thirty, in 1933 (the victim of a botched operation), was a blow to Venuti, who had to wait some thirty years to regain his place in the jazz sun. (Without Joe, there'd be no Stephane Grappelli.)

Another greatly influential player from this crop was Adrian Rollini, the undisputed master of the bass saxophone, and one of the rhythmically most incisive early jazz soloists. A real prodigy, he gave a Chopin recital at four, in 1908; after piano, he took up xylophone (and after he gave up the bass sax, he became an early jazz specialist on vibraphone). Among Rollini's biggest fans was young Harry Carney—listen to Adrian's tone and phrasing on "Davenport Blues," and you'll hear the reasons why.

On that session, we hear Manny Klein at his jazz best. A brilliant all-around trumpeter, he wound up in the Hollywood studios. Born in 1908, he stopped playing some years ago, but at this writing is still alive and well. His work on this date was long mistaken for Bunny Berigan, which made Manny proud. In a recent interview, he fondly recalled the drummer on this session, Stan King, as having unflappable time and one of the best beats of his day. The opening cut, "It Had to Be You," has never been legitimately issued before; it comes to us in pristine sound thanks at least in part to its having been transferred to tape by John R. T. Davies, one of the masters of sound restoration. Ella Logan sounds nice here; not a jazz singer, she's got better time than some so called; she's Annie Ross's aunt, so the genes were clearly good.

I think some of Benny Goodman's finest jazz playing can be heard on this cross section from his first maturity as a soloist. There isn't a cut here on which he fails to swing, and I love his sound from this period, with the grit still in there when he wants it that way—notably on "China Boy." He digs in on "Dinah." But it's when he allows himself to soar on a melodic number that young Benny really tells a story. Hear "Peg o' My Heart," with its passion; the way he floats his lines on "Sheik," a truly inspired solo (unmentioned, like all of these, by both Gunther Schuller and James L. Collier); the minor groove he hits on "Deep Harlem," and how he could breathe; his lyricism on "Davenport Blues" (this whole splendid performance is an early tribute to its composer, Beiderbecke, just three years after his death); and what might be one of Benny's greatest romantic solos, "Someday Sweetheart." Please forget all that political stuff about the King of Swing; this man was one hell of a jazz clarinet player!

No one disputes Jack Teagarden's place in the trombone pantheon, and hearing him go to work on "Dinah" (the piece that represents Big T in the revised Smithsonian Collection of Classic Jazz) shows why: the wonderful ease and swing of the phrasing, the blues lurking not far beneath the surface of those melodic ideas; the propulsion of the riffs on the bridge, and that incomparable tone. There are several other highlights. The "Sheik," of course (a justly famous record in its day, ignored by historians), with wonderful vocal work as well; and his authentic blues playing and singing on "Beale Street," from a session that in its totality achieves some kind of near-perfection of collective empathy. There's the "Strut Miss Lizzie" solo, analyzed by Schuller in his "The Swing Era" and clearly inspired by the presence of Bix; the way he sings the word "gone" in "After You've Gone"; his slide-and-water-glass special on "Sweet Georgia Brown"; the supreme relaxation of the opening and closing "China Boy" cadenzas (and don't Sullivan and Krupa go together on that one!); the lovely work on "Davenport"; and the complete instrumental and creative command on "Riverboat Shuffle," another Bix tribute.

As for Bix himself, the rare next-to-last session, appearing here in full on an American reissue for the first time, doesn't show him at his best, yet only he could have played those lead and solo passages. The two versions of "Loved One" (known as "I Like That" in an earlier Bix-Trumbauer incarnation) have it solo-wise, and we get an unusual opportunity to hear him play the blues, on the main strain of "Deep Harlem," and with superior time.

Goodman and Teagarden clearly inspired each other, but their collaboration was confined to the period covered here. These selections are highlights among dozens and dozens more, including many with small groups from the Pollack band. Jack sat in on the Goodman band's second Victor Records date, and two Metronome All-Star sessions in 1939 and '40 were somewhat impersonal occasions for reunion. A Teagarden guest shot on a Goodman radio show early in 1941 marks the very last time these two played together. They obviously moved in somewhat different musical directions and on very different levels of public acclaim. Despite continued warm personal feelings, nothing brought them together during the final years before Jack's untimely death in 1964—which would seem to increase the value of their limited joint musical legacy.

Come to this music without the excess baggage of historicity, questionable esthetics, and political correctness that seem to becloud much of our present-day perceptions of jazz, and it will pleasurably reward your open ears.

(1992)

Fats Waller

Thomas "Fats" Waller had been making records for almost a dozen years when, just five days short of his thirtieth birthday, he entered the Victor Studios in Manhattan with five fellow musicians in tow. While he no doubt was pleased that his manager, Phil Ponce, had worked out a contract for him to record in this format on a regular basis, neither Fats himself, Ponce, nor recording supervisor (the title "A&R man" had not yet been invented) Eli Oberstein could have known that they were about to embark on one of the most productive and longest-running enterprises in the annals of recorded popular music.

Henceforth known as "Fats Waller and his Rhythm," the sextet, with a changeable (and sometimes augmented) cast, made hundreds of records during the next eight years, many of them substantial hits, catapulting its hefty leader to international fame. But that gets us ahead of the story—the material included in this set did well enough in the marketplace to warrant further activity, but did not yet include any major best sellers.

Not that Fats Waller was an unknown entity when the Rhythm series began. He was certainly no stranger to Victor Records, having already produced a number of piano and pipe-organ solos for the label, as well as several ad hoc band dates. His activities for other labels included a wide variety of settings: accompanying blues, pop, and gospel singers and groups; sitting in for the leader with Fletcher Henderson's band; sharing keyboard duties with his friend and mentor James P. Johnson on several occasions; and participating in some of the earliest racially integrated recording sessions, among them a guest shot with Ted Lewis on which he sang as well as played. But his singing—so significant to his eventual success as a recording artist—had not been well featured; aside from the Lewis items, a little-known single for Columbia (issued in 1931, when the record business had hit Depression bottom) and some banter on an obscure Jack Teagarden date were about all.

Fats had of course already established himself as a songwriter, although he'd relinquished his copyrights to some of his biggest successes, such as "Ain't Misbehavin'" and "Black and Blue," for a song, so to speak. Melodies poured from him with such ease that he didn't take the business seriously; it is said that he turned nine instrumental pieces over to Fletcher Henderson for some hamburgers, number not specified. (Fats's capacity for eating was almost as legendary as his consumption of alcoholic beverages, but it is still certain that Fletcher got himself a bargain.) There is also a long list of famous songs credited to others that supposedly originated with Fats. Many of his best songs came from scores to shows—some that made it to Broadway, like *Hot Chocolates* and *Keep Shufflin'*, and others that just ran for a week at Harlem's Lafayette or Lincoln theaters.

The big man was also known from coast-to-coast as a theater organist— the movie palaces boasted king-sized Wurlitzers, and Fats could massage these monsters into swing like nobody else. Also, he had occasionally been seen on stage, for example as a member (with Edith Wilson and Louis Armstrong) of a trio billed as A Thousand Pounds of Rhythm in *Hot Chocolates*. And from the pit in *Keep Shufflin'*, he and James P. stopped the show nightly with their duets.

It was on the radio, however, that Fats found his first real fame. Younger than the phonograph as a medium for the dissemination of music, radio was still in its infancy in 1924, when Fats first performed over station WHN in New York. By 1930, he was heard three times weekly on WABC, then CBS's New York flagship station. Originally scheduled for fifteen minutes at noon and as a thirteen-week series, his show was expanded to a half-hour format after four weeks, and extended for an additional thirteen weeks. (It is said that Fats had come to the personal attention of William S. Paley, head of CBS, possibly at a party at George Gershwin's home.) In the fall of 1932 (after a short visit to Europe—his first), he repaired to Cincinnati, where his manager had gotten him a contract with WLW, a clear-channel station reaching listeners far beyond the confines of Ohio. Known as "Fats Waller's Rhythm Club," the prime-time Saturday night show was an instant success. He also broadcast during the week on a sister station, WSAI, and played a romantic organ program, *Moon River*, on WLW. In addition, he toured frequently while in Cincinnati, fronting local big bands.

It was when Fats returned to New York early in 1934 that manager Ponce went to work securing the Victor contract. Meanwhile, Fats guested on several famous radio shows, such as Morton Downey's, and in April had his own morning show back on WABC. It was on radio that Fats established his singing as an integral part of his public persona.

When the time came to plan for the first Rhythm date, Fats proceeded with characteristic panache, apparently waiting until just a few days before the session to round up a likely bunch of players. Having been away from New York for quite a while, he had lost touch with the local jazz scene. The only musician he definitely had in mind was a nineteen-year-old guitarist named Al Casey, who had been babysitting for Fats's sons and was the nephew of members of the Southern Suns, a vocal group that had appeared on Fats's WLW show. Finally, he visited Small's Paradise, where Charlie Johnson's band was in residence, to scout out some likely prospects.

The rest of the initial cast came from Small's. Trumpeter Herman Autrey recalled that Waller spotted him doing something unusual during a set break: he had remained on the bandstand to check out his section mates' parts on some new arrangements, moving from chair to chair and humming the parts to himself. This diligence seemed to impress Fats. He also liked the bass work of Billy Taylor, and no wonder. Soon to join Duke Ellington, this was one of the best of the pre-Blanton bassists. Drummer Harry Dial, who was playing in a show at Small's, had been with Louis Armstrong, among others, and was a good reader—a rarity among the era's percussionists. The reedman, Ben Whitted, is the least known of the batch, and, according to Autrey, the eldest. He was the lead alto and clarinet of the Johnson band, had recorded with Clarence Williams and Eubie Blake, and according to the trumpeter, was terribly nearsighted and wore such thick glasses that he "looked like Cyclops."

This cast was rounded up by Waller's friend Bud Allen and gathered at Waller's apartment. According to Dial's autobiography, this was the only rehearsal during his entire tenure with the Rhythm. But Autrey, in a 1975 interview, could not recall any rehearsal at all. Since the record date was his first, one imagines he would have remembered, and he does recall coming to Fats's apartment a few days before the session. It's most likely that Fats just wanted to talk things through with the men and acquaint himself with them, and that no actual rehearsing took place. And thus the stage was set for a most auspicious debut.

THE RECORDING SESSIONS
MAY 16, 1934

I don't think it's a coincidence that Fats began his Rhythm series with a song by his main man, James P. Johnson, and his own closest lyric collaborator, Andy Razaf. "Porter's Love Song" has an attractive melody (quite similar to "Allah's Holiday") and cute lyrics if the listener can put political correctness aside. The methodology for the Rhythm is in place from the start. Fats was phonogenic; like his good friend Louis Armstrong, he was at home in a studio and uninhibited by a microphone. And like Louis, he came across on a record. Moreover, he had a masterful sense of time and timing, and seemed to know exactly how to proportion a three-minute performance, rationing out solos, vocals, and ensembles judiciously. As for his exhortations, exclamations, and asides, he may have taken his cues not only from Armstrong, but also from another performer who'd been making successful records since 1930, Cab Calloway.

Autrey gives us some insight into Fats's routine: "He'd play something . . . he'd say, 'All right, Herman—you come in and do this, play the first sixteen, or the second eight, and Gene [Sedric], you come in and do this and that, we'll try that.' We try it, and ah, pretty good! We do it again, and the engineer says that's pretty good, give us another one. . . . No, we didn't know what numbers we were going to do. They come up and hand them out to Fats. He turns and puts the music on the piano—first time he's seen it—and then he passes out a lead sheet to each one of us, or chords, maybe, and sometimes parts from a stock arrangement. With those—ah, sometimes Fats would hit the ceiling when we started to run through them. 'No! Why did they do that? Bring me that bass part. That's lousy!!' Then he'd change the notes, and it would be beautiful because we had the right notes, the right chords. And he knew. Believe me when I say he knew. He wasn't guessing, he knew!!"

The four tunes on this first session are above average—some of the material music publishers made Fats (and many other recording artists—there was no discrimination when it came to trash) accept was actually fit only for buffoonery, at which, quite fortunately, he proved to be a master. And he certainly could perform feats of alchemy when he wanted to, as with the opening piano chorus of "Do Me a Favor," the weakest in this quartet. All four demonstrate Fats's mastery at setting tempos, a talent rarer than you might think. Whitted is a bit of a problem; clearly he can't improvise. But Fats makes the most of what he has to work with. Autrey, by his own admission nervous on his first date, already demonstrates one of his main strengths, the variety of sounds at his disposal. Thus we get fan-hat business on "Porter's" and "Twins," Harmon mute on "Sweetness," and of course a good open horn tone. Not a technical wizard, Herman had lots of feeling, good time, and willingness to play his part in creating musical textures and theatrics. Young Casey shows his ability with a chorded 16-bar solo on "Favor"; also hear him behind the vocal—like Autrey, he could accompany well. Taylor is fine throughout and Dial is steady. The blueprint is there. Now we need the fine-tuning.

AUGUST 17, 1934

Dial claims Gene "Honeybear" Sedric was his discovery in response to Fats's request for a different reedman. Whoever came up with Sedric should take a bow. Little known at the time because he'd spent more than six years in Europe with Sam Wooding's bands, he was a perfect pick for the Rhythm. Equally adept on clarinet and tenor, and his own man on both, he had a style on the bigger horn that owed nothing to Coleman Hawkins. Born in St. Louis in 1907, he'd been a pro since age fifteen. Unlike the boisterous and extroverted Autrey, "Honeybear" was personally gentle and reserved, but not on his horns. His presence raises the Rhythm's rating considerably, and he would remain to the end.

This session also features pretty good numbers. "Georgia May" is by Razaf with his new partner, Englishman Paul Denniker—a nice gesture by Fats, whose "Yes, well all right then" tag is the first of many. "Then I'll Be Tired of You" is by Yip Harburg and Arthur Schwartz and starts with a fairly straight but swinging Waller vocal followed by some flowery piano and some Louis-like Autrey horn. "Don't Let It Bother You" is set up by Waller-Dial patter of the sort one could have heard at a Harlem theater, a witty vocal, some fine Sedric tenor and a full chorus of Waller stride. "Have a Little Dream" opens with piano and prominent Taylor bass, and offers a supple rhythmic vocal (Fats had terrific diction), some Autrey growling (he was good at this), and Fats phrasing his last eight vocally like a horn. Nice stuff!

SEPTEMBER 28, 1934

An early departure from the norm, with a third horn and a guest reedman. This is one of my favorite Rhythm sessions, with Fats in tremendous form, varied and superior material, and a fine balance between spontaneity and planning. The presence of two white players, Mezz Mezzrow and his

Chicago sidekick, trombonist Floyd O'Brien, continues Fats's penchant for integrated studio gatherings.

Things get off to a rousing start with a "progressive" composition by the interesting British composer-arranger-pianist Reginald Foresythe. The son of a West African lawyer and a German mother, he spent considerable time in the U.S., working in Hollywood and arranging and composing for Earl Hines ("Deep Forrest") and Louis Armstrong ("Mississippi Basin") and being commissioned by Paul Whiteman. "Serenade for a Wealthy Widow" was his most widely recorded piece, and it's in good hands with Fats. "Woman," he declaims, "they tell me you're flooded with currency!" His piano solo pays off, and then O'Brien (a master of the plunger) trades fours with Autrey. The riff that follows is the composer's. "How Can You Face Me" is the first Waller composition done by the Rhythm, and a good one. A great vocal with fine Autrey and Casey backing, during which Fats takes liberties with Razaf's lyric (nothing was sacred with this band), leading to piano in the most relaxed Waller manner—he could swing at any tempo. O'Brien gets funky and Waller responds with "Get out in the street, you dirty dog!" Mezz's bridge isn't half bad. "Sweetie Pie," a 1926 number that has lent itself to improvisation for many years (Stan Getz liked it), starts with another gem of a piano solo, replete with bell tones and other decorative devices. Big as he was, Fats had a delicate touch, and even when he dug in, he never pounded. Mezz is at his best here; maligned by some, overpraised by others, he was a limited but honest player and had a story to tell. "Mandy," a vintage Irving Berlin tune, had just been revived in an Eddie Cantor movie, *Kid Millions*. It seemed made to order for Fats. After Autrey, in peak form, manipulates his plunger, Fats uncorks a vocal including a chorus of scat in his own style and knocks himself out during the piano solo. "Oh, this ticklin' is so terrific," he shouts. And it is!

The mood changes for "Let's Pretend There Is a Moon," a typical period ballad, with Fats crooning in his best romantic style—just this side of satire. The piano solo is a classic, full of Wallerian devices and a joy to the ear. He comps sublimely for Autrey's tightly muted solo, and O'Brien takes a solid bridge. A great session finishes with "You're Not the Only Oyster in the Stew," a sophisticated song that Waller thoroughly enjoys singing and playing. Some unusual (for him) blues touches in the opening eight are repeated in the solo that follows the vocal. And hear that ending—so natural and musical!

NOVEMBER 7, 1934

Another new face: Bill Coleman. According to Dial, he recruited the horn man when Autrey couldn't get out of a commitment. According to the substitute himself (in his charming memoir, *Trumpeter's Tale*), it was Billy Taylor who brought him on board. Already a fully formed stylist who had been with a number of leading bands, he was, at the time, with Teddy Hill (where Roy Eldridge was his section mate). His distinctive sound was light and without vibrato, and his phrasing was elegant and rhythmically unpredictable, though solidly grounded in Armstrong. With Sedric back in the fold, we have a most compatible front line, and the rhythm section responds to Coleman's finesse. A relaxed session results. "Honeysuckle Rose" was a standard by 1934, but this was the composer's first recording of it. His piano is to the fore, but don't miss the laid-back vocal. The horns do the famous Henderson (or is it Hopkins?) riff, and then Fats comes up with a fascinating piano bridge. "Believe It, Beloved," a pleasant little tune, has a happy vocal and a splendid full-chorus Coleman solo (unlike Autrey, he plays open horn throughout) with that characteristic skipping beat. "Dream Man" is a masterpiece, blending sublime music (Fats's arpeggios around Sedric's subtone theme and his ensuing stride; Coleman's melodic, Louis-ish solo) with broad comedy (Fats's second vocal offering, directed at his landlady, who wants the rent) and ending with a *Pagliacci* riff. "I'm Growing Fonder of You" offers more Sedric subtone with piano garlands, a vocal in Fats's natural tenor range, and open Coleman à la Louis. "If It Isn't Love," the least worthy in this batch of tunes, opens with a wonderfully rhythmic piano solo, and then Waller takes care of the vocal in several voices, including a semi-operatic one. Sedric's tenor gets a half chorus. "Breakin' the Ice" is treated more gently, vocally speaking, and then Fats conjures up another jewel of a piano solo—he felt like playing that day. Sedric gets his innings here, on tenor; he grows on you with that punchy phrasing.

January 5, 1935

This session took place in Camden to give Fats a turn at the pipe organ. Victor's Camden studios were in a converted church with a great organ long familiar to Waller. Billy Taylor had just been hired by Ellington, and his replacement was not nearly in the same league. Charles "Fat Man" Turner was a bandleader who'd temporarily lost his gig, and Dial says he enlisted him because he felt sorry for him. Turner was no great shakes as a player, but he knew how to hang on to a good thing; he stayed with the Rhythm until the fall of 1937. Coleman was on hand again; Waller must have liked him, for Autrey was now available. The replacement trumpeter had fond and detailed recollections of this occasion. The band had embarked on the train to Philadelphia with two bottles of whiskey supplied by the leader, who passed the jug every time he felt like taking a swig, which was often enough to cause Fats to buy two more for the subsequent short ride to

Camden. Like Autrey, Coleman notes that the numbers to be recorded were first seen by the band upon arrival at the studio, but "with Fats, we fell into the groove from the start. Of course drinks were passed around between each number . . . and everybody stayed groovy." He recalls that something went wrong with an organ pipe, causing a lengthy break during which "we had a big meal, offered by the recording company, and more drinks." On the way back, Fats bought two more bottles, and when Coleman arrived at home, he had to send in a sub for his Teddy Hill job. He never tried to match Fats drink for drink again, but in any case, this was his last Waller engagement. There might have been more had Coleman not gone home for a visit and then taken off for Europe, where he remained until World War II broke out.

"I'm a Hundred Percent for You" has a Coleman stop-time opening, a relaxed vocal and a cute piano solo. Coleman double-times in the Armstrong manner and dialogues with Sedric's clarinet. The nonvocal version (these were made for export, though also issued at home) substitutes subtone Sedric with Fats accompaniment, divided by a chorded Casey bridge (the guitarist's consistent taste and excellence should not go unmentioned—in his eightieth year at this writing, Casey is the sole survivor of the Rhythm cast), a more rhythmically defined piano spot, and no trumpet double-timing. "Baby Brown," by Waller's friend and associate Alex Hill, also gets two treatments. Both open with peppy piano. The vocal is replaced by a chorus of cup-muted trumpet, clarinet bridge, and trumpet again. On the vocal take, there's a bonus in Waller's scatted bridge in the out chorus and his closing commentary, but the instrumental version gives us extra helpings of Coleman and Sedric in fine fettle.

"Night Wind" has Fats switching to organ; he states the melody with great voicings, prominently accompanied by guitar—surely a unique combination. He obviously likes this tune and swings softly into the second chorus and a pretty straight vocal. Sedric's tenor is active in the background until Coleman takes over for the final 16. "Because of Once Upon a Time" isn't much of a tune or lyric, and Fats treats it casually with many vocal asides. Coleman stays close to the melody but sounds energetic. In contrast, "I Believe in Miracles," which finds Fats back at the organ console, is an inspired performance. Organ doubles subtone clarinet on the melody—how light Fats's organ touch can be—until he embellishes the last eight. For the friendly vocal, Coleman provides a sublime obbligato on open horn, and he leads on the third and final half chorus. Waller and Coleman really get together here. "You Fit into the Picture" is a loose, relaxed conclusion to a productive session, with a nice, lacy piano solo and more of that good trumpet.

MARCH 6, 1935

Between sessions, the Rhythm had made their first tour, although apparently no farther than to Connecticut. Sedric had found a job that was too lucrative to pass up, so he was replaced on the job by Emmett Matthews, an excellent soprano specialist. But for the March session, it was Rudy Powell who came to bat, and he would remain the Rhythm's reedman for almost a year.

"Louisiana Fairy Tale" opens with that favorite Waller device, subtone clarinet melody backed by tinkling piano—but Autrey, in a bucket mute, takes the bridge. The trumpeter's backing of the vocal indicates he'd listened to Coleman's records with Fats. The big man puts the silly lyrics in their proper place, and a further nail is driven into the tune's coffin by Autrey's deliberately corny lead. No plantation stuff for this gang, but you have to listen to catch the irony. "I Ain't Got Nobody," a grand old tune by Fats's friend Spencer Williams, is heard in vocal and nonvocal versions, both delightful. Fats's singing and commentary are essential parts of the first—the vocal is special in humor and drive. We get some Powell alto instead of his reedy clarinet on the nonvocal take, which also presents a Casey solo that might be his best up to now. Autrey's solo is slightly out of focus at first, but his lead on the loose concluding jam is certainly audible. "Whose Honey Are You?" fits Fats like a glove, and he has a good time from the scat intro through the scat coda, with good Casey, Powell, and Autrey along the way. For the instrumental version, an operatic piano introduction subs for the scat and the piano solo strays far from the melody. Casey strums 16 and Rudy's alto wraps the chorus. Autrey, in an open-horn Red Allen groove, takes a full 32 bars, then Fats moves to celeste to back subtone Powell clarinet. A fine rideout follows—this version is thirty-three seconds longer than the vocal one!

The two "Rosettas" must have pleased credited composer Earl Hines (it's really Henri Woode's tune)—the very slow tempo mirrors Earl's first big-band version. Subtone clarinet and celeste bring it on. Fats croons one with his tongue not too far in cheek—how about that "God bless you, honey"? The guitar and celeste coda is special. In this instance, the instrumental version is the shorter one. Celeste is more prominent in the opening chorus. The vocal is replaced by a piano and muted trumpet conversation, Fats embroidering. Turner's shortcomings are quite evident here, but the short rideout is righteous. "Pardon My Love," with melody by Oscar Levant, is given relatively straightforward treatment, except for the vocal bridge, which is pretty zany. "What's the Reason?," another double helping, is the fastest Rhythm offering so far, and it romps. Powell gives his best on clarinet, and Casey's full choruses (one on each version) also stand out.

Some extra piano graces the instrumental, which has a great rideout, but Waller's second vocal is a gem. "Cinders" is one of those songs of Southern tribulations, but Fats treats it fairly gently, backed by Autrey growls. He plays both celeste and piano, offering a brief, delicate solo spot on the former that contrasts strikingly with the growling trumpet.

With "Dust Off That Old Pianna," the session comes to a rousing close. This is one of those perfect Waller 78-rpm cameos, starting with a bit of piano exercise, then taking off like a rocket with Fats and the rhythm section. (Dial is excellent here.) After the entertaining vocal, Powell gets off a good one and Autrey solves the fast tempo by confining himself to Louis-like stabs. Casey strums, egged on by Fats's comments, then a bit of celeste sets up the no-holds-barred rideout. Eight tunes, several of them in multiple versions, ain't bad for a day's work in the studio! Fats and the Rhythm were taking to recording like ducks to water.

MAY 8, 1935

In the interim, Fats had been to Hollywood for his first role in a feature film, "Hooray for Love," in which he appeared in a musical production number with Bill "Bojangles" Robinson. He then went on a tour with an augmented version of the Rhythm.

What was to become a pivotal date began with an instant classic: Harry Warren and Al Dubin's "Lulu's Back in Town." Tailor-made for Fats (who was in exceptionally relaxed form that day), it includes some great vocal work—jocular but not burlesqued—and splendid pianistics. Autrey's up for this. "Sweet and Slow," another good one by the same songwriting team, begins with a fine, laid-back exposition, laced with arpeggios and little funky touches. (Don't miss that bridge.) The sotto voce vocal sustains the mood, and Fats offers some great asides. "Lessons in Love" shows how good he was feeling—the opening piano episode is totally relaxed in a James P. vein, and the vocal is intimate. After the horn solos, Fats opens up, and there's a wild little ending. "You're the Cutest One," a trifle, offers more quality piano, another relaxed vocal, and very active comping behind the horns. (Fats could make anyone sound good.) When things get a bit too agitated during the vocal reprise, Fats admonishes his troops: "Run it to me, but don't bruise me!"

You'll have to wait for the next installment in this complete Rhythm series to find out what happened next, but allow me to conclude on a personal note. I was not quite nine years old when Fats Waller appeared in Copenhagen in September 1938. My mother took me to one of his concerts. I'd never seen or heard anything remotely like Fats in my short life, and even though my English was limited to what I'd heard in movies and on phonograph records, his vitality and terrific beat got through to me. As a child of the swing era, chances are I'd have gotten involved in jazz anyway; nevertheless I'll always be grateful to Fats for sending me off on a lifelong journey of discoveries.

More than fifty years after his untimely death, Fats Waller still spreads joy wherever his music is heard. During his stay in Copenhagen, a journalist asked Fats when jazz would disappear. "Never!" he answered. "It's ridiculous when people say that jazz is a passing phenomenon—it has only just begun. . . . A hundred years from now, jazz will be even more influential." And the Waller legacy will always be a part of it.

Note: I'm indebted to Laurie Wright's Fats in Fact, *the definitive Waller sourcebook (Storyville Publishers, 1992). The Autrey quotes are from an interview with John S. Wilson, conducted for the NEA's Jazz Oral History Project, housed at the Institute of Jazz Studies.*

(1995)

Art Tatum

Genius is inexplicable, but Art Tatum, when asked, usually cited Fats Waller as his main inspiration. "Fats, man. That's where I come from. And quite a place to come from," he once told an interviewer.

Waller, in turn, idolized Tatum. Once, when Tatum entered a club where Fats was performing, Fats stopped the music and announced: "Ladies and gentlemen, I play piano, but God is in the house tonight!"

Tatum was a sort of deity to his fellow musicians—not just to pianists, but to players of any instrument. No practitioner of the music called jazz had (or has) such perfect technical command, in the traditional sense, as did Art Tatum. But it wasn't just his astonishing facility that inspired awe in his colleagues. It was his phenomenal harmonic sense, his equally uncanny rhythmic gift, and his boundless imagination. Technique was merely the vehicle through which he expressed himself. What others could imagine, Tatum could execute, and what he could imagine went beyond the wildest dreams of mere musical mortals.

In almost everything that has been written about Tatum, the point is made that he played his best not in recording studios, nightclubs, or concert halls, but after hours. "After hours" was a very special term in jazz parlance in the days when Tatum flourished. Sadly, one has to use it in the past tense today, for there is no real after-hours scene anymore.

But in the '30s and '40s, after hours was a way of life for the creative jazz musician. An outgrowth of Prohibition (when liquor became legal, many speakeasies turned into places serving it after the prescribed hours), after-hours places sprung up especially in the black urban communities throughout the land. Kansas City under Pendergast was one long after-hours party, but Harlem was the place where jazz legends were made after Kansas City shut down.

After-hours spots ran the gamut from big and fancy to small and plain. Most went into action after the legitimate clubs and bars closed, but others opened when the regular after-hours spots closed (these were known as *after*-after-hours places). All of them had a piano, even if it was just an old upright with some keys, hammers, or strings missing. No jazzman with the spirit of the music didn't frequent after-hours spots, but a few were specialists in the field. These included Roy Eldridge, Hot Lips Page, and Art Tatum. Tatum loved after hours. His very first jobs in his native Toledo were at house rent parties, where he would play solo or back all manner of singers and visiting instrumentalists. It was in such environments, perhaps, that Tatum developed his tolerance for modestly gifted or entirely untalented singers or players, whom he would supply with the most ravishing backdrops. But perhaps not—like Charlie Parker, Tatum was interested in everything he could hear, and he could hear everything: a limited blues pianist who might have a certain feeling; a third-rate cocktail-lounge tickler who might have a special run—anything at all within the vast spectrum of music, popular or serious, was grist for his ears.

And Tatum relished competition. Working in a club might offer an occasional opportunity for combat, but that was rare. After hours, on the other hand, or on Monday nights, when musicians gathered somewhere to exchange ideas and socialize, such opportunities were almost unlimited. Tatum was conscious of his superiority yet had a need to sharpen his wits and chops against all comers.

This unique record reveals, for the first and only time, the after-hours Tatum, the relaxed, informal, completely at ease Tatum. (Yes, I know, there's a marvelous two-record set of stuff recorded at a private party in Hollywood in '55, but Hollywood parties aren't Harlem after hours, and '55 wasn't '41 . . .)

The earliest recordings here were made at Jerry Newman's apartment on November 11, 1940. Tatum liked the enthusiastic young fan and was intrigued by on-the-spot recording, so he allowed Newman to follow him on his tours of Harlem and set up his portable machine.

Many years ago, Newman played some of his Tatum material on a New York FM station, and I recall a few things he said about the circumstances. For instance, Reuben's, at 242 West 130th Street, was a small place frequented by piano players, and the owner, Reuben Harris, liked to play along with them, discreetly, moving two whisk brooms over a folded newspaper placed on a chair. The piano, if I recall correctly, was not a full-keyboard instrument. But Tatum liked the place, and dropped in often.

The Gee-Haw Stables, on Wet 132nd Street, so called because a sculpted horse's head graced the entrance, was an after-after-hours place where the action started around 7 a.m. and would often go until noon the next day. Bassist Chocolate Williams, heard on some tracks here, had the house band.

Near the Gee-Haw was Clark Monroe's Uptown House (198 West 134th Street), a spot that rivaled Minton's in attracting major-league jazzmen for after-hours jamming. It was on the premises that had once held Barron Wilkins's Exclusive Club. (In 1943, Monroe moved to Fifty-second Street where, as operator of the Spotlight, he became the Street's first black club owner.)

Though all these were good-time spots where the noise of partying often got pretty loud, Newman seems to have had little trouble in persuading the customers to maintain a minimum of decorum, and the occasional shouts or sighs of approbation that grace these tracks are a natural complement to the music.

There is no need here to go into detailed analysis of Tatum's style—for the best work in this genre, I recommend Dick Katz's essay on some Tatum records, published in *Jazz Panorama*, edited by Martin Williams—but it seems worthwhile to make a few points.

First, Tatum doesn't seem bothered or inhibited by the condition of the instruments he has to play here. In fact, he seems to adapt himself so well to their various shortcomings that one gets the feeling he enjoyed the challenge—circumventing dead keys or adapting himself to different kinds of out-of-tuneness might well have played a major role in sharpening his harmonic wits and manual dexterity. In any case, he was a wizard, and the relaxed, convivial atmosphere no doubt made up for such handicaps.

Second, Tatum, who has been called the soloist par excellence, the man who needed no others to play with or for, seems inspired by the presence of audiences and other music makers, be they singers or instrumentalists. Certainly, the level of inspiration he reaches on the two tracks with trumpeter Frank Newton and bassist Ebenezer Paul is as high if not higher than in any solo performance here (or elsewhere, for that matter). And the good-natured jive of Chocolate Williams as well as the singing of Ollie Potter brings forth some tremendous playing. Could it be that Tatum, sometimes criticized for not being a "real" jazz musician, in fact was very much that— so much so that he functioned best when he had company?

That may be exaggeration, but it certainly seems that he did function most completely when he had an audience he knew he liked. A performance such as the wonderful "Toledo Blues" would have been impossible in the concert hall. When Tatum was granted the too-rare privilege of playing there, he cast himself, quite logically, in the role of a concert artist—which he played better than any other jazzman, it must be said. And when he played nightclubs, he usually was too annoyed by the inattention of bab- bling drinker-sightseers to really relax and enjoy himself. "Toledo Blues" was for his good friends, and we are privileged to partake of it. But we can also be sure that this wasn't the first or only time that Tatum sang the blues, as witness his surprise chorus on "Knockin' Myself Out."

Two of the first three tracks are little sketches—fascinating fragments. But the third, "Georgia on My Mind," is a full-fledged on-the-spot inter- pretation of a standard, the kind of thing at which Tatum has no equals. And don't miss his breaks in the second chorus . . . what equilibrium! (It was later discovered that this was taken from a broadcast.)

The three pieces from Reuben's (May 7, 1941) are utterly relaxed. "Sweet Lorraine" was one of the pianist's favorites, and this version sur- passes, I think, any others. The final chorus is a compendium of Tatum's improvisatory, harmonic, rhythmic, and technical genius. "Fine and Dandy" is a masterpiece—how he sustains the swing of the fine medium tempo—and, good friend that he is, he gives Reuben a few little breaks at the end. "Begin the Beguine" is a set piece, and Tatum seems to want to play it pretty much as he did on the record. (This was the "arrangement" that Eddie Heywood simplified and became famous for.)

"Mighty Lak a Rose" (from the Gee-Haw) is the kind of piece serious critics don't like Tatum to play; Coleman Hawkins played it, too. Maybe it is nineteenth-century "salon" (as opposed to saloon) music, and pretty shal- low, but what Tatum does with it shows that he didn't exactly revere it. It's when he goes into tempo that things begin to happen—and what a tempo! What chops! The opening sounds to me as if Tatum is feeling out the piano to see where its deficiencies lie. He adapts himself to them almost instantly.

Lil Green's "Knockin' Myself Out" is a charming bit of period jive . . . or maybe not so "period"—getting high on grass has hardly become passé. Chocolate Williams has nice time, and what Tatum does in the cracks shouldn't be legal. He sings a humorous chorus of his own, in that veiled voice we hear more clearly on "Toledo Blues," and then, in response to Williams's "Tatum!" plays a chorus of inspired blues piano. (In his wrap-up verse, Williams calls him *Mr.* Tatum.) "Body and Soul" was a piece Tatum played often; this version is very fanciful (the second bridge!) and full of little humorous touches—Tatum had fun when he played; he enjoyed his own virtuosity and enjoyed others enjoying it. This aspect of his art doesn't sit well with intellectual critics. "There'll Be Some Changes Made," also from the Gee-Haw, shows Tatum's complete harmonic and rhythmic freedom, at a fine tempo. He accompanies the singer helpfully and backs the pleasant bass solo with some startling inventions.

The two final performances, from Clark Monroe's Uptown House, are sensational. Newton is up to playing with Tatum—his ear is sure enough not to be thrown by the unorthodox backing, especially on "Sweet Georgia Brown." On "Lady Be Good," Newton shows us where Sweets Edison comes from. A master of mutes (including the almost whispery one he plays here), he was one of the three great post-Armstrong trumpeters, along with Roy Eldridge and Lips Page. It's good to have these indications of his worth; he was under-recorded throughout his career.

The complexities of Tatum's accompaniments and solos are such that it is impossible to take these two performances in at even several hearings. You'll find yourself listening first to Art, then to Frank, then to both, again and again. "Sweet Georgia Brown," I humbly submit, is one of the most remarkable pieces of spontaneously improvised jazz music ever captured by a recording device.

(1974)

Hot Lips Page: After Hours in Harlem

If ever there was a musician who represented the spirit of the jam session, it was Oran "Hot Lips" Page. It can be said that Lips was the spirit of the jam session incarnate . . . only his good friend Roy Eldridge, who even today is ready to jam at the drop of a note, can approach Lips in that respect.

Today, of course, what goes under the name of jam session is hardly ever the real thing. What you'll hear on this record most certainly is, however. There are many reasons why real jamming has disappeared—social, musical, political, and spiritual—and obviously very little of it was ever captured by a recording machine.

Today, Harlem is a concept that strikes fear in the heart of the tourist, releases floods of verbiage from the mouths of sociologists and politicians, and causes resentment in New York taxi drivers. The unorthodox writer Albert Murray has pointed out that even today Harlem is not a "ghetto," and that far from being an unrelievedly depressing slum, it is a large and varied community with style and flair as well as crime and despair. But his is a lone voice, and I confess that I seldom go to Harlem anymore.

I arrived in New York (and the United States of America) in early 1947—several years after the music on this album was made. Still, if the scene that gave birth to the music here no longer flourished, it still existed. It was my very good fortune that I was introduced to it by no less a guide than its Virgil, Hot Lips Page.

I first heard and saw (and he was something to see as well as hear) Lips at one of the Friday night sessions the late Bob Maltz was then running at the Stuyvesant Casino. These were some sort of jam sessions, too, but of the organized variety—a concept introduced by Eddie Condon at his Town Hall concerts and almost simultaneously developed by Norman Granz with his Jazz at the Philharmonic.

The Stuyvesant sessions could be described as mainstream-Dixieland, but such nomenclature became meaningless when Lips was on the scene. He was a jazz musician—j-a-z-z—and he never took offense at the word. He could play with a bunch of young white kids emulating King Oliver records, and he could play with Charlie Parker. He could play for bejeweled socialites and smart-setters at private parties on Sutton Place, and he could play for the black workingmen and night creatures at barrelhouse joints in Harlem. He could fly high over a sixteen-piece band playing arrangements or sit in the kitchen of an after-hours pad, accompanied only by his own tapping foot, and make sounds you wouldn't soon forget.

And wherever he played and whomever he played with—high and low, good and bad—he came through with the message. What that message was is something I can't spell out in words without sounding corny, but to put it mildly, it was affirmative.

The jam session, the real jam session, functioned as a workshop (though nobody would have thought of using such a term), a testing ground, a chop stretcher for musicians who were making a living, in the main, playing music that required a certain amount of discipline and generally restricted unfettered solo playing to a chorus or two. Of course, famous soloists, like, say, Coleman Hawkins, could work with just a rhythm section in one of the jazz clubs on Fifty-second Street, but that was the exception. On the other end of the spectrum was the non-featured big-band section man, who maybe got a few four- or eight-bar solos, in the course of a night's work, if that.

So, to jam meant a welcome and needed chance to stretch out. Today, when everybody stretches, and experimentation is done in public rather than before select audiences of one's peers, the need for jamming has disappeared. Instead, musicians get together in workshops and rehearsal bands to practice reading and section playing and get away from the monotony of long solos and head music.

It was in the very nature of jam sessions that they should be uneven. Great musicians rubbed elbows with lesser lights; if there was no drummer in the house, you made do without, or somebody would kick a suitcase or swoosh a whisk broom over newspaper. Clowns would get into the act—i.e., cats who didn't know their horns but had no inferiority complexes.

Generally, someone—the leader of the house band, if there was one, or the strongest personality on the stand—would take on some aspects of directing, and Lips was a master at this. To kick it off or take it out, set a riff or settle the tempo, cool a cat off or egg him on—Lips knew just what, when, and how. The jam session was not only a musical but also a social and psychological event, and Lips was a master social director and psychiatric counselor.

The music here stems from two different settings: the house jam and the club jam. The former is more relaxed and congenial (due to the absence of another trumpeter), the latter more unpredictable. But whatever the circumstances, it is Lips who takes command and makes it happen.

On "Dinah," "I Got Rhythm," "I'm in the Mood for Love," and "Tea for Two," we hear, in addition to Lips, the then young Herbie Fields and pianist Donald Lambert, a contemporary of Fats Waller and unsung hero of the Harlem stride school.

Lambert recorded very little, and these samples of his work are an important addition to his slender legacy. Fields recorded quite a bit, if not this early, and while he was far from the worst of tenorists, he was also pretty far from the best. He was, however, a close friend of Jerry Newman, and quite possibly responsible for introducing him to jazz, to the musicians, and to Harlem. At least we know that the two hung out together—Fields is almost always present on Newman's recordings.

Fields's problem is restraint; he'll start out fine in a Chu Berry–Herschel Evans mold, then get carried away. And that's the way things remained with him—when he was featured with Lionel Hampton a few years later, restraint was hardly the reason why Hamp showcased him. Here, he sounds pretty hip for a young white boy in fast company.

"I Got Rhythm," next to the blues the most played set of jazz changes, starts off at a fierce tempo. The "drum"—possibly played by one Pops Morgan—is brushes on newspaper. We pick up the action amid a Fields solo, and then Lips bursts in, with his leather horn case over the bell of the trumpet (fact courtesy Nat Lorber), biting off his notes. This is inspired creating, and the groove is pre-bop, if you will—pretty advanced riffing. Lips's last note is made on the mouthpiece alone. Lambert strides out, and the chicks are with him. Fields, next, is pretty solid here, albeit as always a bit theatrical. What follows is some of the wildest, most spontaneous, hilarious, out-of-sight jamming ever captured on wax, tape, whatever, with Lips doing some insane things—you can hear him breathe. After the fours, etc., he sets a fine riff to take it out. If Jerry Newman had captured nothing else but this "Rhythm," he'd merit canonization.

"I'm in the Mood for Love" finds Lips in a ballad groove. If you know, you can tell he's had a few drinks here, and something to smoke, probably. It's soulful, to say the least. Dig the first bridge. Lambert is pretty here, and gives out with some almost Tatumesque filigree. Lips's cadenza is knockout stuff.

"Dinah" is a mellow groove. A nice Lambert intro, then muted Lips and Fields on the theme. The tenor solos first, in his Chu bag, and Lambert comps very nicely. Lips, still muted, makes the chicks scream with his "talking" stuff. The use of symmetrical phrasing—a hallmark of his style—is evident, as is his genius for building excitement. A lovely Lambert solo, bombastic tenor, and a tenor-trumpet conversation in which Lips goes way up high, then asserts himself. All three are into it on the last bridge, and then comes a Lips cadenza—wow! This is after-hours music, free, unfettered, mellow.

"Tea for Two" is a great vehicle for jamming. Lambert starts it off, with glimpses of his favorite trick—playing two tunes simultaneously. Here it's "Frenesi." After Fields's solo, Lips comes in, muted and in a storytelling mood. This is utterly relaxed playing, a kind of groove almost impossible in a commercial (i.e., working, studio, etc.) setting. There's some double-timing, some quoting ("Louisiana"), and all of it is Lips's own, unique stuff. Lambert is with him all the way, listening, and in his own solo he doubles the time, then brings it back. Lips returns ever so flowingly, and later, doubles it up again. A remarkable three-way cadenza ensues, then Lips has the last word.

With "I've Found a New Baby," we leave the house party and arrive at Minton's. Joe Guy is the first trumpeter, good rhythm behind him (this could be Kenny Clarke). Tiny Grimes has certainly already heard Charlie Christian. Then Lips enters, muted, and raises the swing quotient notably. Guy takes it out quickly, probably because Newman was running out of disc.

"Sweet Georgia Brown," a jam session (and Lips) favorite, starts off with Monk's solo, demonstrating the pervasive influence of Earl Hines, and, by the by, the fact that Monk's unique style evolved by choice, not because, as some would have it, he lacked "technique." The drummer's good enough to be Klook, and this track swings from the go. Lips comes in, and the drummer switches the beat to the cymbal. Lips is not as relaxed here as he could be; some tension was in the air at this session. The tenorist (Newman's notations mention Jimmy Wright, who in 1981 confirmed his presence) is egged on by Lips's riffing, and Guy is audible in the concluding ensemble.

"Old Yazoo" gives us Lips, the jazz singer—and what a monster he was! This is, aside from the opening, pure scat, in a class with the immortal Leo Watson. The tune is one of those jive novelties, à la "Nagasaki," and Lips has fun with the lyric before he throws it away and starts making sounds. The alto solo is by Rudy Williams, then with the Savoy Sultans and a frequent jammer. He's adventurous, strongly influenced by the eccentric side of Willie Smith, and unusually dissonant for this period. The tenorist starts his solo with what later became "I Love the Rhythm in a Riff," and the trumpeter is probably Guy in his Lips bag. Lips returns, vocally, over riffing by the band, and outdoes himself on the bridge.

"Topsy," a tune the "advanced" swing players were very fond of, opens with a pretty strange tenor player who can't handle the changes too well, followed by Joe Guy in his characteristic style—to me, he sounds "sideways," if you dig what I mean—and straining a bit for his high notes. When Lips enters, the difference in sound alone is something. He works out with the drummer, suggesting rhythmic patterns, and then the riffs come in behind him as he clinches his inventions with the background. A slight "battle" between Lips and Guy is the main feature of the concluding ensemble passages.

"Konk" is a fast blues, the title derived by Don Schlitten from a conversation with Lips recorded by Newman in which Lips tells a hilarious tale of Benny Moten's band and a hair straightener called "Konkolene." This is tailor-made for Lips and redolent of Kansas City. Lips sets it up, the others fall in line (the odd drumming might be by Struttin' Sam, a longtime Harlem regular), there's a stop-time drum bit, a fair tenor solo, and then Lips, for nine choruses of sheer joy. Pretty nice piano and a walking bass solo, then Lips hums a figure to the tenor, essays a counter-riff, and then takes off on a soaring ride, creating riffs enough for a dozen tunes.

Here, by the grace of God, is some music unlike any you've heard on record before. It fleshes out the hitherto incomplete portrait in sound of a very great artist and wonderful man.

(1974)

Coleman Hawkins

S ome artists are acclaimed during their lifetimes, then soon forgotten. Others live in the shadows and are discovered posthumously. A lucky few are admired and honored in life as well as in death. Coleman Hawkins (1904–1969) began his professional career in his teens, was the leading practitioner of his chosen instrument by his mid-twenties, an international star (when jazz had just a few) at thirty, one of the very few established greats accepted by the young jazz modernists in his (and the century's) forties, and a universally admired "grand old man" of jazz in his sunset years. Today, he is an unassailable icon of jazz—a landmark in no need of a protective commission.

Hawkins accomplished all this by purely musical means. Growing up in an era when musicians were expected to sing and dance, he did neither; there wasn't a trace of the entertainer in his makeup. Only with the greatest reluctance—and when there was no one around to deputize—would he deign to announce a tune or introduce a fellow performer. Yet he instantly established his authority when he took the stage, before he had even played a note. Though short of stature, he was a handsome, solidly built man, impeccably dressed, with an aura that commanded respect. And once he began to play, his sound alone sufficed to seduce or arouse the listener, depending on the mood and spirit of the music being made.

When he played, Hawkins was the image of concentration, a man totally absorbed in his task. More often than not, his eyes would be closed, and on fast tempos he would stomp his right foot from time to time, as if to kick himself into high gear, his breath intake becoming quite audible (as you will hear at times on this record). His playing mien was mostly stern, brow furrowed, but when he did something special, there might be a quick smile between phrases. And when a colleague played something that met with his approval, he'd beam and maybe utter a loud "uuhmm" in the distinctive voice that mirrored the power of his tone on the horn.

Once you got to know him, though, Hawk was a down-to-earth man. He loved a good laugh (frequently at the expense of others; he was an inveterate and crafty instigator of disputes, which he'd step back from and enjoy, and wasn't above playing practical jokes), a good meal (in his prime, he'd calmly consume the equivalent of three full meals at one sitting, but quality had to equal quantity; he was also a superb cook when he had the patience), good liquor, and good company. He was a connoisseur in every aspect of living; only the best would do.

Of course that held true for music. One of the first jazz musicians to acquire a stereo rig (the best, needless to say), his tastes in home listening ran to classical music. Like so many jazz players, he liked Bach, but his preference was for operas and symphonies—logically, for a great romantic balladeer. Beethoven, Brahms, Verdi, Puccini (Wagner only in moderate doses), Debussy, Ravel, even Tchaikovsky ("I know he's not supposed to be chic, but I like him") were his favorites. He was interested in the moderns, too, but they didn't stir his emotions. His classical library was impressive (he favored boxed sets), but he kept just a few jazz records around—Armstrong, Tatum, Parker, Gillespie, Ellington, and especially Monk, whom he loved, musically and personally.

In 1944, Hawk had been the first "name" leader to hire the iconoclastic young pianist for a "downtown" gig on Fifty-second Street and for a record date (Monk's studio debut), years before Thelonious was discovered. He wanted to take Monk with him to California in 1945 in a group that included Howard McGhee, Oscar Pettiford, and Denzil Best, but Monk, ever the stay-at-home, wasn't ready. With Sir Charles Thompson as the replacement, this was the first band to bring intimations of jazz things to come to the West Coast. In its repertoire were at least two numbers Hawk "borrowed" from Monk—"Stuffy" and "Rifftide"—later borrowed back by their composer as "Stuffy Turkey" and "Hackensack" with no complaints.

Hawk had already presided over what discographers and historians have designated the first bebop record date, on February 6, 1944, with Gillespie, Pettiford, Max Roach (who'd made his recording debut with Hawk some two months earlier), and other cats from Minton's and Fifty-second Street. Hawk not only understood and accepted the new ideas in jazz that would soon be labeled bebop—he encouraged and fostered them.

The "innovations" of bop presented no problems to Hawk's educated ear, always attuned to harmonic sophistication and daring. Himself no mean pianist, he had long since worked out all kinds of harmonic progressions at the keyboard. Rhythmically, it took him longer to adapt, but that didn't really matter, because he was so utterly assured within his own conception of time that nothing could upset his swinging equilibrium. Eventually, he did begin to break up his rather regularly accented fast-tempo phrasing, chiefly under the magic spell of Charlie Parker.

(To digress: In its basically linear conception of jazz history, the critical-historical establishment has paid far too little attention to musical influence as a circular phenomenon. Hawkins is a primary example of the fact that great artists don't reach a plateau and stay there, but continue to listen and evolve.)

Parker's impact on Hawkins had another significant result: for the first time in his distinguished career, he became a convincing blues player. Parker showed him that a sophisticated musician didn't have to simplify his approach when it came to the blues—it was possible to be funky and imaginative in the same breath. The 1956 sessions here show Parker's influence on Hawkins as clearly as anything he recorded, perhaps because Bird's death just ten months prior had freed Hawkins in some mysterious way to fully accept the consequences of what he'd been hearing, now that Parker was beyond rivalry.

After all, Coleman Hawkins had long been accustomed to influencing rather than being influenced—especially when it came to saxophone players. The only clear and direct influence on his own musical development had been that of Louis Armstrong, way back in 1924–25. Armstrong, of course, was then affecting everybody. But Hawkins was a direct recipient of his influence. For nearly sixteen months, the two gifted young men were colleagues in Fletcher Henderson's band. Hawk had mastered his instrument but not yet come to terms with jazz as a vehicle for emotionally and intellectually meaningful musical statements. His sound was powerful but rough, and often disfigured by corny slap-tongue devices. His rhythm was strong but crude; he did not swing. After exposure to Louis, all that changed, if not overnight. Since Henderson's band recorded prolifically and Hawkins was always well featured, we can trace this quite handily. Hawk continued to listen to Louis: it is interesting that the saxophonist's first great ballad performance, "One Hour" (with the Mound City Blue Blowers), was recorded in late 1929, the year Louis returned to New York and made his (and *the*) first great jazz ballad record, "I Can't Give You Anything But Love."

I saw Louis and Hawk together only once—at Newport in the late '50s. Hawk had come backstage to say hello, when a tremendous rainstorm broke out. The two old friends took refuge in Louis's band bus, while I found shelter in a car parked nearby. There was a little light above their seat—the sole illumination in the sudden darkness—and I watched them having a smoke and a chat, struck by what I remembered noting in an old Henderson band photo: in a strange way, they looked alike.

We know surprisingly little about Hawk's formative years. He was born in St. Joseph, Missouri, on November 21, 1904, though he liked to tell people (Joe Venuti also did) that he was born aboard a transatlantic liner. Jokes about Hawk's age, endemic among musicians, always centered on his claims to be *younger* than his official age. (He once laughingly showed me his cabaret card—when those obscene documents were still required in New York—pointing out the date of birth, given as 1912.) His standard biographies state he attended Washburn College in Topeka, Kansas, but the school's records do not show him as a registered student. It's also said he studied music in Chicago, but no school is cited. His first instrument was piano, then cello, and he continued to love the latter; one of his favorite own recordings was Schumann's "Träumerei," a piece he'd played on the cello. (Without doubt the sound of this beautiful instrument affected his conception of tenor saxophone tone.)

By 1920, he was playing in the house orchestra of a Kansas City theater. Singer Mamie Smith was one of the acts he accompanied; she liked what she heard, and Hawkins left town as a member of her touring Jazz Hounds, with whom he made his recording debut in the spring of 1922. Within the year, he'd settled in New York as a freelance musician. His recording associates included Fletcher Henderson, and when a Henderson recording group decided to audition for a job at the newly opened Club Alabam, he was one of the reasons it was hired. He stayed with Henderson for a decade, becoming the band's undisputed star though it was studded with talent. Inspired by Armstrong's recent successes in Europe, he cabled Jack Hylton, England's counterpart of Paul Whiteman, on a whim, expressing interest in guesting with him. The response was swift and positive, offering good money, and since Henderson as usual was struggling to meet his payroll, Hawk gave swift notice. He arrived in England on March 29, 1934.

Six months earlier to the day, he'd made his first records as a leader. It's a clear indication of his fame and stature that Hylton nevertheless knew he would be a sure drawing card. Though not yet dubbed the Father of the Tenor Saxophone, he had long since established himself as the leading voice on that horn. And not just that: he was, excepting Armstrong, the most famous and admired jazz soloist. In later years, Hawk always insisted that he had not invented the jazz vocabulary for his primary instrument (with Henderson, he also doubled on clarinet and bass sax), citing contemporaries Happy Caldwell, Prince Robinson, and Stump Evans, but this was uncharacteristically modest of him—or perhaps just another ploy in the age game. Not only was he head and shoulders above these and other able tenorists, but he was showing players of all instruments what jazz was about.

In Europe, what Hawk had intended as a brief visit stretched into a stay of more than five years. While the brutish refusal of the Nazis to let him tour Germany with Hylton (who, like so many others, caved in and didn't cancel his contracts to Hitlerland) taught him that Europe was no Eden for blacks, he liked what he saw in England and on the Continent. The chilling effect of the German ban was soon alleviated by a warm invitation from Holland's leading jazz band, the Ramblers, to guest-star with them. That association led to some brilliant records, in 1935 and 1937. He also recorded in Paris (twice), London (twice), Zürich, and Holland again (with his own trio, with a pianist, and in an international jam band with his friend Benny Carter). In all, his European stay produced forty-seven issued sides, of which only four (with the Ramblers) were issued in the U.S.; even the most famous of these sessions, in Paris in 1937 with a unique saxophone quartet (Carter and two Frenchmen) and Django Reinhardt in the rhythm section, was not released here until the spring of 1939.

Thus, when he returned home, docking in New York on July 31, 1939, few American musicians and listeners had any clear idea what his playing was now like. The timing of his return, a full month before the outbreak of World War II, was typically shrewd; of the many other American musicians and entertainers active in Europe, most waited too long, had to be evacuated on overcrowded steamers, or missed the boat altogether. (Only Carter had preceded him, but that worthy's return in May of 1938 was motivated by a desire to participate in the swing boom.)

During Hawk's long absence, notable claimants to his tenor crown had been honing their reeds. Chu Berry, an erstwhile disciple, had come into his own with a style that rivaled Hawk in rhythmic thrust and harmonic dexterity. Ben Webster, a comer, was on the verge of liberation from Hawk's influence, while Don Byas was yet known only among musicians. However, Lester Young presented the ultimate challenge—an entirely new and different jazz conception of the instrument, crystallized by juxtaposition with his Count Basie–band section mate Herschel Evans, a leading Hawkins-rooted stylist. Lester wasn't unknown to Hawkins—he had encountered him in Kansas City during his last year with Henderson—but his popularity among musicians and fans was new.

Such things would have been in the back of Hawk's mind when he arrived to a warm welcome. Carter was there to greet him; this good friend had also arranged a homecoming party at Harlem's Savoy Ballroom, where he was then working with his band, opposite Ella Fitzgerald's (the singer had taken over Chick Webb's band after the drummer's death). From uptown, the party moved to Fifty-second Street, where Basie was holding forth at the Famous Door (which of course enabled Hawk to check Lester out). By then, it included old Henderson buddies Buster Bailey and Russell Procope; Ella and Billie Holiday; Jimmie Lunceford, Charlie Shavers, and dancer Taps Miller. By 4:30 in the morning, they returned to Harlem for breakfast at Jimmy's Chicken Shack. As one of the participants noted in *Down Beat*, "We drove through Central Park, witnessing the daybreak of August the 1st, a new era for Coleman Hawkins."

A new era it was. After a legendary Harlem jam session, where Hawkins encountered Berry, Webster, Byas, sundry other tenor gladiators, and finally Lester Young, the consensus was that Hawkins had reclaimed his crown, with only the Lester partisans dissenting. On September 11, a Lionel Hampton date in the Victor Studios brought Hawk together with Carter, Berry, and Webster (quite a reed section!). Also on hand were a couple of youngsters, Dizzy Gillespie and Charlie Christian. By this time, Hawk was working on Fifty-second Street at Kelly's Stables with his own small group, but had already announced that he was forming a big band—the first of his career. It was still in the rehearsal stage when it recorded for Victor on October 11—just nine pieces and a vocalist—and had expanded for its November opening at the Arcadia Ballroom on Broadway.

At Kelly's Stables, Hawk was featuring himself on "Body and Soul," perhaps just because he liked this fine 1930 Johnny Green tune with its demanding bridge and harmonically interesting and challenging change, perhaps also because Chu Berry had created some stir with his recent recorded version (made on November 11, 1938, and issued on a 12-inch Commodore disc). In mid-October, *Down Beat* ran a photo of Hawk, taken, the caption claimed, while he was into "his seventh chorus of 'Body and Soul' at Kelly's Stables," so he was obviously making his mark on listeners with it.

With customary caginess, Hawk always claimed in later years that "Body" was included in his Victor debut date as an afterthought, at the request of the recording director, Leonard Joy. But it stands to reason that a minimum of four tunes were scheduled to be waxed that day, and since his version of the song already was the talk of the town, we should take this tale with a grain of salt.

In any event, Hawk came up with a masterpiece that day, at the end of an otherwise fairly routine record date. The two instrumentals—"Meet Doctor Foo" and "Fine Dinner" (the latter Harlem slang for a pretty girl)—show that the band was still a bit rough at the edges, if spirited, and that the leader's tone had become more forceful and gritty on such relatively fast "jump" pieces. His big sound also dominates the three-piece reed section. Pianist Gene Rodgers is the most interesting sideman; he had recorded with Carter in London in 1936 while touring with a late edition of the revue *Hot Chocolates* and was also arranging for the new Hawkins band. Trumpeter Joe Guy, later to become leader of the house band at Minton's in Harlem, shows some of his Roy Eldridge stuff, and the rhythm section is serviceable if a bit on the heavy side. Thelma Carpenter, all of seventeen, had been performing since the age of nine, but this was not her recording debut, which took place a few months earlier with Teddy Wilson's band; she later sang with Count Basie and then became a successful supper-club attraction in New York. On "She's Funny That Way," she hovers between Ethel Waters and Billie Holiday, but the main feature is Hawk's majestic full chorus and closing embellishments.

But this pales beside "Body and Soul," unquestionably one of the milestones in jazz recording history; one of a handful of perfect records. It's all Hawkins, excepting Rodgers's neat little introduction. By today's post-LP standards, his two choruses and short coda might be considered rather brief, but in those days of mainly 10-inch 78-rpm discs, this was an uncommonly long solo, especially at ballad tempo. The tempo, by the way, is a clue to the success of the performance; just right—not too slow, not a hair too fast, it allows Hawk to establish and maintain a romantic mood, but also permits him to maintain rhythmic momentum. He swings. Another factor is the simplicity of the arrangement: piano intro, first chorus backed by rhythm only, second chorus with soft "organ" harmony from the horns. Nothing to distract us from Hawk; even the rather plodding rhythm back-drop becomes an asset in this sense. Teddy Wilson, say, would surely have devised a more interesting accompaniment than Rodgers's static vamp, but then we would have had something else to listen for, and we're better off without that.

The first coupling to be issued—on Victor's low-priced Bluebird label—was "Doctor Foo" and "Foolish Things," and Hawk's solo on the latter earned him reviewers' praise. But "Body" was an instant sensation. "Hawk Ends Year in Blaze of Glory" proclaimed *Down Beat*'s record review section in a banner headline, and the body of the review noted that Hawk "held an ace in sleeve with customary canniness" and "leaves little doubt about his superiority on the instrument." The latter conclusion was unanimous among musicians and fans—in 64 masterly bars of improvisation, Hawk had reclaimed his undisputed tenor crown. Nearly fifty years later, "Body and Soul" instills awe in new listeners. I have played this record in jazz his-tory classes for young people, and the invariable response is applause and requests to hear it again.

When Hawk opened with his big band, "Body and Soul" was his theme song and in a sense remained so for the rest of his life. But he never played it the same way again, nor tried to. That would have been against his musical nature. Remarkably enough, when he next came to record it, at the previ-ously mentioned "first bebop date" in early 1944, he almost surpassed the 1939 masterpiece, under the title of "Rainbow Mist." And when he played it in person, there were always surprises, to the very end. What puzzled him about the public's acceptance of that first recording was that he hadn't both-ered to state the melody. (It appears only in the first two bars.) It was a gen-eral assumption that the public had to hear a tune "as written" before it would accept variations, but Hawk proved that assumption wrong, perhaps because the new melodies he created instantly engaged the listener's heart and mind. His improvisations were even singable, as Eddie Jefferson would prove years later in his tribute to Hawk.

When Hawk returned to the Victor studios in January 1940, it was for a lighthearted reunion with Carter and some other old friends. Trombonist J. C. Higginbotham and drummer Walter Johnson had been fellow Hen-derson sidemen and clarinetist Danny Polo a fellow expatriate (he spent most of 1927 to 1939 in Europe). The other three were in Hawk's big band,

Gene Rodgers being the only holdover from the October session. The music is happy and uncomplicated with a minimum of arranging touches; all the ensembles are jammed. Carter plays clear and solid lead trumpet (unfortunately, he takes no solos), Higginbotham is in splendid form, Polo's neat contributions show that he'd been removed from the pervasive Goodman-Shaw influence, and Rodgers is in his Wilson-Hines bag. The rhythm section is properly functional.

"When Day Is Done" features superb Hawkins, at a fine medium tempo. Fittingly, this is a tune of European origin, discovered and imported by Paul Whiteman during a 1926 tour. The venerable "Sheik of Araby" is taken for a nice fast ride; a highlight is the lion's roars with which Hawk opens his second chorus. "My Blue Heaven" shows Higgy at his best; Hawk dominates the closing ensemble. The single "original," "Bouncing with Bean," is a themeless jam on "I've Found a New Baby," with Polo at his peak on this date and a fine Carter lead. Hawk gets going and you can hear him breathe. (Note how he sets up his solo with a repeated riff.)

Six years elapsed between this and the next session. Hawk had maintained his big band until February 1941—the fronting role and the business parts of running this kind of musical organization were not to his liking. He scaled down to octet size, then to the sextet format he brought to California. That was just about his last fling as leader of a regular working group. By early 1946 he was one of the stars of the first national Jazz at the Philharmonic tour. The "52nd Street All-Stars" were strictly a studio band, put together by Leonard Feather. Hawk did not solo on two of the four pieces recorded that day, but "Say It Isn't So" is all his, excepting Jimmy Jones's introduction. Here the melody is even more oblique than on "Body and Soul"; I doubt that Irving Berlin would recognize his tune. Hawk is at his most 1946 modern and demonstrates his liberation from standard harmonic procedures, playing "off the chord" almost throughout his chorus and a half at a flowing tempo. His sound has changed again and is now smoother and more mellow, but that old roar is still in evidence on "Spotlite" (a Hawkins variation on "Just You, Just Me"). This fast piece is what might be called a "swing to bop" performance. Trumpeter Charlie Shavers is hot, hitting some freak high notes; the excellent guitar of Mary Osborne is in a Charlie Christian vein; pianist Jones proves himself an original with his unique chordal style, and Shelly Manne seems to wake up behind Hawk as the rhythm section turns boppish.

Hawk's next visit to Victor's studios, nearly two years later, finds him in splendid form and very compatible company. Hank Jones is an ideal pianist for the tenorman, and Max Roach had been working regularly with Hawk in New York. Bassist Jack Lesberg proves his mettle—he could (and did) work with any kind of jazz band, or with the symphony—and Chuck Wayne was in the front rank of modern guitarists. Fats Navarro and J. J. Johnson were among Hawk's favorite modern hornmen, and he'd recorded with both of them (and Jones and Roach) about a year earlier. The gifted Tadd Dameron was on hand to furnish the arrangements, and Feather was again in the booth.

The first and last tunes are features for Hawk, backed by the full band on "April in Paris," where, for a change, he shows his masterly way with a pretty melody, his sound more sensuous than ever. On "I Love You" (not the Cole Porter tune, but a nice old pop song), he's backed by rhythm only and plays with flowing, relaxed imagination; Jones has a solo spot. Hawk's also the whole show on "Angel Face," a Jones-Hawkins original that finds the master in inspired arioso form, and "How Strange," a tune of Russian origin on which he displays his beautiful control of the horn in all its ranges, climbing to the top for a fine ending.

"Half Step Down Please," typically Dameronian in its voicings and melody, is not unrelated to Gillespie's "Woody 'n' You," premiered by Hawk in 1944. Hawk, up first in the solo order, negotiates the changes like a champion, and there are fine contributions by Navarro (a clarion full chorus) and Johnson (a typical 24 bars). "Jumping for Jane," a Feather opus dedicated to his wife, is fast and boppish. It features fleet Wayne, Budd Johnson in a rare alto solo (his main horn was tenor) of a very Parkerish hue, Jones (Bud Powell and Nat Cole still audible as influences), Johnson, Navarro (whose entrance is dramatic), Hawk, and some Roach breaks in the out chorus. Clearly at home among the young men of modern jazz, Hawk must have enjoyed this session.

Five months later Hawk was back in Europe for his first visit since the war, and he returned for a longer stay in 1949–50. During the next decade, he frequently toured worldwide with Jazz at the Philharmonic, also fronting ad hoc groups at festivals and in major clubs throughout the U.S. By 1955 he was again recording prolifically, and the January 1956 dates for Victor included his first sessions with strings. Indeed, he was receiving the full LP treatment for the first time: lavish studio bands with special arrangements and no expenses spared.

Three discrete sessions are involved here: one with brass, woodwinds, rhythm, and strings; one with a big band of standard instrumentation; and a second session with brass, woodwinds, and rhythm but also with a much larger string section. Arranger Billy Byers, a jazz trombonist who'd found success as a player-arranger in commercial TV, was making a return to jazz at twenty-eight—to a degree at least, as we shall see—with this assignment.

That Hawk would respond well to such classy treatment was a given. He shows us just how well right from the start, with "There Will Never Be Another You," first at ballad tempo (gorgeous exchanges with the orchestra), then shifting into gentle swing. At this point one can clearly identify the Parker influence (try speeding this track up to 45 rpm and prepare yourself for a surprise), but he integrated that influence with his own unmistakable voice. He sustains his final note like a great cellist—or opera singer.

The fullness and roundness of Hawk's tone is lovely to hear on "Little Girl Blue"; he stays close to the melody but makes it his own. "Dinner for One, Please James" again shows Hawk's mastery of the full range of his instrument, and on "I Never Knew" Hawk again shows traces of Bird when the tempo goes up. Throughout, there's nice work on piano and celeste by Hank Jones, and the brief trombone passages are played by the late Fred Ohms.

On the big-band date, the accent is on brassy swing. "His Very Own Blues" finds the stellar studio cats in a Basie groove, while Hawk and Charlie Shavers (one of his favorite trumpeters) state the riff theme in unison. Hawk holds his own against the shouting brass with that huge tone and, as he moves along, offers some Illinois Jacquet licks (a legacy from JATP?) and some of the refurbished blues playing we mentioned earlier. He ends with a startling growl. "39"-25"-39"" is actually a Hawkins line known as "Bean and the Boys," based on "Lover, Come Back to Me." There's more of that unison with Shavers and a solo spot for Jones. "The Bean Stalks Again" is a revamping of a riff blues recorded by Hawk as the guest of the Count Basie band, "Feedin' the Bean." Compare this version with the one from 1941 and you'll surely hear what Charlie Parker's beneficial impact on Hawk's blues playing was all about. The Basie disc found Hawk mired in a monotonous groove, riffing with force but little imagination, but here he is creative throughout. We also get little solo spots from muted Shavers, front and back. "I'm Shooting High" finds Hawk and Shavers impeded by a brash arrangement noisily played.

"Opulent" is one fitting adjective for the third and final session with Byers arrangements; another, unfortunately, might be corny—there's a thin line being negotiated here. But Hawk triumphs whenever he picks up his horn. No doubt he liked the cello lead on "Have You Met Miss Jones," responding with a positively lustrous sound and complete relaxation. (Hear Milt Hinton's work here and learn why he's been on more record dates than any other bassist.) "The Day You Came Along," from Bing Crosby's early solo repertoire, was immortalized by Hawk on his first leader's date in 1934. This version's no match, but hear how Hawk responds to the first flute-and-strings bridge and know the difference between corn and artistry. Unflappable, he later shows how that bridge should be phrased, his sound, very gentle here, a joy to the ear. Then, "Body and Soul," revisited seventeen years later. This is a different kind of masterpiece, in a different setting and mood, topped off with a long, brilliant cadenza.

We close with a rarity—a Coleman Hawkins original not based on standard changes. He had considerable gifts as a composer (and arranger, too; he and others recalled a remarkable chart on "Singing in the Rain" he did for Fletcher Henderson, which was never recorded) but never had the inclination to pursue them seriously. Near the end of his life, his friend and frequent pianist Tommy Flanagan would often visit Hawk and try to get him to play things he'd composed on the piano in order to notate them, but these planned working visits would quickly turn purely social. "The Essence of You" is one of the few surviving examples of this side of a multifaceted artist. Based on a repeated undulating and catchy phrase, it's more a fragment than a worked-out piece, but offers a beautiful Hawkins solo, once Byers gets done with the interminable introduction.

About a decade of work that equaled—and sometimes surpassed—what he'd already accomplished remained to Hawkins after 1956, including a fruitful partnership with the undiminished Roy Eldridge. He continued to listen well to new developments in jazz and music in general. Nothing he could make use of creatively escaped his ear. In return, musicians young and old continued to listen to him, amazed at his constant self-renewal. When the final decline came, it was stark but blessedly swift, accelerated by his unfathomable determination not to take care of himself, to speed up the process of aging he'd held at bay for so long. It was revealing but not surprising when, not long after his death, a childhood acquaintance informed me that his father had committed suicide—a hitherto missing clue in the biography of a man who always kept private matters private.

But the mysteries of human personality need not deter us from savoring the products of human creativity. The legacy of Coleman Hawkins, of which this album is a significant slice, is one of the glories of twentieth-century music—body and soul.

(1986)

Ben Webster

This fine collection brings together, for the first time, all the recordings made by Ben Webster for Mercury between 1951 and 1953. Like the other albums in the Mercury V.S.O.P. series, carefully researched and compiled by Kiyoshi Koyama, it includes much rare material, some of it issued only on 78, some newly discovered and never heard before.

All of this music, whether taken directly from the original session acetate discs or digitally remastered from original tapes, has never sounded so good before, thanks to the skill and patience of engineer Frank Abbey.

The early '50s were years of relative obscurity for Ben Webster. Bop and cool jazz were the music of the day, and after leaving Duke Ellington in late 1949, Ben settled in Kansas City, his birthplace. He worked with Jay McShann and other local bands, toured briefly with Jazz at the Philharmonic, and made periodic visits to New York. Most often, however, he stopped off in Los Angeles, where his mother and grandmother lived, and by late 1953, he had settled there for the duration of the decade.

During this time, Ben became closely associated with Norman Granz, who employed and recorded the great musicians of mainstream jazz well before they were rediscovered by the jazz world at large. Meanwhile, we are fortunate that Mercury's jazz producer, Bob Shad (who died in March of 1985), gave Ben a chance to be heard on records in the early '50s.

As the history of jazz grows longer, the tendency is to view the past from a more and more concentrated perspective. Thus, the story of pre-bebop tenor saxophone is frequently summarized under the heading of Coleman Hawkins and Lester Young and their disciples. From this angle, such distinctively individualistic players as Chu Berry, Herschel Evans, and Ben Webster are seen as Hawkins followers, but in reality they were much more than just that.

To be sure, Ben Webster (1909–1973) in his youth idolized Hawkins and did his best to copy the great man's style. But by 1940, when Ben truly had found himself, he was uncontestably an original stylist, and himself a strong influence on younger players. By his own admission, he'd grown tired of being complimented on sounding like Hawk, and turned to two great alto players, Benny Carter and Johnny Hodges, for fresh inspiration. The mature Ben Webster can be said to have had two contrasting musical voices. One was a unique and masterful ballad style, gentle but filled with passion, with a sound that could melt a heart of stone. The other was the voice he used for blues and fast tempos: gruff, hoarse-toned, and sometimes almost violent.

These two voices, in a very real sense, reflected the personality of Ben Webster the man. With friends, Ben could be gentle and kind (those who knew him well have described how lovingly he looked after his grandmother, who lived well into her nineties), but if something aroused his anger—look out! He was a big, strong man and not many were willing to argue with him when he told them to get out of his way.

Considering his size and temperament, it is odd that the violin was Ben Webster's first instrument. He soon exchanged it for the piano, which he played well enough to obtain work accompanying silent movies. It was also as pianist that Ben did his first professional work with bands, touring the

Midwest territory. At this time, he met the slightly younger Budd Johnson, from whom he received his first saxophone lessons. But it was Lester Young's father, with whose band he worked for three months, who taught him enough saxophone for Ben to switch instruments for good. (During this time, Ben also saved Lester from drowning in a river.) Ben never gave up the piano completely, however, and loved to play some stride for his friends. Accuracy was not his strong suit, but he had a terrific beat.

As a saxophonist, Ben made his debut with Gene Coy's band, doubling alto and tenor, in early 1930. Later that year he was on tenor with Jap Allen, and then joined Blanche Calloway's band, with which he made his first records—she was Cab's older sister, and a fine singer and entertainer in her own right. Then came a stint with Bennie Moten, including a visit to New York and a famous recording session for Victor in 1932. After a stint with Andy Kirk, Ben entered the big time when Fletcher Henderson hired him to take the featured tenor chair in his famous band—the chair that had been vacated by Coleman Hawkins and briefly occupied by Lester Young, who now took Ben's place with Kirk. The Henderson men didn't care for Lester's approach to the tenor, but found no fault with Ben, then at his most Hawkins-like. When Henderson disbanded in late 1934, Ben worked with Benny Carter and Willie Bryant in New York, also briefly working and recording with Duke Ellington. (It was, by the way, Ben's solo on Ellington's record of "Truckin'" that inspired a youngster named Dexter Gordon to pick up the tenor.)

Ben next sat in Cab Calloway's busy band for a bit more than a year, went home to Kansas City for a rest, and then rejoined Fletcher Henderson, replacing Chu Berry, who'd replaced him with Calloway. Henderson's band was not what it had once been, and Ben left after some ten months to freelance in New York, where his associations included Stuff Smith and Roy Eldridge. He became a charter member of Teddy Wilson's fine but unsuccessful big band; it lasted from April 1939 until January 1940, and Ben was well featured, also contributing arrangements to its library. Like everyone who played in this band, Ben recalled it as one of the most musically satisfying experiences of his career.

But nothing could compare with the next step in Ben's life. As soon as Wilson disbanded, Duke Ellington invited Ben to join his orchestra. Duke had long felt that he needed a tenor solo voice in his orchestral palette, and he could have made no better choice. Nor could the timing have been more appropriate for Ben, for the Ellington band was about to enter what many believe to have been its peak period. Ellington and Webster served each other well. The tenorist fit the Ellington sound like a glove, and made major contributions to a series of masterpieces, not least among them "Cotton Tail." Ben's choruses on the recording of this piece became one of the most frequently copied solos in jazz history, but he also wrote the unison saxophone section passage, which became equally famous. And Ellington knew exactly how to feature Ben to the tenorist's best advantage, helping him immensely to achieve the mature stylistic identity that had become notable for the first time in his work with the Wilson band.

For Ben, an additional bonus was sitting next to Johnny Hodges, from whom he learned some of the secrets of how to handle a beautiful melody, in terms of both sound and phrasing. Like Johnny, Ben was a "singer" on his horn, and when Ellington gave him a melody like "All Too Soon" to work with, he made it his own. In all of Webster's work with the Ellington band of 1940–42, it's notable how splendidly he interacts with Jimmy Blanton's bass. It was Webster and Billy Strayhorn who heard the brilliant young bassist on a night out in St. Louis and rushed back to tell Duke about their discovery. Ben and Jimmy became inseparable, and the death of the young genius at twenty-three was a devastating blow to the man who'd come to consider himself his older brother.

Ben left Duke in 1943 to settle in New York, where he became one of the stars of Fifty-second Street. After work, he'd often go up to Harlem, and when he heard Charlie Parker at Monroe's, he wasted no time in spreading the news, warning his fellow saxophonists that they'd soon have some competition on their hands. In 1944, Ben was among the handful of black musicians to be hired for network radio staff work, on CBS with Raymond Scott. He also spent two months with John Kirby's little band (adapting himself surprisingly well to its rather delicate style), but he mostly led his own groups. His influence was at its peak, and his disciples included Eddie Davis (nicknamed "Little Ben" before he became "Lockjaw"), Paul Gonsalves (later hired by Ellington because he could play all of Webster's solos), Flip Phillips, Georgie Auld, and Charlie Ventura.

In late 1948, Ben rejoined Ellington for almost a year, but by this time his heavy drinking had become a problem, not helped by the band's heavy work schedule. No doubt, this problem was among the reasons why Ben decided to move to Kansas City, where there was less pressure. As we've already noted, he subsequently settled on the West Coast. When both his mother and grandmother died in 1962, he came back to New York, where he had made frequent visits. Among other things, he brought his kind of jazz to Harlem, where it had long been a rarity. During a long engagement at the Shalimar club on Lenox Avenue, he introduced his latest discovery, a brilliant young pianist named Dave Frishberg, and in 1964, Ben's roommate was another young keyboard artist of great promise, Joe Zawinul.

It was Joe who persuaded Ben to go to Europe. Astonishingly, the great tenorman, now fifty-five, had never been abroad. I vividly remember taking a long walk with Ben a few months before he decided to make the trip across the Atlantic. He explained his reluctance to travel all by himself to countries where a foreign language was spoken. "What if I should get lost on my way from the gig to my hotel?" he asked. "What if I should get sick, or get robbed?" The fact that so many of his good musician friends had long been going to Europe, Japan, and other parts of the world did not ease his apprehension.

In December 1964, Ben finally took off for Europe. He never came home again, finding a degree of warmth and acceptance overseas that was quite a contrast to the struggle for survival in New York. He first made his home in Holland, then in Denmark—both small and friendly countries where the pace of life was relaxed. His jobs became almost entirely a matter of playing with a rhythm section in a repertoire of the standards he loved best. His ballad artistry reached its highest level, and even as his physical powers declined, the feeling with which he could imbue a melody was astonishing. Though he missed his old friends, they often came to visit when on tour, and there were many new ones. The man who had been fearful of foreign lands spent the last decade of his life as a beloved and honored citizen of the world, respected as the great artist he was.

The blues-based music of Jay McShann presented no problems to Ben Webster, who was always at home with the blues. The pianist's jumping little band featured a strong back-beat and plenty of Kansas City–style riffs.

"You Didn't Tell Me" has two solo passages by Ben. After the vocal by Pee Wee Crayton (whose main importance to jazz history is that he fired Ornette Coleman from his band and left him stranded in Los Angeles, where he first became noticed), Ben plays a typical chorus with his own vocabulary of slurs and inflections. Clifford Jenkins takes the boppish alto solo, and then Ben returns, this time for 24 bars of powerful blues playing.

"Got You Begging" (the first take of which has not been issued before) has no solo work by Ben, but he makes his presence felt in the ensemble. Crayton's singing is well backed by McShann. Trumpeter Orville Minor, who was with McShann's big band in its Charlie Parker period, plays simply but well, especially on the second take, where he is encouraged by shouts from the other musicians. Jenkins gets two choruses and employs plenty of double-timing, notably on take two.

"The Duke and the Brute," a minor blues by Webster, is all instrumental and features the composer throughout, as lead voice in the band and in extended solo. His playing here is very emotional, with an almost vocal quality, and he gets fine support from the pianist. "Brute" was Ben's nickname in the Ellington band.

"Reach," also an instrumental blues, was not known to exist until Kiyoshi Koyama discovered it for the Mercury Fortieth Anniversary V.S.O.P. collection. The second take is issued here for the first time. McShann, well featured, begins with a figure from "Yancey Special"; he is in good form, especially on the first take. Ben's two choruses are very different on the two takes. Both are very relaxed, but he is more intense on take one, where he ends with a Webster "snarl."

Two months later, we find Ben in Los Angeles, sitting in as a featured guest star with the band of Johnny Otis. Born to Greek immigrant parents in California in 1921 (his real last name is Veliotes), the drummer and vibraphonist became so involved in black music that he completely identified himself with the black lifestyle. (His interesting autobiography, *Listen to the Lambs*, was published in 1968.) Most closely associated with R&B (he discovered Esther Phillips, and his son, Shuggie Otis, is a fine blues guitarist), Otis often featured jazz, as those familiar with his 1945 recordings for the Excelsior label will know. This fine session for Mercury is almost unknown—nothing from it has ever been on LP—and here we also get some excellent alternate takes, plus a previously unissued and unlisted item.

"Oopy Doo," after some good-natured rhythmic singing by Otis and the band, has a nice vibes chorus by the leader, Ben in two very strong choruses over the band, and more ensemble riffing, with Otis on top. The band tags, and vibes have the last word.

"One O'Clock Jump" is the new discovery, presented in three very different takes. All begin with a vibes chorus by Otis, followed by ensemble with Webster on top for two choruses. Gerald Wilson's trumpet choruses, quite different, are played with plunger mute on the first take, open on the other two. A piano vamp à la Basie by Devonia Williams follows; then Otis leads the band into some exciting riffing, and Ben comes back, hollering and screaming over the band's turmoil. The first take is the longest and has the most Ben, while the third has a noticeably different studio balance, with Ben much more forward of the band's riffing. This is powerfully swinging music—big-band jazz with an R&B flavor.

"One Nighter Blues," slow with an after-hours feeling, starts with saxes and piano fills. Pete Lewis's guitar solo has a B. B. King sound. Then Mr. Webster enters in the upper register and proceeds to preach a mellow sermon; his second chorus opens with a break, and he has a cadenza at the end. This is really the blues.

"Goomp Blues" commences with a piano-guitar boogie pattern over shuffle rhythm—Mr. Lewis and Miss Williams make a good team. The sax section riffs, and then there is plenty of action, including two stop-time sequences from Ben and Otis, more guitar, Ben hollering for two choruses with heavy brass riffs backing him up, Otis again, and Curtis Lowe's baritone, with a burly sound, the band stomping behind him. Then the opening pattern returns. You can dance to this!

"Stardust," a showcase for Ben, is the masterpiece from this excellent session, and the three complete takes—two of them newly discovered—give us a fascinating view of the great tenorman's artistry and unflagging inspiration. Each take is a gem. The first begins with Ben *a cappella*, way up high, answered by Otis's vibes. Then Ben moves gently into the chorus, backed by soft organ chords from the band. He doesn't state the theme, improvising from the start and making wonderful use of dynamics as he builds his solo. A brief Otis interlude sets up Ben's return, the band fuller behind him. He shares the complex cadenza with Otis and concludes with a cascading chromatic run. Take two is introduced by Otis alone. Ben sticks closer to the theme this time, and has only rhythm behind him. This is the big man at his most romantic. Otis's interlude is longer now, and then Ben opens up his sound, takes the cadenza by himself, and gives the band the final chord. Take three (the issued one) follows the routine of take two, but Ben stays even closer to the melody, though he devises a new and lovely ending for the chorus. Otis, obviously inspired by Lionel Hampton's famous record of this tune, takes his few bars, and Ben re-enters softly, then opens up into the most elaborate of the three cadenzas (with a slight reed squeak that doesn't matter at all). The tempo here is the slowest of the three takes, each of which, in varying degrees, demonstrates Ben's unique use of the air escaping from his mouthpiece as part of his total sound. (You can also hear him breathe—the recording quality is excellent.)

The next day, Ben was back in the studio as leader of his own date—his first in more than four years. His old friend Benny Carter was on hand and provided the rhythm section (most sources have given the drummer's name as George Johnson, but as corrected in Edward Berger's monumental Carter discography, he was George *Jenkins*). It is perhaps a bit odd to find Maynard Ferguson in this company, but he probably enjoyed this holiday from Stan Kenton and fits in better than one might have guessed. Sadly, this was one of John Kirby's last dates—the great bassist and bandleader died the following June. He was already ill, and it must be admitted that his playing here is not his best—he seems to have been unfamiliar with the correct changes to the two ballads.

"Randle's Island," a play on the name of jazz disc jockey Bill Randle and Randall's Island in New York City, is a medium-fast blues with a head devised by Carter. We get it here in three complete takes—two of them newly discovered—and a couple of false starts. The first take is the longest and has the bonus of a Carter alto chorus, typically elegant, plus one by Maynard (who appeared on the original 78 labels as "Tiger Brown"). On the other two, Maynard takes two choruses and Carter none. Ben has three choruses after the boppish opening ensemble and two more after Maynard, on each of the takes. He is best on the third, where the rhythm section also is most together, but the second was chosen for issue. It has the best of the trumpet solos, however.

"Old Folks," a beautiful Willard Robison ballad that bears a close resemblance to the much later "I Remember Clifford," is also offered here with two previously unknown takes plus the original master. It's all Ben's show. He plays a chorus and a half plus cadenza. The first take, which has Ben's most tender playing, begins with a piano introduction; this is omitted from the other two. Ben *sings* the melody, not departing much from it, and the tempo on the first attempt is slower than on the two others. On take two, Ben's second bridge is worth noting—a lovely variation. The feeling is less romantic. You can hear Ben asking, "Can you cut another right now?" and he moves into take three. This is his most assured performance, with another splendid second bridge and the best of the three endings, though there is less presence on Ben's sound.

"King's Riff" is a one-take item; apparently, everyone was satisfied. An up-tempo blues, it has two ensemble choruses, then two each by Ben, Maynard, and Benny (then in his most boppish stage, and the outstanding soloist here), plus pianist Gerald Wiggins with some busy bop runs and octave doublings. Ben returns in good form for three more, doing some of his special hollering. The whole performance swings nicely.

"You're My Thrill," a mournful ballad made famous by Billie Holiday, begins with a false start preserving Maynard's dramatic unaccompanied introductory fanfare (his only stratospheric playing on this date). The newly discovered complete first take opens the same way, then Ben swoops into the theme, exposing it in a reflective mood. But the pianist anticipates the ending of the first chorus, and though Ben moves right ahead and doesn't lose his balance going into the second bridge, this flaw was sufficient to call for another attempt. Maynard again executes the demanding intro without a hitch, and Ben, more mellow and relaxed, gives us a great cadenza. The accompaniment is also more relaxed and secure on this master take.

Dinah Washington had been recording for Mercury since 1946, often with excellent jazz accompaniment. In January 1952, she was in Los Angeles with her trio including Wynton Kelly on piano and her then husband Jimmy Cobb on drums. Cobb put together an excellent studio band including two great tenormen, Ben and Wardell Gray. Wardell's presence has been noted by discographers, Ben's previously only by sharp-eared listeners. On Richard M. Jones's classic 8-bar blues, "Trouble in Mind" (first recorded by Chippie Hill and Louis Armstrong), Dinah is in great form and Ben takes a grand chorus, at a relaxed tempo that suits him very well. Kelly's piano is much in evidence, and a good alto sax is heard in the opening band chorus.

In the 1950s, jazz musicians, tenor players especially, were often employed to accompany R&B vocal groups in the studios. Budd Johnson, Al Sears, Sam Taylor, and many others could be heard on many a vocal record, but until now, Ben Webster's presence on a Mercury session by the Ravens was a well-kept secret, and we must thank Bob Porter for revealing it. The Ravens, who started their career in 1945, were one of the very first R&B vocal quartets, with many hits to their credit. The secret of their distinctive sound was the resonant bass of Jimmy Ricks, often employed as the lead voice.

"I'll Be Back," co-composed by Ricks and featuring him throughout, is not a very distinguished song, but it has a nice beat, and Ben is heard both behind the singers and in a vehement solo turn, his tone at its roughest. The real find is "Don't Mention My Name," a slow, sweet ballad featuring lead tenor-singer Joe Van Loan. After the piano introduction by Bill Sanford, the Ravens' arranger, Van Loan sings a chorus, and then Ben comes in, backed by the voices, for a beautiful solo in his most romantic vein, which is the centerpiece of the performance. After the brief vocal recap, Ben can be heard again in a short but lovely cadenza. We repeat: a real find!

A year and one month after his first Mercury date as a leader, Ben was in New York for his second and last. This was a more ambitious undertaking than the Los Angeles session, with the gifted arranger Johnny Richards at the helm of an octet with an unusual instrumentation. Mellophone, trombone, and baritone sax emphasize the lower tonal ranges, with piccolo used for contrast and Ben's tenor moving freely through the middle range. (Experienced listeners will note that this instrumentation and conception is almost identical to the one employed by Richards on a Sonny Stitt date for Roulette in the spring of 1952.)

"Hoot," one of two Richards originals with nice, fast-moving changes, finds Ben leading the ensemble and soloing on the first bridge. He takes the next chorus (Richards keeps things busy behind him), there's an ensemble interlude, and then Don Elliott takes an agile mellophone solo, displaying his fluency in the upper register. Ben comes in at the bridge and completes the chorus. The final ensemble features piccolo lead—a device Richards was fond of and used well.

"Pouting," a minor blues composed by Ben and arranged by Richards, features Ben in four authoritative solo choruses. He demonstrates once again his mastery of the art of building up intensity, and offers a brief cadenza after the concluding ensemble passage, in which Billy Taylor's piano can be heard playing fills.

"The Iron Hat," a swiftly moving Richards piece, brings us the only alternate take from this session—evidence of the professionalism of all involved, for Richards's music was never easy to perform. Ben is featured extensively, in a setting including frequent breaks and complex ensemble writing. In both takes, Ben is in top form, at home with the changes and the fast tempo, swinging to the hilt and in full command. (Those who consider Ben primarily an emotional player with "limited" technique should listen well to his work here—he was a complete musician in all ways.) On both takes, the empathy between Ben and drummer Jo Jones is evident (Jo also has a break to himself), but the drumming is even better on the unissued take, with masterful hi-hat playing and a more relaxed flow. Probably the first take was chosen for issue because the ensemble playing is a shade more precise—and Johnny Richards, after all, was an arranger first.

As a bonus, we get an item from a session led by altoist Marshall Royal (of Count Basie fame) on which Ben made a guest appearance—he does not play on the two other pieces recorded that day. Jo Jones and Milt Hinton— a great team—are again on hand. The pianist is Bobby Tucker, best known as an accompanist (to Billie Holiday and, for more than twenty years, Billy Eckstine).

"'S Wonderful," the Gershwin classic, has a Tucker introduction, and then Royal exposes the familiar theme with his typical sweet tone, sounding quite a bit like Willie Smith. When Ben enters, Jo switches to ride cymbal, and the tenorist plays a strong, gutty chorus. The alto returns and, perhaps inspired by Ben, roughs up his tone quite a bit. Nice playing, but nevertheless, Ben's presence serves to point up the difference between good and great when it comes to jazz improvisation and true originality.

This set is a feast for fans of Ben Webster, among whom you can certainly count the writer of these notes and on behalf of whom I offer thanks to Kiyoshi Koyama for his discovery of so much new music by Old Ben.

(1986)

Jack Teagarden

Jack Teagarden's contract with Verve was the last of his long career, and *Think Well of Me* was the next-to-last album the contract yielded. Though the follow-up (*Jack Teagarden!!!*) was a pleasant romp through contemporary tunes with an all-star sextet, the elegiac nature of *Think Well of Me* makes it feel more like the great trombonist-singer's swan song.

The choice of songs by Willard Robison was singularly appropriate, for it was with this songwriter, singer, pianist, and bandleader that Teagarden made his first records—shortly after his arrival in New York in 1928. This was not the first encounter between these two, however, for Teagarden had done a short stint with Robison's band at a Kansas City hotel in 1924. Moreover, Robison's songs, redolent with a rusticity akin to Hoagy Carmichael's celebrations of nature, were ideally suited to Teagarden's relaxed and gentle vocal style. Producer Creed Taylor may have become aware of this empathy when Teagarden recorded two Robison songs, "Don't Tell a Man About His Woman" and "Peaceful Valley" (bandleader Paul Whiteman's erstwhile theme song), on his first Verve LP, *Mis'ry and the Blues*.

Like all of Teagarden's studio recordings since early 1958, *Mis'ry and the Blues* had been made with his working sextet, a group very much in the mold of Louis Armstrong and his All Stars—of which Teagarden had been a charter member. But for *Think Well of Me*, Taylor had something more ambitious in mind: special arrangements performed by a full complement of strings (with a harp thrown in for good measure) and commissioned from an old studio pro and a bright young star in the Verve stable who also happened to be a trombonist. The latter, of course, was Bob Brookmeyer; this record appears to be his first string assignment. The old pro was Russ Case (1912–1964), a better-than-average trumpeter who had been in an early edition of Benny Goodman's band and in arranger Raymond Scott's experimental sextet.

Case became an arranger-conductor and, during his tenure as director of pop music for RCA Victor, had used Teagarden in his studio bands. (For some odd reason, there's a non-Robison tune—Jimmy McHugh and Harold Adamson's "Where Are You?"—arranged by Claus Ogerman, then a Verve staffer, included in this otherwise all-Robison, all-Case/Brookmeyer venture.)

Perhaps at Teagarden's request, Don Goldie, from his working sextet, was brought along (according to George Hoefer's notes for the original LP, the two were "flown up to New York City from Florida" for the session) and written into the scores with featured spots and obbligatos. Goldie, the son of Whiteman trumpeter Harry Goldfield, was a favorite of Teagarden's. A technically accomplished, versatile instrumentalist who could also do a serviceable Louis Armstrong vocal impression (Teagarden used him as his partner on "Rockin' Chair"), he functions in this context as a kind of minor-league Bobby Hackett whose occasional lapses in taste serve to point up how impeccable Teagarden was in this respect: the man never played a meretricious note in his life.

That perfect taste is also highlighted by the arrangements. While the jazz use of strings shouldn't be reflexively condemned as "commercial," the Case and Brookmeyer charts, not so different from each other as one might have thought, don't add much musical meat to the proceedings. On occasion, the string textures do enhance the Teagarden sound, instrumentally and vocally; he probably enjoyed the status such attention conferred on him. And Robison did often employ strings in his Deep River Orchestra scores (long a feature on radio). Yet Teagarden's conception, sound, and feeling seem to inhabit a different realm from his surroundings—though there are exceptions, such as Case's excellent setting for "Country Boy Blues," one of the highlights of the set.

Diligent research has failed to reveal the identities of the supporting players. Though it wouldn't do any harm, we need not know the names of all the violinists, violists, and cellists. But it would be nice to confirm the identities of the sometimes overly busy pianist (probably Bernie Leighton on at least one of the sessions), the consistently fine bassist (Art Davis on at least one session) and drummer, and the proficient (and frequently prominent) harpist.

But what matters here is Teagarden. Though only fifty-six when this music was made, he had barely two years left to live. His health had started to fail, though there is no sign on this record of any weakening in his instrumental command and creativity. Nobody before or since has played trombone like this. (Though Teagarden was called a natural, in music as in sports this is a meaningless term.)

Teagarden did have instrumental technique that was strictly his own. When he began to play trombone, his arms were too short to execute all seven slide positions, so he taught himself to make do with just four, and even after his limbs were fully grown he never felt the need to extend his right arm beyond the bell of the horn. He could do everything necessary (and then some) in those four positions, and with his embouchure capabilities, this added up to something no player could match.

Then there was Teagarden's sound. Like every truly great jazz player, he had his own, and it was a joy to the ear: never overly brassy or boisterous but strictly mellow, a burnished sound that warmed the heart. He had a timbre that was instantly recognizable, whether he was playing hot or sweet, and it had a bluesiness that was part and parcel of the Teagarden musical profile. (For just one example, hear the last bars of his solo after the vocal on "Cottage for Sale.") He also had flawless intonation; blessed (or afflicted) with absolute pitch, he kept a tuning fork handy and would often spend part of the afternoon before a gig tuning the club's piano. And every note he played had that special velocity called *swing*.

And whatever Teagarden did musically was accomplished with a seeming effortlessness that made it unique. Those trombone codas that he loved to top off a performance with were done with such grace and ease that a listener could forget just how difficult it was to execute those trills, slurs, and bent notes. And it was all done with the barest minimum of movement, all in the wrist and the chops.

The laid-back essence was of course reflected in Jack Teagarden's singing as well; it, too, was accomplished without any strain. There was a time in his career, in the early '30s, when no less a talent spotter and recording director than Victor Young thought that Teagarden had the potential to capture some of Bing Crosby's audience appeal. Young recorded Teagarden as a kind of crooner (on Brunswick, which was also Crosby's label then). The records didn't become runaway hits but did make such songs as "Stars Fell on Alabama" and "A Hundred Years from Today" part of the Teagarden canon.

Those records were made during Teagarden's long tenure with Paul Whiteman, which lasted from 1933 through '38. It was a well-paying job during the Depression but Teagarden always felt that by the time he was free to start his own big band there were already too many in the field. Nor was he cut out to be the combination of businessman and musical director that a successful swing-era leader had to be. His eight years in that position added up to one long headache that was not curable by the medicine that he applied—strong drink. He gave up both the big band (permanently) and the bottle (temporarily), and in '47 he embarked upon four happy years with his old friend and early idol Louis Armstrong, whose music he had first encountered on a Bessie Smith record, "Cold in Hand Blues" ('25). Teagarden recalled many years later that he'd played the record over and over, delighted that such music could exist. (Eight years after that record was made, he recorded with Smith himself.)

It was inevitable that after the Armstrong All Stars began to enjoy great success, Teagarden would once again be tempted to become a leader, and heading up a small group did prove to be less of a burden than the big band had been. And his third wife, Addie, had a good head for business. Nevertheless, the years on the road were taking their toll, and it was the consensus among his peers that he was too kind a man to be a successful leader.

The last time that I saw Jack Teagarden was some three months before his death. He was leading a pickup group at the Metropole, a Times Square jazz spot featuring what must have been the world's longest bandstand. Musicians, perched somewhat precariously atop a bar that stretched the length of the room, dispensed the sounds of traditional jazz and swing at a time when modernism ruled the roost.

Teagarden was still playing well, but when he wasn't playing or singing, he seemed to be in a world of his own. Not that his timing was off—it was still perfect. But he looked, with that big moonface of his, as if he were a million miles away. One night, after the last set, I went to visit a friend at a nearby hotel, the one where Teagarden happened to be staying, and by coincidence I found myself in the elevator with him. At such close quarters, and away from the bandstand, he looked unbelievably tired and very pale. I couldn't think of any small talk, and his faraway gaze didn't take me in. I was almost afraid to get off at my floor, thinking that he might just go on riding that elevator, up and down, up and down, so I decided to bid him goodnight before getting off. And he did respond, with a slow smile and a drawled-out "Goodnight, gate." In Joe Showler's recently completed documentary film *It's Time for T*, Addie Teagarden reflects on the circumstances of Jack's death, alone in a New Orleans motel. "He was just so tired," she said. "He couldn't go on."

But on three days in New York City in January 1962, Teagarden was not tired at all as he brought new life to the eleven songs contained on this disc. On every one of these performances there are magic moments. And some, such as "Old Folks," are masterpieces. That one we know, of course. But hear such rarities as "In a Little Waterfront Café" (now you'll know another song about San Francisco) or "Country Boy Blues," with its challenging lyric (containing the immortal lines "A shoemaker's daughter / Could make a heel out of me") and marvelous blues trombone solo. Or the instrumental "I'm a Fool About My Mama," where Teagarden starts in the upper range of the horn—with that astonishing articulation and perfect intonation, each note a precision product (an accomplished mechanic, he made his own mouthpieces)—and concludes with one of those special cadenzas.

Hear those things, and then you'll agree with Teagarden's old friend, Pee Wee Russell, who said, "He was a complete master—absolutely no doubt about it. He owned it—that thing did his bidding."

(1998)

Pee Wee Russell

I n the early evening of March 29, 1960, I walked into Beefsteak Charlie's, a midtown Manhattan bar frequented by jazz musicians. With
some surprise, I spotted a familiar figure at the bar—familiar, but not at
Beefsteak's.

Pee Wee Russell, who'd turned fifty-four two days before, didn't hang
out there—or in any other bar, for that matter. He'd done his share of that
sort of thing—more than his share—but after his miraculous recovery from
a near-fatal illness some years before, he had stopped.

But here he was, by himself, having a quiet drink. I didn't yet know Pee
Wee well in those days, though I'd been enthralled by him for years, and
Pee Wee was shy with people he wasn't familiar with. But I sidled up to him
and ventured a greeting.

"How do you feel, chum" he acknowledged in that unforgettable *sotto
voce* way of his. "Have a drink." Pee Wee was in a mellow mood, and it soon
became apparent why. "We just made a record," he told me, "and it was a
good one—I think."

That was almost as surprising as finding him there. Pee Wee was not as
self-effacing as some people think, but he was his own severest critic, prone
to shaking his head and waving a hand "no" when his solos were applauded,
and only very rarely satisfied with his recorded efforts.

But about this session, he was not at all apologetic. In particular, he was
pleased with the rhythm section. "It was modern," he pointed out. "And the
piano player is one of the best I've ever played with." Pee Wee was particular about piano players. He was, in fact, particular about everything concerning music, but years of enforced association with contemporaries he'd
outgrown decades ago had made him adaptable. He had learned to endure,
and hold his head above the water.

No such problems this time out, though. No liabilities in this band. And
no Dixieland chestnuts on the program, either. Not even a traditional front
line. It had been more than a year since his last date as a leader, and in this
kind of setting, Pee Wee was ready to do some serious playing.

As for most of the great jazzmen we call, for lack of a better term, main-
streamers, the '50s and early '60s were problematic for Pee Wee. As often as
not, he had to play in settings far from perfect. Buck Clayton, that sensitive
and elegant stylist of classic swing trumpet, was making a living playing at
Eddie Condon's, where the staples on the musical menu were "That's A

Plenty" and "Muskrat Ramble," with an occasional ballad medley for respite. Oh, there was some good music made there, to be sure, and I wish the club were still around, but Buck deserved a less restricting framework. He had it here.

Pee Wee had given up the Condon routine years before, and led some good bands of his own, but the tribulations of leadership soon became more than he was willing to cope with, and so the gigs were infrequent and often less than congenial. Things were to get better in a couple of years, but at the time this record was made, it provided a welcome relief.

Now that Pee Wee's gone, it has become a precious gift. Every note he put on wax is something to be treasured, and fortunately, he managed to get quite a few things down for keeps. This album, however, is special; there are no dull spots to wade through. It's all of a piece.

It has been almost seven months, at this writing, since the bad news. If you love jazz and the people who make it, and have been with the music for a while, you get used to bad news—some expected, some not—and learn to live on as the ranks thin, accepting the inevitable.

Yet it is difficult to be resigned about Pee Wee's death. Every being is unique and irreplaceable, but he was more so. And he still had so much music in him to give. At sixty-two, he was not a shadow of former greatness, but rather the substance of new discoveries; as good as he'd ever been—perhaps even better. And music aside, Pee Wee was a lovable man. A few hours in his company could light you up for days to come. He was no saint, but he was holy.

Some unfortunates couldn't dig Pee Wee's music. Among them are some noted sages of jazz, one of whom only recently complained that Pee Wee spoiled a record that in fact was salvaged from mediocrity by his presence.

To me, he was a permanent revelation. In my early listening days (those days when you first discover the things that make the music part of you), I found a record of "Hello Lola" and "One Hour" by the Mound City Blue Blowers. I picked it up because I'd read Coleman Hawkins's name on the label, and the ballad side made me fall for Hawk for good. But there was something else on that side that made me play it over and over—a solo by a clarinetist named Pee Wee Russell.

He turned the scene around when he started to play on that. It had been recorded in 1929, the year I was born, and I was sixteen when I heard it. But it sounded "modern," strange at first, then as clear and inevitable as something by Louis or Pres [Lester Young]. I still love that solo, and it still sounds as fresh to me as it did those many years ago. It was my real introduction to Pee Wee's world, a world complete in itself and full of rare delights. He was a jazz musician to the core, and he never played an untrue note. Some wrong ones, maybe, though he could make wrong sound right, but never a false one.

He was often called odd, and there were people who considered his way of playing something to patronize. Belittling Pee Wee, however, only revealed the smallness of the belittler. It hurt him, nonetheless, as when a younger clarinetist, whom he sometimes sat in with (and without meaning to, played rings around), said, not softly enough to escape Pee Wee's acute ear, as his guest had left the stand (addressing his pianist), "Well, now we can play some real music."

Pee Wee didn't let on, but he never came back, and he never played with that cat again. What hurt him more than the insult was that he had liked the man and considered him his friend.

Among the many peculiar theories about Pee Wee was the one that he was some sort of natural musician who played his instrument in hit-or-miss fashion, a kind of happy accident. In fact, he was a thoroughly skilled professional, who'd done his share of section work in more or less jazz-flavored dance bands, doubling alto and tenor saxophones. He played the way he did because he wanted to, not because he was without legitimate skills. He was good enough at that sort of thing to have become a studio hack, but he was an artist by choice and temperament, and he cherished his freedom.

Pee Wee was one of the survivors of a generation of white jazzmen (though he was inordinately proud of his Indian ancestry) who discovered, without help or handbooks, the beauty of the black man's music and became part of it. All of these men were (or are) true originals. Some garnered more fame or notoriety than Pee Wee, but in some ways he was the most remarkable of them all. From the start, his music was unique, yet it could fit almost any surrounding. In later years, he never looked back. He was totally uninterested in re-creation, only in spontaneous creativity. While others played the old songs, Pee Wee taught himself new ones, and thus he found new listeners. His work of the last decade, I think, will stand with the finest music from that time—and of the time. When this record was made, Pee Wee, as always, was caught in the act of reinventing himself.

We have here one of the most compatible and relaxed rhythm sections imaginable. Any horn player with a liking for swing could not help but be inspired by such backing, and Pee Wee Russell and Buck Clayton are swingers.

Osie Johnson, whose playing sometimes could be a bit choppy, is flowing throughout; Wendell Marshall plays the right notes in the right places with the right time; and Tommy Flanagan is a jewel.

Buck Clayton is an ideal partner for Pee Wee. Both are melodists, but of pleasantly contrasting styles. Buck is symmetrical and lucid, Pee Wee asymmetrical and oblique. And they both listen as well as play.

There are two great blues on this LP, both originals by Pee Wee (who could write marvelous pieces). "Midnight Blue" is a happy blues, climaxed by some fine 4-bar exchanges between the horns. "Englewood" is a mean blues, opening and closing with splendidly funky clarinet. Each hornman takes a pair of brilliant choruses, and in the last ensemble, Buck's vocalized trumpet essays "West End Blues." This track alone is worth the admission price.

The other pieces are all standards, none of them shopworn. "The Very Thought of You" is the only ballad, and Pee Wee's soulful solo is beautifully complemented by Buck, muted and tender. This song was recorded by Billie Holiday, with a clarinet spot for Lester Young, my second-favorite clarinetist. Pee Wee and Pres had a lot in common—in respect to feeling—and Pee Wee's solo here ends on a Lesterish note. Dig his coda, too, and Tommy Flanagan's half-chorus.

"What Can I Say," etc., starts with some remarkable ensemble playing. All three soloists have spots, and Pee Wee opens his in his special trumpet bag.

"Lulu's Back in Town" has a nice tempo, and Pee Wee displays his lower register, leaping into high for part two of his solo. Buck saves some great glisses for his climax. The closing ensemble demonstrates the virtues of intelligent interplay—no arranger could improve it.

On "Troubles," Flanagan sounds remarkably like a modern Jess Stacy. Buck reaches for some high ones, while Pee Wee goes into his second chorus with a growl that is like a signature.

"Anything for You," a tune Pee Wee liked and recorded several times (once on tenor), has a remarkable clarinet solo, almost entirely based on the opening phrase. Buck is particularly strong and joyful in the collective finale.

Well, those are some things I especially enjoy about this record. It captures some happy moments in the life of a great jazzman. He liked it and so will you.

(1969)

Bobby Hackett

There was a very special aura to Bobby Hackett's music; it can perhaps be defined as purity. He never played a meretricious or unmusical note, no matter what the surroundings—and Bobby, in the course of his prolific career, frequently performed in contexts most jazz musicians would have found alienating. But he was incapable of compromising his musical integrity, and he enhanced whatever he touched.

This fine collection surveys some of Bobby's earliest recorded work. It's interesting to hear what a fellow trumpeter, Benny Harris (one of the unsung pioneers of bebop) had to say about it in a rare 1961 interview. (The opening "we" refers to "Little Benny" and his close friend Dizzy Gillespie.)

"We jumped on a record like Bobby Hackett's 'Embraceable You' because it was full of beautiful extended harmonies and unusual changes. Bobby was a guitarist and knew his chords, just as Dizzy and [drummer] Kenny Clarke knew keyboard harmony." In the spring of 1939, when that record came out, Benny was twenty, Dizzy twenty-one, and Bobby twenty-four. Such vital statistics, combined with opinions from musicians rather than critics, can be enlightening—in a recent biography of Louis Armstrong, Bobby is categorized as a "Dixieland" trumpeter. (Bobby's name for it was "whiskeyland.")

Armstrong, of course, was among Bobby's warmest admirers; so was Miles Davis. When Bobby came to New York in early 1937, his first write-ups drew comparisons with Bix Beiderbecke, and he was even called "another young man with a horn." Bobby liked Bix well enough—he pays fine tribute to the legend on the last two selections here—but insisted that his chief inspiration and idol was Armstrong. His playing bears him out, even at this early stage of the game when the putative links to Bix were most pronounced. In the '40s, he changed his embouchure and attack and increased his range upward, though he never became a high-note man—the story goes that Bobby once offered a trumpet for sale; when a prospective buyer asked about its condition, Bobby replied: "The upper register is brand-new."

Such slightly self-deprecating humor was one of Bobby's strong suits. A slender, gentle man with a laconic New England cadence to his surprisingly deep voice (born in Providence, Rhode Island, in 1915, he died on his beloved Cape Cod in 1976), Bobby was in his later years a chronic insomniac. Tired of staring at hotel room walls on the road, he often felt the urge to talk. If the phone rang at 3:30 a.m., it was almost certain to be Bobby, whose disarming opening gambit invariably was a measured "Gee ... I hope I didn't wake you." Who else said "gee"? That quaint phrase alone triggered instant forgiveness. Besides, Bobby always had stories to tell, laughs to share (even when things could have been better, and they usually could), insights to offer.

In those later years, Bobby was happiest working in tandem with Vic Dickenson, the great trombonist he always introduced as "my co-host." These unique individualists joined forces as often as possible from 1951 until Bobby's untimely death. When a gig didn't pay enough to cover Vic, Bobby worked with just a rhythm section, and he also guested with other leaders. Vic stayed busy. But both men looked forward to those special opportunities, when they could call the tunes and the feeling would be right, on and off the bandstand.

Bobby was famous for his reluctance to speak ill of anyone, and he was one of the world's worst businessmen. Thus, his biggest-selling records, mood-music albums made under the leadership of a Famous Comedian, brought him no royalties, just double union scales for the sessions. That left a bitter taste, but years later the worm turned. The Famous Comedian had received a lucrative offer to perform with his orchestra at a gala affair, but there was a hitch: the sponsor insisted on Bobby as featured soloist. The F.C. bit the bullet and called Bobby, who, with uncharacteristic acumen and toughness, held out for a huge fee. "I had him," he recalled, "and I didn't budge."

Usually, however, Bobby got the short end. Take the big band heard on six 1939 selections on this album. It lasted less than a year and left Bobby in a $35,000 hole—a lot bigger then than today. In desperation, he accepted an offer from Horace Heidt, leader of a show-and-sweet band, with whom he was featured on immortal numbers like "Little Curly Hair in a High Chair." (Occasionally, there was a respite, when Heidt cast him as Bix with a jazz contingent from the band, as heard here on "Clarinet Marmalade" and "Singin' the Blues.") He left after nine months and got a Hollywood gig, soundtracking trumpet-playing Fred Astaire in *Second Chorus*; musicians knew, but the public was none the wiser. He led his own smaller bands for a while, and then had trouble with his teeth. Glenn Miller (usually depicted as a martinet with a heart of steel but a good friend to Bobby, whose playing he loved) came to the rescue, giving him a job on his first instrument, guitar. When the chops started to come back, an occasional cornet solo would enhance a Miller performance—take "String of Pearls," with that beautiful scalar solo, or "Rhapsody in Blue."

Then came a real break—a staff job at NBC, and then one at ABC. Good pay and time to moonlight in jazz clubs and on jazz record dates, or

behind singers who knew what a Hackett obbligato could do for them—
take Sinatra's "I've Got a Crush on You." Tony Bennett used Bobby a lot
later on, after another failed experiment with an unusual eight-piece band
in which almost everyone doubled (or even tripled) instruments. The ideas
were always there, but the breaks weren't. Yet Bobby never lost his love for
playing or his sense of humor. In Chicago in 1969, the Hackett-Dickenson
band opened a new club that had failed to advertise, though they'd printed a
lot of posters. After playing a set for a small group of friends, Bobby told the
owner to forget about the rest of the gig. Then he took a red marker and a
poster and wrote TILT across it in big letters. Then back to the hotel room
for some Armstrong tapes and some laughs. I still have that poster. (And I
miss those calls.)

There's a lot to listen for here aside from that magnificent "Embraceable You"—a model of creative improvisation, and yet (that was part of
Bobby's magic) always in touch with the essence of Gershwin's song. His
chorus on "Poor Butterfly" is another stunner; this cut also has fine Ernie
Caceres baritone. But among the other soloists, Pee Wee Russell stands
out. He tells a story in 8 bars on "Ghost of a Chance," coming in relaxed
like Lester Young. And on "Sunrise Serenade" he follows a rather lame
arranged passage with a jolting definition of jazz. On this and the other big-
band sides, the drummer is Don Carter (who also recorded with Muggsy
Spanier and Jess Stacy), whom the great Dave Tough admired—listen for
his cymbal work and press rolls. There's a glimpse of Pete Brown's unique
alto style on two cuts from a Leonard Feather session (his first in the U.S.);
"Jammin' the Waltz" was inspired by Benny Carter's 1936 "Waltzing the
Blues"—3/4 jazz was still a rarity. The violinist, by the way, is Ray Biondi,
otherwise on guitar. But most of the guitar work is by Bobby's great friend
Eddie Condon, including that worthy's sole big-band recordings. George
Brunies had few peers as an ensemble trombonist, and Brad Gowans had
interesting ideas, also as an arranger.

But this is Bobby's record. "Ja-Da," a feature for him then, is another
masterpiece of scalar poetry—how relaxed he was! That came from Louis,
but Bobby was his own man. How much so we can hear on the Bix tribute
"Singin' the Blues." It opens with a Bix quote and ends with the whole band
playing a transcription of the famous 1927 solo, Bobby taking Bix's break.
But in between, the voice we hear is Bobby's, and on his solo he plays *his*
stuff. With no disrespect to the Davenport kid, Bobby holds his own, and
maybe then some.

Bobby Hackett was special. He's in the pantheon.

(1988)

Ella Fitzgerald

A s in Louis, Frank, Elvis, and very, very few others, the first name suffices. No one's going to ask: "Ella who?" Nor would anyone take issue with the following claim:

"Ella Fitzgerald has been called the greatest and the First Lady of Song and almost every other superlative for so long now that it begins to become one of those accepted bromides like 'an apple a day keeps the doctor away,' etc."

What makes this passage really quotable is that it was written forty-five years ago—by the late Bob Bach in the late *Metronome*, then a leading music magazine. The article also noted that Ella had placed first in the magazine's annual readers' poll as long ago as 1939, four years after her professional debut. *Metronome* is long gone, but *Down Beat* still runs polls, and Ella still wins them, though her reign has on occasion been interrupted by such upstarts as Sarah Vaughan and Betty Carter.

At seventy-five, the redoubtable First Lady has curtailed her appearances considerably, but seeing her at Radio City Music Hall last year proved to this old admirer that the magic is still there. She's frail now, and failing eyesight requires that she be led onto the stage, where she settles onto a stool. But once warmed up, after a couple of songs, the voice still has that essential girlish charm, the vitality still flows, the pitch is still perfect, and she swings as hard and sure as ever. Moreover, and perhaps more important, she still loves to perform, and still has to beg off after who knows how many encores, demanded by a crowd of fans still as committed to her as she is to them and to her art. She remains the First Lady of Song—a title that should be retired with her when the time comes.

This compact disc birthday bouquet covers the period from 1938, the year of Ella's first big hit, to 1955, when her twenty-year association with the Decca label came to an end. During that time span she graduated from band vocalist to bandleader to featured single attraction. These were the years in which she honed her musical and performing skills to the astonishing consistency that has been her hallmark ever since.

The warm personal reminiscences by Milt Gabler have painted a far more intimate portrait of the artist than I could attempt, but, in spite of Ella's great fame, a few inaccuracies still crop up in biographical sketches, so here is a résumé of her earliest years:

Ella Fitzgerald was born in Newport News, Virginia, on April 25, 1918, and never knew her real father. As a young child she moved to Yonkers, a suburb of New York City, with her mother and stepfather. By her own account (Ella is essentially a private person and doesn't talk readily about herself, she made an exception in a long interview with old friend Leonard Feather in 1983); she had a pleasant family life, relatively sheltered from racism.

"Growing up in a mixed neighborhood," she told Feather, "I had mostly Italian friends. First time I ran into a prejudice thing, a boy came in from another school and he called me 'nigger.' Well, I pushed him, he fell down, and the other kids thought I had hit him—so I became a heroine at the school! They made him apologize, and after that everyone looked up to me, thought I was real bad! I was about eleven."

She learned to read music in school, though her first ambition was to become a dancer—her idol was the remarkably flexible (and somewhat sinister) Earl "Snakehips" Tucker. But her mother had records, and Connee Boswell became Ella's favorite singer (she also liked Dolly Dawn, whom she heard at a local theater). She had a few piano lessons, but the money ran out. To supplement the family income, Ella took numbers and for a while worked as a lookout for a "sporting house." As she jokingly told Feather, "Oh yes, I had a very interesting young life."

Ella also entered amateur contests at both the Apollo Theater and its neighbor and brief competitor, the Harlem Opera House. These events, several of which she won, have often been rolled into one, leading to confusion about who did what to eventually get Ella her job with Chick Webb's band. At one of those contests, most likely at the Apollo, she was heard by Benny Carter, who, along with John Hammond, recommended her to Fletcher Henderson. But that bandleader, who never did feature a girl singer, wasn't interested. This may or may not have been the same contest that led CBS to offer the young girl a contract for regular appearances with "The Street Singer," Arthur Tracy, on his popular radio show. But suddenly, Ella's mother died, "and I wasn't of age and nobody could sign for me, so the whole deal fell through," she told Feather. (Her mother's death while she was still a minor has led to the mistaken notion that Ella was reared as an orphan.)

Now living with an aunt, she continued to enter contests. The payoff came in February 1935, when first prize at the Harlem Opera House earned a week's work with the band there, led by drummer-singer Tiny Bradshaw, for $50. "They put me on right at the end, when . . . everybody was ready to leave. Tiny said, 'Ladies and gentlemen, here's the young girl that's been winning all the contests,' and they all came back and took their coats off and sat down again." Among those who stayed on was Bardu Ali, the entertainer who fronted Chick Webb's band. He thought Ella would be great for the little drummer's outfit, which held forth at Harlem's Savoy

Ballroom and had recently engaged a male vocalist, Charlie Linton (who, by the way, is still active in New York at this writing). Chick wouldn't hear of it, though, until Ali smuggled Ella into his dressing room and forced him to listen.

The drummer grudgingly offered to take her along for a prom date at Yale. "If the kids like you, you can stay," he promised. According to legend, the chorus girls at the Opera House chipped in to buy Ella, never noted for stylish couture, a pretty dress. Fortunately, the Eli promtrotters approved, and she got the job, at a starting salary of $12.50 a week—musicians made $75. By the time of Webb's death in June of 1939, she was up to $125 and was the band's undisputed star and primary meal ticket. Ironically, some of the sidemen felt that her popularity was holding the band back from a musical standpoint, although Webb continued to feature plenty of instrumentals. These same musicians, however, soon found themselves beholden to the young singer for their very livelihoods, for she was selected by Webb's manager, Moe Gale (who also ran the Savoy), to front the drummer's band, henceforth known as Ella Fitzgerald and her Orchestra. It lasted a respectable two years, with surprisingly stable personnel. Whatever jealousy there might have been, the musicians affectionately accepted Ella as one of their own. Needless to say, she didn't call the shots for the band and must have been relieved, in the summer of 1941, to start her career as a single. At first she was backed by the band's rhythm section and its last musical director, reedman Eddie Barefield. Then she toured with a vocal-instrumental quartet, the Four Keys, with whom she made her last sides before the August 1942 American Federation of Musicians recording ban.

Her first session after Decca had settled with the union (the first major label to do so) paired her with another vocal group, of considerably greater fame: the Ink Spots.

Decca was enamored of cross-pollinating its contract artists. This had begun almost at the label's birth, leading to such extravaganzas as the 12-inch medley from the film *Pennies from Heaven*, featuring Louis Armstrong, Bing Crosby, Frances Langford, and the Jimmy Dorsey Orchestra. In Ella's case, the producers were high on vocal groups. Aside from the two already mentioned, we hear her with the Delta Rhythm Boys, the Song Spinners, and the Ray Charles Singers (not *that* Ray Charles, but the vocal arranger); others included the Mills Brothers, the Skylarks, and Four Hits and a Miss.

Such a mixed bag indicates that the label was never quite sure how to present a singer of such versatility. She could range from all-out jazz performances like "Flying Home" to what can only be called the outright commercialism of "My Happiness." From a positive angle, this made it impossible to typecast Ella; but on the other hand, it prevented her from

developing a strong identity—which she *did* achieve during her later relationship with Norman Granz's record labels.

   This is not to deny that many pairings with other artists, and much of
the material and settings she was given, did have terrific results. Her encounters with the Ink Spots were engaging, especially when her style and
sound were contrasted with those of tenor Bill Kenny. Creative sparks really flew when she and Louis Armstrong were brought together—"Dream a
Little Dream of Me" is utter bliss! Louis Jordan, who had been with Chick
Webb during part of Ella's tenure, also proved a near-perfect match. (The
two had been an "item" in the Webb band, and he tried to get her to leave
with him when he decided to form his own Tympany Five—or so we are
told in John Chilton's biography of Jordan, *Let the Good Times Roll*.) And
some would claim that Ellis Larkin was the perfect accompanist for Ella: try
"Until the Real Thing Comes Along," the sample collaboration in this
collection.

   Among Ella's regular pianists, a standout was Hank Jones, who put in
some five years with her, starting in 1948. It's interesting to note that a later
occupant of that demanding position was Tommy Flanagan, in many ways a
musical descendant of Jones, and who, like Hank, began his career in Detroit. Playing for a singer is a special kind of musical task, which, among
other things, calls for sublimation of ego. It speaks volumes for Ella's
artistry that two of the greatest jazz pianists of all time spent years working
with her.

   Another great instrumentalist who accompanies Ella on many of these
performances is bassist Ray Brown, but his frequent presence was due to
extra-musical reasons: Brown and Ella were husband and wife from 1948 to
1952. It was her second marriage; the first had been in name only. As she
told Leonard Feather: "I went and got married on a bet. I was that stupid;
the guy bet me I wouldn't marry him. The guys in the band were all crying
when I told them." This was while she was still a bandleader. She got a
quick annulment, and the judge told her, "You just keep singing 'A-Tisket,
A-Tasket' and leave these men alone."

   Ella and Ray worked together often, even after their divorce. One permanent effect of the relationship was that Norman Granz discovered Ella's
magic. She had come to see Brown at a Jazz at the Philharmonic concert in
1948; members of the audience caught a glimpse of her and called out for
her to sit in. Granz was reluctant but gave in, and was converted on the
spot. By 1950, she was touring regularly with JATP and Granz had become
her unofficial manager (she was still contractually tied to Gale). By 1954,
the relationship became official, and a year later Granz was able to get Ella
out of her Decca deal—and thus her *Song Book* era and long affiliation with
his Verve label began. Ella had been linked with Decca for twenty years,

and while Granz was to open many new doors and expand her artistic horizons, that period had laid the groundwork. The eclecticism of Decca's approach had served to put her in contact with every facet of the vast audience for popular music and jazz; she had already, as we have learned, become the First Lady of Song, and had influenced countless singers.

This compilation, a cross section of those first two decades in a truly remarkable career, selected by Milt Gabler, the man who produced many of the numbers, shows us that she was, among other things, unflappable, consistent, and capable of enhancing not only trivia, but also gold. One of her secrets, perhaps, is that she thinks like a musician, always able to find the best in any melody. Another is that she loves what she does, and never has become complacent about it. To this day she's nervous before she goes on, and even after ten standing ovations not sure she really did well. We, of course, know better. As Murray Kempton (a great admirer) once put it, no one else is "at once so simple and so complicated, so innocent and so sentient." This musical trip takes Ella Fitzgerald from girl to woman; to this day, she remains both. That's another of her secrets.

(1993)

Lester Young

There was only one Pres. To say he was unique is an understatement; he was miraculous. And since everything he played contained his unique presence, nothing he has left us is less than precious.

Don't let them tell you how Pres (some spell it with a "z") couldn't play in his later years. Sure, there were times when the strength required to fill the horn just wasn't in him, and then it was painful to intrude. But he usually managed to make the instrument do his bidding, and the power of his imagination was never impaired.

The Lester of 1956 is not the Lester of 1936, but should we want him to be? It is the fate of the artist, as unfair as it is unavoidable, to always be measured against himself; he may be faulted for changing too much as well as for not changing enough.

In Lester's case, we know nothing (except scattered, dimly remembered impressions of musicians who heard him then) of his earlier style or styles, before he finally got to record at twenty-seven (relatively late as great jazz figures go). It surely could have been as different from 1936 as that in turn from 1956.

Lester as the world first heard him, leaping out from "Lady Be Good" and "Shoe Shine Swing," was so pure, so perfect that he became a measure not only for himself but also for all of the music. The perfection of his work with Count Basie, with Billie Holiday—with anyone—during the late '20s and early '30s, is such that it stands on heights inhabited by only a very few other genuine miracle makers.

Yet that perfection is the work of the same man who made the music on the record you are now holding. He was never less than Lester Young, or other than Lester Young. And that was never less than enough.

This is some of the best late Lester Young you'll hear.

The year 1956 had begun auspiciously with the recording—for Norman Granz, who never lost faith in his greatness—of an album, *Jazz Giants of 1956*, which contained things that made even the naysayers take notice. On the following day he did a quartet date that, among other gems, produced a blues named "Pres Returns." The title had reference to a recent bout of ill-ness—general debilitation rather than any specific ailment—from which he had emerged refreshed.

The jazz scribes have painted a so unmitigatedly gloomy picture of Lester's years after his traumatic experiences in the U.S. Army—that is, from late 1945 until his death on March 15, 1959—that one is tempted to overemphasize the positive aspects for the sake of just balance. The only unbiased witness is his music of those years, and while it sometimes speaks of pain and suffering impaired by abuse to which he subjected his body, it often speaks with such power and conviction, humor, and love—even joy—that it is quite impossible to accept the gloom-and-doom reporters' picture.

Their vision is impaired by certain prejudices—not racial, but social and cultural—against his unorthodox behavior that kept them from under-standing and appreciating Lester in his later stages. For instance, his drink-ing and smoking. (Jazz writers, by and large, reflect an astonishingly dense and puritanical attitude toward marijuana—at least, officially—that isn't very different from the average Rotarian's.) Or his eccentric demeanor and speech, which gave rise to all manner of doubts about his sexual orientation (he liked women) and sanity (he was saner than most of us, to the end). Did these petty, mean-spirited attitudes, refracted in far too much of what was and is written and said about him, cause him to withdraw even further into himself? We can only guess.

We—I—do know, however, that when we heard and saw Pres during those years, it was more often than not an exhilarating experience. It is not at all true that he had lost his audience to bop by the late '40s; packed houses at the Royal Roost and Birdland then, and later, would cheer him. He was loved well. It is not true, either, that he was ill at ease and discomfited with Jazz at the Philharmonic because so-called honkers were pitted against him. Listen to "Lester Leaps In" or "The Opener" from JATP Vol. 7, and see if Flip Phillips bothered him. That he wasn't an extrovert didn't mean he couldn't play bold, outgoing music. And don't tell me that these examples (from late 1949) are too early to prove the point: check out "Lester Gambols" from late '53 or "The Slow Blues" and "Merry Go Round" from late '57.

Aside from these JATP things, Lester made a long series of studio albums for Norman Granz, from 1950 to the end, which contain many musical marvels. Sure, he was slowly, tragically destroying himself. But—and this is a large "but"—he remained a powerfully communicating artist. He was, despite the hurts and abuses, still a loving, giving man and artist, still capable of and willing to communicate beauty, hope, even strength. There is a touching sense of resignation in very late Lester. He was tired of fighting ugliness, stupidity, and insensitivity with the only weapons he had: beauty, wit, and total awareness. And there was frequently physical pain as well, fought off with pharmaceuticals that then in turn aggravated it. And yet the message, even in resignation, remained a positive one.

The figure painted by the writers—a pitiful, degenerating man—is denied by the lack of self-pity in his music. Maybe Lester was laughing to keep from crying, as the title of one of his last albums has it, but his was the laughter of the gods. The last time I saw and heard Pres, in his final months, he softly admonished his faltering pianist: "Never give up. Don't ever give up!" It wasn't Lester who failed us.

On the record in hand, Lester is backed by a French rhythm section consisting of pianist Rene Urtreger, bassist Pierre Michelot, and drummer Christian Garros—a trio that Lester also worked with for a two-week stint at the Club St. Germain in Paris that preceded the tour. The package premiered in Paris on November 2, and was in Frankfurt a week later. After the concert, Lester went to a local jazz club (Frankfurt was pretty much the center of German jazz activity in those days), perhaps at the invitation of some of the musicians he wound up playing with. Bassist Al King and drummer Lex Humphries were both stationed at the U.S. Army base nearby as band members, and the Swedish pianist Lasse Werner was active in Germany between 1956 and 1961. (This detailed information, unavailable when this music was first released, comes from the Danish jazz scholar Frank Buchmann-Møller's excellent Young discography, *You Got to Be Original, Man!* [Greenwood Press].) Judging from the audible audience reaction (cries of "work, work," and some rather un-Germanic whistling), a goodly contingent of Americans was in attendance. The piano, unfortunately, was not state-of-the-art.

The recording devices and setups are primitive, but no matter. In recent years, a tremendous amount of privately, non–commercially recorded material, on the spot and off the air, has come into release. When I began to collect jazz more than fifty years ago, there was no tape and the existence of such abundant material was unknown, at least to novices. Now our whole picture of the music of the past is changing. Music from broadcasts, jam sessions, private music-making, nightclub sets, and concerts is shedding much light on what was hitherto known largely through studio recordings—and what light! Some of the greatest music is also some of the worst recorded, but if recording quality were the ultimate criterion, Enrico Caruso would long have been eclipsed.

No, there's enough of the sound of Pres—and what a sound, far from pale—to carry the message. If there isn't always a lot of the other instruments (drums excepted), no matter. Pres is it, and he was in fine spirits. Rather weak support notwithstanding, he stretches out, makes himself comfortable as only he could (Lester was the ultimate in relaxation, another innocent source of resentment from uptight folks), and spins his enchanting tales. He observes, he understands, he laughs—sometimes mockingly but never maliciously—he dances, he sings, he floats.

Lester was a dancer, a dreamer, a master of time and its secrets. Foremost among them: equilibrium. He never stumbles on the tightrope of swing, of tension and relaxation held in perfect yin-yang balance. He is a juggler, a high-wire artist without a net, a diver, a gambler, a gamboler.

The discoveries, the clear profundities, of late Lester have been little understood. Some of his exquisite languor, no doubt, was the result of the need for conservation of energy. But what he made of this necessity! He was indeed a mother of invention, Pres was.

The two final selections, apparently taped directly from a TV set, stem from a Birdland Show concert at an unknown location, probably in late November. Pres and the rhythm section certainly were attuned to each other by then, and even though these performances are fragments, it's good to have them. By the time the TV show was broadcast, on January 2, 1957, Pres had been back home for a month or so; in early December, he played a memorable gig in Washington, D.C., from which a good deal of music was posthumously issued (on Pablo), sustaining the great form he demonstrates herein.

"Lester Leaps In"—what genius it took to make up a piece so simply containing the essence of the jazz spirit. The tempo (you can hear Pres beat it off) is a mite slower than is customary, tailored to the limitations of the rhythm players. "No bombs, please—just 'titty-boom,'" was Lester's standard instruction to boppishly inclined drummers. Humphries is at first more 'boom-chick' than 'titty-boom,' but he warms to his task, as does Pres himself. Dig the stop time. And the tonguing—what a master of that he was. And the humor and gaiety of the performances! Is this the music of a weak, faded, wasted man?

"These Foolish Things"—a favorite of his. He paints a picture, with that warm sound so falsely described as small or thin. It is the perfect sound to convey the inner meaning of the music. He ascends with perfect control into the uppermost register of the tenor for the final half-chorus, picking it up at the bridge. And what a bridge! All great soloists quote themselves on their favorite pieces; here it's done to set up the cadenza.

"There Will Never Be Another You"—a worthy sequel to the 1952 version. He opens with five wondrous choruses, the first doing justice to Harry Warren's fine tune. ("There's not a poorly chosen note in the melody. It's sinuous, graceful, gracious, sentimental, totally lacking in cliché."—Alec Wilder, *American Popular Song*.) He floats, suspended on air. Ingenious use is made of repetition in the fourth chorus; the ultimate in sophisticated simplicity was Lester—soooo concentrated. He had more ideas in 32 bars than some musicians manage to come upon in a lifetime. And note the return to the melody for the climax of the solo—a Louis touch, also in the singing of it. (You can always sing Pres.)

"Lester's European Blues"—a blue fantasy by a master bluesman, a man who made up a whole new thing on the blues. He begins with a wryly happy groove, having a little conversation with himself, trading phrase for phrase (and how many phrases did he imprint into the jazz language?). Before too long, he starts to holler, gets very blue (with a quote from "Blue Lester" and another from "Shake, Rattle and Roll" that cues a sing-along). Then, finally, he darkens, goes way down, and ends as he started out. A ten-minute trip through Lester's beautiful head.

"Lullaby of Birdland"—Shearing's inversion of "Love Me or Leave Me" transformed into Lesterian arcs of sound. Third chorus into it—"Hear me talkin'"—and a nice and typical ending. The drummer is with it here.

"Polka Dots and Moonbeams"—another fine standard by Jimmy Van Heusen. Lester loved it. (Once, on an Art Ford TV show, a certain ballad was suggested. Said Pres: "I don't want to play 'Waterfront,' I want to play 'Polka Dots and Moonbeams,'" stressing the moon. He did. On that occasion he had brought a stray kitten to the studio in his saxophone case.) The main strain, Alec Wilder notes, "is made up mostly of a series of ascending and descending scale lines." Lester, utterly relaxed, gives us 4 bars of the melody, then glides into Lesterland. The coda is superb.

"Lester Leaps In"—faster this time, the support firmer. The fact that the drummer uses his foot makes the kit sound like a different instrument. This is all Pres, strong Pres; a mere fragment, yet a whole. Pres could say it all in 4 bars. Hell, he could say it in a note.

Long live Gentle Lester, who loved life despite what it had done to him, and who never stopped reaching out, gifts in hand. To hell with those who called your strength weakness because you turned the pain inward, upon yourself rather than on others, and offer simplistic explanations for your singular fate. Perhaps they envy you your immortality.

(2000)

Charlie Parker

You are holding in your hands a precious document—one of the most important jazz records ever released. It sheds new light on the art of one of the greatest musicians of our century by making public—after years of clandestine circulation—the earliest recorded works of Charlie Parker. And in addition, there's a fantastic find, a 1942 "Cherokee" embodying Bird's first extended solo captured by recording equipment.

The earliest music here antedates Parker's first commercially issued recordings by a mere five months, but is so different in setting and atmosphere—and gives us so much more of him to hear—that it is indeed a revelation. That this music was recorded, preserved, and uncovered is something of a miracle. It came about as follows:

In the fall of 1940, the band led by pianist Jay McShann had just completed its first major road trip out of its home base, Kansas City, and was playing a weekend date in Wichita. The manager of the local radio station, KFBI, Fred Higginson, knew and liked McShann. Higginson arranged for McShann to make some broadcast transcriptions for KFBI. Either because McShann was playing Wichita with a group smaller than his regular twelve-piece lineup or, more likely, because the station couldn't afford to pay for the full band, the transcriptions were made by an octet.

In any event, the scaled-down instrumentation results in a much looser, more freewheeling kind of music than can be heard on the records made by the full band for Decca in 1941. What we have here, in fact, is a representative cross section of the 1940 repertoire employed by jazz musicians around the country, excepting such regional specialties as "Moten Swing."

There is "Honeysuckle Rose," the favored set of changes to improvise on before its place was taken by "I Got Rhythm." The latter was already popular, but "Lady Be Good" still had an edge because of Lester Young's phenomenal 1936 recording of it with a small group from Count Basie's band. "I Found a New Baby" had been a preferred vehicle for jamming since the late '20s, and "Coquette" is typical of the simple tunes liked by musicians and scorned by critics. As for "Body and Soul," it had been a test piece for advanced players since Louis Armstrong made it a jazz standard in 1930; its position was reinforced by the 1938 Chu Berry–Roy Eldridge version, with Roy's sensational double-time chorus, and of course cemented for good by Coleman Hawkins's definitive 1939 treatment. And then there was (and had been, and is, and will be) the blues . . .

For Charlie Parker, just three months past his twentieth birthday, the McShann band was the best permanent musical company he'd yet found himself in. McShann was an excellent pianist and took his cues for rhythm-section playing from Basie. In fact, McShann's was the most Basie-influenced of 1940 big bands, and in Texans Gene Ramey (bass) and Gus Johnson (drums), he had a couple of young men who'd studied Walter Page and Jo Jones more than well. The horns are more of a mixed bag, but no player is less than competent. Trumpeter Orville Minor is heavily into Roy Eldridge, with touches of Frankie Newton, Lips Page, and Red Allen. His tone is broader than Bernard Anderson's, and that may be why he gets the lion's share of the solo space—a big sound was still valued then.

Anderson is an interesting player. Just twenty-one at the time of these recordings, he had to give up trumpet four years later due to a lung condition. (He switched to piano, gigged for years in Oklahoma City, and is president of the musicians' union local there.) During his stints with McShann, Benny Carter, Roy Eldridge, and finally Billy Eckstine, he much impressed both Dizzy Gillespie and Fats Navarro. Had he been able to continue on the horn, he might well have become a considerable figure. His work here hints of things to come, primarily in terms of harmonic sophistication and speed. But it is absurd to claim, as Ross Russell does in *Bird Lives!* (and *Jazz Style in Kansas City and the Southwest*), that Anderson's work on "Moten Swing" blends "legato and staccato passages in a way that had not been done before." It's a very nice solo, but, just for openers, Russell might listen to Charlie Shavers on John Kirby's "Sweet Georgia Brown." This 1939 recording might also disabuse Russell of the notion that the tempo on "Honeysuckle" was exceptional for the time. For that matter, the 1932 Benny Moten band got into some faster ones.

The two tenorists, William J. Scott and Bob Mabane, are both indebted to Herschel Evans. Trombonist Bud Gould appears to be of a slightly older school; his broad vibrato and solid tone make up for a lack of dexterity. A friend of Higginson, he was the only white musician in the band; he later became a jazz educator. His violin playing on "Honeysuckle" is nice.

And then there is Bird. Only a few years removed from the derision of his peers when he had tried to bite off more than he could chew, and equally few years from becoming the new messiah of jazz, he is *ready*; daring, new, in full command of his horn and his music. The 12- and 16-bar bits previously heard from this early Bird on the McShann big-band sides were tantalizing glimpses of where he stood and what he was as he approached maturity, chronologically and spiritually. Here, his full choruses show the whole picture. The tone is already distinctive; not yet as full, as gleaming as it would become, but different, tangy. The sound is the perfect vehicle for the ideas, which already pour forth with the astonishing fecundity that was to set him apart from ordinary—even extraordinary—mortals.

The most fully realized solos—on "Honeysuckle" and "Lady"—reveal his unique combination of Lester Young's melodic and rhythmic freedom with Coleman Hawkins's drive and harmonic strength; his truly new alternation of stresses on weak and strong beats, of suspended time and double (even double-double) time. The efforts on "Moten" and "Baby" are not far behind—just a bit less poised. (The bridge on "Baby," though, is as stupendous as anything from the session.) On these faster tempos, Charlie Parker, at twenty, is already himself. He has mastered the swing tradition. He is the first alto player to base his style on stronger, heavier tenor models, without ignoring the delicacy and speed of the alto triumvirate of Benny Carter, Johnny Hodges, and Willie Smith—not to mention Buster "Prof" Smith, from whom elements of both sound and phrasing definitely stem (check out "Baby, Look at You" by Pete Johnson and his Boogie Woogie Boys). He is moving, in his blend of what were still thought to be stylistic opposites, toward a new definition of the tension/relaxation, yin-yang principle fundamental to all swinging jazz.

On the slower pieces, we have a Bird not quite on the wing; and that is as it should be, for mastery of the balladic form seems to ripen later than mastery of speed. His "Body and Soul" is moving because of his very special sound, but played straight, especially on the bridge. However, the way he clinches that bridge with the final 8 bars is a hint of genius, and the statement as a whole is graceful, even elegant. As for "Coquette," I must again take issue with Ross Russell, who conjures up Rudy Wiedoft (!) and Carmen Lombardo (!!)—the ultimate in pointless comparisons. As I've said, the tune has traditionally discomfited critics, but the disdain that Russell professes to hear in Parker's treatment of it is simply not there. The solo is a nicely turned piece of "pretty" playing of a kind that remained in Bird's vocabulary (try "Temptation" with the big band), and the conception is much closer to Willie Smith than to Rudy or Carmen, neither of whom ever attempted to play anything remotely resembling jazz. Strangely, Bird does not solo on "Wichita Blues," which features Gould's trombone. But listen to the ensemble countermelody behind Gould's second chorus. An old, churchly strain—or an original melody that sounds traditional? In either case, this becomes "The Hymn" of 1947 . . . at a much faster pace, of course.

And how did all this, miraculously, survive and filter down to us? Gene Ramey remembered the transcription date years later. He told jazz historian Frank Driggs, who made the trek to Wichita and found the acetates intact. Since then, tapes have circulated among the fraternity of heavy jazzheads (and have even made illegitimate appearances on legitimate and illegitimate European labels), but here, for the first time, the music is legitimately dispensed (by special arrangement with Spotlite Records and the Charlie Parker Estate) to the public.

"I Found a New Baby" opens with McShann in a Basie-Hines groove, Gus Johnson really into Jo Jones. Minor has a fiery solo with sax backing, Bird solos with trumpet riffs behind him, trombone solos backed by sax riffs, Scott does nicely, and McShann and the rhythm take it out, the ensemble joining in on the last four. "Body and Soul," after the piano intro, follows the Chu-Roy format: Bird plays a full chorus in medium ballad tempo, Minor's trumpet doubles it up (hints of Red Allen) then halves the tempo again for his last say. Unexpectedly, McShann plays a Tatumesque concluding passage.

"Moten Swing," at a fine K.C. bounce tempo, opens with the famous riff, then Bird enters with a lilt, his bridge a marvelous mixture of note values. A happy, sweet solo. Anderson follows, his last four bars really hinting at bop. Mabane moans à la Herschel, Minor completes the chorus, and trumpets answer saxes going out, riff style. "Coquette" opens with Bird; Anderson takes the bridge, Bird returns; trombone takes a full chorus; McShann opens with the bridge, and they go out with Minor on top, bending the melody toward the blues.

"Lady Be Good" starts in a Jones-Smith Inc. groove via McShann, Johnson, Ramey, and Mabane. Minor solos, a nice riff behind him, and then Bird dances in, very much involved with coming to terms with Lester. He succeeds; the accent is his own. He quotes "Mean to Me"—another Lesterian echo or just a fitting sequence? Anderson opens à la Sweets Edison and plays a well-balanced chorus, and then McShann, in that 1936–37 Basie groove, takes it out. "Wichita Blues" has trombone preaching over "organ" horns; catch that "Hymn" theme behind Gould's second. Straight-ahead tenor is followed by growl trumpet alluding to Bubber Miley's "Creole Love Call" solo. Ensemble with trombone fills ends it. Don't ask me why Bird, so wonderful on the blues, didn't solo—but this was a brotherly band, and Gould doesn't get much space elsewhere . . .

"Honeysuckle Rose" begins with a vocal routine adapted from Alphonse Trent's "Louder and Funnier"; fittingly, Gould's violin recalls Trent alumnus Stuff Smith. McShann has one of his best spots, trumpet-in-cup-mute solos à la Shad Collins (another "advanced" swing trumpeter nobody talks about)—Russell says it's Minor, but I lean toward Anderson. Then Bird: lovely sound, relaxed drive. Ramey; Gus takes the bridge, Ramey returns, and then, in the riffing home, a happy bonus: Bird takes the bridge.

Bird left McShann in July 1942, settling in New York, where he'd already become a regular via his jamming at Harlem after-hours spots whenever the band was at the Savoy Ballroom or the Apollo or another New York location. He made the Minton's scene, but favored another spot, Clark Monroe's Uptown House, which opened at four in the morning. The club had a regular floor show, but the house band also played for dancing and was open to sitting in.

The "Cherokee" that starts part two of our Bird trip comes from the Jerry Newman Collection. According to notations on Newman's tape boxes, it was recorded on a paper disc. Newman's flaw was that he didn't care for Bird; he never recorded him. He also did not use paper discs. So it is reasonable to assume that Newman himself did not record "Cherokee." Obviously, it's not from a jam session. There is a formal arrangement, at least a well-rehearsed "head," for the little band. Producer Don Schlitten, friend and colleague Ira Gitler, and other mavens guessed, proposed, and argued, but there were no clues other than that "Cherokee" was Bird's feature number with McShann. This was no clue at all since neither piano nor band here is in McShann's sound, style, or size.

There was little to go on until Ben Webster posthumously lent a helping hand. In an interview with John Shaw in *Jazz Journal*, Ben reminisced about his first encounter with Bird:

"I first heard Charlie at [Monroe's] . . . there was this guy on the stand blowing weird stuff. It was Charlie. I said to Clark: 'Is that cat playin' what I think he's playin'?' Clark said yeah . . . I was feeling pretty fit, but I wasn't sure; I didn't trust my ears." Ben said he would return the next night to make sure he'd heard right, and Clark Monroe answered: "Well, if you come back tomorrow, I'll put him on the show, and he'll be playing 'Cherokee'!" Eureka! Here was our clue. If Bird played "Cherokee" in the show at Monroe's, which had a small house band led by George Treadwell, this meant there had to be a small-group arrangement. And the music on Newman's paper disc was no longer a mystery. Ben did go back and heard Bird play. "It stopped the place. I never heard anything like that before." At Monroe's, Bird no doubt played longer than on the excerpt we are so fortunate to have. But it's a miracle that we have anything at all.

"Cherokee," of course, is the pièce de résistance of modern jazz, and it had a special role in Charlie Parker's musical development. He has told, in an oft-quoted statement, how he discovered a way of employing substitute harmony while jamming on "Cherokee" in New York in 1939—during his first visit. He was featured on it with McShann and at Monroe's. And he used it to build one of his masterpieces—perhaps *the* masterpiece—"Ko Ko." So this "Cherokee" fragment is of supreme importance. It reveals a harder, more lilting sound than heard on the Wichita sessions—the fuzz is off the peach. There is, in the first bridge, that throaty inflection—almost a growl—that became a key color in the Parkerian tonal palette. And there is increased rhythmic freedom—even though this rhythm section hasn't the drive of McShann's.

Dating the music precisely is impossible, but most likely it stems from the period after Bird left McShann. Though he had frequented Monroe's earlier, he would not yet have had a special spot in the floor show, complete with arrangement, while a casual visitor. I surmise that it stems from the late summer/early fall of '42. The bass and drums, especially the former, give good support, but the piano's vamping under Bird's first chorus sounds a bit awkward. The fade, right after the second Parker bridge, at first seems cruel, but as you get used to it, you'll savor the music that's there and give thanks for its existence.

Clyde Hart, that pioneer of modern piano style, was the leader on five tracks stemming from an interesting date in early 1945. The singer, Rubberlegs Williams, was primarily a dancer (whence the sobriquet), a huge man, and, according to Trummy Young's recollection, not quite sure that Dizzy wasn't putting him on with those (to him) strange trumpet obbligati. At some point during the proceedings, coffee was brought in. Bird, who hadn't slept for a while, dosed his liberally with Benzedrine. Somehow, Bird's and Rubberlegs's containers got mixed up, and the unsuspecting singer soon was high as could be. Perhaps that is why he sings with such ferocity; at any rate, he is said to have admonished Dizzy to play it straight by lifting him off the ground with one arm, addressing him as "Sister Gillespie."

Bird kept his cool throughout, as usual. He plays some lovely stuff in solo and obbligato, giving Rubberlegs no cause for complaint, at home in this atmosphere reminiscent of blues-drenched Kansas City. At that, not all the pieces are blues; the first two stem from Bessie Smith's repertoire and are vaudeville songs with blues inflections. Solo and backup work by all is first-rate, with Don Byas in top form. The session emphasizes that Bird hadn't lost touch with the roots.

The final track with Cootie Williams, "Floogie Boo," is from a broadcast from the Savoy Ballroom, when Bird did a brief stint with the ex-Ellington trumpeter. This is a small group, a band within a band, similar to the Williams sextet that recorded this number with Bud Powell. The overall sound is John Kirby-ish and also owes a debt to the Benny Goodman sextet that Cootie had played with. If you know Sam Taylor as only a honker, his Lester-cum-Jacquet solo may surprise you. Bird announces himself in pianist Arnold Jarvis's last bar, and in a happy mood quotes from "Paper Moon" and, appropriately, "Stompin' at the Savoy." He also plays the hell out of his ensemble part.

(1974)

Thelonious Monk

F ame did not come early or easily to Thelonious Monk, but once it came, it lasted. Jazz, they say, is a performer's art, and audiences are notoriously fickle. ("You've got to keep your name before the public" was Louis Armstrong's *modus operandi* until he dropped in his tracks.) During the last ten years of his life, Monk made all of three public appearances (in 1974, 1975, and 1976, all in New York City), yet his funeral in February 1982 was a media event surpassed in the annals of jazz only by those of Armstrong, Duke Ellington, and Billie Holiday.

He had become a legend, of course, and his prolonged inactivity and invisibility added to the aura of mysteriousness that had surrounded him from the time he first came into view—obliquely and gradually—in his third decade of life. And there were musicians who performed his music in his absence, though Monk without Monk could at best be only a reflection. What kept him alive as a continued presence in jazz, then, were the records, not least the body of work he created for Riverside Records from 1955 to 1960, a period that many (including this writer) consider his peak years, and which was consistently and intelligently kept in view via Milestone reissues put together by the music's original producer, Orrin Keepnews. (For a fascinating and moving account of recording Monk, read Keepnews's notes to *The Thelonious Monk Memorial Album*.)

Many of these albums contained newly reissued alternate takes from which fresh insights into the workings of Monk's mind could be gleaned, but none is more revealing than the music on the fourth side of this double LP. There we can eavesdrop on Monk for almost twenty-two minutes as he shapes and refines a solo interpretation of his most famous composition, "'Round Midnight," a workout that is followed by the originally issued final version of the piece.

No doubt this unique sequence will be a feast for musicologists and serious students of Monk's music. But it also offers many delights to the lay listener, whom it allows to follow the inner workings of Monk's mind as he chisels and polishes those granitic blocks of sound until they assume shapes that please and satisfy him. Until he recently came across the tapes (which have been only slightly edited, and contain some of Monk's verbal asides as an additional bonus), Keepnews had not been aware of their survival. Needless to say, he was overjoyed.

The self-contained panoramic view of "'Round Midnight" is of such significance that it must be considered the album's main event, but it follows a preliminary bout of considerable interest—the only recorded encounter between two very distinctive (and very different) musical personalities, Monk and Gerry Mulligan, brought to us complete with four previously unissued alternate takes.

I suspect that there were few among the multitude crammed into St. Peter's Lutheran Church to witness Monk's funeral who recalled, when Mulligan appeared to pay musical homage, that he had once recorded with Monk. (Gerry played a beautiful "Ruby, My Dear," but was then a bit annoyed to learn that it had already been performed earlier in the proceedings. "I would have played something else," he said. "I know lots of Monk's tunes.")

Mulligan Meets Monk (that was the original title—an indication of where things were at when the album was issued late in 1957, more than six years before Monk appeared on the cover of *Time* magazine) is not one of the more celebrated albums in the Riverside Monk canon. It did get four and a half stars in *Down Beat* (from Dom Cerulli), but there were mutterings elsewhere in the jazz press of a musical mismatch. Those were the days, of course, when the critical game of putting musicians into stylistic boxes was at its height. Monk thus was identified with bebop. That was a mistake, he himself had long since pointed out, telling George Simon of *Metronome* in 1948 that "most bebop sounds like Dixieland to me"—not as cryptic a remark as it might seem, since it pertained to Monk's dislike for just running the chord changes in a solo. Mulligan, in turn, was associated strictly with cool jazz, perhaps less of an error but nevertheless, like all such pigeonholing, misleading and limiting.

Often, early critical dismissal of a record leads to subsequent neglect, and that has pretty much been the fate of this one, referred to, if at all, as one of the few unsuccessful musical meetings either player has been involved in. This canard was no doubt often repeated entirely by rote, since the original album was hard to find, at least until it was reissued in Japan in the '70s. I've always been rather fond of it, though it would be wrong to rank this collaboration as equal to those between Monk and such musical mates as Milt Jackson, Sonny Rollins, Thad Jones, John Coltrane, Art Blakey, and Max Roach. It has its special virtues, however, not least among them the humor and playfulness that Gerry seems to bring out in Monk, in particular on "I Mean You" and "Rhythm-a-ning." Another virtue, albeit not unique to this session, is the presence of a rhythm team uncommonly sympathetic to Monk. While not as famous as Blakey and Roach, rightly considered ideal drummers for Monk, nor associated with him for as long as Frankie Dunlop or Ben Riley, who came later, Shadow Wilson had a marvelous empathy with the rhythmic feel of Monk's music and had recorded with him as early as 1948—the success of the Blue Note version of "Misterioso," one of the first genuine Monk masterpieces, is to no small degree due to his drumming. This becomes all the more impressive when one considers that Shadow had been Jo Jones's immediate successor in the Basie band. He filled that demanding role so well that no less a drummer than Charli Persip could cite "the Jo Jones kick on 'Blue Skies'" as one of his favorite Basie recollections, though the author of that kick had actually been Shadow Wilson. The nickname takes on a certain irony (there had to be a nickname, since the given name was Rossiere), for it was Wilson's fate to always be overshadowed, and he was given little time to rectify matters. He died in July 1959, a few months shy of forty.

Shadow worked hand-in-glove with Wilbur Ware, another tragic figure. Though he lived to be fifty-six, the bassist's career was frequently interrupted by bouts with drugs or alcohol, and in his later years, by advanced emphysema. One of the great natural musicians in jazz, Ware had a totally personal approach to his difficult instrument and was, in addition to his brilliant section work, one of its most remarkable soloists. His influence on better-known fellow bassists was great, but his individuality of ideas and homegrown technique was uncopiable. Ware's association with Monk brought out the best in him, and there was no musical reason for it to end at a time when Monk was just beginning to come into his own in terms of public acceptance. But end it did, with characteristic abruptness. As Keepnews tells it, Ware walked out of the studio after the last of the two afternoon sessions with Mulligan without more than routine goodbyes, left his bass at the Five Spot, but failed to materialize there for work with the regular Monk quartet that evening. When there was no message and Ware proved impossible to find, Ahmed Abdul-Malik was quickly recruited and became his permanent replacement. That the music here represents the last collaboration between Monk and Ware gives it an added dimension of musical and historical interest. The Monk-Ware-Wilson team was indeed a marvel.

For Mulligan, his visit with Monk & Co. was a considerable departure from the pianoless, rhythmically smooth and understated approach he had been favoring since the great success of his 1952 quartet featuring Chet

Baker. Of course, it was a Mulligan axiom that he could play with anybody, and he was an inveterate sitter-in with groups and players of all persuasions, in clubs and at festivals. Nevertheless, recording with Monk was a challenge. Not only was Monk a pianist with a most definite touch; he was also a leader who truly led, and in fact insisted that any improvising soloist who came to play with him must play the music his way, all the way. Though Monk liked to lay out for long stretches when a horn soloist got going, anyone straying too far from the melody and structure into the forbidden realm of aimless noodling on the chord changes would be sharply called back onto the track. There are moments here when this almost happens, but Gerry is quick to get the message. Clearly, Monk is in charge, and just as clearly, Gerry doesn't mind being led, for a change.

As a result, Gerry's playing here is very concentrated. The discursiveness that on occasion crept into his work at this stage of the game—after all, he was not much past his thirtieth birthday, almost a full ten years Monk's junior—is absent. And on the two ballads, "Sweet and Lovely" (one of those romantic tunes Monk was so fond of, and which he made his own) and "'Round Midnight" (in a group version that adds to our perspective on the solo workout), he brings out the passion in the baritone saxophonist. Clearly Gerry is more at ease with "Midnight" than with the other Monk originals, and it is not insignificant that it was included at his request.

As almost every musician who has worked with Monk points out, he had a gift for bringing out something new and perhaps unsuspected in them. Even in a rather casual encounter such as this, Monk makes Gerry play with uncommon assertiveness and with a sound as strong and deep as he has ever produced. What Monk seems to be telling him is "Follow me, but be yourself," and it works. It works also on the one original Mulligan brought to the date. "Decidedly," as the title gives away, is a pleasantly disguised variation on "Undecided," a standard by trumpeter Charlie Shavers that was not part of Monk's repertoire. Monk has fun with it, playing longer and more flowing lines than usual in his first solo chorus on the originally issued take, and giving most of the solo space to Gerry and Ware (who shows what he can do with an ostensibly simple walking bass pattern). Monk even responds to Gerry's invitation, in the out chorus, to engage in a little of the contrapuntal interplay that is a Mulligan trademark. (Elsewhere, he usually stands off, obviously preferring the horn to play thematically along with him when the melody is stated, so that in the out chorus of "Straight, No Chaser" the baritone's part is reduced to background noodling.) Yet even here Monk's stamp is clearly on the take selected for original issue, where the tempo is more stately and the improvisation more focused on the melody.

Speaking of tempos: Monk almost invariably plays his own pieces more slowly than others do. A case in point is "Straight, No Chaser," obviously conceived as a medium blues rather than the horse race it usually becomes in other hands. He was never shy of speed when it fit, as shown on "Rhythm-a-ning." Speed for its own sake, however, never interested him, another distinction between Monk and bebop.

The three takes of "I Mean You" are quite instructive in this regard. As every connoisseur of alternate takes well knows, they invariably get consecutively faster, as the players become more familiar with the tune, the routine, and each other. The tempo goes up not necessarily by intent, but almost instinctively. Not so with Monk here. To be sure, take two is just a mite faster than take one, but the issued take is considerably *slower* than the first. The only other musician of whom such a thing was true on occasion was Duke Ellington, with whom Monk had more than just that in common. (I remember a Newport Jazz Festival in the early '6os—a time when public endorsements by established jazz figures could still make a difference—where, during a Monk set, Duke came out on stage to lean over the piano and watch Monk play, with fond approval written all over his face.) The three versions of this tune also offer a wealth of other differences, especially in the piano solos—the one on take two being especially unpredictable and venturesome, albeit with an air of speculation about it.

In retrospect, this meeting with Mulligan offers very satisfying music. It's good to have it back in circulation, especially with the four fresh takes added. Now that we will get no more new music from Monk, everything he left behind takes on new importance, and it is good that so much unissued material has been prudently saved, for Monk never played a meaningless note.

The "'Round Midnight" in progress proves how much each note meant to Monk. He never wasted any—few players have been more economical than he—especially pianists, whose instrument by its very nature tempts the player to extravagance and displays of dexterity. But not Monk; he was too conscious of the specific gravity and weight of each note he culled from the instrument, and its relationship to the next one. (I was pleased to learn, from Ira Gitler's eulogy of Monk, that he had excelled in physics and mathematics at Stuyvesant High School—then as now one of the best and toughest in New York—but not surprised. His keen awareness of relationships was evident in everything he played and everything he did.)

To Monk, the piano was a sounding board. A study should be made of his use of the pedals, both the damping and sustaining one. He used his feet as unorthodoxly as he did his hands, and as percussively. He *struck* his notes, aware that the piano is a percussion instrument, a big, tunable drum. His technique may have been eccentric, but it was intensely functional—to borrow a word from the Monk canon (not so coincidentally, the title of a piano solo). He knew exactly what he wanted from the instrument.

Much as I love Monk's ensemble music—would that he had been able to explore further the possibilities of tonal and textural combinations implied by "Carolina Moon" and "Brilliant Corners"—it seems to me that when you hear him playing solo, you hear the essence of Monk. It is in this role, by himself, that he is free to explore fully what is in his mind, free to bend notes (he could do that on the piano), free to suspend meter, free to shape the music as he wanted it to sound. He is also free to lurch forward in those sudden clusters of sound that so resembled the manner in which he sometimes "danced" by himself. (I remember one night in the little room just off stage at the Village Gate, crammed with musicians and all manner of hangers-on, when Monk, waiting to go on at a benefit, heard some inner muse that wanted him to dance. And so he did, big as he was, nimbly picking his way between sitting and standing bodies, utilizing every inch of shiftingly available space and never stepping on anyone's foot.)

Here he is, in 1957, working on a solo version of a piece of his own, his most famous composition, that even then must have been part of him for almost fifteen years, a piece he had played perhaps a thousand times. In the hands of almost any other pianist, it would long since have become a set piece, a showpiece, perhaps subject to refinement in detail, but not to changes in overall design.

Monk, however, approaches "'Round Midnight" as if it were a brand-new challenge. In his hands, it becomes a vehicle for new explorations of melody, harmony, rhythm, sound texture, and structural and spatial relationships. In overall design and smallest detail, the encounter with the familiar becomes an occasion for renewal and discovery. And how he knew to use space and silence!

Monk used words even more sparingly than he used notes, but everything he said was fraught with meaning. There is a marvelous moment, early on in the progress of "'Round Midnight," where Monk stops and says: "I can't hear that right . . ." Not hit; not get. *Hear.* He has to hear himself right, satisfy his mind's inner ear, bring forth what must be. There are no shortcuts.

If there could be a single word for Monk's music, that word might be "integrity," in all its levels of meaning. Since words are treated rather cavalierly these days, it might be worth our while to define these levels. Integrity means "the state or quality of being complete, undivided or unbroken; an entirety." That fits. It also means "an unimpaired or unmarred state; entire correspondence with an unmarred condition; soundness; purity." That fits too. And it further means "soundness, honesty, freedom from corrupting influence and practice." That also fits. And it finally means "an unimpaired moral condition, a state of innocence." And that, insofar as music can be moral (and it can; any art can), fits again.

Thelonious Monk never played a meretricious note, never let his music or himself be used for any nonintegral purpose. Yet he achieved acclaim, even success. He could not have done this all on his own, yet he never asked for help. He took it when it was offered unconditionally, and he survived as an artist and a man because he inspired such offers. Yet he didn't use people, like some artists—great ones—have done. He was no saint, yet there was something holy about him, as there is about those rare beings who are all of a piece, all unto themselves.

Some day, perhaps, we will find out why Monk withdrew from the world in his last years of life. Was it by choice, or was it imposed by conditions (physical, mental) beyond his will? Did the private world he had built for himself, and which for so long seemed to make him almost invulnerable, break down? No matter what the answer might be, no matter how sad it is that the music he could have made (and must have heard) in those years will never be, it is a miracle of sorts that he was here at all, that he accomplished what he did with such integrity.

"'Round Midnight" in progress affords us a rare glimpse of Monk's private musical workshop, and makes us understand just a little bit more about his art and craft.

(1982)

Sarah Vaughan

The combination of Sarah Vaughan's glorious voice and the burnished swing of Count Basie's band is such a natural one that it's hard to believe it has been nearly twenty years since they last got together in a recording studio. Outside the studio it's been a different story: Whenever Sassy finds herself in Count's vicinity and the schedules work out right, she drops by and sits in for a few. It was my good fortune to be present at one such occasion a few years ago, and it was a delight.

This album is a delight as well. Sarah usually works with a trio (her current one is on hand here as the rhythm section, augmented by the one and only Freddie Green) and that's just fine—she could carry off a performance with no backing at all—but the resources of a big band, not to mention a working band as supple and versatile as Basie's, can provide a very special setting for her very special voice.

And what a voice it is! After more than thirty-five years of full-time professional singing, it remains a flawless instrument, its three-octave range intact, and even extended downward into astonishing baritone terrain. Some popular singers (so called for lack of a better term) could not survive without the microphone, but Sarah has no such problems. Had she chosen a career in opera, she would no doubt have reached the top as well, but it is our good fortune that she was drawn from gospel to jazz, an area of music where her exceptional gifts of invention could find full expression.

And while the voice has lost nothing, Sarah Vaughan the improvising musician has grown in stature. She always had an exceptional ear, and this enabled her to become the first (and perhaps the only) singer who could utilize the harmonic subtleties introduced to the jazz language by Charlie Parker and Dizzy Gillespie—not so coincidentally among her first fans and boosters. In terms of rhythm, she was able to keep up with the innovations in jazz as well. But in her earlier days, her playfulness sometimes interfered with the sense and intention of the songs. No such dangers now—she has become a great interpreter of great songs as well as a great singer, and she has accomplished this without giving up her sense of humor, which remains as delightful and unpredictable (and girlish) as ever.

If proof should be required, listen to her new version of "If You Could See Me Now," a song that occupies a very special place in the history of Sarah Vaughan. She was present when its composer, Tadd Dameron, got it into shape at his apartment (the main theme was inspired by Dizzy Gillespie's cadenza to "Groovin' High"), and she recorded it in 1946 with an all-star band under Dameron's direction. It became her first recorded masterpiece, and has held a place in her repertoire ever since.

However, to the best of my knowledge (and discographical research), she has not ventured to record it again until now. The results are worth the thirty-five-year wait. It is a wonderful performance from the first note, climaxed by what she does with the last 8 bars of the second chorus and the cadenza based on the lyric's final word. What she accomplishes with that "now" is worth the album in itself.

There is much else to savor, of course. Here is the definitive Vaughan version of "Send in the Clowns," long a showstopper in her live appearances; a "When Your Lover Has Gone" at a tempo that would challenge most horn players but which Sarah handles with ease, interacting with the band as an instrumentalist would (she gives us a fine sample of her scatting here, and on "Just Friends" and "I Hadn't Anyone Till You" as well); marvelous interpretations of two great Harold Arlen standards, "I Gotta Right to Sing the Blues" (with fine assistance from Booty Wood's plunger-muted trombone and a matchless last chorus) and "Ill Wind"; a gorgeously nostalgic "Indian Summer"; and a dazzling display of that startling low register on "All the Things You Are," taken not as a ballad, but as a jazz tune. And much more for the listener to discover.

A word about the band. Even without Basie at the keyboard, those tempos stay firmly in place. Drummer Harold Jones, now with Sarah but a Basie alumnus (1967–72), sounds as if he'd never left, and pianist George Gaffney ventures a few Countish figurations here and there. Bassist Andy Simpkins makes himself at home, too. This being Sarah Vaughan's record, there is not much display of the band's solo resources, but in addition to the aforementioned Booty Wood, tenorist Kenny Hing gets off a fine full chorus on "All the Things You Are." And the band provides a splendid carpet of sound and swing for the magnificent voice and imagination of Sarah Vaughan, who, as you may recall, started her jazz career as a big-band singer.

(1981)

Sonny Stitt

S onny Stitt made more records as a leader than any other jazz instrumentalist.
   This sweeping statement may seem incredible, but it is literally true, provided only that you join me in applying the term "jazz instrumentalist" strictly to individual artists, excluding from the category prolific and nearly immortal bandleaders like Duke Ellington and Count Basie. On his way to his world record, Stitt rarely signed an exclusive contract with a label and preferred a simple and sweet cash deal to any royalties. And while he wasn't averse to providing input on the matter, responsibility for picking sidemen belonged to the producer. His live appearances usually followed the same pattern: he'd book himself as a single and let the club owner or concert promoter take care of hiring the rhythm section.

Only rarely during his long career, which began in the 1940s and lasted into the '80s, did Stitt lead or co-lead organized groups. Notable exceptions were his partnership with Gene Ammons in the early '50s and his regular employment of organist Don Patterson and drummer Billy James in the following decade. The two leading producers of jazz concerts, Norman Granz and George Wein, did manage to snare him briefly, Granz for Jazz at the Philharmonic tours and Verve recordings in 1957–58, and Wein for the 1971–72 Giants of Jazz package that co-starred him with such colleagues as Dizzy Gillespie, Thelonious Monk, and Art Blakey.

This self-styled "lone wolf of jazz" was a complete professional who could play with anyone, anywhere. Equipped with magnificent technique and iron chops, and gifted with an innate ability to swing, he could turn on the music seemingly at will. He knew every musical trick in the book and the changes to hundreds of songs, could make up instant heads on the blues and "I Got Rhythm" sequences, and never had to warm up or break in a new reed—he just picked up either one of his horns and blew. (Equally at home with alto or tenor, he had his own signature on each.) He had tremendous endurance—like Dexter Gordon, he specialized in marathon solos long before John Coltrane came on the scene—and blistering speed, and thrived on competition from other horns. Even in his partnership with Ammons, the nightly tenor battles they staged could turn serious, and unlike Gene, Sonny was capable of mean tactics.

Not until the final years of his life—born in 1924, he died in 1982—did alcohol have a noticeable effect on his playing. (He had put other substance abuse behind him.) But when he was tired, or bored with his musical surroundings, or both, he could operate on automatic pilot. He could in effect turn himself into a musical machine that could, as if by rote, produce uncannily effective performances, even though they would consist entirely of licks, phrases, and gestures stored in his memory bank. (It would not surprise me to learn that Sonny had been able to play in his sleep.) On the other hand, when things were right he could use that unflappable technical command and vast storehouse of musical knowledge to create dazzling and inspired music.

Stitt's huge recorded output—in the 1960s alone, certainly not the best decade for marketing his brand of straight-ahead jazz, he made forty-two LPs—reflects both of these sides of his unique personality. Fortunately, the compilation at hand finds him in fine fettle. All three of the sessions from which this program was culled took place in Chicago, a town with a special jazz ambience, where Stitt could be sure of a deep pool of talented accompanists, a loyal and responsive audience, and hip promoters, club owners, and record producers.

Three such individuals involved on these occasions were Joe Segal, who for more years than seems possible has been presenting great jazz in the Windy City; Esmond Edwards, who has produced an impressive number of very good jazz records for various labels; and Mike Pierpaoli, who owned the Plugged Nickel (in its heyday one of the country's great jazz nightclubs) and had a special "thing" for tenor players.

Thus the notable encounter between Stitt and Zoot Sims came about when Zoot had already been booked into the Nickel, and Sonny, just back from a European tour, called Pierpaoli and told him he was available. The owner felt the two would be compatible and moved quickly to create the dual booking. Indeed, their two-week stint at the club turned out so well that Cadet decided to record them using the backing they'd had on the stand—the excellent working trio of pianist John Young, bassist Sam Kidd,

and drummer Phil Thomas, which had backed Stitt on several previous occasions. (All this logistical information is derived from Segal's notes on the
original LP.)

Similarly, the studio union of Stitt and Bennie Green was the upshot of
a joint live appearance. In this case, it was on a jam-session-styled bill at another well-known Chicago club, McKie's. It had been a case of instant rapport, so much so that the two men decided on the spot to tour together. A
bit later, Segal arranged for them to appear together at his annual Charlie
Parker Memorial Concert (an event that's been going on, at this 1997 writing, for a mere forty-two years), and the recording session took place the
next day, again with appropriate local backing.

For the earliest date of the three, excellent accompaniment for Stitt
came as if made to order: Barry Harris had recorded for Argo just the day
before, making his debut album as a leader. The pianist and the saxophonist
were by no means strangers. During Barry's days in residence at the Bluebird in Detroit, Stitt was among the many visiting stars he'd played for.

Of the five selections taken from this album, "Koko" stands out as a daring tour de force. Stitt's relationship to and with Charlie Parker was complex. When the younger man first came into view as an alto player, it was as
Bird's replacement in Dizzy Gillespie's group—a fact that threw into bold
relief his kinship with the master. (I clearly recall hearing Stitt's solo on
Dizzy's recording of "That's Earl, Brother," on Symphony Sid's radio program, and finding it hard to believe that it wasn't Bird.) Stitt often claimed
that he'd arrived at his conception independently of Parker, but trumpeter
Willie Cook, who knew him early in his career, has provided an interesting
perspective on the matter. Stating that Stitt was the first to make him listen
to Parker, on a jukebox (saying, "This is going to be the man"), Cook notes
that Stitt at that time "played like Johnny Hodges when he was drinking
and Benny Carter when he wasn't. He was good at both of them." He adds
that "Sonny was very intelligent, and he was always fast, even when he was
just a kid. He could analyze and dissect chords. He knew what everybody
was doing when they played." (These remarks are from the chapter on
Cook in Stanley Dance's book, *The World of Duke Ellington*.)

Stitt has claimed that after hearing Parker on the first records he made,
with Jay McShann's band, he was determined to meet him, and sought him
out when passing through Kansas City with Tiny Bradshaw's band. He reports that they met and had a quick noontime session together, after which
Bird told him, "You sound like me." This tale, however, may be taken more
as wish fulfillment than as reality, largely because by the time Stitt was on
the road with Bradshaw, Parker had already left Kansas City.

More credible is what Sonny told Great Britain's *Melody Maker*—that he
first heard Parker live in 1943 in Washington, D.C., and that "he was elec-

trifying." Stitt then went on to define his relationship to the master in very cogent fashion: "No one is a successor to Bird because he was out there by himself—if a fellow has a style on the order of the artist he idolizes, and he can use his own ideas, then he can build something out of it." This was in 1959, and comes as close as anything I've ever read or heard from Stitt on this question to an admission that he did "idolize" Parker and had not independently arrived at a similar place.

As amazingly close as Stitt could come to Parker in terms of sound (perhaps a bit edgier), speed (as fast, and more accurate in hitting each note in the sound-stream clearly on the head—though more mechanical and less maniacal), and vocabulary (he spoke Bird fluently, like a native), there always was a fundamental difference, originality aside. Stitt thought in bar-length phrases and always remained a symmetrical improviser, while Parker darted across bar lines and where a phrase might land was never at all predictable.

Take this "Koko" as an example. It's a masterly re-creation; Stitt amazingly replicates some of Bird's exact phraseology, and intermittently does his own takes on Ray Noble's melody, but the end result is much smoother than the original. In fact, the most exciting moment for this listener is the Harris piano solo, short as it is. It's Barry at his most Bud-like, and since Bud Powell had been a no-show at the Parker session, this is a little taste of what might have been! Barry is also excellent when playing the Gillespie trumpet parts in Stitt's rearrangement of the introduction and conclusion of the piece.

With "Easy Living," we come to the "other" Sonny Stitt—the tenor player. Some say he took up the instrument to ward off the constant comparisons to Parker, but I think he just liked the variety and challenge, and it certainly better equipped him for his "lone wolf" role to have another horn in his arsenal. When he announced himself as a tenorman in 1949, it was with a bang—on a recording session with Bud Powell that produced an immortal version of "All God's Children Got Rhythm." On tenor, Stitt had few peers. He takes his cues from Lester Young, but there's not a trace of cloning. On this axe, he is indisputably his own man. On the very relaxed "How High the Moon" (by 1959, no longer as ubiquitous as it had been), the cheerful original "It's Hipper Than That," and the thoughtful "Lover Man" (another Parker special, but in this case *not* a masterpiece to emulate), with its stunning cadenza, Stitt plays alto.

The set with Zoot also opens with Sonny's alto as he states the melody of "Fools Rush In" with aplomb. ("The melody—that's what it's all about" is another revealing quote from Stitt.) John Young offers the first of several eccentric but appealing solos—he's one of Chicago's several unsung piano originals, with a long career going back to Andy Kirk's band, in which he replaced Kenny Kersey—and Zoot has a lovely, loose solo spot before

Sonny wraps it up. It's tenors all the way on the other numbers. Zoot solos first on the cooking "Lonesome Road" and also initiates the exchanges. The tag ending was a favorite Stitt device, and Zoot finds it to his liking. It's Stitt first on his own "Katea," both on the split bridges and the solos; this is a nice original by Sonny, who also penned the "Preacher"-like "I Want to Go Home," where both tenors show the way to go, Stitt leading off. The humorous vocal ending there is an indication of how well these two got along; I saw them at the Nickel on a later occasion, and have rarely caught Sonny in a happier tenor matchup.

With a trombonist for a frontline partner, there was no possible feeling of rivalry, and the session with Bennie Green is clearly a friendly encounter. There's a lot of bossa nova flavor to this session; we tend to forget what an impact this rhythmic-melodic approach had on jazz in the wake of Stan Getz's tremendous success with "Desafinado." This would also explain the presence of a guitar, not so much as a voice in the rhythm section but for added melodic spice. Joe Diorio was an excellent choice. Although far from a household name in jazz, Diorio has become a guitarist's guitarist and is greatly admired as a teacher and theoretician. After many years in Chicago, he now makes his home in California. Bobby Buster was one of many good organists to be found in the Windy City—he displays a light touch and some tasteful ideas, as well as the requisite swing. Good drummers were another Chicago commodity, and Dorel Anderson acquits himself well in what was then a new bag.

On "Flame and Frost" we learn that producer Esmond Edwards had a knack for songwriting. We also can hear that Green, although most often found in the company of bebop musicians, was a very direct descendant of Trummy Young and really a player with a swing conception and a droll sense of humor much like Trummy's. Stitt shows here that bossa was a tenorman's meat. (Although he actually did play alto on some selections in the original album, the reissue producer has chosen to focus on the tenor numbers.) The long-lined "The Night Has a Thousand Eyes" lends itself well to the Brazilian vein; Stitt is very fluent here, followed by fine Diorio. "Our Day Will Come," a pop hit for Ruby and the Romantics, is a less obvious choice for transplantation to South America, but these cats make it work, and Bennie shines. "My Main Man" is the blues, a staple item in the Chicago jazz diet, and a piece of cake for this crew. Sonny gets deeply into it, tipping his cap to Lester Young; Green seems closest to the J. J. Johnson vocabulary here, but in his own down-home way. Overall it's a good note on which to end this visit with Sonny Stitt in three different settings—all of which illuminate his ability to take charge of any music situation in which he might find himself, and to keep it swinging.

(1998)

Dexter Gordon

Dexter Gordon is of course the man who first created an authentic bebop style on the tenor saxophone. He is also the man who profoundly influenced young John Coltrane (the roots of what became Coltrane's characteristic modality are plainly evident in Dexter's unusual and very personal harmonic accents) and, to a lesser but still significant degree, Sonny Rollins. But above and beyond such historical credits, Dexter Gordon was one of the great players in jazz, a man who made music that is vital, direct, and emotionally satisfying. This collection of some of his earliest recordings shows that, from the start, Dexter was a great communicator. They stand up as music, not just as history.

Dexter Keith Gordon was born in Los Angeles on February 27, 1923. His father was a prominent physician whose patients included Duke Ellington and Lionel Hampton. When the boy took up the clarinet, his father suggested that he also study theory and harmony. As Ira Gitler, the noted bebop historian, points out in his indispensable book, *Jazz Masters of the Forties*, "these were subjects that most jazzmen of that period took up much later, if at all," and the solid foundation Dexter thus acquired, when combined with his natural ability—there is no doubt that Dexter, like all natural improvisers, was gifted with great ears—gave him a superior knowledge of "changes." That such knowledge came in handy as the new jazz called bebop began to flourish should be obvious.

Dexter's teacher was a man named Lloyd Reese, with whom Charles Mingus also studied. Both men gave Reese great credit. (His chief instrument was trumpet, but he played all the brasses and saxophones, as well as piano. Although he rarely recorded, he did take part in a 1937 Art Tatum and his Swingsters session that coincidentally also included Marshall Royal, the other man cited by Dexter as a salutary early influence.)

Dr. Gordon died late in 1940, when Dexter was seventeen. In Duke Ellington's autobiography, *Music Is My Mistress*, he specifies the date by recalling: "I had made a date to meet my Los Angeles doctor . . . Dexter Gordon's father, in the bar of the Dunbar Hotel on Forty-first and Central at four o'clock Christmas morning. A friend came in right on the hour and told me the doctor couldn't make it because he had just died of a heart attack."

In that same month, Dexter, who had quit school earlier in the year to join a local band called the Harlem Collegians, became a member of Lionel Hampton's newly formed big band. "We went right on the road without any rehearsal, cold. I was expecting to be sent home every night," Dexter remembered.

In the band, his section mate and the featured tenor saxophone soloist was another youngster, just up from Texas. Illinois Jacquet, four months Dexter's senior, undoubtedly had an effect on his colleague, and it is an interesting though little-noted fact that two players who would become the most influential tenor stylists of the later '40s sat in the same big-band section for several years.

Jacquet's style combined elements of Lester Young and Coleman Hawkins (the latter via Illinois's idol, Herschel Evans) with a special Texas spice, and led directly to the "jump" and R&B approaches to tenor. Much has been said about Jacquet's honking and lack of taste, but while his theatricality and excessive grandstanding no doubt had much to do with his considerable success, there has been too much emphasis on these aspects and not enough on his very considerable positive musical qualities. The fact is that even the honking and overblowing in which he indulged were a part of a genuine contribution to saxophone techniques—if only because Dexter Gordon, for one, was to make good use of these devices, not to mention their impact on John Coltrane and his followers.

Until recently, no recorded evidence of Dexter's Hampton period had surfaced—not even his one known feature, a tenor battle with Jacquet called "Po'k Chops." But in 1996 a piece from a September 1941 aircheck, "Train Time," turned up, including a 16-bar Gordon solo. Short as it is, it contains no less than two quotes from Lester Young's famous "Jive at Five" solo; and in a session with Nat Cole and Sweets Edison that has not been authoritatively dated but is probably from 1943, he is still clearly under Lester's spell, although the sound is already his own. He can next be heard during a brief stay in Fletcher Henderson's band in the spring of '44; well featured, he plays with striking authority for a twenty-one-year-old. This was back in his hometown, and it was there, soon after, that Louis Armstrong caught Dexter at a late-night jam session.

Forty-five years later, when I interviewed him at his New York apartment for a television documentary, Dexter vividly recalled that he had just come off the stand and—still wringing wet—sat down at a table, when from behind someone gripped him in a hug, declaring "Man, I dig your sound! I want you in my band!" The voice was unmistakable; it was Satch himself, and the next day, Dexter reported for work, which turned out to be a movie shoot. He spent six months with the great man, whose big band left much to be desired but whose own work made a lasting mark on the youngster. Louis featured him well ("Take it, Brother Dexter," he commands on the several airchecks on "Ain't Misbehavin'") and they developed a personal relationship based on shared affection for a substance Satch sometimes called "Miss

Mary Warner." When Dexter gave his notice, the leader offered him a substantial raise, but the lure of a berth in Billy Eckstine's band was too strong.

Taking the chair vacated by Lucky Thompson, Dexter joined a section that included Sonny Stitt and Leo Parker. When Gene Ammons came on board, replacing John Jackson on tenor, they became known as the "Unholy Four." This of course was the first big band to play bebop, and Dexter recalled that at first Art Blakey's bomb-dropping disconcerted him. Rough at the edges but filled with fabulous talent, the Eckstine band was Dexter's finishing school.

It was "Blowin' the Blues Away," featuring a Gordon-Ammons tenor exchange, that put Dexter on the map with the jazz public. He and Ammons even had the benefit of not only label credit but a kind of "singing commercial" on the recording of the tune: in Eckstine's vocal, he sings "Blow Mr. Gene, blow Mr. Dexter, too" not just once but twice.

By the time he joined Eckstine, Dexter had heard Charlie Parker and he had heard him pretty early, when he first came to New York with Hampton in 1942. "I heard a couple of young alto players who were nice—Bird and Rudy Williams," he told Ira Gitler. That was also the point at which he first heard Coleman Hawkins and Don Byas in person, which made a greater impression than the records he'd been exposed to. Lester Young he'd heard as early as 1939, in Los Angeles.

During that first visit to New York, Dexter had just listened, he didn't sit in. He didn't feel he was ready, but when he came to the big town with Eckstine, it was a different story, and he found himself on the bandstand at Minton's, the fabled birthplace of bop, wedged in between Lester Young and Ben Webster. And when he left Eckstine after eighteen months, he came straight to New York and started to work on Fifty-second Street. His credentials were good: in addition to the stay with Eckstine, he had been featured on Dizzy Gillespie's second record date as a leader. Only one number from that session, "Blue 'n' Boogie," was issued at the time—the reverse side, "Groovin' High," was from a session without Dexter. But in 1975, quite incredibly, a copy of that Guild 78 turned up, *looking* just like all the others but containing a "Groovin' High" from the date with Dexter; the long-lost version was promptly included on a reissue LP.

The fact that Dexter was a handsome six-foot five-inch giant with a personality to match his looks didn't hamper him in acquiring fans on the New York scene. He had a special kind of magnetism, despite the personal troubles the young tenorman had by then gotten himself into. For the moment, though, he was able to deal with the habit he shared with so many other young jazzmen of that day.

On the Street, he worked in a band with Parker and Miles Davis, plus a shifting rhythm section that might include Bud Powell and Max Roach. He became a figure at the bop sessions that were beginning to proliferate in New York, and he made records, including, for Savoy, the first under his own name.

In the summer of '46, Dexter returned to Los Angeles, did a stint in Hawaii, and then teamed up with a tenorman who had preceded him in the Eckstine band, Wardell Gray. They jammed a lot together, and eventually one of their tenor battles wound up on record. It was the famous two-part "The Chase," further cementing Dexter's popularity with fans of the new jazz.

Back in New York in 1947, he again recorded for Savoy, this time with the wonderful trumpeter Fats Navarro, with whom he also worked in Tadd Dameron's band at the Royal Roost, and with baritonist Leo Parker of the Unholy Four. In 1949 he was back in California. The '50s began promisingly, with some more work with Wardell, but in 1953 and '54 Dexter was off the scene, an inmate of Chino—California's experimental "prison without bars." During his stay there, he participated in a movie, *Unchained*, about the facility. He is seen playing tenor, but in typical Hollywood fashion, someone else's music is heard on the sound track. (Just a few days after Dexter's release, his old sidekick Wardell Gray was found dead in the desert outside Las Vegas, where he had been working with Benny Carter's band.)

In 1955 Dexter recorded for the first time in three years. The music is fine, but not much attention was paid to it then, in the heyday of West Coast jazz. In 1960, by which time other fashions in jazz had become dominant, Dexter was chosen to act in and write the music for the Los Angeles production of *The Connection*, Jack Gelber's successful play about junkies. It was well received. Cannonball Adderley produced the first Dexter Gordon album in five years, for Riverside; and in 1961 he once again returned to New York, to record some more.

Later that year, he was reunited in Chicago with Gene Ammons. Chicago jazz audiences (as I learned a bit later when I spent some years in the Windy City) have a special kind of warmth, and Dexter had already been a special favorite there. In the club he was playing at, a sign in the window read: "Dexter—We Love You." And in an interview that I published in what unhappily turned out to be the last issue of *Metronome*, he told Brooks Johnson: "Since I've been here, nearly everyone I talk to tells me how much they've missed me. It's a very good feeling, knowing that you've been missed. It's inspiring."

There were more recordings, all of them excellent, revealing a new strength in the work of a man who had always been among the strongest players, and new dimensions of wisdom, warmth, and wit in his approach to the art of playing ballads. In 1962, Dexter decided to settle in Europe. Copenhagen became his home base, and unlike many expatriates he thrived and grew as a player abroad. In a roundtable discussion that appeared in *Down Beat* after he had been in Denmark for a few years, he put his finger on some of the reasons for living there. "Since I've been over here, I've felt that I could breathe, and just be more or less a human being, without being white or black. . . . I've played for months on end at the Montmartre in Copenhagen . . . now I've never in my life played three or four months continually at a place in the U.S. The opportunity to work regularly in the same spot gives you the kind of feeling you need to stretch out, relax, and at the same time develop musically without having those job-to-job worries hanging over your head."

He became one of Copenhagen's most popular adopted sons, raising a family, learning some Danish (he had a gift for languages), teaching jazz in schools, appearing on TV, picking up flute and also adding soprano saxophone to his roster of instruments, and cutting a familiar figure riding his bicycle through the streets of the friendly Danish capital. He recorded regularly, both in Denmark and during his fairly frequent visits to the United States, where he and his records were always warmly received.

His 1976 visit—one of several billed as a "homecoming"—was so resoundingly successful that he made the decision to repatriate in the following year, a decision no doubt bolstered by a contract with Columbia Records and many offers of work. He formed a quartet, frequently augmented by the addition of trumpeter Woody Shaw, and had what amounted to a long honeymoon with American audiences. In 1983 he celebrated his sixtieth birthday with a memorable party at the Village Vanguard in New York, one of the clubs at which he appeared regularly. When he called to invite me, he said—with that unique cadence of his, pauses that grew longer with the years—"Dan, I never ever thought, back in the olden days, that I would make it to sixty, and if anyone had suggested it I would have roared with laughter."

As it turned out, Dex made it to a bit past sixty-seven, and in those final years, though plagued by declining health, he enjoyed his greatest fame outside the confines of the jazz world when he starred in Bernard Tavernier's film *'Round Midnight*, released in 1986. In it, he portrayed a character based in roughly equal parts on Bud Powell and Lester Young; but while he borrowed some of Pres's mannerisms, he was basically playing himself, with marvelous presence and peerless timing. He received an Oscar nomination for his efforts—no mean accomplishment for an amateur actor. But, after all, he had been in the spotlight for most of his life, and to the very end, even when his physical strength had ebbed, he retained that uniquely magnetic presence—and that unconquerable sense of humor.

(1998)

Jimmy Rowles/Stan Getz

This album is a listener's dream come true.

The lovely music it contains is of a very special kind, seldom if ever captured in a recording studio. It is pure, intimate music, with a certain ambience that usually only comes about when great players get together for their own pleasure—late at night in a club, perhaps, or at somebody's home. There are no obstacles here between the artists and the music.

Sometimes, music of this kind has been preserved by some stroke of luck, under rather primitive recording conditions. But this album was made in a studio, with all the advantages that environment has to offer in terms of the best possible reproduction. The secret of this rare and happy combination of inspiration and technology is that the album was conceived and produced by a musician, and a very great one at that.

Stan Getz had already made his official debut as a producer with the splendid *Captain Marvel*, though, in effect, he had been acting in that capacity on record dates with his own groups for more than twenty years. It was Stan's idea to present his old friend Jimmy Rowles in a context ideally suited to illuminate the unique talent of this remarkable artist. It isn't easy to devote oneself fully to playing and at the same time taking care of the business demanded of a producer, but Stan has brought this feat off with flying colors.

The friendship between Stan and Jimmy dates back to the late '40s, when they worked side by side in one of Benny Goodman's bands, participated in some Woody Herman sessions, and freelanced in the Los Angeles area. Some years later, they recorded together on a memorable Getz quartet date.

The stage for this overdue reunion was set when Jimmy, who'd spent more than twenty years laboring in the musical vineyards of Hollywood, was persuaded to come to New York in the spring of 1973.

At the time, Jimmy was what is known as a "musician's musician." He enjoyed an enviable reputation among his peers. In his youth, he'd been a protégé of the great Ben Webster and held one of his first important jobs with Lester Young. He paid his big-band dues, became one of Billie Holiday's favorite accompanists, and served in the same capacity with, among others, Sarah Vaughan and Peggy Lee. He worked with Charlie Parker, did every conceivable kind of studio playing, and kept up his jazz chops playing in clubs and on occasional record dates that gave him a chance to show his mettle. In the process, he amassed an awesome repertoire of more than a thousand tunes, including many obscure gems. And, being quite a singer himself, he knew the lyrics to many of them.

To the broad jazz public (and many critics), however, Jimmy Rowles was not exactly a household name. For better or worse, New York remains the place where one must make one's mark. Predictably, when Jimmy descended upon Manhattan, appearing at the 1973, 1974, and 1975 Newport Jazz Festivals and enjoying long runs at such noted spas as the Cookery, Bradley's, and Michael's Pub, he was "discovered." He was profiled in *The New Yorker*, interviewed in the *New York Times*, highlighted in *Newsweek*, and recorded by several small jazz labels. But it is this album (made, incidentally, before any of the others) that best showcases the varied aspects of this gifted player, singer, and composer.

We have here Rowles, the solo pianist ("Body and Soul"); the wondrously affecting singer ("I'll Never Be the Same," "My Buddy," "This Is All I Ask"); the remarkable composer ("The Peacocks"); the wry humorist ("Rose Marie"); the splendid combo pianist ("Lester Left Town"); and, in what makes this album so special, Jimmy Rowles, the complete soloist and accompanist, in a series of unique duets with Stan Getz. These masterful collaborations are unlike anything either artist has previously recorded; a kind of summation of their respective accomplishments, and prime examples of the art of jazz in its most mature and pristine state.

While this is Stan and Jimmy's album, the supporting cast enlisted by Stan is by no means secondary. Bassist Buster Williams worked with Jimmy during a long engagement at the Cookery. His big, deep sound, perfect intonation, supple beat, and musicality are qualities that have been appreciated by, among others, Miles Davis, Art Blakey, McCoy Tyner, Herbie Hancock, and Sarah Vaughan. Elvin Jones, of course, is a true master of the drums and a seminal figure in the development of modern jazz rhythm. Elvin is seldom heard as a sideman these days, and rarer still in a setting as intimate as this one, which is precisely why Stan wanted his good friend to be on this date. He is a player of great subtlety as well as towering strength, and a man of rare sensitivity. It is a joy to hear him in this setting.

There is a surprise vocal contribution on "The Chess Players," and thereby hangs a tale. Jon Hendricks was so taken with this version of the Wayne Shorter tune when he heard a tape of the session that he couldn't resist the impulse to set it to his own brand of poetic wit. He found the words to go with the music, enlisted the vocal aid of his wife, Judy, and daughter Michelle, and also of Beverly, Stan's daughter (who'd been singing with Michelle and Buddy Rich's daughter Cathy in their group Hendricks, Getz, Rich), shepherded his flock into a studio, and overdubbed his creation.

When Stan returned from a gig in London, Jon innocently asked him to listen to the Rowles session tape. Though Stan had already done so a number of times, he acquiesced. He was amused and surprised, and got in touch with his friend Wayne Shorter, who had no objection to the inclusion of a vocal version of his tune.

"I'll Never Be the Same," a charming 1930s ballad immortalized by Billie Holiday and Lester Young, introduces Jimmy Rowles, the singer. His time, phrasing, and intimate, smoky delivery are indescribably delicious—the epitome of jazz singing. Stan's beautiful 16 bars of solo and subsequent obbligato to the vocal reprise sustain and deepen the mood of the performance. Total communion!

"Lester Left Town," Wayne Shorter's tribute to the departed Lester Young, is the album's hardest-swinging track. Stan, propelled by Elvin's infectious brushwork, takes charge and makes the piece his own. Jimmy's solo, potent support, and exchanges with Elvin show his strength as a group player.

"Body and Soul" is Rowles alone. The art of playing solo piano brings into focus the artist's inner core. This great standard has become a sort of test piece—after all, Art Tatum, Earl Hines, and Teddy Wilson have put their personal stamps on it—and Jimmy's interpretation is one of the best. It moves flowingly from rubato into gentle swing (his time is something to marvel at), offers a hint of stride, shifts to improvisation of the highest order, and returns to the melody for a perfect landing, all imbued with his marvelous touch.

"What Am I Here For?," a metaphysical question posed by Duke Ellington in 1942, comes from Jimmy's treasure trove of Ellington-Strayhorn works. The first of the instrumental duets, it approaches perfection. Without the support of a rhythm section, the two masters handle the beat like expert jugglers, stating it, suspending it, always implying it.

"Serenade to Sweden" was inspired by the warmth and affection of the Swedish fans who helped Ellington celebrate his fortieth birthday during the band's 1939 tour of Europe. The experience is reflected in the haunting melody, here lovingly "sung" by Stan, one of the master melodists in jazz. There are startling harmonic moments in Jimmy's solo, and he flavors the piece with aptly Ducal keyboard touches. Utterly relaxed music-making, yet with a spring-like inner tension. The seeming ease with which it is done is something only true masters can attain.

"The Chess Players" opens with Elvin. Stan's solo is echoed in unison by the singers, and Jimmy inserts a sneaky quote from *Chloe* in his statement. A stirring drum solo is punctuated by the piano, and there's a concluding vocal "amen."

"The Peacocks" is a Rowles composition, and I've been fascinated with it since I first heard him play it. Unlike many jazz "originals," it is a genuine piece of music, and has the impressionistic ambience of a Debussy prelude. Stan, the master melodist, does it full justice. Notice the ending, where Stan musically conveys the futile attempt at flight of the peacocks by letting the air flutter through the keys. This is a masterpiece of rare beauty, and you'll want to hear it again and again.

"My Buddy," done as the waltz it originally was, has more of Jimmy's warm singing, not a bit mawkish, yet respecting the song's sentiments. Stan's chorus is just about perfect, sustaining the mood with that inimitable sound and melodic grace. He also embellishes the vocal reprise, in which we once again are made to marvel at the singer's time.

"The Hour of Parting" is the art of ballad playing exemplified. In contrast, "Rose Marie," the old Jeanette McDonald–Nelson Eddy warhorse, is given what the British call a "send-up," done in bossa nova time. Elvin whips his cymbals, Jimmy gives us a sample of his satiric wit in his vocal, and Stan seems to be taking revenge on all the bossa nova requests he's had to cope with. Jimmy lends some Monkish touches to his brief but pithy solo. The music fades out with echoes of "Indian Love Call," and some hilarious exchanges with Stan assuming the role of "Jeanette" in his responses to "Nelson Eddy" Rowles's gaily romantic propositions.

(After this take, the cozy studio audience, which included such friends and fans of the performers as Alec Wilder, Helen Merrill, Charlie Bourgeois, and the undersigned, was in stitches. And Stan Tonkel, the engineer who did such a fine job on this date, was wiping tears from his eyes in the booth.)

"This Is All I Ask" opens with Jimmy accompanying his own singing with spare grace. In his own *sotto voce* way, he has quite a vocal range (the key demands it), and his interpretation of this song should be the envy of many a singer. Stan and the rhythm section enter on tiptoes, and Stan fashions a soulful half chorus, then backs the singing in perfect taste. Another gem.

"Skylark," one of Hoagy Carmichael's finest melodies, has seldom been in such good hands. Stan and Jimmy caress the melody and find new ways of enhancing it, taking turns in solo roles like old friends in deep, easeful conversation. Stan paints the song blue in the second chorus, and he and Jimmy distill its romantic essence. Stan's bottom note is the perfect finishing touch, contrasting with the lovely upper-range sounds that precede it.

To close this marvelous recital, Jimmy offers a little sign-off gesture—a finely wrought miniature, a gracious farewell. As throughout, the sound of the piano is captured with a brilliance rare on records (and the same can be said for Stan's tenor). Natural sound, with no artifice.

Listening to this record over and over while working out these comments (almost superfluous for music that speaks so directly for itself, and severely taxing my supply of superlatives), I've fallen in love with it.

I think you will, too.

(1978)

John Coltrane

This is the fourth Pablo album of previously unissued music by John Coltrane and the best group he led, as culled from tapes made during a tour of Europe in the late fall of 1962. Like its predecessors—*Afro Blue Impressions*, *The Paris Concert*, and *The European Tour*—it is an important addition to the recorded legacy of one of the most influential and enigmatic musicians in jazz.

Some fourteen years after his death, Coltrane continues to cast a powerful spell on jazz, and that is not strange, since no jazz voice of comparable influence has appeared in his wake. From the perspective of early 1981, it is even possible to suggest that John Coltrane may have been the last of the spellbinding jazz giants who decisively reshaped the language of jazz. These chosen few—Louis Armstrong, Lester Young, and Charlie Parker being the others—differ from the many other great musicians jazz has produced in that the music could never be the same after they had made their presence felt; their impact was subliminal as well as direct.

(Since it is all too easy to be misunderstood, let me make it clear that this is not a qualitative judgment, and that it does not diminish the stature of, say, an Art Tatum or a Roy Eldridge, a Johnny Hodges or a Dizzy Gillespie to claim that the four artists I have named played a unique role in the music.)

Of these four, Coltrane is by far the most problematic, both in terms of his art as such and its influence. Unlike the other three, he was not a "natural" who found his own voice early on, but a late-blooming seeker of true identity. And unlike the others, he approached both music and instrument self-consciously, analytically, and not at all with serenity and self-assurance.

Moreover, once he had discovered a way that seemed right for him, and within which he achieved mastery of content and execution and invented a language that gave him recognition and made him an influence, he abandoned this way just as he began to have perfection within his grasp. Instead, he searched anew (this time in the limelight, which took great courage), and the search became the essence of his new self, with perfection no longer even an issue, much less an achievable goal.

On this record, we find John Coltrane in transition. Just barely still in touch with the harmonic universe of *Giant Steps* and its relentless exploration of the changes, dense, vertical, and with a unique, running rhythmic gait—mastery within the style about which Miles had told him, "You don't have to play *everything*"—he was already off in the direction set by *Chasin' the Trane*, recorded just a year and two weeks before this music.

That was just before Coltrane embarked on his first European tour (also under the banner of "Norman Granz Presents"). At that time, McCoy Tyner and Elvin Jones were already with him, but Reggie Workman was on bass, and he was leading a quintet with Eric Dolphy as the second horn. *The* quartet, with Jimmy Garrison coming over from Ornette Coleman's group, was born in the spring. As it shook down, the urgent sting of Dolphy gone, there was a temporary easing of tension. In late summer, Coltrane recorded with Duke Ellington, who inspired him to create a masterpiece, "In a Sentimental Mood," in which he achieved, for a moment, balance between serenity and despair. And just before leaving on his second European tour, he recorded an album of ballads, showing those who'd not yet heard that he could *sing* on his horn (no great jazz player is *not* a melodist). But there were powerful undercurrents, churned up by Elvin Jones (responding to what he could hear in Coltrane, implicitly and explicitly), implying the radical dissolution of the forms and textures and pulse and tonality of the common jazz language as even Coltrane still spoke it.

Perhaps because of these growing undercurrents, Coltrane chose to play at this performance (and in several others documented from the 1962 tour) the two pieces heard here, neither of which he had played in years. ("Bye Bye Blackbird" not since with Miles in 1958, and apparently never with his own groups; his own blues, "Traneing In," not since he'd recorded it on his second issued album as a leader in August of 1957.)

"Blackbird," the 1926 pop tune brought into jazz by Miles Davis (born that same year, and God knows where he picked it up), begins deceptively like a Davis quintet interpretation in classic '50s style. Coltrane is liltingly melodic and swinging, with that unmistakable tone and tonality. But by the fourth chorus, he's into harmonics, and unleashes a wild but logical sequence of riff-like phrases in the uppermost, false range of the horn. His fifth chorus offers polyrhythmic interplay with Elvin—how they could work out together—but in the sixth, interplay has turned to battle, and Elvin whips while Trane screams. Tyner settles things down with four swinging choruses (traces of Silver and Garlandish octave voicings, then more and more real McCoy, still swinging in 4/4), Elvin adapting instantly to the changed climate. Jimmy Garrison's solo serves as a pleasant but emotionally neutral interlude, and then comes part two of this "Blackbird," prime late-1962 Coltrane, riding on a vamp as he builds from a fragment of the melody through what starts as a tag (he sounds like Dexter for a moment), to seemingly impossible things: multi-phonics (producing several notes simultaneously from an instrument not built to do this), and a duet with himself in alternating falsetto and bass voices. And here he is in charge—even Elvin can only follow. Coltrane ends on a startlingly lovely phrase, and then Elvin thunders, all by himself, as if to protest that he didn't get a solo. There is no comparison, but to hear Coltrane on the Miles Davis "Blackbird" done in 1956 is instructive after this.

"Traneing In," a blues with a bridge, starts (just like the 1957 version) with a long piano solo, followed by equal space for the bass. At a swinging medium-up tempo (faster than five years before), Tyner plays delightfully, with a light touch and happy feeling far removed from his present mode, drums and bass in firm support. After Garrison's solo walk, Coltrane pipes himself aboard with a memorable call, starting his marathon solo with another echo of his Dexter roots. But by the second chorus, he's off and running in strictly Coltrane territory, through riffs and maximum swing (it was Coltrane who once said, "Nothing swings like 4/4") to chordal extensions, modality, breaking up of the time (with Elvin, miraculously, with him into space-time yet keeping the pulse steady), vocalized cries and groans, new sounds and patterns. When it seems as if he's running out of steam, he soon recaptures the drive and intensity, buoyed by the hardworking rhythm section. (Elvin is the epicenter, but Garrison's unflagging, steady-walking presence is the stabilizer; McCoy lays out a lot—the time of the pentatonic drone had not yet come.) No matter how "outside" things at times become, "inside" remains the point of reference, and throughout, this is the blues (with a bridge), and it swings. Coltrane still comes back to touch home base, though the circles he makes around it are widening.

Eventually, the center could no longer hold. Not all who had followed Coltrane this far were able to follow him further, and indeed quite a few had stopped at *Giant Steps*, or rather just short of that vertical *tour de force*, still unsurpassed of its kind. And still further on (or out), the quartet splintered, bursting apart of its own centrifugal force.

When Coltrane was appointed standard-bearer of the jazz avant-garde (perhaps more of a burden than an honor, but one which, good and charitable man that he was, he bore patiently, almost dutifully), he was made responsible for more than his share of "innovations." Who knows what his next stage might have been? We do know that wherever he was at any given time never seemed to satisfy him or quench his restlessness. In that search, and the uncharted terrains it led him into, Coltrane reflected the turmoil of his time. And the degree to which his uncompromising musical adventures were accepted (an acceptance made possible only by his first having strongly established himself within the jazz tradition) made it possible for others to take risks.

Today we have become accustomed to the unaccustomed. The shock of the new has long since worn off. The charlatans who attach themselves to any new movement in the arts have, where jazz is concerned, long since disappeared, while players who had something genuine to say have endured. There is no longer any singular voice that pulls the music along in its direction. Instead there are many voices, some old, some new, some telling old stories in new ways, others vice versa, and some, as at any time, saying nothing at all though seeming to, and loudly. There are many ways to play jazz, and few nowadays claim exclusive legitimacy for their preferred kind.

Where would Coltrane have stood in this calm, eclectic musical climate, and would it have come about had he been with us through the strange decade of the '70s? Chances are it would, for the absence of charismatic leader-figures is emblematic in all the arts today. The flame that was so abruptly extinguished might in any event have simmered down, lest it devour itself.

But in this absence of new guiding lights, Coltrane—and especially the Coltrane of *Giant Steps*—continues to inspire countless budding saxophonists and players of other instruments as well. His sound, once so harshly criticized and even branded ugly, has become part and parcel of the sound of jazz, and his extensions of the possibilities of his instruments have been absorbed into the working vocabulary of the music, though some of the things he could do with a horn remain out of reach.

Someday, jazz may spawn another Coltrane, but as of now, he is the last of the spellbinders. Everything he left for us to hear and rehear is a welcome gift.

(1982)

Tommy Flanagan

Tommy Flanagan is indeed a jazz poet—a title bestowed upon him by Whitney Balliett, himself a poet and thus not likely to use the term loosely. A poet, of course, is a kind of magician, and what Flanagan can do with a piano is akin to magic. From this most intractable of instruments, which some players try to beat into submission, he draws the most astonishing and irresistibly luminous array of colors and textures, seemingly able to transform everything his fertile mind imagines into tangible musical reality.

And what his imagination conjures up is sheer musical poetry, sounds and thoughts that, insofar as they can be translated into words, require such superlatives as pure and sublime. But let the reader of such words not fall into the trap of equating poetic sensibility with the ethereal and the introspective. Tommy Flanagan is no shrinking violet of the piano. There is strength and sinew in his music, as well as gentleness and grace. His touch, a marvel in and of itself, can coax from a piano the most amazing dynamic range, with a clarity that matches the lucidity of his ideas. And hand in hand with this tonal wizardry goes a rhythmic sensibility of the highest order. No matter how lyrical, Flanagan's playing always reminds us that the piano is a percussive instrument, and Flanagan has absorbed the rhythmic discoveries of the greatest hornmen in jazz, perhaps most notably those of Charlie Parker. He makes the piano sing, and he also makes it swing. While he is never obvious, he commands a full range of emotions, from tenderness to exultation. Like the poets of old, he can exhort as well as beguile. He is a presence to conjure with.

For too many years, Flanagan, the most modest of men, was inclined to hide his light under the bushel of the demanding but unsung role of accompanist. Musicians and cognoscenti knew how much he had to offer, and never took his brilliance for granted, as even a partial listing of notables who made use of his gifts to enhance their records will show: Coleman Hawkins, Sonny Rollins, John Coltrane, Miles Davis, Thad Jones, Dexter Gordon, Milt Jackson, and on and on. But far too rarely did he let the public at large in on what he could do on his own, especially during two long stints with Ella Fitzgerald, first from 1962 to 1965 and then, as accompanist and musical director, from 1968 to 1978.

Toward the end of that long decade, those of us who were longing for Tommy to make records of his own finally got some succor. In 1975, the master made three albums in trio settings—fifteen years (!) after the last such morsel, and that only the second one since 1957. A couple of others followed before he sprung himself loose from Ella, and since then there's been at least a handful of discs (four of them Grammy nominations) in what is the most fitting format for the Flanagan magic.

All of them are marvels, but I think this new one is special, for a number of reasons. For one, Flanagan, like all truly great artists, keeps getting better, perfecting his skills. For another, this is by a working trio—bassist George Mraz, Tommy's first choice in that role, has been with him, on and off but mostly on, since their first encounter more than fifteen years ago. Mraz is astonishing. He has perfect time, and an ear to match that perfection. Add to that a command of his instrument that enables him to execute instantly and flawlessly whatever comes into his mind, and you have the perfect partner for a pianist of Flanagan's harmonic and rhythmic subtlety and imagination. At times it seems as if telepathy is involved, for Mraz does much more than merely provide a walking bass line; at times he meshes with Tommy's right-hand inventions as if the two minds were one. In Kenny Washington, the trio has acquired that rarity, a drummer who really listens and plays for the cause, and whose ego doesn't demand a solo on every number. He swings, too.

The program presented here differs from most of Tommy's other trio albums, in both the number and the variety of selections. We get the full spectrum of Flanagan's range, though any one album can of course only hint at the true breadth and scope of his amazing repertoire—he could play for a month without repeating a piece, and he *knows* everything he plays, including the lyrics, if any. And Rudy Van Gelder, that prince of jazz engineers, has captured the multiple hues of Tommy's sound. Clearly, he too is a member of the Flanagan fan club.

Some of the pieces have appeared before in the extensive Flanagan discography, but either long ago or in different contexts. Others are new; all are fresh.

"Raincheck," from the pen of Billy Strayhorn, one of Tommy's very favorite composers ("I find myself listening more to Ellington and Strayhorn music than anything else," he said), is a Flanagan first, though he did a Strayhorn album while still with Ella. Written for the Ellington orchestra, it retains its full flavor in Tommy's translation to the keyboard. His attack is so crisp you can almost feel the raindrops fall, and at this demandingly fast tempo one marvels at the precision of his articulation—no blur of notes here; each stands out. Mraz is up to this speed in his solo, which maintains the flowing conception. After the bass spot, Tommy sets up the exchanges with Washington in Ellingtonian fashion. The reprise of the theme is beautifully voiced.

"Lament" is one of J. J. Johnson's most attractive compositions. (Tommy was a member of the trombonist's 1957–58 group, with which he visited Europe for the first time.) This very personal interpretation features Tommy all the way. His ad lib exposition of the moving theme is lovely; he moves into a gentle rhythm for the lyrical variations in a shimmering rainbow of textures, returning to rubato for the reflective ending.

More than thirty years have passed since Flanagan's first trio recording of "Willow Weep for Me." This Ann Ronnel classic has long been a favorite with jazz musicians, and Tommy treats it with the respect he brings to all good tunes. The tempo is utterly relaxed but unfailingly swinging. There's a hint of Tatum in the exposition (less ornate, to be sure), and as he moves into improvisation, there's a fine mix of octave and single-note line touches, all colored by hints of the blues. Mraz's solo has something to say (some bassists just play notes) and sustains the groove. Tommy returns, devising a perfect ending—love those last chords!

"Caravan" is such a warhorse that one must marvel at Flanagan & Co.'s ability to turn it into something quite unhackneyed. The pianist uses appropriately Latin octave voicings to present the theme, over lively work by the rhythm team, and makes them sound tasty, not trite. Kenny's fine here as the trio shifts into vigorous 4/4, and Tommy's ideas keep coming—dig his second bridge, and how he clinches it with the last eight of the chorus. Mraz displays his amazing articulation and flawless intonation in a flying-fingers solo, with some slower spots for contrast. Tommy returns with an incisive treble figure and does some educated bopping before returning to the theme, again voiced in octaves, but with a different flavor than in the opening. It ain't what you do but the way that you do it!

Matt Dennis's "That Tired Routine Called Love," a fine but little-known tune, was recorded by Tommy with J. J. Johnson way back when. It has nice long lines that lend themselves well to the pianist's flowing, continuous conception. Tasteful brushwork by Washington underpins this liltingly swinging performance, and Tommy displays an astonishing variety of colors. He skips and dances through an amazing third chorus, each note perfectly placed in the rhythmic stream. Mraz takes a very melodic full chorus, and then Tommy returns with still more ideas. The recapitulation of the melody is the epitome of elegance.

"Glad to Be Unhappy" was previously recorded by Tommy as part of a Billie Holiday medley, but it is fully developed here, in tribute to Lady Day and also in memory of a friend, Bradley Cunningham (the owner of Bradley's in Greenwich Village and a true lover of fine piano jazz). "Bradley requested this when I was at the Village Vanguard," Tommy recalled. "Usually I hate requests, but that one came at just the right moment, and it got a wonderful reception." Small wonder, if it came off anything like here. He opens solo, with the verse and first chorus ad lib, and you can *hear* the lyrics, so songful (and soulful) is the playing. Almost subliminally, the rhythm section joins in, and a serene, stately tempo is established, Tommy coaxing bell-like, shimmering sonorities from the treble. He stays close to the melody, enhancing it with subtle harmonic touches. The rubato feel returns for the ending, and a crystalline cadenza concludes a masterpiece.

The venerable "St. Louis Blues" is another much-traveled musical road newly illuminated by the special Flanagan perspective. He opens alone, with an out-of-tempo paraphrase of the first strain, weaving in an echo of "Parker's Mood," then moving into tempo with an octave touch. The tango strain swings gently, with funk underneath, and then we're treated to blues improvisation of the first order—blues that sing and swing, blues that show how deeply the pianist has absorbed and transmuted the special blues language of Charlie Parker, that synthesis of the basic and the abstract into a blues epiphany. Mraz uses walking patterns in his solo, spiced with double-stops, and duets with Tommy on the return of the tango strain. Kenny's in there too as some educated riffing ensues; the fine ending just grows naturally from this spontaneous unity.

"Mean Streets," a Flanagan original named for Kenny Washington (it was Philly Joe Jones's nickname for the young drummer, who fittingly took over the drum chair with Dameronia after his mentor's death), threatens to break all speed limits. Kenny's brushes fly under Tommy's lightning figure-eights—a tempo like this is hard enough to hold, let alone make music at, but these three manage. Riffs lead to a short bass flash, and then the drums take it for a long but meaningful outing that builds to a fine climax, with tap-dance patterns on the snare and sound-streams on the cymbals. Tommy returns, and the tempo's where it was before—quite a feat.

"I'm Old Fashioned" is treated to a warm, happy ride. Felicitous touches abound, and again one marvels at the multiplicity of colors Flanagan can elicit from the piano as he dresses up this fine old tune in sparklingly fresh harmonies and textures. With Flanagan, technique is never employed for display, always at the service of the musical content. Not only does he never strike a wrong note—he seems incapable of even thinking a tasteless one. This is a luminous performance; it elevates the listener.

"Voce Abuso," by singer-composer Ivan Lins, is a lovely Brazilian song Tommy brought home from Rio in the early '70s. Once again the pianist shows his mastery at delineating a melody, and then he improvises at his most romantic, but with that special purity—you never hear a clichéd phrase or sentimental notion in his music. He returns to the melody with a full, resonant touch, adds a gentle, humorous ending, and lets that last note ring.

There are few greater pleasures in life than spending time in the company of Tommy Flanagan. Long a master of his demanding art and craft, he has reached a level that only a chosen few can attain. The beautiful stories this poet of jazz has told us here should be cherished, but they are just a prelude to what's in store when hearing him in the flesh.

(1990)

Martial Solal

What marvelous, mesmerizing, yes, even miraculous music Martial Solal has brought us here! Twenty masterpieces, two hours selected by the artist himself from forty half-hour concerts (or, as André Hodeir has aptly dubbed them, "recitals of improvisation") presented on Sunday afternoons from September 1993 to June 1994 and broadcast live at France Musique.

A daunting challenge, such a series, especially for an artist who sets such high standards for himself, who never permits himself to coast or play by rote, who has no repertoire of "licks" to fall back on when inspiration falters, who approaches each performance as a journey of discovery, and to whom the concept of improvisation is as rigorous a discipline as composition, but composition where decisions must be made on the spur of the moment and without the luxury of correcting and revising the score.

It is a challenge that Solal met triumphantly, though he has said that in the beginning he wasn't sure he could stay the course. What we have here is contemporary music of the highest order, music that is a joy to the mind and the heart of the listener, music that combines astonishing instrumental virtuosity (the word "technique" is insufficient to describe what Solal can bring forth from the piano) with equally astonishing imagination. We can only be grateful that Solal has the patience and discipline that has enabled him to hone his skill to such a point that he can instantly realize on the keyboard what comes into his mind. And that mind is one that seems to contain the whole history of music, beyond categories. Not as a bag of tricks to dip into, but as a mastered vocabulary from which the artist has created his own language, in which he tells us stories that are fresh and new and totally surprising.

With instrumental command as awesome as Solal's, lapses in taste could have disastrous results. But he never indulges in gratuitous effects. Even his most dazzling runs resolve into musical messages; there isn't an iota of meretriciousness in his artistry; not a single false or empty note is struck. But this purity does not result in austere music; not in the least. Solal leads us on fantastic journeys, taking chances at every turn in the road. He is a trapeze artist working without a net, a juggler who keeps a dozen balls in the air, an inventor of gorgeous musical kaleidoscopes.

Every performance here is, as I've said, a masterpiece, and there's no need for the kind of commentary that too often prevents listeners from making their own discoveries. But it's hard to resist pointing to some particularly joyful moments. "Cheek to Cheek" would no doubt have brought a smile to the face of Art Tatum; "Ah non" (Solal is also an outstanding composer of subjects for improvisation) contains astonishing displays of independence of hands; "Cuivre à la mer" conjures up the sounds of the harp, for which Ravel, to whom the piece is dedicated, wrote so masterfully; "Somebody Loves Me" surpasses the great (and also live) 1966 trio version; "Tout va très bien" is a marvelously extravagant "deconstruction" of a Paul Misraki hit from Solal's (and my own) youth (it was even popular in Denmark); "Hommage à Tex Avery" offers fascinating differences to the longer version on the splendid Stefanotis Solal collection; "Lover Man" is perhaps the definitive exploration of a great standard—and in terms of spontaneous composition, would it be possible to improve on that wonderful ending?

But one could single out felicities in every piece, sudden but seamless and logical changes in key or mode; the resolution of every idea, no matter how daring (there are no loose ends in this music); the spellbinding voicings; the crystal-clear touch; the masterful pedaling—in sum, the total command of instrument and ideas. This is music in which hands and head have become one. Martial Solal has been creating great music for decades, but I don't think he's ever played better than now. He has said that he will not wear his heart on his sleeve, yet he does not hide it from us. Hearing Solal in all his many facets is to be in the generous presence of one of the very greatest of living musicians, an artist who continues to surpass himself.

(1994)

Ruby Braff/Dick Hyman

This lovely music was created in the course of a miracle on Tenth Avenue—the location of Clinton Studios in Manhattan—where, during four consecutive days in the early summer of 1994, Ruby Braff recorded enough material for this and several other CDs.

Why a miracle? Because, just a few months before, the great cornetist had been so gravely ill with emphysema that it was feared he might not only never play again but perhaps not even survive. But here he was, sounding as glorious as ever, and his old feisty self (albeit some pounds lighter) as well, bless him! Miraculous indeed—even more so since music played a major role in Ruby's recovery. Specifically, *Essence of Armstrong* (Blue Decca brand), prepared and administered in cassette form by that noted Satchmo specialist, Jazz Dr. Jack Bradley (on hand at these sessions as well as Ruby's designated driver). Could one imagine a more appropriate medicine for a patient who has stated that "anything you hear on this planet of any musical use at all comes from Louis Armstrong"?

Most fittingly, the redoubtable duo of Ruby Braff and Dick Hyman was born in a Satchmo setting, at a salute to the immortal King of Jazz at Carnegie Hall in 1974. Thus Ruby and Dick in effect celebrate their twentieth anniversary with this auspicious CD. Theirs has been a most productive creative association, fortunately well documented on records (including two with Dick on pipe organ). I cherish them all, but this one's special—not least because it is so relaxed and tuneful. These are indeed "nice tunes." Some of them might even be called great tunes. Of course, our two alchemists can make any song sound good, but fine material gives them more to work with.

It may be a coincidence that half the songs herein have Armstrong affiliations, but I don't think so. The first of these is "I Want a Little Girl," done by Pops in 1946 and first put on the jazz map by McKinney's Cotton Pickers in 1930, with a great George Thomas vocal. Ruby *sings* on his horn and right away seduces the listener with that opulent sound. He and Dick split the first chorus, painting it blue. Then they trade fours and other subdivisions in their inimitable way. Dick gets Hinesian on the last bridge, and Ruby makes two references to Louis's "Melancholy," early and late.

Among Cole Porter classics, "My Heart Belongs to Daddy" is infrequently adopted by jazz musicians, but not because it is unsuitable, as this romp proves. Dick puts a catchy figure into play and repeats it under Ruby's entrance, later turning it into a little fugue. The tempo's pretty free here, and Ruby floats his phrases over active piano accompaniment. The cut-time ending is effective, and this is the first of several minor-hued tunes. (It's been suggested that these particular minor hues are Porter's clue to the Sugar Daddy's ethnic identity.)

"Sweet Savannah Sue," a Fats Waller opus, stems from the 1929 Broadway musical *Hot Chocolates*, in which Louis stepped up from pit to center stage, never to leave again. Ruby's opening chorus romances the melody, Dick moves from lacy double-time touches clothed in 1920s harmonies to full-fledged stride, Ruby rhapsodizes, and then the two friends trade fours, feeding each other ideas, before Ruby soars to a climax.

Dick sets up Ruby for his imaginative paraphrase of Jerome Kern's "Why Was I Born?," then gets into a contemporary Teddy Wilson groove. A dialogue in fours ensues, and the cornet takes it out. Kern didn't care for jazz treatments of his songs, but I doubt he'd have balked at this one.

"Lotus Blossom" was Duke Ellington's favorite Billy Strayhorn piano piece, and the duo takes it at Duke's chosen keyboard pace. Ruby makes outstanding use of his cello-like lower register on this lovely ultra-romantic melody, and he and Dick display perfect taste.

Seldom heard these days, "Joseph! Joseph!" was a hit for the Andrews Sisters in 1938. A 1920s Yiddish theater tune converted to Tin Pan Alley, it was also popular in Europe, ironically even heard in Nazi Germany, and I remember it well from my childhood. Our team gives it the proper Russo-Jewish flavor. Dick wanders into strange keys; Ruby *davens* and Dick responds. Then they trade fours and work up to a spontaneous ending that couldn't be bettered.

A vintage Armstrong Blue Decca item, "Thanks a Million," is a 20-bar song launched by Paul Whiteman in the eponymous film. It becomes an intense dialogue here, with full choruses by both men, plus plenty of parsing. The treatment conjures up the spirit of the master.

"By Myself," a fine Arthur Schwartz melody in a minor mood, was Maxine Sullivan's signature song. The tempo's fairly up, Dick gets into some interesting bass stuff, he and Ruby trade a lot, really swinging, and the "free" ending on Ruby's low note is special. There is such togetherness here that they could change the title to "By Ourselves."

Most of us think of "I Can't Give You Anything but Love" as the first pop ballad recorded by Louis Armstrong, but another Jimmy McHugh–Dorothy Fields tune beat it by some three months. Of course "I Must Have That Man" wasn't sung by Pops. It was on a Lillie Delk Christian date that he got to play it. Here, Ruby starts with beautiful phrases, building. Dick maintains the Louis groove, playing with much feeling.

There are echoes here of "Sleepy Time Down South," a not-too-distant harmonic cousin, from time to time. An impassioned 16 cornet bars are answered by Dick, digging in. Then they ease up for the gentle ending. A masterpiece!

First heard as part of Ellington's *Black, Brown and Beige*, the theme of "Come Sunday" was stated by the incomparable Johnny Hodges in one of the suite's greatest moments. Since then, it has established itself as a free-standing Ellington standard, and Ruby and Dick treat it with the dignity it warrants—just two choruses say it all.

From the canon of the Second Hot Five stems one of Don Redman's nicest tunes, "Save It Pretty Mama." Our duettists are at their most relaxed and conversational here, and the tempo's perfect. This is music you'd expect to hear after hours in somebody's living room, not from a recording studio. Thanks for letting us listen in!

Benny Carter has often said that the trumpet is his favorite instrument, and when he plays it, it's not hard to figure out who his favorite trumpeter is. He has seldom played that horn better than on his own "Once Upon a Time," recorded in 1933, with among others a young Teddy Wilson in one of his first great solos. It's a performance steeped in Armstrong. Astonishingly, this pretty Carter melody has been revived just once on records—on an obscure 1955 British date led by reedman Bertie King, a Carter alumnus. So, in effect this is a "first," and Ruby and Dick give it the royal treatment.

Eubie Blake's "You're Lucky to Me" was instantly immortalized by Louis in 1930, which means that Bix Beiderbecke would still have heard it. Why bring that up? Because our heroes get on a Bix kick here. Both men improvise from the start, and soon Ruby plays a descending phrase that subliminally conjures up Bix. Dick picks up on it, elaborating it into a quote from Bix's cadenza to "I'm Coming Virginia," and Ruby echoes and extends it. Then Dick reuses it, throwing in some more oblique Bixisms, and Ruby keeps Bix in view, though Louis shines through on the final bridge. A delightful romp. What ears these guys have!

"Sleepy Time Down South" was one of Ruby's earliest recordings—a live one, from a Boston festival in 1954, with the great Vic Dickenson doing vocal honors. This is not Ruby's first version with Dick on records—they did it on one of the pipe-organ albums. But it's wonderful to have this new and quite different duet—yet another love letter to Pops. From Ruby's opening cadenza (note how seamlessly he eases into tempo and Dick falls in) to his perfect Louis coda and strictly Ruby downward flourish, this is sheer delight. Dick's fine solo chorus is no letdown, and it's high time for us to point out how important his accompaniment is throughout these collaborations: always the right choices to allow Ruby to breathe and think.

Ruby and Dick—you're lucky to us. Thanks for making us believe in miracles.

(1994)

Dick Hyman

D ick Hyman is a marvel. His ability to delight and surprise is, it would seem, unceasing. A musician of well-nigh incredible range and versatility (a listing of his accomplishments would take up the space of these notes and include references to Broadway shows, film scores, works in the major classical forms, arrangements and accompaniments for a host of stellar singers and instrumentalists covering almost the entire spectrum of jazz and popular music; leadership of a variety of jazz repertory companies and ensembles, which is to say re-creation and, relatedly but quite differently, imaginative recastings of the works of Jelly Roll Morton and James P. Johnson; and, not last and by no means least, the pianistic skills of a true virtuoso combined—and this is truly rare—with a profound understanding and deep knowledge of musical content and meaning), he continues to reveal new facets of his talent.

Consider this marvelous record: it is, astonishingly, Hyman's first solo piano LP of traditional jazz repertory—astonishing at least to a listener who has heard Dick perform so much traditional jazz piano live. He has, of course, recorded much from this repertory before, but either interspersed with other material or not in a solo setting (as in an excellent, overlooked 1973 album with Don Butterfield, tuba, Tony Mottola, banjo, and Ron Zito, drums). He has made solo recordings of ragtime, foremost among them his unequalled five-record set of Scott Joplin's complete piano works. But that's a different idiom, as is his recording of Eubie Blake songs arranged in a variety of Hyman approaches. So this is the first Dick Hyman recording of its type, with the added distinction of being devoted to the work of a particular composer.

From a purely pianistic perspective, Clarence Williams might seem an odd choice, since even his most ardent admirers would not claim that he was a distinguished performer at the keyboard. Adequate might be the word. But Williams was not first and foremost a pianist. As Hyman points out, "he was not a remarkable pianist and perhaps not even a remarkable composer in the sense that Ellington and Morton were. But he was a remarkable organizer—like Eddie Condon, in a way. Both managed to do remarkable things in the recording studios."

Williams's rich and remarkable career has been lovingly and meticulously detailed in Tom Lord's hefty bio-discography (published in 1976 by Storyville Publications). He was, among other things, one of the first and certainly one of the most successful black music publishers. And he was the man who convinced OKeh Records to start a race catalog, the man who first got Bessie Smith into a studio, and the man who organized, supervised, and played on a most remarkable series of records with sound and instrumentation all their own. There were many kinds of Clarence Williams records. The quintessential ones I have in mind are those anchored in Cyrus St. Clair's tuba and spiced by Floyd Casey's washboard.

(Permit an aside—pertinent, I hope. Around 1950, I was fortunate to hear and see a re-creation, for one night only, of the Clarence Williams Blue Five, assembled by producer Bob Maltz at New York's Central Plaza: Ed Allen, cornet; Buster Bailey, clarinet; James P. Johnson, piano; Cy St. Clair, tuba; Floyd Casey, washboard. Alas, nobody had a recording device handy. It was indeed the past recaptured.)

It was in Breda, site of a fine traditional jazz festival, that Dick Hyman heard European bands perform Clarence Williams–style music. "I was surprised at the repertoire they played," he said. "Quite different from American bands. No warhorses, but lots of good, overlooked material. So when Bob Erdos—we'd been talking about an album for Stomp Off for a year or so—suggested my doing Williams-associated tunes, I was intrigued. I was familiar with the Williams reissues, of course, and in terms of this project I've tended to adopt some of the performance values I heard in the records and base my versions on them."

Thus, interestingly, Dick's models here are mostly band performances, not piano music, and that accomplishes at least two important things: it frees him from "re-creating" a particular pianist's style, and it enables him to bring to bear the full resources of his imagination, on a superb grand piano that responds gloriously to his awesome technique and touch. Listeners who know the original recordings will be especially pleased at points where Dick comes up with particularly felicitous allusions, but it should be stressed that what is at hand here is freshly minted music. While Dick's approach is infused with his empathy for and mastery of the jazz keyboard styles and expressive manner of the period with which this music is associated, he always applies these skills and sensibilities in strictly his own manner. This needs to be said because, in jazz, the relationship between creativity and stylistic orientation has been needlessly obfuscated by ill-defined notions about "improvisation," "spontaneity," and "originality," all of which, in their truest sense, are represented by what Dick Hyman does here.

We're off to a good start with "Organ Grinder Blues," recorded by its composer as a piano solo, as accompanist to Victoria Spivey (with King Oliver on board) and Ethel Waters, and twice with his own band. It's the 1928 band version that serves as the model here. Dick's piano arrangement refers exactly to the band record in terms of spirit, pace, and form. The fine, deliberate tempo becomes the springboard for a performance infused with blues feeling and hints of boogie-woogie.

Though "Achin' Hearted Blues" was recorded by a 1923 Williams group, the rather undistinguished results are not what Dick turned to for inspiration. Rather, it's the slightly earlier recording by Charles Matson's Creole Serenaders of "It Ain't Nobody's Business If I Do," which contains an interpolation of "Achin' Hearted." "I used *that* tempo," said Dick. "It's a charming record." The same adjective can be applied to Dick's version, with its hints of ragtime, touches of Jelly Roll in the concluding choruses, and fine breaks.

"I'm Going Back to Bottomland," from a Broadway musical and recorded by Williams bands for Paramount and Columbia in 1927, is also, Dick said, "a re-creation of an orchestral version—I like the tune quite a bit." This is a very relaxed performance, with some lovely "chime" effects and a James P. Johnson touch.

"Wild Cat Blues" was one of the first really great Williams records, and also Sidney Bechet's debut on disc. Dick wanted to capture some of "the feeling of Bechet," and he did—his right hand conjures up Bechet's brilliant lead and breaks, against a solid left-hand rhythm, and in its concluding passages, there's some striking contrapuntal stuff that reflects the ensemble climax. And Dick has also captured the special, rocking swing of the original performance.

"You Don't Understand," co-composed by James P. Johnson, is a peppy tune that inspired Clarence to sing on his band's recording (something he did quite frequently), but he let James P. accompany his wife, Eva Taylor, on her record of it. Dick, however, decided to perform this number in what he calls "piano-roll style." That particular "roll" rhythm is present, but Dick imbues it with more swing than the mechanical playback is capable of rendering. There are some Waller touches here, and an effective change of key. The pleasant verse appears midway through, and dig the fancy ending.

The once prominent bandleader and pianist Tim Brymn and the gifted arranger-pianist Alex Hill co-wrote "Shout, Sister, Shout" with Clarence. It became a hit and was adopted by the Boswell Sisters as their theme song. Clarence made numerous recordings of it, including one that has been suggested as Roy Eldridge's debut. Dick treats this jaunty stride piece in what he describes as "standard 'Minor Drag' fashion," but he's too modest; there's nothing "standard" about this imaginative interpretation, and few pianists can handle this kind of tempo so well. One of Waller's favorite riffs appears here.

"What's the Matter Now?" was done by Clarence as a piano roll; he also backed Bessie Smith and a couple of other singers on it, while Don Redman did the vocal on his band version. The tune reminded Dick of "Weather Bird," the King Oliver piece made famous by Louis Armstrong and Earl Hines. "It has similar changes, so I do some Hinesian stuff," Dick elucidated. Indeed he does, and he evokes Louis as well in this brilliant rendition—to me, one of the album's high points.

"Gulf Coast Blues" is about the only piece on this collection that could be described as a standard. It was a big hit for Clarence, especially as done by Bessie on her first date, with the composer at the piano; they did it again a few years later with refurbished lyrics as "The New Gulf Coast Blues," and in 1934, Clarence kicked off the new Decca label's race series with a band version that had Willie "The Lion" Smith on piano and Clarence on jug. And he performed it in 1947 on his last recorded appearance, with his daughter Irene doing the singing and Baby Dodds on drums. Dick has picked a perfect tempo for his rendition, which features some remarkable trills and more of that Hines-Armstrong flavoring.

Louis was present on Clarence's first recording of "Papa De-Da-Da," as was Sidney Bechet; Clarence revived it in 1930 and made a number of new versions, including one with Lil Hardin Armstrong. Dick takes the famous first record as his point of departure, using "a lot of the arrangement." Again, he picks a perfect tempo, not as fast as most bands tend to do this pleasant piece. Terrific stuff!

"Let Every Day Be Mother's Day" underwent a slight change in title with Mom losing out to "Sweetheart," for reasons unknown. No matter what you call it, this is a snappy piece in which The Lion had a hand. The 1935 record, with Ed Allen, the great Cecil Scott, Cy St. Clair, and Casey on board is one of my personal favorites in the Williams canon, and Dick's too. "I like the tempo on these records," he points out. "I do this one in my own style, trying to get the sound of the band on the keyboard, with single-note lines and contrapuntal clarinet things. I used to play the clarinet, you know. Those single-note lines were a bit too modern-sounding for Bob Erdos at first, but he relented!" We can be glad he did, for this is a delightful and tremendously spirited performance that swings from first to last note and really captures the ensemble feeling, with some surprising hints of Erroll Garner in Dick's left-hand strumming. This is a masterpiece.

"Nobody but My Baby (Is Getting My Love)" was done by Clarence with a number of singers (Eva Taylor had Eddie South on her date), but

Dick has based his version on Fats Waller's great 1927 QRS piano roll. "I stay very close to Fats for the first half, then modulate and follow up with my own interpretation," he commented. It's done seamlessly, and again, with more swing than a roll (even a Waller roll) can supply.

We conclude with another rouser, "Cushion Foot Stomp." Clarence did this twice with his Washboard Band in 1927. Dick sparkles here, trotting out some great stop-time stuff and building up to a Jelly Roll finale. There's a surprise in store here, and I was tempted not to give it away: Dick offers a chorus of scat. It's idiomatic, and reveals yet another facet of the Hyman personality.

In the gifted hands of Dick Hyman, the music of Clarence Williams and his time takes on new life here. I'm certain Clarence would have loved this record; his good friend James P. Johnson would have, too. I can think of no higher praise than that.

(1986)

Dave McKenna

I t's a joy to have this record reissued, finally. In its first incarnation, it became an instant collector's item, so rare that many Dave McKenna fans have never laid eyes on it. It wasn't even reviewed in *Down Beat*. It was only the pianist's second LP as a leader, and his first trio date. (His debut, a solo effort, appeared in 1955.) More than a decade would pass before Big Dave got to record regularly on his own, but since 1973 there has, happily, been a fairly steady supply of albums from one of our most distinctive keyboard stylists.

Putting musicians in neatly labeled stylistic pigeonholes is endemic to jazz appreciation, but McKenna is a hard man to pin a label on. In some ways, he's a lineal descendant of the two-fisted pianists that sprang from the Fats Waller–Earl Hines school, but he came up during the bebop era, and there's a flavor of that in his approach. His own utterances have not been helpful to the classifiers at all. "I'm more of a song player than a jazz player," he told John S. Wilson in 1980. "I'm a saloon player, a cocktail player. I don't want to stretch out the way jazz pianists do." McKenna is too modest: that powerful left hand shakes a mean cocktail indeed. When he wants it that way, he can be a whole rhythm section by himself.

As for stretching out, that's become more of a vice than a virtue in jazz today.

He claims few direct pianistic antecedents, but it's a clue to his style that he loves trumpet players and has wished he were one himself. "You can *bend* notes on a trumpet," he points out, adding that Nat King Cole was the only pianist who could do that, "and maybe Ray Charles." His trumpet heroes are Louis Armstrong, Roy Eldridge, and Buck Clayton, so it figures that he values melodic improvisation and plenty of swing. He has a right-hand attack like a trumpeter, while his left sometimes strums like a guitar (something he says he was doing before he heard it from Erroll Garner) but more often punches out percussive, pile-driving bass lines.

Born in Rhode Island, he joined the musicians' union at fifteen and first came to national attention at nineteen, with Charlie Ventura's hip little band. Woody Herman grabbed him, but his career as a Herdsman was cut short by Uncle Sam, who sent him to Korea; since he was a musician, the Army made him a cook. Dave loves to eat, but in Italian restaurants; he told Whitney Balliett that his Army biscuits were "like rocks." (Perhaps they took after his beat.) Free again, he rejoined Ventura, then worked in succession with Gene Krupa, Stan Getz, the early Al Cohn–Zoot Sims group, and Buddy Rich. Next came a lengthy association with Eddie Condon, and a lasting one with Bobby Hackett, who called him "the greatest piano player in the world" and meant it. During the '70s, McKenna could most often be found on Cape Cod, where he'd settled with his wife and two sons, with time out for the "jazz parties" in Colorado, Texas, and California. More recently, he's toured worldwide with the Concord Superband, and if you're lucky, you may catch him at a jazz festival or, best of all, at a piano room, like Bradley's in New York.

That is the ideal venue for McKenna's singular artistry, which rolls into one personal mode of keyboard expression the whole vocabulary of jazz piano from stride to bebop. On such gigs, he often unfolds his large repertory of songs in medleys related by titles (moon or water songs, for instance) or composer (an unforgettable Rodgers and Hart medley, at the late lamented Hanratty's, included a ravishing "A Ship Without a Sail," and how often do you hear that one?).

Like any musician worth his salt (of which there's plenty on Cape Cod), McKenna has grown and matured, particularly as a ballad interpreter, in the nearly thirty years since he cut this record, but he already had his style well in hand in 1959—this is unmistakably McKenna. His gift for choosing good tempos and keeping them firmly afloat is well in evidence, as are his supple touch and choice of unhackneyed repertory. And when he goes to work on a standard like "Way Down Yonder in New Orleans," he transforms it, in this instance by choosing a racehorse tempo and sounding like a whole band.

He's more than ably assisted by a famous drummer and a little-remembered bassist, both unfortunately no longer with us. Osie Johnson had worked with, among others, Earl Hines and Illinois Jacquet when he settled in New York in 1955 and very quickly established himself as one of that competitive city's most in-demand studio drummers. Until his death at forty-three in 1966, he appeared on hundreds of sessions, all of which he enlivened with his terrific swing and fine musicianship (he was also a gifted composer and arranger, and could sing some mean blues).

John Drew, born in Liverpool in 1927, came to the U.S. in 1954 with a reputation as one of England's best bassists. He soon got a job with Gene Krupa (where he met McKenna), and also played with Stan Getz and Les Elgart; by the time of this recording, he was a busy studio man, valued for his firm, swinging time and big sound. Tragically, he contracted cancer of the lymph nodes and died in early 1962. This date was one of his best; Dave gave him plenty of solo space, and those fast tempos, not easy to hold, show his mettle.

From the start, McKenna's penchant for unusual material is evident. "This Is the Moment," from a Betty Grable movie, is taken for a typical McKenna ride; at times, he reminds of the great, forgotten Eddie Costa, who had a similar way of creating plunging, percussive, and relentlessly swinging two-fisted patterns in the bass end of the keyboard. Dave and Osie have fun here. "Silk Stockings," from the eponymous Cole Porter musical, was new then, is seldom heard now, and has that Porter flavor. The pianist respects the melody but also turns it blue. We've mentioned "Way Down Yonder"; it moves, and shows how well McKenna can speak his piece in a short span.

"Fools Rush In" sounds to me like Dave's tribute to Garner, in tempo, mood, and touches of humor—a little double-time, too. "Expense Account" is a happy swing-to-bop opus by trombonist Bennie Green. Dave gets a Basie-band feel, and there's a nice bass spot. Irving Berlin's "Lazy," seldom used as a jazz instrumental, opens with the bridge to "Jive at Five"; McKenna's vocalized, behind-the-beat phrasing swings to the hilt at this relaxed tempo. Two fine McKenna originals follow. "Splendid Splinter" is a tribute to Ted Williams (Dave is a stone Red Sox fan); a fast blues with plenty of fireworks, some boppish riffs, fine interplay between the three men, and excellent fours with Osie. "Lickety Split" is even faster; a 32-bar pattern that sounds to these ears like "I May Be Wrong," with an "Idaho" bridge—but I may be wrong. Does it move? Please, Dave, don't tell us you're not a jazz player!

"Along with Me" by Harold Rome is another good, unusual choice for a jazz vehicle. It goes from a samba-feel head into 4/4 for some splendid improvisation, a neatly negotiated return to the theme, a bit of unaccompanied piano, out of tempo, and then home with the samba. "Secret Love"

opens with a Parker lick, recasts the tune's harmony, and has vigorous exchanges with bass and drums. "Da-Da-Da-Go-Dig-It," a blues by Osie
Johnson, shows that Dave is at home with the basic jazz text. Osie works out
some interesting cross-rhythms in front and back, Drew shows his Blanton
roots, and Dave treats us to some stop-time. The wrap-up, "I Should
Care," is treated with sentiment but without sentimentality; as always,
McKenna plays a ballad with a beat. Dig the key change and Dave's own
way of voicing chords. Osie and John are right with him when he slips into
a double-time feeling—this was a real trio.

As a bonus, this record is an example of early stereo at its best; all the
nuances are captured. But then, this music wears its years without wrinkles
in every respect.

(1988)

Svend Asmussen

S
vend Asmussen? A hell of a musician," said Benny Goodman recently.
"I've known him for about thirty years, and he's always been kind of a
favorite of mine. Marvelous taste in what he plays."

We open with this praise from a king because the name may not be familiar, though the brilliant Danish violinist, active on the jazz scene since
the 1930s, has long been a top attraction in Europe. While he has had numerous chances to come to the U.S.A. (Goodman, who first heard Asmussen in 1950, wanted him to join his group then and there, but Svend
had his own successful band and politely turned down the flattering offer),
his working visits have been rare.

In 1959 and '60, he toured here with the Swe-Danes (himself, guitarist
Ulrich Neuman, and singer Alice Babs), but not on the jazz circuit. A wonderful duet album with Neuman, recorded in Los Angeles, was issued on
Warner Bros. but didn't make a ripple. In 1962, he recorded another fine
album in Stockholm with another great admirer, John Lewis, and in 1967,
he appeared at the Monterey Jazz Festival in a violin summit with Ray
Nance and Jean-Luc Ponty. A record was cut at a European summit a year
before (with Stuff Smith, Stephane Grappelli, and Ponty). And in 1976, yet
another summit (with Nance and Grappelli and Duke Ellington) was
briefly available on the U.S. market. Later recordings with Lionel Hamp-

ton, Toots Thielemans, and the Indian violinist L. Subramanian have sneaked in as imports.

One hopes that this wonderful record—Asmussen's first made in this country with American jazzmen—will bring him the acclaim in U.S. jazz circles he so richly deserves. Producer Bob Thiele, who'd first become aware of the Danish fiddler's talent when he heard him play "June Night" on a 1940 recording issued here on the obscure Hit label just before Pearl Harbor, has long had it in the back of his mind to add Asmussen to his roster of great jazz names. In the late summer of 1983, Thiele brought Asmussen to New York and put together a top-notch group of sympathetic players to back him up: pianist Derek Smith, guitarist Bucky Pizzarelli, bassist Milt Hinton, and drummer Oliver Jackson.

The result is an ideal showcase for a world-class player. Since I grew up in Denmark, I've long been an admirer of the great Dane, who was a star in his homeland before he was out of his teens. Not just a great jazz player but also a master showman (he sings, plays guitar, bass, piano, and vibes, and is a gifted arranger), he soon began to reach audiences beyond the inner circles of jazz, appearing on the musical stage, in films and in vaudeville.

I hadn't seen Svend since Monterey '67, and was both pleased and surprised to note that he hadn't changed a bit. No one would guess that he made his professional debut as far back as the fall of 1933, when, at seventeen, he appeared at a student gala in Copenhagen. By then, he had studied violin for ten years, acquiring a solid classical background, but been aware of jazz only about a year or so. His first inspiration was Joe Venuti, and his first group was patterned on the Blue Four. In 1935, he made his first record as a leader; it was reviewed in *Melody Maker* by Leonard Feather, who praised him, and even more so after a visit to Denmark in 1938. (On that latter occasion, Feather judged him superior to Grappelli. I won't get into comparison games, but to my ears, the greatest violinists in jazz are Eddie South, Venuti, Stuff Smith, Grappelli, and Asmussen—Ponty is lost to rock, and young Didier Lockwood, whom Asmussen much admires, has yet to reach maturity.)

It wasn't until 1937 that Svend decided on music as a full-time career, having also studied dentistry and sculpting. During the next few years, he worked in Denmark with Fats Waller, the Mills Brothers, and Josephine Baker, as well as various Scandinavian stars. His 1939 visits to London, Hamburg, and Paris created quite a stir, but the outbreak of World War II aborted other projected tours. Ironically, the Nazi occupation of Denmark brought local jazz activity to an unprecedented peak, perhaps because jazz symbolized America and freedom and was hated by the Nazis. Another factor was the cessation of visits by top foreign artists and the unavailability of American records. In any case, Danish jazz flourished, and Asmussen became its top star. Eventually, the Nazis arrested him, and for a while he was incarcerated in Berlin.

After the war, Asmussen focused his activities on Sweden, where there was always more work than in Denmark, and where jazz was becoming increasingly popular. By the early 1950s, he had, according to old admirer Feather in *Down Beat*, "his pick of the highest priced night club, vaudeville, radio and movie jobs in almost every country in Europe; his records are constant best sellers," and was not tempted by offers from America. Yet he greatly enjoyed his infrequent visits, such as one in the spring of 1955, when he was leading the band aboard the Swedish liner *Kungsholm*, and got a nice write-up in *The New Yorker*'s "Talk of the Town" section.

It was the presence in Denmark of an old idol, Stuff Smith, that fully rekindled Asmussen's commitment to jazz. At a memorial concert for Stuff in 1967, he said: "Stuff gave me inspiration once more, and courage and self-confidence, which I had halfways let slip years ago."

Svend is in top form here, in a typically relaxed and swinging program of jazz standards (some evergreens, some less known) and a sprinkling of originals. He has always been at home in the classic jazz repertory, and handles himself like a native, with just a dash of Continental charm. Immediately evident is his assurance, both as a player (his technique, perhaps the most violinistic, in the classical sense, of all the great jazz fiddlers, is absolutely secure) and as a leader (he has a special knack for setting the right tempos and devising tasteful routines that impose structure on what might in other hands have become an occasion for run-of-the-mill jamming).

In other words, Asmussen has the authority that is a hallmark of a great jazzman, and a conception of his own, which he was able to transmit readily to his American colleagues. These, needless to say, are all seasoned pros, with illustrious careers far too long to summarize here. (I'm counting Derek Smith, who settled here in 1957, as American, though he was born and bred in England.) Together, they make up a formidable rhythm team (they all love to swing, and so does Asmussen), but their roles call for more than support, and each man steps front and center from time to time.

All told, this is wonderful music: swinging, inventive, relaxed, and tasteful, featuring a player of true world class. Nice to have had you in New York, Svend Asmussen! Come back soon. . . .

(1983)

Joe Lovano

There seem to be no limits to Joe Lovano's musical horizon. Each new encounter with this remarkable player and composer—live or on record; in a big band or small group—brings surprises, all of them pleasant. Impressive from the start (this listener first caught Joe, amazingly, some twenty years ago, with Woody Herman), his instrumental mastery continues to expand: on this album, we hear him on tenor, alto, and soprano saxophones, alto clarinet, and wood flute—not to mention tuned gongs and percussion. And as a composer (all but one of the pieces here are his), he is finding an identity that may become as unmistakable as the one he already has as a player.

Joe wants us to hear this record as "a concert set; each tune has a different form, there are different settings, and we cover a lot of ground. There's been a conscious effort to create a flow." Each of Joe's compositions, and even the single standard on the program, has a specific meaning and identity *vis-à-vis* his own musical and personal history.

The many and often lasting musical environments in which Joe has found himself have taught him that music at its best and deepest is a matter of awareness of others as well as yourself. "All the great ensembles I've been lucky to play in have had a band sound," he said. "Relationships make the music great; we all had awareness of each other." As anyone familiar with the career and music of Joe Lovano will know by now, important associations have included the Herman Herd for three years; the Mel Lewis Jazz Orchestra (now the Village Vanguard Monday night band) for thirteen years; Charlie Haden's Liberation Music Orchestra since 1987; the John Scofield quartet, and, for more than a decade, Paul Motian's splendid trio. And, of course, Joe's earliest musical association with his father, Tony "Big T" Lovano, a prominent and committed jazzman on the Cleveland scene.

Music continues to be a family thing with Joe; featured on this album is his wife, Judi Silvano, an experienced singer adept at both jazz and classical music. "Judi and I have been together since 1980," Joe said. "She has a sound and creative input that I've never experienced with any other player, and I say 'player' because we use her voice as an instrument—something I don't think has been properly explored yet."

There are other longtime associates involved. Scott Lee, one of three bassists heard here (and particularly impressive on "Worship"), has been a friend since Joe's Boston days in the '70s ("We often played together every day"). Pianist Kenny Werner also goes back to that decade with Joe. Steve Swallow and Joe were together in the Carla Bley band in 1983, and also worked in Europe with bassist Henri Texier's foursome, the Transatlantic Quartet ("another two-bass band," Joe pointed out). Trumpeter Tim Hagans, a Kenton alumnus who spent time in Europe with Thad Jones and Ernie Wilkins, has been a friend since the early '80s. The association with Charlie Haden has already been mentioned. "It's been a thrill to play his music," said Joe. "It's fantastic to have him play mine. He's one of the most creative players in jazz." Joe has worked with some fabulous drummers: Motian, of course; the late Mel Lewis, and another fallen hero, Ed Blackwell. Now we can add the fabulous Jack DeJohnette. "The rhythm section didn't rehearse," Joe explained, "so everything was fresh, and Jack and Charlie's reactions were amazing."

Our concert, which Joe describes as a kind of "culmination of my life as a player till now—people and places; feelings about music and scenes; Cleveland, Boston, New York," begins with "Luna Park," named for a Cleveland amusement park in operation from the 1920s into the 1930s. "Everybody talked about it, if they were old enough," Joe said. "It had been right across from where my grandma lived. I tried for a carnival feeling here, like the early days of Pres." This is a showcase for the band with Judi and Tim, with collective ensemble effects (Joe is on soprano, on which, as on all his horns, he has a great sound, and which, unlike many practitioners, he keeps in tune at all times); a fine open-horn Hagans solo; Swallow sounding like a guitar (well, electric bass is also known as bass guitar, right?), and, as throughout, a very active role for the drummer.

"Sculpture" changes the mood and texture. Inspired, Joe said, by Coltrane's "Expression," it has form, Joe explained, "but really takes its shape from the playing of the rhythm section, spontaneity through tempo. With a different rhythm section, it would be completely different." The atmosphere is modal, meditative, sometimes declamatory. The piano solo is marked by unusual voicings. ("Kenny's the perfect piano player," said Joe, whose tenor is authoritative here.)

"Josie and Rosie," Joe's mother and aunt, "were my biggest critics and fans. Aunt Rose was a singer; she knew tunes, was hip to Ella, and prepared me for lessons. My mother loved music. This is based on 'Woody'n You,' and I did it as a dedication to Dizzy; now it's become a memorial tribute. I play alto here, my original horn." With the alto, the blend of trumpet, voice, and saxophone takes on a different hue from "Luna Park." There are some Monkish touches in this swinging, up-tempo ride. A drum solo early in the proceedings brings to mind Joe's live performances, in which the solo order is never predictable, thankfully—another one of those things that make his music so fresh. He has his own conception on alto, too. Hagans is fleet and crisp, clearly someone to hear more from; Werner has great ears and takes no rests. Hear Judi's high-note ending!

"This Is Always," put in the books by Bird, Garner, and Earl Coleman, was a tune Joe's father played; he has a tape of him doing it with organ trio. The tempo's brighter than usual for this tune, and Joe calls it "a walking ballad, in two; Dad played it like that." There are two basses here, and Joe pointed out that Steve Swallow plays "a chordal part, with a pick, in the register of the piano's left hand; very supportive of the tenor." Steve takes an interesting solo, and Joe's very relaxed here, with a fine rhythmic-melodic flow, climbing into the upper register for the last eight, and an effective ending. (Joe, who also plays in the Smithsonian's Jazz Masterpiece Orchestra, is clearly at home with the tradition but infuses it with a natural non-reconstructive feeling.)

"Worship," "about meditation and peace," features remarkable interplay between Joe, Judi, and Scott Lee's bowed bass. Joe's on soprano here, but also plays the gongs, something he's been into for a while. In fact, the piece is written in the key of the gongs. Prayer-like, incantatorial, this music is wholly original. The two sopranos alternatively entwine and separate, harmonize and merge in unison. Throughout, the arco bass maintains a solid foundation—and stays in tune.

"Cleveland Circle" is dedicated to Joe's Cleveland connection, to Boston's Cleveland Circle, where Joe lived while attending Berklee School of Music in 1971, and to New York, where Joe would rather live than anywhere else. It explores, the composer said, "different dimensions of rhythm and tempo. Jack sets a new tempo for his solo, which I take up, and I hand over to Tim . . . not just one solo after another, and not just playing free, but staying within the structure of the song." Lots of activity here, rhythmic and harmonic. At times, DeJohnette gets into an Elvin Jones groove, while Joe's overblowing (he goes "out" here, but always musically) reminds of later Trane. Hagans's good solo starts up high and stays there, and there are some interesting tenor-piano unison figures. Silvano again blends well with the other horns.

"The Dawn of Time" is a warm, expansive ballad. "Tunes like this," said Joe, "are the foundation of my playing. Ken and Charlie and Jack play so open here." And Joe is authoritative, building, painting a picture. This story has a lovely ending, with Jack's word the last.

"Lost Nations" is dedicated to the late Jim Pepper. "We played together with Paul [Motian], and I learned a lot from him about Native Americans. This is a kind of a folk song." Joe plays both soprano sax and alto clarinet here. The latter instrument, he explained, "has tenor range but goes lower—like an extension of the tenor sax. James Farber, our engineer, set me up so that I could switch horns in midstream." On soprano at first, Joe improvises freely over a bass-drum figure, which is taken up by trumpet and voice as Joe continues, exploring all registers, including the warm middle. A three-way unison theme appears; then each voice goes its own way, contrapuntally before they come together once more. The alto clarinet adds yet another tonal color. The bass figure is there throughout; we fade on it.

"Hypnosis" does achieve a "kind of hypnotic feel," Joe said, pointing out that Charlie Haden "plays a fantastic solo." Perhaps not least due to Haden's strong role, there is an Ornette aura to this performance, free in form yet song-like in pattern, with a fine collective spirit. It also swings (as does much of Ornette), Joe's tenor contributing greatly to the rhythmic flow.

"Chelsea Rendezvous," a 12-bar theme, was on Joe's second record for Soul Note, in a tenor-piano-drums version. This one is much extended, though the only original tune not specifically written for this album. "This is about my New York scene," Joe said (Chelsea is the part of Manhattan where he makes his home), "playing with Judi and Tim and Scott. Think of it as our encore." Joe is heard here on tenor, alto clarinet, wood flute, gong, and percussion (the flute and percussion are overdubbed, the only such technology employed on the album). Joe opens on tenor with bass and drums only and a ballad feel. As he goes into harmonics on the horn, his sound doesn't seem distorted but is pleasing to the ear. Judi joins him, and as they duet; they take turns leading, drums very inventive behind. As muted trumpet enters and Judi scats, Joe switches to flute, and after Hagans's Miles-like solo, Joe does his gong thing, then solos on alto clarinet (odd that such an attractive instrument should be so seldom used, but maybe it takes Joe Lovano to make it sound this good). Judi joins Joe for an "echo" effect, and then Joe returns to the tenor, harmonizing with Judi, taking it home, thematically.

If you feel like me about this music, one encore from Joe Lovano won't be enough. Fortunately Joe travels widely—during 1992, he was heard all over Europe, in Japan and Hong Kong, Latin America, and throughout the U.S. And aside from his own records, he is much in demand as a featured guest and continues as a regular with the groups we mentioned at the start of these comments. So you won't have much trouble getting to that encore, and many more.

As the 1990s move along, Joe Lovano's strong and beautiful music is bound to become ever more prominent on the jazz scene. To hear this marvelous musician unfold his gifts is a never-ending pleasure for the ears—and the heart!

(1992)

RECORD REVIEWS

Bessie Smith:
The World's Greatest Blues Singer

This handsomely packaged double album, the initial release in Columbia's reissue of the complete recorded works of Bessie Smith, contains the first 16 and the last 16 of the singer's glorious legacy of 160 songs. Eight single LPs to come will complete the chronology.

There can be no quarrel with the album title: Bessie Smith is indeed the greatest of blues singers. But perhaps "blues" says too little. Bessie did all kinds of songs, not just blues, and a good case could be made for calling her the greatest *jazz* singer of all time, with only Louis Armstrong to challenge her sole right to the title.

Bessie had it all: a marvelously rich, powerful, and perfectly placed voice; mastery of inflection; an infallible sense of swing, and clarity and unaffectedness of diction. But these great gifts, perfected by years of hard work, were merely the means through which she projected her feelings. To say that she had "soul" would be an understatement; she was soul personified, and all woman.

In this age of so-called sexual liberation, which in effect means unbridled vulgarity, Bessie Smith's unsurpassed directness, honesty, and genuine sexuality should come as a revelation to those raised on what currently passes for the real thing. She could transform even the tawdriest, most suggestive lyric into an expression of a love of life and its realities that turned pornography into poetry.

That is not to imply that her repertoire was limited to suggestive songs that required transformation, or was exclusively concerned with love or sex.

But these, after all, have ever been the main themes of blues and pop songs. The point is that everything she touched she made real and alive.

Such artistry is not bound by changing fashions, and thus Bessie Smith's voice, stilled for more than thirty years, communicates to us directly, without the adjustment required to enjoy some sounds from the past. It must be pointed out, however, that the acoustically recorded pieces (the first sixteen tracks here) do need an adjustment of the ear—for technical, not spiritual, reasons. Good as the job on the recorded sound is, that very sound erects a time barrier: tinny and remote, it feels dated until the ear accustoms itself to it and allows the emotions to follow.

It is suggested, then, that the newcomer to Bessie's art begin with the later works. Even more so since they not only have the advantage of electric recording, but also reflect a growth in Bessie's artistry. I cannot go along with those who claim that her voice declined. She was, after all, no old woman in 1930–33, just in her middle thirties, and even though years of singing without the benefit of microphones, and indulgence in alcohol (not good for the voice), did bring about a coarsening of her vocal equipment, time also added new dimensions of depth, poignancy, and power. The story Bessie had to tell just kept on unfolding, and there can be no question that she was influenced by the new swing brought to black American music by Louis Armstrong and his disciples.

Thus, this wonderful record, offering works from 1923 and from seven to more than ten years later, shows striking advances in style and projective powers, aided but not caused by improved recording techniques.

It would take more space than available here to describe in detail the thirty-two songs presented. They range from tender to violent, from funny to profoundly sad (though never approaching self-pity), from interesting to fascinating.

Aside from Charlie Green's trombone, a marvelously apt foil for Bessie's singing; James P. Johnson's piano, heard only on two tracks (and then in the background behind a vocal group); and the final all-star jazz date that closed Bessie's recording career, the accompaniments here are just suggestions of things to come. On future albums, we shall hear the masterful complementary work of cornetists Louis Armstrong, Tommy Ladnier, and Joe Smith—the latter perhaps the ideal accompanist for Bessie—and more revealing samples of James P.'s piano. But that is all right; there is nothing in Clarence Williams's or Fletcher Henderson's functional piano parts on these records that distracts the listener from what Bessie is doing.

My own picks among the early tracks are "Beale Street Mama," "Mama's Got the Blues," and "Keeps on A-Rainin'" (Billie Holiday, who loved Bessie, did the latter so beautifully), but these are in the main intimations of things to come. Of the later, greater works, one might single out

"Baby, Have Pity on Me" to show what Bessie could do with a non-blues; "In the House Blues" for the kind of blues power that could match "rural" blues at its most basic; "Black Mountain Blues" for surrealistic humor and for Bessie's ability to make lovely music from the simplest singsong blues melody; "Need a Little Sugar in My Bowl" for sheer beauty and almost overwhelming poignancy, plus superb relaxation of phrasing and time; the famous "Gimme a Pigfoot" for projection of persona equal to Armstrong and Fats Waller, who came across on records like nobody—except Bessie— and for shouting power; "Do Your Duty" for its stop-time passages that swing as much as anything in jazz, past and present, and this track and "Down in the Dumps" for the fine solo and obbligato work by some of the era's great young jazz stars, notably the unjustly forgotten trumpeter Frankie Newton; and the two semi-spirituals, "Moan You Mourners" and "On Revival Day," Bessie's only known attempts in this melismatic genre, yet sufficient to place her among the greatest of gospel singers and show where Mahalia Jackson comes from—as that great artist herself readily admits.

But this is music to hear for yourself, to discover for yourself. If you're interested in what Bessie was able to achieve as a musician, in terms of subtleties of melodic and rhythmic nuances, read the chapter on her in Gunther Schuller's *Early Jazz*. All I need to tell you here is that listening to Bessie Smith is one of the greatest experiences America's unique music has to offer.

These being times of little service to gods other than Mammon, let us thank Columbia for making this project a reality. Credit co-producer Chris Albertson with a fine essay and liner note, plus the painstaking work on the technical aspects of the production, and thank John Hammond, who made possible Bessie's last session, for also making possible this monument to her artistry, which, on the evidence of such an auspicious beginning, will stand as a model for creative, intelligent revitalization of the jazz legacy.

(1970)

The Original Dixieland Jazz Band

The ODJB, as every student of jazz knows, made the first jazz records in early 1917 and became a sensation. The combined and unsuspected powers of the phonograph, press agentry, and a "strange" new music catapulted the band to fame. Though the sobriquet "Inventors of Jazz" was hyperbole, they were the first popularizers of the music and of the term, initially spelled "jass."

After nearly fifty-two years, what does their music sound like? Though the primitive acoustic recording process does not fully convey what the band must have been like in person, a fairly accurate portrait in sound does emerge, especially since this LP brings out all there is to get from the ancient records. To the unschooled ear, the music sounds jerky, shrill, crude, and perhaps closer to marching-band music than to anything now thought of as jazz. Yet, if one is at all familiar with other popular dance music of the period, there is an enormous difference.

That difference is chiefly based in the rhythm—two-beat, yes; jerky, yes; but much more lively and rousing than the stiff, metronomic beat of one-steps and most ragtime—but also in the exuberance and energy generated by the five-piece ensemble with its prototypical cornet-trombone-clarinet front line. Cornetist Nick La Rocca, trombonist Eddie Edwards, and clarinetist Larry Shields were all well versed in the collective ensemble style that already was a tradition in their native New Orleans, and pianist Henry Ragas and drummer Tony Sbarbaro (later Spargo) knew exactly how to back them properly. The routines were well worked out. These young men were not, as their publicity had it, some new species of musical primitives, but rather, by the standards of the day, accomplished professionals—several cuts above the imitators who almost instantly sprang up in their wake.

In contemporary terms, none of the men except Shields and Spargo were really improvisers. They followed a fairly rigid formula, and their music was an ensemble music with no solo excursions, as a rule, except short breaks. Most of the latter were handled by Shields.

La Rocca played a steady, syncopated lead, usually sticking close to the melody. Edwards played a bass line, and did it expertly. His "tailgating" (with its broad smears and glissandi) may at times seem clumsy to the modern ear, but his notes were perfectly placed. Shields embellished freely with agility and a liquid tone, piercing but not shrill. Ragas, under-recorded, supplied a steady vamp and occasional fills, and Spargo used woodblock, cowbell, cymbals, and snare (bass drum did not record well in those days, but I can't agree that it wasn't used at all, as it seems clearly audible at times) to create an intricate but steadily propulsive beat, using swinging patterns that still sound fresh.

Most of the band's early repertoire was of their own making, though much of it certainly was pieced together from traditional New Orleans materials that earlier jazzmen in turn had borrowed from diverse sources (marches, polkas, quadrilles, etc.). But they put it together well, and no doubt Shields and La Rocca and Ragas also had a flair for original melodies. The earliest pieces on this album, among them "Tiger Rag" and "Clarinet Marmalade," have remained staples in the traditional jazz repertoire to this day, along with such other ODJB originals as "Fidgety Feet," "At the Jazz Band Ball," and "Ostrich Walk."

The ODJB, in the first phase of its history, recorded until 1923, and disbanded in 1925. Ragas died in the influenza epidemic of 1919 and was replaced by J. Russell Robinson (composer of "Margie"). In 1920, a superfluous saxophone was added. The ODJB, which had been such a great influence, was in turn influenced by new fashions. The once fresh repertoire was (at least on record) largely replaced by pop tunes of the day. (Does this sequence of events sound familiar? It's the archetypal jazz success story, isn't it?)

Four examples of this decadent stage of the ODJB are included here. One would have sufficed, and it is odd that "Ostrich Walk," to my mind the best of all ODJB records because of its fine tempo and relaxed performance, or the swinging "Jazz Band Ball" were not selected instead.

The last six tracks stem from the 1936 rediscovery, re-formation, and brief return to the limelight of the ODJB. Some of the men came out of semi-retirement, and it shows, though the revived "Tiger Rag" still has plenty of punch, and "Bluin' the Blues" is an excellent performance. Though there was now considerable solo work, the music of the ODJB had become an anachronism, and the reunion was a premature prelude to the New Orleans revival of the '40s, which, ironically, would spurn the legacy of the ODJB—because it was white.

Overpraised and ballyhooed at first, then neglected and underestimated, the ODJB's pioneering records, viewed objectively, contain enough of musical value to be assured of a meritorious place in jazz history. They are more than curiosities, and it wasn't the ODJB's fault that no authentic black New Orleans jazz was recorded until the early '20s. (According to legend, cornetist Freddie Keppard didn't want the Original Creole Band to record because others might "steal their stuff," but other sources deny this, claiming that he merely wanted more money than Victor was prepared to pay.)

Be that as it may, the fact remains that such Negro dance bands as James Reese Europe's, Wilbur Sweatman's, and W. C. Handy's recorded before, during, and after the ODJB's reign but produced little if anything that can be called jazz. It was not until King Oliver recorded in 1923 that jazz substantially superior to the ODJB found its way to wax, Kid Ory's 1921 Sunshine records notwithstanding.

Generally, historians have been kindest to Shields, perhaps because his role in the ensemble allowed for the lion's share of improvisation (he's fine on "Lazy Daddy"). Spargo's sterling contribution has been neglected (he is the band's sole surviving member, by the way). Edwards was greatly admired by as fine a musician as the late Brad Gowans, and for good reason. La Rocca, finally, claimed so much credit for himself in later years that it became absurd. The fact that he was Bix Beiderbecke's admitted idol is generally written off as merely because Bix taught himself to play jazz from ODJB records. But listen to him in the opening and closing choruses of "Margie," and you'll hear that there was more to it than that.

By a combination of luck, proper timing, and brashness, the ODJB changed musical history. Perhaps the ODJB were not the ideal candidates for bringing the jazz message to the masses, but they got there first. All things considered, they didn't do a bad job.

(1969)

The Chicagoans (1928–1930)

Justly, this album is subtitled "Frank Teschemacher, His Influence." The name of Teschemacher may mean little or nothing to the current generation of jazz enthusiasts, but to many older fans "Tesch" was a hero; a legend. His untimely accidental death at twenty-six in March 1932, a little more than six months after that of Bix Beiderbecke, marked the end of an era and cut down a great promise.

Tesch played the clarinet (and occasional saxophone), and was associated with the talented bunch of young white Chicagoans in search of the jazz grail who would become known as "The Austin High Gang." On this record in Decca's new reissue series, some of the best in his small but significant recorded legacy of twenty-five sides is once again made available, alongside some oddments of the period that will be gobbled up by collectors due to their extreme rarity, though they are musically disappointing.

Tesch is present on all but four of the fourteen tracks. The Chicago Rhythm Kings sides are among the most famous of the school, recorded in April and May of 1928. The 1930 Cellar Boys session was the last Tesch made, and the final installment in the recorded saga of authentic Chicago style. Today, disregarding the niceties of musical hairsplitting, one may conclude that there indeed was such a style: what it was, in effect, was the first deliberate attempt by white musicians to play their own kind of jazz in an authentic (i.e., Negro) manner. For many reasons, it was not an entirely successful attempt, but some very laudable music was created in the process, and most of the players involved—those who survived—maintained their commitment to jazz throughout their subsequent careers.

The best performances on this album have a freshness and rough-hewn enthusiasm that stands the test of time. They are spirited and decidedly uncommercial, despite the occasional period vocals, and they swing in their own freewheeling manner. They remain unique.

Among them are "There'll Be Some Changes Made," with its solid Muggsy Spanier lead and fine Tesch solo—it can almost stand as a definition of his style: the slightly sour tone, the definitely blues-inflected intonation, the urgency of plentiful ideas not always under control, the inventions and turns of phrase that influenced such diverse personalities as Pee Wee Russell and Benny Goodman. Red McKenzie's vocal, albeit a bit corny, has a nice feeling to it, and is certainly several cuts above the customary male white vocalisms of the day. "I Found a New Baby" is all instrumental. Tesch gets carried away in his solo (it is said that he hated all his records, and would break any that he came across), but it's not bad, and there is a sample of young pianist Joe Sullivan feeling his oats (dig teenaged Gene Krupa's bass drum behind him), plus a rare tenor solo by Mezz Mezzrow, very well constructed and with an appealingly archaic sound. Jim Lanigan's bass is righteous. "Baby, Won't You Please Come Home," the third item from this session, went unreleased until 1943, and is an interesting failure. The ensemble hovers on the verge of collapse, and Eddie Condon's vocal is pure camp, but his banjo had found the beat he was to keep.

"Jazz Me Blues" is taken from a test pressing that miraculously survived from an unissued date featuring an all-reeds-and-rhythm lineup. The reedmen are Tesch and Rod Cless on clarinets and altos, and Mezz on tenor. Tesch takes alto and clarinet choruses, both good, and there is a short glimpse of Cless—one of the unsung heroes of the bunch.

"Trying to Stop My Crying" and "Isn't There a Little Love to Spare" are sprightly versions of pop tunes, with Wingy Manone's New Orleans horn and jazz vocals to the fore. Tesch has fine solos on both; he *improvises*, especially on the former, and he seems relaxed here. There is also a brief glimpse of young Art Hodes, who does very well in the ensembles, and already had the makings of a very personal piano style.

One of Tesch's very best solos occurs in the Elmer Schoebel band's "Prince of Wails"; more like his idol, Jimmy Noone, than any other he recorded, and very relaxed, flowing, and rhythmically free. This date was more arranged and organized than the others, but George Wettling's good drums and Charlie Barger's nice guitar moved the beat along smoothly. Dick Feige's cornet is in a Bix groove, especially on "Copenhagen," one of the favorite "jam" tunes of the period.

The Cellar Boys session is something else again. The band played in a small speakeasy, and the music is rough and ready. An unknown accordion player is on hand, as well as Frank Melrose's barrelhouse piano, and Manone is in a lowdown mood. Young Bud Freeman takes two of his best early tenor solos here, especially on "Barrelhouse Stomp." He swings and growls. His break on "Wailin' Blues" is something else. Tesch's solo on "Stomp" opens with some liquid lower register, then switches into high gear for a joyous 12 bars, the notes punched out with an almost trumpet-like edge. Wingy's solo features some drag-tempo in the best New Orleans manner. These were among the very last "hot" records issued before the Depression closed the studio doors to such uncompromising efforts.

The four remaining tracks have only their rarity to recommend them. The Husk O'Hare Footwarmers sides were never issued; the personnel is unknown, but a lineup suggested by John Steiner includes only one fairly well-known name: banjoist Lou (Lew) Black of the erstwhile New Orleans Rhythm Kings. A passable cornet is featured, as is a rather nasal vocalist; it was once rumored that Tesch was on clarinet, but he is definitely not. As examples of jazz-flavored midwestern dance music of the period, the tracks are of interest to historians.

The Manone "Downright Disgusted" and "Fare Thee Well" were issued but have become extreme rarities. They prove that rare not always equals good: the rhythm plods awfully; Manone sings a lot, not at his best, and Freeman tries hard but doesn't get anywhere. The best moments come from Wade Foster's clarinet; he seems to have been an Omer Simeon man and had a nice sound.

It's good to have this material available again to flesh out the obscure legend of Frank Teschemacher, whose music still has a message. If today's youngsters wonder what that message might be, let them consider that Tesch was in his early twenties when he made these records: a middle-class white boy who started on violin but crossed the tracks when he heard other voices. Few tried harder to make the music their own, and when he made it, it was something special.

(1968)

Earl Hines: A Monday Date/ Quintessential Recording Session

The neatly simultaneous reissue of Hines's fabled 1928 solo piano performances and release of his 1970 reinvestigation of the same material offers a unique perspective on one of the greatest pianists in jazz.

The 1928 solos rank with his greatest achievements of that rich decade, together with the four solos recorded for Columbia later that year. The eight reissued here were made for the QRS label and received only very limited distribution at first (they were subsequently reissued on 78 by HRS and on 10-inch LP by Atlantic—in both cases with better sound quality than this new reissue on Milestone).

Hines, then not quite twenty-five, was the first important pianist to break with the ragtime and Harlem stride traditions and establish a new language for jazz piano. He based his style on the linear playing of jazz horns, due in part to his early training on trumpet, his youthful admiration for trumpeter Joe Smith, and his encounter in 1926 and subsequent playing experience with Louis Armstrong. Fittingly, Hugues Panassié labeled it "trumpet-style piano."

However, Hines had already mastered the earlier styles, and utilized elements of them to fashion his new approach. His sparkling technique, ear for unusual harmonies, and uncanny mastery of time, combined with a rich musical imagination and highly developed sense of contrast and drama, made his impact on the instrument's future role in jazz decisive.

Forty-two years later, these revolutionary solos still sound fresh and vital, and are often startling in their rhythmic freedom and sudden flights of fancy. How they must have struck the tradition-bound ears of his contemporaries is difficult to imagine!

Perhaps the most beautiful of the pieces (all Hines originals, some of them based on standard patterns) is "Blues in Thirds," with its lovely melody and relaxed, reflective mood. "Monday Date," a performance charged with vitality, and "Panther Rag," a near-surrealistic romp through "Tiger Rag" procedures, are also standouts, and none of the other six is far behind—the high level of inspiration is sustained throughout.

Reinvestigating these youthful achievements forty-two years later, Hines brings to them a lifetime of musical experience and a pair of hands even nimbler at sixty-six. Though he consistently has surrounded himself at every opportunity with bands big and small, with vocalists, and with the trappings of showmanship so dear to him, Hines is and was at his greatest when he works with just a piano and his own boundless imagination. Thus we must be grateful to Marian McPartland, who produced the date, for coming up with this brilliant idea and realizing it. There can be no doubt that Hines enjoyed the task hugely—among the many solo albums he has cut in the past seven years, none seems as charged with enthusiasm and spirit.

The album abounds with staggering displays of virtuosity. At times, indeed, the music threatens to overflow boundaries of form and development and spill over into unrestrained excess, but whenever this is about to happen, Hines pulls in the reins and returns to the structure of the piece, only to take off again.

Since the 1928 solos were restricted to the three-minutes-plus of 78 recording, they have more consistent formal structure. In that sense, and that sense only, they are superior; each seems to stand as the last word on its theme. The contemporary versions, on the other hand, though not as well thought out or rounded off, enable the pianist to stretch his powers to the limit—and they are awesome powers. If, at times, there are lapses of taste (the introduction of a superficial riff here, of a run for run's sake there) where the older versions were unblemished, the many moments of brilliance and true inspiration more than make up for them, and there is the added spice of freedom to do as he pleases.

Essentially, Hines has remained himself. The most striking change is the much greater independence of the left hand. There are also things here and there that Hines has picked up from others—a Tatum run, a locked-hands passage, a Bud Powell lick, a Garnerism. But all are synthesized into pure Hines, with that remarkable touch and dynamic range that no other hands can duplicate.

The Milestone album contains an added bonus in Hines's very first recorded performances, dating from 1923. Exceedingly rare (and dubbed from originals in less than mint condition), they offer a fascinating glimpse of a nineteen-year-old on the threshold of genius.

Four are vocal accompaniments, and Lois Deppe's singing, while showing a good voice, is mainly of historical interest (the rolling r's, articulated consonants, and "proper" pronunciation are strictly in the nineteenth-century salon tradition). But Hines's solo flashes are delightful, showing how well he had mastered the essentials of the Eubie Blake–Lucky Roberts–James P. Johnson school (one of Johnson's favorite licks shows up several times). The Deppe band side, "Congaine," is rhythmically spirited but corny (Vance Dixon's saxophone work is quaint indeed), but when Hines comes in for his solo chorus, the scene changes.

Not since Louis Armstrong's 1957 remakes of past landmarks has a jazz musician produced such startling evidence in support of the too often overlooked fact that this music is not a neat series of historical progressions but a creative continuum. The music Earl Hines has created here—yesterday and today—is music for the ages.

(1971)

Art Tatum: Piano Starts Here

J azz has produced a number of astonishing virtuosos. The majority of these invented new approaches to and techniques for their chosen instruments (trumpet, trombone, the saxophones, guitar, string and brass bass, and drums). Sometimes they even invented (or modified) the instrument itself (the amplified guitar; the jazz drum set). Few, however, brought to jazz a virtuoso technique from an already established tradition, and the piano has the most elaborate virtuoso tradition of them all.

Art Tatum was a bona fide virtuoso in this tradition—the greatest jazz has produced. To conclude from this, as Leonard Feather does in his notes to this album, that Tatum "was the greatest soloist in jazz history, regardless of instrument," is to furnish grounds for debate. One could certainly argue the cases for Louis Armstrong and Charlie Parker. But none could argue that Tatum was not the greatest virtuoso pianist in jazz history.

This is not to say that Tatum wasn't more—much more—than a great technician. Had virtuosity been all he had to offer, he would most certainly have become a kind of Jose Iturbi, for even though he was black and almost sightless, his gifts were such that a career in the popular concert field would have been open to him. (Attempts, in fact, were made to steer him in this direction.)

But Tatum was a black man and heard the music his people were making. Born in 1909, he was exposed in his formative years to a creative ferment, a musical revolution, and the path he chose was one of commitment to that revolution.

It was not an easy path, for jazz was first and foremost a collective music, and Tatum was first and foremost a soloist. Furthermore, his formal studies and phenomenal ear enabled him to imagine and execute musical ideas of a sophistication beyond the grasp of almost all his contemporaries. Even the most gifted and skilled among them were awed by his presence and in-hibited by his almost monstrous (and almost always pitiless) displays of brilliance.

Thus, Tatum had to go his own way, though he was the most sociable and competitive of musicians and loved nothing better than cutting con-tests and jam sessions. He had to go his own way, too, in the world of com-merce, for once he had committed himself to be a jazzman first, he had to carve a niche for his unusual and demanding art within the constricting framework of the jazz marketplace.

It is ironic and embittering that Tatum never made a concert tour as a solo attraction, that he played most of his engagements in nightclubs (where he would often have to suspend playing until a decent level of back-ground noise had been established), and that his sole visit abroad was a brief one to England in 1938, where he played (like his idol, Fats Waller) in "va-riety," not in concert, halls. It is no solace to suggest that this happened not because Tatum was black but because he was a jazz musician.

But Tatum in any circumstance was remarkable, and while it is not quite correct, as *The New Yorker* recently had it, that "all of Tatum" is on this record, there is a considerable part. What there is becomes even more in-teresting because the only Tatum material available to Columbia stems from the pianist's first solo session in March 1933 and from an outdoor con-cert in Los Angeles more than sixteen years later. The album provides samples of a great artist at twenty-three, when he was still working out his style, and at thirty-nine, when all aspects of that style had crystallized.

On both occasions, we hear Tatum, the master stylist, playing pieces he had polished and mastered. Like all virtuosos, Tatum delighted in astonish-ing and dazzling his audiences, and like all virtuosos, he had many set pieces in his repertoire.

Tatum's bravura style exhibited an elegant surface (unlike other great jazz improvisers, he rarely departed totally from the theme, and he never failed to state it as a point of departure) beneath which boiled a fantastic imagination. It is underneath the surface and especially in its cracks and fre-quent suspensions (Tatum loved breaks) that one hears the master of rhythm and harmony as well as the master of technique and melodic expo-sition. He was not unlike a great painter whose luminous, balanced compo-sitions reveal, on closer scrutiny, a mysterious and apocalyptic inner vision.

Each track on this album contains staggering moments. Of the four early pieces, only "Tiger Rag" fully stands the test of comparison with later Tatum—perhaps because it is inspired by Armstrong's treatment of the tune, which makes it the piece least indebted to other pianists. Also, it fully brings to bear Tatum's orchestral conception of the piano, and is taken at a frightening tempo (about a bar per second) sustained by a combination of rhythmic finesse and firmness of time that can only be described as incredible. One can imagine what a weapon such a piece must have been to Tatum in his beloved battles with other pianists—who would have dared to follow it!

In "Tea for Two," we recognize two great influences: Fats Waller and Earl Hines—the former in the steady stride of the left hand and the rippling, calm arpeggios in the contrasting right, and the latter in the rhythmic suspensions and "strange" harmonies of the breaks in the second chorus. Interestingly, he does not yet swing as much as either of these men already did (though he outdoes both on "Tiger").

"St. Louis Blues" is immature compared to the version recorded for Decca six years later. Tatum, from Toledo, Ohio, and inspired by Eastern pianists, had apparently not yet discovered (or not yet fully absorbed) the essence of the blues, and his approach to it here is a surface one. Though his only other blues on this set is a display piece at breakneck tempo ("Tatum Pole Boogie"), it shows how much Tatum had learned about the blues. (For his lovely, deeply moving slow blues, one must look elsewhere, and to later and late Tatum especially.)

"Sophisticated Lady," then a brand-new tune (Ellington's first version had been recorded only a month before), must have intrigued Tatum with its harmonic subtleties, which he handles masterfully. But there isn't much depth in his playing, except in the break that links the first and second chorus and in the remarkable harmonic interventions during the latter. Near the end, there is even that extreme rarity, a corny idea; i.e., the "chime" chords, for which he atones with a dazzling coda.

The 1949 "How High the Moon" that follows illuminates drastically how Tatum had grown. First of all, there is his touch—by now a magic combination of gossamer and Bessemer. In a dynamic spectrum that ranges from whisper to roar, each note is articulated with the clarity of a bell. There is a startling rhythmic freedom, allowing Tatum to play with time in the most astonishing manner. Even the out-of-tempo first choruses of which he was so fond suggest a beat, or rather several shifting beats, and he was an unequalled master at transitions from rubato to swing. His independence of hands was the envy and frustration of other pianists.

On "How High," there are passages that strikingly prove Bud Powell's ancestry (third chorus), while the employment of a wide variety of technical, rhythmic, and harmonic devices from Tatum's vocabulary suggests that he was using this as a warm-up piece (he misses a few notes in a run; later in the concert he executes far more complex ones without dropping a stitch).

Dvořák's "Humoresque," which Tatum loved to play, has caused certain critics to frown. Approaching Tatum with a European bias, they fail to understand his liking for this shopworn staple in the semi-classical repertoire, but how they could fail to appreciate his treatment of it, which combines just the right amounts of affection and liberty, is mystifying.

"Someone to Watch Over Me" is a fond and relaxed performance; Tatum and George Gershwin formed a mutual admiration society. He is taking a breather here, playing a melody he likes, ornamenting and embellishing rather than improvising. But watch those harmonic inventions that made him such an important influence on the incipient boppers.

"Yesterdays" is a masterpiece. This is serious Tatum, not merely decorating but transforming his material. The beguine pattern, the startlingly effective broken-chord passage, the octave unison fingering in fast tempo, the kaleidoscopic display of ideas, and their coherence and structure add up to a breathtaking musical experience.

"I Know That You Know" returns to pure display—but what a show! Experimenting with all kinds of time (straight, halved, doubled) and all kinds of rhythm, Tatum imbues what might have been merely gratuitous with a disarming lightness and joy—and does he swing!

"Willow Weep for Me," a lovely piece, is not quite as perfect in this version as in the less florid Capitol recording from the same year. "The Kerry Dance" is a little throwaway employed by Tatum to beg off after several encores, full of wit and charm and of the briefest duration. It should have been placed last on the program. "The Man I Love" is, again, a piece for which Tatum had genuine affection. His theme statement is lovely—in fact, the opening half chorus is the high point of the rather reflective performance—and the final bridge is pure bop.

Listening to Tatum in depth temporarily spoils one for all other pianists. His like will not be heard again, for he was a phenomenon. Others have emulated his technique but lack both his excellence and his musicality. Surface elements of his style (the extensive rubato; the arpeggiated runs; the decorative embellishments) have been adopted by untalented lounge pianists all over the world, as well as by a few players more than that but far less than Tatum. The only pianist of stature who borrowed extensively from Tatum and emerged with his own intact style was Nat King Cole, whose textures could be amazingly Tatumesque. Bud Powell, of course, drank deeply at the well, and others have used Tatum elements to creative advantage. But Tatum remains an inimitable, unsurpassable, and inexhaustible delight.

(1968)

Jimmie Lunceford: Lunceford Special

L unceford's unique band has been overshadowed in critical acclaim
and continued attention by the durable Basie and Ellington and the
much-lauded Fletcher Henderson, but it was without question of
equal caliber. Though it had passed its zenith by the early '40s, it exerted a
powerful influence on big band styles through the ensuing decade, and definite echoes can still be heard today in the work of Basie, Kenton, Harry
James, and many a studio band.

Lunceford's was an arranger's band—an ensemble—rather than a
soloist's launching pad, though it did have outstanding individual players.
But it was the fabulous reed section and the powerful brasses, anchored in a
very personal and powerful rhythm section, that gave the band its stylistic
profile.

Discipline, polish, and sometimes flashy showmanship characterized the
band's work. It had wit and flair and many moods, but only rarely did it
achieve the profoundly moving dimension of "Uptown Blues," a masterpiece that—perhaps significantly—was a "head" arrangement emphasizing
soloists (Willie Smith's alto and Snooky Young's trumpet).

However, even its most lighthearted (and, by contemporary standards of
utter seriousness, perhaps superficial) moments were so musical that they
remain enjoyable and interesting. Even today's expert craftsmen would
have trouble with some of the old Lunceford charts, particularly the brilliant saxophone scoring. There were few personnel changes, and the band
was a unit as few seen before or since.

The first two selections, never previously issued, are from May 1933,
and show the band at the threshold of stylistic identity. The influence of the
Casa Loma still looms, especially on the fast "Flaming Reeds and Screaming Brass"; "While Love Lasts," a ballad, is prettily scored. Both arrangements are by pianist Eddie Wilcox, along with Sy Oliver the founding
father of the Lunceford style.

The remaining tracks date from early 1939 to early 1940. The band's
material, in the main, were either originals or unlikely revivals of old, seldom "jazzed" numbers. Oliver was in his creative prime; how much the
band owed him was tellingly demonstrated when he became a staff arranger
for Tommy Dorsey in late '39—suddenly, T.D.'s band became Lunceford.
His ideas flowed profusely, and he had taste.

Taste, in fact, was a hallmark of the band, and this is one of the reasons
why it hardly ever sounds dated. (Such judgments, of course, are of neces-

sity subjective. Don Ellis finds Charlie Parker "old fashioned." Clearly, there is taste and taste, and we all apprehend the past differently.)

If you listen to the entire album, you will be struck by the discovery of just how many of swing's favorite licks originated with (or were first widely disseminated by) this band. Voicings and devices, too.

Billy Moore, who took Oliver's arranging place, was also greatly gifted. (His talents have been buried, for many years, as pianist-arranger for internationally touring vocal groups; currently the Delta Rhythm Boys.)

Several of the band's instrumental stars doubled as vocalists: Trummy Young, Willie Smith, Joe Thomas, Oliver. Sweet singer Dan Grissom doubled tenor sax. Everybody contributed to the fullest.

The outstanding soloists were altoist Smith, the Youngs (Snooky, trumpet, and Trummy, trombone), and tenorist Thomas, a much underrated man, who loved Hawkins and Chu Berry but had his own thing going. Smith could play fine clarinet, too ("What's Your Story, Morning Glory"). Altoist Ted Buckner (not to be confused with the trumpeter of West Coast fame) was also a fine player; credit for some of his solos has often gone to Smith. Dig him on "I Wanna Hear Swing Songs." (Stanley Dance's as usual exemplary notes give full solo details.) Trumpeter Paul Webster, a high-note specialist, had musical range as well.

Jimmy Crawford stands with Chick Webb, Sid Catlett, and Jo Jones among the giants of classic big-band drumming. He was (and is) a master of time, the bass drum, and cymbals. His colleagues in the section were not of the same stature, but as a unit, it functioned admirably indeed.

Aside from "Uptown" and "Morning Glory," two exceptional pieces, and the marvelous arrangement and performance on "Swing Songs" (the later "Monotony in Four Flats" might have been included, for it was crafted from the concluding ensemble passages and vocal backgrounds of this track), "Baby Won't You Please Come Home" offers a sample of the band's flair for the unexpected; "Ain't She Sweet" and "Cheatin' On Me" its great ways with old songs and relaxed tempos; "Lunceford Special" its flag-waving forte; "'Tain't What You Do" its (and composer-singer Trummy Young's) special "novelties"; and "Bugs Parade" its pioneering "modernism"—that's where vintage Kenton came from.

Band instructors as well as young and old pros might profitably investigate the true Lunceford sound. For a decade, from 1934 to 1944, this was a band in a class by itself. It still is—class will tell.

(1968)

Count Basie: Basie's Beat

The Basie band is an institution, and institutions are often taken for granted—or criticized in noninstitutional terms. The question isn't what the band should be or ought to play, but what it is and what it represents. This doesn't have to be explained to Basie fans, who are legion; those who are not might listen to this record—one of Basie's best in years—and ask themselves why they aren't.

For happy, delightful, swinging big-band jazz, nobody can touch this outfit, and even though the competition in the field ain't what it used to be, that is an accomplishment for which no excuses are needed.

On this album, there is no gimmick—no salutes to Bond, Broadway, or Hollywood, no machine-tooled arrangements crafted for the occasion— only straight-ahead Basie music, stuff the band likes to play; some new, some older, but none previously committed to wax.

There are several gems, but the album stands up as a whole—no track is weak. The subtitle reads "Introducing Richard Boone," and this able trombonist is featured in two hilarious vocal excursions: "I Got Rhythm" and his own "Boone's Blues."

Boone has his own brand of jazz vocalese and is a bright new light in a line of singers that began with Leo Watson, who was a genius and one of the great American humorists of this century. The tradition, what with Clark Terry's mumbling and now Boone, who is something else, shows signs of continued life, and that's good news. Eric Dixon's arrangements of Boone's two features are nice.

Dixon is also responsible for the charting of "Only a Paper Moon," which features Basie's piano in a melodic vein; "St. Thomas" (the same territory visited by Sonny Rollins), a happy romp with witty saxophone scoring and a rare spot for Wallace Davenport's bright, Armstrong-touched trumpet, and "Frankie and Johnny," a fresh look at an old chestnut. His solo talents are not on display, except in a flute obbligato on "Boone's Blues."

"Squeeze Me," a new Nat Pierce setting of the Fats Waller classic, features Harry Edison's trumpet and Basie, as well as the ensemble. It's a groove, and Sweets sounds fine back home with the band. He has no other solos on the set, but walks off with top honors nonetheless. Basie's introduction shows how much piano he can play when he lets himself. It smacks strongly of Willie "The Lion" Smith, and that's only as it should be, since the tune is claimed by him as "The Boy in the Boat."

The Count's keyboard fancies are also well displayed on "St. Louis Blues." This loose and rocking head arrangement, one of the best in the book, should have been recorded long ago. Among other things, it affords a glimpse of Freddie Green's guitar in a non-rhythm role; he furnishes lovely backgrounds for Al Grey's plunger-muted trombone introduction—just the two of them. The trumpet riffs (in Harmon mutes) swing to the hilt, and then Eddie "Lockjaw" Davis takes over for eight choruses of stomping tenor blues. A great track.

Bobby Plater, unsung hero of many years in Lionel Hampton's band, contributed "Happy House," an excellent arrangement in a contemporary blues bag. He plays clean, Willie Smith–flavored alto on it, and Al Aarons has a bright trumpet spot. Aarons is in special form, though, on "Frankie and Johnny" (which also has a Plater solo), showing that sitting next to Roy Eldridge for a spell has had its effects. (Aarons, by the way, is a fine musician long due for general recognition.)

Thad Jones scored "Makin' Whoopee," a vehicle for Grey. There is some stunning saxophone writing, superbly played, and the slow, utterly re-laxed tempo enables Grey to discover new depth in the old tune. His humor, sometimes too broad, is subtle here, and he really plays.

But the best arrangement of the lot is Frank Foster's "Hey Jim," a good bebop line by Babs Gonzales that he sang with James Moody's swinging little band. This is a swinging big-band version, though, and this track cooks. The trumpet section is in fine fettle, and the soloists are Lockjaw, Grey, and Mr. Basie himself. If they still had "battles of the bands," Basie would score quite a few points with this one.

A few words about the sections. The reeds are the backbone, and the section with the fewest personnel changes. Lead man Marshall Royal and anchor man Charlie Fowlkes have been aboard for some years, and there are few better men. It's quite a sound they get, and it's most certainly to-gether. The trumpets kick. Gene Goe is a good lead replacement for Dav-enport, and Sweets adds some marrow, but both sections (the bulk of the album was done in November 1965; the four later tracks in February of this year) are excellent. The trombones, with Bill Hughes's bass horn adding bottom, are mellifluous.

With Basie and Green around, no bassist or drummer need look far if he develops pulse problems. Norman Keenan's bass is wedded to them by now, and his somewhat dry sound has a pleasantly penetrating edge. Rufus Jones is perhaps a more musical and certainly a less erratic drummer than Sonny Payne, but when Payne is right, he gives the band (this band) something extra—his fills, for example.

Drummer Ed Shaughnessy, who often records with Basie, knows what the job requires and does it impeccably. It's odd that the Basie band of the

'30s was so notable for its looseness while the Basie band of now (and since the '50s) is so notable for its tightness. But both emphasize swing, and a glance at Basie in the '40s may reveal that the transition was not really abrupt.

Today, the Basie band, in a sense, incorporates two great traditions of the swing era: their own and that of Jimmie Lunceford. Not the Lunceford sophistication, perhaps, but the Lunceford ensemble unity. At any rate, we have spent some time on this record because it is such a good one, by a fine band.

(1966)

Thad Jones–Mel Lewis
Live at the Village Vanguard

To followers of this great band, its first album, good as it was, did not quite indicate just what these guys are capable of—perhaps because it was a studio effort. This one, recorded live at the band's stomping ground, New York's Village Vanguard, before an enthusiastic audience, does give a true picture in sound of what I believe to be the finest and most important big jazz band to come along since the old giants got their thing together.

Through some miraculous alchemy, this ensemble of men who are both soloists and section players combines the best elements of freedom and discipline in an amalgam that retains the power and excitement synonymous with the big-band jazz tradition but adds to it the freshness and surprise of today and now. That is quite an accomplishment, and it has been achieved as a labor of love. Maybe that's the secret—along with, of course, extraordinary talent and perseverance, and teamwork in the truest sense.

One could write a book about this album and this band, but annotator Ed Beach has done nearly that in his excellent, detailed notes, so I'll confine myself to some of the highlights.

"Little Pixie II," composed and arranged by Thad Jones, stars the reeds. As a section, they have no peers other than their Ellington counterparts, with whom they share the ability to breathe as one. And can they get around their horns! Look out!

As soloists, they have a variety and individuality that is equally astonishing. Lead man Jerome Richardson, doubler *par excellence*, is spotlighted here on the soprano, of which difficult horn he is one of the prime practitioners. His choruses climax a round-robin of solos by, in order, Joe Farrell, Jerry Dodgion, Eddie Daniels (clarinet), and Pepper Adams, all of them first-rate, and backed by a variety of rhythmic and coloristic devices. This track is a gas—and to me not least because it shows what can still be done after all these years with one of the most basic sets of changes in jazz.

The album's other Jones original, "Don't Git Sassy," has a fabulous reed passage led by Richardson's soprano, a great Farrell tenor solo, stunning ensemble work, fine Roland Hanna piano, and as the filling in the pie, exuberant trumpet solos (with plunger mutes) by Jimmy Nottingham and lead master Snooky Young.

Bob Brookmeyer's two charts are contrasting in nature; both are gems. His setting of Fats Waller's pretty "Willow Tree," featuring co-leader Jones in his soloistic role, is distinguished by warm, lovely voicings, colored by Dodgion's and Farrell's flutes. There is also a solo interlude by the remarkable bassist Richard Davis. Thad's coda tops it off. The other Brookmeyer opus, the punningly titled "Samba Con Getchu," is a graduate seminar in Latin. It features superb Thad, Daniels (on tenor this time, and hot), Richardson (alto), and a rare Lewis drum solo. But the thing is not the parts but the whole, a twelve-minute romp that sweeps you along and lifts your spirits. Intermittently, the hornmen double on percussion of all sorts, and issue vocal exhortations. Everybody has a ball.

Trombonist Garnett Brown is featured on "Ah' That's Freedom," a brotherly collaboration between composer Hank and arranger Thad Jones. Fittingly, the trombone section plays an important role in the chart. Brown's six choruses show that he is up there with the best, and he further impresses with "Bacha Feelin'," which he wrote and arranged. A modal piece, it generates a lot of heat, with solos by Brown and Farrell (in great form), the fires stoked by Lewis. (The drummer is consistently excellent throughout, but on this track, he outdoes himself.) A startling touch near the end is the 8 bars of total freedom—every man just blowing for himself.

It comes out together, as does everything in this remarkable album. I love this band because when I hear it, I know that jazz has a future. It makes real music on a grand scale, music that has all kinds of feelings—passion, joy, and humor. This record (beautiful sound and balance, technically, too) captures the band at its finest, and if you like music, it will capture you.

(1968)

Benny Carter: The King

To the best of my knowledge, this splendid album is Benny Carter's first LP of his own in a decade—since *Additions to Further Definitions*, recorded in February 1966.

Of course, the great man has not been inactive as a player all these years. He appeared at several Newport Festivals, played with Jazz at the Philharmonic at Montreux '75 (the fine results can be heard on Pablo 2310-748), and on an album (and in person) with Maria Muldaur. And this writer has been more fortunate than most, having heard him in several appearances at Princeton University (one with a fantastic big band) and at Dick Gibson's Colorado Jazz Party. In addition, Carter headed up a small group including Sweets Edison for a little-publicized State Department tour of the Middle East last year, on which he was joined by Professor Morroe Berger of the Princeton faculty, a sociologist, expert on Arab affairs, and probably the world's number-one Carter fan (though he has strong competition from his son, Ed, who is preparing what promises to be the definitive Carter discography).

Just before this album was released, Carter spent a month at Michael's Pub in New York at the helm of a group comprising Ray Bryant, Milt Hinton, and Grady Tate—his first club appearance in the Apple in thirty-four years. For this occasion, Carter also unwrapped his trumpet, and no matter what the remaining months of 1976 may bring, and in spite of the discomforts of listening to music at Michael's, a noisy and noisome East Side watering hole, this visit must stand as one of the highlights of the year.

Carter is a perfectionist, which undoubtedly is one reason why he waited so long to make a studio session. Another is that Norman Granz was not available to produce such dates for some time; the relationship between these two is special, and so are Granz's powers of persuasion when there is something he wants done. Lovers of good music owe Granz a debt of gratitude for getting Carter back on wax in proper style, for he is among the handful of surviving giants from the golden age still at the height of their creative powers.

As Leonard Feather points out in his informative notes, this is Carter's first album consisting entirely of his own compositions—a tribute to the modesty of this true gentleman of music. But while Carter is one of the greatest arrangers in jazz history, he has relatively few standards to his credit (one of them a piece from 1931, "The Blues in My Heart," is not included here; neither is "When Lights Are Low".) That this is the result of circumstances having nothing to do with ability is made evident by the material on display here. It is consistently superior.

The key characteristics of Carter's writing (and playing, for one is a reflection of the other), melodic grace, balance and logic of structure, and elegance and ease of execution, are apparent throughout this well-paced program of eight pieces, including ballads, swingers, and a basic blues. The latter, "Blues in D-flat," is the only work specifically created for this date. The others have all been heard before, but several only ephemerally, and none in this instrumentation and atmosphere.

This is a studio group, but with Carter in command, it performs as if it were a working unit of long standing. Carter is an inspiring leader; I know not one musician among the dozens and dozens who've played with him who does not sing his praises at the mere mention of his name. The cast is impressive: Milt Jackson, vibes; Tommy Flanagan, piano; Joe Pass, guitar; John B. Williams, bass; Jake Hanna, drums. Carter gives ample solo space to Bags, Tommy, and Joe, featuring himself just enough to always make a complete statement, saying what he wants to say without a wasted note or redundant phrase. His solos are gem-like: perfectly poised, masterfully executed, yet never sounding premeditated. It is part of Carter's very special charm that he is able to combine musical intelligence of the highest order with the quality of spontaneity so essential to jazz. In Jackson and Flanagan, who turn in some of their most inspired work here, he has companions who share this characteristic. It is a special pleasure to hear the pianist in such fitting surroundings. (Please, Norman, let's have a Flanagan solo album!) And Hanna, noted for his driving big-band work, here also proves himself a drummer of rare taste and sensibility.

The selections include the beautiful "Blue Star," in a performance as memorable as that on the *Further Definitions* date; the catchy "Easy Money" (written for the Basie band); the moody "Malibu" (also originally a big-band score, for Benny's own great 1945 crew); the sophisticatedly funky "A Walkin' Thing"; the slightly Latinesque "Green Wine"; the haunting "My Kind of Trouble Is You," and my personal favorite, the exquisite "I Still Love Him So," introduced on a 1955 Roy Eldridge and Benny Carter LP, and also to be found on Roy's latest Pablo disc.

The grapevine has it that two more Carter dates are already in the can, one with Oscar Peterson, the other with Dizzy Gillespie. That's something to look forward to. Meanwhile, this lovely album celebrates the return of Benny Carter, truly a king of jazz, to the world of active recording in proper style.

(1976)

Lester Young: The Pres/Pres

Both albums stem from home recordings made in an "uptown" atmosphere, and the disembodied sounds of good times emerge now and
then in the form of shouts of encouragement, laughter, and the tinkling of glass. These are not "jams"; the groups have basic routines worked
out. The pianos are all out of tune; the trumpeters (excepting the cat on
"Destination Moon" and "Sunday") are indifferent and datedly boppish,
and the drums on one side of the Savoy record are overbearingly loud. The
sound is surprisingly crisp on the Savoy, more muddied on the Parker. The
latter is very handsomely packaged in a double sleeve, and marks an auspicious beginning for the new Charlie Parker label in all respects but for the
amateurish liner notes. But all this is secondary; the main thing is that these
are fresh performances by Lester Young and that he comes through.

   The message of Lester Young was intensely personal. Pres *spoke* into his
horn, and what came out was always a story. As one listens to these creations torn from the womb of indifferent time, one marvels at the measure
of this man, who in his own gentle way had the strength of a giant and the
patience of an angel. What marks these moments from the life of Lester
Young as the heritage of genius? The warm, breathy, life-filled sound; the
marvelously relaxed, flowing conception utilizing so subtly all the possibilities of time; the innate sense of form that shapes each interpretation—or
the message that is the sum of all the describable elements of what was truly
a *style*? Whatever they may make of it on paper, the sounds spell Lester
Young—and there never was and never will be another Pres.

   The music on these records comes from, at a rough guess, somewhere
between 1950 and 1953. The Savoy is perhaps the earlier, and the two
longest tracks, "Destination Moon" and "Sunday," are perhaps later than
the rest. Those who like to fragment artists into periods have declared that
Pres "declined" after, say, 1945. All this reviewer can say is that Lester always played himself, and that he of course grew older, perhaps lonelier, and
certainly more troubled as the years went on. But he never stood still, and
the important thing to bring to the post-war Pres is an understanding of his
music as part indivisible of the man. When Pres was in control of the physical prerequisites for playing (and he often was—up to the very end), the
beauty and power of his message showed no symptoms of decline. On the
contrary, Lester Young went on and on making discoveries. What he did in
later years with phrasing and time has not yet been comprehended or as-

similated by other musicians, who, after all, were slow even to pick up on what Pres had already left behind.

There are many dimensions to Lester's music: fantastic humor and high comedy (dig the stop-time business in "Lester Leaps In," here taken at lightning speed); passion and yearning ("Body and Soul"); near resignation ("I Cover the Waterfront"); surrealistic happiness ("Lester's Blues No. 2," better known as "Neenah"); preaching in the great tradition ("Lester's Blues No. 1"); and relaxed, gentle strength ("Sunday"), to name a few. No note Lester played was wasted or meaningless. Technique is a term that has little function here. Lester knew what he wanted and how to get it out of the horn. Technique. Who swings more than Lester? He was a master of the dramatic entrance. The now conventional idea of beginning a solo on a break was reintroduced to jazz by Lester, within the context of swing. Tonguing is an act he raised to perfection. His tone *was* large and vibrant, in its own unique way. Sub-tone playing, a lost art these days, is admirably demonstrated on the opening choruses of "Waterfront." Melodic imagination, without which there can be no great jazz playing, is present here on every track. Lester's ballad improvisations were always involved with the creation of new and fresh melodies, which, miraculously, never tore asunder the underlying original. And although these were free sessions, Lester never solos at grotesque length—he leaves you knowing there is more, and wanting it.

(1961)

Dexter Gordon: The Panther

Since Coleman Hawkins made it so in 1939, "Body and Soul" has been *the* test piece for tenormen. There have been some pretty heavy entries in this special sweepstakes since then (including Hawk outdoing himself on "Rainbow Mist" five years later), but this new one by Dexter is a landmark. From a nonhistorical perspective, it is simply one of the loveliest ballad performances you'll ever hear.

There used to be a myth (and it still has adherents) that jazz was primarily a young musician's art, and, to be sure, some flames burn themselves out quickly. Also, music is the only art in which genius can appear fully fledged in mere infants. Still, the process of ripening plays no less a role in music than in other realms of life.

Suffice it to say that if Dexter Gordon was heavy when he came on the scene, he is heavier today than ever before. This album deserves a place alongside *Go* and *Our Man in Paris* among the best of Dexter on record.

"Body and Soul" is the supreme masterpiece, and in a class by itself, but the rest is not far behind. In fact, every note Dexter plays is a joy to hear. His music has strength and conviction; it is a celebration of life looked straight in the eye. There is no excess of any kind in it: no sentimentality, no self-pity, no posturing, no striving for effects. It is music that flows with the natural ease of speech, and every inflection is uniquely personal and direct.

Dexter's tone is like a certain kind of fine red wine: full-bodied and slightly tart, at once warm and coolly refreshing, with a flavor that lingers. In every register throughout the range of the horn, his sound is round and full. The notes are superbly articulated—only the greatest musicians have such command of the instrument and only the greatest of jazzmen have such command of the music's language.

In a time when some of even the best of contemporary music is singularly lacking in poise and control, too often reflecting the disorder of everyday existence rather than the sense of logic and balance implicit in the act of creation, music like Dexter Gordon's seems truly revolutionary. Instead of draining the listener, it enriches him.

Jazz being a music of interaction, it goes without saying that a session as nearly perfect as this was not the work of one man alone. The presence of Tommy Flanagan, Larry Ridley, and Alan Dawson creates a climate of understanding and empathy, for each of these men is an artist in his own right.

Flanagan, far too seldom heard in a creative context such as this, is a masterful accompanist—enhancing, underlining, feeding, supporting. His solos and introductions are radiant—just flawless. A pity that there isn't more of him on records. It is a compliment to Ridley and Dawson that they match Flanagan's impeccable taste—in addition to providing the solid rhythmic foundation Dexter wants and deserves. Dig the two of them in the "strolling" choruses on the potent "The Blues Walk," and their solo spots.

Of Dexter's three originals, I especially like the moody "Valse Robin," a typical Gordon melody. "Mrs. Miniver" is also appealing, and both are much more than the mere sketches that often pass for jazz "compositions." The third, the title track, is a minor blues with a subtly contemporary beat. The practice of "quoting," which can become a bore in lesser hands, is something Dexter is a past master at, and he indulges himself here.

If someone asks you what jazz is, and where it can still be at today, put on this record. That it was made is a mitzvah.

(1971)

Lee Konitz: Duets

An album of this quality does not come along often. It differs from the run-of-the-mill jazz LP in many ways: based on an original and venturesome concept, it was planned and executed with care and craftsmanship, and it is free from all extramusical trappings. For once, an undertaking in the realm of jazz was carried out from start to finish in a worthy manner.

What is involved here is artistry of the highest order standing on its own merit; nakedly, so to speak. Lee Konitz has always been a completely honest musician, incapable of meretriciousness and false pride. At times, this obstinate courageousness may have been a hindrance to his progress as a performer (i.e., a breadwinner), but this album is proof positive that it has been no hindrance to his development as an artist, which here reaches a new plateau.

The idea of this album (it was Lee's) was, like all great ideas, startlingly simple: the creation of a number of playing situations with a number of different players whom he felt drawn to play with, but one at a time, in strict duet settings—the most intimate possible way to make music together.

This basic concept is departed from just twice: in the "Variations on Alone Together," which begin as pure solo, become a series of duets (with drummer Elvin Jones, vibraharpist Karl Berger, and bassist Eddie Gomez, Konitz playing tenor on the first and third), and end as quartet; and on the final piece, "Alphanumeric," where all the participants (except Ray Nance, who was late for work) join together. Both exceptions are entirely in context and serve to round out the gestalt of the album.

One could hold forth at length about the many beautiful and fascinating things that happen here. No two of these "confrontations" are alike; they differ not only in such elements as outline and texture (some are free improvisations, others are based on predetermined materials), but also in ambiance. There are dialogues and there are conversations.

Each listener must discover for himself the many delights to be had from this music. One of its most marvelous aspects is that it never sounds the same twice. The two voices may complement each other, may become entwined, move apart, come together again; one may become dominant, then the other. If the listener wishes to interfere, he can bring forward at will one or the other by adjusting the stereo balance, then bring them back together and hear them differently.

Another remarkable feature is the spectrum of jazz covered here. Twice there is specific re-creation: Louis Armstrong's "Struttin' with Some Barbecue" solo from the 1927 Hot Five version is played by valve trombonist Marshall Brown and Konitz (in octaves, over a pre-recorded stop-time background), and Lester Young's famous "Tickle Toe" solo from the Count Basie record is played in unison by Konitz and Richie Kamuca on tenors.

In the latter case, this comes as a fitting climax to a very Pres-inflected conversation. In the former, what is most astonishing is that Konitz, in his brilliant playing prior to the quotation, suggests Louis in spirit and sound (!) to such a degree that the quoted music actually sounds less Louis-like.

Another surprise is tenor saxophonist Joe Henderson on "You Don't Know What Love Is," really getting together with Konitz, in sound and feeling. What is surprising is not that the two could get together in this way, but how they did it.

"Erb," though based on "a graph containing instructions as to dynamics and range," by guitarist Jim Hall (according to Gunther Schuller's good liner notes) is more abstract in quality than the duet with Nance, which is completely free improvisation. In "Erb," there are moments when Konitz uses pitchless key-clicking in a way that is meaningful, and if such a thing is possible, beautiful.

"Duplexity" is fascinating. Nance, on violin, becomes so absorbed in improvising in a classical context (he plays, with beautiful expansiveness, what sounds like a series of cadenzas) that he resists Konitz's repeated suggestions to enter into jazz dialogue, including a rapid-fire quote from "Lester Leaps In." Yet they are together.

Since I don't want to turn this review into a play-by-play, let me just say that of the "Alone Together" variations, I like best the duet with Berger, whose sensitivity and clear, pure sound were an overdue revelation, and that "Alphanumeric" is a lot of fun, with superb Elvin Jones (on the duet, too) and extraordinary multivider and/or overdub effects by Konitz, including a duet with himself. But my favorite is "Checkerboard," the duet with Dick Katz (who produced this album).

Konitz and a piano, of course, bring to mind Lennie Tristano, and Dick and Lee, without imitation, at moments seem to re-create that long relationship that meant so much to Konitz but from which he eventually had to liberate himself. That, however, is not the essential thing about "Checkerboard," which contains some of the loveliest and strongest lyrical playing I've heard, and on which two musicians come together as closely as seems possible.

As Schuller mentions, this piece makes one think of the great Armstrong-Hines duet "Weatherbird," one of jazz's true masterpieces. Entirely different, "Checkerboard" is also a true masterpiece. Both are joyful affirmations of love—of the best man is capable of.

This album is such a remarkable achievement that two others directly involved—supervisor Orrin Keepnews and engineer Elvin Campbell—should not go unmentioned. If you only get one record this year, make this the one.

(1969)

Houston Person: Trust in Me

S tyles come and go, but certain basic ways of playing the music, once established, happily remain. They do so, one suspects, because the players feel comfortable and right within them, and because they are indeed basic, in the essential sense.

One of these basic ways established itself as a mainstream after bebop had ceased to be regarded as revolutionary, but it existed both before and during the bop era. It generally involves a saxophonist—a tenorman, mostly, though there can be additional horns—and a rhythm section. Both major components swing. The repertory consists of standards old and new, a mess of blues at various tempos and with different dance beats, and jazz originals from the late '40s on. The melody is always stated to establish a point of departure, and a tap-your-foot, shake-your-head beat is never absent. Sometimes an organ may be involved.

This music has been, still is, and more than likely will continue to be one of the most viable types of jazz, providing bread-and-butter jobs for many musicians of both national (or international) and purely regional repute. It encompasses players whose reputations were established as far back as the dawn of swing; ex-beboppers; would-be new-thingers (a few), borderline rhythm-and-blues players, and newcomers.

Houston Person is among the latter, relatively speaking. He's been around long enough to have served in the Army with Leo Wright, Eddie Harris, Don Ellis, and pianist Cedar Walton, who's with him here, and to have spent three years touring and recording with organist Johnny "Hammond" Smith, and another three leading his own group in New England. This is his second straight-ahead jazz album as a leader and shows increased confidence and presence over the first, which was far from unimpressive.

His approach resembles Gene Ammons's, with touches of classic Rollins here and there (particularly in his wry, terse way of stating themes). He is strong without being swaggering, which many lesser tenors tend to be when given their own head.

He has a knack for choosing his material intelligently: good R&B tunes ("One Mint Julep," "Trust in Me"); quality pops of not too distant vintage ("Hey There," "The Second Time Around"); seldom done Birdlore ("My Little Suede Shoes"); and basic soul ("Sometimes I Feel Like a Motherless Child"). He does little things with each tune that reveal thought and planning, but the routines are fitting, not cute. And he is just as honest in his playing, which is free from phony effects and never meretricious. He is backed by some of Prestige's best house men, plus ringer Ralph Dorsey, whose conga drums are not intrusive, though they add most to "Shoes," which is home territory (a nice solo here).

Walton, bassist Paul Chambers, and drummer Lenny McBrowne would be hard to top as a section for this kind of groove, though they are far from being restricted to it. They are paragons of togetherness and other rhythmic virtues, and they support. The pianist has several fine solos, his most impressive to these ears being the exploratory one on "Child."

Chambers is a prime example of the fickleness of the jazz public. While with Miles Davis he was enormously popular; today, he's often overlooked when the bass honor roll is called. Ironically, he has grown in the intervening years and is a joy to hear and (I'd venture) a gas to play with. McBrowne never has had due recognition, but increasing exposure should bring this about. He is one of the steadiest and most musical drummers on the set these days.

Person is at his best on "That Old Black Magic," where he digs in, and on "Child," which he turns into a deep-blue sermon of considerable weight. "Julep" is also in there, and while I'm no dancer, it had me doing some stepping. "Trust" is a mite too fast to bring out the genuine lyricism of the melody (Hawk did it up just right on a Prestige album of a decade ago, *Stasch*). But in general, no complaints.

The rating of three and a half stars would be higher if Person were not so promising. He didn't blow his all on this one, and neither did we. He's a comer.

(1968)

Barry Harris: Magnificent

This is perhaps Barry Harris's finest album to date, which is to say that it is an event, for Harris is as good as they come. Though still a young man, he was a father figure to most of the gifted players who came out of Detroit in the '50s. Today he is one of the standard-bearers of a musical tradition sometimes called bebop—I prefer the term "Charlie Parker music." Even in a music to which honesty is so basic as jazz, artists who never yield to the temptation of betraying their gifts are rare. Harris is such a man.

On this remarkable album, which maintains an uncommonly high level of inspiration, we find all the facets of a complete musician. There is no shucking and jiving, no cute concessions to hip fads, nothing but pure, honest music.

For openers, Harris salutes the memory of a close friend and frequent musical associate, Coleman Hawkins, with a broiling, one-take-perfect assault on "Bean and the Boys." Harris's marvelous swing and unceasingly inventive horn-like single-line style are to the fore as he builds and sustains excitement for six and a half minutes with sterling rhythm support. The well-paced program continues with two Harris originals, the minor-hued, almost Monkish "You Sweet and Fancy Lady" and the pretty, sweet (but never saccharine) "Rouge," nostalgic in mood and spotting a little gas of a Tatum run in the final bridge. (I'd like to hear this scored for the Ellington band.)

Charlie Parker's "Ah-leu-cha," opening with some deft contrapuntal work, is a lesson in melodic improvisation in the composer's mold; Harris's lines even seem to "breathe" like a horn's. "Just Open Your Heart" is a gentle, happy melody stated by the composer at a relaxed, pulsing tempo. It evokes a mellow mood. Harris again creates superb variations, and there is a full solo chorus by Ron Carter—melodic bassing at its best. "Sun Dance," another Harris original, is a Latin-flavored blues with a catchy theme, splendidly performed by the trio; a most cohesive unit.

On "These Foolish Things," Harris demonstrates how to play a standard with a master's touch. His second chorus is a marvel of lucid construction and development, and the elaborate, romantic cadenza is touched with gentle humor at the end. "Dexterity" takes us back to Bird—a passionate, swinging conclusion to a generous forty-minutes-plus of uplifting music. Harris begins his solo in the bass register and gradually climbs higher; his intelligent utilization of the full resources of his instrument, without frills or excesses, is a joy to hear. Harris is one of the very few pianists who never allow the fingers to fill in when the mind falters. There are no clichéd runs in his book.

That Ron Carter should be a perfect partner here comes as no surprise, but Leroy Williams is a name new to me and a most welcome acquaintance. He is a listening drummer, agile of mind, hands, and feet, and everything he does here seems just right. The engineering is first-rate and the piano good and properly tuned: one of those rare dates where everything seems to have gone well, produced by the intrepid Don Schlitten—like Harris a believer in honest music. Ironically, there'll be no follow-up. We hear that Prestige is cutting back on noncommercial jazz, and Schlitten will no longer be producing live dates for the label. This is 1970 . . . grab this while you can!

(1970)

Jaki Byard: Solo Piano

S olo albums by pianists are rare these days, perhaps because few (except the old masters) are really capable of playing a full, two-handed keyboard style—the inevitable result of working with bass and drum support far more often than alone. Byard, however, has always had two hands, and even when working with a rhythm section, he thinks pianistically. He is a fascinating musical personality and among the very few major figures who have been able to combine eclecticism and originality to create an intensely individual style.

One hears in Byard elements of the entire jazz piano tradition, from ragtime to Cecil Taylor, but always from a unique perspective. Like most true solo pianists, he is also a composer and here, left free to select and develop his material, he shows just how wide a range he can span. Byard is not a very tidy musician; he may miss a few notes in a run, or go on to a new idea before having fully explored his last one. Good for him. Neatness is not a prerequisite for jazz or any good music, and Byard can afford to drop ideas midway—he's got plenty to spare.

This is not to say that Byard can't be orderly when he chooses. The very lovely "Spanish Tinge No. 2," with its impressionistic harmonies, is an example of lucid development, and "New Orleans Strut," Byard's impres-

sion of a Crescent City street parade, never falters through almost six minutes of evocative and imaginative music-making.

Byard's love of ragtime and stride piano is displayed on the delightful
"Top of the Gate Rag." There is humor here, but not of the patronizing
kind one sometimes encounters in re-creations of older styles by younger
players. That's because Byard feels these musics; he doesn't play with them,
but on them. "The Hollis Stomp" is another lighthearted piece, a furiously
paced game with "I Got Rhythm" changes; an exuberant tip of the cap to
Art Tatum. Like Tatum, Byard often plays show tunes. "Hello Young
Lovers," one of just three of nine tracks not using original material, is an
example of his imaginative treatment. He almost re-composes the tune, and
in the process (perhaps because he really likes it) strips it of Broadway
pathos, investing it with genuine feeling.

Even better is his "Do You Know What It Means to Miss New Or-
leans," graceful and nostalgic. Here, and in "Strut," there are echoes of
Garner, and as in the previously mentioned cases of ragtime and stride,
Byard uses the style creatively, not as pastiche.

These are my favorite tracks, which is not to say that the rest is not of
equal interest. "Seasons," for example, shows the romantic side of Byard
the composer, and the medley of "I Know a Place" and "Let the Good
Times Roll" romps and rolls with great spirit. "A Basin Street Ballad" is
more reflective and introspective than Byard usually is. But then, he is a
man of many moods.

This is the kind of record too rarely made today: no gimmicks, just
music as the musician wants to play it. That, of course, is a challenge, and
Byard is up to it. Don Schlitten, who produced, is also responsible for the
cover—one of the best and most original of recent times. Things being
what they are, one assumes that this fine record won't sell a million copies,
but it is sure to be remembered when a lot of the stuff that does has long
been rotting on the compost heap.

(1970)

Wes Montgomery:
Down Here on the Ground

L ike all jazz artists who've made it big, Wes Montgomery has a
sound—hear that good, ye squealers and brayers—a lovely sound.
Like all jazz artists who've made it big, he is a superb melodist—
hear that, ye runners of tuneless runs—a singer. And like all jazz artists
who've made it big, he swings—hear that, ye twisters of time. And not least,
of course, Wes Montgomery is a musical personality: his own man.

You can't manufacture that, but you sure can market it, and one of jazz's
most harmful myths is that if you do market it, and it sells, some mysterious
essential change takes place: art is tainted by success.

Wes Montgomery is very successful these days, yet he is not one iota less
the artist he was when only his fellow musicians and a few of the initiated
knew that he was great. If anything, he is even better, for it is also a myth
that an artist must suffer to create. Do *you* do your thing best when you are
suffering? Is an artist not human?

This splendid album is, I guess, what the purists would call "commercial." That means, in the present case, that the selection of tunes is varied
and tasteful, that the tracks are not overly long, that arrangements have
been thoughtfully crafted, that excellent musicians have been provided to
interpret them and back the featured artist, that the music has been carefully recorded and mastered, and that the packaging is handsome. (Take the
opposite of almost all these ingredients, and you'll have a pretty good description of what some people consider honest, untainted "art.") At the risk
of being labeled a middlebrow philistine, I'll take the commercial concept.
You see, I believe in communication.

And so, apparently, does Wes Montgomery. His music, aside from the
virtues already cited, has the additional qualities of logic, clarity, form, and
feeling—feeling that communicates directly, without that ambiguity that is
so much in fashion everywhere today, and which so often simply hides inability to feel and inability to think.

But I don't want to make of this album a brief of beliefs it happens to
confirm while losing sight of the subject itself. It is a most pleasant subject.
Though the selections aren't long, almost every moment is the soloist's.
The arrangements, all but two by Don Sebesky and a third probably a
"head," are there to enhance his work, and almost always do.

The strings, in number and instrumentation, equal the classic string quartet, and no better sound for strings has yet been devised for intimate contexts. (That sound is best represented on "When I Look in Your Eyes," but is always the antithesis of that cloying schmaltz that marks commercial string writing at its most common and worst.) Flutes and oboes are used with tasteful discretion. The flute trio on the bossa nova "Know It All" is delightful, and the solo oboe on Lalo Schifrin's "The Fox" is superbly played (by Romeo Penque or George Marge). Mike Mainieri's vibes add coloristic touches—the chromatics on "Fox" are a bit trite, but that's not his doing.

As for the rhythm section—just read the names, please. Herbie Hancock, though he doesn't solo, adds many fine touches. On "Georgia on My Mind," the title tune, and "Know It All," he is particularly apt. Ron Carter is merely one of the best, and his sound records wonderfully well. Grady Tate is felt rather than heard, which is just right under the circumstances. When more presence is called for, as on the romping "The Other Man's Grass Is Always Greener," he's in there.

My own favorites (no track is less than very good) are "Greener," a good tune; Wes's own two blues, the slow "Up and At It" and the medium "Goin' On to Detroit"; "Georgia," hauntingly nostalgic; "When I Look," a tranquil ballad; and the title tune, a fine melody by Schifrin, which I'd like to hear Carmen McRae sing—provided the lyrics are good.

Though this is not a blowing session, there is plenty of blowing. Wes flies on "Greener," and stretches out on "At It," hypnotically repeating a phrase, kneading it into you, and later echoing his own octave riffs on single string (not fake echo; the real thing). His brief unaccompanied passages on "Look" sound as full as a harp, his theme statement on "Georgia" is glowingly golden, and his two opening notes on the blowing section of "Detroit" are startlingly trumpet-like.

But these are sketchy details. Let your ears fill in the gaps, and be glad that Wes Montgomery has made it big—good and big. To give due credit, the album was produced by Creed Taylor. As they say in the trade, it's a superior package.

(1968)

CAUGHT IN THE ACT

Erroll Garner at the Village Gate

For a nightclub season haunted by dwindling attendance for jazz attractions, Garner, in his first New York club appearance in some four years, proved that a great jazz artist with a loyal following can still pack in the crowds.

No wonder—for Garner gives his listeners full value, sharing with them his joy in making music. He is one of those rare beings who is able to achieve total communication through his art. Moreover, he can do this consistently—a seasoned Garnerite will know when the pianist is really inspired. But even on an "average" night, hearing Garner is an extraordinary experience.

Because Garner has committed the sin of being accepted by the general public, certain jazz critics have attempted to dissect and downgrade his art.

Such attempts invariably fail to convince the listener who exposes himself to the music. He will then hear that what they call "mannerisms" is really style—and true style has secrets that defy dissection. What they have called his "limitations" are actually his very strength, for every note he plays bears the unmistakable stamp of his unique and personal conception. (A great jazz pianist, recently reported to admire Garner but "with reservations," because he "follows only one line of the piano's potential," is himself an object lesson in the difference between a stylist and a player who in spite of his phenomenal equipment has failed to create a music truly his own.)

First, Garner is one of the great melodists in jazz. He knows how to make a line sing. Second, he has a flawless sense of time and rhythm, enabling him to play at any tempo he chooses without loss of swing. Third, like all great jazzmen, he is an architect of sound, a master at shaping and building phrases.

Classic jazz (and Garner surely belongs among the classic players) is the art of the phrase, of concentrating a maximum of invention and emotion into a minimum of musical space. Garner doesn't waste notes, and he can tell a compelling story in one chorus or eight bars.

No windy orator, he crams an hour on the stand (Garner never plays short sets) with as many as sixteen selections, each a perfect statement, a fully explored and developed piece. When he is through—having had to beg off with a minimum of three encores—the listener has had an experience that has involved his emotions, has lifted him out of everyday existence, has given him something he can keep: in short, the kind of experience true art gives.

Sure, Garner can be unashamedly and nakedly romantic. Why not? The theory that music is not supposed to sing and laugh and cry is an invention of our death-obsessed century. Lucky the artist who is not touched by it.

These points need to be made, for many self-styled sophisticates in jazz take Garner's art for granted, assuming that its popular appeal is proof that it must be lacking in the complexity they so adore. In reality, Garner is much more complex and sophisticated an artist than those who substitute obscurity for lack of invention, whose "modernism" cloaks paucity of spirit or inability to communicate.

One could choose almost at random from several hours spent listening to Garner at work at the Village Gate:

A lovely "Moon River," building from a *misterioso* introduction (Garner's introductions, in which the theme plays hide-and-seek with the ear, are as free as anything the "new thing" has to offer) into a softly rolling theme statement and then a series of improvised passages, each contrasting with the previous. The passages are rippling, seemingly out-of-tempo arpeggios; single-note, right-hand inventions backed by those steady "guitar" chords from the left that only Freddie Green could match for firmness of time; and then the clean, sweeping, big-band riffs that are building blocks to a climax. Finally a gentle coda, stopping the flow.

Or a "One-Note Samba," seemingly at first just unadorned melody, until the listener discovers that each bar has a subtly different voicing, growing steadily away from the original line, until it suddenly has become dissonant—even though the melody is still present. While this is happening, the beat is changing, too—and when the song has been entirely reshaped (but always in terms of itself), it softly returns to its original form.

Or a "Where or When," at a wild, way-up tempo that yet doesn't rob it of its song. First it is smoothed out, like a streamlined missile moving through space; then rocky and craggy, with those big, crashing chords to the fore, but still retaining its momentum; then, quite suddenly, a half chorus of unaccompanied piano, almost surrealistic in its free gyrations; then, right on the beat, a return to the smooth opening flow.

Or a "Surrey with the Fringe on Top," with pounding bass notes on the loose, the melody outlined in broken chords. And midway along into the fiery tempo that never gets frantic, a delightfully unexpected two-bar quote from "Lester Leaps In," so fitting that it doesn't seem to be a quote.

And all this is performed with such graceful aplomb, with such enjoyment, and with such a variety of dynamics and sound patterns that the piano seems transformed into an orchestra—an impression bolstered by that marvelous sound, big and strong or soft and gentle, but always a true piano sound.

A word, too, for Garner's loyal supporters, bassist Eddie Calhoun and drummer Kelly Martin. Theirs is a selfless but ultimately gratifying task, which both of them approach with all the considerable skill and musicianship they have to offer. The trio is indeed an organic entity.

To catch Garner in person, especially in a club, is one of the most gratifying and joyous experiences in jazz today.

(1965)

Erroll Garner at Carnegie Hall

G arner's first Carnegie Hall concert in eight years was a resounding success—popular as well as artistic. It also was the pianist's first concert appearance in more than a decade with accompanists other than bassist Eddie Calhoun and drummer Kelly Martin.

There had been little rehearsing with the musicians present; so there was a welcome aura of the impromptu, though the accompanists had little difficulty adapting themselves to the pianist's requirements. Guitarist Wally Richardson and Latin percussionist Jose Mangual did not play on all numbers, and Richardson's amplifier failed early in the evening, so his contribution was more visual than aural. The promising opportunity to hear Garner's famous "guitar" left hand in conjunction with the real article did not really materialize.

Mangual, on the other hand, made his presence felt in a most tasteful and musical way; in fact, it was he, of all the sidemen, who seemed to have the most rapport with Garner. Milt Hinton also did well; his fat sound and fine ear were much in evidence. Herbie Lovelle, on the other hand, was almost too self-effacing and tentative in his playing; working mostly with brushes, he was often nearly inaudible.

But Garner could have carried the night by himself. In fact, the high point of the concert was his two unaccompanied solos: a reflective, lovely "Someone to Watch Over Me" and an untitled original, made up on the spot, that at times echoed "King Porter Stomp" and "Carolina Shout."

On this second piece, Garner played all kinds of piano; a burst of stride, some delicate chording, a bit of near-ragtime, and a startling demonstration of hand independence that rivaled Art Tatum at his best. It was a condensed encyclopedia of jazz piano, an example of spontaneous invention that probably no other pianist today could equal.

If this was the peak, there were many other moments that scaled the heights. There were those delightful, often witty, and always surprising "free" introductions, which the listener always wants to hear again, once he knows what the tune is going to be. Among the finest were those to "That's All" and "Lulu's Back in Town" (a splendid performance from start to finish).

One of the joys in listening to Garner is that you can play the game of anticipating his ideas and still always be surprised; this, in my opinion, is one of the great pleasures in hearing jazz, a much greater pleasure than merely being startled without a foothold in a familiar context.

Another joy is Garner's ability to choose the right tempo—right for the tune and for the creation of fully formed and freely flowing ideas. He never gets soggy on slow pieces and never rushes into the frantic and inchoate when the tempo is up. Each note counts, and each note is fully articulated.

And what a piano *sound*! There is a full range of dynamics, but at all volumes the sound is clear and round and musical.

As always, Garner relied on standards and current hits for the bulk of his program. No well-known melody is too hackneyed, no hit of the day too trite for him to use as a vehicle for invention and surprise. He is a romantic but not a sentimentalist, and even such a tune as "More" can serve him.

Such choice of material, unpalatable to the snob, is one of Garner's ways of keeping in touch with his audience. He does not play down to the people, but he helps them come up to him.

Garner has become an institution, but he has not stagnated. His formation of a new working group shortly after this concert, and his brilliant performance at the concert itself, indicate that there are still many surprises to come from the little giant of the piano, whose playing is one of the purest joys to be found in music today.

(1967)

Bud Powell

Wen Bud Powell mounted the bandstand at Birdland for his first appearance in his homeland in more than six years, the packed house gave him a standing ovation. It was a spontaneous and moving vote of confidence in a musician who has had more than his share of trouble and whose eagerly awaited return had been accompanied by persistent rumors that this once great player was now just a shadow of his former self.

As soon as Powell sat down to play, however, it became apparent that the expression of faith was justified. For, while it would not be fair to Powell or his admirers to say that this was "the old Bud," there can be no doubt that the Bud Powell of 1964 is still a creative jazzman and pianist of the first rank. If the fire and abandon of youth are no longer, one now finds in their place a deliberate and lucid crystallization of the chief elements in the piano style that has been so enormously influential since the mid-'40s.

As might be expected from a man only recently recovered from a long and severe illness (tuberculosis), there were moments when fingers would not do the bidding of the mind, but after two weeks of steady playing, these moments had been reduced to occasional missed notes in up-tempo runs. On opening night, it was evident that the trio (with Horace Arnold on drums) had not rehearsed long. Nor was the support given by the sidemen really adequate, though bassist John Ore, who worked with Powell some years ago, was steady and firm.

Nevertheless, from the opening "The Best Thing for Me Would Be You" (with a beautifully voiced block-chord ending) through a rhapsodic "Like Someone in Love" (with unaccompanied opening and closing choruses played in a suggestion of 3/4 time) to a delightful, romping "John's Abbey," there were moments of inspired music-making.

Not the least moments were Powell's readings of two selections from the Thelonious Monk canon: Monk's own "Epistrophy," and Denzil Best and Monk's "Bemsha Swing." Powell was among Monk's earliest admirers, and no other pianist except Monk himself can get to the marrow of Monk's music like Powell. This would seem especially true today, since Powell's approach to tempo has become more deliberate. During his third week at Birdland, when J. C. Moses had taken over the drum chair, Powell played Monk's "I Mean You" in absolutely masterly fashion, his inventions bolstered by Moses's expert phrasing and time. Powell's sense of humor (like all great players, he has one) was evident here.

On his own originals, of which there seemed to be fewer than in earlier days, Powell displayed some of the fireworks of yore, particularly on several versions of "Collard Greens and Blackeyed Peas" (otherwise known as "Blues in the Closet"). The famous horn-like right hand came to the fore, as Powell would improvise a string of blues choruses with a melodic inventiveness and swing that proved him still master of the "Bud Powell school." "Oblivion" (which sounded much gayer than its title) and the aforementioned "John's Abbey" were the only other Powell compositions heard by this reviewer.

The pianist's repertory, as always, included a number of standards. The aforementioned "Someone" seemed to be a particular favorite, the pianist obviously relishing in the rhapsodic flourishes in the rubato solo passages. There also were a Latin-flavored "Old Black Magic," a fast and very exciting "Nice Work If You Can Get It," and a charming "I Hear Music." A bouncy and easygoing "Just You, Just Me" and a fine-tempoed "Hot House" brought back nostalgic memories of the bebop days, with Powell's improvisations on the latter recalling Charlie Parker's in approach and feeling.

At times, the trio achieved real integration, with the proper emphasis on support for the pianist. But far too often, the sidemen indulged in lengthy solos that, no matter how interesting, only served to disrupt the continuity of a given piece. An occasional solo of two or three choruses from bass or drums ought to suffice to keep the players happy, though it must be said that Ore here revealed himself to be a much more adventurous and inventive soloist than indicated during his long tenure with Monk. One longed for the kind of empathy Max Roach and George Duvivier might have given Powell, who was a model of patience and endurance during his sidemen's solos.

Despite these drawbacks and an understandable unevenness of inspiration, it is a gratifying experience to hear Powell play. His mere presence testifies to the triumph of the human spirit over adversity and suffering, but he needs no excuses or apologies. The purity of his conception, the joy he still can find in making music, the unmistakable identity of those horn-like melodic lines and those characteristic minor sevenths, the logic, clarity, and sheer musicality of his ideas—these speak for themselves, and with moving eloquence.

(1964)

Bill Evans

S urprisingly, this was Evans's New York concert debut. The happy results made clear that the concert format is perfectly suited to Evans,
whose work invites and rewards the kind of concentrated listening
possible in such a setting.

Evans's music is a delight—in good measure so because it utilizes the basic
traditional materials of jazz without distorting or abusing them and with
almost classic restraint and simplicity. Because of his mastery of the song
form, Evans is able to inject into his work a wealth of nuance, re-creating the
familiar, and uncovering endless possibilities in a realm others have discarded
in favor of a "freedom" that too often becomes self-indulgence.

This Town Hall concert was a model of intelligent organization. It presented Evans in three distinct settings: at the helm of his trio (surely one of
the best integrated units of its kind), as a soloist, and as a functional sideman
and soloist in a big-band format.

The trio segment came first and consisted of eight selections—two originals, four standards, and two superior ballads of recent vintage. Of the latter, Evans wrought a near-miracle with the much-abused "Who Can I Turn
To?," avoiding all bombast and sentimentality in his delicate rubato exposition of the theme, accompanied only by arco bass, and then moving into
tempo with relaxed and flowingly swinging ideas. "Make Someone Happy"
also became a vehicle for discovery, from the unaccompanied introduction
to the bracing Bud Powell–like run at the end.

The originals were "Very Early," a gently melodic air with a light waltz
lilt, and "My Lover's Kiss," a beautiful ballad. "Spring Is Here" became a
shimmering impressionistic canvas. "I Should Care" brought out the full
contour of the fine melody at a surprising medium-bounce tempo. And
"My Foolish Heart," usually a cloying thing in the hands of singers, was the
premise for a very free and ingenious improvisation that barely sketched in
the outlines of the tune.

"Beautiful Love" concluded the first segment. It was taken at an up
tempo and featured Arnie Wise. Originally an East Coast substitute for
Larry Bunker but now a permanent member of the trio, Wise is the best
drummer Evans has had. Working mostly with brushes, he was a model of
good taste and comprehension of Evans's musical aims, unintrusive but always there.

Bassist Chuck Israels, with Evans some five years, has more than filled
the shoes of his illustrious predecessor, the late Scott LaFaro. Israels is a

fine technician, with a full, rounded tone, but the most impressive aspect of his work with Evans is his seemingly intuitive feeling for the direction of the pianist's improvisations. Israels soloed on nearly every selection, and it is a compliment to his gifts as a melodic player to note that these spots maintained the lofty level set by Evans.

Evans opened the second half of the concert with a new composition for solo piano titled *In Memory of His Father, Harry L. Evans,* 1891–1966. A three-part piece, it consists of a prologue, an improvisational section based on two themes in song form ("Story Line" and "Turn Out the Stars"), and a brief epilogue.

On the basis of a single hearing (it was the kind of piece one immediately wanted to hear again), it is Evans's most impressive achievement as a composer. The prologue, not in a strict jazz idiom, was reminiscent of a Ravel piano piece, without being in the least derivative.

The middle section, played with jazz feeling and time, introduced a theme ("Stars") of astonishing loveliness, developed in what surely was Evans's most remarkable playing of the evening. The startlingly brief epilogue, less than a minute in duration, crystallized the mood and feeling of the entire piece. It was the kind of music about which it is difficult to comment because it was a complete and totally absorbing experience. (The audience was asked to refrain from applause at the conclusion of this section.)

The orchestral pieces ("What Kind of Fool Am I?"; "Willow, Weep for Me"; and Evans's "Funkallero" and "Waltz for Debby") were performed without interruption, with brief transitions between tunes by either woodwinds or piano. Al Cohn's writing for woodwinds was particularly attractive and imaginatively colored. There also were brilliant brass passages sparked by Ernie Royal's immaculate lead.

Though Evans was well featured, the arrangements were not piano showcases. Solos by Clark Terry, Eddie Daniels, Jerry Dodgion, and Bob Brookmeyer added excitement, with Terry particularly outstanding in a vehement plunger spot on "Fool." Daniels, an excellent tenorist and clarinetist, shone on "Willow" with a dramatic tenor solo, and the theme of "Waltz" was introduced by Terry and Brookmeyer in their inimitable duo style. Evans dug in on the bright "Funkallero."

Don't come to Evans looking for flash, funk, and surface emotion. But when it comes to creating *music* at the piano, Evans has few peers.

(1967)

Cecil Taylor

A benefit for the New York University chapter of the Congress of Racial Equality in June was billed as Taylor's second annual Town Hall concert. The pianist introduced four new pieces, two utilizing the septet, one performed without the horns, and one by the group without trumpeter Eddie Gale. Each piece was approximately twenty-five minutes long and was followed by a lengthy intermission.

The intermissions were a good idea, for they allowed the listener to collect his senses between the often furious onslaughts of the music.

There can be no question that hearing Taylor's music is a unique and often compelling experience. I know of no other contemporary music of such immense and concentrated energy or comparable density of texture. At times, it has the force of an erupting volcano, and it is impossible to withstand its almost elemental power.

On the other hand, such sustained tension and high velocity may reduce the listener to a passive, non-receptive state. Having been drained and exhausted, he no longer is able to respond and is left merely to marvel at the energy on display, without being moved by it.

This, however, may well be a matter of conditioning—for me, passivity did not come about until the last piece was under way. Prior to this, the music was fascinating, sometimes exhilarating, sometimes almost grotesque, and always full of surprises.

With the exception of the quartet piece, each selection included arranged as well as improvised passages.

The writing was most extensive and interesting in the opening piece, "Enter, Evening" (subtitled "Soft Line Structure"). It began gently, the reflective opening section scored for Harmon-muted trumpet, oboe, and alto saxophone. There ensued a partially unaccompanied dialogue between Gale and Jimmy Lyons; a transitional section with the piano and Alan Silva's arco bass to the fore; a trumpet solo with remarkable backing by Taylor; a brief plucked bass solo by Henry Grimes; some beautifully played oboe, with soft, mallet-struck drum backgrounds; a long solo from Lyons; and, in climax, an astonishing Taylor solo utilizing all the resources of the piano.

Taylor's solo grew from a subdued opening to a roaring crescendo of sound; then it leveled off to the opening mood, led into a return of the ensemble theme, and ended on a long, sustained collective note.

This was the most nuanced and developed of the pieces heard. It was at times—especially in the ensemble passages and during those moments in Taylor's solo when he played delicately and shimmeringly—almost Debussyesque, creating impressionistic and haunting hues.

The balance of the concert displayed a different aspect of Taylor's personality.

Here, the emphasis was on constant, turbulent motion, physically reflected in the pianist's fantastic gyrations at the keyboard. At times, Taylor seemed to assault the instrument, but significantly his touch, even at its most violent, never failed to produce a pianistic and thoroughly musical sound.

He never descended to mere banging (as is sometimes the case with would-be avant-gardist practitioners), and he always maintained control. Even when great, roaring waves of sounds were produced, each note in the cascade was clearly and cleanly struck and articulated.

This amazing technique, combined with a quicksilver temperament, is perhaps behind Taylor's tendency to heap climax upon climax, to the point where the total effect becomes diluted, and one begins to long for some contrast and moderation.

This was most apparent on "Steps," which featured Lyons and Ken McIntyre in lengthy alto solo forays and Taylor at his most vehement.

McIntyre was the more agitated of the saxophonists. His solo was replete with hoarse cries, frenzied swoops, and vocal inflections—in interesting contrast to his work on oboe but similar to his later excursion on bass clarinet. McIntyre is a most accomplished musician, with expert command of all his instruments.

"Steps" also contained interesting unison passages for saxophones, a vigorous bass duet (throughout, Silva played arco, while Grimes plucked and strummed; both bassists performed with impressive dexterity), and some stimulating interplay between Taylor and Silva, including excursions into the uppermost range of the bass, which were often eerie but never shrill and scraping.

The quartet piece, "Tales" (subtitled "Nine Whisps"), began with Taylor shaking a tambourine and then venturing inside the piano for some strumming of the strings; the performance also emphasized the remarkable teamwork of the two bassists and their sympathetic communication with the pianist. During this selection, effective use was made of lighting, alternating between deep red and brilliant white.

Andrew Cyrille was functional; his role, for most of the concert, was mainly that of percussive colorist rather than timekeeper. The shifting rhythms were cued by Taylor, and there was no steady metric pulse as such.

Gale, a trumpeter with strong chops and good facility, was heard on open horn in the final piece, which also featured McIntyre's bass clarinet and Lyons's alto.

Lyons, throughout, was the most melodically oriented of the hornmen, projecting his fluent ideas with an attractive tone and with few of the extreme effects favored by most saxophonists of the "new" orientation.

Though it is certainly related to some of the current trends in jazz, Taylor's music is unique. It is perhaps the most striking example of the increasing inappropriateness of categorizations and labels like "jazz" and "classical," and Taylor's situation in American music today is one of the most lamentable results of this outmoded system of classification.

This is music that, for lack of better venue, belongs in the concert hall. Yet, while academic hacks and fashionable modernists reap the necessary grants and fellowships without which no "serious" musician can sustain himself in our time, Taylor, regarded by the establishment as a "jazz" musician, is left to shift for himself.

In view of this, it is not surprising that Taylor, when given the all too infrequent opportunity to present his music properly, attempts to pour everything that is straining to be expressed within himself into each performance, thus sometimes causing an overflow of creative energy uncontainable within such limitations of time and space.

Given his rightful opportunity to create and perform with that minimum of security that our society now grants talents much lesser than his, there is no telling what Taylor might accomplish, considering what he already has achieved in spite of the unfair odds against him.

(1966)

Harry Edison

Among the many fringe benefits of the recent Newport Jazz Festival (carping critics often forget to take into account just how much adrenaline the festival stirs up on the New York jazz scene as a whole) was the welcome presence of master musicians seldom seen in these parts under optimum conditions, and for more than a fleeting moment.

Harry "Sweets" Edison had been around in recent years as comedian Redd Foxx's musical director, which gave him the opportunity to take one or two featured solos before that very funny man and his co-stars would come out and do their stuff. The only other times Sweets came to town was for record dates. This time, he could be heard not only at the Newport jam sessions at Radio City Music Hall (an exceptional night of music) and the Roseland Ballroom, but also on two occasions at Eddie Condon's, for a weekend at Gulliver's (a jazz room in West Paterson, New Jersey), and, some six weeks later, after a visit to Europe, for two weeks at Hopper's, a fairly new Greenwich Village club.

At Condon's, Sweets first guested with the house band on a Tuesday night. Balaban & Cats vary in quality, and on this night were not at their best. Sweets's old Basie colleague, Vic Dickenson, was on leave, and while Dick Rath did a nice job, there were no special vibrations. (Vic, by the way, celebrated his seventieth birthday on August 6, without fanfare and on the job. "They didn't even have a cake for me," he said a few weeks later, when, crestfallen at having forgotten such a landmark date, we bought him a be-lated birthday drink. Vic is a marvel.) Herb Hall, that underrated gentle-man of the clarinet, was able to offer the visitor some inspiration, and pianist Jimmy Andrews fit in nicely, but the rest of the rhythm section was feeble. Still, it was something to hear that great open horn sound of Edi-son's live and at close range, and he got off a lovely "Georgia on My Mind," a solo feature with a long, suspenseful, beautifully resolved cadenza. And it was interesting to hear him lead a "traditional" front line on "Sweet Geor-gia Brown."

It was a different story the following Sunday, when Sweets led his own group at Condon's, with old Californian sidekick Jimmy Rowles on piano, Victor Sproles on bass, Walter Bolden on drums, and another Californian buddy and rare and welcome visitor, Teddy Edwards, on tenor. (The last time we'd seen Teddy here was in 1964, at the World's Fair with Benny Goodman.) The first set, caught after attending a Newport concert, found the band getting it together. Several musicians, including Joe Newman and Roy Haynes, were in the house. Sweets's bandstand manner, new to us, is most engaging, especially his long, humorous, and informative introduc-tions of the sidemen (and himself) at the end of each set. The cadences of his speech, accompanied by some gentle but funky Rowles ramblings, were as well timed as one of his muted solos, and he threw in comments about musicians and other friends in the house.

The music was so good that we came back for more after the second Newport concert of the night, arriving just in time for the last set. That was about 2 a.m., and the atmosphere was different now—reminiscent of old Fifty-second Street. Roy Haynes, who'd played the Newport concert, was back. Zoot Sims and his sweet Louise were at a table opposite the band-stand. Basie altoist Danny Turner, who'd been sitting in, we were told, was still there. Marilyn Moore, who, as Sweets pointed out in his closing oration, can sound remarkably like Billie Holiday, was there, as was singer-pianist Daryl Sherman. And so were such seasoned hipsters as Elliot Horne, publicist for RCA Records, and Ed Fuerst, former George Shearing road manager and ace Rowles fan.

Everybody was ready for some music, and Sweets & Co. delivered. Sweets has that certain presence, and so does his sound. The famous Edison blues, "Centerpiece," was a lesson in relaxed, laid-back swinging. Edwards, in wonderful form, offered an extended solo on a way-up "Love for Sale," building excitement in a manner reminiscent of his contemporary and one-time tenor battle partner, Dexter Gordon; as Sweets said later, he is one of the pioneers of that style. Rowles, a truly great man of music (as we've come to learn since he, happily for New York, decided to settle here a couple of years ago), displayed mastery, in the role of both accompanist (no wonder Billie loved his work) and soloist. He goes exceptionally well with Sweets; both men have perfect time, are masters at crafting musical epigrams, and care about the tunes they play. Bolden and Sproles listened well and worked hard.

But on "'Round Midnight," it was all Sweets and Jimmy. The trumpeter, playing open horn with a sound no record has yet done full justice, explored the famous Monk melody in a manner that became increasingly abstract, Rowles following his intricate but always logical path with astonishing empathy. They were like two mountain climbers sharing a rope. Rowles's fearless solo didn't lose the continuity established by Sweets, and when the trumpeter came back in, they went further out together. Eventually, bass and drums dropped out, intuitively sensing that this was a climb for two, and the free duet that ensued revealed a rarely heard aspect of Sweets. After-hours music!

At Hopper's, Sweets looked even better. His sartorial style is strictly California, but he is the sort of man who can wear a bracelet and necklace and get away with it. That he is nearly sixty-one is difficult to comprehend; he is in his prime as a player. I've never heard him in better form, once again with Rowles, plus Earl May (sitting in for Bob Cranshaw) on bass and David Lee on drums. As the only horn in the group, it was up to Sweets to set the pace, and he wasn't coasting. (All players, great and small, coast sometimes, and Sweets is a master at it; he can make a routine phrase glow and let one note do the work of ten. But there was none of that now.)

The set was all standards, and Sweets was in an up-tempo mood. Even "Out of Nowhere" (which ended as Tadd Dameron's "Casbah," by the way) was nowhere near ballad tempo, and on every number, Sweets took at least three choruses in front and rode out in style after the obligatory piano and bass solos. Rowles was with him all the way, and like Sweets, never wasted a note. His suspensions of the pulse are quite different from Earl Hines's, but just as surefooted, and he always tells a story. He explores the piano, and not the least interesting aspect of his style is its combination of harmonic audacity and rhythmic sophistication, which might be called "modern" traits, with a left hand that is no stranger to stride. He keeps you on your toes.

Lee, my candidate for greatness among young drummers, was a bedrock. He is from New Orleans, where Dizzy Gillespie found him, and he has got that certain thing special to drummers from the Crescent City, from Zutty Singleton to Ed Blackwell. He lays down the time, keeps it firm, and *listens*. He was always there when Sweets came up with one of those phrases that demands a rhythmic answer, and their eights and fours were true conversations.

(1976)

Dizzy Gillespie

T he degree of purity in your hearts is astounding—especially with this damn cold weather outside. For it would take the angel Gabriel himself to get me out of here tonight . . . or money; not necessarily in that order."

Thus Dizzy Gillespie thanked his small but enthusiastic London House audience for an especially warm round of applause on one of the coldest Chicago winter nights in recent memory.

Perhaps it was the circumstances—obviously, anyone who braves below-zero cold reinforced by strong winds must be a true music lover, or crazy—but, whatever the reason, Dizzy and his brand-new group made this a memorable night.

The new group is not yet complete; Phil Upchurch, better known as a guitarist but equally accomplished on bass, was just filling in during this engagement. James Moody, the trumpeter's stalwart frontline associate for more than six years, is gone, as are longtime drummer Candy Finch, and Jymie Merrit, the last in a series of relatively short-term bass players.

Moody is missed, of course, but after so many years of working together, he and Dizzy easily fell into established routines. Furthermore, in Moody, Diz had more than a featured sideman. He was almost a co-star.

Now, at the helm of a young group, with only pianist Mike Longo as a holdover, the leader has to carry the ball himself most of the time. He more than rose to the challenge.

If there had been nothing else (and there was plenty), two pieces would have sufficed to lift the evening into the realm of the extraordinary.

The first of these was a new Gillespie composition, "Brother K.," dedicated to the memory of Dr. Martin Luther King. It is a lovely melody, not at all maudlin, but intensely lyrical. Opening with a Harmon-muted theme statement and elaboration with only the barest suggestion of stated time, it moved into tempo with a slight Latin inflection during Longo's solo, maintaining it through Diz's flowing improvisation to the fade-out ending. This ranks with Gillespie's finest compositions, and the elegiac mood was beautifully sustained.

If this was an example of the master at his best, Dizzy's next offering was even more—the kind of musical experience that sustains one's faith in jazz' enduring power.

It was a slow blues—a Longo original called "Let Me Out of Here, You Hear?"—and during the pianist's introduction, Diz sat down on the apron of the stage, adjusted the mike, picked up his horn, still muted, and closed his eyes. Then he began to blow, building a blue sermon that had the message from the first note.

The solo contained all the key elements of Gillespie's remarkably individual style: his harmonic and rhythmic wizardry (what that man can do with time, and how he can swing at a tempo like this); the almost unbelievable runs, each note fully articulated with breath control that would amaze a master of Yoga; the glissando wails; the characteristic half-valve-accented swoops into bottom register, and, during the exciting double-time passage, the staggering rhythmic freedom and criss-crossing of bar lines that, because swing is always maintained, are far "freer" and more astonishing than the new-thing experiments.

But these observations are made in retrospect. While Dizzy played, there was only the content of the music, not the means by which it was conveyed. And that content was the essence of the blues, as deeply as we've ever heard Diz get into it. (The great ones grow greater, and don't you forget it.)

Dizzy is a master of abstraction, yet never a maker of merely abstract music. The feeling for melody, the sense of form, the soul are always there. This blues was something to remember, and when I say that the groove reminded me of Hot Lips Page, Diz and a few others will know what I mean.

There were other things: Longo's "Alligator," a loping blues with a good solo from the composer, who, during his long tenure with Dizzy, has developed into a confident and convincing soloist and a gifted writer; and "Soul Kiss," with a rock beat, some humorous smacking sound effects from Diz, and a memorable contribution from guitarist George Davis, who gets around on his instrument, has an unusual, slightly echo-chambered sound and a fine beat, and comps and blends effectively.

David Lee, like Davis a New Orleanian, has very relaxed, swinging time, plays for the group, and seems a truly natural drummer in a way resembling Ed Blackwell, his landsman. Upchurch laid down a good foundation, and his solos displayed guitar-like facility and invention—not surprisingly.

The group is already together, and with the right permanent bassist, and more new material of the caliber already demonstrated, it should give much pleasure and inspiration to the leader, and vice versa.

It was a nice evening in other respects. Between the two late sets, Dizzy was warmly greeted by an array of fans with different stories.

First was the man who told him he'd been his fan since the days of "Salt Peanuts." This prompted a bearded gentleman at an adjacent table to volunteer the information that *he* had been listening to Dizzy's horn since the broadcasts with the Teddy Hill band (that would be 1937, kiddies) and had come out this night "to see if you could still play." Needless to say, he was disappointed only in his own lack of faith.

Then appeared a jovial Englishman to request an autograph and tell Dizzy that he'd not seen him since a memorable concert at the Salle Pleyel in Paris in the mid-'50s. The international note was sustained by the next visitor. "Guess where I saw you last," he asked, in a voice with an Eastern European accent. "Athens?," ventured Diz. "Not quite," the man answered. "It was in Aleppo, Syria . . . we went out together after the concert and had dinner, remember?" Dizzy did, beamingly. The man said that he was with a lady from the Soviet Union whose son was a jazz fan, and would he please come and say hello.

Dizzy, always friendly and accommodating with his public, obliged. Returning after a long and seemingly animated conversation, he reported with genuine pleasure that the lady had told him she'd been unhappy about her son's liking for jazz until hearing and meeting Dizzy on this night.

She picked a good one.

(1970)

Miles Davis

In his first New York appearance since his recent recovery from hip and leg ailments, Miles Davis proved the old magic hasn't waned. The long lines of people waiting outside the Village Vanguard—not a common sight on today's nightclub scene—testified to Davis's drawing power, and the music more than justified the turnout.

Though he has lost weight, Davis appeared to be in good physical condition, and his playing certainly reinforced this impression. Featuring open horn for the most part on opening night, Davis was probing, fiery, and strong, playing like a man happy to be back in his element.

There were no stage-waits before or between sets, no displays of moodiness and no letdowns in the caliber of the music. From start to finish of each set, Davis and his men were taking care of business.

The Davis repertoire hasn't changed (there had been little time for new additions at this stage), but it is varied enough to sustain interest. Like most of the great players, Davis has found a number of tunes that are to his liking, and he continues to discover new aspects and dimensions in them.

So one heard, with undiminished interest, the standards ("'Round Midnight," "If I Were a Bell," "When I Fall in Love," "I Thought About You") and the Davis originals ("Four," "So What?," "All Blues," "The Theme"), and, as an added treat, a spontaneous blues, on which Davis dug deeply to roots, toying with phrases from "Royal Garden Blues" and "Easy Rider."

Among Davis's most moving performances was a finely wrought solo on "I Thought About You," developing from a slow, muted opening statement into a flowing, medium-tempo, open-horn improvisation, plus a near-perfect opening chorus on "When I Fall in Love," which was a masterly distillation of the essence of the melodic line.

Davis was in driving mood on a way-up "Four," displaying beautiful tonguing in his fast runs, and inserting a fitting quote from "Skyliner." Not less exciting was his work on "All Blues," for which he again discarded the mute after the atmospheric opening and unleashed some piercing, crying high notes, filled with a strange kind of painful joy.

Wayne Shorter was the other prominent soloist and acquitted himself well. His playing was often understated and at other times presented more ideas than he seemed able to order well. His tone was hampered (perhaps by a cold horn) early in the evening but became fuller as the night went on.

Interplay between Shorter and Tony Willams often gave rise to interesting structures, as on the ad lib blues, in which Shorter went "outside" in a more decisive manner than in the occasional avant-garde departures inserted in his more conservative solos.

One of Shorter's best moments came on "Four," when he opened his solo with intense drive and swing for a chorus or two before beginning to break up the time (and, unfortunately, the flow). But Shorter is never dull.

Herbie Hancock confined himself to short solos (one of the best came on "I Thought About You,' on which he concluded with some striking Ellingtonish clusters). In accompaniment, his sensitive choice of notes and space never interfered with the logic of Davis's lines. He seemed more aggressive behind Shorter, and there were intriguing exchanges of ideas between these two.

Reggie Workman is a potentially ideal bassist for this group, in which teamwork really counts. He has a big, beautifully articulated sound, an extremely versatile and fluent instrumental technique, and an excellent ear. His time-sense cannot be faulted. He had little solo space, but when he took the spotlight, he was impressive. His flawless sliding notes made a considerable contribution to "All Blues."

Drummer Williams is the backbone of the group and a complete delight. Few drummers, and none so young, combine astonishing instrumental dexterity and ease of execution with such a high degree of musical sensitivity. Williams never lets the band down, and what he plays, even when it is at its most original and unexpected, always seems right. He swings—and make no mistake, this is a group of men who like to swing. Even when they indulge in liberties with steady tempo, the musicians never lose the pulse that is so essential to continuity within a piece, that something that used to be called a groove. Williams is largely responsible for this.

Among his other virtues is his sound, which is subtly shaded to fit whatever he is backing. He has power to spare, but he doesn't waste it, and he doesn't impose.

After this prolonged involuntary absence, it is indeed a pleasure to welcome back Davis & Co. There has never been a greater need for the musical virtues this group represents so well. Among these are taste, disciplined freedom, swing, concise expression, and beauty.

(1966)

"Jazz at the Philharmonic"

Ⅰf the return of JATP to its homeland after an absence of eleven years was an occasion for nostalgia, it also was proof of the viability of Norman Granz's conception of what a jazz concert should be and an eloquent testimonial to the matchless pleasures of maturity.

Jazz, it has been said, is an art of the young. But among the stars of the current JATP, some were past sixty, several in their fifties, others in their forties, and none under thirty. Yet, with a few unimportant exceptions, the music was full of vitality, creative energy, and freshness.

No beginners or amateurs here—only seasoned professionals. They showed that they still can't be beat when it comes to making music that swings and communicates and stirs the emotions. There wasn't a performer on the stage who hadn't mastered his instrument. Levels of inspiration, of course, varied; but nobody was shucking or jiving.

The concert—one of two in New York that were the beginning of a nationwide tour—was a jazz banquet. There were the JATP standbys: jam sessions (when Granz first made the inspired move of putting such sessions on the concert stage, it was said they were not the real article; now, the JATP sessions, and an occasional festival get-together, are about the only remaining examples of the genre), ballad medleys, and a set by the Oscar Peterson trio. But freshness was brought to the session formula by adding Ellington saxophonists Johnny Hodges and Paul Gonsalves, and a further innovation was the appearance of Zoot Sims and Benny Carter with the Ellington band.

The Peterson trio warmed up the full and enthusiastic house with three numbers, best of which was the opening "The Lamp Is Low." The trio has by now achieved that organic unity that has been the hallmark of Peterson's groups, and the leader was in excellent form. As is so often the case with Peterson, there was a bit too much dazzle and not enough variety in mood and tempo—but it was brisk and swinging music.

Clark Terry and tenorists Gonsalves and Sims joined the trio for "Perdido," done without grandstand displays. Gonsalves, who was certainly one of the night's stars, was "Perdido"'s spark plug.

A ballad medley followed: Sims played a mellow, reflective, and very moving "Memories of You"; Gonsalves did an abstract, intriguing version of "Gone with the Wind," Terry an impeccable "Misty," Carter an elegant "I Can't Get Started," and Hodges a most inventive "Don't Blame Me."

Coleman Hawkins ended the medley with "September Song" (first chorus unaccompanied, his big sound filling the hall with warmth). Hodges, Carter, and Hawkins then rendered "C Jam Blues," each man telling his own story in front of the hardworking rhythm section.

Then it was the Ellington band's turn—and with a new program. Russell Procope's burnished, full-toned clarinet was featured on "Swamp Goo," the latest entry in the Ducal jungle series; in contrast, Jimmy Hamilton's sophisticated approach to the same instrument was showcased in an up-tempo swinger with pretty chords. For trombonist Lawrence Brown there was the appropriately romantic "Rue Bleu" and for Harry Carney's masterly baritone saxophone a beautiful "Chromatic Love Affair," a piece one immediately wanted to hear again.

After a sample of the standard Ellington—a brilliantly performed "Rockin' in Rhythm"—there was still another new piece, this one for Cootie Williams, who was introduced by Ellington as playing "the role of the shepherd who watches over the night flock." It was a piece in the manner of *Echoes of Harlem*, and Williams's majestic sound (mostly plungered, but also briefly open) and stately phrasing were something to hear.

Next it was guest time. Sims joined Gonsalves and Hamilton (on tenor this time) in an extended blowing session with long solos by each and closing rounds of fours. The band, aside from occasional punctuations, remained inactive, which was a bit disappointing.

But there was nothing disappointing about the two masters of the alto saxophone, Hodges and Carter, sharing solo honors on "Prelude to a Kiss" in the standard Ellington setting. Hodges, on home territory, had a slight edge, but after Carter plays this for a while, it will be hard to pick a winner. This masterpiece concluded the long first half of the concert. (According to Granz, there will also be Ellington showcases for Terry, Cat Anderson, and Hawkins as the tour progresses.)

Part two was devoted entirely to Ella Fitzgerald, who was backed by Ellington's band and her trio. It was readily evident that drummer Sam Woodyard made the band sound better than did Rufus Jones, though the latter had been most conscientious. Miss Fitzgerald was in rare form—even for her. Though slightly hoarse, she gave everything she had—which was plenty.

There wasn't an uninspired moment in the dozen songs she sang, which included a wondrously relaxed "Don't Be That Way," an emotion-charged "You've Changed," a leaping "It Don't Mean a Thing," and a witty and charming "Let's Do It."

But the climax was a fantastic version of "So Danco Samba," on which Miss Fitzgerald gave a lesson in the art of vocal improvisation and displayed a sense of time, a range of imagination, and a variety of timbres and sounds that were the equals of any master instrumentalist's. Her duet with Wood-yard, in which she imitated drum sounds and patterns, was a delightful and novel experience. It brought the audience to its feet. An encore was in order.

For that, Ellington reappeared to spell Jimmy Jones at the piano for a rousing "Cotton Tail." Gonsalves, who had played brilliantly all night, out-did himself in an extended exchange of eights and fours with Miss Fitzger-ald, topping off his performance with a scissor jump, and the night ended in a burst of joy.

(1967)

Phil Woods

Opportunities to hear Phil Woods in person are far too rare these days, so it was indeed a pleasure to see him leading his own quartet at a Jazz Interactions Sunday session.

On today's agonized (and often agonizing) jazz scene, Woods's playing comes as a ray of sunshine and sanity. He knows where he's at and isn't trying to prove anything, other than perhaps his desire and ability to communicate.

From the first ("What Is This Thing Called Love?" at medium-up tempo), the group struck a relaxed, swinging groove, sustained without let-down through three long sets. Everybody had ample room to solo, and there was a feeling of musicians coming together to play for their own pleasure and that of the audience.

Since this was not a permanent group, the material consisted mainly of staples. It was perhaps no coincidence that many of the tunes came from the Charlie Parker era.

Woods was inspired by Parker, and he is not ashamed of his ancestry. There are players who, in striving for originality, jettison what comes natu-rally, succeeding only in cramping whatever style they might have had. Happily, Woods is not among these, and because he is comfortable with his roots, he has achieved his own identity and become his own man within a great, lasting musical tradition.

He plays with conviction and fire, and with a beautiful, ringing, singing tone. His command of the horn is complete, his ideas concise and coherent (but also full of welcome surprises), and he knows the all-important secret of building a solo. And his flowing music has muscle and sinew as well as beauty; Woods is never strident, never maudlin, always tasteful. He is an improviser as well as a melodist, and his playing has shape and contour as well as harmonic interest and rhythmic suspense. Best of all, it possesses warmth and life.

Woods was in top form on Miles Davis's "So What?," taken at a crazy tempo that held together all the way. His relaxed phrasing on the melody would have pleased the composer; after that, he plowed into his long solo with rare balance between abandon and control. His "hollering" and rhythmic freedom indicated that he has not ignored recent jazz.

In a different mood, Woods shone on two ballad performances, "Lover Man" and "How Deep Is the Ocean?" On the former, his upper-register sound was lovely and perfectly controlled; he inserted a fitting quotation from "Parker's Mood" at the end. On "Ocean" his theme statement was superb; the ensuing improvisation was a masterpiece of construction, especially the second chorus, with an elegance of style reminiscent of Benny Carter.

"Too Marvelous for Words," one of Woods's favorite tunes, was given a joyful workout. Woods demonstrated his ability to tie together choruses into a continuous statement, and here he played a little catalog of phrases that are his alone (every great player has such a vocabulary).

His solo on "Groovin' High" had a rhythmic strut that brought to mind the infectious Fifty-second Street jump style of such altomen as Pete Brown and Don Stovall—happy memories.

Everybody had fun with a long version of the group's theme, "Doxy," at the end of the middle set, with all hands, pianist Hal Galper in particular, going into an "outside" bag.

Woods had excellent support throughout from Galper, Richard Davis, and Dotty Dodgion. Female drummers being something of a novelty, a number of customers registered initial surprise at seeing an attractive woman behind the drums. But Mrs. Dodgion's playing needed no visual aid. It is supposedly a compliment to say a female musician plays like a man; Mrs. Dodgion certainly had a swinging drive and confidence comparable to a male drummer, but her playing also had an intuitive quality that seemed distinctly feminine. With commendable modesty, she restricted her solo excursions to some good four-bar exchanges, taking only one long solo all night.

Davis played with his customary total command and presence. Of his several intriguing solos, perhaps the best was on "So What?" It was an index of bass history, from walking in four to some fabulous drones at the climax.

Galper is a promising young pianist, who, at present, hears more than he can play; i.e., his ideas are sometimes ahead of his fingers. But that is a positive quality. The obverse only leads to Peter Nero. Galper was excellent on "Ocean" and "Doxy."

For the two final selections, guests were invited to join the group. Randy Brecker, a young trumpeter with a bold, bright sound and good ideas, was impressive on an up-tempo "There Is No Greater Love" but committed a sin common among young players—his solo was far too long. Woods, who followed, showed him how to say what one has to say succinctly.

For the concluding piece, a vintage Parker line, valve trombonist-fluegelhornist Brian Bate joined. The tempo was too rough for him, but he managed to make a kind of impression by playing simultaneous riffs on his two horns. Musically more to the point was Davis's astonishing solo.

The Jazz Interactions Sunday Top of the Gate sessions, held in what has become, after numerous alterations, one of the most pleasant jazz rooms in the city, are commendably broading their approach. With Woods, they scored a touchdown.

(1967)

Ira Sullivan/Sonny Stitt

Ira Sullivan doesn't get a mention in *Modern Jazz: The Essential Records*, and there is but one passing reference (albeit a nice one, by Alun Morgan) to him in *Jazz on Records*. To be sure, his recorded output isn't huge, yet he can be heard on some fourteen LPs (six of them under his own name).

Ira has mastered all the saxophones and the flute, but his main horn is the trumpet. He is a phenomenal musician. I'd been vaguely aware of him through his work on two Red Rodney albums, and through my friends Ira Gitler and Don Schlitten, two walking, talking encyclopedias of bebop. But it wasn't until I came to Chicago in 1967 that I began to realize just how much there was to Ira Sullivan.

It was in Chicago, from 1952 through 1962, that Ira made his mark. Except for a brief journey to New York and other places with Art Blakey's Messengers in 1956, Chicago was his turf, and he remains a legend there.

Joe Segal, the promoter who has been a one-man bebop movement in the Windy City for more than twenty-five years, is his greatest booster, but just about every jazz musician there speaks of him with awe and admiration. Ira moved to Miami in '62, and the legend has continued to grow through periodic reports from visiting sitters-in and writers. Last year, Ira's first record date in a decade was released.

These comments are prompted by a recent visit to Miami (not, I regret to say, to bask in the sun, but to promote my new book). Though I was there a mere twenty-eight hours, I did manage to catch Ira. It was only the second time I'd heard him in the flesh (the first was in 1971, at the Kennedy Center Jazz Festival in Washington), and it was a joyful experience.

The setting was a newly opened and very pleasant jazz room in the Airliner Motel, operated by veteran disc jockey Joe Rico (to whom Stan Kenton long ago dedicated his "Jump for Joe"). Every visiting artist who doesn't bring his own group to the club has the good fortune to be backed by a house band that includes Ira. On this occasion, the guest was Sonny Stitt.

Of late, Sonny hasn't always been on the beam, but he was in fine form; with Ira on the stand, he had to be. He played mostly tenor, and Ira mostly trumpet, but there was also quite a bit of Sonny's alto, and some samples of Ira's soprano, the saxophone he's been favoring for the past ten years or so. The rhythm section was surprising (or perhaps not; there are first-class players in every American city of some size). Maybe I should have written "rhythm sections," since there were two pianists. They happen to be twin brothers: Tony and Dolph Castellano; look-alikes, but each with his own style. Don Koffman was on bass, and Steve Bagley on drums.

The musical fare included such standbys as "Groovin' High," "Lover Man," "Secret Love," and the blues, but there were surprises, too, such as a happy, swinging version of "I'm an Old Cowhand" (a result of Sonny having been presented with a beautiful ten-gallon hat by Tony Castellano on this, his closing night); a Stitt vocal on "Pennies from Heaven," with a good-natured takeoff on Louis; a gorgeous "Moonlight in Vermont"; and two farewell offerings, "Please Don't Talk About Me When I'm Gone" and "For All We Know." (You didn't know that Sonny is a sentimentalist at heart, did you?)

Ira's trumpet sound is full and strong; on more than one occasion, it brought to mind Fats Navarro. But he is an original, one of those rare players whose every note means something. He played a stunning chorus on "Lover Man," making use of the lower register in a manner seldom heard these days. Using a cup mute, he retained that big, singing sound in flowing, melodic solos on "Pennies" and "Talk" that positively gleamed. His eights and fours with Sonny became friendly duels in which the two elaborated on each other's inventions, especially on the fast blues, following one of Sonny's marathon displays of swing and stamina. The endings tended to become cliff-hangers. Sonny loves to "tag," and he is sly, trying to catch his companions off guard. A few times, Sonny broke up Ira so much that he couldn't catch him, but on "Groovin' High" the trumpeter took charge with a brilliant cadenza based on the classic Dizzy model, ending with a dazzling high note.

"Secret Love" was a tenor-soprano duet full of delights. Ira's solo, which contained very unusual and wholly original displacements of accents, was rhythmically free but maintained melodic continuity. Sonny, who thrives on competition, responded with a display of harmonic ingenuity, gobbling up the changes. His alto sound on "Lover Man" would have pleased both Johnny Hodges and Charlie Parker. This was top-drawer Stitt, and so was his long unaccompanied cadenza on "Know." Ira's half chorus on "Moon-light" was yet another gem. Tony Castellano held his own with a sparkling solo on the blues on which he uncorked some plunging bass passages worthy of Eddie Costa. He also inserted some delightful Basie touches in the riff ensembles.

The closing portion of the last set reflected the good feelings engendered by Sonny's week in Miami. A young boy (there with his father) had been treated to some saxophone lessons by Sonny, and reciprocated with a fancy saxophone stand. Sonny made a pleasant speech and offered "For All We Know." After he'd left the stand, Ira made a speech and dedicated "My Reverie" to Sonny. A soprano-piano duet (it can be heard on the aforementioned Horizon LP), it was an emotional conclusion to a happy night.

It was now nearly 3 a.m., and though there was to be a little party for Sonny, I had to catch an early flight and regretfully declined the invitation. As I was saying goodbye to Ira and the friendly management, a young saxophonist who'd dropped in after his gig at a local strip joint asked Ira which of his instruments he preferred to play.

"Trumpet," was the unhesitating reply. "That was my first instrument, and I picked up the saxophones primarily because it was easier to find work on them. As much as I enjoy playing them and the flute, the trumpet is the real challenge, and I always come back to it."

I hope Ira plays more trumpet on his next album, and that we won't have to wait another ten years for it. He is content to stay in Miami, which is that city's gain and everyone else's loss. Aside from his irregular work at the Airliner, he plays twice a week in a church (where he also sings in the choir), and he seems relaxed and happy. On the basis of what I heard that night and my previous knowledge of his work, I'd say without much hesitation that Ira Sullivan is one of the finest jazz players around today.

(1977)

Joe Turner

J oe Turner's month-long sojourn at the Cookery created quite a stir in the press. Whitney Balliett, John S. Wilson, and Gary Giddins heaped praise upon the big man in *The New Yorker*, the *New York Times*, and *The Village Voice*. As a result, Barney Josephson's pleasant Greenwich Village café did capacity business. Even on the coldest December third in New York history, people were standing on line waiting to get in.

Big Joe hasn't been in the best of health of late, but he looked just fine, and the dry weather was kind to his arthritis. He doesn't really need a microphone, and holds the gadget at a respectful distance from the source. Though he sings everything in the key of C, and what he sings is mostly familiar and almost all blues (the sole exception, "Corrine Corrina," was a close relative), his mastery within those limits is supreme. His ability to project that nasal, somewhat high-pitched yet undeniably masculine voice is awesome, and the fine gradations of inflection, phrasing, and pitch he employs to lend variety to the repeated lines are uncanny. His beat is stupendous.

His repertoire includes "Ain't Gonna Be Your Lowdown Dog No More," "I Took the Front Door In," "Cherry Red," "Gimme All You've Got," "Shake, Rattle and Roll," and "Stormy Monday Blues." To make sure that the message gets across, he usually repeats the first three stanzas after the piano and/or guitar solos, and unlike some practitioners, he doesn't swallow any of the words.

Joe's accompanists were Lloyd Glenn at the piano and Wayne Wright on guitar. Glenn, whom Turner brought along from Los Angeles, is just about the best conceivable replacement for old sidekick Pete Johnson. He is a splendid blues and boogie-woogie player, though unlike most specialists in that genre he is an all-around musician of considerable accomplishment. (Some readers may recall his arrangements for Don Albert's big band of the '30s.) He has a crisp, sure touch and a rock-steady, swinging beat, and is a skilled accompanist. Wright, perhaps best known for his recent stint with the Ruby Braff–George Barnes quintet, is a seasoned New York session man, and while this kind of work is new to him, he seemed quite at home in it already.

The two instrumentalists have a fifteen-minute set to themselves, in which Glenn offered "Old Time Shuffle," "After Hours," "Frankie and Johnny," and a rolling "Honky Tonk Train Blues," while Wright got into some different changes in an unaccompanied "Skylark." Then there is an intermission, after which Big Joe and the duo do some forty minutes. Joe's patter between numbers is an added delight. "I sound like grandpa's mule," he joked after having done some hollering. He gave Wright a special introduction, noting that "he's been playing with all these society people— Peggy Lee, Tony Bennett—and now we're trying to teach him to play the blues." He talked about having had Thanksgiving dinner with Lloyd at Wayne's home, listening to Fats Waller records while watching a football game on television with the sound off, and "talking all kinds of stuff." (Wayne told us it was a pleasure to watch the big man eat. "He earned that stomach," he said.)

Joe started his career as a singing bartender in Kansas City, and he still gives you the feeling that he is singing for his own enjoyment and to entertain his friends. ("He's so down-home, it's unbelievable," said Wayne.) Big Joe is one of the last of a vanishing breed, and it is good for the soul to have him around. We were not at all surprised to hear from Josephson that Joe will be back at the Cookery, this time for eight weeks, starting next March.

(1977)

Ornette Coleman

Ornette Coleman returned to his cradle of fame, the Five Spot, after a year's absence with a completely new group for a month's stand. The single most important fact that emerged from this occasion should give Coleman's detractors some food for thought: this was a wholly new group, but the music was unmistakably and undilutedly Ornette Coleman's personal brand of jazz. In other words, Ornette's music is a music with its own principles and its own logic, which can be conveyed to any musician in sympathy with its aims. Bobby Bradford's execution of unison passages with Ornette was no less symbiotic than Don Cherry's.

It was also obvious that Ornette had not been idle during his semihibernation. The sound, always the most immediately communicative element of any musician's playing, has become fuller and richer. And his technique (though unorthodox, it is a technique) has become more assured and reliable. It's no news that Coleman's playing is emotional, blues-based, and often marked by *vox humana* characteristics. Although he sometimes blows with almost overbearing intensity, Coleman knows dynamics and also maintains interest by varying the rhythmic accents within the phrase. Ferocious, hollering bursts of rapid, multi-noted passages alternate with calm, spacious, and often lyrical interludes. He knows how to build a solo. There is much melodic charm in his writing; the tunes are often reminiscent of Mexican mariachi songs. Bradford, a young trumpeter from Texas who worked with Coleman back home, plays a regular-sized trumpet and is an improvement over his predecessor in other respects as well. He solos only as long as he has something to say, and his work shows evidence of thoughtful lyricism and a sense of construction. He does, however, tend to rely too much on stock phrases and seemed to be holding back. Greater confidence will undoubtedly come with experience.

Bassist Jimmy Garrison, well established in more conventional jazz frameworks, seized the opportunity for greater freedom with enthusiasm and contributed some astonishingly bellicose bowed work, as well as supplying a big-toned, firm, and inventive background for the soloists. Drummer Charles Moffett also tackled his part with great zest and has a fine, infectious beat. On the whole, this group was more of a cohesive unit than previous versions of the Coleman quartet—more bent on staying together than being individually "interesting." Some of the wild freshness of the first days is gone, but in its place we have a more mature Coleman, set off to best advantage by sympathetic collaborators.

Structurally, Coleman's jazz seems a little too specialized, being an emotional rather than a formalistic phenomenon, to have widespread effect. The bar line, the given chord, and other such *seeming* restrictions are here to stay: jazz is what it is. But total, fearless experiments are not only permissible but necessary. What is perhaps more important is that the music of Ornette Coleman is often beautiful. It is a pity that some ears remain closed to that.

(1961)

Ornette Coleman at the Village Vanguard

Coleman never sounded better than he did at the Village Vanguard in his first public playing engagement in more than two years. The strikingly personal conception of this extraordinary musician has seemingly not undergone any radical changes, but it has matured and crystallized, has become at once more economical and more expressive, more controlled and more emotionally affecting.

On his opening number, an untitled ballad of compelling melodic strength that he performed on a metal alto (his plastic horn also was on the stand), Coleman played with impassioned lyricism and a big singing sound, his control of the instrument as remarkable as the lucid flow of his invention. There was sadness in his song, and joy as well, but more than anything, there was serenity—an aspect of expression that has become exceedingly rare in modern music.

Though the tempos ranged from slow and stately to fast and furious, the balladic mood was sustained throughout. Tempo changes and playing out of tempo are commonplace in so-called advanced jazz, but in the hands of lesser practitioners, such devices too often break the flow and mood of a piece. Coleman, with the near-intuitive aid of his accompanists, is able to make both gradual and abrupt adjustments of tempo without ever ceasing to maintain the swing so essential to jazz. He can do it because his phrases swing from within and because his sense of melodic continuity rarely fails.

There could be no greater contrast produced by one musician than the contrast between the almost classic and measured flow of that opening ballad and the near-frenzy of the violin passages during Coleman's third selection, on which he also played trumpet.

Between these extremes came a simply constructed up-tempo piece based on a repeated, riff-like phrase, on which Coleman again played alto exclusively. This performance, consisting almost entirely of runs, licks, and phrases from the jazz vocabulary—mostly Coleman's own but also including a quote from "All God's Chillun Got Rhythm"—was wholly invigorating and played with tremendous drive.

Coleman attacks (there is no better word) the violin with intense concentration. His playing cannot be judged in terms of conventional violin technique. For one thing, he plays the instrument left-handed—but without reversing the order of the strings. For another, his bowing technique is unorthodox—a rapid, circular arm motion that almost enables him to touch all four strings simultaneously.

Coleman rarely plays one string at a time. He produces a cascade of sounds—sometimes surprisingly pleasing to the ear, sometimes almost abrasive, but never with the scratchy uncertainty characteristic of incompetent violinists. He seems to have tuned the instrument in his own manner, but it is, so to speak, in tune with itself.

Coleman may not know the rules, but he knows the point of the game. The music he produces on the violin is idiomatically his; there are patterns and passages reminiscent of his work on alto. And he swings ferociously. His playing might best be described as a mixture of Stuff Smith at his wildest and an old-time country fiddler at a way-out hoedown.

His trumpet playing, on the other hand, left this listener a bit cold. For the most part, he stays in the upper range of the horn, which gives his playing a high-pitched quality that is not aided by his uncertain articulation, possibly caused by mouthpiece problems. The character of the music, again, is strictly Coleman, but rather jagged and fragmentary in expression. When, on occasion, he descended to the middle range, his tone was round and appealing.

Both David Izenzon and Charles Moffett were with Coleman at his last public appearance at Town Hall in December 1963. Throughout his hiatus, they have remained in touch with him, playing, talking, growing together. Their sympathy and understanding for Coleman's music is deep, and the trio at its best functions almost as one organism.

The sidemen are very different from each other.

Izenzon, classically trained, has phenomenal technique and an uncanny ear. He can run all over his bass, plucking, strumming (sometimes with both hands on open strings), sliding, and bowing with truly remarkable tone and pitch. His unison work with Coleman on the opening ballad and his bowing in fast tempo behind Coleman's violin created unique shapes and sounds. His solos were engrossing, his time solid and firm.

Moffett isn't polished, isn't slick, but he has more important qualities. He is solid as a rock, and he knows where the music is going. At times, he sounds refreshingly "old-fashioned," playing press rolls and rim shots, even banging on a cow bell. Some time ago his dynamics left something to be desired, but now he has learned to control them. His occasional solos were bouncy and engaging, and he never covered up his teammates.

As interesting as Coleman's excursions on the other instruments may be, one can hypothesize that the restlessness engendered in a musician as creative as Coleman by a long period of private or semi-private music-making may have led him to wrestle with these other horns but that the return to professional activity will result in an increasing emphasis on the alto saxophone, unquestionably his best means of expression.

Whatever he chooses to do, it is good to have Coleman back. We hope he will not withdraw again. His presence is needed: first and most important, because his music is strong and fresh and joyous and good to hear; second, because it may have a salutary effect on the "new thing." But the jazz community must not allow itself again to make of Coleman's music a political issue or a critical football. Such strategies, however sincerely motivated, erect unwarranted barriers in the minds of potential and actual listeners and obscure the music. Coleman, after all, did not develop his unique and beautiful music in order to "revolutionize" jazz; he did it because he had to, because that was the way he heard and felt it.

Some may like his music, others may not, but all owe him the respect of allowing him to be himself, not a symbol of something he may or may not be part of. Ornette Coleman is a musician, not a movement; a man, not an abstraction.

(1965)

Mary Lou Williams/Cecil Taylor

"Mary Lou Williams and Cecil Taylor Embraced" was the optimistic title of an unusual experiment that took place recently at Carnegie Hall. It was Mary's idea, and she deserves great credit for intrepidity. But the embrace was a precarious one, executed across a musical chasm.

Any two-piano collaboration is dependent for success on a great deal of give-and-take by both artists, but on this occasion neither party seemed able to adjust to the other, though it must be said that Mary Lou seemed to be trying hard.

On the other hand, it was at her insistence that a rhythm section (Bob Cranshaw, electric bass; Mickey Roker, drums) was brought into play at intervals during both halves of the concert, though Taylor, according to inside information, had stated that he was unwilling to play with such "support."

During the first half—some forty minutes long—it often seemed as if the two pianists were simply playing at the same time on the same stage, nothing more. There were moments of conjunction, and these were exhilarating, but might have been aleatory rather than premeditated. Due to a quirk in amplification, it was difficult to sort out the two players: on one side of the hall, Taylor seemed to dominate; on the other, Williams was on top. This was rectified for the second portion, which in any case came off better. Instead of the dense and unceasing onslaught of notes that characterized part one (momentarily relieved by some sprightly ragtime sounds from Williams, soon obscured by Taylor's fusillades), there were prolonged periods of gentle, lyrical playing by both pianists. But this piece, too, ended in disarray, and Mary Lou exited abruptly after a heavy Taylor barrage, thus ending a noble experiment that failed.

Norman Granz recorded the concert, and it is entirely possible that stereo separation will enable listeners to sort out the two piano parts properly. Certainly I would want to hear this music again, if only for the opening passages of the second half and those moments in the first when, after the rhythm section's entrance, Cecil began to play strong blues chords, subsequently engaging in a percussive dialogue with Roker. And there will also be Mary Lou's encores (Cecil did not reappear, despite the chanting of his name by a considerable portion of the audience), including a lovely, reflective unaccompanied "I Can't Get Started."

Could it have worked better? I doubt it, considering Cecil's iconoclasm. I think he tried; I know Mary Lou did. But each, to a greater or lesser degree, lives within a well-defined musical spectrum, and the two are just too far apart to merge in a manner that makes musical sense. To put it more bluntly, Mary Lou will always swing no matter what she plays, while Cecil's rhythmic impact derives from anything but a 4/4 pulse. If they had been able to meld rhythmically, the boundaries of individual style might have melted away, but this was impossible. Come to think of it, the record might work best if heard one channel at a time.

(1977)

FESTIVALS AND EVENTS

Newport 1960

I missed the first three Newport Jazz Festivals, but from 1957 on I was on hand every year, through 1971, after which Newport morphed into Newport–in–New York and its successors, Kool and JVC, all of which I've also managed to catch. But after the move, the festival became an entirely different event, with multiple venues instead of a single stage, and complete coverage by one observer became impossible. I did write about almost all the "real" Newports I attended, more often than not at great length. We did consider a Newport section for the book but decided that it would add up to too much minutiae to hold a reader's interest. What follows is a sample, of particular interest because 1960 was the year of the first so-called riot—a disturbance that pales compared to what happened eleven years later, yet at the time left the future of the event in serious doubt. Of course it survived, but it should be noted, for the record, that the 1961 festivities were produced not by George Wein, still persona non grata, *but by Sid Bernstein, better known as the man who brought the Beatles to America.*

It isn't very likely that Newport will ever again be the site for a jazz festival. Unless Louis Lorillard is a man who can work miracles, the seventh Newport Jazz Festival, cut off *in medias res* by the boorish and boozy products of progressive education, was the last. It would be a pity if history, in its preoccupation with the riots and their causes, should fail to put on record that this seventh Newport Festival also was one of the best.

. . .

The afternoon programs at Newport have always been labors of love. In 1960, they were produced by Dr. Marshall Stearns. The second afternoon was pleasant, the fourth had to be cancelled. But the first and third rank among the most pleasurable, well-planned, and interesting jazz shows of our times.

Even the weather seemed to be against Newport in 1960. On Friday, July 1, gray skies and a brisk breeze held the threat of rain. A small but attentive crowd was on hand when Rudi Blesh, the old stalwart, beard fluttering in the breeze, bestrode the stage to introduce Danny Barker and his Strolling Trio and pianists Eubie Blake, Donald Lambert, and Willie "The Lion" Smith.

It began with a demonstration of stride piano by a master of the style. Don Lambert looked as abstracted and unassuming as ever when Blesh gave him his cue. He arose, gravely and deliberately, to make his way to the piano. That instrument was a first-rate concert grand with the capacity to respond fully to the Lambert touch. Lambert played "Sweet Lorraine"; first straight, then with the accents of Harlem. It was an utterly relaxed performance without fireworks, but when Lambert got up to take his bow, the applause was strong enough to elicit a swift promise from Mr. Blesh: "We'll hear more from Donald Lambert." And we surely did.

But first there was Eubie Blake. Eubie Blake, composer of "Charleston Rag" (1899), "I'm Just Wild About Harry" (1921), and "Memories of You" (1930) is, at seventy-seven, a charming old gentleman with a razor-sharp memory and ten nimble fingers. He reminisced for a while: about the genesis of ragtime; about his great Broadway success *Shuffle Along*; about how "Harry" was originally conceived as a waltz. Eubie has been everywhere and he knew everybody; we could have listened to him for hours. Among the things we learned from Eubie that afternoon was the not uninteresting fact that one of his early influences was the Hungarian operetta composer Franz Lehar.

Eubie didn't just talk. He sat down and played his own composition "Black Keys on Parade," and played and sang a pop hit from 1909, "Lovie Joe," in the style of the period. The vocal gave more than a hint about the origins of Al Jolson. The difference is that Jolson, a great showman, was corny. Eubie is not. His piano playing is (in his own words) not what it used to be—but that is still plenty more piano than an ordinary pianist could come up with. Eubie has beautiful hands with long, slender, and graceful fingers. He isn't a stride pianist; his style is more elaborate and flowery than James P. Johnson's or Donald Lambert's. But he swings, and has a powerful touch. What the years have taken in accuracy he makes up for in enthusiasm. And there is a fine, subtle sense of humor in his approach.

Danny Barker is another great raconteur. He can tell a story on the banjo, or on the guitar—and he can tell a story in lyrics or in prose. His role at Newport was that of banjoist, lyricist, vocalist, and leader of the "strolling" trio. Strolling bands were generally made up of more than three musicians; the instrumentation, while mostly strings, was quite variable; their habitat the streets of the Negro quarters of cities large and small. This reincarnation of an almost vanished brand of folk-jazz had Danny on banjo, Bernard Addison on mandolin, and Al Hall on bass. Addison, a fine guitarist, had purchased a mandolin especially for this occasion, and he was much concerned about the sound. "Could you hear me all right?" he asked after the concert. We could, and the sound was delightful. Al Hall's swinging bass laid a firm foundation. But the star was Danny Barker. He opened "as requested" with "Take Me Out to the Ballgame"; first chorus sung and played straight, then with swing and some special Barker lyrics. "Muskrat Ramble," too, had a new set of words. They were fabulous, telling an animal story in the vein of the Uncle Remus fables. Danny's wit is steeped in authentic southern Negro lore, with a special accent: that of an educated, highly aware and much traveled artist who digs everything that goes on— around him and in the world at large. Danny is also a master banjoist. The banjo is not a rewarding instrument; its highly percussive sound doesn't blend well in ensembles. But in the hands of Mr. Barker it becomes as expressive as the guitar. "The World Is Waiting for the Sunrise" is Danny's showpiece; it starts off slow, builds to a whirlwind tempo and winds up with a flurry of notes. It's good fun and good music. Even more fun was "Tiger Rag," which features Danny playing the banjo behind his back.

A few isolated drops of rain had begun to fall, but everybody made a wish, and the crisis passed. A large Navy helicopter circled Freebody Park and temporarily drowned out the voice of Mr. Blesh. When the noise had subsided, Blesh quipped: "Well, the Navy closed up Storyville—I hope they don't have any ideas of continuing the tradition." Moments later the helicopter circled the scene at Cliff Walk Manor, down the road a piece, where the secessionists were holding *their* jazz festival. Charlie Mingus, who was on the stand, pointed to the whirlybird and shouted: "That's Lorillard!" Well, there's nothing like a little persecution complex to keep a man happy.

Now it was time for the pièce de résistance. Donald Lambert, who had been sitting with Eubie and The Lion; sitting with them and yet sitting by himself—for Lambert, in a way similar to yet utterly unlike that of Thelonious Monk, is a man who seems to carry his own self-contained universe around with him—Donald Lambert got up and walked to the piano. Rudi Blesh talked about "ragging the classics," told us that this was one of Lambert's specialties, and introduced "Anitra's Dance." Grieg never had it so good. It was Lambert's day. He had a good piano, he was at Newport, and there were a couple of good piano players in the house. In jazz as in the other arts, there is the mediocre, the good, and then there is the great. Words can describe many things, but in music only the ear can define greatness. In Lambert's case, it is a matter of touch, of authority, of conception—a sense of form of the highest order that infuses everything he plays—and perhaps most important, of beauty. "Anitra's Dance" is not a great piece of music, and we have all heard it innumerable times. Lambert, without violating it or breaking it apart, transformed it. "Tea for Two" is Lambert's showpiece. He uses it as a basis for displaying a special talent: the superimposition of countermelodies—"Tea for Two" goes on in one hand while the other plays a medley of standards ranging from "April Showers" to "Because of You." It's all done with excellent taste, subtle humor and outstanding technique. But as music it didn't compare to the next item, "Liza," played way "up" and with infectious swing. Lambert's left hand is a phenomenon—and it is a small hand. One noted jazz enthusiast and critic always complains that Lambert doesn't play tenths. Without tenths, he seems to imply, it's not real stride piano. Well, "Liza" made even him forget about the tenths.

They wouldn't let Lambert go, but it was time for The Lion. Willie is a temperamental performer, and sometimes his temperament gets in the way of his judgment. It had been planned for him to play one of his own inimitable pieces, "Morning Air," or "Echoes of Spring." But no. If Lambert could jazz the classics, so could Willie. So after some wonderful chitchat from The Lion, who with his inevitable cigar, straw hat, cane, and vest, is a superb entertainer and a personality in the best sense of that word, we were treated to Chopin's "Polonaise Militaire," à la Willie. It was a mistake. Lambert had made him nervous; not just the sheer impact of Lambert's prowess, but Eubie's delight and constant nudging of Willie while Lambert played. And alas, it wasn't one of Willie's good days. The polonaise came out as Polish ham. Undaunted, Willie went on to the most spectacular of the cutting contest pieces, "Carolina Shout." Guts he has. But the hands wouldn't quite do what Willie had in mind. Finally, wisdom came to the fore. The Lion did a vocal rendition of "Ain't Misbehavin'," in that lovable singsong style of his, and retired to the bench to the sound of warm applause.

Lambert returned and, not being a man who gloats over minor triumphs, played a gentle and perfectly conceived Waller medley. And after that, from his vast repertoire of James P. Johnson classics, he trotted out "You Can't Do What My Last Man Did," and the old master's spirit was never better served.

Then, for a special treat, Eubie and Lambert got together in a four-handed version of "Charleston," joined in the last chorus by the strolling trio. Twenty fingers flying; and of course they had to do it again, this time with Willie aboard—first reluctantly, then joining in the spirit of fun. Willie remained to pay tribute to the legendary Tim Brymn with a piece entitled "Sparkles." It would have been better if Willie had done one of his own pieces. "Sparkles" was nothing more than a variation on Grieg's "Morning," however well played.

As was right and fitting, the star returned to finish it off. There could have been more, but the rain was beginning to fall in earnest now, and all we got from Donald Lambert was "I Know That You Know." All? It was plenty.

Donald Lambert is certainly the greatest living exponent of stride piano, if not more. Eubie Blake put it right. Shaking Lambert's hand, and beaming like a youngster, he told Don: "You're one of the greatest damn piano players I ever heard—and I'm seventy-seven years old—I've heard them *all!*"

If there is any justice in the world of jazz, we will be hearing more from Donald Lambert in the near future.

Friday night, the rains came, and we got soaked to the skin digging Louis Armstrong. We were in the best company conceivable, on stage and off, and loved every minute of it. How could one catch cold with that much warmth around? Saturday afternoon rolled along, and the clouds, gone from the skies, were gathering elsewhere. There was an intangibly ominous mood in the streets. Yet, when Ruby Braff, Pee Wee Russell, John Kenny (bass), Buzzy Drootin, and George Wein swung into "Fine and Mellow" as a tribute to Billie Holiday, things were in the groove again for a while. Ruby remains himself: true to the jazz he loves; warm, full-toned, and seemingly undaunted by capricious fortune. Pee Wee is a unique musician. It is always good to see him and to hear him; somehow, he always manages to surprise. This was, praise the Lord, no Dixieland group. They played "Rosetta," "Mean to Me" and "Three Little Words," swingers all. The groove was not unlike that of the wonderful Frankie Newton's Bluebird session—warm and swinging. Much was due to the presence of Buzzy Drootin, who is a great drummer. He reminds of Davey Tough—they are about the same size—in his solid swing and in his ability to get into any kind of jazz groove. He has big ears and a big beat.

As for Mr. Wein, he has been subjected to a good deal of unfair criticism. It's easy to see why—there aren't many people on his side of the jazz fence who play an instrument well enough to appear on the other side as well. George has improved a great deal in the past couple of years. He is not much more than competent, but competent he is. This was the first time he played at Newport, and he needn't apologize. It is true that he occasionally sits in where he isn't welcomed with open arms, but he isn't the first cat to do that. It's only that the other guys can't say no to him very well. It would be nice if the gentlemen of the press could forget the sour grapes and judge George Wein, the pianist, as just that and forget about his other roles. And perhaps this is as good a time as any to state that the accusations leveled against Wein by Messrs. Mingus and Roach *in re* Jim Crow are just so much hogwash.

After Ruby & Co. came the Newport Youth Band, which has become an amazingly professional aggregation. It's a good band, with plenty of spirit. The arrangements, while not outstandingly original and mostly in a safe modern Basie groove, are much better than the unfortunate pretensions of a few years ago. There are good soloists in the band, and the trumpet section is a killer. On this occasion, Cannonball Adderley joined sixteen-year-old Andy Marsala in an Ernie Wilkins original called "Party Line," and the kid more than held his own. It is to be hoped that the band will survive the aftereffects of the riots. Some good musicians are being incubated here, and credit goes to bandmaster Marshall Brown, who knows how to discipline the kiddies without making them lose the swing.

Also on the bill Saturday was the Herbie Mann sextet: flute, vibes, and a Machito-styled rhythm section. In their own way, they swing—but we'll take Frank Wess or James Moody for our flute diet (small doses, please); Hamp or Red Norvo or Bags on vibes, and Machito for the Afro-Cuban jive. The popularity of this group has always been a puzzle to us. They never get into a *jazz* groove, and convey to these ears no emotional message whatever. The rhythm moves—but on top there is only twitter and chatter. Strictly for stereo bugs.

Came Sunday. The beer cans had been swept away. The town, bathed in brilliant sunshine for the first time since Thursday afternoon, seemed almost deserted. All the undesirables had been chased out. At the Viking Hotel, festival headquarters, small groups of insiders awaited the outcome of a meeting of the city council. Rumors and guesses were flying. George Wein looked like a man who has seen a ghost. At last the word came: Sunday night and all of Monday had been cancelled, but the city fathers would allow the afternoon session to take place.

That afternoon, perhaps the last chapter in Newport's jazz saga, was appropriately an afternoon of blues. And what blues! Langston Hughes as narrator and master of ceremonies. Muddy Waters and his band. John Lee Hooker. Sam Price. Al Minns and Leon James. And Willie Thomas and Butch Paige, an extra-special treat.

A sober audience gathered in Freebody Park that afternoon. It was also, ironically, the largest audience ever assembled at a Newport afternoon concert. For once, the press and insiders were outnumbered by the general public. The concert began without formal announcements, other than an explanation from Hughes that Sammy Price, who had been reported unable to get through the blockade, would be replaced by Otis Spann, Muddy Waters's pianist, as demonstrator of the various blues forms.

The blues began with Muddy Waters, who sang a plain and basic 12-bar blues. Muddy and his band were dressed in their Sunday best; Muddy and Otis Spann in black suits (Muddy with a sharp pair of black-and-white shoes); the rest of the band in their neat beige uniforms: James Cotton on amplified harmonica, Pat Hall on guitar, "Andrew" on bass, and Francis Clay at the drums. Muddy sang one; then he walked off and let the boys take over. Otis Spann played a boogie; he played "How Long" and he played "St. Louis Blues." Otis Spann is quite a pianist. Again, the superior quality of the instrument at his disposal may have had something to do with it—or perhaps it was the atmosphere. Whatever it was, Spann dug in with both hands, playing a rolling, rocking blues piano with a way-back beat— blues, pure blues. No gospel borrowings here, no jivey phrases—just bottom blues. Langston Hughes asked Spann to play "about twelve bars" of "How Long," but Otis played four choruses. Perhaps he didn't understand; it is more likely, though, that he felt that 12 bars wouldn't tell much of a story. He was right, and Hughes got the message. The narration was excellent: never condescending, and informed with a true respect for the performers. Hughes is a poet, an educated man, but he has found no reason to reject the better part of his heritage or to patronize its bearers.

For "St. Louis Blues," Leon James and Al Minns, the superb dance team whose lecture-demonstration of jazz dance history was one of the high spots of last year's festival, were added. They performed, solo and in tandem, with humor, ease, and grace. The kind of dancing they did is akin to contemporary rock and roll, but devoid of any trace of vulgarity. It isn't even suggestive—rather than suggesting, it *is*, period.

For a taste of folk blues, Langston Hughes introduced John Lee Hooker. No showmanship here. Just a man on stage with his guitar. Hooker opened with a blues about a girl named Molly; a good chick, but he didn't treat her right. How many times has that story and its opposite been told in the blues? It is an eternal story, and when it is told as well as John Lee Hooker tells it, it is always new. Hooker did five numbers in all, but had us so entranced that we didn't make notes of the titles. One was about a flood in a small Mississippi town, Tupelo; it was a declamatory blues—half talking, half singing—and it described the essential, unchangeable facts of human suffering without a trace of sentimentality or false pathos. The song was as basic as the event it described. And while this was Newport, and a stage, and a fine summer afternoon with everybody there well fed and not wanting for any of the necessities of life, the experience of hearing Hooker's story was immediate and natural. It carne across without barriers. Another blues, "I Wish (That You Were Here with Me)," was about loneliness and didn't require any translation either. Throughout, Hooker's guitar served as a second voice, underscoring the message and keeping the rhythm going.

One wished he would have played his unique brand of amplified guitar, with which he seems more at home. But that was a concession to the archeologists, who believe that old-fashioned equals authentic. Hooker was the real thing. His voice is essentially a soft one, and he uses understatement to a greater extent than other contemporary blues singers. For contrast, he will break out with an occasional shout or holler, which becomes all the more effective in this restrained context.

After Hooker, who, authentic as he is, also is a professional, came the surprise of the afternoon. Butch Paige, eighty-four years old, was born in Mississippi but now lives in Florida. He plays the violin and sings. His partner, Willie Thomas, is a mere youngster of fifty, also from Mississippi, who plays the twelve-string guitar and sings. Neither is a professional musician, but they have played for country dances and get-togethers all their lives. Thomas, who is a lay preacher, was taught to play and sing by Paige. Paige is tall, white-haired, and mahogany-colored. He wore a gray suit and a panama hat. Thomas is very short and very dark and was dressed, as becomes a preacher, all in black: black suit, black tie, and a large, wide-brimmed black hat. The guitar seemed as large as he; Paige's fiddle seemed small and frail in his hands. There was on hand a professor, a folklorist, who had discovered these two and brought them to the attention of Dr. Stearns and Mr. Hughes. He introduced them, and we were off.

Paige and Thomas began with a blues, "Woke up this mornin' with my shaw-nuff on my mind." No one present had ever seen or heard anything like these two. Paige's fiddle (which he held, alley style, on his chest) swung like crazy. It had some kinship with hillbilly fiddle and some relation to the violin but seemed like an entirely new instrument. Thomas, who sang lead, strummed his guitar with such intensity that it seemed at times as if the guitar played *him*. His voice, rather high-pitched and thin, was clear and had plenty of carrying power. Paige, who sang the responses like instrumental fill-ins, had a much deeper and rougher voice, which contrasted perfectly with his partner's. That the two of them had worked together for years was evident; their music seemed wholly spontaneous, yet they never got in each other's way. The response of the audience was electrifying, and if the two had been nervous at the start they warmed up instantly. Thomas looked out from under his brim with an intense gaze; so far he hadn't cracked a smile. The old man, on the other hand, was smiling broadly and benevolently; he didn't have a whole lot of teeth, but his smile was beautiful. The professor introduced the next number, which was a spiritual. But no sooner had he gotten through than Thomas began to speak. His voice didn't need amplification—it was the voice of a man accustomed to addressing crowds. He spoke loudly, clearly, and distinctly. "How do you do," he said. "Perhaps you people won't understand me too well. I'm from down South, you know.

But I want to tell you something about this next song and how it got its name." And he did. "Pick Up the Slack and Hew to the Line" takes its imagery from construction work, and Thomas drew a parable between building a straight road and living a straight life. It was a little sermon, and he meant every word of it. At the end, when the applause came warmly and spontaneously, he flashed a quick smile. Now he was convinced that the audience was laughing with him, not at him. The spiritual turned out to be a fast, rocking piece that illuminated the roots of contemporary gospel singing; the rhythm was there, but the thick harmonization had not as yet come in. The next number, "Hen Cackle," was a barn dance and featured Paige's fiddle. It was very similar to hillbilly dance music, but purer and with more swing. Paige and Thomas wound up with another spiritual, the famous "He's Got the Whole World in His Hand," again done faster than is customary, and "we've got some different words of our own in there." We wanted more, but in the meantime the lost Sammy Price had arrived, so our friends begged off to an ovation. It is rumored that Paige and Thomas will be recorded, probably on Folkways. We hope so, indeed. One would be hard put to get closer to the roots than this, and there is something very refreshing about such roots.

Sammy Price came on to play some good, rocking Texas boogie, accompanied by drummer Dave Pochonet, an unlikely but adequate entry in this congregation. Lafayette Thomas, a wild-haired young guitarist and singer who is a discovery of Sammy's, sang a blues, "Things I Used to Do," in a style not unlike B. B. King's, and played some very metallic but good guitar. Sammy also brought along Miss Betty Gennett, a very pretty young lady who unfortunately couldn't sing too well. But she looked sweet, so everybody gave her a nice hand.

Now it was Muddy Waters's time. Muddy works. He came on with "I've Got My Brand on You," followed it up with "Baby Please Don't Go" (don't see how she could have after that); "Soon Forgotten"; a rocking, vehement "Gonna Put a Tiger in Your Tank"; a tribute to Big Bill Broonzy, "I Feel So Good"; and finally, the climactic "I've Got My Mojo Working," which called for an encore. Muddy sang all kinds of blues—these are city blues, but with a difference—mostly about love: sad love, happy love, lost love, tender love, violent love, exasperated love. To say that Muddy has a beat would be an understatement: he has you rocking before you even know it. Once or twice he did a little dance, a few time-steps; sometimes he played his guitar and sometimes he just sang. His band backed him to perfection: Spann's rolling piano, Cotton's moaning harmonica (he came on like a tiger in a few solo spots), the hum of the guitar and Fender bass, and Clay's superb, steady drums. (We'd like to hear Clay with a jazz band.) Muddy had his mojo working that afternoon, no doubt about it.

Now it was jam session time. Everybody got on stage, Muddy gave a downbeat, and while Leon and Al danced and the singers formed a swaying line, everybody took a turn singing two choruses of blues. Little Jimmy Rushing, who had been scheduled for Monday night, had come up early and was in the audience. He was persuaded to join in. Sammy Price turned out to be a pretty good singer. Even Betty Gennett sounded fair, and Dave Pochonet beat it out on one of Clay's cymbals. Butch Paige's fill-ins on violin were perfectly timed. It was a happy session.

But Newport was not to end on a happy note. The bad news was now made official. Willis Conover, the voice of Newport, who has done such an excellent job of emceeing all the festivals, came on to make his final announcement. Conover is a sincere man, and he was visibly shaken. His farewell speech was not without bitterness, and justly so. It was the end of Newport 1960, and perhaps of Newport jazz. But not yet: when the bad news broke, Langston Hughes was moved to write a blues, the "Goodbye Newport Blues." He wrote it in the press tent, on the back of a Western Union telegram blank, and gave it to Otis Spann, who made up a melody to go with the words. And after Conover's statement, with everybody still on stage, Otis Spann began to play a minor blues, and the rhythm joined in. Then Spann began to sing, in a nasal, mournful voice: "It was a sad, sad day at Newport. . . ." It was the perfect ending.

When it was all over, and the crews of workmen had begun to strip the tenting and take apart the equipment, we spotted a familiar figure standing inside the press tent.

Miff Mole is sixty-two years old; his health hasn't been too good in recent years. And work has hardly been abundant. His contribution to jazz history is well remembered by musicians and by those in the know, but to the larger audience his name is hardly a household word. This year Miff Mole had been asked to Newport, to play—not in the afternoon but on the more glamorous Sunday evening program—with exposure to radio, TV, and perhaps recordings.

Early Sunday morning, not having heard the news, Miff Mole, with his cane and his heavy trombone case, boarded the bus for Newport. Miff arrived at Freebody Park after the blues concert. He tried to find John Hammond, but all the big shots were off to a board of directors meeting. The musicians had packed up and gone. A few stray writers and photographers with a sense of history remained.

"Do you know where I can reach John Hammond?" Miff asked us. We didn't know. We offered our inane condolences.

"I've been practicing for weeks for this thing," Miff Mole said. He had misplaced his cigarettes and apologetically asked us for one. We had some, but on this sad afternoon we were surrounded by nonsmokers, and both matchless from the wastes of the wind.

"My lip is in good shape; whatever that means now," Miff said. "You don't know where I can get hold of John Hammond?"

Mitch Miller walked by, and we collared him.

"John's at a meeting right now," said Miller. We introduced him to Miff.

"You don't remember me, do you," Miff said.

"Oh, sure I do. Of *course*," said Miller, and produced the phone number for Miff. Then he was off to supervise the demolition. An unhappy job for Mitch, who had persuaded CBS to take a bigger-than-ever slice of direct broadcasts from Newport this year. Now they were sitting pretty, with sold time and no music.

Miff Mole is a proud man. Since no one seemed concerned about his presence, he could take himself home.

"I'll take the bus back, I think," said Miff. The Newport bus station is a good ways from Freebody Park. And on that sad, sad Sunday in Newport, cabs were not so easy to procure.

"I'd been looking forward to this," Miff said. He said it like a man to whom looking forward to things had become a rare event, but he wasn't sorry for himself. Jack Bradley found Miff a cab, and he went back to New York with his good lip, his heavy, old-fashioned trombone case, and his cane.

(1960)

One Night in Birdland

Would you like to spend a night at Birdland in the company of Charlie Parker and his Giants? Hop aboard the musical time machine and take a trip you won't soon forget. You'll hear an hour and a half of some of the greatest jazz ever captured by a recording device, just as it happened one night in 1950—a precious moment of living time preserved for posterity.

Jazz is the most ephemeral of arts, created in the inspiration of the moment, here and gone. While thousands of hours of the music have been made permanently reproducible through the miracle of recording, they are as a drop in the ocean compared to all the music that has been played.

Most, by far, of the jazz that has been recorded was made in the studio; for the record, so to speak. But from about 1930 on, at first rarely, then with increasing frequency, bits and pieces of live performances have been captured, and these are of immense help in rounding out our comprehension of the music's past. Initially, these were so-called airshots (home recordings of broadcasts) or airchecks (official radio recordings for reference purposes).

Because the equipment—a 78-rpm disc recorder—was cumbersome and primitive, there were few location recordings, but when first wire then tape recording came on the market in the late 1940s, these began to proliferate. (The great exception to this generalization, of course, was Jerry Newman, who brought his equipment to important Harlem jazz spots in 1941. God bless him.)

There is a big difference between music captured live and music made in the studio. To be sure, there have been spontaneous studio happenings. But the fact that you are making a record and that you can work out and polish and re-do what you aim to set down creates a mind-set different from the one operative during a public performance. One isn't necessarily "better" than the other, just different. And in the period we're dealing with here, there was another significant distinction. Until the advent of long-playing records, a studio performance was limited to slightly more than three or at most nearly five minutes.

Thus, most of Charlie Parker's studio recordings feature him in solos of a few choruses, a fact that has led some misguided historians to claim that he seldom played long solos. His live recordings tell a different story, though even they haven't captured the kind of really stretched-out playing he occasionally indulged in, mainly at jam sessions. One must bear in mind, however, that in Parker's heyday, which is to say at the acme of bebop, jazz players did not practice the kind of marathon soloing that we associate with a John Coltrane. Bop was highly concentrated music, packing a lot of drama and vitality into the basic framework of variations on a 32- or 12-bar theme. So listen well.

In 1950, Charlie Parker was at the peak of his popularity. Late in 1949, he had made his first recordings with strings, including his own favorite side and only near-hit, "Just Friends." The critics, then and now, frowned on the string things, considering them lapses into commercialism, but to Bird, they were a dream come true. It is undeniable that he played magnificently with the strings, reaching a new audience with those records.

On December 15, 1949, he was present at the opening of a New York nightclub named for him, Birdland. Located on Broadway between Fifty-second and Fifty-third streets, it was a nicely appointed basement room, decorated at first with suspended bird cages containing a variety of feathered creatures. But the poor birds soon died from smoke inhalation and air-conditioning, and were replaced by not-so-terrific portraits of jazz greats hung along the walls.

Like its direct spiritual ancestor, the Royal Roost (four blocks further down Broadway), Birdland was, in a sense, a slice of uptown transplanted. Most of the staff was black, the menu featured polite soul food (no chitterlings, but chicken in the basket), and the clientele was well integrated. On Fifty-second Street, at least until the later war years, black patrons were an exception. But the move west, which coincided with the rise of bop, changed the complexion of jazz clubs.

Owned by Morris Levy, who with his partner Ralph Watkins had changed the Roost from restaurant to jazz club, Birdland catered to the night people. For people watchers, the Christmas–through–New Year stand by Count Basie's band was prime time. During this season the club was always packed, with everything from hustlers to genuine celebrities, and, as Fats Waller put it, "the joint was jumping."

A special feature of the club (as it had been of the Roost) was the "bleacher" section, stage right from the bandstand and adjacent to the long bar. Here, impecunious customers could perch all night, required only to pay the door charge, but able to procure drinks from the bar if desired. It was a treat for young fans short on cash and for many old-timers as well, and you could hear and see better than from many a table toward the back of the room.

Table service at Birdland was brisk. The waiters did not encourage nursing of drinks and were not always polite about it. A night at a table could empty one's pockets, but I certainly didn't mind going for broke on the occasion when I found myself seated next to Ava Gardner's party and was favored with several dazzling smiles.

The master of ceremonies was the redoubtable Pee Wee Marquette, a shrill-voiced, self-assertive midget of indeterminate age. He'd been in show business all his life, was an expert at screening out undesirables, and extracted a fee from the sidemen in the bands in exchange for announcing their names—something leaders didn't always attend to in those days. He also worked the bandstand lights, and this became another power base for him. Dinah Washington was perhaps the only performer who wasn't a little bit afraid of Pee Wee, who knew it well and showered attention upon "The Queen" when she was in residence. Lester Young, coiner of apt phrases, once called him "half a motherf——."

Opening night featured a brace of bands, including Charlie Parker's, Lester Young's, Hot Lips Page's, Lennie Tristano's, and a traditional group led by Max Kaminsky. The leaders, assisted by Max Roach and a bassist I can't recall, all jammed together. The management soon abandoned attempts at covering all the jazz bases and concentrated on modern jazz and its bigger names. Mondays were so-called jam session nights; sometimes, that was indeed what took place, but more often than not, they provided showcase opportunities for new and/or lesser-known groups. Up-stairs, right next door, was a little bar that went through several name changes (I best recall it as the Magpie), and this was where many of the Birdland performers hung out between sets, if not trapped by fans at the Birdland bar or secluded in the relative privacy of the not-so-elegant dressing rooms.

To the left of the entrance, there was a glass broadcast booth, from which Symphony Sid Torin conducted his radio show. For one hour most nights, he switched from records to live transmission, emceeing the show from the stand in his inimitable manner. Somehow, Sid, who'd spent his life around jazz and must be credited for being the very first disc jockey to feature bop on the air, always managed to garble musicians' names, facts about their careers, and song titles. but he had a great, syrupy radio baritone, was nothing if not hip, and certainly enjoyed his role. (He eventually graduated to network radio but was bounced off the air when he made an obscene comment over an open mike. Sid was unique. At this writing, he is enjoying retirement in Miami.)

There were times when Bird himself was *persona non grata* at Birdland, barred from the premises named after him. This was due to financial problems, since Bird sometimes would run a tab that exceeded not only his own wages, but those of his sidemen as well. The ban also applied when he was going through a psychological crisis and would behave in a bizarre or unpredictable manner.

But I remember Bird at Birdland taking care of business. I remember him with the strings, sharing solo honors with Dizzy Gillespie, annoyed with Diz for milking laughs by conducting the ensemble with exaggerated gestures and slightly indecent body movements, but having to laugh himself after a while. (When Bird conducted, he was dead serious.) I remember him gently trying to get a very far-out Bud Powell to complete a solo on "The Man I Love," which had been going on and on, without Bud ever returning to the bridge as he gazed into space in the direction of the audience, face like a mask. Bird put his arm around Bud's shoulder, nudged him slightly, and whispered, "Bud . . . Bud . . . the channel," and Bud came out of it, looking up and saying, "Okay, okay, I got you covered." That was a tough night, but Bird played like an angel.

And I remember my only one-on-one encounter with Bird, at the Magpie, on a day when he wasn't working but just hanging out, recuperating from some bout with the demons, refusing a drink but sipping Coca-Cola, walking with a cane, in one of his heavyweight stages, neatly dressed in topcoat and open-neck white shirt. I was so carried away by my unexpected tête-à-tête with the great man that I've forgotten most of what we talked about, but I do recall distinctly that his manner was that of a much older man, much more like that of the jazz veterans than of his bop contemporaries.

Bird crammed several lifetimes into his brief span on earth, and you won't learn what he was about from such sensationalistic and biased accounts as *Bird Lives*. Hooked at fifteen, he was, as he once said, never a child. He consumed life, and it consumed him in turn. But make no mistake, he was a disciplined artist and a very hard worker, deeply serious about his music. Like Billie Holiday, another self-destructive genius of jazz, he was truly himself only when there was music to be made. And the music that poured, ejaculated, out of him, was an affirmation of the life force.

Bird's song reached every open ear. Only Louis Armstrong, who forged the vocabulary and syntax of jazz as an individual expression, had a comparable impact on all who heard him. Bird has been called a rebel, a revolutionary, an outsider, a victim; but he was inside his music, which was solidly built on the tradition that spawned him. His life was a constant struggle, and he lost control over it early on, but when it came to the music, he was in command, and victorious.

There will never be another Charlie Parker, and here you have him, large as life, hard at work creating astonishing, beautiful music, holding together a band of competing egos, making it all mesh—just a night in the short, turbulent, fantastic life of a master jazz musician.

The band over which Bird presides here is a marvelous one. The place has been established, but the most meticulous research has failed to nail down the exact date. The current consensus, June 30, 1950, is a bit difficult to accept, since Fats Navarro is present, playing very well indeed. The trumpeter died of tuberculosis on July 7, 1950, and it seems unlikely that he should have been capable of such playing just a week before his death. Ira Gitler, who saw Fats at Birdland in 1950, recalls him as a shrunken, pitiful figure, racked by coughing spells and playing feebly. But available clues have been checked and rechecked, and June 30 is the date that comes up. In any case, it matters not when but what.

Fats was the ideal trumpet for a Parker quintet. He had the ear, speed, execution, and sound to match Bird's flights of fancy, and Bird's music was in his soul. Only Dizzy equaled him among Bird's trumpet mates—with all due respect to Miles Davis, Kenny Dorham, and Red Rodney. Listen to Fats here, and you'll know where Clifford Brown came from. Fortunately, nearly all of Fats's best work is currently available on records, and his true stature can once again be properly assessed.

Bud Powell is in fine shape here. *The* bop pianist, he has no peers when it comes to this kind of music, and here there is none of the tension sometimes evident in his studio recordings. Among many fine moments, I'd single out his solo spots on "'Round Midnight" and "I'll Remember April," but that's a personal choice. All of this is prime Powell, with no lapses. No jazz musician, I'd wager, fought against greater psychic and somatic odds than Bud, and Birdland was the scene of many triumphs and defeats. Sometimes he battled with Bird. Here they seem in harmony.

Art Blakey needs no introduction to the contemporary jazz audience. Still very much on the scene, he has operated one of the great finishing schools of jazz, his Messengers, since what seems like time immemorial. Two generations of great players have been propelled into maturity by his driving beat. Art will make you play; there's no coasting possible with him behind you. These are his finest moments with Bird; they didn't team up often.

Curley Russell is the unsung hero of bebop rhythm. He had worked with the big bands of Don Redman and Benny Carter, recorded with Dizzy and Bird in 1945, and from then on became one of the busiest and most frequently recorded bassists on the modern jazz scene. His warm, resonant sound recorded well, and he kept perfect time. Keeping time, not soloing, was his forte, and as bassists gradually became co-featured soloists and virtuoso performers, Curley dropped out of the jazz mainstream, doing club dates and such. Little has been heard from him since the late 1950s. He's a bedrock here.

Some program notes:

"Wahoo" is Tadd Dameron's riff on "Perdido" changes, barely stated before Bird roars out of the starting gate with three fiery choruses, followed by three from Fats, who is warming up. Bud takes two, Bird and Fats trade fours (hear Bird's last!), and they riff on out. Not bad for openers.

"'Round Midnight," on which Fats lays out, has Bird stating the theme in his most melodic manner. What a melody player he was! A songbird. His second chorus is a marvelous piece of improvisation, and then Bud proves his affinity for Monk's music in a lovely solo passage. Bird returns with the interlude (created by Dizzy, by the way), and the performance fades out.

"This Time the Dream's on Me," a pop tune favored by Bird, is also done without Fats. Bird's three opening choruses take wing—no one could (or can) match him in combining speed and beauty. Bud, perhaps bedazzled, enters late for his two choruses, backed strongly by Blakey's brushes. Bird and Art trade fours, and Bird takes it out. A lesson in mastering changes.

"Dizzy Atmosphere," an "I Got Rhythm" variant, is taken at a wild tempo, and it speeds up at that! Bird's five choruses find him maintaining his equilibrium in the manner of a man racing across a tightrope. It's to Fats's credit that he makes the tempo and maintains continuity too, though he confines himself to a shorter statement. Bud, on the other hand, takes five and thrives on the tempo, gobbling up the changes. Bird starts off the fours with Art, joined by Fats. The chase sequence gets scrambled, and the ending is a cliff-hanger. This is definitely not a studio performance: no re-takes. Quite a ride, and a veritable definition of bebop.

"A Night in Tunisia" is Fats's feature; Bird lays out. Fats skips the sec-tion of the piece that leads up to the famous break. This is an excellent track to prove the point of Clifford Brown's parentage; the opening 8 bars of Fats's second chorus could very well have been played by Clifford, who also loved this piece. Bud phrases like a horn in his solo, and Curley Russell takes the final bridge—his only "solo" of the night. Fats's cadenza is brief but lovely, and his beautiful sound is well displayed.

"Move," yet another "I Got Rhythm" offspring, takes off at a tempo al-most comparable to "Dizzy Atmosphere." Fats is alone on the theme and solos first. Then Bird enters vehemently, with a darker sound than before, and offers five staggering choruses, of which the third is the standout. Bud, with driving Blakey behind him, digs in for four, and there are some spirited exchanges between the horns. To finish up, the horns transpose the theme to minor. No wonder some players switched to cool behind this kind of wizardry!

"The Street Beat" was concocted by pianist Sir Charles Thompson for a date on which Bird joined Dexter Gordon and some swing players. It's what was known as a mop-mop piece, named for the rhythmic device that recurs at the end of each 4-bar phrase. This, too, is not far removed from the "I Got Rhythm" pattern. Fats solos first, on mike for a change, giving us a sample of his ability to construct long-lined phrases; he finishes the solo with some effective runs. Bird's six choruses (he enters as relaxed as Lester Young, then starts to build) are stupendous, and Bud maintains the level, Art displaying some fancy hi-hat stuff behind him. Three full rounds of ex-citing fours between the horns, and then a scramble back to the theme (I think Bird wanted Art to take a solo, whence the delayed entrance).

"Out of Nowhere," taken at a brighter tempo than on Bird's earlier Dial session, and making for fascinating comparison to the several takes surviv-ing from that date, starts with Fats, who loved this tune and is at his most lyrical, first paraphrasing the melody, then inventing his own. Bird's two choruses are perfect; nothing stands between him and the horn. The way he abstracts the theme in his opening statement recalls, momentarily, Lee Konitz's approach to melody. Bud shows that he too is a melodist of the first rank; this is the Powell whom Barry Harris comes from. The horns take 8 bars apiece, then go out together in collective improvisation rather than the customary unison. Like Sidney Bechet, Bird leads, not yielding to the trumpet.

"Little Willie Leaps," based on "All God's Children Got Rhythm," out-does "Dizzy Atmosphere" in terms of speed and brilliance. The two horns are as one on the theme, then Bird leaps in on a break and hurtles head-on through five breathtaking choruses. Fats is short but pungent, while Bud stretches out a bit more; this piece, under whatever name, was a staple of his. Listen to Bird on this track and hear what Ornette Coleman picked up on—in fact, the unison playing here also hints at Coleman-Cherry things to come.

"52nd Street Theme," Bird's standard set closer, is heard in a capsule version here—more to come.

"Ornithology," the national anthem of bop, is, as if you didn't know, a variation on "How High the Moon." Again, there is fine ensemble playing on the theme. Bird leads off with authority, Fats follows with a thoughtful, finely conceived solo, Bud digs in with both hands, and then come two rounds of terrific fours by the horns.

"I'll Remember April," another Parker favorite, is just Bird and the rhythm section—no Fats. After some splendid Parker, Bud continues in Bird's idiom. He starts his solo with a Monk phrase and refers to Monk again in the final 8 bars of his three choruses. Bird skips and dances in for two rounds of fours with Art, who plays like a pile driver. In the out chorus, one of Bird's favorite licks links the bridge to the last eight.

"52nd Street Theme" comes in for fuller treatment this time. This tempo is absurd, but Bird, in two whirlwind choruses, hits every note right on the head—perfect definition! The ensemble interlude is followed by some volcanic Blakey action.

"Embraceable You" opens with Bird in splendid voice, the beauty of his sound fully captured. The Dial versions of this tune are among the undis-puted masterpieces in the Parker canon, but what he does here is on the same high plateau. A gorgeous solo! He abstracts the essence of the theme in a few bold melodic strokes, subtly works in a quote from "If You Could See Me Now," and makes Birdland a shrine. Then, in the kind of abrupt, extreme contrast unique to jazz, comes a vocal episode, after which Fats takes a half chorus with a veiled, cloudy sound. The vocalist reprises, the horns come in under him, and Bird swoops into his patented "Country Garden" coda.

"Cool Blues," the only blues of the night, has eight choruses by Bird, of which the fifth and sixth are veritable compendiums of Bird lore, and seven fleet ones by Fats (if this really is his swan song, what a way to go out!). Bud's outing is unavoidably marred by a mechanical defect in the original recording, but this momentary slip is bracketed by some spotless playing. A sequence of fours in somewhat random order, involving the horns and Blakey, again show the great empathy between Bird and Fats.

"52nd Street Theme" (one could make up an entire album of Bird's versions of this piece), again way up, is one of the best. In addition to the first bridge, Bird takes three choruses, and elevates us once again to elysian heights.

This is what it's all about.

(1977)

Lester Leaps In

Monday night is jam session night at Birdland. The regulars are off, admission is lowered to a dollar twenty-five, and there is no minimum at tables. On these nights, Symphony Sid, a unique disc jockey, presides over meetings of the loyal devotees of the style of modern jazz known as hard bop, an un-euphonious but surprisingly fitting description. Hard bop is big-city music, and to the juvenile delinquents who inhabit the lower depths of the cities, a "hard bop" is a rough, free-for-all fight.

It is on Mondays that newly formed groups and little-known musicians are given a hearing. There are always a few "names" present, but more often than not they appear in supporting roles. Drum battles, flute battles, and unusual instrumental combinations are regular features. On this particular Monday night, however, there was to be something else, something quite different. There was to be an anniversary party for Lester Young, to celebrate his "Thirty Years in Show Business." The guest of honor, who was to appear fronting a group of his own choosing, was said to be in a Parker mood. Three weeks ago he had opened and closed at Small's Paradise in Harlem on the same night. After arriving late he had fallen asleep on the bandstand. It was said that he had the "No Eyes Blues," and bad. Thus it was a noble and missionary gesture that Marshall Stearns and Nat Hentoff, the sponsors, Morris Levy, the club owner, and Sid, the promoter, were making. In the world of jazz, such gestures are frequently made too late; more attention is paid to the dead than to the troubled living.

Would Lester be there? And if he did show, would he remain on his feet? And if he stayed on his feet, how would he blow? Faith and doubt contended.

And Lester did come—graceful sleepwalker, Pres hat and Lester face, beat but on the scene. The house is full. The Lester Young quintet is on the stand—a young band, as Lester's bands have always been. A promising supporting cast: Curtis Fuller on trombone, a young hard bopper but not looking hard at all; Nat Pierce on piano, the unbilled member of Count Basie's Home Runners; Doug Watkins on bass, very young but already a name; Willie Jones on drums, even younger, but already a veteran of the Bohemia and the Charlie Mingus "Quo Vadis" club. Lester mounts the bandstand. The downbeat is soft, the tempo medium. "Pennies from Heaven" is a haunted song. Not a mild summer rain, this, but a gray November drizzle. The pennies are few and worn thin and smooth. The tone is choked, the phrasing halting . . . not from inability, but from pain. The last note dies, and Lester looks up from a troubled sleep. Silence. The faces of the musicians who have backed him so gently, so sympathetically, are intent and serious. Then the applause, warm and strong and friendly, not the applause of a concert audience.

"Mean to Me" is not a lament but a quest, climbing in uncertain terrain, gaining a foothold and finally reaching solid ground where one can walk once more. And Pres smiles, and the young band, having helped to cause that smile, is in turn infected. From then on, it's walkin' and talkin'. Pres, having prayed, is now ready to preach. "Up 'n' Adam" jumps. The master starts softly, gaining volume and heat with each successive chorus (can one speak of choruses where there is unbroken continuity?), coming up shouting like the old Pres (did they say he was no more?), and suddenly there is a new astonishing Pres as well!

Back of him, cool Doug Watkins, elegant in his double-breasted Ivy League suit, new in approach as well as clothes, is coming on like Slam Stewart's little brother, singing, bowing, and having a quiet ball. Shy Willie Jones, knowing how to drum softly yet hotly, knowing how to join the party without slamming the door and grabbing all the whiskey, uncorks a drum solo that has the message—the first of a triad of uniquely original excursions into time and timbre. With humor, whimsy, and a good strong foot, he is the first young drummer to bring Zutty, the old master, to mind. Nat Pierce, laying down the right changes in the right places as if he's there to help; striding out on his own, having listened to Erroll and Count.

And Pres . . . walking over to whoever is speaking his piece, saying "yes," "ahem," "yeah," digging everybody, before taking it out with a "catch me somewhere along the way." Someone shouts, "Yeah, Prezzerini" . . . there's been some hand clapping, too. And then it's over and everybody's happy, Sid beaming from inside for a change and Pres hugging his horn as he retires to his corner.

The other group makes its appearance. Three Bones and a Quill consists of Gene Quill, alto; Jimmy Cleveland, Frank Rehak, and Jim Dahl, trombones; Red Garland, piano; Chet Amsterdam, bass; Charlie Persip, drums; and four music stands. "In a Mellotone" by Duke Ellington. But where is Duke, where the mellow tones? Loud, man . . . and I do mean loud! Still, it's hard to hear anything. Quill is an aptly named feather, having heard the Bird, but only when he spoke in anger or frustration. The bones have heard J.J., but have they heard Teagarden, Vic, or Dicky? All machine-gunning—Cleveland chief gunner, triple-tonguer; Dahl burp-gun champ; Rehak placing third but running fast. There is no attempt at contrast in mood or volume, and had there been, it would have been effortlessly demolished by the perpetual drum solo played behind it all. And everybody blowing so long—oh, baby, how long! Everybody drumming, nobody singing, everybody driving, nobody swinging . . .

Off go the music stands and Lester Leaps In. Horn up high, tempo solid, rhythm gentle but firm behind him. Then those stop-time things: stop time, suspend time—go around it, behind it, in front of it—always on time and on to time. Lester leaping in and bouncing back, spiraling up like a diver in reverse, joining time and space in sound. Can Pres still blow? Oh, baby! "Waterfront, Pres baby," someone calls out when the last leap has returned us to earth with 4 bars of half-time for a gentle landing. The plea in the voice is explicit. "Right now," says Pres, who has just made Curtis Fuller blow like he never blew before—and didn't even know he could. He'll forget, not too much later, but undoubtedly never will forget. Pres covers the waterfront, all of them, covers them with a tenor saxophone sound that vibrates right through everything and everybody, giving us the message from so deep within himself that it is beyond word-meaning, merging all, as he and his instrument have merged. This is what jazz can be, what jazz can do. (Only the greatest arts can do it, and how rarely it is done in our time!)

Almost without pause Lester glides into "Tea for Two," fast, fast, but unhurried. Surging like a river, like blood through the veins—runs and cascades of notes and tones whole and sustained. That good old tension-relaxation riff. Tea for two, me an' you . . . tea for we.

Return of the music stands: Three Rasps and a Shrill? Rattle 'dem bones, crash that cymbal. Off we go! To where? To Lostville: too much sound and no true fury. Good hands, good skill. Good will? Yes, but frustration as well. Tense, not relaxed, alone, not together. Not together is not jazz. Many notes is not much music.

Let's go back to Pres! The sponsors and their guests, having arrived amid the boning, are now ready for the ceremony. Lester is on the stand, perhaps wanting to blow, but ceremonies must proceed on schedule. Big cake and champagne brought on. Lester attempts cake ritual from stand. Impossible. Descends into space between stand and table and blows out candles, smiles, shakes hands. Symphony Sid announces members of party and Lester cuts cake. Birdland camera girl takes picture. Pop! goes flash-bulb. "He didn't look up," says camera girl, plaintively. Lester plays few bars of "I Didn't Know What Time It Was." Dr. Steams breaks up. "Got the message?" Pres asks. Lester picks up knife, makes like cutting cake, looks up and says "Cheese." Flashbulb goes pop. Success! A toast. Exchange of pleasantries. Party members attentive but vaguely reminiscent of philanthropists at a benefit.

Pres beats off "There'll Never Be Another You." It is nostalgic, wistful, and tender, but somehow removed. A part, who can say what, of the whole Lester is no longer involved. The spell is breaking. During trombone solo, distribution of cake commences. Guests at table on left begin conversation—not loud, but it spreads. Nat Hentoff is digging. The party was a wonderful idea. The cake should have been cut later, the guests should have arrived earlier. Did they want to give Pres ample time to warm up? Doug Watkins plays his first plucked solo of the evening. Pres gently whispers out. Pres and band deliberate next tune. Familiar face appears on stand. Roy Haynes asks to sit in. He was with Pres some years ago. Willie Jones leaves stand, slowly. Pres plays "Jeepers Creepers." Fantastic tone. Haynes seems a little stiff. He is louder than Jones.

And now something very strange is about to happen. A familiar figure is being guided to a ringside table. Clad in brown suit, red sport shirt, and blotchy beard, Bud Powell takes his seat. He hunches over. He digs Lester. He digs Lester. Thirty seconds pass. Bud leaps from chair to stand, gives Nat Pierce a hug, and takes over the piano bench. It was a rather gentle hug, to be sure, but sudden. Nat, now sitting at the vacated table, looks as if he has seen a ghost. Lester, too, has seen him, but it is reflected only in his playing. In the middle of his solo, he searches for Bud, but Bud is hard to find. Lester plays three choruses, under strain, but he will not hurt Bud's feelings. Bud solos. He is trying to play everything he can hear. The fingers cannot always follow, so he sings. He sings a weird song, yet he is happy—he is possessed. Lester, gazing upon Bud, is gradually withdrawing. He doesn't show displeasure, only regret. From the back, a little man is looking at Bud with an indescribable expression on his face. His name is Erroll Garner. He has been present since early in the evening but did not leap on the bandstand. Where he lives that isn't done.

Bud goes into a locked-hands passage that gains in coherence but is interrupted by the entry of the drums. A long solo, and Bud, leaning over the keyboard, seems to dig it. He digs everything. Lester raises and lowers his horn, moves his lips, and politely waits the drummer out. He re-enters with the bridge, takes it out, and then turns to the mike for the first time. "Ladies and gentlemen," he says, "I would like to introduce my trombonist, Curtis Fuller. He will play a slow-motion number for you." He acknowledges the sporadic applause and steps down. The blues begins. Fuller is caught out twice by Bud's introduction. Then he just moves in, and Bud falls into line. His playing is much clearer now. He no longer sings, and he adopts his characteristic pose, legs crossed, eyes fixed on faraway places, smile frozen like a mask. His solo is moving. Perhaps he understands and is sorry, in his own way. He just wanted to blow. Fuller plays much better than any of the music stands. Maybe he's angry.

Pres sits at the musicians' table far off the bandstand, where he also sat between sets. His companion is a lady dressed in black. She was not present at the cake-cutting. The party is restless. Nat Hentoff is digging Curtis and Bud. The tempo doubles. I think of "Up 'n' Adam." How long ago was that? Pres will play no more that night. The music stands return. The party rises, bids Pres goodbye. They should have come earlier. They did a great thing.

I will never forget the celebration of Lester Young's Thirtieth Anniversary in Show Business. Some business. Quite a show.

(1958)

Eubie Blake in Session

Twentieth Century Fox is musically noted for the brief flourish accompanying the familiar trademark with the searchlights. Other sounds, however, will soon be associated with the name. The film company has entered the recording arena with its own label (the sort of thing known hereabouts as "expanding its interests in the communications field"), and it promises to be an enterprising newcomer. Trade secrets that cannot be revealed at this time prevent me, etc., but there is something underfoot that has already included the recording of American Revolution songs by a small jazz band led by Claude Hopkins and including Buster Bailey, and the reunion of the famed team of Noble Sissle and Eubie Blake.

We had the pleasure of being present at two of the three Sissle and Blake sessions. Actually, it was Eubie Blake's date. He had been coaxed out of retirement, at first unwillingly but spurred on by the incentive of a huge collection of sheet music covering Negro "Americana" from the Civil War days to the early 1900s, and the promise of a free hand in matters musical. At seventy-five, Eubie Blake may look like a grandfather, but a very spry one. He is bald and wears green "police type" suspenders, but there is nothing old about his eyes and hands. The composer of "Memories of You" and other hits, the writer and musical director of *Shuffle Along*, the first successful all-Negro revue on Broadway, has a pair of hands that not yet lag behind the tapping of his foot. At the first session, Eubie was exuberant and his playing bubbled over with the joyous stride accents of Harlem piano as it should be played, with more of a jazz feeling than his early records ever displayed. On this date there were—in addition to Noble Sissle—Buster Bailey, George Duvivier, Bernard Addison, and Panama Francis. Perry Bradford assisted Mr. Blake with the musical direction in inimitable fashion.

The session kicked off with "Wild About Harry," a Sissle and Blake composition and vehicle to success. It jumped, from the Lionesque intro to the last happy note from Buster's clarinet, in spite of some reading trouble occasioned by the somewhat confusing fact that the written arrangement was *not* the arrangement to be played. After some tossing around of terminology that might have set some of our "educated" youngsters on their ears, everything went smoothly. Sample dialogue: Blake: ". . . and then I go into this thing" (plays a paraphrase of Liszt). Buster: "Oh, you mean the Second Hungarian Rhapsody?" General breaking up.

The second number was "Maple Leaf Rag," in which Eubie included a strain usually left out in jazz versions. George Duvivier, who plays with Bud Powell when he isn't busy arranging and recording for big bands and studio groups, did very well in the ragtime climate. Bernard Addison had begun with an amplified guitar, but it was soon decided to give him a mike and disconnect the amp. Addison played fine rhythm guitar throughout, but unfortunately he did not solo. He had just returned from a tour of the Southwest with one of the current editions of the Inkspots.

Next was a selection mysteriously titled "Bulldyker's Dream," but not to be released by that title. According to general consensus of opinion, there would be protests. As Eubie put it: "Every Negro in the United States over sixty years old knows what that means." It isn't really that bad: the word is a slang term for lesbian. "Spanish Rag" was the bowdlerized title selected for this unusual piece: a slow rag with a Spanish tinge in melody and rhythm, a Jelly Roll flavor and an intriguing out-of-time passage that reminded Panama of Dave Brubeck. "You mean Brubeck reminds you of Eubie . . . he came first," said Bailey. The final selection recorded that day was a medley of ragtime hits from the early 1890s. "Your mother and father weren't even born when that one came out," Eubie informed Addison. The vocal duets between Sissle and Blake were delightful, as were the tunes themselves. They should have made a movie to go along with this one.

The second date saw two replacements: Milt Hinton on bass and Charli Persip on drums. Dizzy Gillespie's drummer may seem an odd choice for such a date, but if we forget our carefully nurtured prejudices, isn't it quite wonderful? Persip drummed well, showing that he knows how to use snares as well as cymbals and explosive foot pedal. Contrary to general opinion, more young musicians are learning to take pride in mastering all styles of jazz, from motives intrinsically economic but often becoming sincerely musical in the heat of things. Persip has subbed for Cozy Cole at the Metropole ("They sure create some excitement in there," he said, wonderingly—having no doubt been led to believe that this was the home of Dixieland) and was on his way to a rehearsal of the Johnny Richards band as he left Messrs. Sissle and Blake. Rudi Blesh and Barry Ulanov should know about this double agent! "Which side are you on?" may yet become an obsolete question in the jazz world—but we must be dreaming.

Eubie was a wee bit tired on this session, and after a romping "Eubie's Boogie Rag" (actually a medium-up blues), which featured a fine slap solo by Milt, who was enjoying himself immensely, the boys ran into some trouble with "Jubilee." This was a fine piece with a long Sissle vocal and some duet routines. After a number of false starts and a take-five interlude (during which Eubie gave out with "Rustles of Spring"), it finally came out right. Buster's part on this—intro, behind vocal, under piano, in brief solo, and back behind the vocal—was not the easiest in the ensemble, but he executed it faultlessly most every time. He is an exceptional musician. Recently, he acquired a bass clarinet. The outcome of this meeting should be interesting.

"Mobile Rag," with a floor mike to pick up Eubie's foot-tapping, was painless and mobile. But the closing medley of the first nationwide ragtime hit (according to historians) and its follow-up, both dating from 1891 and titled "Mr. Johnson, Turn Me Loose" and "The Bully Song" (concerning a feud between an indigenous and an out-of-town bully), was the occasion for timing complications. With just two minutes to go, however, they did a perfect take, and everybody left in high spirits. The final session, with Panama resuming the drum chair, came out well, according to earwitness reports. As Panama said after the first session: "Seventy-five years old and doesn't sound corny. That's something." It is.

(1958)

Jazz Goes to Washington

Viewed in the light of such advance publicity images as "America's first national tribute to jazz," and the listing of high-ranking cabinet members among its sponsors, the First International Jazz Festival, held in Washington, D.C., from May 30 through June 3, turned out to be somewhat disappointing.

Though there were such fancy trimmings as a concert of "symphonic jazz" at Constitution Hall, a reception and champagne supper at the State Department, and a concert of chamber music at the Library of Congress, no less than half of the eight main musical events took place at the Washington Coliseum—a wrestling and ice-hockey arena particularly ill suited for the presentation of music. Subjected to the Coliseum's stifling heat, awful acoustics, and truly miserable amplifying system, artists and listeners could not but doubt the sincerity of this tribute to jazz as an art.

Withal, there was much interesting music to be heard at this festival, which was presented by the president's Music Committee of the People-to-People Program, with all proceeds going to the committee's international program. The festival emphasized the current rapprochement between jazz and modern concert music (no less than six original compositions, commissioned by Broadcast Music, Inc., received premiere performances in Washington), but one listener, at least, came away with the renewed conviction that the future of jazz is in the hands of those musicians who continue to work within the traditional framework of jazz, which seems far from having been exhausted.

The first major event of the festival was the concert of "symphonic jazz" at Constitution Hall. The National Symphony Orchestra performed the opening selections under Howard Mitchell, after which Gunther Schuller, composer and leading proponent of "third stream" music, took over the baton. The first work to be heard, James P. Johnson's *Yamekraw*, was a nostalgic echo of the "jazz age" and of the earliest attempts to merge jazz and concert music. As edited and orchestrated by Schuller, *Yamekraw* emerged as a light piece somewhat in the vein of *Rhapsody in Blue*, quite charming and likely to be heard again.

After Dinah Washington's characteristic renditions of "Summertime" and a Duke Ellington song with the composer at the piano, the full Ellington band joined forces with the National Symphony for the performance of a 1955 Ellington composition, *Night Creature*. Though not one of the outstanding works in the Ellington canon (it lacks the homogeneity and conviction of *Black, Brown and Beige*), this proved to be the high point of the concert. Ellington's unique use of instrumental colors, his melodic grace, his unpretentious originality, and the superb work of his brilliant orchestra combined to give this rather slight piece a flavor quite different from what was to follow. This was especially so in the driving finale, where Ellington drummer Sam Woodyard (whose work throughout the festival was outstanding) generated sufficient rhythmic intensity to "swing" the whole array of musicians into a climax that shook the walls of the staid auditorium.

Subsequent to this demonstration of authentic jazz sound and feeling, the remainder of the program seemed rather dry. André Hodeir's *Details*, one of the commissioned works, contained no element of improvisation. Scored for solo vibraphone, supported by a jazz bassist and percussionist plus symphony orchestra, this short work was rather more conservative in harmony and structure than one might have expected from Hodeir, who, as a critic, is a staunch supporter of extreme modernism. The jazz elements here consisted of sound (the cool, airy sonorities of the vibraphone) and an occasional passage in jazz rhythm. Eddie Costa, the vibraphone soloist, performed his part with great skill and intelligence.

Improvisation played a considerable role in the young Californian composer Larry Austin's *Improvisations for Orchestra and Jazz Soloists*. A sprawling, eclectic work in three sections performed without interruption, *Improvisations* was lively but unorganized. Its main attraction was the brilliant work of young trumpeter Don Ellis, ably supported by bassist Ron Carter and drummer Charles Persip. But the restless tempo changes and occasional torrents of sound from the orchestra prevented the jazz soloists from displaying more than occasional glimpses of their capabilities. Austin's effective use of percussion indicated that he has listened to the work of Edgard Varèse.

Whatever its faults, the Austin work at least had vitality. In James Louis Johnson's *Scenario for Trombone and Orchestra* (also a BMI commission), in which the composer appeared as trombone soloist, there was little but earnest craftsmanship and utter solemnity. Johnson, known in jazz circles as J.J. rather than James Louis, is one of the most gifted instrumentalists in modern jazz, and from a technical standpoint his playing was remarkable. As a composition, however, *Scenario* merely proved that a jazz musician is capable of acquiring certain academic skills in the handling of musical materials as well as any conscientious conservatory student. Throughout the evening, what impressed the listener was the high caliber of musicianship displayed by the performers which stood in marked contrast to the relative shallowness of the music to which they applied themselves so diligently.

Schuller appeared in the role of composer as well as conductor at a concert of Jazz for the Young Audience on the morning of June 2, again at Constitution Hall. Here, Schuller introduced a work tentatively entitled *Journey into Jazz*, a children's introduction to jazz set to a narration written by critic Nat Hentoff. Scored for small jazz ensemble and a "straight" contingent of sixteen strings and one trumpet, this proved to be a charming, unpretentious piece well suited for its purpose. In spite of Hentoff's somewhat didactic narration, the music had genuine warmth and humor. The jazz passages were allowed to emerge unobstructed and there was good work from trumpeter Don Ellis, bassist Ron Carter, and drummer Charles Persip (these three were the workhorses of the festival), as well as tenor saxophonist J. R. Monterose and alto saxophonist Eric Dolphy.

On the same day, a program of Jazz for the Small Ensemble was presented at Cramton Hall, a splendid modern auditorium on the campus of Howard University. Though three hours of music without an intermission seemed rather too much of a good thing, this concert was the most rewarding and best integrated single event of the festival. The climactic event was the performance of tenor saxophonist Sonny Rollins, who, having recently emerged from a two-year period of voluntary retirement from the jazz scene, without a doubt is one of the leading exponents of jazz today. Displaying staggering musical imagination combined with virtuoso control of his instrument, Rollins's two performances at the festival were unforgettable. The key to his music is improvisation, but unlike some other modern jazz practitioners who seem to lack control over their material, Rollins is always in full command. He is neither afraid to state the melody on which he bases his flights of fancy, nor of returning to it as a guidepost to the listener before plunging into further investigations. Though often extremely long, Rollins's improvisations maintain the hearer's interest without letup by virtue of their clarity, logic, and coherence. And though his playing is technically astonishing, he never loses sight of the content of his music. In the best jazz tradition, Sonny Rollins always "tells a story" when he plays.

Though Rollins was ably supported by his quartet, notably the excellent guitarist Jim Hall, his personality dominated the proceedings. The music of composer-pianist George Russell, on the other hand, came to life as a collective effort. Performing with his sextet, Russell seemed able to extract the best from each member of the group, allowing their individuality free play within the framework of his conception of jazz. Russell, who is the inventor of his own system of tonality (set forth in his treatise *The Lydian Concept of Tonal Organization*), introduced a commissioned work, *D.C. Divertimento*, which was a refreshing indication that he took neither himself nor the occasion overly seriously. Russell's use of the Lydian mode, based on ancient Hellenic concepts, is pleasing to the ear and facilitates jazz improvisation.

The *Divertimento*, a short piece, featured several tempo changes but never lost its rhythmic impetus. But it was a slow, moody piece, *In a Lonely Place*, that made the most lasting impression. Trombonist Dave Baker's inspired playing, filled with joy and zest, was outstanding. Trumpeter Don Ellis here found, and took advantage of, the freedom that his other appearances seemed to deny him, and came through with playing both technically brilliant and musically meaningful. George Russell seems to me a composer in the true jazz sense: i.e., his personal conception is strong enough to impose unity on the performance of his music, and the music itself is free enough to give the players ample opportunity for jazz expression.

Another highlight of the afternoon was the appearance of Duke Ellington as pianist. Supported by his first-rate bassist and drummer, Aaron Bell and Sam Woodyard, Ellington played his famous band theme, "Take the A Train," and a lyrical piece dedicated to Queen Elizabeth II, "Single Petal of a Rose," and romped through *Slightly Dukish* before turning things over to Woodyard for a lengthy exhibition of jazz drumming at its best.

Also on the program were baritone saxophonist Gerry Mulligan and his relaxed, well-integrated quartet—though Mulligan seemed distressed and somewhat listless at the loss of his large orchestra, which recently disbanded due to the vagaries of the current band business. The audience was also treated to a recital by composer-pianist John Benson Brooks, assisted by Don Heckman on alto saxophone and Howard Hart on snare drum and cymbal (an outfit referred to by Brooks in his introduction as "tubs"). This was the sole example of truly avant-garde music offered by the festival. Brooks believes that silence is an integral part of musical performance, and he did some rather startling things with time.

The three concerts and the Sunday morning session of gospel music that took place in the Turkish-bath atmosphere of the Coliseum can be evaluated only as major achievements in valor and endurance on the part of both performers and audience. The music came through as if it had been played into a tin tub on an acoustic phonograph with a blunt needle. The musicians on the stand were often unable to hear one another. The whole atmosphere was drenched in heat and humidity: barkers hustled cold beer and other beverages, and the audience milled about in search of one spot where the music might be heard.

Under such circumstances, it is truly amazing that so many of the performers tried to give their best. Jazz musicians are well accustomed to adversity, but in this case they were not led to expect it. Nonetheless, they delivered. The programs were unevenly balanced between musical validity and so-called name attractions. Among the worthwhile performances were Thelonious Monk's iconoclastic renditions of three original pieces, Horace Silver's peripatetic set of warmly swinging feetwarmers, Oscar Peterson's display of pianistic fireworks, a surprisingly professional and idiomatic set by a Polish quintet, tenor saxophonist Tubby Hayes's demonstration that it is possible to lose one's British accent when playing jazz, and the sincerity and good will of the Chris Barber band.

Outstanding performances were contributed by the aforementioned Sonny Rollins, who took a tune from *Camelot*, "If Ever I Would Leave You," and used it as building blocks for a magnificent improvisatory structure, and by two jazz veterans, trumpeter Roy Eldridge and tenor saxophonist Ben Webster, who played their uniquely personal and convincing brand of mainstream jazz with undiminished authority and vigor.

The First International Jazz Festival, in spite of its many good features, emerged as another chapter in the uphill trek of jazz toward adequate and responsible presentation. If the jazz festival is to become a valid genre (and there is every reason that it should), the people involved in planning and executing these events must learn to draw the line firmly between what is musically valid and commercially expedient. There are plenty of reasonably good auditoriums in the nation's capital, even if they don't accommodate 7,500 people. If we are to have experiments, let them at least be noble. If there is to be a festival in Washington next year, let it truly be a tribute to the men who make jazz, instead of an odd mixture of artistic pretension and inept presentation.

(1962)

Swinging at the White House

I n the royalty of American music, no man swings more or stands higher than the Duke."

The reader was Richard Milhous Nixon, President of the United States of America. The scene was the East Room of the White House, the date was April 29, and the occasion was a gala evening in honor of Edward Kennedy Ellington, who was celebrating his seventieth birthday.

It was a night few of the 180 guests—government officials, members of the Ellington family, fellow musicians, friends, and members of the press—will ever forget. Though there were moments of appropriate solemnity, the tenor of the evening was one of cheerful warmth and friendly informality, set by the president himself. As a veteran observer of state functions put it: "I haven't had this much fun at the White House in forty years."

The evening had begun with a dinner hosted by President and Mrs. Nixon for Ellington and eighty guests, including his sister, Ruth, his son Mercer, and his wife, and Duke's two grandchildren. Also present were Vice President and Mrs. Agnew, several cabinet members, other prominent government officials, members of the clergy and judiciary, and leading representatives of various branches of the arts.

From the world of music, there were composers Richard Rodgers and Harold Arlen; Mahalia Jackson, Benny Goodman, Cab Calloway, Mrs. Count Basie (representing her husband, who was on a European tour), Dizzy Gillespie, Dave Brubeck, Billy Eckstine, Lou Rawls, Willis Conover, Stanley Dance, the Reverends John Gensel and Norman O'Connor, and former Ellington guitarist Fred Guy. Harry Carney, Duke's closest friend within the band, and Thomas Whaley, his longtime musical right-hand man, were there, and Johnny Hodges would have been, had he not been recuperating from a sudden illness that had struck him earlier in the month. The dinner culminated in an exchange of toasts.

Following the dinner, President and Mrs. Nixon and Ellington and his sister received the after-dinner guests at the top of the Grand Staircase, after which the party adjourned to the East Room.

There, Mr. Nixon presented Ellington with the Presidential Medal of Freedom, the highest civilian medal the government can bestow. The president showed the night's first glimpse of his sense of humor by pausing significantly between the first names and the last of the recipient.

"Edward Kennedy Ellington," the citation read, "pianist, composer, and orchestra leader, has long enhanced American music with his unique style, intelligence, and impeccable taste. For more than 40 years, he has helped to expand the frontiers of jazz, while at the same time retaining in his music the individuality and freedom of expression that are the soul of jazz." It concluded with the words quoted above.

In response, Ellington, characteristically, first kissed the president twice on each cheek. Then, in his formal acceptance speech, he expressed his gratitude and went on to quote as his credo the "four freedoms" of his fallen comrade-in-arms Billy Strayhorn:

"Freedom from hate, unconditionally; freedom from self-pity; freedom from fear of doing something that might help someone more than it does me; freedom from the pride that makes me feel I am better than my brother."

Then the president spoke. "We all know," he said, "that Duke Ellington is ageless. But after all, this is his birthday, and in looking over the fine program of music that has been prepared, I noticed that one work is missing."

Mr. Nixon then made his way to the piano, and removed a saxophone from the stool. "Don't go away," he told the guests. "Earlier, Duke asked me if I was going to play . . . Would you join me in singing 'Happy Birthday'—in the key of G, *please*."

It was now time for the more serious musical portion of the evening, and Willis Conover, who had selected the musicians and prepared the program, took over as master of ceremonies.

The ten-piece band was an impressive one. In addition to three ex-Ellingtonians, trumpeters Clark Terry and Bill Berry and drummer Louis Bellson, there were trombonists J. J. Johnson and Urbie Green; saxophonists Paul Desmond and Gerry Mulligan; pianist Hank Jones; guitarist Jim Hall; and bassist Milt Hinton.

They swung into Strayhorn's "Take the A Train," and were off on a more than hour-long panorama of Ellingtonia. Among the highlights: a joyous Terry-Berry dialogue on "Just Squeeze Me," which delighted even non–jazz fans in the audience; a highly original Mulligan arrangement of "Prelude to a Kiss," and the baritonist's own salute to Harry Carney, "Sophisticated Lady"; J.J.'s bluesy "Satin Doll"; Desmond's gentle "Chelsea Bridge"; and Bellson's exciting "Caravan" solo.

Midway through, three guest pianists appeared. Billy Taylor essayed a medley of "Drop Me Off at Harlem," "All Too Soon," and "It Don't Mean a Thing"; Dave Brubeck asked Desmond and Mulligan to join him and the rhythm section in "Things Ain't What They Used to Be." But it was Earl Hines who broke it up with just three choruses of a romping "Perdido," assisted by Hinton and Bellson—a moment of musical magic.

To conclude the musicale, two singers joined the band. First, Mary Mayo, pure-voiced, straightforward, and possessed of very accurate pitch, did a medley of Ducal standards. Then, Joe Williams. Singing as movingly as I've ever heard him, he did "Heritage" and a lovely "Come Sunday," and concluded the formal musical proceedings with a rousing "Jump for Joy."

The president, after the musicians had taken their individual bows—each acknowledged by Ellington with a blown kiss—got up to say that no one could possibly top the performance everyone had just heard "except one."

"I think we ought to hear from the Duke, too," he said. Ellington graciously dedicated his reflective, romantic improvised piano solo to Mrs. Nixon.

It was now past midnight, and when Mr. Nixon again rose to speak, most of the guests thought it would be to bid them goodnight. What he did say, however, was that the East Room would be cleared for a jam session and dancing, and that everyone was invited to stay. Loud cheers greeted his announcement.

The session that ensued was not remarkable from a musical standpoint, but very much so in terms of joy and warmth. Eckstine, Rawls, and Williams joined forces in an impromptu blues sparked by Gillespie's horn and wound up with their arms around each other; a series of four-handed exchanges at the piano bench featured, in order, Billy Taylor and Leonard Feather; Dave Brubeck and George Wein; and Willie "The Lion" Smith and Ellington himself (the guest of honor, however, spent most of the session on the dance floor with a succession of charming partners); members of the Marine and Navy bands stationed at the White House sat in with the stars, tenorist Phil Dire being most impressive; Marian McPartland joined the fray, and Leonard Garment, a former law partner of the president, played a nice clarinet solo and later lent his horn to Dr. Harold Taylor, former president of Sarah Lawrence College and a member of the National Council for the Arts, who had a ball with "Tin Roof Blues."

While all this was transpiring, we discovered that presidential assistant Daniel P. Moynihan is a great Mulligan fan; decided that the fashions on display were rather conservative and that our best-dressed vote should go to Mrs. Whitney Balliett and Mr. Billy Eckstine; noted that the White House is a remarkable example of the superiority of eighteenth-century architecture in terms of airy elegance of interior space; drank lots of lovely champagne; and came to admire the unfailing courtesy and efficiency of the White House staff, which seemed to consist of Ellington fans.

Behind-the-scenes credit, aside from Conover, must go to Charles McWhorter, a lawyer, Nixon campaign strategist, and lifelong jazz fan, who, according to no less an authority than the *New York Times*, conceived the idea and helped to realize it. It was indeed a night to remember.

(1969)

The Blues Comes to Ann Arbor

The mass media had plenty to say about the profound implications of the great Woodstock Happening—prime-time TV news coverage, editorials in important papers, etc., etc.

While the communicators were making the great discovery that pot smokers are nonviolent, they had nothing to say about the first major blues festival held in this country. (The sole exceptions, the *Chicago Tribune* (!) and the *Washington Post*, devoted space to the event as a result of the personal initiatives of staffers Harriet Choice and Hollie West, respectively.)

This particular happening did not attract even one-tenth of the 300,000-plus that Woodstock could boast. Total attendance for the three evening and two afternoon concerts at the Ann Arbor Blues Festival was around 20,000. But everyone there had come to hear the music—not to make the scene—and the enthusiastic response was a joy to behold.

Organized from top to bottom by students at the University of Michigan, the festival presented a most impressive and truly representative cross section of the real blues, from deepest roots to latest branches.

Perhaps most significantly, the festival was a sincere and honest tribute to a great black American art form and its makers, organized and attended by young people almost all of whom were white. Though there was much free and easy camaraderie between artists, production staff, and fans, the performers—especially the veterans—were treated with a respect that bordered on reverence. It added up to a kind of recognition that blues artists have seldom, if ever, received from their own people—for reasons too complex to pursue here.

In this fact—and in the astonishing receptiveness and knowledgeability demonstrated by the audience—there lies much hope. The blues is the seminal music from which springs nearly all the rock, pop, soul, C&W, etc. sounds consumed in such vast quantities by young America. Perhaps the time will come when at least a sizable segment of that audience will wake up to the real thing, and we may yet see a B. B. King, a Muddy Waters, a Lightnin' Hopkins, and even a Big Joe Williams gain their rightful share of the public adulation and economic rewards currently reaped by their variously gifted students, imitators, and plagiarizers.

The setting for this historic event was Fullerflatlands, a grassy piece of land belonging to the University of Michigan. There was a sturdy, workmanlike stage, a good sound system, some improvised refreshment stands—and lots of green grass to sit or lie on. No chairs, but nobody seemed to mind. The young people brought their own blankets, pillows, loaves of bread, jugs of wine, etc., and beyond the fenced-in festival area, there was plenty of land on which to camp.

The festival got under way (on time) Friday evening with the inimitable Roosevelt Sykes, a master of blues and boogie-woogie piano, and an enjoyable singer. His solo stint, including two of his big hits, "Driving Wheel" and "Sweet Home Chicago," as well as a rollicking boogie instrumental, triggered the first of many standing ovations and demands for encores. Like several of the "single" acts, Sykes returned later in the festival, and as in most of these repeat performances, his second outing was the more relaxed and impressive.

He was followed by Arthur ("Big Boy") Crudup, a venerable singer-guitarist whose primary talent is not so much performing as writing. He has many a classic blues to his credit, and his avid followers include Elvis Presley. After a long and successful career, he dropped out of the performance field in 1960 and was only recently rediscovered and recorded by Bob Koester of Delmark Records.

His first set, though including such solid numbers as "Look on Yonder Wall" and "I Stay in the Mood for You," failed to catch fire. Crudup's singing is effortless and relaxed, and he has great dignity as well as unusually clear and excellent diction, but the spark was missing.

It was there, however, when he returned on Saturday afternoon to do a fine set including "That's All Right Baby," "Sittin' by My Window," and a piece that included one of my favorite lines of poetry at the festival:

> . . . that's where a blind man seen my baby
> and a dumb man called her name. . . .

Next came the first of many contemporary Chicago blues bands, J. B. Hutto and the Hawks. An excellent guitarist and an engaging singer, Hutto represents modern blues at its best. His guitar work is influenced by the late Elmore James and has swing and vitality. His band boasts a good lead guitarist, Lee Johnson; the reliable Hayes Ware on bass; and Frank Kirkland, a great blues drummer. (Jazz fans not yet hip to the blues should find Hutto's music a good place to make a start, by the way.)

The next group, also from Chicago, was led by Jimmy "Fast Fingers" Dawkins, whose strong guitar work is rooted in the tradition but also very contemporary in sound and feeling. Vocally, he was at his best on "I've Been Down So Long," sung in a plaintive, high-pitched voice that went well with his somewhat sharp playing. Two tenor saxophonists gave the group an R&B flavor; Mickey Boss turned in some serious playing, but the other hornman came on with some tasteless, annoying gyrations. Dawkins was more impressive at a jam session later that night at the Michigan League, and in a second set on Sunday.

There followed one of the festival's big-name attractions, Junior Wells. Blues purists found his exciting set too commercial, and with numbers like "Harper Valley PTA" and "What Did I Say," they might have had a point. However, this listener found Wells's fiery harmonica playing (he calls the instrument his "Mississippi saxophone") and strong singing, backed by a really together band, infectious and enjoyable. The musically most meaningful piece was "Help Me," dedicated to Sonny Boy Williamson (No. 2), and featuring a beautiful harmonica cadenza. "I'm gonna tickle my baby now," Wells announced, and he did.

After an encore, Wells begged off to the biggest hand so far, but what followed to close the evening was, to me, the festival's peak set. It was B. B. King, and they don't call him the King of the Blues in vain.

King combines, in a highly personal way, the best elements, past and present, of the blues tradition. He is a sensational guitarist—the peer of the best jazz has to offer—a moving singer, and an outstandingly gifted performer. From start to finish of a long set (the audience would not let him go, and one felt he could have played into the wee morning hours without losing a single listener), he made beautiful music, communicated warm emotion, and gave fully and freely of himself.

His fine backup band (John Browning, trumpet; Louis Hulbert, tenor saxophone; Booker Walker, alto saxophone; Onzy Matthews, organ, arranger; Kenneth Board, bass; and twelve-year man Sonny Freeman, drums) kicked off with a jumping instrumental; then B.B. came on with his standard opener, "Every Day," followed by "How Blue Can You Get" (written years ago for Louis Jordan by that noted blues composer, Leonard Feather), on which he played seven fantastic slow choruses of guitar, displaying astonishing time and masterly instrumental control, solidly backed by the rhythm section. A jumping "That's Wrong" featured some intriguing turning around of the time, and then B.B. introduced each member of the band with a personal and informative statement (other leaders, blues and jazz, please note).

"Someday Baby" had some more lovely guitar. ("Can I do one more?" asked B.B. after the first chorus, answered by a resounding "Yeah!" from the crowd, and a heartfelt "Do ten more" on its heels.) His guitar work here, as strongly jazz-flavored as any heard at the festival, bore a more than passing resemblance to prime Django Reinhardt.

"Why I Sing the Blues" brought the crowd to its feet for a true standing ovation, and King accepted it gracefully with a little speech about his pleasure at this support for the blues, and the fact that this year so far had been the best of his career. "You make us feel like Americans," he said. "I wish I could shake hands with all of you tonight." He followed this with a simple and eloquent "Please Accept My Love," which stepped the vibrations up a bit higher.

King spoke again, about people. "They went to the moon," he said, "but they didn't find no people there. Look around you. Touch somebody next to you. That's what it's all about. People." He finished up with one of his biggest numbers, "Sweet Sixteen," and there was communion in the summer night. B. B. King is a great artist, and while he is a showman second to none, there is not one iota of sham in anything he does. After the end of the program, he lingered backstage for nearly an hour, signing autographs and taking time to chat with every young fan who'd come to see him. (His kindness and grace reminded me of that of another great artist, Louis Armstrong.) Still later, he got the jam session off to a good start, retiring from the stand only when a succession of harmonica players showed the same appalling lack of musical courtesy that, alas, has become common at similar jazz jams.

Saturday afternoon started with one of the greatest of traditional blues-men, Big Joe Williams, his gravelly voice, and his nine-string guitar. Though not at his best, he still was something to hear, with "Baby Please Don't Go" the capper. On the next afternoon, however, he hit his true stride and got a deserved ovation for the beautiful "Vernita." Big Joe is more in his prime than most other elder statesmen of the blues, and seemed like a veritable embodiment of the strength, directness, and vitality of the blues tradition. One had the feeling that what he played and sang was himself; there seemed to be no distance at all between art and artist.

This was to have been a "workshop" afternoon, and emcee Dick Water-man, head of Avalon Productions and manager of some of the greatest blues artists in the world, gave informative and apt introductions to Williams and Arthur Crudup, summarizing their careers and contributions. He was filling in for his colleague, Bob Messinger, who arrived in time to introduce Muddy Waters and his band.

Muddy's current group is one of the best he's had in recent years, and Messinger, in a well-worked-out attempt to delineate different blues styles, introduced members of the band and let them do their thing. In succession, we heard from pianist Pinetop Perkins, a worthy replacement for Otis Spann, who demonstrated boogie-woogie (Albert Ammons style) with a fine, rolling "Boogie Shuffle," sang some pleasant city blues, and offered "Caldonia" in tribute to Louis Jordan; guitarist Pee Wee Madison, who did "Sweet Sixteen" in B. B. King style (he is a more interesting guitarist than singer); bassist Sonny Wimberly, who impersonated Wilson Pickett more ably than he did James Brown; and lead guitarist Sammy Lawhorn, who is a great player when the spirit moves him. The small but enthusiastic audience made it clear, however, that they preferred just plain music to didactic musical examples, and wanted Muddy most of all. Both harmonica player Paul Osher and drummer Little Willie Smith got plenty of opportunity behind the leader when he came to bat.

Muddy, in a splendid mood, did "Train Fare Home," "Hoochie Coochie Man," "Long Distance Call" (with a sterling guitar solo), and, of course, "Got My Mojo Working"—one of the all-time surefire blues killers. Osher, a young white musician, did some of the best harp work heard at the festival. He has a natural blues feeling, good facility, a pleasing sound, and excellent time.

Muddy and the band were on that night as well, and did basically the same set. Because Howlin' Wolf had overstayed his allotted time (he was on for eighty rather than forty-five minutes) and his welcome, they were forced to do just a half hour (the program was already into overtime when Wolf went on) and did just that, almost to the second, without any shortcuts or strain. It was a brilliant demonstration of true professionalism, and "Mojo" brought one of the biggest ovations of the three days.

The evening concert had begun with a rare treat: Sleepy John Estes and Yank Rachell, partners in blues for forty years and legends in their own time. Blind and frail-looking but full of vinegar, Sleepy John is one of the greatest of blues poets. To the uninitiated, his diction can be hard to grasp, but close study of his lyrics is more than worth the effort.

Though Rachell, the world's only blues mandolinist, at times seemed to overpower his older and more subtle partner (in part due to lack of balance in respective amplification), Sleepy John scored strongly, particularly with "Divin' Duck Blues." A sample of the happy blues was "You Shouldn't Say That," with a joyous refrain and a melody line quite similar to the jazz standard "Shake That Thing." The team also demonstrated a sukey jump, and with Rachell switching to guitar, did a stomping "Goin' Down the Highway."

How well the youthful audience received these traditional performers! All the ridiculous nonsense about generation gaps was thrown into a cocked hat by this festival. Would that jazz could boast of a similarly receptive, understanding, and generous audience!

Accordionist Clifton Chenier, with his zydeco music from Cajun country in Louisiana, was not happy or relaxed without his customary backup band. Though most of his material is derivative and highly eclectic, encompassing Ray Charles, "Pinetop's Boogie Woogie," and "Shake, Rattle and Roll" as well as traditional blues fragments, he is a sincere and interesting performer. But a logy drummer got in his way, and the sudden appearance of a tenor player (Chenier eventually chased him off) didn't help. He was so unhappy with himself that he insisted on going on again the next night, but this was a mistake.

Howlin' Wolf's rather unfortunate marathon followed. After a hilarious entrance on a motor scooter (Wolf is a huge man), he essayed a couple of fair numbers climaxed by "Smokestack Lightning," on which his fierce harmonica was at its best. Though he followed up with two other hits, "Spoonful" and "Little Red Rooster," the sameness of the tempos he picked and the seeming apathy of his normally excellent backup band combined to make the set relatively boring.

Otis Rush and his Chicago band was another story. From the opening number, on which Jim Conley's hoked-up but exciting tenor brought memories of Big Jay McNeely and Wild Bill Moore, to the closing "I'm a Cross-Cut Saw," this was a swinging, intense set of modern blues at its best. On "I'm So Glad You're Mine," the band generated a great, rocking beat that flowed irresistibly, and on "I Can't Quit You Baby," Rush's singing was something to hear. He is also a fine, fleet guitarist in the B. B. King tradition, but with a penchant for chording that is his own and a bright but never piercing sound. This is another group that jazz fans would readily enjoy.

The Sunday program got under way a half hour before noon and continued almost uninterrupted until 11:30 p.m. Yet it never was too much of a good thing. Among the highlights were an afternoon stint by Big Mama Thornton, an irrepressible performer who sings, plays harp and guitar, and also did a not-bad turn at the drums. Her big numbers, "Ball and Chain" and "Hound Dog," on which she was backed by a jazz-flavored little band, were predictable audience rousers, but she showed another side of her nature when she sat down with Fred McDowell, the great bottleneck guitarist, to do a moving, way-back rendition of "Heavy Load." McDowell, whose guitar work is exceptional, also did his own set earlier in the program.

A quite different kind of guitar was represented by T-Bone Walker, one of B.B.'s admitted idols, and a superb musician—when he wants to be. He is, however, heavy on showmanship, and upstaged his own playing with jumps and gyrations. But when Luther Allison, a brilliant young Chicago guitarist, came on to challenge him, some exciting exchanges ensued, and T-Bone showed what his reputation is all about. He is, by the way, closely allied to the jazz tradition, and one wonders if Charlie Christian might not have heard him in his early days.

I found Allison's two sets with his own band a bit disappointing, but he showed his mettle at the jams, and left no doubt that he is a player to contend with.

A pleasant job was done by drummer Sam Lay's little band, which features another good white harmonica player, Jeff Carp. Their repertoire is derivative ("Tell Me Mama" was Washboard Sam's "Back Door"; "Key to the Highway" is a staple and their "Mojo" wasn't up to Muddy's by any stretch), but the solid time of the leader, the togetherness of the band, and the conviction with which they played made the set jell.

Lightnin' Hopkins, on the other hand, is anything but eclectic. His style, both vocally and on guitar, his demeanor, and his material (though he, of course, also dips into the traditional well) are genuinely original, and he was a joy to behold. *Sharp* from dark glasses to yellow shoes, he seemed determined to have a good time and take the audience with him. "It's good out here in the prairie like this," he told them, launching into "Mojo Hand." Among the things that followed in a set that seemed to end too soon (Lightnin' knows how to pace himself), the standouts were "Don't Wanna Be Baptized" and a long anecdote about a girl who stole his brand-new second-hand Cadillac.

Magic Sam scored the biggest success of the day and was one of the indisputable hits of the festival. A talented guitarist and convincing singer (his rather soft, somewhat tremoloed voice reminds a bit of Lonnie Johnson's), he was expertly backed by Sam Lay on drums and a good bassist, the threesome generating more heat than many a larger band. "Need You So Bad," "If You Love Me," and "Sweet Home Chicago" were fine, but the climax came with "Lookin' Good," propelled by a strong eight-to-the-bar beat and featuring a thrilling, expertly executed stop-time segment. This number really broke it up, and the festival's inept emcee (a Chicago disc jockey named Big Bill Hill) had a great deal of trouble getting the show moving again. Cries of "Magic Sam" recurred throughout the rest of the night.

Charlie Musselwhite, the festival's sole white leader, headed a mixed band including the first-class drummer Fred Below, pianist Skip Rose, and the festival's only steel-guitar player. Musselwhite is a good harpist, a pleasant singer, and a sincere, ungimmicked performer. "Help Me" and "Long Way from Home" featured his vocals, but the emphasis throughout the set was on instrumental work. He closed with the festival's only obvious reference to jazz, a swinging version of "Comin' Home Baby."

Freddie King came on strong and tried hard—too hard—to break it up. He has personality and power, but his blatant imitations of B. B. King (to the point of calling his guitar "baby") and rather cute routines did not score heavily with the crowd. "Have You Ever Loved a Woman" (also known under various other titles) was his most convincing number, but on the whole, this was a jive set.

There was quite a bit of jive in James Cotton's performance as well, but if there can be such a thing, it was sincere jive. Not a brilliant harp player nor a particularly gifted singer, Cotton works tremendously hard to get to an audience, and he succeeded that night, even though he had to jump down from the stage, sing while lying on his back, and eventually resort to removing his shirt, displaying a scarred potbelly. It was all good fun, however, and "Turn On Your Lovelight" really did it, what with R&B effects, ceaseless repetition of lines, and a well-organized backup band. When he let up, pandemonium ensued.

In stark contrast—and one could have thought of no more fitting way to end this festival—was the finale. After quieting down the audience, Dick Waterman spoke. "You've heard all kinds of blues," he said, "but we thought it appropriate to end this festival without horns or amplified guitars. We want to go back to the roots."

And he brought on an aged, stoop-shouldered black man, simply but neatly dressed in white shirt, blue pants, and a blue string tie. The old man sat down, gingerly grasped a steel-body National guitar, and, after the mikes had been adjusted, began to talk about the blues. This was Son House from Mississippi, friend and companion of Charley Patton, teacher of Robert Johnson, and sometimes called "Father of the Blues." That might be hyperbole, but there can be no doubt that there is no purer living representative of the source.

Son House spoke in a soft voice, but clearly, like a grandfather telling a story to attentive ears. And it was as quiet as in church. He talked about Robert Johnson, and then he began to play and sing. His bottleneck stroke was slow and deliberate, but the sound rang out pure and strong. The voice quavered a bit, but it still had power, and the words were clear. "Death Letter Blues." Many verses, each beautiful, and the guitar accompaniment—phrases of uneven length—full of unexpected twists and turns. When the last note died, there was silence, and then, terrific applause—not of the kind that greeted James Cotton, but just as emphatic.

The old man smiled and shook his head, as if in disbelief. Then, joined by his wife, he told another story, leading into: "the church says Lord have mercy when I come to die, but I say, Lord have mercy *before* I die." And they did the song—a spiritual as much as a blues—Son House keeping strong time with his foot and digging into the strings with surprising energy. Another ovation. Then his wife sings "Precious Lord, Take My Hand" *a cappella* in an unschooled but rich voice, and then, together, they sing "This Little Light of Mine."

When they finish, many people have tears in their eyes. It has been an immensely moving and wholly appropriate finish to a great festival—a stroke of genius on the part of Dick Waterman, whose idea it was to end it this way. It was a gamble—some people backstage were concerned about anticlimax and such—but the audience proved itself worthy.

The Ann Arbor Blues Festival did not make headlines. Yet it was without doubt the festival of the year, if not the decade. We hope it becomes a permanent institution and that it will live up to the standard it has set for itself. To producer Cary Gordon, Jim Fishel, Janet Kelenson, and the other youngsters who worked so hard and well to bring it off—more blues power!

(1969)

Breakfast with Champions

The promoters had wisely refrained from playing favorites and advertised their function at New York's Americana Hotel immediately following the most widely publicized fight in history simply as "Breakfast Dance in Honor of the Champion." (For those too young to remember, a breakfast dance is an affair that starts anytime around midnight and goes on from there. In the old days, it could last well into day-light; this one happened from 11 till 5—a rare enough treat.)

Nevertheless, Joe Frazier had his victory party around the block at the Hilton with Duke Ellington's band featured, so that's where his close people were—at first. But the Americana event was the more public one (and at $25 a head, a ten-spot cheaper) and could boast three bands (Count Basie, Buddy Rich, and King Curtis), so the good-sized crowd on hand was not a partisan one.

Estimating that neither Count nor Buddy would hit much before 1 a.m., I arrived around that time. Though it was a chilly, gusty night, the Americana's spacious lobby was packed with celebrity watchers. Most of them were probably hoping to catch a glimpse of the champ or his fallen adversary but seemed quite willing to settle for whatever else might come along.

In the checkroom area, things were more quiet. The first familiar face I spotted was the bearded one of ex-Rich pianist David Lahm, who informed me that he'd been visiting the band room and that Buddy's men were kind of down because they were on location in Toronto and this was their night off—the trip back was booked on a 7:30 a.m. flight. I suggested that the unusual nature of the occasion might compensate, but David, who is a marvelous pianist but not very sanguine in outlook, countered that the Basie band hadn't been playing much the last few times he'd heard them (which he admitted was some time ago). We fell to talking about Duke, a subject for which we share enthusiasm, after I had suggested that playing a breakfast dance for a crowd that I'd been able to identify as predominantly Harlem (they call it "ghetto" nowadays, but it is also a style and a feeling and a tradition) might be something quite different.

The Imperial is a huge rectangular room in contemporary hotel style. It lacks the warmth of the cheerfully ugly, gilt-edged, stuccoed, and muraled ballrooms of another day, but a good-time crowd creates its own atmosphere, and the feeling inside was already happy. Basie's set had begun, and as I got my bearings and made my way toward the bandstand, the blues (was it "Splanky"?) wafted through the air, lubricated by that special Basie oil.

Some dancers were on the floor, and the cluster of bobbing heads and swaying bodies confronted the bandstand, but most people were still coming in or getting settled (and primed) at the tables.

The bandroom across the hall had been sparsely populated when I checked it out, and sure enough, a number of Rich bandsmen, easily recognizable in their casual but neat uniforms of striped long-sleeved sport shirts and complementing vests, were checking out the sounds and sights.

There were other things to check out, among them a sprinkling of hot-pants outfits, a style to which I have no objection, plus other sartorial factors of lesser impact. There was much young blood in the well-integrated yet predominantly Harlem crowd, but I can't recall seeing many Afros.

Seeing Basie & Co. again after a while (I'm ashamed to admit that in this case it was quite a while—late summer of '69, to be exact) is like running into a pretty girl you used to know and finding that she's still got it all together. A few details may have changed, but the glow remains.

The feeling of constancy within change is amplified by the presence of new faces and the absence of some anticipated ones, the latter balanced by the surprise of seeing Al Grey and Frank Foster in their old chairs.

And then of course, the core presences of Mr. Basie, looking marvelously fit presiding over his chargers, and Freddie Green, keeper of the pulse and embodiment of the tradition.

Two of the Rich boys are attempting to sort out the familiar and the new faces among themselves when one of their questions from a few moments ago is spontaneously answered by the familiar voice of a big-band freak who has just joined the diggers with a broad smile on his welcome face.

"That's Paul Cohen up there," Dizzy Gillespie said delightedly, identifying the lead trumpet. "Paul Cohen . . . you remember him. He goes back to the days with Benny Harris and everything . . . he's a hell of a man."

Meanwhile, and this by ESP, Cohen has been the first in the band to spot Dizzy, waving and smiling and hunching the others. The trumpets get it first and then it goes through the band.

The second tune now under way, "In a Mellotone," and the big hand Al Grey gets for his robust solo, in which the Rich boys join, makes them and some others miss the marvelous entrance of the reeds for their soli chorus—a bitch from way back, and executed with a flourish that spells high class. Bobby Plater has a lead alto tone slightly less ripe than Marshall Royal's but just as powerful, and Cecil Payne's bottom, while not as fat as Charlie Fowlkes's, is in there.

Sure, Basie isn't playing anything new, and on the two sets that night there is nothing that isn't warmly familiar in outline . . . but new and novel are not the same, and everything is novel: the setting, the personnel, the certain something. It's a pity that only age fully reveals the pleasure of familiarity combined with renewal. Basie is like the seasons, like a strong old tree that greets each spring with fresh foliage.

Al Grey gets out his plunger for "Makin' Whoopee," the band swinging softly behind him at a tempo no other big band has mastered (or dares to attempt), and the older dancers are with it, gliding with the glisses of the reeds. Frank Foster gets his first innings on "Corner Pocket," Mr. Green's permanently pressed and sharp contribution to his band's wardrobe.

Almost the entire Rich crew is on hand by now. Buddy himself appeared not long after Dizzy. As I noted with pleasure a few weeks before, on a stomping night at Barney Google's, he looks so well and relaxed these days. He'd been looking forward to this particular occasion then, and he's beaming now, digging the band. Basie is one of Buddy's great loves—the man and the music—and it's a two-way thing, as we will soon see.

Buddy's been to the fight, naturally, so we ask him. "It was a very good fight," he says, adding that there can be no question that Frazier won. (At this time, many who neither watched nor listened but only heard "decision" were still a bit doubtful, for which they couldn't be blamed.) Buddy knows a bit about boxing, having done some in the Marines, both in and out of the ring, and I don't want to misquote him concerning his other comments— this being neither time nor place to take notes.

"One O'Clock Jump." Already? Lots of shouts for more—from Buddy, too—but there's lots to come yet. Basie takes the mike, thanking the folks and telling them that they are about to hear a great band, a great *young* band (his emphasis), "a band that's fiery and exciting . . . I believe it's the last word in big bands today." You can hear Basie now as well as feel him—the piano was badly undermiked.

Meanwhile, the object of this affectionate introduction has been setting up. The stand is very long, with Basie set up on the left and King Curtis's paraphernalia on the right, leaving just enough room for the Rich brass on the stage. Reeds are on the floor, and Buddy's drums on a platform to their right. Not an ideal setup, but there are no complaints.

The crisp sound of the drums that sound like no others, and they're off at "Moment's Notice." It's a different groove, yet part of the same tradition. The brass bite, the reeds kick, propelled by a jetstream of rhythm. Basie is like a coiled spring, Rich is the spring uncoiled. Two kinds of tension and release.

There are some new faces around the bandstand now, including that of Ed McMahon, who'd been on the scene a few weeks back, too. (Johnny's missing, hospitalized with hepatitis.) Big Ed's attention is divided between the music and looking for his son. "I don't want him to miss this," he says repeatedly.

There is new life on the dance floor, too, especially after the contemporary rhythms of "Norwegian Wood" have begun to vibrate through the room. All kinds of dancers, mostly good, now mostly young. The best (now and for the night) is a tall, slender (but not skinny) blonde, not in hot pants but in neck-to-ankle slinky black, with a matching feather boa. She moves, despite her corny partner, shedding feathers as she goes. The other couples make a bit of room, and Buddy digs the action. (For the remainder of the night, the lady just listens up close. She made her statement.)

The band's fine new chart on "La Ronde," an entirely fresh reworking of what was once "Two Bass Hit," is the climax of the set. "Midnight Cowboy," which follows, presents the dancers with some hurdles, what with the changes in time and tempo, but they are a minority anyway. The listening crowd, however, has swelled.

Main solo kicks of this set have come from Pat La Barbera's strong, swinging tenor, Bruce Paulsen's trombone (also first-rate in lead), and Danny Hayes's sparkling trumpet. George Pritchard, a fantastic guitarist who upset the joint at Google's, is back home in Milwaukee where he has a steady thing. I hope I'll hear him again someday.

The set is over. A disc-jockey type, dropping so many names that I missed his, points out that Aretha Franklin is in the house, and Al Grey shows me where: at a table with a family air, wearing a dress that matches her hat—an out-of-sight creation of, I would guess, North African design, though it has an Oriental look—like something a Tartar princess might have worn.

James Brown is mentioned, too, but I can't find him in the sea of tables. A Motown-styled male quartet is going through its paces now, but, having been lucky to get in, and noting the increased security at the door (not a cop in sight but just cats who can't be jived with and know all the stories), I decide to stay, chatting with Frank Foster near the door, joined later by Mel Wanzo, Basie's lead trombone, who was with Woody when I last saw him. We're digging the constant flow of newcomers, like two tall studs in floor-length white fur coats with matching belts and brimmed hats that must have cost a fortune if they're real, and some more hot pants.

A familiar face whisks by. Frank Sinatra and party, ten or so, including trusted friend Jilly Rizzo, whom I just manage to greet. By the time they get seated, the deejay is on again, about to introduce King Curtis's band. When he hears that Sinatra is in the house, he doesn't give up until he has cajoled him to the stand—a difficult proposition for Sinatra, since his table is now surrounded by gawkers. The people with him appear to be just friends, no show-offs, wanting to relax and have a good time. But the lot of a star is a wearying one, and Sinatra pleasantly comes up to the stand, says a few words, and politely wards off requests for him to sing. He's looking extremely well, better than in his recent photos, face fleshed out a bit but still youthful, and he's being very gracious. Through the rest of his stay, the gawkers never let up, and Jilly doesn't get to sit down at all. I hope Frank got to dig some of the music.

King Curtis, a powerfully built man, has put together quite a band. One of the two trumpets is Joe Newman, one of the four saxes (including the leader) is Ronnie Cuber, and the drummer is none other than Pretty Purdie—and can he play that stuff! There is also an organ, two guitars, and electric bass.

This is dance music—none like it in the world—and soon the floor is packed with swaying bodies. Curtis plays tenor on the first piece, a rocking blues (what else?) on which Newman sets most of the background riffs. The music is loud but not piercing, and the beat is irresistible.

King plays alto on "Ode to Billie Joe," a slower tempo that gets the dancers into body contact. On the last number (all three are long), he features the saxello, with a nasal but interesting sound. A job—to play dance music—superbly done, but the cat who came up to the band and yelled "changes" had a point. Curtis (not to mention Joe and Ronnie) can play those, too. But not tonight.

Basie's second set begins while I'm distracted, greeting Leon Thomas, with whom I had spent the previous weekend judging at the Collegiate Jazz Festival at Notre Dame, and it's only when I look (the band is into a medium blues that has some Sweets Edison riffs in it) that I see the drummer is Buddy Rich. If you don't think that's a compliment, let me assure you it's the highest I can give. Paul Cohen has a solo on this, not a lead man's type of solo but one with splendid jazz conception and great chops.

The band is grooving, stretching back with heels dug in, and Buddy's smile is of a sort you don't see too often. There's constant communion between him and Freddie Green, who, when necessary (which isn't often), discreetly alerts the drummer to upcoming cues. Buddy is at home here.

Next, "Discommotion," a way-up thing by Frank Foster with strong echoes of "Cotton Tail." It's cooking now, and Eric Dixon's long solo is in keeping with the Ellington echoes, recalling Paul Gonsalves in its litheness. Harold Jones, the best drummer Basie's had since Gus Johnson (and I do like Sonny Payne), should not be the least concerned about the fact that Buddy makes the band catch fire, and I'm sure he's not. This is, after all, something else.

"Shiny Stockings." This brings back the dancers, and gives Sonny Cohn a chance. In front of me is Nat Pierce, wedged into a corner above the band is the beaming face of Phil Leshin, ex-Rich bassist of many moons ago and a good PR man, Bob Thiele is in the crowd, and to Basie's left is Al Hibbler, his sightless face reflecting the music as if it were a light, conducting with his arms and trunk, and not missing a cue. Norris Turney is there, too. Duke's gig is over, and Norris is the only one who made it here—there's an afternoon record date coming up. It's good to see him. Buddy's almost gentle on this. He's got a few bags.

"Whirlybird." Frank Foster front and center on this, giving his old solo spot new hues. Then, that great climax, with the band shouting and the drums responding, Basie getting up to conduct in that easy yet authoritative manner, opening up the spaces for Buddy to fill. And how he fills them! Total concentration and control, plus that fire that makes him not just a phenomenon in terms of speed and skill and unbelievable coordination, but a phenomenal *jazz* musician.

"One O'Clock Jump"—the gag version this time, marking the last set. And suddenly, the sound of another drummer up front, at Buddy's set, Jo

Jones, with some of his unique offbeat things. I didn't even know he was there, though I should have.

As much to give Buddy a well-earned rest as for the fun of it, Jo remains at his perch while the Rich band gets into "Basically Blues," as a tribute to the master, and just the thing for now. If Jo doesn't cut the chart like Buddy did Count's, it's because the one book is a known quantity and the other isn't. And Jo does some delightful things, especially at the end, Buddy cueing him.

Back in the saddle, the leader calls for "Groovin' Hard," and Pat La Barbera gets off a long solo that brings shouts from the people, still gathered around though it's now nearly 5 a.m. Though passions should be spent, the trumpets, with John Madrid's strong lead, still kick. Buddy conjures up an extra ounce of energy for the ending, and that's it.

While chatting with Pat La Barbera, who is the first musician we've talked to in years who says he *likes* to travel and who says he had a ball, we're introduced to a very pretty young lady who still looks radiant at this late hour (which can be done when you're sixteen). Miss Cathy Rich is going on to Toronto with her father and seems delighted at the prospect.

I convey greetings from Jim Szantor to his old acquaintance John Madrid, who is helping to clear the stand. I ask him if he enjoyed himself. "Oh," he says, "it was great to work with Mr. Basie around. I love that band— I've got most of their things on tape, and I listen to them all the time."

Mr. Basie. It suddenly makes you realize just how young Buddy's band is, and how a night like this will be something to remember for some who were there long after most of us have checked out and how this music is a living chain of being, of interlocking links that convey the message and pass it on.

In the lobby, we meet Ray Nance, who made it over from his gig just in time to miss all the music but also in time to greet Dizzy and Hibbler and other old friends.

It's early in the morning. A champ has been dethroned (Ali was the champ, no doubt about that, until tonight), a new champ has been born, and on that occasion, two all-time champions and their great seconds and corner men and fans have had a chance to get together and trade not blows but embraces. It's been a good night, and there should be more nights like it, for jazz is a music that thrives in a social setting.

Once, the many big bands that roamed through the nights of this land often met, in serious battle or friendly jousts. Today, the few surviving giants seldom cross paths. When they do, it brings them and all of us a little closer together, and in these times, that counts a lot.

(1971)

Woody's Fortieth

Not all the guests announced for Woody Herman's fortieth anniversary concert at Carnegie Hall materialized, but the absen-
tees were not missed.

Woody, who always considers his current band his best, kept his young
crew on stage throughout. Not surprisingly, the emphasis in the historical
portions of the concert was on tenor saxophones, as represented by Flip
Phillips, Al Cohn, Stan Getz, Jimmy Giuffre, and Zoot Sims. The rhythm-
section guest contingent was also strong: pianists Ralph Burns, Nat Pierce,
and Jimmy Rowles; guitarist Billy Bauer; bassist Chubby Jackson; and
drummers Jake Hanna and Don Lamond. Sam Marowitz led the saxes with
the authority he brought to the First and Second Herds—an unsung hero.
Mary Ann McCall, recently embarked upon a welcome comeback, sounded
as fine as ever on "Romance in the Dark" and "Wrap Your Troubles in
Dreams," and trombonist Phil Wilson and trumpeters Pete and Conte
Candoli rounded out the guest list.

The opening and closing numbers, "Apple Honey" and "Caledonia,"
were the most exciting offerings of the night, the former with solos by Flip,
Wilson, and Pete Candoli, the latter featuring all the tenors (except Zoot,
who left early for a gig), the Candolis, and a most promising young trumpeter, Al Vezzuti, who almost stole solo honors and made the Candolis
work harder than they had anticipated. Jackson, in fine form, set a murderous pace for the rhythm section.

Flip's warm ballad style was showcased on "With Someone New" and
"Sweet and Lovely." Now that Ben Webster is gone, it seems better than
ever to have Flip around to keep that great tradition alive. Bill Harris was
honored by Wilson on "Bijou" (certainly one of the gems in the Herman
book) and by Jim Pugh, the outstanding lead trombonist of the current
Herd, on "Everywhere." (It was Pugh's last night with the band, by the way;
he is settling in New York and should do well.)

Getz came up with an entirely new solo on "Early Autumn," the piece
that launched his fame, and was in peak form on his feature, "Blue Serge,"
the Mercer-Ellington classic as arranged by Gary Anderson, the Herdsman
responsible for most of the current book, and no mean tenor player himself.

Of course, there was "Four Brothers," with extended soloing from
Cohn, Getz, Sims, and composer-arranger Jimmy Giuffre. Cohn took honors, evoking the spirit of Big Brother Lester. Woody sang "Panacea," and

Pete Candoli re-created his solo and showed some of his old power. The current Herd did a number of contemporary selections, including Freddie Hubbard's "Crisis," and pulled out all the stops on a long, showy arrangement of good old "Blues in the Night."

When the Four Brothers first came into view, an ecstatic fan in the front row jumped up and scattered folding money on the stage. Zoot wasted no time in picking up the bills (which, we learned, were of large denominations) and unceremoniously stuffed his pockets. (He shared the "take" with his compatriots backstage.)

After the concert, there was a party, co-hosted by RCA and Columbia records. No one was able to recall a precedent for such collaboration between the two industry giants, who normally are very competitive. But the current presidents, RCA's Ken Glancy and Columbia's Bruce Lundvall, are serious jazz fans, and this gesture toward Woody was evidence of their sincerity.

The whole night was an outpouring of affection for Woody, who was visibly moved more than once. It is characteristic of the man that the anniversary celebration did not become an exercise in nostalgia, but rather was an affirmation of the role he continues to play on the jazz scene.

(1977)

Trumpet Encounter

My friend Gary Giddins, a young man whose writings on jazz (along with those of Peter Keepnews and Stanley Crouch) make me believe that jazz criticism has a viable future, told me that Lester Bowie had dropped in at Jimmy Ryan's to catch Roy Eldridge, and that, when he disclosed that he was a trumpeter, Roy suggested he stop by with his horn some night. Gary promised to alert me when the time came, and duly did so.

When I arrived, Gary was on hand, but there was no sign of Lester. We chatted with Roy, whose interest was piqued by the presence of two critics on the same night. We didn't let on, however, but when Lester, accompanied by Stanley Crouch, walked in, and a photographer from *The Village Voice* also materialized, Roy knew his suspicions had been well founded. His famous combative instincts told him that Lester's presence was a challenge.

In fact, Lester is in awe of Roy and had no intention of entering into a cutting contest. But Roy will never be ready to accept the role of an out-of-reach father figure of jazz. To him, bless him, any person entering the premises with trumpet in hand is an antagonist—friendly, perhaps, but nonetheless to be sized up and taught a lesson.

The band was playing when Lester came in, but Roy, during one of the sideman solo features strategically placed through the night's work to allow for breathing spells, came over to say hello. We found a table—not a good idea at Ryan's—near the outer reaches of Siberia, and listened. The set was routine, but Roy got off a few stunners.

Lester, for whom I've always had great respect as a player but had never heard in circumstances such as these, unpacked his horn in time for the next set. Requests are common at Ryan's, and when accompanied by folding money (Roy calls it "lamb's tongues"), even the most arcane are honored. As luck would have it, "Bei Mir Bist Du Schoen," with lamb's-tongue garnish, was tendered right off the bat. Roy, with fluegelhorn (a stratagem), reached into his capacious memory bank, and led a somewhat tentative ensemble. Lester got the first solo call (another stratagem) and proved that his ear is quick. He'd never heard, or heard of, the tune, but came up with a competent chorus. "Black and Blue," another request, was next. Years ago this might have caused some flinching, but Lester backed Roy nicely during the vocal and found a suitable second trumpet voice for the out chorus.

He'd proven himself with these observations of the ground rules on Roy's turf, and the leader now granted him the spotlight with a nice introduction of "our special guest" and a query as to what he would like to play. Lester responded with "Now's the Time," and Roy yielded the stand to him. The blues, at a nice, swinging tempo, ensued. Lester played very well, not stretching out for too long, Joe Muranyi offered a nice soprano solo, the rhythm section got into a good groove, and Roy climbed back on the stand, switching to trumpet, to grab a few choruses. In the jam ensemble that concluded the piece, a small trumpet battle took place, Roy showing his bristles for the first time with some of his high-note stuff.

Next, Roy stomped off a very fast "Apple Honey." Lester was at home with the "I Got Rhythm" changes, but Roy had the last word with a surging, crackling solo and sudden ending. The closing theme, a combination of "Fish Market," "Yard Dog," and other Eldridgian blues riffs, sometimes turns into a nice bonus, and this was one of those times, the two trumpets interweaving effectively (Lester had obviously been listening well from the table earlier on).

This was the extent to which the trumpets battled. In the following set, Roy didn't give his guest much elbow room. He opened with "Little Jazz," on which the advantage of familiarity was all his, though Lester did well enough while learning the changes. (Incidentally, any doubts I might have had, and they were slight, about Lester's ability to play this kind of jazz had been thoroughly dispelled by then—he is a complete musician.) A ballad medley was next, with Lester assigned the leadoff spot. He called for "Misty," a very appropriate choice, and made almost his best showing of the night on this pretty melody. His intonation was impeccable, his tone bright and clear (if lacking the burnished warmth of Roy's), and he worked out some fancy passing tones to run between melody phrases. It was a stylish performance, poised but not brash, and it drew warm applause. After interludes by Muranyi and trombonist Bobby Pratt, Roy turned to the fluegelhorn again and built himself a beautiful solo on "The Man I Love." Mastery of the art of ballad playing comes with maturity, and Roy offered incontrovertible proof of this dictum. To finish off the set, there was "Chinatown," done Louis style (how else?) and allowing only Muranyi to solo, aside from the leader. Roy hit those high ones smack on, and I always get a special kick from hearing him do this number, which has become a Ryan's staple through persistent requests in years past from Jack Bradley and myself.

After a final exchange of pleasantries, Lester took his leave. Roy had given him the respect due a fellow pro, but I can't help thinking that the encounter would have held greater warmth if the press hadn't been so obviously on hand. The piece Gary wrote for the *Voice* the following week had a nice big photo, but his thesis—that this had been an example of the supposedly lost art of the cutting contest—is one I find it hard to subscribe to. It is perhaps more to the point to see it as a friendly but guarded encounter between generations, and I think Roy would have appreciated Lester's work even more if he had been familiar with his "regular" style. As it turned out, his comments after Lester had left indicated that he thought him to be a Freddie Hubbard–type stylist. Roy loves to indulge in some special avantgarde playing of his own, and had he known that this was Lester's bag, they might have had some real fun.

When Roy was complimented on his "Man I Love," by the way, he shrugged it off. "The other night," he said, "I played 'Body and Soul,' and it was one of those things. I *cried* on the horn. Then I played it the next night, and I cried because I was so bad. . . ."

(1977)

Return to Birdland

I t was the oddest feeling—walking up Broadway toward Fifty-second, coming close enough to see the marquee. "Birdland," it said, not on a makeshift signboard, but in big white letters stitched on blue, on a regular cloth drape. Columbia, the world's leading record company, does do things in style.

The date was November 3, and the occasion a "Celebration of the inaugural release of the Contemporary Masters Series," in the form of a press party on the premises that used to house Birdland. The basement space is currently occupied by Casablanca 2, a Latin disco club. The layout has changed (the bandstand is now at the opposite end of the room, the "bullpen" is no more) and so, of course, has the ambience (not sleazy, like so much of the neighborhood's entertainment has become, but just a bit tacky). But for one night, it was a sort of shrine.

Having been privy to some of the preparations, I was not as surprised as I might have been at encountering Pee Wee Marquette upon descending the familiar stairs. Good to see you, Pee Wee, in your green Hawaii Kaii uniform. (When he was working here, rather than at the nearby Hawaiian nightclub, the tough, inimitable midget greeter-host used to wear an impeccable tux.) To see the beaming countenance of Bob Altshuler, Columbia's VP for press and public information, was no surprise at all, for this party was his brainchild, enthusiastically adopted by Bruce Lundvall, the company's president and a committed jazz fan, especially jazz of the Birdland vintage.

Ted Curson's cap stood out in the cluster of familiar figures gathered near the entrance inside. Don Schlitten and his wife, Nina, guarded the best table in the house, front and center, saving seats for friends. (Sorry, Dan—all booked up.) Being only about the tenth guest in, I had no trouble finding an only slightly less advantageous observation post. By and by, the place filled up. Identifiable faces, almost one and all—excepting the ever-changing rock-press cast. Musicians, scribes, record people (nice touch to have invited the heads of several smaller jazz labels), hipsters, flipsters, ladies and gentlemen of the royal court of King Bird, and even a genuine baroness.

The sound of Bird was the background music—including some sounds first played right between these walls, eons ago—culled from the three Parker albums in the release we were here to celebrate. The friendly specter of Bird. But there was nothing ghostly about the presence, in the spotlight, of grizzled, yacht-cap adorned Sid Torin. Yes, Symphony Sid, none other than, looking fit and tanned. The Florida Keys are the present habitat of this rara avis, genus jazz. It's been a long time, Sid; guesting on your last radio series, then in its sunset phase, reminiscing about Birdland and the Royal Roost.

King for a night, basking, as disc jockeys must, in the reflected glory of past associations, Sid was right at home, expansive as ever. He still garbles the names of musicians and gets their instruments and past affiliations messed up. He still calls them, one and all, "great gentlemen of jazz." And he still has no bandstand manners—his attempts to get musicians to come up and play when a lull in the music arose were decidedly counterproductive in tone. It wouldn't have been the same without you, doll.

Nor were these apparitions from the past: Dexter Gordon, Kenny Clarke, Percy Heath, Jimmy Heath, Barry Harris, Jo Jones, Horace Silver, Randy Weston, Roy Haynes, Buddy Tate, Billy Taylor, Buck Clayton, Helen Humes, Helen Merrill, Dick Katz, Peck Morrison, Dave Bailey, Slide Hampton, George Wallington, George Duvivier, Billy Mitchell, Jimmy Rowles, Don Elliott, Al Haig, Cecil Payne, Dick Hyman, Charlie Rouse, Frank Wess, Earl Coleman, Henri Renaud from Paris, Gil Evans, most of whom worked here, a lot or once or twice.

And the ranks were augmented by players too young to have performed here, though not to have listened: Howard Johnson, George Cables, Rufus Reid, Jual Curtis, Woody Shaw, Curson. And others we may have missed, or failed to jot down on the notepad.

Dexter, Slide, Cables, Reid, and Klook Clarke were on first, opening with "Green Dolphin Street." Not exactly a Bird or Birdland tune, but then, Bird would no doubt have played it, and I also recall when he was barred from the joint. So, maybe, right after all. Anyhow, good music, if not startlingly so. Klook, steady as always, looking great at a grandfatherly sixty-three, last played here at forty, with the MJQ, original edition. He just happened to be in New York, passing through on his way home to France from his native Pittsburgh, where he had been participating in a seminar at the university. Welcome, 'fess.

There was some stretched-out jamming, with marathon solos, especially from Payne and Mitchell, on "Now's the Time." Blues jams, on heads by Bird and others, were standard Birdland fare, and so were long solos. Don Elliott, Curson, and the legendary Ray Turner (off mike) were other participants. But it fell to Barry Harris, always keeper of the flame, to bring to life the true legacy of Bird and bebop, in a rousing trio performance of "A Night in Tunisia."

Then Buddy Tate, who, along with Buck, had been summoned to the stand by Sid from time to time, made his way up there at his own command, not with Buck, who sat things out, but with Helen Humes. Attired in a bright red flowing gown, Helen wasted no time. She charged into "He May Be Your Man (But He Comes to See Me Sometimes)," and within seconds had the room mesmerized. For the first (and only) time that night, everyone's attention was riveted on the music. Helen belted out the blues, in tremendous voice, with Buddy playing rich fills, then taking a few on his own without letting the tension level down. They followed up, after the evening's first ovation, with "All of Me" (I think—who was taking notes?), and got the only other. (Incidentally, or perhaps not, Pee Wee Marquette emceed that set.)

Breaking it up in no uncertain terms, Buddy and Helen acted as emissaries of the absent Count Basie. Next to Bird himself, Basie and band were the essence of Birdland, as anyone who ever spent a night, especially a Christmas holiday season night, in their company there will agree. Among those particularly pleased by this well-earned triumph of the older jazz generation were a couple of decided non-boppers in the audience, Messrs. Stanley Dance and Frank Driggs.

A tough act to follow, and while Earl Coleman did his baritone best, including (naturally) "This Is Always," the evening had peaked. It ended, after some desultory noodling by a tenorman who once had his picture taken with Bird, with Jimmy Rowles playing after-midnight music, surrounded by a cluster of rapt listeners and impatient Casablanca minions.

As the invitation had claimed, Birdland lived for one night. It was a nostalgia trip on a first-class ticket.

(1978)

RECORDING JAZZ

Recorded Jazz

Jazz and the phonograph were made for each other. Without the medium of recording, a music so defined by spontaneity of invention, individuality of instrumental sound, and rhythmic complexity that defies musical notation could not have been so rapidly or widely disseminated, nor lent itself so readily to rehearing, studying, and copying. Without recordings, jazz might have remained a temporary regional phenomenon.

Yet the ideal union between two near-contemporaneous artistic and technical inventions took time to be consummated. The fledgling record industry saw jazz as strictly a salable new kind of dance music and had not the slightest awareness of or interest in its potential as art. (Nor, admittedly, did any but a handful of its practitioners.)

The first genuine jazz captured by a recording device was played by the Original Dixieland Jazz Band in the New York studio of Columbia Records on January 30, 1917. Just two weeks earlier, these five young white New Orleans musicians had opened at a midtown Manhattan spot for dining and dancing, creating more of a stir than during an entire previous year in Chicago. But when Columbia's managers heard the sounds they had recorded, they cried "cacophony" and shelved the masters. Less than a month later, the band recorded two numbers for Victor, which promptly issued them. "Livery Stable Blues" and "Original Dixieland Jass [sic] Band One-Step" became one of the best-selling records of its day.

It may be an irony of history that the first jazz band to record should have been white, but this was not the result of racism. In 1913 and 1914, Victor had issued four 12-inch discs by James Reese Europe's Society Orchestra, then the rage of dancing New York. The music was ragtime, not jazz, as was that recorded by the black clarinetist Wilbur Sweatman in 1916. In the summer of 1917, Columbia recorded three productive sessions with W. C. Handy's Memphis Orchestra (also still playing ragtime) and followed up by signing Sweatman, now leading an ODJB-styled band, which made some thirty sides for the label over the next few years. A similar number was recorded by Europe's erstwhile associate Ford Dabney in 1919, when Europe himself made his final records, directing the civilian version of the Army band with which he had scored such resounding successes in France. Several of these were considerably more jazz-influenced than his earlier discs, and all were more interesting than the repetitious, military band–styled Dabneys.

The ODJB continued to make records, some of the best during a year-long stay in England in 1919–20 for the British branch of Columbia, but a session by a band that included Sidney Bechet made in London around the same time was never issued. A white New Orleans group led by clarinetist Alcide Nunez, the Louisiana Five, recorded prolifically in New York at the turn of the decade, while trombonist Tom Brown, first to bring jazz to Chicago from New Orleans, was busy in the New York studios, recording mainly with groups directed by Harry Yerkes. And the New Orleans Creole clarinetist Achille Bacquet (brother of George) worked and recorded in New York at this time with Jimmy Durante's New Orleans Jazz Band, passing for white.

By far the most prolific and durable of the ODJB-styled recording bands was the Original Memphis Five (four from Brooklyn, one from Long Island), co-led by cornetist Phil Napoleon and pianist Frank Signorelli and often including the fine trombonist Miff Mole. Between 1922 and 1931, they made hundreds of sides for dozens of labels under a variety of pseudonyms—a common practice in the industry during the 1920s, when masters were routinely leased nonexclusively.

Another feature of the record business in this period was the existence of special ethnic series catering to every conceivable nationality. Arabic, Danish, Greek, Irish, Polish, Italian, Yiddish, and Hebrew records were sold in the appropriate neighborhoods or available on special order. There was also an "old time" series, later renamed "hillbilly," for what would later (and more flatteringly) become country music. Thus it was only logical that African-American music should be added to the list, once demand became demonstrable. The enterprising songwriter, music publisher, and sometime vocalist and pianist Perry Bradford accomplished this, first persuading OKeh Records to allow a black singer, Mamie Smith, to record his "Crazy Blues," and then promoting the record assiduously in Harlem. Within less than a month of its release in September 1920, it had sold more than seventy-five thousand copies.

Smith now began to record regularly, accompanied by her Jazz Hounds, a touring band that then included the Memphis-born cornetist Johnny Dunn. (The band's instrumental from January 1921 of the standard-to-be "Royal Garden Blues" has been proposed as the first genuine jazz recording by a black ensemble.) Later in 1921, OKeh introduced its "race" series of blues, gospel, and jazz aimed at black customers. ("The race" was then the preferred term for African-Americans, consistently used by the black press, public spokespeople, and advertisers, and is mistakenly perceived by later generations as pejorative.) Other labels soon followed suit, and 1921 also saw the debut of the first black-owned record label, Black Swan. Its major discovery was singer Ethel Waters, and Fletcher Henderson made his first records for it, but it was short-lived. Meanwhile Columbia had signed Johnny Dunn, whose clever use of muted effects and showmanship made him a popular attraction. His replacement in the Jazz Hounds was Bubber Miley, another master of mutes, and a teenaged tenor saxophonist Mamie Smith had picked up in Kansas City named Coleman Hawkins made his recording debut with the Hounds in 1922.

Solo piano recorded well in the acoustic mode. Two great stride pianists, James P. Johnson (who had been cutting piano rolls since 1917) and his protégé, Fats Waller, made solos for OKeh in 1922. The label's race series was now in the good hands of the New Orleans–born pianist-songwriter-publisher Clarence Williams, who also had considerable influence at Columbia (the two labels would come under joint ownership in 1926). He first brought the great Bessie Smith to OKeh, then, when they declined her services, placed her with Columbia. Though her first record was a "cover" of an already established song, "Downhearted Blues," recorded by its composer, Alberta Hunter, and other singers, Bessie's version sold more than three hundred thousand copies. She became Columbia's most consistent seller, billed as "The Empress of the Blues."

Smith's debut came in early 1923, a watershed year for the recording of important black jazz and blues artists. Jelly Roll Morton, Sidney Bechet, King Oliver's Creole Jazz Band, and Ma Rainey now became able to reach a wider audience. Oliver's band included a young cornetist from New Orleans named Louis Armstrong and made its (and his) first records for a small label, Gennett, located in Richmond, Indiana, which for a decade would produce an extraordinary amount of notable jazz and blues records. The best white jazz band in Chicago, the New Orleans Rhythm Kings, had recorded for Gennett in the summer of 1922, and about a year later, they were joined in the label's studio (a rickety barn-like structure adjacent to a railroad siding and thus subject to sudden interruptions) by Jelly Roll Morton for the first deliberately integrated record date in the United States. (The first such event occurred in England in May 1921: the American clarinetist Edmund Jenkins recorded with a band led by the soon-to-be-famous Jack Hylton.) And in early 1924 a band from Indiana, the Wolverines, with twenty-year-old Bix Beiderbecke on cornet, made their first session for Gennett.

Bechet's debut inaugurated a long and distinguished series of records issued by the Clarence Williams Blue Five, though it was often more than a quintet. In 1925, while Armstrong was in New York with Fletcher Henderson's band, Williams paired him with Bechet, and the results, notably on "Cake Walking Babies from Home," were spectacular. The cornetist also accompanied several blues singers, including Bessie Smith and Ma Rainey (the latter for Paramount, an important blues label that also recorded jazz and was headquartered in Wisconsin), and made many sides with Henderson. If he was less prominently featured than one might expect, there were such exceptions as the 1925 "Sugar Foot Stomp," one of the first great jazz records made by the newly introduced electrical process, which much improved sound quality, if not consistently so from the start. (The acoustic method lingered on for a while, like silent films after sound had come in, but by the end of 1927, it was gone for good.)

The new technology worked particularly well for large ensembles, and Henderson's was by no means the only big jazz band now sounding better on discs. Duke Ellington first recorded in late 1924 at the helm of a sextet. Two years later he had ten pieces and was in the process of becoming the first jazz artist to realize that the medium of recording was fundamentally different from live performance. In the mid-1920s, recordings of popular music still ran a distant second to sheet-music sales as a source of income for publishers, and many performers also saw them mainly as an extension of song-plugging and a tool for promoting in-person appearances. (This attitude explains to a degree why so many artists accepted relatively low fees for making records.) Not so Ellington, who soon made himself the master of the three-minute musical gem and paid close attention to the proper placement of players in the studio and to the special tonal characteristics of that new contraption, the microphone.

Armstrong, who late in 1925 began the extraordinary series of Hot Five and Hot Seven recordings for OKeh in Chicago, now became the first jazz artist to demonstrate the true power of the phonograph record. Musicians throughout the United States and abroad (his records were soon issued in Europe; the record business was international) learned Armstrong solos by heart, and his way of phrasing a melody or parsing the rhythm caught on with arrangers as well as instrumentalists.

But perhaps the single most influential record in this period was made by an ad hoc recording unit, drawn mainly from the ranks of the Jean Goldkette band, under the leadership of C-melody saxophonist Frank Trumbauer and featuring solos by himself and Bix Beiderbecke. The profound impact of "Singin' the Blues" on musicians black and white was due to the quality and length of the two solos (both complete choruses), the relaxed tempo (slower than customary for the tune, a standard in the repertory of jazz and dance bands), and the fact that neither soloist stated the melody— for 1927, this was extended improvisation.

The Goldkette band was subject to a very different kind of musical power: that vested in recording directors (now called A&R men). Famed for its jazz soloists and the fine "hot" numbers featuring them, the band was prevented from recording all but two of these by Victor's Eddie King, who disliked jazz but favored the treacly vocalizing practiced by singers of the pre–Bing Crosby era that mars so many 1920s band records.

(It stands to reason that recorded jazz of any era can reflect only a minute fraction of the music actually performed; aside from many deserving players and bands who never entered a studio, those who did record were not always captured at their best. Since it is inevitable that our picture of the music's history is so strongly colored by what exists on record, this should be kept in mind.)

The opposite of the Goldkette situation applied to the New York–based musicians who often recorded under the leadership of cornetist Red Nichols, a very successful record and radio studio player and contractor. (Radio's role in the dissemination of all kinds of music grew as the decade moved on, and almost all that music was made live; the disc jockey was a 1930s phenomenon.) Under a variety of band names, famously as Red Nichols and his Five Pennies, these gifted instrumentalists, including many bandleaders-to-be, between 1926 and 1932 made records of jazz played for its own sake, often quite experimental in nature. These records were very influential among musicians. (A special offshoot of this jazz branch was the charming chamber music of violinist Joe Venuti and guitarist Eddie Lang.)

Chicago was a comparable recording nexus of black talent. Transplanted New Orleans players ruled the studio roost. Clarinetists Johnny Dodds and Jimmie Noone recorded frequently in a variety of settings, Dodds in a mostly traditional idiom, Noone more contemporary, his popular Apex Club Band featuring a front line of clarinet and alto sax, with Earl Hines at the piano. Jelly Roll Morton never led a band in public in Chicago, but his carefully rehearsed and handpicked Red Hot Peppers made a brilliant series of discs for Victor that can be considered the artistic apotheosis of New Orleans style. His later New York–based groups were less successful, musically and commercially.

While recording activity was centered in New York and Chicago (and late in the decade in Los Angeles as well), several labels regularly sent mobile recording units on field trips to capture local talent, primarily to stimulate regional sales, but also in hopes of unearthing acts of national potential. Cities visited included New Orleans (Columbia's 1927 trips preserved the unique Sam Morgan band, and there were other fine catches); Kansas City (OKeh got hold of Bennie Moten early on; his later Victors were made in Chicago or Camden, while Brunswick caught Andy Kirk's fledgling Clouds of Joy); Dallas, Houston, and San Antonio (with a good yield of Texas blues and territory bands, but Alphonse Trent's, the state's best, recorded for Gennett in Indiana); St. Louis (another jazz center, where OKeh and Vocalion documented such riverboat-associated bands as Charlie Creath's and Dewey Jackson's); and the blues centers Atlanta and Memphis (the latter the source of the intriguingly archaic sounds of Williamson's Beale Street Folic Orchestra on Victor, a label that also ventured to Savannah and even Seattle).

All told, an amazing (and amazingly varied) amount of music was captured by recording devices during the first dozen years of jazz recording, even pipe organ solos by Fats Waller, who managed to make the monster swing in Victor's Camden studios.

On Black Thursday, when the stock market first began to crumble, an unknown band from the Midwest, managed by the Goldkette office and called the Casa Loma Orchestra, recorded its first of many sides for OKeh in New York. With its well-tooled section work and riff-laden hot arrangements and romantic ballads, it would pave the way for the swing era, an event also forecast by Ellington's "It Don't Mean a Thing If It Ain't Got That Swing," introduced in 1932. Between those dates, the Great Depression cut deeply into the record business, sending annual sales from more than a hundred million units to a rock-bottom ten. Race records were among the worst-hit markets—even the great Bessie Smith stopped making records in 1931. Yet Armstrong and Ellington (not confined to the race lists) and newcomer Cab Calloway, who had replaced Ellington at the Cotton Club and also was managed by the shrewd music publisher and recording director Irving Mills, all continued to record with surprising frequency.

In 1932 a new chapter in the story of jazz on records began when John Hammond became active as a producer. Motivated solely by a commitment to the music and its makers, regardless of race, modified only by strong personal preferences, he was young (twenty-one) and fearless (his mother was a Vanderbilt, and he was not beholden to any employers). Hammond had been writing about American jazz for Britain's *Melody Maker* and now started to produce records for Columbia's London-based branch (they were soon also issued in the United States). His talent roster included Benny Carter (in small-group and big-band settings, the marvelous young pianist Teddy Wilson involved in both), Fletcher Henderson ("Talk of the Town" featured Coleman Hawkins's longest recorded solo to date), a Joe Venuti–

led all-star group, and Benny Goodman with Jack Teagarden (and in 1933 with an unknown teenaged singer named Billie Holiday). By 1934 Goodman was leading his first big band and recording with it, Hammond serving as his adviser.

These names would loom large during the swing years just around the corner, helping to revive the record business, slowly but surely. And a new element now came into play: the jazz record collector. Opera, and to a lesser degree instrumental classical music, had long since attracted dedicated listeners who sought out favorite performers and performances deleted from active record catalogs. Such seekers after "collector's items" were still rare in jazz during the 1920s, though there was a nucleus of knowledgeable collectors at Princeton University. In Europe, affiliated labels issued U.S. masters, including items culled from the race lists, which gave local fanciers easier access than their American counterparts, who had to visit stores in black neighborhoods or special-order the discs. By 1930 the eighteen-year-old Frenchman Hugues Panassié was already writing surprisingly astute record reviews for the short-lived *Revue du Jazz* and the longer-lasting *Jazz Tango Dancing*. And in New York City, a young record-store manager began to stock cutout jazz and blues items, catering to a small but growing clientele of collectors, among them musicians, songwriters, and journalists from the staff of nearby Time, Inc. This was Milt Gabler, his store was the Commodore Music Shop, and one of his best customers was John Hammond. Soon, Gabler was ordering custom pressings (minimum order: three hundred) of deleted material from the American Record Company, which had gobbled up a host of bankrupt or near-bankrupt labels during the early Depression days (Columbia, OKeh, Brunswick, and Perfect among them) for release on his own white-label Commodores.

Meanwhile, the accelerating popularity of swing, spurred by Benny Goodman, prompted a steady flow of new releases, mostly by big bands but also by small groups. These might be working units, such as bassist John Kirby's "biggest little band in the land," a versatile sextet, or ad hoc all-star studio gatherings, such as the splendid series for Brunswick under the leadership of Teddy Wilson, produced by Hammond, and for Victor, headed up by Lionel Hampton. Wilson's records often had vocals by Billie Holiday, who also recorded under her own name for Vocalion; the difference was that with Wilson, she would sing one chorus, framed by instrumental work, while on her own records, the players got the middle passages. Hampton handled his own vocals, as did the popular and prolific Armstrong-inspired New Orleans trumpeters Wingy Manone (on Victor's thirty-five-cent Bluebird label) and Louis Prima (Brunswick).

But the most prolific and popular singing instrumentalist was the irrepressible Fats Waller, who between 1934 and 1942 made more than three hundred sides for Victor and Bluebird with his six-piece Rhythm, not counting piano solos and occasional big-band ventures. Discs like Waller's were prime fodder for the by now ubiquitous jukeboxes, a boon to the record industry and a thorn in the side of the musicians' union, since no royalties were derived from this kind of public performance. The rapidly growing popularity of the disc jockey was also viewed as a threat to live music on radio, though there was as yet no shortage of that, not least in the form of "remotes" from ballrooms and nightclubs all over the land, carrying the sounds of swing.

By the later 1930s the record industry, dominated by RCA Victor, ARC, and the upstart Decca—founded in 1934 and, unlike the competition, retailing all its popular output, even by such top performers as Crosby and Armstrong, at thirty-five rather than seventy-five cents per disc (three for a dollar)—was still under the considerable influence of the music publishers. They wanted quick recordings of the songs, mostly ephemeral, issuing forth in a steady stream from Tin Pan Alley. No big band recorded more of these than Tommy Dorsey's, led by a man with publishing interests. But Dorsey's biggest hits of the decade, "Marie" and "Song of India," were sparked by the trumpet solos of Bunny Berigan, who had also lit up Goodman's seminal 1935 "King Porter Stomp." Inevitably, Berigan wound up as leader of his own band, and with it he recorded one of the swing era's most enduring works, "I Can't Get Started." All these bands recorded for Victor, and so, by 1938, did an ambitious young clarinetist named Artie Shaw. He had just switched from ARC's Vocalion label to Victor's Bluebird imprint when he struck gold with an instrumental version of Cole Porter's "Begin the Beguine," a song neither new nor popular. Its stunning success was yet another demonstration of the phonograph's power; in its wake, Shaw became Goodman's chief rival in the swing sweepstakes. The Goodman band never had a comparable hit record, though "Sing, Sing, Sing" sold well for a 12-inch record. That size was still rare for jazz, but Berigan's "I Can't Get Started" also was of that diameter.

Both discs were part of Victor's somewhat pretentiously named *Symposium of Swing*, an album set of four 12-inchers, to which Decca responded with *Five Feet of Swing*, going Victor one disc better. The usual jazz album contained four to six 10-inch discs. Victor led off in the genre in 1936 with a *Bix Beiderbecke Memorial Album* that set high standards. It contained several so-called alternate takes. Routinely, more than one version of a selection would be recorded, sometimes at a single session, sometimes at different dates; one was chosen for release, but others might be saved as "safeties." In the case of significant soloists, such alternative versions might be quite different and of great interest to specialists and collectors. The Beiderbecke album also came with a booklet of excellent annotations by the pioneer discographer Warren Scholl. Subsequent Victor albums were mainly compilations of hits until the label launched its *Hot Jazz Classics* series in the 1940s. Decca was more enterprising with its anthologies of white and "colored" jazz, instrumental surveys such as *Sliphorn* (trombonists), *Blackstick* (clarinetists), *Saxophobia* (tenor saxists), and *Drummer Boy*. And Decca's 1939 *Chicago Jazz* was an innovation: the first jazz album of newly recorded material, produced and conceived by nineteen-year-old George Avakian, who would become a notable record producer. Columbia, though in financial doldrums, was persuaded by Hammond to issue a Bessie Smith memorial album in 1938.

A year before, Hugues Panassié and his co-editor at the French magazine *Jazz Hot*, Charles Delaunay, who in 1936 had published his unprecedented *Hot Discography* (a slightly earlier British book, *Rhythm on Records*, was not a proper discography since it omitted exact recording dates, complete personnel listings, matrix numbers, and original issue), launched the world's first record label exclusively dedicated to jazz. Called Swing, it made an auspicious debut with a session starring Coleman Hawkins and Benny Carter, joined by leading French practitioners such as Django Reinhardt and Stephane Grappelli (on piano) and another American in Paris, drummer Tommy Benford.

Meanwhile Milt Gabler had continued his reissue program, now on the UHCA label (the initials stood for United Hot Clubs of America, patterned on the Hot Club de France, best remembered for the sponsorship of a quintet that bore its name and starred Reinhardt and Grappelli), but he had long wanted to record freshly minted jazz of the kind closest to his heart. In early 1938 his Commodore label made its debut as the first American jazz label, with a session under Eddie Condon's leadership, featuring Bud Freeman, Pee Wee Russell, Jess Stacy, and newcomer Bobby Hackett in a latter-day Chicago-style setting. Shortly after the first Commodore release, Gabler's friendly rival Steve Smith, who ran the Hot Record Shop and its Hot Record Society reissue label, launched HRS Originals with a session led by Pee Wee Russell, but now in the company of James P. Johnson, a couple of Count Basie sidemen, and drummer Zutty Singleton.

The Basie band, one of Hammond's happiest discoveries, had first been heard by the jazz proselytizer on his powerful car radio, broadcasting on a shortwave station from Kansas City, where he promptly caught them in person. He meant to sign them to Vocalion, an ARC label, but Decca's Jack Kapp jumped in with a contract. Hammond did manage a preview, recording a small Basie group including the leader and Lester Young, billing it as "Smith-Jones, Inc." (Smith and Jones were on trumpet and drums.) But he had to wait two years to produce records by his favorite band.

The existence of an independent jazz label like Commodore made it possible to record, when Hammond's bosses turned down the idea, some of the finest small-group swing music of the decade, a kind of follow-up to the

Smith-Jones date, which had introduced Lester Young to records. Now another Basie spinoff, this time without the leader, or any piano, but with two guitars—one electric—and Young doubling clarinet (Gabler's idea), recorded for Commodore as the Kansas City Six some jazz gems that have seldom been out of circulation since. The label also played a key role in Billie Holiday's career. She was still contracted to Vocalion, now owned by CBS, and Hammond was still her producer, but they were most reluctant to let the singer record a very unusual song recently added to her repertory at Café Society, the country's only nightclub catering to integrated audiences. This was "Strange Fruit," which dealt in unsparing terms with lynching. Holiday approached Gabler, long her friend, who persuaded Hammond to loan the singer to Commodore for one date. As it turned out, the controversial song's flip side, a blues, "Fine and Mellow," concocted by Holiday and Gabler for the occasion, became the label's first modest hit.

Under new ownership, the Columbia label once again became a major player in the record business. In 1939 Hammond helped to lure Goodman away from Victor, where the clarinetist's trio and quartet records had become catalog staples. With Lionel Hampton as the sole holdover, he now formed a sextet including yet another Hammond find (with help from Mary Lou Williams), the electric guitarist Charlie Christian, who, not least due to his Goodman sextet records, would change the role of the guitar in jazz (and popular music) forever. Another youngster had a similar effect on his chosen instrument, the bass. This was Jimmy Blanton, whose 1939 arrival in the Ellington band coincided with a new creative peak in Ellington's career and a fruitful new association with Victor (whose engineers were still the best). The unprecedented Ellington-Blanton duets launched the bass as a solo voice in jazz.

Simultaneous with such new developments, the rediscovery of jazz's past continued apace. Hugues Panassié, visiting the United States, was invited to supervise sessions for Victor's Bluebird label and enlisted his friend and mentor, the clarinetist Mezz Mezzrow, to assist him. The results, while uneven, helped to launch Sidney Bechet to his first fame in his homeland and gave New Orleans trumpeter Tommy Ladnier his last chances to record. "Revolutionary Blues," featuring these two, announced what would become the New Orleans revival movement. Jelly Roll Morton, aided by Alan Lomax's documentary recording project for the Library of Congress in 1938 (not issued until nine years later, on critic Rudi Blesh's small Circle label), was recorded solo in Washington, D.C., by the Jazz Man label, formed by Neshui Ertegun, son of the Turkish ambassador to the United States, and subsequently brought to New York to record for Bluebird with a band including Bechet and other veterans from Morton's hometown. The year 1939 also saw the publication of *Jazzmen*, an influential book that became the sacred text of the revival, soon further spurred by the discovery in New Iberia, Louisiana, of the legendary trumpeter Bunk Johnson, rumored to have taught young Louis Armstrong.

Johnson did not record until 1942, but in 1940, music by a band made up of New Orleans elders, led by trumpeter Kid Rena and performing in a pre-Oliver Creole Jazz Band style, was issued on the Delta label. This had appeal to the still limited circle of serious collectors and students of jazz history. Considerably more resonant was the not-so-archeological music recorded for Bluebird by the short-lived but excellent Muggsy Spanier Ragtimers. Small independent jazz labels now began to proliferate. Some, like Solo Art, dedicated exclusively to blues and boogie-woogie piano, did not last, but others, like Blue Note, which also began life as a boogie-woogie piano label, survived the century. By 1942 the list included Bob Thiele's Signature; Collector's Item, and the aforementioned Jazz Man, now relocated to California and introducing Lu Watters's Yerba Buena Jazz Band, a bunch of obscure San Franciscans attempting to copy classic Oliver and Morton—two cornets, banjo, brass bass, and all.

On the swing front, such Kansas City–based bands as Harlan Leonard's Rockets (with a young arranger named Tadd Dameron) and Jay McShann's (with a young altoist named Charlie Parker), recording for Bluebird and Decca respectively, were pointing in new directions, as were the remarkable Art Tatum (prolific on Decca since 1934) and fellow pianist (and singer) Nat King Cole, at the helm of a swinging trio (at first on Decca's "Sepia Series" race list, then signed by Capitol, a label formed in 1942 by a Los Angeles triumvirate including songwriter Johnny Mercer and record-store owner Glenn Wallichs). Since 1938 Decca also had been the home of Louis Jordan's Tympany Five, a hip little band that godfathered rhythm-and-blues and by the early 1940s had "crossed over" to the general catalog. And it is impossible to ignore the effect of an instrumental record that became an unexpected hit and re-established Coleman Hawkins as the rightful king of the tenor saxophone shortly after his return from Europe in 1939. "Body and Soul" remains a jazz landmark, its two choruses of improvisation (the melody stated only in two opening bars) a lesson in solo construction—a kind of successor to "Singin' the Blues."

But there was trouble ahead for the record business. Effective August 1, 1942, the mercurial president of the American Federation of Musicians, James Caesar Petrillo, ordered a ban on all recording by instrumentalists, the labels having failed to agree to a demand for royalties to musicians for broadcast and jukebox play. Changes wrought by World War II, such as the shortage of shellac and the effects of the draft, were already a burden on the music industry, and the ban had a profound impact on jazz. With new instrumental records, the singers, already growing in popularity, might not have prospered with such rapidity, though Frank Sinatra would undoubt-edly still have made his impact. In any event, a ray of jazz recording light emanated from the V Disc program of special records made solely for dis-tribution to the Armed Forces, with union dispensation and a surprisingly high percentage of jazz, most of it produced by jazz critic George T. Simon. A bit later on, transcription sessions made for radio use only were permitted by the union and also yielded a fair amount of jazz. (Decades later, the release of music from broadcasts made for the Armed Forces, notably the Jubilee series aimed at black troops, added to the slender record of jazz made during the ban.)

It took more than two years to fully rescind the ban. Decca was first among the majors to settle, late in 1943, but Victor and Columbia held out longer. In the interim, independent labels sprang up all over the land, mak-ing their own deals with the union and issuing country music, gospel, rhythm-and-blues—and jazz. These upstarts, and the older independents, would document new trends in jazz well before the majors came on board. Among the first was Savoy, located in Newark, New Jersey, and, like Com-modore and HRS, the offspring of a retail store dealing in radio parts, used records, and other "dry goods." After an inauspicious debut, Teddy Reig, an enterprising habitué of Fifty-second Street and the Harlem jazz scene, was hired as producer, adding to Savoy's roster such budding stars as Erroll Garner, Don Byas, and above all Charlie Parker, who made his first leader's date for the label. Parker's earlier discs with Dizzy Gillespie had been made first for Guild, then for the older independent that gobbled it up, Musicraft, which also launched Sarah Vaughan: the producer here was veteran Albert Marx, first to record Art Tatum in 1933. Musicraft also recorded Gillespie's big band, later signed by Victor, but the trumpeter's first own date was made for another Newark-based label, Manor. The two fathers of bebop also recorded for Continental, not a jazz-only label but also the home of such es-tablished artists as Mary Lou Williams, Hot Lips Page, and Slam Stewart.

Williams did most of her sessions for Moe Asch's Asch and Disc labels, later to become Folkways Records. The first of Norman Granz's Jazz at the Philharmonic live concert recordings appeared on Asch and Disc; it was an influential innovation in jazz recording and, with its 12-inch album re-leases, a prelude to the long-playing record. Behind many of the small-label modern jazz sessions was the enterprising critic, broadcaster, concert pro-ducer, and prolific songwriter Leonard Feather, who had been producing dates of his own since 1937, beginning in his native England. An early booster of bebop, he was responsible for getting the new sounds through Victor's door. That label also recorded the annual Metronome All-Star dates, sponsored by and featuring the poll winners of *Metronome* magazine, second only to *Down Beat* among jazz periodicals. Other jazz names on Victor included Coleman Hawkins, the most bop-friendly among established stars, who also recorded modern sessions for Capitol, Joe Davis, Sonora, and Apollo—the latter yet another record store–associated label, this with the Rainbow Music Shop in Harlem.

Capitol was for more than two decades the home of Stan Kenton, whose self-styled "progressive jazz" had a big following that enabled the pianist-arranger-bandleader to include in his voluminous recorded output much music of a highly experimental nature. Another big-band leader to find success in the post-war era was Woody Herman, long a Decca artist with his Band That Plays the Blues, but then leader of his First Herd on Columbia, the more boppish Second Herd on Capitol, and several more to follow. Many other leaders disbanded in the mid-1940s, at least temporarily, as television and the growth of suburbs cut into nightlife, and swing was replaced as the number-one dance music by rhythm-and-blues and then rock-and-roll.

By 1946 Charlie Parker was recording for still another label spawned by a record store, Ross Russell's Dial, based in Los Angeles. Dial also signed a former Savoy artist, Dexter Gordon, whose double-sided 78 "tenor battle" with Wardell Gray, "The Chase," transcended bop and appealed to the same listeners who responded so well to Hampton and Basie alumnus Illinois Jacquet, the tenor spark plug of early Jazz at the Philharmonic.

Parker's marvelous quintet recordings for Dial (and Savoy, to fulfill old contracts), with Miles Davis on trumpet and Max Roach on drums, became bebop classics, but Parker's biggest sales resulted from his somewhat later sessions with strings, produced by Norman Granz and distributed by Mercury, like Capitol a new label with major ambitions. Chicago-based, Mercury at first recorded blues and boogie-woogie, in the process discovering tenorman Gene Ammons, the son of famed boogie-woogie pianist Albert. The son would score his biggest hits with a new jazz label, Prestige, also a record store offshoot, founded in New York by Bob Weinstock. Mercury soon spawned EmArcy as a jazz subsidiary, with Bob Shad as producer. This brings us to the dawn of the LP era, which began in 1948 and would profoundly change the nature of jazz recording.

The LP, introduced in a 10-inch format, was initially perceived primarily as a boon to classical music, since long works could now be recorded (or remastered) without the annoying pauses or cuts mandated by 78s. For jazz and popular music, the LP was seen mainly as a compact compilation medium, in the image of the 78 album. This format had become increasingly popular for jazz reissues (including unreleased masters and alternate takes) during the recording ban, but lingered on beyond it. Columbia led in this field, but Victor as well as Decca and its subsidiaries also had been active, and now these labels all converted them to LP, sometimes adding material.

It was one of the new independent jazz labels that pointed the way to creative use of the new technology. Prestige included an eight-minute excursion by tenorman Zoot Sims, "Zoot Blows the Blues," as a track on an LP—a prelude to the "blowing sessions" the label would soon specialize in. This formula called for gathering a bunch of compatible horn players, bringing them together with a strong rhythm section, and maximizing studio time to generate several lengthy, jam session–like pieces, sometimes taking up an entire side of an LP (the soon-prevailing 12-inch format included). Columbia also launched a series of studio jam sessions under the leadership of ex–Basie trumpeter-arranger Buck Clayton, produced by George Avakian with Hammond. Blue Note, which gradually had moved from revivalist jazz to swing, now entered the modern field with a coup, courageously and successfully recording pianist-composer Thelonious Monk in his debut as a leader. Excepting a lingering loyalty to Sidney Bechet, greatly admired by the label's founder, Alfred Lion, and his partner, Francis Wolff, Blue Note now focused on modern jazz; loyalty to favorite artists remained a label characteristic, most fully expressed in more than two decades of association with Horace Silver, one of the founders of the hard-bop style that Blue Note mined with great success.

Monk would find this kind of affiliation, after a brief Prestige interlude that followed his Blue Note period, with the third of the "big three" jazz independents, Riverside. Founded by Bill Grauer and Orrin Keepnews, it began as a reissue operation, having obtained rights to the classic Gennett and Paramount catalogs, and then joined the modern sweepstakes. Keepnews nurtured Monk, played an essential role in the career of a very different pianist, Bill Evans, and became the legendary guitarist Wes Montgomery's first and best producer. He was aided in the latter coup by Riverside's leading seller, altoist Cannonball Adderley, whose quintet specialized in hard bop, and whose role as highly valued informal artistic adviser reflected a unique relationship between producer and artist. The veteran tenorman Ike Quebec played a similar role as talent scout and facilitator at Blue Note. This kind of involvement by musicians in the recording process had begun with Eddie Condon and Milt Gabler and became more direct with pianist Art Hodes's Jazz Record, Mezz Mezzrow's King Jazz, and bassist Al Hall's Wax, all short-lived. The longest-lasting and most visible of musician-owned (or operated) labels was Charles Mingus's Debut (1952–57), entering auspiciously with the famous Massey Hall concert LPs, starring Parker, Gillespie, and Bud Powell, and living up to its name by introducing a number of artists.

Prestige's leading players were Miles Davis and Sonny Rollins. The trumpeter was lured away by Columbia's Avakian in 1955, and the tenorman (after fruitful Blue Note and Riverside albums) was signed by the selfsame Avakian, by now with Victor, to what was claimed to be the most lucrative contract offered a jazz artist. It is safe to assume, however, that Davis's two-decade-long association with Columbia, resulting in such landmarks as *Kind of Blue*, *Sketches of Spain*, and *Bitches Brew*, yielded much more. Teo Macero produced the latter two LPs and also worked with Monk when the pianist came to Columbia in 1962. Columbia was most committed to jazz of the majors, not least due to the unusually enlightened presidency of Goddard Lieberson (and later, and more briefly, Bruce Lundvall), but also thanks to the resounding success of Dave Brubeck, brought to the label by Avakian after the pianist's quartet had proven its appeal with a California independent, Fantasy. The fortunes of the California-based jazz labels were not at all limited to so-called West Coast jazz. With Richard Bock in the producer's chair, Pacific Jazz developed such leading West Coast lights as Gerry Mulligan and Chet Baker but also nurtured Gerald Wilson's big band and much else. The most consistently interesting Californian label was Lester Koenig's Contemporary, put on a solid business footing by the unanticipated and huge (for jazz) sales of its jazz version of the score from *My Fair Lady*, performed by André Previn, piano; Leroy Vinnegar, bass; and Shelly Manne, drums. It spawned a long-lived genre: jazz versions of Broadway musicals. Koenig, unlike other producers also a first-rate engineer, was guided by excellent and wide-ranging taste. His sizable catalog included much of Art Pepper's best work, a pair of superb Sonny Rollins LPs, Ornette Coleman's first studio recordings, and most of Phineas Newborn, Jr.'s output. He also tended to traditional style on his Good Time Jazz label, much of it supervised by Neshui Ertegun, who subsequently took charge of the Atlantic label's jazz wing.

Atlantic, like Contemporary, mirrored its producer's tastes. Ertegun's commitment to the Modern Jazz Quartet (and other John Lewis ventures) lasted for twenty-five years. He had a fruitful association with Coleman, worked patiently with Charles Mingus, and presented Ray Charles in jazz settings. And he took risks with trumpeter Tony Fruscella and the gifted vibist-composer Teddy Charles that paid off artistically if not commercially. Some of Mingus's most politically outspoken work was done for Candid, aptly named but short-lived, which also brought out the most agitprop of civil rights–related jazz pieces, Max Roach's *Freedom Now* suite, and some striking early Cecil Taylor (who had also recorded for Contemporary). Writer Nat Hentoff was Candid's producer, but it was a subsidiary of Cadence Records, home of the popular singer Andy Williams, who years later acquired and reissued much of the Candid catalog on his Barnaby label.

No jazz label was more prolific or prolix than Norman Granz's Verve (which absorbed its antecedents, Clef and Norgran), or less tied to the bottom line. His multiple Jazz at the Philharmonic releases included the first jazz LPs to be marketed in boxed sets, and he commissioned fine cover art, notably from David Stone Martin. Some of his ventures, such as the Ella Fitzgerald *Song Book* series, were commercial successes (and prime examples of how intelligent record production and packaging and promotion can boost an artist's career) while others were not, among them several first-rate LPs featuring the altoist Lee Konitz and those starring veteran jazz violinist Stuff Smith. But Granz recorded who and what he liked—no one more frequently than the pianist he had first brought from Montreal to Carnegie Hall, Oscar Peterson. Granz's loyalty to great jazz figures no longer in their prime (Lester Young and Billie Holiday, and later Coleman Hawkins) has no parallel. Possibly his crowning achievement was his Art Tatum project, which over the last four years of the great pianist's life yielded more than a dozen solo piano albums as well as great encounters with peers Benny Carter, Roy Eldridge (a special Granz favorite), Ben Webster, Lionel Hampton, Buddy DeFranco, and Buddy Rich. Granz sold Verve in 1961 but returned to the fray in 1973 with Pablo, for which he bought back his Tatum masters, re-signed Fitzgerald, Peterson, and Eldridge, and continued to behave more like a patron of the arts than a businessman.

Duke Ellington was among Granz's Verve and Pablo artists but enjoyed his longest LP-era relationship with Columbia. Among the first established recording artists to grasp the potential of the new medium, he was now able to comfortably record a long work like *Harlem*, combining it with an extended version of "Take the A Train" in an LP he called *Ellington Uptown*, and giving similar expanded treatment to such staples as "Mood Indigo" and "Solitude" for *Masterpieces by Ellington*. By the mid-1950s, when stereo recording had arrived, Ellington was specializing in suites, a genre well suited to the LP. He continued in this vein, including his term with Frank Sinatra's Reprise label, until the sunset of his half-century recording career, when the Sacred Concerts (all three on record) had become his main pursuit. A Columbia LP that played a pivotal role in Ellington's later career was also one of the best-known samples of yet another LP genre, the live recording. This was *Ellington at Newport*, recorded at the 1956 festival, which, when reissued in expanded form on CD in 1999, turned out to have been only partially "live." But there is no doubting the authenticity of another live Columbia LP that had a most positive effect on an artist's career, Erroll Garner's *Concert by the Sea*, an album with great initial success and longevity. The pianist had been recording for all comers, but once he had entered the major leagues, he became the first jazz artist to exercise complete artistic control over his product, à la Horowitz.

These were festival and concert recordings, but perhaps the most significant live LPs were those that captured music made in nightclubs. New

York's Village Vanguard is primary among these venues, the site of classic performances by various Bill Evans trios (notably the first, on Riverside), by Sonny Rollins in a very different trio format (Blue Note), and by the John Coltrane quartet and quintet, caught in the act on the Impulse label in 1961, near the beginning of the influential saxophonist's lengthy relationship with veteran producer Bob Thiele. As the decade moved on and rock music came to dominate the record business, Coltrane was among the few jazz performers to still enjoy a solid contract and steady sales. He was even able to bring out the unique *Ascension*, a continuous spontaneously improvised ensemble performance stretching over an entire LP (and unintentionally issued in two versions).

There was, however, another saxophonist whose recording fortunes were not ill affected by the 1960s. This was Stan Getz, once cited by Coltrane as a favorite and among the Verve artists held over after the label's sale to MGM. The new producer, Creed Taylor (incidentally the man who had signed Coltrane to Impulse), got off to a good start with Getz by way of the unusual *Focus* LP, a work for strings and rhythm section ingeniously conceived by Eddie Sauter to provide a backdrop for the saxophonist's improvised solo part. This was an artistic triumph for Getz, but his next venture would make him one of the most commercially successful of all jazz musicians. At the behest of guitarist Charlie Byrd, Getz joined him in a program of recent Brazilian tunes in a style known in its homeland as bossa nova. While the LP was issued as *Jazz Samba*, it put bossa nova on the musical map to stay and also spun off a single (the 45-rpm configuration had long since replaced 78 for such discs) that would become the only jazz instrumental of the decade to place in the trade magazine charts, "Desafinado." (Getz and the bossa nova gave birth to an even bigger hit, "The Girl from Ipanema," but this had a vocal by Astrud Gilberto.)

Taylor eventually left Verve to start his own CTI label, which employed effective packaging and marketing to gain a goodly share of what remained of the jazz record market by the 1970s. Its leading artists included trumpeter Freddie Hubbard, flutist Hubert Laws, and tenorman Stanley Turrentine, all engaged by Taylor in accommodations with rock, while another three-letter label, the German-based ECM, nurtured such newcomers as keyboard players and composers Chick Corea and Keith Jarrett and later came to specialize in so-called world music. Other European labels would make significant jazz contributions, among them the Danish SteepleChase, Italian Black Saint/Soul Note, Danish Storyville, the German Enja, the Swiss Hat Hut, and the Dutch Criss Cross. Without these labels, many gifted musicians would have gone unrepresented on records. An American label that consistently attended to deserving jazz and blues artists was the Chicago-based Delmark, founded by Bob Koester, with his record store as the base of operations; it was first to record the music of the city's 1960s avant-garde, including several members of the Art Ensemble of Chicago, and Anthony Braxton in his recording debut.

The last years of the LP exhibited the sort of gigantism associated with an earlier vanishing species, the dinosaurs. ECM presented a ten-LP box, *The Sun Bear Concerts*, of Keith Jarrett solo concert performances in Japan—a haven for jazz in the lean years. But it was reissues that weighed in heaviest, as with *The Complete Keynote Recordings*, twenty-one LPs celebrating an independent jazz label of the 1940s, produced by a jazz expert from Java, Harry Lim. The reissue set was lovingly produced by one of Japan's foremost jazz authorities, Kiyoshi Koyama, whose penchant for large-scale projects earned him the nickname of "Boxman."

A pioneering and still-unique multi-LP project (later available in a five-CD format) was *The Smithsonian Collection of Classic Jazz* (Smithsonian Collection of Recordings), released in 1973 and revised in 1987. This collection, selected and annotated by critic Martin Williams, has not been without its detractors, but it still stands as the best survey of recorded jazz history.

When the CD was introduced, forecasters anticipated a decade-long co-existence with the LP, but the handy new format established itself in half that time. "Vinyl," as the LP is called in the CD era, survives in occasional limited editions aimed at collectors and audiophiles (in 1999, the Japanese branch of Blue Note issued two dozen 10-inch LPs in exact replications) and at second hand in a lively international collectors' market. The LP's reign was shorter than the 78's, and at the turn of the century it seems certain that the days of the CD are numbered. The format, however, has long since made its mark on jazz. With disc duration averaging an hour, it confronted the artist with the very real problem of how to sustain sufficient listener interest, notably when he or she was expected to record with some frequency. A result has been the proliferation of original compositions, many of which are neither. Another, since CDs are much easier than LPs to store, carry, and even produce, is an abundance of self-produced records. There are very many small labels as well, usually specializing in niche markets.

And there is a cornucopia of reissues, some approaching the scope (if nowhere near the heft) of the latter-day LP boxes. These include the eighteen-CD Bill Evans box and the sixteen-CD Ella Fitzgerald *Song Book* set, both on Verve, and an eighteen-CD Nat King Cole box issued by Mosaic, a mail-order label specializing in complete sets of various kinds, licensed for limited editions from the record companies created in the mergers of the last three decades of the twentieth century that now control the bulk of the recorded legacy of jazz. A notable and happy exception is

Fantasy Records, which, thanks to the success of the rock band Creedence Clearwater Revival, was able to acquire in turn Prestige, Riverside, Milestone, Contemporary, Pablo, and some smaller labels, and is keeping a commendably large percentage of its huge catalog in circulation.

At the turn of the century, the amount and variety of recorded jazz readily available, now also via the Internet, is staggering. It encompasses almost everything of significance from every era, and in constantly improving sound quality. There are of course regrettable gaps at any given moment, and every connoisseur has favorites that remain un-reissued. But when one considers such vintage 1999 bonanzas as *The Complete Duke Ellington on RCA Victor* (twenty-four CDs with extensive annotation) from the perspective of more than fifty years of listening to and acquiring jazz records, the advantages of the present are undeniable.

(2000)

Discography: The Thankless Science

Today's jazz record buyer, accustomed to finding full personnel listings and recording details neatly laid out on the back of most LP jackets, and taking the availability of such information so much for granted that he is likely to complain when it isn't furnished, can hardly be expected to consider the problems that confronted his much hardier predecessors.

Nonetheless—and especially if he collects reissues of historic recordings—he is the beneficiary of that unsung breed of researchers and enthusiasts who practice the science of discography.

Current editions of the better dictionaries define discography as "a descriptive, classified catalog or listing of phonograph records, usually including dates, and names of performers," which is neat and accurate enough, but as little as ten years ago, the word could not be found even in the most complete versions of Webster's big, fat *International Dictionary*.

No discographer ever has received a foundation grant, even the tiniest one, though researchers in the most obscure cracks and crevices of esoterica, such as the correspondence of a fourth-rate nineteenth-century poet, or the travels of a long-forgotten mannerist painter, regularly are awarded financial assistance.

Though a considerable literature has developed in the field of jazz discography since Hilton Schleman published his *Rhythm on Records* in 1936, few works in this genre have sold well enough to be published by commercial houses. Generally, after years of unpaid work in his spare time, the author has to publish his book privately, and he is fortunate if he is able to recover the printing and distributing costs.

At this point, the reader might well ask: What of it? Is discographical research really of any importance? And what could be so difficult and time-consuming about compiling listings of old phonograph records? Why shouldn't this kind of musical bookkeeping, as one disparaging critic has called it, be left to those mad enough to plow through dusty piles of 78s and pore over old record-company ledger files?

The answer is that the tireless and thankless work of the discographers has in fact produced a painstakingly detailed body of factual data that constitutes an invaluable tool to jazz historians and researchers, and which has made it possible for the beginning student of jazz to become, in a short time, as well informed about who played what chorus on an important record as the expert of yesterday was after years of devoted studies.

In order to appreciate the achievements of discography in the jazz field, it is necessary to point out that, up to its fairly recent rise to the status of an art, jazz was simply a form of popular entertainment—at least as far as record companies were concerned.

In the early 1920s, when jazz records first were manufactured in sizable quantities, few if any consumers of the product were the least interested in the identity of the musicians in the various bands. In many cases, they were not even interested in the identity of the band, and it was the general practice of record companies to issue discs under various pseudonyms, which often offered no clues to the artists involved. Another common practice was to lease the masters of such recordings to other companies, which then would issue the record under yet another pseudonym.

The matter was confounded further by the fact that any given pseudonym was often indiscriminately applied to a variety of bands. The discovery, for instance, of a record by the Dixie Daisies that included Jack Teagarden and Benny Goodman in the personnel was no assurance that other records under this band name would be worth acquiring, for they might turn out to be by Fred Hall and his Sugar Babies, a band of decidedly mild jazz interest, or by a truly anonymous studio group of no jazz interest whatsoever.

It is well to bear in mind, too, that the hobby of collecting jazz records was practiced by a mere lunatic fringe of devotees, until the advent of the swing era. There were no stores specializing in this music, and by the time jazz collectors had become an in-group of some size, the records they were after generally could be found only in junk shops, Salvation Army and Goodwill stores, or among old dealer's stock on a back shelf.

It was no trick, of course, to discover an OKeh record by Louis Armstrong and his Hot Five—Armstrong's name was on the label. But things became more complicated when the Armstrong collector listened to a disc by Lil's Hot Shots and found it to be by the Hot Five, recording for the rival Brunswick label. There was some logic to this, since Lillian Hardin was the Hot Five's pianist. But why should Armstrong's OKeh recording of "Ain't Misbehavin'" turn up on Odeon as by Ted Shawn and his orchestra?

If our collector knew that Fletcher Henderson's orchestra, featuring Louis Armstrong, had recorded "Everybody Loves My Baby," he could then search for it—and find it—plainly labeled as by Henderson, on the Regal, Banner, Ajax, Apex, or Imperial labels. But he might well pass up the same title on Domino, as by "Hal Whyte's Syncopators," or on Oriole, as by "Sam Hill and His Orchestra," little knowing that these, too, were what he was looking for. Short of listening to the records, his only clue would have been a tiny series of numbers engraved in the shellac near the label.

This so-called master or matrix number was the only constant factor in the puzzling picture confronting the jazz researcher. It not only revealed the origin and, after still more research, the approximate date of the music. Then the even smaller number, letter, or Roman numeral following the master number itself, was found to be the "take" number, making it possible to visually identify those "alternate takes" that were, and are, the delight of the serious jazz-collecting enthusiast.

But it was not only because of the puzzle of pseudonyms, or the discovery of alternate takes, that discography came into being. The need for it evolved because the growing interest in the music required some kind of guide to what jazz was available on records.

The catalogs published periodically by record companies were a help, of course, but these did not list discontinued items or give details about personnel other than the leader and, perhaps, the featured vocalist. (The latter, more often than not, was the most uninteresting thing about the record.)

In 1936, when the first well-informed book on jazz published in the United States, Hugues Panassié's *Hot Jazz*, came off the press, the two first jazz discographies saw the light of day.

Both were published in Europe, where serious interest in jazz was more widespread than in its homeland. Schleman's *Rhythm on Records*, published by the British music weekly, *Melody Maker*, was the work of a record company publicity man who was the owner of a distinguished jazz collection. It was the pioneer work in the field, but it did not confine itself to jazz, including much material on dance music of the period, and though it gave valuable personnel information, it was not detailed; it simply listed all the musicians who were known to have worked with a given band. (Schleman, according to Stanley Dance, who assisted in the compilation of the book, was a born collector rather than a jazz enthusiast; after the book was finished, he turned from records to cigarette cards.)

More significant and permanently valuable was a book published later that year in Paris, Charles Delaunay's *Hot Discography*. This was the book on which all future works in the field were to base themselves—the first open sesame to the musical riches preserved in the grooves of jazz phonograph records.

Delaunay, today the editor of France's *Jazz Hot* magazine, was then a gifted young graphic artist and journalist, a close friend of Hugues Panassié, and an avid record collector. His book bore the stamp of his tastes and opinions, for it was arranged according to a plan that served to emphasize the work of artists he considered important. This layout also reflected, in retrospect, the then prevailing view of jazz development.

Rather than a straightforward alphabetical listing by artists, Delaunay grouped his material under diverse headings.

The first, "Originators of Hot Style," included the Original Dixieland Jazz Band, the New Orleans Rhythm Kings, King Oliver, the Wolverines, Doc Cook and his Dreamland Syncopators (an early large band with cornetist Freddie Keppard and clarinetist Jimmie Noone in the personnel), the Bucktown Five (a 1924 recording group including Muggsy Spanier and clarinetist Volly DeFaut), Bix Beiderbecke, Louis Armstrong, and blues singers Bessie Smith and Ma Rainey.

Then came "The Great Soloists," among whom Armstrong and Beiderbecke had primacy. The others were Sidney Bechet, Tommy Ladnier, Noone, Jimmy Harrison, Jack Teagarden, Earl Hines, Coleman Hawkins, Frank Teschemacher, Fats Waller, and Johnny Hodges—not such a bad list for 1938. (The first edition being exceedingly rare, this summary reflects the second, published two years later.)

The "Prominent Orchestras" section had Fletcher Henderson, Duke Ellington, Count Basie, Jimmie Lunceford, McKinney's Cotton Pickers, Don Redman, Luis Russell, Mills Blue Rhythm, Jean Goldkette, Paul Whiteman, Ben Pollack, Casa Loma, Benny Goodman, Bob Crosby, and Tommy Dorsey. This was followed by a miscellaneous listing, and a listing of "Special Studio Combinations," i.e., recording bands as opposed to regular working units.

The first edition of this groundbreaking tome had 271 pages. The second had grown to 408, reflecting the tremendous interest stirred up among jazz enthusiasts throughout the world, who sent in additions and corrections, as well as the natural two-year growth in recorded jazz. The first U.S. edition of the book was published in 1943, under the auspices of the Commodore Record Shop.

Delaunay had not gone it alone. In the compilation of information, he had consulted and corresponded with numerous collectors and experts and, not least important, with as many jazz musicians as he could persuade to help him. Cooperation from record companies was scant; it wasn't until some time later that company files were opened to inspection and then often only grudgingly. (An early, and lasting, exception to this attitude was Columbia's Helene Chmura, a veritable discographer's angel. Special thanks and credit to this helpful woman have been a constant feature of all works in the field.)

Naturally, the margin of error was wide. But an amazing amount of accurate and hitherto unknown information had been unearthed and compiled. Moreover, Delaunay's remarkable energy and enthusiasm had fired the interest of other like-minded researchers. Far from being a dry and dusty collection of names, dates, and numbers, the book was found to be a guide to fuller enjoyment and deeper understanding of jazz—in retrospect, a far more substantial contribution to jazz literature than the bulk of critical and historical writing from the period.

Working with facts and figures, the discographer, of course, faces the danger of becoming more interested in dates and numbers than in the substance of his labor, the music. But Delaunay was no antiquarian. His approach is best reflected in his own words, from the introduction to the 1938 edition:

"Despite the strict aridity of my work, I must confess that, at times, my research was pursued with real passion. . . . I cannot conceive of this work as an immobile mass; it is a new and living substance."

With the swing era in full bloom, "collecting hot" soon became a less esoteric pursuit. *Down Beat* reflected this changing climate when it introduced, in October 1939, George Hoefer's *Hot Box*, a column devoted to research and discography, which soon became an important medium for contacts and exchange of information. A typical early column, from the issue of August 1, 1940, contains information about the recording career of pianist-composer Richard M. Jones a reference to the Hal Whyte–Henderson "Everybody Loves My Baby" item, and mention of two avid collectors, John Hammond and George Avakian.

The war years disrupted discographical research, which had become a truly international phenomenon. It also had an adverse effect on the future of collecting, since hundreds of thousands of old records were lost in the scrap drives—the shellac supposedly contained valuable strategic materials.

Nonetheless, 1942 marked the appearance of an important addition to jazz literature: *The Jazz Record Book*, edited by Charles Edward Smith, with the assistance of Frederic Ramsey, Jr., Charles Payne Rogers, and William Russell. It was not, strictly speaking, discographical work but, rather, a guide to jazz collecting.

Inspired by David Hall's best-selling *Record Book*, a classical guide, the work contained personnel and catalog numbers of 1,000 carefully selected records, with discussion and analysis of the music, and a 125-page historical survey. The closest thing to a success in jazz book publishing, the work went through six printings and remains readable today.

Though it surveyed the entire field of recorded jazz, the book was marked by the traditionalist orientation of its authors. It was blasted in a *Metronome* review by the then influential critic Barry Ulanov, whose most strenuous objection seemed to be that it praised Sidney Bechet and Jelly Roll Morton. It was, however, a child of the times. The blues and boogie-woogie section consisted of 48 pages, while 106 pages were devoted to big-band music.

This book, which greatly helped and stimulated the taste for jazz of many budding enthusiasts, would have been an impossibility without the foundation of discographical research.

The saga continued. The U.S. answer to Delaunay came in 1944 with the publication, once again privately, of Orin Blackstone's *Index to Jazz*, a four-volume alphabetical listing far more inclusive than the French work.

However, Blackstone listed records in sequence of catalog rather than master numbers, which made for jumbled chronology, and often his personnels were collective rather than individual. A second edition of the work was published in 1947 by *The Record Changer*, the leader in a then growing field of "little" jazz magazines, published by Bill Grauer and edited by Orrin Keepnews.

In the following year, *New Hot Discography*, a revised and greatly expanded U.S. edition of the Delaunay work edited by George Avakian and Walter E. Schaap, made its appearance. It was a departure from the discographical norm in terms of production, being a well-bound and beautifully printed hardcover book, published by a trade house.

In other respects, it was somewhat of a disappointment to the collecting fraternity. In spite of the obvious advantages of alphabetical listing, as demonstrated by *Index to Jazz*, the new book followed the erratic arrangement of Delaunay's original work and, in fact, compounded the clumsiness of this approach. In addition, a number of important records listed in the previous edition were omitted for no good reason. But in many respects—not the least of which was the complete artist index, down to the lowliest third alto man in an obscure big band—the book marked a step forward.

Interestingly, the critical bias is reflected in the book's layout, which had changed considerably since 1936.

The "Pioneers of Jazz" were now Oliver, Johnny Dodds, Ladnier, Bechet, Noone, Keppard, Kid Ory, Morton, and Armstrong—Dodds, Ory, and Morton had come into their own. The blues singers were still just Bessie Smith and Ma Rainey (blues being the major weak spot in all Delaunay's works), while the bands selected for special treatment had been pared down to Henderson's, Ellington's, and McKinney's.

The ODJB and the New Orleans Rhythm Kings, once honored as pioneers of jazz, were now relegated to a section headed "Early Dixieland Jazz," in company with obscure white bands of the early '20s. A Chicago section was simply Beiderbecke and Teschemacher, nothing more. New York included Red Nichols, Miff Mole, the Original Memphis Five, and other less significant artists. And the book's chief weakness, a section headed "Other Early Bands and Musicians," was simply a grab bag of pre-1930 recording artists. Post-1930 jazz, listed alphabetically, made up the balance of the 608-page tome, which has recently been reprinted in an unchanged edition—an indication of slow but steady demand for its services.

The next step set new standards for the field. This was the publication of the first volume of Dave Carey and Albert McCarthy's long-awaited *Jazz Directory*, in July 1949. The preface described the work as "presenting the subject more broadly and in a more lucid form than has hitherto been attempted," and that was exactly what it succeeded in doing.

Arranged alphabetically by artist, and chronologically by master numbers within the chapters, including blues and gospel artists, and employing extremely clear and legible type and intelligent layout, the *Directory* promised to become the definitive reference work so long awaited by serious students of jazz.

Unfortunately, the project so well begun had to be abandoned following the appearance of volume six in 1957.

During the eight years of the project's published life, many reversals had been encountered. The publisher had been changed; the response, in terms of sales, had been less than expected; and the workload was staggering. With volume six, the alphabet had been covered, in 1,112 pages, only from A to Lo, and the contemplated seventh volume was to be a revision of volume one (A–B), so much new material having been issued and/or uncovered. The two hardy Englishmen were willing to continue, but the publisher was not.

Most of the volumes are now out of print, and *Jazz Directory* remains an unfinished masterpiece, a saddening monument to the indifference encountered by discographers in a world abounding with cheap and temporal products in the music and book marketplace.

However, the labors of Carey and McCarthy (the former is the proprietor of London's Swing Shop, a first-class record store, and the latter is one of Britain's leading critics and the editor of *Jazz Monthly*) had pointed up one basic stumbling block in the compilation of definitive discographies: the element of time. Continuing research and the never-ending flow of new record releases made a book obsolete before it appeared.

The next great discography avoided this pitfall by limiting itself to a specific historical period. This was another British work, Brian Rust's monumental *Jazz Records, A to Z: 1897–1931*. Published privately in 1961 by the author after a lifetime of work, the original edition was a weighty loose-leaf tome of 884 pages, including blues and gospel records. Though priced at $16.95, it sold out quickly.

The second edition, well bound but shorn of blues and gospel, gave birth to another great work, devoted solely to these aspects of jazz, *Blues and Gospel Records*, compiled by John Godrich, encompassing the years from the beginning of recorded Negro folk music to 1942. That year also marks the break-off point of Rust's second edition of *Jazz Records, A to Z*, the author frankly admitting that he has not sufficiently deep and abiding interest in later jazz developments to take his labors further afield.

Rust's work represents the most thoroughgoing and complete approach to jazz discography hitherto accomplished. Every record Rust could lay his hands on was checked by him personally. He made several trips to this country, solely to inspect rare and obscure records and recording company files.

No record with even the remotest connection to jazz was left unaccounted for, though the reader is often warned that the jazz content of a given record may be slight or nonexistent. If anything was omitted, it was because its existence was unknown to the discographer.

In his search for completeness, Rust included even rejected and never-issued master recordings, many of which have undoubtedly been destroyed or lost. But having them listed at least makes a search possible, and several such items already have come to light. In addition, these listings often make fascinating footnotes to jazz history.

Perhaps the most interesting of Rust's uncovered rejects is a test recording made for Victor on December 2, 1918, by the famous Creole Band, which included cornetist Freddie Keppard (the title is "Tack 'Em Down"). This overthrows the legend that Keppard refused to record because he was afraid that other musicians would "steal my stuff" and that the opportunity for the first recordings of authentic Negro jazz thus was lost.

Rust's discovery rather confirms composer-singer Perry Bradford's statement (in conversation with this writer) that Keppard refused to record because Victor didn't offer him enough money. This is one indication of how discographical research can help jazz history. Research of personnels also presents the historian with countless traces of the careers of now-dead or obscure musicians.

The scope and accuracy of Rust's work makes it a landmark in the history of jazz discography that is not likely to be surpassed. Within the territory he has cut out for himself, only addenda and corrections remain to be contributed.

But other areas are still wide open.

In the wake of Rust and *Jazz Directory*, the Danish discographer Jorgen Grunnet Jepsen is hard at work on filling in the gaps. During the last two years, he has published three volumes of his *Jazz Records*, 1942–62, taking up where Rust left off in terms of time, and where *Jazz Directory* left off in the alphabet (his first volume was M–N, his second O–R, his third S–Te).

Jepsen's volumes, averaging 350 pages, are the product of sound research. He includes blues and rhythm-and-blues recordings but omits gospel and borderline pop material. His projected goal is eight volumes, and when he is done, having reached M once again, the jazz world will have, for the first time, a nearly complete index to all recorded material from 1897 to 1962.

So far, I have surveyed only works that have attempted to cover the whole field or a complete period. But there are other examples of the discographer's work, some of them quite outstanding.

There are, for instance, the discographies limited to the work of a single artist. In their simplest form, these are merely listings, with complete personnel, master, and catalog information, of all known recordings in which a given artist participated.

Jepsen has published a series of these small, practical volumes, including artists like Armstrong, Ellington, Gillespie, Morton, Art Tatum, Bud Powell, Lester Young, Charlie Parker, Lee Konitz, Fats Navarro, Clifford Brown, Count Basie, and Billie Holiday.

Swiss discographer Kurt Mohr prepared several such volumes devoted to lesser-known artists, including Hot Lips Page, Lucky Millinder, and Tiny Bradshaw, published by the now-defunct magazine *Jazz Statistics*. These are all useful, especially to the collector with specialized and not all-encompassing interests.

An exemplary work of this kind, though larger in scope, since it is devoted to one of the most prolific recording artists in jazz, is Benny H. Aasland's *The Wax Works of Duke Ellington*, published in Stockholm, Sweden, in 1954.

But two "name" discographies go beyond the bounds of a mere listing of records and are best described as bio-discographies. The first of these was D. Russell Connor's *B.G.: Off the Record*, published in 1958. It traces the career of Benny Goodman through his recordings, including all known transcriptions, broadcasts, film and television appearances, and concert checks.

The book, arranged chronologically, gives complete recording details, including solo information, interlaced with relevant biographical commentary. Though a commendable work, it is so Goodman-focused that it seems the work of a fan rather than a researcher.

This is not the case with Howard A. Waters's *Jack Teagarden's Music: His Career and Recordings.*

Published in 1960, it crams into 222 pages all the information conceivable concerning Teagarden's musical life. Not only is there a complete discography, with solo details, of every record Teagarden had made up to then, including his broadcasts, transcriptions, films, etc., but there also is a listing of records with Teagarden-like trombone solos, with indications, when known, of who was actually responsible for them.

In addition, aside from a forty-page no-nonsense biography, and many rare photographs, there is an itinerary of Teagarden's engagements from the inception of his career. Thus, the interested reader can ascertain that the trombonist was working, from February to April 1928, with Billy Lustig's Scranton Sirens at the Silver Slipper Club in New York City or can trace the laborious strings of one-nighters Teagarden worked with his struggling big band for nearly a decade.

Such abundance of detail might seem pointless to some, but it gives as complete a picture of the working life of a great jazzman as we have ever had and does so by virtue of fact rather than sentimental fancy. The labor involved in this outstanding work is staggering to contemplate, but, of course, the book made no profit.

An outstanding work of yet another kind is Dan Mahoney's *Columbia 13/14000 Series,* a truly remarkable feat of scholarship. This series was Columbia's so-called race product in the years 1923–32, including blues, jazz, gospel, and comedy records.

In eighty pages, Mahoney not only lists the 689 records issued in the series with complete and accurate standard discographical information, but he also indicates the quantity of each record shipped and ordered, as well as giving statistical breakdowns of releases by category, complete details of label designs (the series underwent twelve changes during its life span), an index of tune titles, and a complete index of supporting artists.

But is such information of any practical use, or is it merely a kind of indulgence in a passion for research?

It all depends on how one uses the material. The quantities of records shipped, for example, show how many records an artist like Bessie Smith could sell at the peak of her career and how such sales compare to today's. The figures also provide striking illustration of the toll the Depression years took on the record market, particularly the Negro market. From a peak of more than 20,000 copies an issue, the total dwindled to 400 in the last months of the series.

Mahoney presents his material lucidly and succinctly. Had he been a sociologist rather than a discographer, his booklet would have been published by a university press or credited as an exceptional master's thesis. But he is a discographer, and so it was published, probably at a financial loss, by Walter C. Allen, himself a member of the fraternity.

There are other discographical works, such as Ernie Edwards's current series of big-band volumes and George I. Hall's *Nat King Cole, a Jazz Discography*, that deserve mention, but the scope of this survey is limited. Two magazines, the British *Matrix* and the U.S. *Record Research*, are currently eking out an existence, publishing much valuable material. The latter keeps itself alive through record auctions.

Though it can be said that jazz discography is a field of limited and specialized interest, the same has been said of jazz itself, and with no more justice.

If it has contributed nothing else, the hard and unselfish labor of the discographers has unearthed much music that might otherwise have remained unknown, has given perspective and foundation to the history of an art form that sorely needs it, and has snatched from the grinding jaws of time facts and details that illuminate the checkered course of jazz, instructing and enriching the willing student.

Jazz discography has come of age, and the hardest work has already been done, by men who have sought and gained no material profit from their enterprise. The least they deserve is a heartfelt thanks from all who profess to love jazz.

(1966)

Enormous strides have been made in jazz discography since 1966. Jepsen completed his work with the eleventh volume, published in 1970 and covering issues through 1969. His fellow Dane, Erik Raben, took on the task of updating Jepsen, but extending coverage only to 1980; the work, painstakingly accurate but excruciatingly slow, had only arrived midway through letter G, in seven volumes, by 2002; there have been separate volumes covering Miles Davis and Duke Ellington.

A sixth edition of Rust appeared in 2003, unfortunately bereft of a tune index; this work continues to be the touchstone for recordings through 1942, but its territory has also been covered by two monumental efforts aiming at completeness. First came the Belgian Walter Bruyninckx with *60 Years of Recorded Jazz*, published in loose-leaf form between 1978 and 1982 and attempting coverage of all jazz, blues, and gospel recordings through 1977. After a misguided effort of individual volumes arranged by styles, instrumentation, and era, he resumed his earlier format with *70 Years of Recorded Jazz*, which was completed in 1999, whereupon he began a CD-ROM update encompassing an additional fifteen years.

Also available on CD-ROM, with many convenient search features, as well as in twenty-six volumes, Tom Lord's *The Jazz Discography* was completed in 2002, with periodic updates promised for CD-ROM. A computer expert, Lord managed to extend his coverage to recordings issued just months prior to the closing of each volume; his is the most up-to-date discographical work. However, since it is wholly derivative except for the recent material, Lord's work incorporates almost every error made by his predecessors and also includes redundant entries apparently not noted by the compiler. His methods aroused considerable controversy, but the usefulness of the work is indisputable.

In the realm of bio-discographies, the late Walter C. Allen's *Hendersonia: The Music of Fletcher Henderson and His Musicians*, self-published in 1973 and long unavailable, stands as a landmark of dedicated research and minutely detailed information, including identification of soloists, bar-length of solos, arranging credits, etc. Connor's Benny Goodman work, thrice updated and much improved at each step, is now known as *Listen to His Legacy*. Laurie Wright's King Oliver and Fats Waller books are first-rate, as are Chris Sheridan's on Count Basie, Cannonball Adderley, and Thelonious Monk; Tom Lord's (not the discographer) on Clarence Williams; Vladimir Somosko's on Eric Dolphy and Artie Shaw; Ben Young's on Bill Dixon; and Manfred Selchow's on Edmond Hall and Vic Dickenson.

So-called name discographies, without the biographical component, have become so numerous that only a handful can be mentioned: Koster and Bakker's on Charlie Parker; Fujoka, Porter, and Hamada's on John Coltrane; Westerberg's on Louis Armstrong; and Pirie and Mueller's on Stan Kenton. But the favorite subject by far has been Duke Ellington and his huge legacy, explored by Timner, whose *Ellingtonia* has seen four editions, and Massagli and Volonte, who updated their *Duke Ellington's Story on Records*, published in individual paperback volumes beginning in 1966, with two massive hardbound tomes titled *The New DESOR* and leaving no disc or tape undocumented. Each year brings a basketful of new name discographies, the work greatly aided by computers.

And so is a relative newcomer to the genre, the label discography. This had its start with Max Vreede's Paramount (1971), and then, a year later, Michel Ruppli's first of many, with various collaborators, which have covered Prestige, Savoy, Clef and Verve, Blue Note, and, branching out to labels of a general nature, Brunswick, Decca (six volumes), Atlantic, Mercury, and MGM. A very fine work in a special area is the late Richard Sears's *V Discs*.

It should also be noted that Goodrich's pioneering *Blues and Gospel Records* has gone through four updates, with collaborators Dixon and Rye, the most recent, in 1997, having the distinction of being the only discographical work published by a major house, Oxford University Press.

Thus, huge output notwithstanding, one essential fact has remained unchanged: discography, be it jazz, blues, country, or classical, is a labor of love—a science still thankless from the standpoint of remuneration.

(By the way, that test pressing purportedly by the Original Creole Band but listed as "Creole Jass Band" has never come to light, a fact made somewhat less disheartening by research proving beyond dispute that the OCB had long since disbanded by late 1918. And Freddie Keppard of course did begin to record in 1923, when it was no longer a novelty for jazzmen.)

The Commodore Story

O nce upon a time there was a record store in midtown Manhattan called the Commodore Music Shop. It was run by an enterprising young man named Milt Gabler, who loved jazz, and by the mid-1930s, it had become, in the words of George Frazier, "a wondrously cluttered hole-in-the-wall where you would go at lunchtime or after work to hear tumultuous talk and brave new music. . . . By and large, the Commodore clientele was made up of individuals who were awfully bright and shiny in their particular lines of endeavor."

The store was on East Forty-second Street, opposite Grand Central Station, and in those days the offices of Time, Inc., were in the nearby Chrysler Building, and Wilder Hobson, author of the first history of jazz published in the U.S., Frank Norris, Alexander King, and cartographer Richard Eades Harrison were among the Luceites hanging out at Commodore. When Gabler branched out into record production, it was Harrison who designed the Commodore label, Norris who wrote it up in *Time*, and King who saw to it that *Life* did a photo-essay on an early Commodore session.

But we're getting ahead of our story, which begins in 1911, when Milt Gabler was born at 114th Street and St. Nicholas Avenue in Harlem. His father owned a hardware store that had branched out into the newfangled electrical stuff, and by the time Milt was attending Stuyvesant High School (then as now one of New York's finest), it had a radio department, where Milt helped out after school. Milt's uncle Sid talked his older brother into opening an exclusive radio store around the corner on Forty-second Street. It was Milt's idea to install a speaker over the door and play music from radio stations to attract customers.

Pretty soon, they started asking if the store carried records, and Milt got his dad's okay to branch out into this area. Milt had first heard live music at dances in Throgs Neck, where the Gablers had a weekend bungalow. "It was an open-air dance pavilion," Milt recalled, "and they hired a black band of six men that played jazz." There was also a military band at Fort Schuyler with jazz-minded members who'd moonlight as a hot unit. "Then, in the store, I took in records around 1926—I was all of fifteen years old. So I got to hear the bands." At first, he liked Ted Lewis best; then he began to discover Duke Ellington, Louis Armstrong, Fletcher Henderson, and one record that particularly knocked him out, "I Found a New Baby" by the Chicago Rhythm Kings.

As Milt's interest in jazz progressed, he began to seek out and stock records that were hard to find, and also bought "cutouts" from jobbers. Then he discovered that he could have records pressed to order from discontinued masters, and put out some of his favorites, such as the Rhythmakers (a 1932 unit that included Red Allen on trumpet, Pee Wee Russell on clarinet, and Eddie Condon and Zutty Singleton in the rhythm section), on a plain white Commodore Music Shop label.

None of these musicians were listed on the original labels, and of course there were no discographies. Milt found out who was on these and other jazz discs by asking the musicians when he encountered them at ballrooms or nightclubs, and some of them began to come to his store. Among these was Condon, and the intrepid guitarist-hustler and Milt became lifelong friends. Another regular was a tall, dour-looking graduate student from Yale, moonlighting as a jazz correspondent for *Variety*. That was Marshall Stearns (who later founded the Institute of Jazz Studies), and he and Milt decided to form the United Hot Clubs of America and invite another Commodore customer, John Hammond, to be president.

The UHCA became the umbrella for Milt's second venture at issuing records; its monthly releases, licensed from various catalogs, included rare jazz and blues, by King Oliver, Bix Beiderbecke, Jabbo Smith, and other legends. And as a "first," the labels gave complete personnel and recording information. As the UHCA proved the marketability—limited yet real— for vintage jazz, the major labels from whom Milt licensed got the idea that they could issue the stuff themselves, and the well ran dry. Meanwhile, Milt had attended his first recording session in 1933 (supervised by Hammond, it was a Benny Goodman date featuring Coleman Hawkins and Mildred

Bailey) and had already decided that he would start a label to issue freshly minted music of his own choice.

Commodore *almost* became the world's very first jazz record label, but Milt had to postpone his first session several times until his favorite pianist, Jess Stacy, was available, enabling two Frenchmen (Charles Delaunay and Hugues Panassié, both Commodore mail-order customers) to steal a march on him and start their Swing label a few months earlier. Gabler had been of great help to Delaunay in the gathering of information for his pioneering *Hot Discography*, first published in 1936. (The first American edition was brought out by Commodore in 1938.)

On January 17, 1938, when Milt supervised Commodore's debut date, Condon was the leader, as he would be again several times during Commodore's life span. And, as Milt pointed out, "every time Eddie and I gathered some of our favorite musicians and songs . . . if my man Condon was on the date, he ran the show in the studio. He set the time and kept it there. He tapped it off. I took care of things on the other side of the glass. I chose about ninety-five percent of the tunes; that was my business—selling songs and the people that made them. I also set the balance."

Milt was also a pioneer in that regard. To him, recorded small-group jazz (of which there was precious little at the time) rarely sounded right. From his first date, he made sure that all the musicians could be properly heard. To Milt, jazz was an ensemble music as well as a soloist's art, and he saw to it that all the elements were in proper balance.

The first Commodores were the first independently produced American jazz records, at a time when the record marketplace was totally dominated by less than a handful of major labels: RCA Victor, the undisputed giant; Decca, a surprisingly successful upstart (founded in 1934); Columbia, fallen on bad days and recently acquired by the American Record Corporation; Brunswick and its subsidiary, Vocalion, also owned by ARC. (In 1939, Columbia would be acquired by CBS and soon regain its stature.)

Once Milt had shown the way, others gingerly entered the field. The Hot Record Society, operated by Steve Smith, also was a collector's store and reissue label enterprise; its HRS label started cutting sessions in Milt's wake. Alfred Lion and Frank Wolff's Blue Note label made its debut in 1939 with advice (and distribution) from Gabler. A lover of boogie-woogie piano named Dan Qualey launched Solo Art, and not much later a teenaged Bob Thiele jumped into the fray with his Jazz Records. It is typical of Milt that during the war years he took care of things for most of his "competitors" while they were away in uniform. To him, jazz was not a business but a communal cause. "We tried to stir up the world about this great American music, and I guess we succeeded," he said some fifty years later.

Milt promoted jazz in other ways. Even before the first Commodore date, he'd begun to organize Sunday afternoon jam sessions, first at recording studios, then in Fifty-second Street clubs. Eventually, he settled on Jimmy Ryan's, and the Sunday sessions became a fixture, well into the 1940s. From the start, these sessions were integrated, and featured musicians of a variety of stylistic persuasions—as long as they could swing. And in the Commodore store's backroom was a mimeograph machine on which was produced a feisty little magazine, *Jazz Information*, edited by a triumvirate of Columbia University students: Ralph Gleason, Ralph De Toledano, and Eugene Williams.

Milt's knowledge of who played on jazz records was the cause of his branching out in yet another direction. Martin Block, the first real disc jockey, asked his listeners if they knew who took the trumpet solo on a new Red Norvo record; Milt called in with the answer: Bunny Berigan. Soon he was supplying Block (and eventually other deejays, as the trend spread) with the weekly new releases (daft as it may seem, in those days, record companies did not furnish free samples to radio stations), making a little extra cash for the Commodore till (frequently tapped by musicians on what Condon called "transparent hamburger diets").

Producers involved with the major labels came to Milt with their problems. When Leonard Feather (on a visit from England) produced a four-side date for Vocalion and only two were issued, Milt took the remains for Commodore. When John Hammond had a session featuring members of the Count Basie band nixed by the same label, Milt came to the rescue. And it was Milt to whom Billie Holiday turned when Vocalion wouldn't let her record "Strange Fruit."

Inevitably, Milt was eventually induced to join a major label. It was Decca, and Milt negotiated an agreement that allowed him to continue producing for Commodore—with the proviso that he was to turn out no hits for his own label! During his long stay with Decca, Milt created a string of hits for them with such artists as his first idol, Louis Armstrong (who dubbed him "Angel Gabler"), Bing Crosby, the Mills Brothers, the Andrews Sisters, Louis Jordan, Ella Fitzgerald, and so many others. He made the first rock-and-roll hit, "Rock Around the Clock," beefing up Bill Haley's weak rhythm section with the great jazz drummer Cliff Leeman. Of course, he was able to sneak in some real jazz here and there, and during the early 1940s recording ban imposed by the American Federation of Musicians, he made a string of terrific small-band jazz dates for Decca's transcription service, World Broadcasting System.

But Milt had plenty of time left over for Commodore, and after settling with the musicians' union in late 1943, the label enjoyed a burst of activity that lasted into the spring of 1946. After that, recording activity was only sporadic, and the final Commodore sessions were produced in 1954, not by Milt but by his younger brothers Barney and Danny, with old buddy Leonard Feather in on the last two dates, which featured Frank Wess in a modern-mainstream setting. In 1958, the Commodore Music Shop closed its doors. For a while, there had been two stores—the other was on Fifty-second Street, from 1938 to 1941—but by the 1950s, the record retailing business was changing: Sam Goody had opened a superstore not many steps away.

But the Commodore catalog continued to live, and over the decades, selective reissues appeared on a variety of labels, in the U.S. and abroad. The crowning glory to date has been the gigantic, limited-edition release by Mosaic Records of the entire Commodore output in chronological order, including all extant alternate takes. Now out of print, it added up to sixty-three LPs, housed in three boxed sets.

It is fitting that Milt Gabler's extended labor of love now has found a permanent home under the aegis of the present successors to Decca, the major label that recognized and utilized his remarkable talents as a record producer. Here's how Milt, not long ago, summed up his feelings about the music:

"If you love jazz, you cannot stand still. Your interest can only go forward as the new performers and innovators appear. By the same token, if you have an open mind and are serious about the subject, you must go back to the source, the mouth of the mother river, the root. You must hear the men and women who came before, the creators and stylists and writers who inspired and taught the young people of today. There it is—on the record, to be enjoyed and listened to."

Milt Gabler's contribution to the record of jazz is something we should all be thankful for. He never put a note on Commodore that he didn't care about. He had the guts to go to bat for something he loved, and he showed others the way.

And now for some Commodore highlights:

"Love Is Just Around the Corner" was the first tune recorded at the first Commodore session, on January 17, 1938—the day after Benny Goodman's famous Carnegie Hall concert. Milt Gabler had already postponed his label's debut several times because he insisted on certain players—especially B.G.'s pianist Jess Stacy—and it almost didn't happen again. The clarinetist had scheduled a record date for his band, but Milt pleaded with him (they were on good terms), and he relented. It didn't just hinge on Stacy. This was the swing era; Bud Freeman (who was with Tommy Dorsey) and George Wettling (with Red Norvo) were on the road most of the time. The others were easier to pin down: George Brunies, Bobby Hackett, leader Condon, and the star of this piece, clarinetist Pee Wee Russell, were all regulars at Nick's in Greenwich Village by then.

Pee Wee had his own sound and conception. One of the great originals in jazz, he was a Commodore regular and a special favorite of Milt's. The balance is fine—all the ensemble voices are clearly heard, and the rhythm section is perfectly balanced; among other things, we can hear just how good a rhythm guitarist Condon was. As Milt put it: "If I'm paying eight guys to play, I want to hear them all!" Commodore was off to a fine start with this gutsy, honest music with a tart Chicago flavor.

The second number changes the mood drastically. In 1939, Billie Holiday was working a long stint at Café Society, the Greenwich Village nightclub that not only featured integrated bands but encouraged integrated audiences. A schoolteacher, Abel Meeropol, whose pen name was Lewis Allan, brought club owner Barney Josephson a song he'd written, suggesting it might be suitable for Billie, although its topic—a lynching—was far removed from the usual world of popular song. (Meeropol, who also wrote the words to "The House I Live In," later adopted the orphaned sons of Ethel and Julius Rosenberg.) At first the singer didn't take to "Strange Fruit," but when she included it in her show at the club, audiences sat in stunned silence, then burst into ovations. She wanted to record it, but her label, Vocalion, declined (as did her producer, John Hammond, but in his case for esthetic reasons only). Billie turned to Milt Gabler; to her surprise, Vocalion was willing to lend her to Commodore for four sides.

Frankie Newton's hushed trumpet, with a backdrop arranged by him, sets the stage for Billie's entrance. It's been a half century since I first heard this searing performance, but Billie's melismatic moan on the word "rot" still gives me gooseflesh. "Strange Fruit" remained in her repertoire to the end, but this is the definitive version.

"A Good Man Is Hard to Find" was one of those 1920s songs beloved by Gabler; both Bessie Smith and Sophie Tucker had featured it. Here it became the occasion for a notable Commodore experiment. Milt wanted to capture the feeling and scope of a typical jam-session performance at his Jimmy Ryan's Sundays, and was willing to devote four 12-inch sides to the effort. In those pre-tape days, each segment had to be recorded separately, so the assembled troops (four brass, three reeds, four rhythm) had to be on their toes. Unfortunately, several of the participants decided to stay up all night to make the 10 a.m. studio call, fortifying themselves with appropriate "medication," while some others arrived with plentiful supplies of "eye-openers." No less than fifty-two takes and/or false starts were required to complete the task at hand, even though Milt had the foresight to record the most demanding final part right after the one-take first portion. Decades later Milt reflected: "I love these sides, but I shall always recall the frustration. It was my dream band, and almost a nightmare." Judged on its own merits, part one is an excellent performance, from the moment Stacy's rolling piano kicks it off in a good groove. The centerpiece is Russell, telling a story with two spectacular breaks.

"You're Some Pretty Doll," a New Orleans opus vintage 1917, was later rudely parodied in a Brunies vocal as "Ugly Child," but while Fats Waller is on hand here, there is no singing. Fats was a surprise present from Condon to Gabler, who had no advance notice of the great pianist's appearance. Fats and Eddie were old friends who'd first recorded together in 1929. Eleven years later Fats was a star, but still a team player when he wanted to be. Few could match him in a rhythm section, and even at this relaxed tempo his great time tells. He opens with a delightful solo chorus (hear those trills) and later backs the only other soloist, Russell (displaying his lower register), to perfection. This is George Wettling's third appearance, and we can tell by now why Milt valued him so. Not as famous today as his contemporaries Gene Krupa and Dave Tough, he was nonetheless their equal as a thinking man's drummer.

"Indiana" was startling in 1945 and is still anything but routine. This tenor and bass duet was recorded at a Town Hall concert produced by the Danish baron (genuine—the family name appears in *Hamlet*) Timme Rosenkrantz, who loved jazz and America so much that he gave up a secure life in Denmark for a hand-to-mouth existence in New York. Nothing ever worked, financially, for Timme, although he was full of ideas. He ran a record store in Harlem, started a jazz magazine (one issue only), worked in radio, produced records (mostly culled from sessions at his legendary pad near Fifty-second Street), and was almost always broke. The Town Hall concert was his most ambitious venture; it was a great artistic success, but few of the musicians got paid, none for the recordings, which Timme had turned over to Milt—but had also peddled to other labels! Gabler of course paid all the players when he discovered the truth, but remained friends with Timme—it was impossible to stay angry with the baron, who in his own way did a lot for music.

Don Byas was at his peak in 1945, a veteran of the Count Basie and Andy Kirk bands and a fixture on Fifty-second Street. Though not a bopper, he was in on some early bop happenings with Dizzy and Bird. (The following year he would leave for Europe, returning home only once before his death at fifty-nine in 1972.) His skills at execution, his sophisticated harmonic sense, swing, and beautiful tone placed him in the front ranks of tenormen. This performance proves his mettle. It opens with Slam Stewart, picking and slapping; then Don eases in with that mellow sound and perfect command of the horn. After a while he lets his melodic invention flow—and could that man tongue a mouthpiece! Stewart, inventor of singing and bowing in harmony—voice an octave above strings—does his thing, humorous yet very musical, before Don comes back, floating his lines, his harmonic ideas as "advanced" as any contemporary's. Then he returns to the melody, building *down* to close with a perfect little tag. Slam is with him all the way, and both tempo and intonation hold throughout. A masterpiece!

"At a Georgia Camp Meeting" is from the last session Gabler supervised for Commodore, the only one to feature one of his favorites (and frequent Ryan's jam participant), the great Sidney Bechet. He had been a Blue Note artist, and Milt didn't want to trespass on Alfred Lion's turf. But now the New Orleans veteran, recently returned from France, was a free agent. Gabler must have really wanted to plan this one properly, and he did: Bechet was picky about trumpeters, but had frequently teamed with Wild Bill Davison, so that Commodore regular was a safe choice. Wilbur De Paris was a Fifty-second Street fixture by 1950, and young Ralph Sutton had appeared with Bechet on *This Is Jazz* radio ventures. Bechet liked old numbers, so this vintage cakewalk is, shall we say, a piece of cake for him. His soprano solo and ensemble work is what counts here—but don't fail to notice Sutton, then as now a rock-solid master of the idiom.

Lester Young came to Commodore by Milt's special request. John Hammond had done a session for Vocalion that was found unsuitable by higher-ups, and had placed it with Gabler. It featured an unusual quintet of trumpet, electric and acoustic guitar, bass, and drums, all drawn from the ranks of the Basie band. But there were only three sides, so to even things up for two-sided 78-rpm singles, Milt requested and got another session with the same band, plus Lester Young. Milt asked Pres to bring his clarinet, having been knocked out by his solo on that horn on Basie's "Blue and Sentimental." Bless Milt! Lester's clarinet, of which there is precious little on records, is nothing less than sublime on this date, originally issued under the group name Kansas City Six, directed by electric guitar pioneer and champion arranger Eddie Durham, and as a whole certainly a jewel in Commodore's crown.

"Way Down Yonder in New Orleans" features Lester on tenor, but his clarinet is heard in the opening and closing ensembles, first in harmony with Clayton's muted trumpet, then in free improvisation around Buck's equally free lead—a kind of angelic counterpoint. Lester's tenor is on the same immortal plane—is there anything more relaxed and swinging in the annals of jazz?

Coleman Hawkins was Young's predecessor, the man who first created a viable jazz language for the tenor saxophone. Some jazz commentators think of Hawk and Lester as opposite poles, but they share a romantic attitude toward ballads. Hawkins had been back home for ten months, after a five-year stay in Europe, when he cut "Dedication" at an all-star date featuring Fletcher Henderson alumni. Leonard Feather, himself a recent U.S. arrival, organized this session and wrote out these ballad changes for Hawk to blow on. And that he does, in the manner he had set down some six months earlier on "Body and Soul." Backed only by guitar, bass, and drums, he displays his sound—one of the landmarks of jazz—and harmonic flexibility, with no indication that he misses the piano, or the other horns. This spare accompaniment—Big Sid Catlett's cymbal work is the epitome of tasteful support—set the stage for Hawk's eventual unaccompanied soloing.

Lee Wiley was a stylist of song. Born in Oklahoma (like Pee Wee Russell, she had some Cherokee in her ancestry), she ran away from home at fifteen, came to New York, passed for older, and was working and recording with Leo Reisman's band within the year. Inspired by Ethel Waters, she developed her own sultry style, and became a favorite of the musicians around Eddie Condon, who otherwise had little use for singers, male or female— Louis Armstrong, Hot Lips Page, and Billie Holiday excepted. Wiley was the first to make albums devoted to individual songwriters: Gershwin, Porter, Arlen, Rodgers and Hart. "Sugar" was a Wiley staple. No singer could ask for more sympathetic backing than is provided here by Jess Stacy, whom she'd marry three years later (a brief union, not made in heaven), and Muggsy Spanier, who proves that romantic cornet music can be created with the aid of a plunger mute. Lee does the pretty verse, and her tempo is just right—few singers would dare it that slow, but it works.

Almost five years had passed since Billie Holiday's "Strange Fruit" date, but the great song stylist (which is what she had become by 1944) was back at Café Society, free of her Columbia contract and able to record for Milt once again. At the club, she was backed by Eddie Heywood's tight little band, but "Billie's Blues," one of her infrequent forays into blues country, is a less formal trio number, with Heywood on piano and the great Sid Catlett giving a lesson in *musical* drumming. The number was suggested by Milt, who had loved her 1935 version with Bunny Berigan and Artie Shaw. Here the tempo is much more deliberate, each word fraught with meaning. The way she sings her own name and the way she drags out "I" are priceless moments. This is from Billie's last session as a Commodore star; from here she went to Decca, under Milt's tender care. On their first session there, with the strings she'd asked for, they came up with "Lover Man," the biggest record of her career.

Art Tatum's sole appearance on Commodore was as a member of a group of *Esquire* magazine poll winners—and some "placers," not all winners being available. But the two stars on "My Ideal" certainly were in the winner's circle. It has been said that Tatum was a one-man show, but listen to his accompaniment to Coleman Hawkins, whose work here ranks with his greatest ballads. He caresses Richard Whiting's pretty melody, enhancing it in his opening statement and then, after Tatum's solo, rhapsodizing with that authority reserved for a chosen few. But don't for a moment forget our man at the piano. His chorus is sheer joy, and you can clearly hear where Nat Cole and Oscar Peterson come from. That touch alone is, as they say, worth the price of admission, not to mention the incredible nonchalance with which he tosses off those arpeggios.

Ben Webster would be featured on Tatum's final record date; a pianist himself, he adored Art. As coincidence would have it, the piano bench in the quartet led by Sid Catlett in which Ben was working at the Onyx Club on Fifty-second Street when he took part in his one Commodore date was occupied by a Tatum protégé, Marlowe Morris. Ben had begun his saxophone career as a Hawkins disciple, though he had his own individual gruffness from the start. By 1944 he had graduated from Duke Ellington's academy of jazz and become an influence in his own right. His ballad style, as heard on "Memories of You," was not yet the serene, reflective, and achingly nostalgic manner of his late years, but more florid and outright romantic, even passionate.

Teddy Wilson was, from the time he hit New York in 1933 with Benny Carter, and then through his exposure with Benny Goodman, the trendsetting jazz pianist of the decade. Though influenced by Earl Hines and Tatum, he was less extravagant than either. Clarity, structure, impeccable harmonic syntax, infallible time, and admirable touch all added up to a style remarkable for its musicality. It was a great disappointment to him that his big band failed so quickly and decisively—formed in 1939, it disbanded within a year. When he guested with Commodore, he had long been involved with Barney Josephson at both the original Café Society and its uptown satellite. Clarinetist Edmond Hall, from New Orleans but a swing stylist with his own spiky sound, had been a Wilson sideman but also led his own groups. On "Night and Day," Teddy sits in with Ed, comping magisterially and offering a lucid solo spot.

Roy Eldridge (widely known as "Little Jazz") was the trumpet trendsetter in jazz by the time he joined forces with his "running buddy" Chu Berry in the Commodore studios; the two seemed equals, so Milt billed the band as "Chu Berry and His Little Jazz Ensemble," a nice touch. Roy and Chu had been together in the bands of Teddy Hill and Fletcher Henderson. They both loved the jam-session environment; they were challengers by nature. In the absence of Hawkins, Chu had become the leading contender to the tenor crown, and Roy was playing notes on the trumpet that were faster and higher than what Louis Armstrong had hit. "Body and Soul," recorded a year before the Hawkins version, set the jazz world on its ear. Chu's rhapsodizing, his mastery of breathing, his sheer ability as a saxophone player, were something special, but Roy almost steals the record with his daring, doubling the tempo (something new then on a ballad) and flexing his chops. He cuts smoothly back to the original tempo, handing over to Chu but dominating the ending. He had fire—and never lost it, because he loved to play.

Benny Carter was one of Roy's idols. (The other was Coleman Hawkins; he wanted to play changes on trumpet like those two great saxophonists did, with that kind of mobility.) Here they are together, at the Henderson alumni date from which we've heard Hawk's "Dedication." Carter is the star of "Smack." (Fletcher's nickname, for the sound of a kiss—and not yet a slang word for heroin, lest someone should get the wrong idea), and Benny comes right on, as if shot from a cannon. For two choruses, he conducts a swinging seminar on how to structure a solo and play fresh changes; the way he constructs his bridges and clinches them is special. After solos by Roy and Hawk, he comes back with another sterling bridge, staying in front for the jammed ending. Benny Carter is a marvel—still active as he approaches ninety, and playing and writing at the level of creativity he set for himself so long ago.

Benny Goodman, by 1942, hardly ever appeared as a sideman. So it was truly something when he consented to guest on his young pianist Mel Powell's first date as a leader. Mel was a week shy of his nineteenth birthday, but had been playing and arranging for the King of Swing for a while. He was special, and Benny knew it; the two remained friends until the clarinetist's death. Young Mel didn't just know about music, he also had a psychological insight. On this date, everybody was treated equally; Benny was one of the boys, and he responds with some of the most inspired and creative playing he ever put on record. "The World Is Waiting for the Sunrise" was one of his favorite tunes, wisely picked by Mel to showcase him on the date. The other horns are all B.G. sidemen; the rhythm section includes Al Morgan, the great New Orleans bassist who preceded Milt Hinton in Cab Calloway's band, and Kansas Fields, who'd been with Eldridge and Carter. Pros of this caliber were needed for the tempo Mel had picked: pretty damn fast. I think that, for this kind of groove, this is perhaps the greatest of Goodman solos—maybe because for once he didn't have to worry about being the leader and could just relax with the music. Benny was one of Gabler's three favorite clarinetists (the others being Pee Wee and Ed Hall), and it was quite a coup to get him on Commodore; the label identified him as "Shoeless John Jackson," but nobody was fooled.

Jelly Roll Morton had been rediscovered in the wake of his monumental documentary recordings for Alan Lomax at the Library of Congress in 1938. Victor, his label during his glory years, had recorded him twice in

1939, and then a small label that specialized in ethnic stuff, General, did two—one solo, one with band—co-produced by Lomax and apparently also guided in part by the legendary jazz critic Charles Edward Smith. When General went under, Milt acquired the Jellys. Morton died in 1941; otherwise he would no doubt have become an icon of the traditional jazz revival lurking just around the corner. But it was not to be, and "Mamie's Blues," though not his final recorded say, has always seemed to me an appropriate swan song. It is certainly his last great record, and one of the most beautiful blues ever made. At that, it is simplicity itself: from the spoken introduction to the piano's last note, this is music stripped of all pretense, the purest distillation of the blues, and the essence of the man, who sings and plays, one feels, as much for himself as for us.

Bunk Johnson personified the traditional revival. Discovered during research for the seminal book *Jazzmen* (1939), he cunningly told his naive and romantic white interviewers just what they wanted to hear, and to make his role as a pioneer feasible, added ten years to his age (he had just turned fifty in late 1939). But Bunk was a genuine discovery and a musician of limited but not inconsiderable gifts. Ironically, his own tastes were much less antiquarian than his sponsors'; he preferred the company of trained musicians. "Franklin Street Blues" is part of another Commodore rescue operation. The session was the work of Eugene Williams, a founder of *Jazz Information*, and was issued by him on a short-lived label of the same name. Milt picked up the pieces. Bunk was a good bluesman, in that melodic New Orleans manner, and while his chops improved later on, his ideas here are intact and logical. ("Where my boy Louis goes up," he once said, "Bunk goes down.") Clarinetist George Lewis would become the standard-bearer of revivalism after Bunk's death in 1949. Contrary to what Williams and likeminded others thought, this brand of music was *not* the old style but something newly minted. It would prove quite resilient.

Bob Wilber was the catalyst among a group of jazz-minded teenagers who had discovered the music of Oliver, Morton, early Armstrong, and Bechet, and first became known as "The Scarsdale High Gang" (a sobriquet inspired by the Austin High Gang of 1920s Chicago). He would soon become Bechet's pupil. Milt invited them to perform at some Ryan's Sunday sessions and gave them their first record date, which included "Willie the Weeper." These kids were no flashes in the pan: Wilber, pianist Dick Wellstood, and the baby of the band, trumpeter Johnny Glasel (sixteen at the time; Wilber was not quite nineteen, and Wellstood had just reached that ripe old age) all became respected professionals, while Charlie Treager, after some years of playing in the major leagues, became a noted bass "doctor." The youngsters show a solid grasp of the idiom—the number is in a Clarence Williams Blue Five vein. Glasel is surprisingly secure and has his

Louis phrases well in hand, and Wellstood already is somebody—that great beat is in place. Wilber is amazing. He has absorbed Bechet's vocabulary and speaks it fluently, and he plays with authority. Of all the revivalist players, these were the best—and they would soon leave mimicry behind.

The Original Dixieland Jazz Band, first to record jazz, was first reunited in 1936 and enjoyed a brief flurry of publicity—all but one of the original members had survived. When Gabler, a man with a sense of history, got the idea of re-creating their music for Commodore, he had already been involved in such a venture for World Transcriptions. Brad Gowans, a gifted multi-instrumentalist best known for his valve-trombone work, recruited his idol, ODJB trombonist Eddie Edwards, and the band's drummer, Tony Sbarbaro (now known as Spargo), and cast himself in the role of clarinetist Larry Shields. When they recorded for World Transcriptions, neither perfectionist Gowans nor Milt was satisfied, and they got on the case again in 1945. "Lazy Daddy" is typical of the ODJB's intricate ensemble style: a peppy multi-strainer with plenty of breaks. Edwards had his own ensemble style—it's more intricate than the kind of tailgate Kid Ory or Honore Dutrey played; Brad does a decent Shields impression (he knew every note of the ODJB's records); and Spargo, who appears on other Commodore dates, was a solid New Orleans drummer with a good sound. The ODJB is often unjustly blamed for having been first with jazz on records. It wasn't their fault, and they did a pretty good job at that. This was the last authentic re-creation of their music.

There's no great difference between trumpet and cornet to the listener, but players may prefer the stubbier, wider-bored cornet (a direct descendant of the bugle) to the longer, narrower trumpet with its more brilliant upper range. Some guys kept changing, like Bobby Hackett; others, like Wild Bill Davison and Muggsy Spanier, were strictly cornetists. Louis Armstrong switched to trumpet in 1925 and stayed with it.

Wild Bill Davison was an amazing man. Though he was an awesome drinker, his professional career lasted almost seventy years, and he blew his horn hard. Born, appropriately, in Defiance, Ohio, in 1906, he was active on the Chicago jazz scene in the '20s and early '30s, but from 1933 to 1941 worked almost exclusively in Milwaukee, and was known only to a handful of musicians when he finally moved to New York. From then on, his star rose swiftly, and he and Eddie Condon soon became inseparable, musically and personally. Bill could lift even a tired band with his gruff tone and rhythmically driving phrasing—a style once described as "damn the torpedos." But he was also capable of caressing a ballad in a highly emotional manner derived from Armstrong. He was unique, and he went on blowing his horn all over the globe until his death in his eighty-fourth year. "That's A Plenty," from the Wild One's debut date for Commodore, is one of the hottest records ever made, and one of Milt's own favorites. The Davison-Brunies-Russell front line is potent and compatible—when reasonably sober, these were hard to beat at what might be called New York–style Chicago jazz (if you called it "Dixieland," Eddie would take you off his list). Earlier in 1943 they had been a fixture at Nick's; two years later, when Condon's own Greenwich Village club opened, this unit would be one of the foremost house bands. From the first explosive ensemble note of this number, you can tell they are *on*, all cylinders hitting together, and things remain hot throughout its more than four-minute duration, down to a spectacular rideout, with Chicagoan dynamics setting up the climax. If Wild Bill had left us only this record, he'd have made his mark.

Bobby Hackett was greatly admired by both Louis Armstrong and Miles Davis, which shouldn't surprise anyone who has really listened to Bobby's music. He had a marvelous ear for changes (an excellent guitarist, he knew harmonic foundations), a lovely sound, perfect time, and an imagination second to none. He could make himself felt in any musical setting. When he came to New York in 1937, he was quickly adopted by the gang at Nick's, but while he and Condon were lifelong friends and associates, Bobby branched off in many directions, including his own ill-fated big band and a stint (on guitar and cornet) with Glenn Miller. His happiest association, he once told me, was as co-leader of a quintet with Vic Dickenson; musically and personally, they were an ideal match. "New Orleans" is a fine Hoagy Carmichael tune, in an effective arrangement probably written by Hackett. He has a four-horn front line to work with, Ernie Caceres's bartitone providing a full foundation. Jess Stacy proves once again that he was a great band pianist. Front and back is Bobby in his ballad vein, getting to the heart of the tune—and of the listener.

Muggsy Spanier, one of ten siblings, started playing professionally at fifteen to supplement his salary as a messenger. Quite soon his steady horn was in demand on the Chicago dance-band scene, and Muggsy never wanted for work even when his less disciplined jazz chums were scuffling. He was proud all his life of the fact that King Oliver let him sit in at the Lincoln Gardens (the other white kids were just listening), and Oliver remained his idol. Muggsy was a master of the plunger, and like the King he loved the blues. His 1939 Ragtimers were a terrific band and made some excellent records, but lasted less than a year; Muggsy had to go back to the Ted Lewis orchestra. By 1944, he was a fixture at Nick's. He starts off "Memphis Blues" with a fine modulating cadenza and sets the right tempo for W. C. Handy's old tune—most bands play it too fast. Then Pee Wee Russell scores with a blues statement delivered with an incredible sound— "growl" is an understatement—and deep feeling. Muggsy responds with two of his best, linking them well, the second in his Oliver-Armstrong mold. Muggsy Spanier never played an insincere note in his life.

Sidney De Paris, like his older brother Wilbur, got his musical start in his father's carnival band. In the '20s and '30s, he was featured with some of the best big bands, including Charlie Johnson, Benny Carter, and Don Redman. His 1939 records with Jelly Roll Morton and Mezz Mezzrow, and with Bechet the following year, gave him revivalist credentials, but he was essentially a swing trumpeter, with his own skipping, whimsical phrasing. The band he co-led with his brother when the "Sheik of Araby" was made was a swing outfit, but in 1951 Wilbur formed his New Orleans band, which enjoyed considerable success and fixed Sidney in a musical setting that restricted his lively imagination. With Ed Hall added by Milt, this little Fifty-second Street band offers a sample of Clyde Hart's educated piano, good bass-drum work, and Wilbur's slightly archaic trombone. The ever-dependable Hall and lithe Sidney are what make this record memorable.

Oran "Hot Lips" Page was a regular at the Ryan's sessions and everywhere on Fifty-second Street, at the Town Hall concerts produced by Eddie Condon, at the fabled Minton's jams in Harlem, and anywhere else uptown where jazz was made. Lips could ignite a session with his big-toned trumpet, his infectious singing, and his inexhaustible bag of riffs. And he had the kind of presence—like Louis, whom he loved but didn't copy—to spread joy wherever he went. Fate did not reward him for such gifts; Lips was always knocking at the door but they never let him in. For this Commodore session, Lips had himself the kind of little band he liked—Kansas City by way of Harlem—his own blend of jump and jive. Three saxes to give a nice cushion, riff and take solos, and a solid rhythm section. "You Need Coachin'," a Page original, has lyrics that mix passion and humor; he sets up his vocal with a clarion trumpet intro, and Don Byas follows with his smoothly melodic approach to the blues, backed by good riffs. Then Lips blows, with that broad, gliss-laced sound, perfectly poised, strong as a bull, first phrasing symmetrically, then with unpredictable accents. Now Earl Bostic jumps in (the later-to-be-famous altoist often worked with Page then) with an amazing solo. His two choruses are a single entity, linked with astonishing breath control—a saxophone virtuoso, from whom John Coltrane learned a lot, technically, as a sideman when Bostic had his own band later on. Lips died in 1954—just forty-six years old. Had he survived into the era when blues became big, that elusive fame might have been his at last.

Jack Teagarden was still trapped in the rather sterile vastness of Paul Whiteman's orchestra when Milt snared him for the second Commodore session. "Diane" was his showcase—a lovely waltz too seldom played by jazz musicians, it seems made to order for Teagarden's signature sound and subtle inflections. Just by stating a melody, he could make it his own. Bud Freeman sustains the mood, tempering romanticism with a dash of blues. Jack returns after the relaxed ensemble passage for a special 8 bars and cadenza—he has such control he makes it sound easy, but just ask a fellow trombonist! Teagarden created his own technique—when he started on the horn, his arms were too short for the correct slide positions, so he used his chops instead. He was unique, and his artistry transcended stylistic categories. Even at the height of the sniping between moderns and moldies, he had everyone's respect. (Although it is not heard here, there should be at least passing mention of his warm, blues-steeped singing voice, quite comparable to that of his friend Louis Armstrong, with whose All Stars Teagarden was featured on both horn and voice in the late '40s and early '50s.)

George Brunies, oldest of the trombone triumvirate here, came from a musical New Orleans family (three brothers were also professionals). He came to Chicago at seventeen, and at nineteen was a founding member of the New Orleans Rhythm Kings. A co-composer of "Tin Roof Blues," he first recorded it in 1923. That solo (one of the first extended trombone solos on record) still sounded good twenty years later when played as the second of his two choruses here. But it was as a master of traditional ensemble playing, rather than as a soloist, that Brunies made his mark. He was also quite a showboat—at Nick's, he'd sometimes play trombone lying on his back. At Condon's club, Eddie discouraged such tricks, but when the boss wasn't looking, George might do it anyway.

Miff Mole was the trombone king when Teagarden came to New York in the fall of 1927 (Jack was subbing for Mole when he recorded his first solo). His supple technique made Miff, in the words of no less a master of slide than Dicky Wells, "the J. J. Johnson of the '20s." On first call in the record and radio studios, he worked in all kinds of situations (in the '30s, he even did a stint in the NBC Symphony under Toscanini) and was featured on hundreds of records, including many with his own "Little Molers." Some of Teagarden's bluesiness crept into him, and by the time he made "Peg O' My Heart," he was ensconced at Nick's, after a year on the road with Benny Goodman's band, featuring a rougher approach to the horn than in his earlier days. This was his showcase number at the club, and he offers a big-toned, mellow exposition of the old tune. The other soloists are vintage Commodore stars: Pee Wee, with a gem of a solo (he could make you cry), and Hackett, leading a perfect transition into an octave jump for the ensemble.

We've already met our two clarinets and two tenors. Russell was at Commodore from the start; it's hard to believe that it was more than six years before Milt gave him his own date, but leadership wasn't Pee Wee's strong suit. It was only after his miraculous recovery from a liver ailment in 1950 that he began to front his own groups, and even then reluctantly. He's among friends here, and Stacy is in particularly fine form on Fats Waller's "Keeping Out of Mischief Now," a 20-bar tune with a fetching melody. Pee Wee exposes it nicely, then Stacy invents some interesting stuff, bassist Sid Weiss (he had a fine sound) and drummer George Wettling trade fours, and Russell growls himself back in, moving upward gradually, and also becoming more intense. This is Pee Wee's last appearance on this program, so let's say it again: he was one of the heroes of the Commodore saga, and one of the true jazz originals.

Ed Hall was a classy gentleman—the first musician I knew to drive a Mercedes (a convertible, yet). Though he was on some great records in the '30s, a decade that found him mostly in big bands (he was a great baritone player), it wasn't until the next decade that he came into his own, mainly at Café Society, where he worked with Red Allen, Teddy Wilson, and his own hip sextet. From 1950 to 1955 he was in the house band at Condon's and then joined the Louis Armstrong All Stars. One of Benny Goodman's favorite clarinetists, Ed liked show tunes, and "The Man I Love" is up his alley. Typically, Hall doesn't deviate much from Gershwin's melody, using his distinctive sound and well-timed embellishments to create a personal interpretation.

Bud Freeman had been present on the very first Commodore session, and on that day he and Stacy and Wettling had stayed on to make some trio sides. The three had known one another as youths in Chicago and spoke the same musical language. "There was a great feeling among the three of them," Milt has recalled. "The Benny Goodman Trio was like salon music, but the Freeman trio was *saloon* music." "The Blue Room" is not from that very first session but rather from the third by this distinctive trio. Bud was an individual stylist—he didn't copy Coleman Hawkins, and any similarities between his approach to the horn and Lester Young's are strictly coincidental. As a featured soloist in such notable swing bands as those of Goodman, Ray Noble, and Tommy Dorsey, Freeman had quite a few followers himself. Here he starts right off with variations, not bothering to state the theme. His sound is his own, and so is his rhythm. The trio sounds like a whole band. (Listen to Wettling, here and elsewhere. Drummers were doing other things than just timekeeping long before bebop, folks.)

Three years after his "Body and Soul"—and only two months before his tragic death in a car accident—Chu Berry is back with Commodore. He was two weeks shy of his thirty-first birthday, just reaching his prime. "Sunny Side of the Street" is less ornate than "Body," and his mastery of the horn, already impressive back in 1938, has become even more so—hear those beautiful high notes at the end. Berry has fine support, notably from pianist Clyde Hart, whose solo suggests why he was one of Dizzy Gillespie's favorites. Chu's up-tempo style was something else; Coleman Hawkins himself suggested that if Berry had lived he would have rearranged the top seedings on tenor. Hawk rarely used the term "genius," but he applied it to this man.

Piano players were a Commodore specialty. We start this segment with three "Chicagoans." Actually, Jess Stacy was born in Missouri and Art Hodes in Russia, but all three cut their musical eyeteeth in Joe Sullivan's hometown. Hodes was not part of the Commodore crowd, although he was no stranger to the record store and regularly worked at the Sunday jams at Jimmy Ryan's. But Art had his own agenda; for a while he had his own label (Jazz Records) and edited his own magazine (*The Jazz Record*). He also had a radio show on WNYC (producer Orrin Keepnews says that's probably where, as a boy, he first heard recorded jazz), ran sessions, and in general proselytized for the cause—as he would continue to do until his death, at age eighty-nine, in 1993. Art's first and last love was the blues, which he played with no trace of a Russian accent—strictly South Side Chicago. "A Selection from the Gutter" is a case in point: tempo, feeling, and touch all add up to the real thing. This was recorded by young Bob Thiele, who then got drafted and asked Milt to put it out. It's nice to have Art at Milt's table.

Sullivan made several band sessions for Milt, including a great one with Pee Wee and Zutty Singleton, after which he stuck around to do some solos. Joe had been in on the earliest recordings by the Chicagoans, worked with a bunch of big bands (including Bob Crosby's) and accompanied a bunch of singers (including Bob's older brother Bing); he also led his own integrated band at Café Society. But Joe was above all a soloist, and a splendid one; inspired by Fats Waller and Earl Hines, he had his own thing, infused with his Irish temperament. Joe had imagination: you've heard "Summertime" a hundred times by a hundred players and singers, but Joe does it his own way. He could make a piano sing.

So could Stacy, Milt's favorite, and the subject of several Commodore solo sessions. "Ec-Stacy," a 12-incher, stands out. It's a blues, reflective and nostalgic, with much dynamic and textural variety (including some charming chime effects—Jess had played the steam calliope on the riverboats early on). Through chorus seven we get straight blues, albeit with sophisticated harmonic augmentation, but the concluding passages hint of Carmichael's "Washboard Blues." Bob Haggart later scored this piece as a feature for Jess with the Bob Crosby band, retaining some of the Beiderbecke spirit of this great solo.

Eddie Heywood's slick little band (Doc Cheatham on trumpet, Vic Dickenson on trombone, the underrated Lem Davis on alto sax) had much success at Café Society, but despite the fine horns, the leader basically featured himself. Adept at highly stylized playing, once he made up a solo he kept it that way. "Begin the Beguine" was his biggest number and almost got Gabler in trouble (remember his Decca contract that said no hits on Commodore?), but Milt recorded it as a 12-inch single—denying it the big commercial market—and later, having brought Heywood into the Decca fold, remade it as a "normal" 10-incher, which did become a hit! The clever trick that makes this arrangement click is the unexpectedly slow tempo combined with a repeated bass figure (borrowed from Art Tatum's 1939 version, but Art's had been *fast*)—a kind of boogie beguine.

Albert Ammons also worked at Café Society—as part of the famous tuxedo-clad boogie-woogie threesome with Meade Lux Lewis and Pete Johnson. To this listener, Ammons was the greatest of the three—he had a fabulous beat and a real feeling for jazz. "Jammin' the Boogie" finds him at the helm of a band, which in 1944 was no novelty for him; he'd recorded for Decca back in 1936 with a fine little jazz band in his native Chicago. This time Milt grabbed Albert just before he was due to join the Army. The flavor here is a combination of Kansas City and Fifty-second Street; thanks to Hot Lips Page, it's a lesson in riffing, but first we get a sequence of great blowing choruses, with the leader framing solos by Byas, Page, and Dickenson. Big Sid Catlett, partnered by Chicago bassist Israel Crosby, provides a splendid bottom. And if you didn't know: yes, Albert was Gene Ammons's dad.

George Zack goes well after Ammons. A two-fisted barrelhouse player, he was a special favorite of Milt's ("He had a spirit I loved") but was a problem in the studio. The difficulty wasn't Zack's talent (Gabler saw him as a "missing link between Jelly Roll Morton and Earl Hines") but his love of the grape. Although he made no less than six attempts, the producer felt he had failed to capture Zack at his best. Even so, "Lazy River" sounds fine to me. Zack adored Armstrong and captures the spirit of Satchmo (the pianist also sang à la Louis and claimed to have shared an apartment with the great man in Chicago in the '20s).

With Willie "The Lion" Smith we come to piano royalty. Along with Fats Waller and James P. Johnson, he held court in Harlem in the '20s, showing kids like Eddie Ellington how it should be done. (Actually, Willie was just two years older than Duke, but he had started early.) Unlike Fats, who thrived in the recording environment, Willie made few records that do him justice. "Finger Buster" is from a Commodore session in 1939 that produced his finest work on wax. No fewer than fourteen pieces were recorded; this was the next-to-last and the pièce de résistance for stride dexterity—the Lion's answer to James P.'s "Carolina Shout" and other such display pieces. Multiple strains, interludes, modulations, and left-hand panache are all in evidence; the final appearance of the "A" strain in a new key is a nice touch. This is the great Lion at his best.

Willie claimed to have composed "Squeeze Me," though it is credited to Fats Waller. Truth told, its melody stems from an old (even by the early '20s) bawdy song, "The Boy in the Boat." Fats and Clarence Williams cleaned it up; Fats may have "borrowed" the descending chromatic melody that is a refinement of the tune (and became known as "the escalator" among pianists) from Willie. Ralph Sutton loves both Fats (his original inspiration) and Willie (his friend), and with him, "Squeeze Me" is in good hands. Big hands—strong hands. According to his good friend Dick Wellstood (who did the liner notes for a 1982 reissue of Ralph's Commodore sessions—Dick wrote as well as he played), Ralph plays the third chorus double-timed "the way Willie the Lion used to do it." Dick pointed out that, on listening to these 1950 Sutton solos, "it's easy to hear why he had such an impact on musicians and critics alike. In addition to strength, accuracy and swing, his playing possessed a naturalness and sense of inevitability that marked him a star from the first. And then of course there was his 'Fatsness.'" Dick has left us, much too soon, but Ralph is still doing his thing; having him conclude this survey of Commodore's rich history lends it a nice sense of continuity.

Milt's still with us, too, to witness this reincarnation of his legacy. He was around at a very special time for jazz—a time that will never be equalled—and thanks to his initiative, integrity, and imagination, some precious aspects of that time can be recaptured. This is music that will live as long as there are ears to listen.

(1997)

Milt Gabler died in 2001, aged ninety.

The Hot Record Society

T he initials "HRS" stand for Hot Record Society (amended in later publicity to "High Recording Standards"), an organization of collectors formed in 1937 under the leadership of Stephen W. Smith, himself among the founders of the United Hot Clubs of America in 1935. The impressive advisory board included the ubiquitous John Hammond; George Frazier, Charles Edward Smith, Marshall Stearns, Wilder Hobson, Warren Scholl, and William Russell, plus the Europeans Hugues Panassié, Charles Delaunay, and Sinclair Traill.

Initially, HRS was centered on mail-order auctions and sales of collector's items, many of them provided by Russell, then touring the country as musical director and percussionist-flutist with a group of dancers called the Red Gate Chinese Shadow Players (some may have been red, but none were Chinese). George Avakian recalls that he had "a photo of Bill, unrecognizable in a black robe and black skullcap with a woven pigtail, cross-legged at stage left, blowing a flute amid a modest array of percussion instruments. The [three] dancers are in silhouette, backlit behind . . . a white sheet. During the day, Bill would scour the area for junk shops and other time-honored sources of discarded records, which he would then ship back to Steve for listing in the next auction."

Russell is of course famous today in jazz circles as the guru of the New Orleans Revival, sometime manager of Bunk Johnson, founder of the American Music label, violinist with the New Orleans Ragtime Orchestra, author of a small but distinguished body of musically literate articles on jazz, compiler of the huge, posthumously published Jelly Roll Morton sourcebook *Oh, Mister Jelly!*, and noted avant-garde classical composer (his contemporary John Cage called him "the most gifted of all of us") who gave it up for the cause of jazz. (He died in 1992.)

Steve Smith, on the other hand, can certainly qualify for the title his erstwhile partner Heywood Hale Broun bestowed on him: "The Forgotten Man of Jazz." Ironically, much of Russell's early reputation was based on his contributions to the seminal 1939 book *Jazzmen*, edited by Charles Edward Smith and Frederic Ramsey, Jr., in which Steve Smith was also represented, by an insightful and witty essay, "Hot Collecting." The book has been in print more often than not for more than sixty years, but Steve Smith is not a name we encounter in most other jazz literature. A recent exception is the fascinating but sprawling *Jazz by Mail: Record Clubs and Record Labels*,

1936–1958, by the veteran collector Geoffrey Wheeler (Hillbrook Press, 1998), in which a thumbnail sketch of Smith and a partial history of his label appear. Another is John Chilton's excellent *Sidney Bechet: The Wizard of Jazz* (Oxford University Press, 1987), which quotes from the author's correspondence with Smith in 1984. And he appears in *Oh, Mister Jelly!* (Jazz Media, 1999).

From these we glean that Smith not only produced the wonderful Bechet-Spanier sessions for HRS, but also had previously been in the studio with the king of the soprano sax in his role of de facto producer of the famous Jelly Roll Morton comeback session for Victor's Bluebird label in 1939. Among other things, it was Smith's idea to have Bechet and Albert Nicholas share solo honors on "High Society," thus avoiding potential ego trouble—and realizing great music.

As he told Chilton, a year earlier he and his wife, Lee (who by all accounts was a big help to Smith in his various jazz endeavors, though she also worked as a legal secretary), had been at Nick's, the popular jazz club in Greenwich Village, to hear Bechet, Wellman Braud, and Zutty Singleton. "In walks Jack Teagarden and his wife; they took a table right next to the trio and listened for a while. Then Jack went outside . . . and came back with his trombone. [He] played a duet with Bechet for more than an hour, the trio not even stopping to take a break. Lee, I and Nick heard some of the most beautiful and inspired music that I am sorry to say the world will never hear. The voices of the trombone and soprano sax stayed with me, so that when I was doing the Jelly Roll sides for Victor I had Jelly put in a spot [for Claude Jones and Bechet]."

In the spring of 1940, Decca enlisted Smith to supervise the New York sessions for their New Orleans Jazz album set, inspired by George Avakian's pioneering Chicago Jazz set of the previous year, according to Avakian, at his suggestion. This included no less a summit than one of the rare encounters between Bechet and Louis Armstrong. But Steve Smith's important role has been eclipsed; until I took a closer look, even I thought that it was the other Smith, Charles Edward, who'd been responsible, since he wrote the booklet notes. (These do contain a footnote crediting Steve Smith, and there's even a photo of Steve in the montage of faces that adorns the inside cover of the 78 album. But these clues did not survive on the LP reissues.)

And speaking of photos: Steve's name appears in the index to the fine collection of Charles Peterson photos published in 1994 as *Swing Era: New York* (Temple University Press), but when you look for his image under the caption "Stephen Smith, a New York record store owner and co-producer of the [HRS] label, chats at Nick's bar with Bobby Hackett and Sharkey Bonano," the gentleman depicted looks nothing like our man. Fortuitously, I found a clipping in the Institute of Jazz Studies' HRS file of the identical photo with caption from a 1938 issue of *Tempo* magazine, which correctly identifies the subject as Park Breck, a member of the HRS advisory board. Forgotten man of jazz, indeed!

Avakian describes Smith as "a quiet, private sort of person who kept to himself—a short, wiry fellow with dark, curly hair . . . and the appearance and mien of a slowly aging bantam-weight boxer." Both Avakian and Wheeler identify Smith as a commercial artist who made his main living by turning out cover paintings for pulp monthlies like *Flying Aces* and *Real Detective*. Avakian describes his work as "colorful and realistic," but when he once praised a work in progress at Smith's studio, calling him an artist, the response was: "Picasso's an artist; I'm a commercial painter."

Avakian was present at HRS's first live recording (the label had been turning out monthly reissues since May of 1937, hard on the heels of Milt Gabler's UHCA; the first issue was two masters of the rare "Three Blind Mice" by the Chicago Loopers with Bix and Tram); it was the first record date he ever attended, and he wrote about it in *Tempo* under the headline "HRS Stages Black & White Disc Session." Describing HRS as "fast-growing," he wrote that Smith "picked the men, brought them up to the American Records studios, and turned them loose without a written note in the house," adding that "Pee Wee [Russell] himself ran the show," and concluding the piece with the prediction that "after that trio disc gets around, Pee Wee will come into his own."

A few months before that memorable first live HRS date, Smith had launched the first issue of a magazine, the *HRS Society Rag*. Its editors were the two Smiths, Bill Russell, and Dick Reiber, and the debut issue contained the latter's profile of George Frazier. Published irregularly (a total of eleven issues appeared, the last dated March 1941), such profiles were featured often, including Otis Ferguson's famous (and not wholly flattering) one of Hammond. There were also nice graphics—not, as one might have thought, by the publisher (though he may have been responsible for some uncredited art) but, from the fourth issue on, by the Chicago-based John Groth—and interesting photos, criticism, and news. Broun took over as editor with the fourth issue; veteran collectors will remember him as the producer of a fascinating album featuring some of the oldest surviving New Orleans musicians, under the leadership of Kid Rena, for his own one-shot Delta label. Aside from his early jazz activities, Broun is a noted author, broadcaster, and actor. Another editorial spark plug of the *HRS Rag* was Russell Sanjek, who became one of the founders of BMI and wrote an exhaustive (and exhausting) history of the popular music business, and Charles Peterson was the staff photographer. Altogether, the *HRS Society Rag* was the closest thing to a "little magazine" on the jazz scene—a cut above *Jazz Information*, though that publication was produced by Columbia undergraduates.

In 1939, Steve Smith opened the HRS Record Shop at 827 Seventh Avenue, following in the footsteps of Commodore. Avakian recalls helping out in the store in the summer of 1940 ("two customers a day meant we were busy") and spent a couple of days listening to Jelly Roll Morton, who, like many older musicians, dropped in for a chat from time to time. Clearly, Smith was someone Morton trusted. A younger musician acquaintance was Rex Stewart, who probably was brought into the HRS fold by Smith's Eddie Condon, the guitarist, arranger, sometime bandleader (and later in life, very successful copyist) Brick Fleagle.

These two were contemporaries (Smith born in 1907, Fleagle a year earlier) and shared a love for the music of Duke Ellington. Fleagle, whose given names were Roger Jacob, had first met Rex in 1930, when the cornetist was with Alex Jackson's band in Cincinnati, as he described in a profile of Rex written for the *HRS Rag*'s August 1940 issue. He is present as guitarist and/or arranger on most of Rex's 1930s small-group Ellingtonian dates, and also arranged "Smorgasbord and Schnapps," which he and Rex composed, for the Ellington band. (Brick also scored his "Pixie from Dixie" for Fletcher Henderson.) Originally a banjoist, Fleagle made the switch to guitar in the late '20s, touring with various bands (Hal Kemp and Orville Knapp among them), sometimes leading his own, and also writing for Jimmie Lunceford and Chick Webb. From the 1950s on, he ran his own copying and arranging service; I often encountered him at such watering holes as the Copper Rail, Beefsteak Charlie's, and, later on, the last Eddie Condon's, but he was always too much in his cups for me to ask him serious questions, which I now regret not having found a way to do. He was a happy fellow with a curiously high-pitched voice.

As for their shared love of Ellington, here is a tribute to Duke penned by Smith sometime in the 1940s: "Staying up after the folks had gone to bed to hear Ellington's Cotton Club Band down in Harlem, on the crystal set we made ourselves . . . The Brunswick record we bought of 'Black and Tan Fantasy' by the Washingtonians, with the fine Bubber Miley horn . . . The big tone and solid beat of Wellman Braud's bass that for us will never be surpassed . . . Sonny Greer, the first to drum up that broad curtain of sound in back of the band and his beat that went Do De Do De Do De Do DEET . . . Dapper Freddie Jenkins . . . Breakfast dances . . . And the Duke's touch always in there, keeping things alive and jumping, constantly fresh and new . . . Tricky Sam's growl on 'Tishomingo Blues' . . . Listening to the lyrical Hodges at friendly record sessions . . . Packed like sardines at the Savoy as the Duke presents Cootie at his best to an appreciative audience . . . Rex and Barney and Lawrence Brown working hard to make (solid rock) one of our best records . . . Ben Webster on our next one, high, happy and soulful with the Blues . . . And always the Duke, with 'Black and Tan Fantasy,' 'Stormy Weather,' 'Mood Indigo,' 'Creole Love Call,' 'Sophisticated Lady,' 'It Don't Mean a Thing If It Ain't Got That Swing' . . . Thank you, Duke Ellington."

This love letter to Duke also gives us some insight into Smith, whom Avakian recalls as "a practical guy who seemed anxious to hide a strand of romanticism that was in all of us fans and collectors." It came out there. Avakian observes that "when Peter Falk arrived on TV with his trench coat, I was reminded of Steve, who usually wore a beat-up leather jacket but had the same quizzical, ready-to-doubt air. He was a Socratic arguer whose questions were meant not to be answered, but to provoke thought."

The war years put a stop to HRS's recording activities. (The label had put out some twenty-seven reissue discs but discontinued the series when both RCA Victor [on its Bluebird subsidiary] and Columbia [with its vault material collated by Avakian] became serious about restoring classic jazz to the catalog.) New recording became problematic, what with the union-imposed recording ban and the shellac shortage. From scattered correspondence (with George Hoefer) in the Institute's files, it appears that Smith had made a deal with Keynote Records to press his masters (this fits with a Stewart date issued on Keynote) but was disappointed with the results; there was also some sort of arrangement with BMI to distribute the discs that ran into problems. By 1944, Smith was involved in a music-publishing venture, first under the name of Roger West Publishers (Roger likely for Fleagle, West perhaps Smith's middle name), then as Onyx Publishers; BMI (probably via Sanjek) was in the wings here, too, according to a music-press clipping, but nothing seems to have materialized.

In 1945, HRS resumed recording activities, with Broun as Smith's partner. In a *Washington Post* story by Bill Gottlieb, of photo fame, headlined "Steve Smith Can't Stand a Tie—and Disc Competitors Know It" (the date is August 25, 1946), a photo of a pugnacious-looking Smith, cigarette in hand and dressed in a checkered short-sleeved shirt, is captioned "Tieless Steve Smith, Daddy of the Independents." The story notes that HRS "rents studios, jobs out record pressing and handles sales and deliveries by mail. These operations are typical of independents, except that HRS works on a higher plane. Steve figures he can afford to. His finished products are timeless."

Gottlieb's conclusion was correct, as this collection proves, but Smith's tolerance for the vagaries of the record business was wearing thin. He threw in the towel, probably not long after the final HRS session, and moved with his wife to a farm in Valley Falls, New York, northeast of Troy. He didn't cut himself off completely from the past—his great-nephew recalls that he visited Rex Stewart, who was active in the 1950s as a disc jockey in the Albany area. Sadly, he eventually had to part with his record collection, and he spent his final days in a nursing home, having suffered a stroke.

George Avakian recalls Steve Smith's thinking as "touched with cynicism." This could only have been reinforced by what happened to his HRS masters. Some material surfaced on LP labels designed for the five-and-ten-cent-store trade. The Russell and Teagarden sessions appeared briefly on Atlantic. Then Riverside got hold of the catalog, and one would like to be able to say that they treated it well. But while the label did issue a good deal of the material, the transfers were so poor that those of us who had access to the 78 considered ourselves lucky, and few new ears could have been snared for this fine music.

But now, at last, Steve Smith's legacy has been treated with the kind of care and respect it deserves, and one may hope that this pioneer of independent jazz recording and independent jazz journalism will no longer be the forgotten man of jazz.

(2000)

The Birth of Blue Note

On the first day of what was to become a legendary jazz label, Alfred Lion brought to a rented recording studio in New York two of the great masters of boogie-woogie piano, Albert Ammons and Meade Lux Lewis.

Two weeks before, he had attended the first of John Hammond's famed Spirituals to Swing concerts at Carnegie Hall, at which the two piano giants were featured along with a host of other performers representing what Hammond considered the pure jazz, blues, and gospel idioms. It was a powerful experience for the twenty-nine-year-old jazz fan, a recent refugee from the murderous thugs who had seized power in Germany and made even his beloved Berlin, where he had discovered jazz at sixteen, at a performance by Sam Wooding's Chocolate Kiddies, a place fraught with danger.

Lion had a special touch from the start. His maiden session produced an astonishing nineteen usable masters, twelve of which were issued on the extra-length 12-inch 78s that would become a Blue Note trademark—no other jazz label of the 78 era issued so much of its output in this more costly format that gave the artists more time to create. From day one, Blue Note had class.

Lion made the two Chicagoans in New York (where they would spend considerable time appearing at Café Society, etc.) feel at home in the studio, providing their favorite food and drink, and they responded with an outpouring of creativity that made this first day a landmark, not only for the quantity of music produced, but also for the quality. In early 1939, boogie-woogie had yet to become the fad that would bestow upon us such jewels as the Andrews Sisters' "Boogie Woogie Bugle Boy," disinterred by Bette Midler, Freddy Martin's "Bumble Boogie," and sundry other gems designed to make a true jazz and blues fan take flight. But there had already been some valid swing adaptations of the style, such as the Tommy Dorsey band's "Boogie Woogie," well crafted by arranger Deane Kincaid from pianist-singer Pinetop Smith's 1929 hit record of "Pinetop's Boogie Woogie," which gave the style its lasting name.

Prior to that, the piano blues style marked by a steady, solid ostinato bass, most often of eight beats to the bar, had been known variously as Fast Western, Texas Piano, or other designations pointing to its presumed geographic origins. It was a music made for dancing and partying, powerfully rhythmic and well adapted to the out-of-tune and otherwise impaired uprights usually available to its practitioners. This most percussive of piano styles uses the blues as its main text; a skilled performer can produce the most complex and driving patterns within a seemingly restrictive vocabulary.

Ammons (1907–1949) and Lewis (1905–1964) have no peers when it comes to making boogie-woogie take wing. Even Pete Johnson (from Kansas City rather than Chicago), who also played at Hammond's concert, recorded for Blue Note, and later teamed with Ammons, cannot match the inventiveness and power of these two, while such acknowledged originals as Jimmy Yancey—considered the father of the style by some—and Cripple Clarence Lofton were not as versatile and accomplished pianistically. Ammons, whose son, Gene, became a famous jazz tenor saxophonist, could play excellent jazz piano and led fine little hot bands in Chicago in the '30s and '40s. Lewis was somewhat less at home with jazz changes but liked to try his hand at standards (he also sang). He was a terrific whistler. We get a swinging sample of their jazz chops on the duet "Nagasaki" (erroneously listed as "The Sheik of Araby" on previous issues); the Harry Warren tune had also been recorded by Ammons with his 1936 band.

But of course it's the blues that's the main course here, and this wonderfully varied program is a lesson in the inexhaustibility of this "simple" form that has produced so much of our century's music, including many a hybrid.

Here we have the real thing. From the first day, Alfred Lion wanted no commercial concessions.

Generally speaking, Ammons is the more forceful, swinging, and pianistically accomplished of our heroes, Lewis the more inventive. As Max Harrison has pointed out, Lewis's prolonged essay *The Blues* (the fifth part, discovered by Michael Cuscuna, was first issued in 1983; the other four, on two 12-inch discs packaged in a cardboard sleeve with art cover and brief liner notes, constituted the first jazz record album ever issued of a single artist's work) "shows the variety of figuration, the different levels of intensity, and the depth of expression which can be drawn from simple harmonic progressions. It is a splendid instance of how stylistic limitations, *willingly accepted* [my italics], can heighten the impact of a music discourse."

These insights are applicable to most of this music. On this first day, Ammons and Lewis knew how to get the maximum yield from their chosen stylistic mode—or from the choices they willingly made at the behest of their host. Alone and together, they made music still startling in its inspiration and purity. In vulgar or meretricious or merely silly hands, boogie-woogie became a noisome cliché, but no amount of vulgarization has been able to rob these performances of their inherent grace and power.

On that first day, Alfred Lion could not have had even an inkling of what this enthusiastic experiment would lead to. He only knew that he wanted to capture for posterity (and immediate dissemination) some music that seemed special and remarkably beautiful. That first day's rich harvest did show that he was able to create a proper climate for recording—a process fundamentally different from other performance modes.

He saw that what he had done was good and continued his labors in the fertile vineyards of jazz, soon abetted by his boyhood friend and fellow fan and émigré Frank Wolff. Because they knew what they wanted to hear on a record, they eventually made it heard around the world. This was the start of the lasting romance between Blue Note and the blues.

(1992)

Notes on Keynote Sessions

Keynote, one of the very few pre–World War II independent labels, was founded by Eric Bernay, who, in his role as publisher of *The New Masses*, had sponsored John Hammond's Spirituals to Swing concerts. But Keynote was not a jazz label—it recorded Paul Robeson, Josh White, folk music, and left-oriented material—until, in late 1943, Harry Lim came on board as producer. Born in Batavia, Java, in 1919 and educated in Holland, where he encountered jazz, Lim was in the middle of a visit to the United States when war broke out and had the good sense to stay put, leaving behind his precious record collection and files of the English-language jazz magazine *Blue Rhythm*, which he had edited as cofounder of the Hot Club of Batavia.

In the United States, he first made a name for himself as producer of weekly jam sessions, in Chicago and then in New York, at the later-to-be-famous Village Vanguard. When he took charge of Keynote, he produced, in the span of about three years, some of the finest jazz recordings of the era. An ill-advised investment in a pressing plant led to Keynote's downfall in 1947, and the masters were sold to a newcomer, Mercury. In 1986, the enterprising Japanese jazz writer, editor, and record producer Kiyoshi Koyama decided to resurrect Keynote, combing Mercury's archives for every trace of its output, uncovering in the process a host of unissued material.

The resultant boxed set was one of the most massive of the then fading LP era, and the annotation the most massive assignment of my career, though subsequently eclipsed by the three-times-larger complete Commodore collection. What follows are some Keynote highlights.

The Lester Young quartet session of December 28, 1943, was the real debut of Keynote jazz—and what a beginning! Young's first date as a leader (the trio session of 1942 was privately recorded by Norman Granz and not issued until 1945) found him in brilliant form and in the friendliest of company (Johnny Guarnieri, piano; Slam Stewart bass; Sid Catlett, drums). The result was inspired music: one of the greatest and most productive record dates of Lester's career.

Prior to the release of this complete Keynote box, alternate takes to three of the four tunes had been issued, but the alternate take of the fourth, "Sometimes I'm Happy," is one of Mr. Koyama's great finds. It is a lovely performance, even more relaxed than the famous original version. At 3:41, it runs too long for a 10-inch 78—thirty-six seconds longer than the issued take. The tempo is a mite slower, creating a dreamy mood, and Guarnieri takes a full chorus. To Lester students, the most interesting discovery will be that the famous tag by Pres, based on a quote from "My Sweetie Went Away," was a spontaneous invention; it is absent from the "new" take.

This marvelous session begins with "Just You, Just Me," one of Thelonious Monk's favorite tunes. The routine for both takes is the same: a Slam Stewart introduction, two choruses by Lester, one each by Stewart and Guarnieri, and a 4-bar tag by Lester. Solo differences aside, the main difference between takes is the slightly slower (and more settled) tempo of the second, which rightly was chosen for issue—it's a perfectly balanced performance. The rhythm section is an ideal one for Lester, and he and Big Sid Catlett work so well together that it's a pity they didn't meet on records again. (The only other surviving collaboration was in the film *Jammin' the Blues*, on just one number.) The tempo picks up for "I Never Knew," which Lester had recorded with the Basie band. He takes the introduction himself and plays three superb choruses. Piano's next with one, followed by 4-bar exchanges between bass and drums. All's gone well up to this point, but the first take breaks down during the ensuing Catlett solo, with stop-time punctuations from the band. But that's all for the best, since take two is even better from the start. Pres dances through his solo, and Catlett (on brushes) creates brilliant rhythmic patterns.

"Afternoon of a Basieite" is a fast blues. (Lester didn't like the title and always referred to it as "Afternoon of a Baseball Player.") Piano starts this one off, backed by Catlett's hi-hat, à la Jo Jones. Then Lester leaps in, his five choruses a textbook of his style. Slam takes two good ones, and then Big Sid solos. Pres and Slam trade fours, and the leader sails out with two choruses that define swinging. The first take is flawless from a musical standpoint; the sole reason for a second try was that Lester's final choruses are slightly off-mike. But we must be thankful for that since the second take is equally wonderful, with Sid's solo even better and Lester showing us that his powers of invention on the blues were limitless. Two masterpieces in a row!

We've discussed take one of "Sometimes I'm Happy." Take two, like everything from this session, is a gem. Slam Stewart plays one of the best solos of his career (years later, when visiting with me, this was the first record he asked to hear), Guarnieri is perfect, and Lester weaves his magic spell. Seldom has so much fine music resulted from a single afternoon's work by four musicians who met in a recording studio and then went their separate ways, never to work again as a unit. A very special chemistry was present here.

. . .

It is difficult to choose the ultimate Keynote session, but the one by the Cozy Cole All Stars would certainly be a contender. It was the first of the label's many 12-inch dates, a format allowing for up to a bit more than five minutes of music per side—the maximum for good 78 sound. The extra time made things more relaxed and flexible, as well as allowing for extra solo space.

The term "all stars" would soon become debased, but here it is perfectly justified. It was a Lim coup to obtain the services of Earl Hines, still leading a big band and rarely willing to record as a sideman. The great Fatha is here reunited with his former trombone star, Trummy Young, who appeared too infrequently on records. Nothing needs to be said about Coleman Hawkins's star qualifications, but trumpeter Joe Thomas never did become a famous name, though truly a great player and perfectly at home in these surroundings. A Lim favorite, Thomas did some of his finest work for Keynote. Ex-Ellingtonian Billy Taylor has been unjustly overshadowed by his successor, Jimmy Blanton, but as an ensemble bassist, he ranks with the best. Guitarist Teddy Walters, the youngest and least-known member, was the son of drummer Danny Alvin and also an excellent singer; he died tragically young. He rises to this occasion, contributing solos in a fluent Charlie Christian idiom that are no letdown whatsoever. Leader Cozy Cole was justly one of the most admired of swing-era drummers.

The discovery of no less than six previously unheard alternate takes from this brilliant gathering is more than welcome; we now have almost fifty minutes of sublime music from a session representing classic swing in its mature prime, hinting at but still unaffected by brewing things to come.

"Blue Moon," at a fine middle tempo, serves well to get everyone properly acquainted, with solo spots for all but bass and drums. From his introduction on, Hines makes it known that he has come to play; his solos on both takes are superb. Young, too, is inspired. But this is just a warm-up for the fireworks of "Father Cooperates," a fast romp through "I Got Rhythm" changes. Each of the four (!) takes is a masterpiece; astonishingly, the players continue to outdo themselves, though they start off at the highest level. Hines is simply dazzling. His ideas flow unceasingly, and he never repeats himself. His forays into uncommon harmonic corners tempt us to adjectives like "modern" and "futuristic," but Hines is just doing what he's always done, albeit in uncommonly inspiring circumstances. Hawkins, always responsive to a challenge, fine-tunes elements of his climactic two-chorus rideout until he has perfected it, yet retains a feeling of spontaneity. Young, on the other hand, is always willing to take chances—he's a spur-of-the-moment player. The effective use of riffs on this piece should be mentioned.

After this display of energy, it's time to settle down with a ballad. "Just One More Chance" features Hawkins, nearly unsurpassable in this kind of romantic mood, but there's also room for a striking interlude from Hines (those famous tremolos) and a tasteful bridge passage by Walters. Both takes are perfect, but there's more perfection to come. Trummy Young's "Through for the Night," a very attractive variation on "Honeysuckle Rose," is taken at perfect middle tempo (the kind one almost never hears in jazz anymore), creating a mood of sublime relaxation and easy swing. Everybody responds, but it is the composer who comes up with the most startling effort—his solo on the second (issued) take is one of his greatest on record and shows why he was the most influential jazz voice on trombone between Jimmy Harrison and J. J. Johnson. Truly a super-session—and let's not forget the sterling work of Taylor and Cole.

This was a hard act to follow, but Lim came up with another super-session, exactly a month later (on March 22, 1944), featuring the cream of Count Basie's band, with Lester Young as the star. This Kansas City Seven date was another 12-inch session, allowing the soloists (Lester; trumpeter Buck Clayton, also responsible for the arrangements; trombonist Dicky Wells; and Basie himself, appearing under the pseudonym of Prince Charming) plenty of room. An interesting aspect of the session is the unusually active keyboard role taken by Basie, who plays in a fuller style than his wont and seems to be having a wonderful time. There are two newly discovered takes here, a special treat for Lester fans since the tenorman is well featured on both "After Theater Jump" and "Six Cats and a Prince." Doing a fine job in the rhythm section is the unsung bassist Rodney Richardson, who'd recently joined the band and manages to fill Walter Page's big shoes surprisingly well. Close listening reveals that Jo Jones didn't bring his bass drum. He works with just snare, hi-hat, and ride cymbal. This was a late-night session, and he probably didn't feel like lugging his heavy bass-drum case to the studio from the Times Square movie theater where the band was appearing. Or perhaps he'd been thinking of the famous Smith-Jones, Inc., date of 1936, Lester's debut on records, when he also worked without a bass drum.

We begin with a new take of "After Theater Jump," a nice Clayton line. The tempo is faster than on take two, and after solos by Basie and rhythm and the three horns (guitarist Freddie Green making himself felt, as always), we get an unexpected bonus: a chorus of exchanges between Buck, Lester, Dicky, and Basie. Lester's two choruses are completely different from those on take two—and not just due to the tempo. And note how Wells, using his homemade buzz mute, starts his solo with an echo of

Lester's concluding lick. Though the second take is more precise in ensemble passages and the tempo has a special relaxed quality, it must have been difficult to decide which take to issue. I prefer the first, for its spontaneity, and the exchanges. The second take of "Six Cats and a Prince" was already known, albeit only to some lucky Swedes (it was issued on the Metronome label in that Scandinavian country) and Pres collectors, but the first had never been known. Thus we now have three takes of this Clayton piece ("'S Wonderful" with a "Honeysuckle Rose" bridge). The new take is somewhat slower than the others and a full minute and ten seconds longer than take two, allowing for an extra chorus by Wells, in particularly fine form that night. Lester also takes two, as he does on all the versions, and the bridge of the closing ensemble. To this listener, his take one solo work is the best of the three—there is a special glow. Basie and Wells take solo honors on the second, where Pres seems less involved, but he regains his inspiration on the third, with Basie again outstanding. Clayton takes his best of three here, and Wells tops his fine earlier efforts with a shouting, happy statement.

"Lester Leaps Again" required no retakes; it came off perfectly. A spontaneous blues by tenor and rhythm, its highlight is the interplay between Lester and Basie. We may never know just why Pres left the band on that Friday the thirteenth in December of 1940, but whatever the reason, no ill will lingered between Count and Pres—the way they get together here proves that, and Lester obviously felt at home again in the Basie fold. Just as obviously, subtle changes had taken place in his style, and they are more closely revealed here than on his first Keynote date. That ought to prove that it was not his subsequent unhappy experiences in the Army that changed his musical approach, but that it was a natural development. Two takes of "Destination K.C." (an "I Got Rhythm" variant) conclude the session. The first, originally issued, finds Lester in an exuberant mood. The second, almost a minute longer (and faster), allows for two extra choruses, taken by Basie, who didn't solo on take one. Buck and Dicky are both excellent on both takes. Lester's take two solo, though just a bit less outgoing, is also a joy. This was indeed a real Kansas City session, not least due to the great work of Jo Jones, his empathy with Lester especially evident here. That bass drum isn't missed one bit!

Though the bulk of Keynote sessions were done in New York, Harry Lim made a productive West Coast trip early in 1946. For perhaps the most interesting of these California sessions, he revived the band name "The Keynoters," which he'd invented for a leaderless New York gathering. The indisputable keynoter here, however, was Nat King Cole, on one of those too rare occasions when he allowed himself to be a pianist first—and what a jazz piano player he was! Willie Smith, the former Jimmie Lunceford alto sax star then with Harry James, was a great Lim favorite and gets to shine in this quartet setting (the bassist is Red Callender, the drummer Jackie Mills), but Cole steals the show. The session found him in peak form, and what a blessing that we now have alternate takes of three of the four numbers, each every bit as good as the issued ones, as far as Nat's contributions are concerned.

The new take of "I Can't Believe That You're in Love with Me" is just a mite too slow compared with the second try, where the tempo is exactly right, but Nat's solo chorus is a delight, completely different from the later—relaxed, airy, and with a delicious turnaround coming out of the bridge. Smith's far better the second time around, though his first-try solo following Nat is excellent up to Callender's bridge. But what can one say of Nat's second take solo, and his work as an accompanist? Had he been unable to sing, we would rank him next to Tatum—truly a King! This is a fantastic performance, but he was just warming up for "The Way You Look Tonight." Smith positively oozes here, stretching his long, sweet notes to the point just before getting sticky, milking the most from Jerome Kern's lovely melody. But Nat's a wizard. On the new first take, he is fabulously inventive, but just getting acquainted. On the issued take, he is phenomenal. What a sound he got from a piano—so musical a touch—and how he varies it, with the bell-like doubled notes he features here, and that unique little glissando run—something he perfected from Mary Lou Williams's idea. This is stunning playing—not a long solo, just the bridge and the last 20 bars (the song has a 4-bar tag), but packed with ideas and telling a wonderful story. Here you have Oscar Peterson's inspiration in a nutshell. After such headiness, the fun and games of "Airiness à la Nat," a bright-tempoed romp on "Rhythm" changes, is a perfect contrast. (The title was a clue, if needed, since Nat appeared on the label, for contractual reasons, as Lord Calvert.) Here, too, we have a new take. The routine's the same on both. A chorus by Smith on the head (surely devised by Nat, and charming) with an improvised bridge; a chorus by piano, another by alto, one by bass, 16 bars of Smith-Cole fours, a walking-bass bridge, and riffing out, with a "Salt Peanuts" drum tag. But the second take is much more intense; though the tempo isn't faster, the listener feels it must be. I like Smith best on the gentler first outing, but there's no choice possible between Nat's contributions. Both are perfect—and don't miss his ensemble and accompaniment touches. They enhance everything, spreading joy. "My Old Flame," in just one take, is mostly Smith, intonation not always quite on the mark. One longs for more piano than just the first bridge, but that's a little gem, quite abstractly conceived and light-years beyond the altoist's paraphrase of the rather banal melody. Quite a session! Quite a piano player! (Nice work, too, from drummer Mills, a Barnet and Raeburn alumnus.)

Keynote's contribution to jazz ended with two marvelous trio sessions by one of the music's most remarkable figures, his first as a leader (excepting a slightly earlier V Disc date). Lennie Tristano, twenty-seven, had come to New York from his native Chicago just two months before the October 8, 1946, record date. It is interesting to contemplate what Tristano's place in jazz might have been had he not coincided with bebop, which certainly affected but was not the wellspring of his conception. Tristano was a unique musical thinker. Harmonically he was closely related to bop, rhythmically he was not, melodically he was his own man. His primary pianistic influences were Hines and Tatum (the latter also important harmonically); his great loves Lester Young, Roy Eldridge, and Billie Holiday; and he certainly knew Louis Armstrong's music. Later he was profoundly affected by Parker and almost as much—perhaps even more—by Bud Powell. But like Thelonious Monk, if in a wholly different way, Tristano was his own man. He was also by nature a theorist and teacher who had, perhaps in part due to his sightlessness, a strong urge for disciples, from whom he expected, and sometimes demanded, undivided loyalty. A complex and difficult man, then, with a powerfully individual vision of music and a sense of mission. All that aside, he was a truly remarkable pianist, and it is in this role that we can enjoy him here, captured at a time when playing was still his main pursuit.

In guitarist Billy Bauer, Tristano found his first (or at least first recorded) partner. Both men had an acute harmonic ear, and both thought in long melodic lines. The empathy between them is evident from the opening bars of the first take of "Out on a Limb." How fortunate we are that Mr. Koyama's patience and good ears uncovered so many new takes in the archives from Tristano's two Keynote dates, plus an unknown master— eleven fresh performances in all. How significant these are will become evident to the listener as he or she realizes that Tristano not only never repeats himself, but that he also is a true improviser, from whose fertile imagination each solo arrives as a new experience. Take "Out on a Limb," based, I think, on a tune associated with Louis Armstrong, Earl Hines, and Lester Young, "You Can Depend on Me." Aside from the brief but original arranged introduction and ending, differences abound. The first take, after Bauer's melodic solo chorus, has Tristano using parallel-octave voicings for a full chorus (he was master of this device) and linear improvisation for the next 16 bars; then Bauer resumes the lead as the chorus is completed. On the slower take two, there is more interplay between guitar and piano. Tristano adheres to the same pattern for his solo, but the octave voicings, the touch, and the ideas are entirely fresh, and his single-note-line half chorus rhythmically freer, his harmonies more "boppish." For take three, the tempo settles between the first two, there is counterpoint dialogue with Bauer, and the piano solo is structured differently. It still begins in octaves, but after 16 bars we get long, limber runs on the bridge that remind of Tatum in ease of execution, and the next 8 are in the same mode. Then the pianist resumes the octave mode but (as in the opening of the solo) with a lighter touch and more transparent voicings.

We cannot describe each piece in such detail, but close listening will yield similar findings. "I Can't Get Started" is above all an exploration of the famous song's harmonies, but the rhythmic approach is distinctly different on take two—much looser—and the keyboard textures not as thick. One is an extension of the other, and that can also be said for Bauer and Tristano. "I Surrender Dear" (two new takes, the second of which breaks down) seems a mite less inspiring as food for Tristano's thoughts, but there are remarkable moments. The untitled, fast, and themeless "Blues" (which may be the hitherto elusive "Ghost," a title previously wrongly applied to a take of "Interlude"), on the other hand, is a masterpiece, running for almost four minutes—until there was no more wax. The abrupt ending doesn't matter. It almost seems right, for this is a continuous, seamless stream of swinging invention, with passages that take one's breath away. Since Tristano rarely played blues (but when he did, watch out—think of "Requiem"), this is a doubly significant find, and should be required listening for those who think Lennie didn't swing.

No fewer than six (!) takes of "Interlude" (the Dizzy Gillespie composition later known as "A Night in Tunisia") are presented here, five of them new, all of them different, though the tempo remains remarkably stable. The usual break strain is omitted; we just get the theme and a string of blowing choruses, with Bauer well featured. The arranged first chorus, Bauer employing glissed notes à la Oscar Moore (certainly an influence on his sound, too), reminds us that this instrumentation is the King Cole Trio's, and that Cole was from Chicago. There are no concessions made here, but this is more "accessible" Tristano. We note that the first take was chosen for issue, and that it and the last are most similar in timing and outline, while the second and fifth takes are incomplete, both stopped by the leader for reasons of his own. In conception and execution, the long lines and runs tossed off by Lennie with such deceptive ease were beyond the ken of all but a handful of contemporaries. They remain remarkable even by today's standards of high-speed facility. A stupendous debut session! (Bassist Clyde Lombardi does what is required—keeping time and stating the basic harmony—very well.)

Seven and a half months have passed. Bauer is still on board; the bassist is now Bob Leininger. Tristano's touch seems even more assured, his thinking more clearly articulated. Two pieces come to us in single takes. Bauer's "Blue Boy" is based on "Fine and Dandy," and on this, Tristano's pianistic approach is most like what it would remain for the next few years in terms of fast-tempo playing. It's a lucid performance. "Atonement" exemplifies the kind of increased harmonic density Tristano loved to apply to romantic ballads. I'm not yet sure what this is based on, but it flows in such a natural way that it doesn't require decoding. The tempo picks up again for "Coolin' Off with Ulanov," dedicated to Barry Ulanov, the then influential jazz critic and co-editor of *Metronome* magazine, who championed Tristano's music with true (and remaining) dedication. The new second take is shorter by a chorus but delightful to have. It is appropriate that the final Keynote session was such a significant one, pointing to the future rather than the past.

(1986)

Review of *The Essential Jazz Records, Volume 1: Ragtime to Swing,* by Max Harrison, Charles Fox, and Eric Thacker

Guides to recorded jazz have a history almost as long as jazz discographies. In the beginning, they were sponsored by record companies; Leonard Hibbs's *21 Years of Swing Music on Brunswick Records* (1937) was one of the first and best. The same year also saw publication, in Buenos Aires, of Juan Rafael Grezzi's *Estudios sobre la "New Rhythm Style Series," Disco Odeon*, a meticulously annotated survey of one hundred sides issued in Argentina in a series that paralleled English Parlophone's of the same name.

The real birth of the genre, however, came about in 1942 with Charles Edward Smith's *Jazz Record Book* (in collaboration with Frederic Ramsey, Jr., Charles Payne Rogers, and William Russell), an offshoot of David Hall's successful *Record Book*, which dealt with classical music. In print for more than a decade, this admirable work (reprinted by Greenwood, by the way) holds up very well, though its publication prompted one of the first salvos fired in the war between traditionalists and modernists, by way of Barry Ulanov's critical review in *Metronome*. Among other perceived flaws, Ulanov singled out the emphasis on Jelly Roll Morton and Sidney Bechet, though from today's perspective, the book seems much more balanced than Smith and Ramsey's *Jazzmen*.

Ramsey's *Guide to Longplay Jazz Records* appeared in 1954. By then, the first version of Hugues Panassié's *Discographie critique des meilleurs disques de jazz* was three years old. Though strictly confined to Panassié's perception of "the real jazz," this book (enlarged and revised in 1958) is of particular value for its nearly always accurate solo identifications. John Wilson's *The Collector's Jazz* (in two volumes, respectively devoted to "traditional and swing" and "modern") appeared in 1958, objective and sober in typically Wilsonian style. The same year saw Rex Harris and Brian Rust's *Recorded Jazz: A Critical Guide*, strictly confined to traditional jazz and rather idiosyncratic at that. This is not to be confused with a book of the same title published in 1960, with Charles Fox, Peter Gammond, and Alun Morgan as joint authors. The latter took a far broader view and was the ancestor of *Jazz on Record: A Critical Guide to the First 50 Years* (1967), with Albert McCarthy, Morgan, Paul Oliver, and Max Harrison as the principal authors, assisted by twelve additional contributors. In between, in 1962, came *Jazz Era: The Forties*, by Stanley Dance, with Panassié and Harrison among his seven collaborators (an unlikely combination, as will be seen). Harrison, with Morgan, Ronald Atkins, Michael James, and Jack Cooke, was also responsible for the more specialized *Modern Jazz: The Essential Records* (1975).

As will be noted from this incomplete survey (it omits, among other things, works in relatively inaccessible languages), Harrison and Fox come well equipped to the book under review here, to be followed by a companion volume dealing with modern jazz. Both men will be well known to readers of this publication, but Eric Thacker is less prominent, though his activities as a writer on jazz began with the late, lamented *Jazz Monthly*. He holds his own, though he tends to be more effusive than his colleagues, perhaps because he is a clergyman and a poet. In general, Harrison is the most incisive of the trio, Fox the most evenhanded. More often than not, opinions dovetail neatly; but areas of disagreement, it is refreshing to see, have not been glossed over.

An astonishing quantity of music is dealt with here. Merely to state that the authors evaluate 250 LPs in great detail would be deceptive; a number of these are anthologies or two-record sets, and since relatively few are from the LP-era, most contain many tracks. Some 425 tune titles are listed in an index, but that figure is also deceptive, since many entries refer to multiple versions (16 of "After You've Gone," 17 of "Bugle Call Rag," 15 of "Honeysuckle Rose," 14 of "Tiger Rag," and so on). I would estimate that roughly 3,500 performances are surveyed. Discographical details include complete personnels, recording dates and locations, and labels and catalog numbers.

For the latter, both European and American issues are cited, as often as feasible, and additional record references appear in the text.

Expectations of yet another journey through familiar terrain are quickly dispelled. Scarcely fifty pages into the book, one has encountered, among many others, Sousa, James Reese Europe, the Original Memphis Five, the Georgians, A. J. Piron, and Wooden Joe Nicholas, as well as the anticipated Joplin, Morton, Original Dixieland Jazz Band, and Bunk Johnson; and if the overview of ragtime is somewhat skimpy, the first section, "Origins," provides fresh perspectives on both black and white New Orleans jazz, including appropriate examples from both the "revival" period (though this is also dealt with later) and the neglected early New York "Dixieland" music.

The next section, "The Twenties," first takes on the emblematic classics: Keppard, Oliver, young Armstrong and young Bechet, Dodds, Noone, young Hines, the New Orleans Rhythm Kings, and the white Chicagoans. The inclusion of Luis Russell and the Rhythmakers makes sense. There are fresh insights, mostly from Harrison, but it is the next chapter, dealing with "styles other than New Orleans" from the same decade, that offers the most welcome revisionist perspectives. These stem from the inclusion of representative recordings by Lang-Venuti, the Dorseys, the California Ramblers, and, most important, the Red Nichols–Miff Mole units. Overestimated in its own day, this music has unjustly been ignored by jazz critics and historians—even Gunther Schuller's admirable *Early Jazz* writes it off in a footnote—since the advent of modernism. Harrison is right on target when he says of Nichols's Five Pennies that "these performances are, in various ways, strikingly exploratory with regard to material and treatment, while the best of the players are engaged in extending the range of improvisation and the jazz capabilities of their instruments." Such reassessments, long overdue, help explain why so many gifted black musicians of the day were avid listeners to these experimental recordings. This long chapter also has room for Tiny Parham, Clarence Williams, lots of Beiderbecke, and an interesting selection of early big bands, among them Charlie Johnson's and Lloyd and Cecil Scott's, whose output, Thacker justly says, "captures the seething vitality of Harlem in a time of transitional experiment which achieved art largely because its creative spirits were not encumbered by high-faluting artistic principles." Early Ellington is also perceptively dealt with at length here, as is Fletcher Henderson. As a kind of afterthought, we get a selection of blues singers, including Bessie Smith (of course), as well as a perceptive essay on Ethel Waters by Fox.

The chapter "Jazz in Europe" serves as a transition to the next decade. It opens with the neglected Arthur Briggs and takes a brief look at Britain in the 1920s, quickly moves on to Benny Carter, Coleman Hawkins, and Bill Coleman in the 1930s, and covers Django Reinhardt and the Quintet of the

Hot Club of France in addition to such relatively obscure figures as Herman Chittison (a great favorite of Harrison's) and Oscar Aleman, among others.

The brief but interesting "Interlude: The Influence of Jazz on European Composers" is a solo effort by Harrison. Three of the five LPs he discusses are of Czech origin, one devoted entirely to Bohuslav Martinů's jazz-inspired compositions, another to Czech interpretations of Stravinsky's jazz- and ragtime-flavored works, the third an interesting anthology of piano pieces by Debussy, Satie, Copland, Hindemith, Auric, Gershwin, and the Czechs Martinů, Burian, and Schulhoff. (What with the recent travails of the Czech Jazz Section, it is useful to recall how important a position this unfortunate country occupied in European music and how receptive it was to jazz influences from the start. But Harrison overestimates Burian's 1928 book *Jazz*, which, though musically literate and vaguely aware of African roots, shows no sign of acquaintance with real jazz and cites Paul Whiteman, Ted Lewis, Vincent Lopez, and Ross Gorman as notable figures. Josephine Baker, W. C. Handy, Shelton Brooks, and the touring revue Chocolate Kiddies are the only black artists I've found in the text. Thus, Harrison's sneering aside that this book was published "a decade before anything of value appeared in America" is typical of European hubris; at the very least, Abbe Niles's introduction to Handy's *Blues: An Anthology* [1926!] was far superior to anything then written on the subject in Europe; Niles was aware of race records and cites Ma Rainey, Bessie Smith, Clara Smith, and Lovie Austin, among others.) The other composers examined by Harrison are Milhaud, Weill, and the British quartet of Lambert, Bliss, Goosens, and Walton. Though he is kind to Gershwin and Copland in passing, he discusses no other Americans, though Antheil, Carpenter, and Gruenberg might have equal claims to attention. Yet this is a stimulating interlude on a subject that some enterprising musicologist might well consider mining further.

Allotted fully 242 pages, "The Thirties and Swing" is the book's longest segment—and rightly so. Here we appropriately begin with Armstrong's 1929–33 recordings and conclude with the section "Swing Continues," of which more later. All the accepted landmarks are here, but also such nuggets as Harrison's intelligent comments on the Casa Loma Band (another bête noire of jazz criticism), Fox's apt evaluation of Spike Hughes's American recordings and good essay on the Savoy Sultans (he is also right on target in his appreciation of Jimmie Crawford's value to the Lunceford band and in singling out guitarist Bus Etri among Charlie Barnet's soloists), and Harrison's outstanding analysis of Armstrong's Decca period—one wants to applaud after having read it. Ellington, Basie, and Goodman are given exhaustive treatment (justice is done to the Sauter-Powell stage of Goodman), and Redman, Hines, Henderson, Webb, Kirk, Tommy Dorsey, and Shaw are all accounted for. But Harry James deserves better than an LP of sides made with pickup groups, and Lionel Hampton's big band is ignored (as is Buddy Johnson's), though Hamp's small-group work is well considered within the generally good selection of non–big band swing. This list includes such welcome entries as Red Allen and Frankie Newton (and Putney Dandridge—an acquired taste), and lots of Ellington small-group work. A good selection of pianists and singers also comes into view here. The time frame is not strictly observed: many 1940s records are included, and the Ella Fitzgerald LP (with Ellis Larkins—a good choice) takes us all the way to 1954.

Such liberties are to be expected from "Swing Continues," which looks at twenty-one LPs ranging from 1953 to 1972. All are well chosen, but one hopes that at least some consideration will be given in the follow-up volume to other examples of this sturdy genre. Such gems as Carter's *Further Definitions*, Ellington's *Such Sweet Thunder*, the Tatum-Carter trio records, Hines's *Quintessential Recording Session*, and *Swinging with Pee Wee Russell* are right here, but Ellington's *Money Jungle* (with Mingus and Roach) seems to belong in the next volume, and the inclusion of Herman Chittison's 1962 solo LP in such a limited field strikes me as odd.

"Against the Current: Traditional Survivals and Revivals" returns us to the 1940s, with a few forays into the surrounding decades. Lots of Bechet is here, from the 1932 Footwarmers to the 1940s Blue Note recordings and the 1957 sessions with Martial Solal. We also find later Jimmie Noone, Eddie Condon and associates, Muggsy Spanier's Ragtimers and Bob Crosby's Bobcats, Louis Armstrong on V Disc and at Town Hall, Willie "The Lion" Smith, Bobby Hackett, Jimmy McPartland, and (surprise!) Louis Prima (the early small groups on Brunswick, unfairly ignored in the standard literature). Also welcome is the fair treatment of Mezz Mezzrow (by Thacker) in the context of his King Jazz sessions with Bechet. In contrast, Fox has not much good to say about Mezzrow's playing (though he is positive about his musical aims) in an appraisal of the Panassié 1938–39 New York sessions. In a sense, the emphasis throughout on Bechet is a vindication of *The Jazz Record Book*'s perspective.

The final section, "The Transition to Modern Jazz," is very brief and mostly relies on anthologies—three of the five selections are Savoy's *The Changing Face of Harlem, Vol.* 1, Capitol's *Swing into Bop*, volume four of Epic's *Swing Street* set (valid but imperfect choices) as well as Red Norvo's 1950–51 trio (with Charles Mingus and Tal Farlow) and Charlie Parker's earliest recordings. One might have opted for the inclusion of this material in the modern volume, if only to make room for a few more deserving items in the "Swing Continues" section, but that strategy might not have solved the problem of dealing adequately with post–swing-era mainstream jazz—

what, for one example, of Roy Eldridge's work after 1940, none of which is included? Yet such questions are perhaps unfair: there are limits to what can be covered within a reference work of reasonably practical size, and the choices for inclusion are consistently valid.

With such a wealth of material under analysis, a few mistakes inevitably have crept in, mainly in the area of solo identifications. They are mostly of minor importance but can be amusing, as when Thacker credits Lester Young with sustaining "largeness of tone" in a solo that is Buddy Tate's (Basie's "Moten Swing"). Rather than display erudition in these pages at the expense of the hardworking team, I have passed on my findings to them. An entertaining divergence of opinion between the authors can be found on facing pages: while Fox finds Jerry Blake's "clarinet playing a distinct improvement upon [Buster] Bailey's genteel correctness," Thacker tells us that "high praise must be reserved for Bailey, whose ecstatic, reedy tone soars in numerous agile and expressive flights." Less enjoyable is Harrison's failure to appreciate Vic Dickenson, whom he finds "vastly overrated" and damns with faint praise in citing Armstrong's "Sugar" as "one of the few postwar recordings on which [Dickenson] plays in a responsible manner."

There are useful notes (page references would have been helpful) and a good bibliography, in regard to both of which a comment must be made. The world of jazz criticism and research is a small (if growing) one and has always been somewhat inbred and contentious, perhaps particularly so in Britain and France. Early in this review I cited Harrison and Stanley Dance as an unlikely combination of collaborators in one of the predecessors to this book—they have been at each other's throats for many years. No less than six footnotes hold up Dance to ridicule (without identifying him in the text) by means of quoting from some ancient reviews in which he offers opinions diametrically opposed to those with which he's long since been identified. This is a game of dozens we could all play, given access to arcane sources, but one not worthy of the level on which this work is conceived and executed—the more so because the bibliography studiously omits any books by Dance, though the value of these, even when regarded purely as reference sources, is indisputable. That, as an old teacher of mine used to say, amounts to spitting in your own soup.

But even with this tiny, self-inflicted mustache, *The Essential Jazz Records, Vol. 1* is the Mona Lisa of its genre. To initiate and novice alike, it provides an enlightened and enlightening overview of the music it surveys—a rich and enormously productive period in the history of jazz. The work indeed accomplishes what Harrison suggests in his introduction, which is to say that when used in conjunction with careful listening it can "lead to comprehension of jazz as a single, indivisible entity" and further "suggest the network of relationships, many of them generally unacknowledged, which unite the many strands of this music." Unlike far too much said and written about jazz, this book is not parochial or narrow-minded, and in its often unorthodox and unexpected choices and juxtapositions it sheds light and stimulates much-needed thought. One looks forward to a sequel of like strengths, but no matter what may be forthcoming, this book stands on its own as one of the handful in the literature of jazz that can truly be called essential.

(1988)

Note: The sequel, The Essential Jazz Records, Modern to Post-Modern, *by Harrison, Thacker, and Stuart Nicholson, did not materialize until 2000.*

A New Standard for Reissues

J azz reissuing in album form began in 1936 with RCA Victor's Bix Beiderbecke memorial set, but got under way in earnest during the ban on new recording imposed by the musicians' union in the summer of 1942. By coincidence, this was also a time when interest in the history of the music had become sufficiently strong to create a market for vintage jazz materials.

Enterprising jazz scholars/aficionados like George Avakian at Columbia and Eugene Williams at Decca not only restored to circulation classic performances that had been out of print for years, but also unearthed previously unissued masters in company vaults, among them the alternate takes so dear to serious collectors and students of jazz. For the record companies, no more committed to jazz then than now, such reissuing was an inexpensive way to get freshly packaged material to the marketplace.

The advent of the LP seemed tailor-made for reissues, but the major labels didn't catch on until the pioneering pirates, such as the aptly named Jolly Roger, had shown the way. With the exception of occasional periods of enlightenment—such as the one at Columbia that produced those marvelous boxed and prodigiously annotated sets of the late '50s and early '60s—they still haven't caught on, leaving the field to their European and Japanese affiliates, to the pirates, and to such lessors as the Smithsonian Institution, Reader's Digest, Franklin Mint, Book-of-the-Month, and Time-

Life. Those in the latter category have the advantage of being able to lease across the board from labels big and small, something that really counts when it comes to compiling representative anthologies.

To veteran collectors like myself, the richness and variety of historic jazz materials available today seems staggering, but we have also learned from experience that records of any kind often have a short shelf life indeed. If you don't grab them when you can, you'll soon be looking for them—at premium prices—and cursing your indolence. This is especially true of major label–generated reissues, which are subject to the whims of computers that toss out of the catalog anything that fails to sell above a certain dollar level.

The experienced producer with a serious interest in jazz will, needless to say, become very frustrated when confronted with such practices. Recently, two such producers, Michael Cuscuna and Charlie Lourie, came up with a brilliant idea. They formed a company, Mosaic Records, which makes deals with major labels allowing it to lease vintage jazz materials and issue them in limited-edition boxed sets.

Well, you might ask, what's new or brilliant about that? Isn't that in essence what the Smithsonian et al. have been doing, though their editions are limited only by marketplace demand? Yes, but there's more to the Mosaic story than that. For one thing, their deal gives them access to the vaults of the companies they lease from and the rights to use unissued materials. Of course, they can't just browse around willy-nilly, but that's where the vast discographic knowledge and firsthand conventional reissue experience of a Cuscuna come in handy, for he knows where the nuggets are buried and can cite the chapter and verse that provide the location of the tapes or discs.

For another thing, Cuscuna and Lourie are able to make fresh transfers of these materials from the best available sources. And they have the taste and know-how to get the best results. Also, judging from the initial releases on Mosaic, they have a very good conception of what is not merely rare but also musically valid.

The first release consists of three handsomely boxed sets: *The Complete Blue Note Recordings of Thelonious Monk* (MR4-101); *The Complete Pacific Jazz and Capitol Recordings of the Original Gerry Mulligan Quartet and Tentet with Chet Baker* (MR5-102), and *The Complete Blue Note Recordings of Albert Ammons and Meade Lux Lewis* (MR3-103)—containing five, four, and three records respectively. Each set comes with a well-produced booklet containing informative historical and musical annotation, photographs (frequently rare), reproductions of contemporary press materials, and complete discographic details. The pressings are first-class.

The Monk set is of primary significance, for it not only brings together, in chronological sequence, all of the pianist-composer's work for Blue Note (the first label to give him record dates of his own), but also provides substantial helpings of hitherto unheard music. Not only are there eleven previously unissued alternate takes, including one each of the masterpieces "Criss Cross" and "Hornin' In," but there are also two entirely new pieces. One is a delightful trio version of the pop tune "I'll Follow You," which Monk never recorded before or again, the other (in two takes) a Monk original, "Sixteen," from the memorable sextet date of May 30, 1952. These discoveries alone make this Mosaic issue a major event, while the intelligent presentation and clean, ungimmicked sound (happily without the fake stereo that mars all other extant LP issues) and Cuscuna's extensive notes, which include much new information about Monk's early career, are additional points in its favor.

The Mulligan/Baker set is also a classic of its kind. Though it does not include the quartet sides waxed for Fantasy (which are currently available on Prestige 24016), it surveys, in sixty-two performances, a major period in Mulligan's career and reminds us that the music of the quartet, while not in fashion today, was of seminal importance in the establishment of West Coast jazz—a direct offspring of so-called cool jazz, in the birth of which Mulligan played a major role.

Here, too, there is an abundance of previously unissued material: fourteen selections (one listed as unissued—"I'm Beginning to See the Light"—is in fact not, but considering the discographic morass created by Pacific Jazz's Richard Bock, that's certainly excusable). Also, two items are issued here for the first time in unedited form (Bock liked to cut and paste), and five others have been only on 10-inch LPs or anthologies.

Again, the presentation is a model of systematic intelligence. The sound is first-class, and Pete Welding's notes are typically thorough and informative. As for the music, it speaks well for Mulligan's multiple gifts as a player, thinker, and organizer, and should bring about a reassessment of Baker's early work, which is often and unjustly labeled as derivative of Miles Davis. Chet had his own voice on the horn, and this was an ideal setting for it. Without slighting the others, however, one must conclude that the most vital and moving music in this set is provided by Lee Konitz, present on thirteen tracks, one of them ("Bernie's Tune") previously unissued. The altoist was in especially inspired form on the session recorded live at the Haig in L.A., where he was the centerpiece, and where the softly propulsive swing of the Mulligan quartet gave him perfect support. This is music that can't be circumscribed by stylistic pigeonholing; it's simply classic jazz.

Albert Ammons and Meade Lux Lewis were two of the greatest masters of boogie-woogie piano—a style that may seem simple (or even simplistic) on the surface but in fact is as infinitely variable and even subtle as the blues form on which it is based.

Their set contains nine Ammons solos, four of them never issued before; twenty-three Lewis solos (he was Blue Note's favorite in the label's early days), three of them previously unissued; and two duets, one never heard before. In addition, thirteen of the cuts have previously only been on 78s, and ten only on 10-inch LP. For boogie-woogie fanciers, then, this is a must, but others will find the music interesting, satisfying, and anything but monotonous (though sampling is preferable to nonstop listening).

While Lewis was perhaps the most inventive of the boogie-woogie giants—as borne out in such ambitious undertakings as the five-part *The Blues* (the fifth part issued here for the first time) and the fascinating four-part *Variations on a Theme*, performed on the harpsichord—Ammons was the most consistently swinging. To these ears, he was the champion, and one of his new pieces introduced herein, "Changes in Boogie-Woogie," with its frequent modulations, is a masterpiece. Why it remained unissued for forty-four years is a mystery. Also masterful is the newly issued duet on "The Sheik of Araby," not in boogie-woogie style, but a sterling jazz piano performance. Yet another treat is Lewis's "Blues Whistle," on which Meade shows himself to have been quite a siffleur—it cuts his earlier "Whistling Blues." (Speaking of earlier Lewis, the set also includes his 1935 "Honky Tonk Train Blues," offering interesting contrast to the 1940 Blue Note version—one was a 10-inch 78, the other a 12-incher, but length is not by any means the only difference, and the piece, a genuine composition, is rightly considered the crown jewel of originals in this genre.)

In addition to Max Harrison's very fine notes, the booklet has some annotation by yours truly, written in 1981 for a projected but never issued single Lewis LP in Blue Note's now defunct reissue series, and a reproduction of William Russell's 1940 review of some Lewis sides for the *HRS Society Rag*, one of the first American "little" jazz magazines. It's a gem. (It would have been nice to see a credit somewhere on these sets to the Institute of Jazz Studies, where most of the old clippings reproduced were found.)

I mentioned that these Mosaic boxes are limited editions; that's part of the deal and no jive. The Monk and Mulligan sets have a run of 7,500 numbered copies, the boogie-woogie set only 5,000. The records are available only by mail from Mosaic Records.

Mosaic has added something new and fine to the jazz reissue field. One looks forward to more, and hopes that the worldwide serious jazz audience is by now big enough and mature enough to make such a state-of-the-art venture viable.

(1983)

In the twenty years that have passed since Mosaic's impressive debut, the label has steadfastly held to the course it set for itself. With only two exceptions, its releases are still limited editions (the two are the Charlie Parker location recordings made by the legendary Dean Benedetti, to which Mosaic obtained rights, and a Phil Woods retrospective culled from the artist's own tapes); its remastering, discographical research, and annotation still state-of-the-art; and the copious and well-reproduced booklet photos almost always previously unpublished.

While Mosaic's one constant has been the mining of Blue Note's deep catalog, the music offered has ranged far afield, from Kid Ory's output for Verve to the Atlantic recordings of Lennie Tristano, Lee Konitz, and Warne Marsh; from the OKeh and Columbia nuggets by Joe Venuti and Eddie Lang to the Blue Note experiments of Andrew Hill. There have been such unexpected and brave ventures as a ten-CD Mildred Bailey box, bringing that great, neglected singer back into full view, and a set of Stuff Smith, the demon fiddler, of all his work for Verve, including many unissued gems.

The tragic death, late in 2000, of co-founder Charlie Lourie, after a long and bravely fought illness, could have been a mortal blow, but Michael Cuscuna soldiered on, aided by Scott Wenzel, who, while considerably younger, brought his 78-collector perspective to the label, resulting in such sets as the one devoted to the parallel 1930s careers of New Orleans trumpeter-singers Wingy Manone and Louis Prima (the latter's vintage Brunswicks, notably those with Pee Wee Russell, much underrated for jazz kicks), and another surveying Bunny Berigan's recordings, mainly as a sideman, from 1930 to 1936.

Aside from the sixty-three-LP complete Commodore boxes (three of them), Mosaic's largest single effort has been the eighteen-CD *Complete Capitol Nat King Cole Trio* box, a revelation to those unaware of Cole's pianistic prowess. Jack Teagarden has had his innings—two sets of his own, one shared with Bobby Hackett, and one shared with Bix Beiderbecke and Frank Trumbauer. Duke Ellington's complete output for Capitol and Reprise, respectively, illuminated generally underestimated periods in the master's career, and Stan Kenton's early Capitols, and a set focused on arrangers Bill Holman and Bill Russo, were feast for fans and something of a revelation to reflexive anti-Kentonians. And for those who savor classic R&B, Mosaic presented Amos Milburn and Charles Brown.

In an age when everything on record more than fifty years old is fair game for reissue in Europe, it hasn't been easy for a label that does everything according to the book, but Mosaic has prevailed, won many awards and much praise, and continued to set standards for the proper presentation of the jazz heritage.

THE OUTREACH OF JAZZ

A—Jazz and the Arts

Hot Chocolates

Connie's *Hot Chocolates* opened at the Hudson Theater, Forty-fourth Street east of Broadway, on June 20, 1929. It was a slice of Harlem nightlife transposed from Connie's Inn to the Broadway stage; it had a cast of eighty-five, new songs by Fats Waller, Andy Razaf, and Harry Brooks, all kinds of dancing and singing, and Louis Armstrong in his Broadway debut.

The show's run of 219 performances was more than respectable, placing it seventh from the top in a field of thirty-four Broadway musicals opening in 1929. (Old-timers think it could have run even longer if its producers had not been so eager to take it on the road.) In 1929, Broadway theatergoers had plenty to choose from. Among the most memorable musicals were Cole Porter's *Fifty Million Frenchmen* (254 performances), Jerome Kern's *Sweet Adeline* (with Helen Morgan; 234 performances), Arthur Schwartz's *The Little Show* (with Fred Allen, Libby Holman, and Clifton Webb; 321 performances), Rodgers and Hart's *Spring Is Here* (104 performances), the Gershwins' (and Gus Kahn's) *Show Girl* (with Ruby Keeler, Clayton, Jackson and Durante, and Duke Ellington's orchestra; 111 performances), and Vincent Youmans's *Great Day* (which could have had Fletcher Henderson's band and Louis Armstrong, but dropped them; just 36 performances). A year of great songs, great performers, and great shows—but also the year in which Wall Street's Black Thursday and its sequels leading to the Great Depression dwarfed any drama played out on the boards.

Hot Chocolates was one of only two all-black shows to open on Broadway that year. The other, *Messin' Around*, with a score by Waller's teacher, James P. Johnson, closed after 33 performances. *Hot Chocolates* was the last solid hit show in a line sired by *Shuffle Along*, the 1921 smash (504 performances) that launched a new era for Afro-American artists in the American theater.

Unlike *Shuffle Along*, *Hot Chocolates* was not a book show of any sort. It was, quite simply, a nightclub floor show adapted and elaborated for the Broadway stage. In this special genre, its most notable predecessor had been *Blackbirds of 1928*, which had Bill Robinson in his "legitimate" debut, Earl "Snakehips" Tucker, and a run of 518 performances. It, in turn, was descended from Lew Leslie's first *Blackbirds* revue, which in the spring of 1926 had moved from the Plantation, a downtown nightclub featuring black shows, to Harlem's Alhambra Theater for a six-week stand, and then sailed for Europe, doing five months in Paris and six in London. Its star was the incomparable Florence Mills. *Blackbirds of 1928* was to have been another Mills vehicle, but her death on November 1, 1927, put a sudden end to what might well have become the most dazzling career of any Negro performer of the era.

That era marked the third stage in the theatrical development of black Americans, and in order to put *Hot Chocolates* in clear focus, it is right and proper to take a brief look at this evolution.

The first stage, according to the authoritative James Weldon Johnson, in his book *Black Manhattan*, published in 1930, began in the late 1860s, when "the full entry of the Negro himself upon the professional minstrel stage" took place. As Johnson states, minstrelsy was, "on the whole, a caricature of Negro life, and it fixed a stage tradition which has not yet been entirely broken."

Thus, *Hot Chocolates* had its leading male performer, eccentric dancer and comedian Jazzlips Richardson, in the blackface makeup and battered frock coat that were stocks of the minstrel trade. And supporting comedians Billy Higgins and Billy Maxey, photos show, also appeared in the blackface makeup.

Minstrelsy, however, did provide invaluable stage experience and training for black performers—training which at the time could not have been obtained in any other way. The most gifted and enterprising of this first generation of performers became the founders of the second stage. This began in earnest with the *1890 Creole Show*, which, while in the minstrel pattern, was free from plantation trimmings, "gave great prominence to girls, and was smart and up to date in material and costumes." It was a sensation in New York; not quite on Broadway as yet, but in a theater near that coveted zone.

The next milestone, *The Oriental Show*, interpolated grand opera, draw-ing on a tradition that had spawned "The Black Swan" (Elizabeth Taylor Greenfield) and "Black Patti" (Sissieretta Jones), both of them outstanding operatic singers. *A Trip to Coontown* (1898), despite its somewhat suspect title, was another forward step: the first black musical comedy with a cohe-sive plot, and the first black show to be organized, produced, and managed by blacks—in this case, Bob Cole and his first partner, Billy Johnson.

Then came *Clorindy or The Origin of the Cakewalk*, with music and lyrics by the great team of Will Marion Cook and Paul Laurence Dunbar, the first show to make intelligent use of ragtime and prove that music's great potential. It ran an entire season at the Casino Roof Garden and was, John-son writes, "the talk of New York."

That was in 1898. In 1902, Bert Williams and George Walker, pioneers of post-minstrel black comedy, finally broke through on Broadway. Their vehicle was *In Dahomey*, by the Cook-Dunbar team, and it made "Negro theatrical history by opening at the very center of theaterdom, the New York Theater in Times Square." (Johnson again.) The two stars subse-quently took the show to London and made the cakewalk a social dance fad in Europe (where, by the way, it became the model for the Parisian can-can).

Walker retired due to ill health in 1907, and Williams, now on his own, soon became a star of the annual Ziegfeld Follies, starting in 1910 and re-maining for nearly a decade. He was an exception; black performers did not star in white shows until years later.

The gifted Bob Cole, who had formed a new partnership with another Johnson, J. Rosamond (brother of James Weldon), launched several hit shows, notably *The Shoofly Regiment* (1906) and *The Red Moon* (1908), both full-fledged operettas. But by the end of the first decade of the new century, the center of Negro theatrical activity had moved from Broadway to the growing new black metropolis of Harlem.

During what Johnson calls "the Negro exile from Broadway," from 1910 to 1917, a genuine black theater grew up in Harlem. It had every-thing, from its own versions of downtown hit shows to classics in repertory, and it had musical shows so good that Flo Ziegfeld bought whole numbers from them (like the finale to the *1913 Darktown Follies*). A title like *Dark-town Follies* engenders a certain queasiness in the modern liberal psyche, but it ought to be remembered that this show and others with similarly quaint titles and themes were produced by and for blacks. And it should also be noted that these shows helped stamp out such taboos (already whittled down in *Red Moon*) as the one against depicting romantic love between blacks on the theatrical stage.

A potential Afro-American theatrical renaissance downtown was nipped in the bud by the entry of the United States into the World War. This took place on April 6, 1917—the day after the Coloured Players had opened at the Garrick Theater with an ambitious bill of three serious plays written, produced, designed, and acted by blacks. Still, Johnson marks this date as the beginning of the third period of the Negro in the American theater.

This continued in 1919 with *Abraham Lincoln*, featuring Charles Gilpin as a character based on Frederick Douglass, followed by Gilpin as *The Emperor Jones*, then passed through stormy waters with O'Neill's controversial *All God's Chillun Got Wings* (starring Paul Robeson), and culminated, according to Johnson, in *Porgy*, which, he wrote, "loomed high above every Negro drama that had ever been produced" and *Green Pastures*, which "established conclusively [the Negro actor's] capacity to get the utmost subtleties across the footlights, to convey the most delicate of emotions, to create the atmosphere in which the seemingly unreal becomes for the audience the most real thing in life."

Today it is fashionable to dismiss these plays with a contemptuous shrug or a polite shudder, and *Porgy* is suspect even in its reincarnation as *Porgy and Bess*. It has been forgotten how far these plays went beyond the limitations imposed on Negro actors by the minstrel tradition (and by outright racial prejudice). In the long view, Johnson's opinion might well be the one to stand.

From our particular perspective, the landmark event of the third period was *Shuffle Along*. The musical show entranced Broadway audiences and eventually went around the world. It almost didn't get to Broadway, since it was conceived and executed entirely by blacks with almost no funds at their disposal, but it triumphed, and established black musicals on Broadway as a fact of American theatrical life for almost a solid decade. It opened the gates for an outpouring of original creative talent in music, dance, and song the likes of which had seldom been seen in the annals of theater.

The presence of such an astonishing pool of talent in New York can be explained only by the phenomenon of Harlem. As we have seen, a Negro theater had flourished there from 1910 on. As the influx of blacks continued, accelerated by the war, and Harlem's boundaries expanded, whites began to take notice. Beginning with *Darktown Follies*, a sizable number of whites attended Harlem theatrical productions. And as a prospering community, Harlem had other entertainment to offer. Cabarets and nightclubs of all descriptions, catering to all social levels, began to spring up, and Harlem in New York became a magnet for black actors, singers, dancers, and musicians from every corner of the land. By 1920, the budding phonograph industry had become an additional spur, and the Volstead Act had brought about profound changes in American mores and entertainment.

Prohibition, that last stand of benighted puritanism, speeded up the changes already set in motion by the war, and as the Jazz Age got under way,

Harlem became a focal point for whites in search of new and hitherto illicit pleasures. Today, when words like "ghetto" (a singularly inept application, as the perceptive Albert Murray has pointed out) are bandied about in relation to Harlem, and the social and economic ills common to our great cities have exacerbated the conditions under which some citizens of Harlem suffered even in the 1920s—while most of the black bourgeoisie was driven out by the Depression—it is difficult to conceive of this black metropolis as a glamorous place.

The glamour, of course, was only part of the Harlem story, but it was genuine nonetheless. "The world's most glamorous atmosphere. Why, it is just like Arabian Nights," said young Duke Ellington in 1923, just up from Washington, D.C., but not exactly a babe in the woods. Per square foot, Harlem in the '20s could boast of more great music, singing, dancing, and acting (and of more poets, painters, writers, and thinkers as well) than any black community on earth. The lid that had been clamped for so long on the creative gifts of black Americans was being lifted, at least to a degree, and the light that had been hidden under it was dazzling.

Harlem, even as whites were able to perceive it, was not merely an outlet for hedonistic impulses. The special genius of Negro Americans elevated nightclub entertainment to the level of true artistry. And while there were places that catered to various lusts, addictions, and vices, there were many more that solid citizens and heads of state could attend without qualms, and where they could enjoy the finest shows imaginable. Soon, these spots would be infiltrated by mobsters, but even they trod softly on this turf.

The big three of Harlem nightclubs in the '20s were the Cotton Club (for white audiences only, expensive, though not a clip joint, and featuring the most elaborate floor shows), Small's Paradise (the only club still in existence today of the hundreds that sprang up during the decade, the stamping ground for some of the world's greatest jazz players, and home of a sterling troupe of singing and dancing waiters), and Connie's Inn (established in 1921 as the Shuffle Inn, named for *Shuffle Along*, and taken over in 1923 by Connie and George Immerman).

Small's and Connie's were "black and tan," meaning that they allowed black and white customers to mingle freely. The Immerman Brothers had operated a delicatessen on 125th Street, where young Fats Waller had worked as a delivery boy. By 1919, he was mostly delivering "packaged goods," and by 1923, the newly rich Immermans could afford to acquire and extensively renovate the big basement cabaret on the corner of 131st Street and Seventh Avenue. Next door was the Lafayette, a 2,000-seater that was Harlem's finest theater, and in front of Connie's stood the Tree of Hope, a modest elm that had, for performers, magic powers to bring luck if rubbed lovingly. (The stump, adorned with a plaque, remains today.)

Two months after Connie's opened with Wilbur Sweetman's band in residence, the club was advertised as Harlem's largest, and LeRoy Smith's Green Dragon Orchestra from Detroit had been installed. This band, which later played in the pit for *Hot Chocolates*, was not a hot-jazz band, but a Paul Whiteman–styled black dance and society band. The band at Connie's had to be versatile to back the elaborate floor shows, staged by the talented and energetic Leonard Harper. Connie's chorus line was second to none (the lightest and prettiest girls went to the Cotton Club, but there was plenty of talent to go around, and then some). Its headliners included the sensational Snakehips Tucker—whose extraordinary gyrations and ominous sexuality are preserved, in a fleeting glimpse, in the 1935 short subject "Symphony in Black," featuring Duke Ellington's orchestra, and who was part of the Connie's Inn version of *Hot Chocolates* but left for Europe with *Blackbirds of 1928* prior to the Broadway opening—along with other dancers, singers, and entertainers of the highest caliber.

The Immermans, by all accounts, were decent bosses. Fats Waller had a standing invitation to perform, hired or ad hoc, and a white Estey organ had been installed at the Inn for his exclusive use. The Immermans also managed to keep the gangsters at arm's length for a time. But when George was kidnapped and held for ransom by Mad Dog Coll's gang, the handwriting was on the wall, and by 1933, Connie's Inn had moved downtown, as the Cotton Club was soon to do. Repeal and the Depression had in any event finished off the glamour phase of Harlem nightlife, though it continued to attract the best in black talent, especially jazz talent, for years to come. The action had moved to the ballrooms and after-hours spots.

Leonard Harper had staged many fine shows at Connie's, but his 1929 *Hot Chocolates* was special. When the Immermans decided to take it to Broadway, they first tried out a stage version at the Windsor Theater in the Bronx. As a program from that weeklong engagement (starting June 3, 1929) reveals, changes in casting and programming took place prior to the Broadway opening. Some members of the cast doubled in the floor show at Connie's (which began after midnight), and *Variety* reported on June 26 that, after the Bronx opening, many revisions had to be made since members of the cast "complained that doubling to the floor show was too arduous."

The show had all the traditional elements, but above all it had style and pacing, energy and drive. The chorus line, the 16 Hot Chocolate Drops, was augmented by an all-male team, Eight Bon Bon Buddies. (For a change, the men almost stole the show.) The Six Crackerjacks, a team of acrobatic dancers, were billed as "the greatest team of singers, dancers and tumblers in the universe"—and, according to Marshall and Jean Stearns's authoritative *Jazz Dance*, that description was not hyperbole.

Dancer-singer Baby Cox was one of the headliners. Best remembered today for her growling vocal duets with Bubber Miley's trumpet on a couple of classic Ellington records, she was, in the words of Emerson Harper, a reed player in LeRoy Smith's band, "a petite, cute dancer who went into a shake number that would make some of these modern twisters look like they were standing still." Another dancer, Louise "Jota" Cook ("what she did with her stomach," said trumpeter and sometime dancer Ray Nance, "would make you seasick"), was featured in "The Rain Dance," which, according to the reviews, she performed with great seriousness. "Little Egypt," wrote the *Evening World*'s Bide Dudley, "had nothing on Louise Cook, who . . . had very little on herself."

Jazzlips Richardson, the male lead, "enthralled" Stephen Rathbun of the *Sun*: "How that man can dance." He added that "the show can boast of the liveliest ensemble to be seen on Broadway," an opinion echoed by most other reviewers, and further noted that it "was presented with the ease, informality and lack of artificiality of a first-class night club entertainment." In that evaluation, we may have the secret of *Hot Chocolates'* success.

The singing star Edith Wilson, only twenty-three but already a veteran, had come to New York at fifteen in 1921 to replace Mamie Smith in *Put and Take*, and made the first of her many records a bit later that year. She had been to England with *Dover Street to Dixie* in 1923, and toured the Continent as vocalist with Sam Wooding's band. Margaret Simms, partnered by Paul Bass, did the romantic singing (Miss Wilson specialized in blues, but also introduced the serious "Black and Blue"). The stylish dance team of Paul and Thelma Meeres handled the ballroom specialties, such as "The Waltz Divine"—which, if it was written by Waller, one would like to hear.

The chief comedy writer, doubling as a performer, was Eddie Green, composer of "A Good Man Is Hard to Find," and the other comics were Billy Higgins (aka Jazz Casper), a patter specialist who often acted on records as a comic foil to female blues singers, and Billy Maxey. Choral director and musical arranger Russell Wooding's Jubilee Singers struck a traditional note with their "Southland Medley," a mixture of spirituals and "Dixie songs" (including "Old Black Joe"!) that must have been reassuring to conservative whites in contrast to the smart (and often quite blue) material of the blues songs and comedy sketches, and the general modern vitality expressed by the company.

This vitality, as apprehended in the quaint language of the time, was what impressed even reviewers who had little comprehension of the true value, nature, and seminal impact of the Afro-American contribution to twentieth-century performing arts. Thus Wilella Waldorf in the *New York Post*: ". . . that peculiar brand of rhythmic enthusiasm achieved only by a troupe of Negroes on a rampage." Or the *Brooklyn Daily Eagle*'s Arthur Pollock: "But the old colored good will is always there, the speed and vitality. *Hot Chocolates* ought to do well in the world."

Others did a little better. The *Evening Telegram*'s review, by Robert Garland, was headlined "Marvellous Dancing Stunts Feature Tan-Skinned Revel" (it was thus that *Hot Chocolates* billed itself). Garland observed that "if the rest of *Hot Chocolates* lived up to its dancing, it would be the show of shows [but] some of it is plain ordinary torso-tossing from the downtown burlesque shows. Some of it is childish prattle . . . some of it is dubious, not to say dirty, wisecracks."

Almost to a man and woman, the reviewers expressed distaste for the ribald humor of the skits and double-entendre songs, and it appears that some of these were trimmed or toned down as the run progressed. But the producers knew only too well that such material found favor with audiences if not with critics, and most of it seems to have been retained.

Garland was alone in singling out "Black and Blue," in which he rated Edith Wilson "excellent," and also liked the sketch "Sending a Wire." Miss Waldorf and Mr. Dudley liked "Big Business" best among the skits. The score, however, was unanimously rated rather weak. If we think better of it, we should keep in mind that 1929 was a banner year for good show scores, and that Waller himself had done better, as with "Willow Tree" from *Keep Shufflin'*, one of his finest songs.

"Ain't Misbehavin'" was readily identifiable as the one potential hit song of the show. The producers knew it, too, and it was heavily plugged. The song, wrote H. P. Dunne, Jr., in the *World*, is one "on which much reliance is placed." To the *Herald Tribune*'s Howard Barnes, it was "the only song that can command more than passing attention—although there is a piece called 'Sweet Savannah Sue' which gives the Bon Bon Buddies their best concerted performance of the evening." He summed up the show as "woefully lacking in tunes, and a magnificent orchestra is left to struggle gallantly with a few snatches of familiar melody." But his headline proclaimed *Hot Chocolates* "Best Negro Revue Since *Blackbirds*."

Mr. Pollock did not like the songs or the band at all: "The music is just noise arranged for voice and instrument and played and sung noisily." The anonymous *Times* reviewer was the most perceptive about the music. "Cornets and saxophones," he wrote, "blare an adequately torrid musical setting for the stage proceedings." And he was the sole reviewer to remain in his seat long enough to catch the entr'acte, which was well worth catching. He wrote: "One song, a synthetic but entirely pleasant jazz ballad called 'Ain't Misbehavin'' stands out, and its rendition between the acts by an unnamed member of the orchestra was a high light of the premiere." That unnamed member had gotten himself identified by the time the second week's program was printed: "Entr'acte: Trumpet solo by Louis Armstrong," it read.

We can hear what Armstrong's interpretation of the song sounded like. But we don't have a record of his only other appearance in the show, on stage, as part of a trio known as the Thousand Pounds of Harmony. With Edith Wilson and Fats Waller, he performed "My Man Is Good for Nothing but Love," but this song was recorded only by Miss Wilson as a solo. The trio version probably was introduced after opening night: it is hard to accept that a combination of such ebullient personalities could have escaped every reviewer's notice.

Waller's own opinion about the score may not have been far from that of the press. In an interview profile that ran in the *Post* on June 18, a week before the show's opening, and which might well be the first such feature on a black jazz musician in an important white daily, he is identified as "one of the leading lights in the field of Negro popular music. When Connie's *Hot Chocolates* comes to the Hudson Theater next week, Waller makes his formal bow to a Broadway that has already heard much of his music."

The article also makes mention of the practice for blacks to sell songs "to white songwriters, who would vary them slightly and re-sell them as their own. The average rate for such a song, [Waller] says, was $250." One song of Waller's, the piece continues, became "the best seller of its season and netted $17,500 to its 'composer' who paid Fats $500 for it." (Waller's professional nickname is rendered as "Fatts" throughout.) Waller didn't learn his lesson; in 1929, he sold outright to Irving Mills all the *Hot Chocolates* songs for $500.

But perhaps the most revealing paragraph is the final one: "In *Hot Chocolates*, Waller says he has made no attempt to break rules, or even to vary a formula." His facility was already legendary. Mary Lou Williams, the pianist and arranger, who attended an early rehearsal at Connie's Inn, recalls how Waller improvised the music to one of the dance routines as Harper put the chorus through its paces, winding up with a finished piece of music. "Ain't Misbehavin'," we have it from no less an authority than its lyricist, Andy Razaf, was tossed off in forty-five minutes, the last song of the score. The bridge was confirmed via telephone, not having been written down at the time.

Razaf, Waller's closest collaborator, was the son of the Grand Duke of Madagascar, who was assassinated prior to the child's birth. His mother fled to the United States, and he was born in Washington, D.C., as Andreamenentania Paul Razafinkeriefo. His output was prodigious, and ranged from things like "My Handyman" to "Black and Blue." Among his other notable associates were Eubie Blake and Edgar Sampson.

A third name appears on the songs for *Hot Chocolates*: Harry Brooks. His role has been clarified by Emerson Harper, who was quoted about Baby Cox. In the same interview (with Bertrand Demusey in a 1967 issue of the now defunct British periodical *Jazz Monthly*) this member of LeRoy Smith's band, in which Brooks was the pianist, states that Brooks "collaborated with Fats Waller and Andy Razaf . . . generally writing the verse of the song while Fats wrote the chorus. One of the collaborations produced a hit, 'Ain't Misbehavin',' which was featured by Louis Armstrong in the show, and Brooks also wrote a special number for Louise Cook, 'The Rain Dance.'"

When the producers decided to close the Broadway run and take *Hot Chocolates* on the road, further changes were made. Armstrong, whose band had held down the Smith crew's place at Connie's Inn, left the show and went to California as a single. The band broke up. Waller himself performed the entr'acte, billed as "the Rachmaninoff of Jazz." A comparatively unknown singer and entertainer, fresh from Chicago, was added to the cast: his billing, Cabell Calloway. Muriel Rahn replaced Margaret Simms, and a gifted eighteen-year-old dancer named Roland Harper replaced Paul Meeres.

In 1933, the Immermans launched *Hot Chocolates of 1934*. A road show from the start, it had Baby Cox (again) and Louis Armstrong (for a while only, backed by Chick Webb's band), and dancer Peg Leg Bates as the headliner. It toured for two seasons, with LeRoy Smith's band replacing Webb's early on.

By then, as we have seen, the era of black musicals on Broadway had come to an end. Broadway would not see Armstrong again until 1939, when he was featured in the ill-fated *Swingin' the Dream*, loosely based on *A Midsummer Night's Dream* and also starring Maxine Sullivan, Benny Goodman's sextet with Charlie Christian, and Bud Freeman's Summa Cum Laude Band, playing intermission music from a box. Armstrong played Bottom. It was his last engagement on Broadway. What a waste of opportunity!

Fats Waller's next Broadway venture did not come until 1943. He composed the music for *Early to Bed*, a show centered on a house of ill repute on the island of Martinique (book and lyrics by George Marion, Jr.). It was a hit, not least due to Waller's fine score. It opened in June and ran for a healthy 382 performances, but Waller wasn't around to see it close. He died on December 15, 1943, aged thirty-nine.

The post–*Hot Chocolates* careers of the other principals are often obscure. Eddie Green, who among other things participated in Armstrong's 1936 Fleischmann's Yeast radio shows (the first sponsored radio series to feature a black headliner and an all-black cast), went on to become Eddie the waiter in radio's *Duffy's Tavern* and Stonewall the lawyer with *Amos 'n' Andy* from the mid-1940s on. Billy Maxey rates a footnote in jazz history, for he was responsible for the vocal on "Lay Your Racket," one of the numbers recorded by Sidney Bechet's glorious 1932 New Orleans Feetwarmers.

Jazzlips Richardson was featured in *Blackbirds of 1930*, but from then on, his trail gets cold. The Six Crackerjacks worked steadily until breaking up in 1952, and were again featured on Broadway, in *Hellzapoppin'*. Baby Cox, as noted, toured in *Hot Chocolates of 1934*. Paul Meeres retired to his native Bahamas and opened a supper club there.

Of all the Hot Chocolates, Edith Wilson, alive and well in Chicago at this writing, enjoyed the longest and most varied career. After *Hot Chocolates*, she toured with a Bill Robinson show, *Memphis Bound*, and visited England with *Blackbirds of 1934*. She appeared with Armstrong on radio and sang with the bands of Noble Sissle and Jimmie Lunceford. In the early '40s, she settled in California, working in vaudeville and taking acting lessons. She landed bit parts in films (including *To Have and Have Not*) and was a regular on radio. Then, for some eighteen years, she portrayed Aunt Jemima, the living trademark for pancake mix, first on radio, then also on television and in personal appearance tours, mainly to promote fund-raising pancake breakfasts. This stage of her career came to an end in 1966, due to pressure from civil-rights groups. Miss Wilson has remained active, made several recent recordings (an album of her own, and guest spots on discs with Eubie Blake and pianist Terry Waldo), and in 1974 she appeared on television in France. Her voice and sense of time are still sure and strong.

With all its shortcomings, the era that spawned *Hot Chocolates* and so much else established a record of achievement that one might expect to be honored by the supposedly enlightened present. But the recent success of a show called *Bubbling Brown Sugar* raises some doubts about that. On the night I attended this supposed tribute to the past, Eubie Blake, composer of *Shuffle Along* and dean of ragtime pianists, was also in the audience. I chatted with him during intermission, and he did not feel honored. Deeply disturbed by Avon Long's portrayal of Bert Williams in a frayed, dirty tuxedo, he said, "Bert Williams never set foot on a stage unless he was impeccably dressed. Wrinkled, maybe. Ragged and dirty, never." And he bemoaned the show's general lack of style and precision, implying that most of its cast would never have made it to Broadway in his day.

Whatever *Hot Chocolates* may have lacked, we can be sure that it had style, precision, and professionalism. Everyone had his or her best foot forward. The Tree of Hope did not stand in front of Connie's Inn for nothing. *Hot Chocolates*, ushered in by the era of the Harlem Renaissance, was inspirited by a *joie de vivre* and optimism very much of its time. We will not see its likes again.

As a postscript, let us note that *Hot Chocolates* was mentioned in an editorial in the *Herald Tribune*, flagship paper of the Republican Party. On October 18, 1929, under the heading "The Negro Arrives," the editorialist took his text from an article in the current *Atlantic Monthly* by the German popular philosopher Count Hermann Keyserling.

> The American Negro, Count Keyserling tells us a little grandilo-quently . . . "is a purely American type, and much more convincing as such than any living white type." . . . He appears also to argue that Negro dancing and music are, with the exception of Christian Science, the only American *articles d'export* which have really swept the world. The good Count enjoys his own intellectual dancing so much that it is sometimes hard to tell when he is pirouetting and when he seriously means to philosophize, but his point seems to be that the Negro soul is something profoundly American and profoundly important.
>
> With *Porgy* playing its third return engagement on Broadway, *Blackbirds* just going off after playing a solid year, with *Hot Chocolates* going strong and *Hallelujah*, the first all-Negro full-length motion picture, turning Hollywood into a cotton field it would seem that the impetuous public agreed with the world philosopher. And that, in its way, is a very convincing fact. . . . When Broadway sets its sign and seal upon a movement it is made. . . . It means that the Negro, not merely as a vaudeville joke and not merely as a highbrow cult, has arrived.

Not bad for a transplanted Harlem nightclub floor show!

(1978)

Jazz and Dance

For today's jazz audience—especially its younger members—the music is entirely for listening. Whether it is heard in a concert hall, a club, or on a record, jazz, like classical music, has come to exist only for its own sake. But there would be no jazz for us to listen to if not for the dance.

There can be no doubt that music began as an accompaniment or response to physical movement—so in a very real sense, all music is rooted in dance. Even the icons of Western European concert music employed dance forms, and by no means only for ballet scores. Jazz, however, is literally unthinkable without its link to dancing.

From Congo Square and the New Orleans "second line" to Funky Butt Hall, where the legendary Buddy Bolden held forth, to the bars, honky-tonks, nightclubs, and ballrooms of Chicago, Kansas City, and New York, jazz functioned as accompaniment to dancing. Indeed, social dancing was the conduit through which jazz entered the mainstream of popular culture. And beyond that, it was dancing that shaped the new music's special character. The rhythmic genius of African-American culture expressed itself in the organic relationship between music and dance, and while this relationship is no longer symbiotic, every time a jazz musician moves his body or taps his foot—and a listener responds with similar physical movement—it still manifests itself.

Yet one can read jazz history and criticism without encountering more than passing mention of this fundamental connection. This is no doubt because jazz still suffers from a cultural inferiority complex, and social dancing lacks sufficient stature as an expression of human creativity. Sitting on your behind and listening to music is regarded as a more elevated response than getting up and moving that part of your anatomy. But anyone at all familiar with the marvelous expressiveness and invention of so-called "vernacular" dance—especially in such forms as tap and Lindy Hop—would question that such a response is inferior to listening.

No less a master than Lester Young stated that good dancers were an inspiration to musicians, and anyone lucky enough to have witnessed what transpired when a good band appeared at the Savoy Ballroom in Harlem could attest to that fact. So let us briefly survey the historical relation between jazz and dance, a subject that one hopes will attract more scholarly attention in the future. (*Jazz Dance*, by Marshall Stearns, published in 1968, remains the best source, but deals only with dance.)

James Reese Europe, whose importance to jazz pre-history is only now beginning to be appreciated, became a dominant force in New York's musical life in the years from 1914 to 1917 mainly due to his association with the dance team of Irene and Vernon Castle, who popularized the fox-trot and forever changed the nature of social dancing. The Castles were white, but they found their ideal accompanists in Europe's black musicians, and before long Europe's bands (so much demanded that he needed several) were playing for the Astors and the Vanderbilts, and were hired for dances at prestigious universities. It was the World War, in which both Vernon Castle and James Reese Europe enlisted, that brought this period in American music to an end, and enabled the Original Dixieland Jazz Band (from New Orleans via Chicago) to bring a new kind of dance music to New York in 1917.

It was the dancers' response that brought fame to the ODJB and caused their records to become best sellers; we need only to consider some of the titles of their recorded pieces to realize that: "Original Dixieland One-Step," "Ostrich Walk," "Fidgety Feet," "At the Jazz Band Ball." And Reisenweber's, where the band broke through in New York, was a place for dining and dancing, not listening.

The next black bandleader after Europe to make a name for himself in white New York was Fletcher Henderson, through his long engagements at the Roseland Ballroom on Broadway. It was the band's popularity with dancers that made it possible for Henderson to bring in young Louis Armstrong from Chicago, and to hire and keep the finest jazz instrumentalists of the period. (Let us remember what Armstrong told us about his first rehearsal with Henderson: "They were playing a medley of beautiful Irish waltzes." What we have come to think of as jazz bands had to play a repertory including not only waltzes but also tangos, maxixes, and rumbas—even a polka, if requested.)

When we think of Duke Ellington's first big success, at the Cotton Club (in Harlem, but catering to whites), as being due to people listening to his fabulous music, we would be wrong. Ellington succeeded because his band was excellent at playing for social dancing, and for the special shows that the club was famed for, which featured a chorus line of girl dancers and individual dancing stars (as well as singers). It was as a great dance and show band that Ellington established himself—and then people started to *listen*, too.

In Chicago, King Oliver at the Lincoln Gardens was playing for dancing—the young white musicians who came to listen were considered an anomaly. When Armstrong came back from New York, he was soon featured at the Sunset, a ballroom. Sometimes the dancers would be so fascinated by his trumpeting that they would stop dancing and gather in front of the bandstand, but he wasn't giving concerts. Even the famous Hot Five and Hot Seven recordings were advertised (as were all records we now think of as jazz, black and white) as music to dance to.

Chicago was famed for its great ballrooms—the Dreamland and the Aragon were huge structures capable of accommodating thousands of dancers. Their decor rivaled that of the major film theaters—both venues were places where ordinary people could leave everyday drabness behind and live, for a moment, in a world of luxury. And while so-called "sweet" bands were the most popular, there was also room for "hot" music, frequently served up by black bands, such as Doc Cook's Doctors of Syncopation. And at the Grand Terrace, Chicago's counterpart of the Cotton Club, a brilliant young pianist named Earl Hines led the band—playing, like Ellington, for dancing and elaborate stage shows. (Musicians have told us that they learned much about tempo, swing, and precision from the chorus girls they played for, not only in places like the Grand Terrace, but in the many theaters where they had to accompany stage shows.)

This was all before the swing era, a period in the history of jazz when the music reached its height of popularity. It was dancing that made this possible. The band that paved the way, the now largely forgotten Casa Loma Orchestra, found its primary market for its special mixture of sweet and hot among college students, who loved to dance. When Benny Goodman made his breakthrough, it was at the Palomar *Ballroom* in Los Angeles, where an unexpected audience had grown for his music through the band's appearance on a weekly radio program called *Let's Dance*. And while some of that audience came up front to listen to Bunny Berigan, Goodman, and Gene Krupa, the other 95 percent were dancing.

Big-band swing gave rise to new dancing styles, chief among them what was originally known as the Lindy Hop ("Lindy" was the nickname of the enormously popular aviator Charles Lindbergh, whose "hop" was crossing the Atlantic) and then as jitterbugging. This very acrobatic (and in the right hands—and feet—very creative) dance had its origins long before the swing era's official debut. It began at Harlem's Savoy Ballroom, which opened in 1926, was an entire city block long, and is perhaps the dance palace most synonymous with jazz. It was here that legendary "battles of the bands" took place. Chick Webb, the fabulous little drummer, led the house band and was the local favorite. He won over Goodman, on a legendary night when more than seven thousand people jammed the room and thousands more stood in the street, but could only get a draw against Count Basie, who brought a new kind of rhythm from Kansas City that dancers loved—for it was they, *not* the listeners, who decided the outcomes of such battles. And speaking of Goodman, we recall that when he set new attendance records at New York's Paramount Theater—the largest movie palace in Times Square—the teenagers who had stood on line for hours to get in began to dance in the aisles when the band started swinging.

Even Fifty-second Street—generally regarded as the venue where jazz established itself as a music for listening—originally also catered to dancers. Small as the clubs were, each had a dance floor, and it was only when it became evident that more customers wanted to listen than to dance that more tables were put in. Perhaps ironically, the first instance of this was at the Famous Door, when Count Basie was booked there—the dance band *par excellence* performing for listeners only!

There were many reasons for the decline of ballroom dancing, which eventually caused the breakup of all but a few big bands, but the changes within jazz itself were one. The music was becoming more complex, certainly from a rhythmic standpoint, and even though the first response to bebop from the dancers at the Savoy was the creation of new variations, it soon became evident that most young jazz musicians no longer had a desire to play for dancing—for a while, at least, they too were affected by perceptions of "high" and "low" culture—but there were many other factors involved. The big bands that remained continued to play for dancers, however, and if you caught Ellington or Basie, even at the very end, in such a situation, it could be a revelation.

Ellington, of course, also wrote ballet music, notably for Alvin Ailey's *The River*, and with Ailey's choreography, and that of Twyla Tharp, among others, we come to a new chapter in the relation between jazz and dance. (What is called "jazz dance" in America, however, mostly is just a kind of Broadway approach with practically no real jazz elements.) It is that chapter of which the performance you are about to see is a part. Dexter Gordon, by the way, was a terrific dancer—as were Armstrong, Ellington, and even Goodman (who used to go to Harlem to dance long before he was a bandleader). And how about Thelonious Monk? When Monk got up to dance, it was either because the music was really feeling good to him, or because something was missing. Either way, it was a wonderfully fitting affirmation of a relationship that has become much less direct, yet remains essential to jazz.

(1998)

Jazz on Film

Jazz and film—the two arts truly indigenous to our time—should, by rights, long since have consummated a fruitful marriage. They have much in common: humble and obscure origins in the final years of the nineteenth century, a long and noble line of ancestors, and belated official recognition as legitimate forms of artistic expression. Most important, they are both popular arts, in the best sense of that stigmatized term.

It is through jazz and the motion picture, at their best, that the feeling and spirit of our century is most tangibly captured and reflected. Both, in their different ways, are storytelling arts that most effectively have their say through movement in sequence. That is to say, they are dependent upon time and timing, and in this, too, they are very much of our time.

Furthermore, both depend on mechanical reproduction—one entirely, the other to a great degree. (The diffusion of jazz would have been impossible without phonograph records and the radio, and had there been no diffusion, jazz would not have developed.)

Of course, it was not until the advent of "talking" pictures that conditions for this logical relationship between jazz and film existed. But even here, the parallel holds: the invention that made sound film possible also liberated jazz from the prison of acoustic recording. Both, of course, had achieved greatness before then.

Ironically, these preconditions for mutual inspiration have resulted in little.

Not a single jazz film—whether documentary or fictional—that could be called a masterpiece has been made. What does exist is almost purely of interest from a historical point of view. Whatever artistry shines through is almost wholly due to the marvelous "presence" and unquenchable communicative powers of the jazz musician with a message.

A detailed and accurate listing of jazz in film does not yet exist. Scattered information is available, from various sources. Only a few persons have seriously concerned themselves with the subject, chief among them two U.S. jazz-film collectors, John Baker and Ernest Smith.

If not for the efforts and enthusiasm of such men, much irreplaceable footage might already have been lost. Much of the film is perhaps already gone, though their search often bears unexpected fruit. But, as has been the case with other important aspects of films and with jazz recordings, irresponsibility has already ravaged unchecked. We have a mania for collecting, cataloging, and preserving trivia, while squandering the major creations of our own time.

Yet, in spite of the absence of organized research and preservation, the list of existing film jazz documents is unexpectedly long. It has many facets and holds many surprises—as well as disappointments. This survey, which makes no claim to completeness or authoritativeness, will attempt to give an overview of a fascinating field in which much further research is needed.

By the late '20s, when jazz and film first touched significantly, both forms already had created a viable language of their own, without benefit of theory or academic schooling. Though serious work was being done, and though there were people who took this work seriously, neither jazzman nor filmmaker could afford the luxury of pure creation, since both forms were popular entertainments, tied to the marketplace.

Not surprisingly, then, the first manifestations of film jazz took the most easily marketable forms. Jazz was used either in the "short subjects," which were employed as program fillers, or as special acts or attractions within the framework of a full-length feature, almost always in the "musicals" that were then just beginning to develop.

The first major talkie was *The Jazz Singer*, but this Al Jolson vehicle had jazz only in the title, which reflected the parlance of the times: the last days of "the jazz age." But it wasn't long before actual jazz came into film use.

Among the 1929 Vitaphone short subjects was one featuring Ben Pollack's band with Jack Teagarden and Benny Goodman in the lineup. Even earlier, Chick Webb's band, seen on screen, provided the music for a Lindy Hopper's contest in a feature film starring James Barton, a famous vaudevillian. Barton was white, but the dancers were Negro.

In these cases—there must have been others—jazz was incidental. But in two short films made in 1929 by an imaginative director named Dudley Murphy, jazz played the lead.

These works, *St. Louis Blues* with Bessie Smith and *Black and Tan Fantasy* with Duke Ellington and his orchestra, stand out in the annals of jazz films. It would have been difficult to miss with such artists, but Murphy did an excellent job besides. (He later directed *Emperor Jones*, starring Paul Robeson.)

Both films were created for the Negro market, and both have story lines: sentimental vignettes that could have become tawdry in lesser hands. Both also contain dialogue situations and characterizations that may offend contemporary viewers. (Throughout this article, references will be made to situations and circumstances that raise the specter of Uncle Tom. To deal here with the historical, sociological, and cultural aspects of these phenomena would take us too far afield. The general comments made in passing should not be interpreted as reflecting unawareness of the issues involved.)

In spite of this, we must be grateful that the films exist. Ellington would be seen on the screen again—not enough but quite often. But this was his earliest appearance. Miss Smith was never in another movie.

The story of *St. Louis Blues*, the stronger of the two films, is simple. Bessie (this is the name of the character she portrays) is in love with and keeping Jimmy (dancer Jimmy Mordecai), who is two-timing her. Returning to her boardinghouse (where a crap game is in progress in the hall—Perry Bradford is one of the players), she surprises Jimmy and the other woman in her own room.

Bessie chases the rival out and then pleads with Jimmy to stay with her. He is contemptuous. Trying to block his exit, Bessie is shoved to the floor. Jimmy leaves, laughing, stepping on Bessie as he goes. Still on the floor, she reaches for a bottle and begins to sing the blues, *a cappella*: "My man . . . My man . . ."

The scene shifts to a nightclub. Bessie stands at the bar, still singing the blues: ". . . my man's got a heart like a rock cast in the sea. 'St. Louis blues.'" As she sings, she is backed by a band led by James P. Johnson (including trumpeters Joe Smith and Sidney De Paris and drummer Kaiser Marshall) and by the Hall Johnson Choir, whose members portray the club's customers.

The singing ends, and the band breaks into double tempo. A waiter does an acrobatic dance while twirling a tray on one finger. Bessie, morose, stares at the glass before her. Jimmy, sharp as a tack, enters, seen by all but Bessie. The band breaks the time in half, and Jimmy greets Bessie. She is overjoyed. He grabs her, and they begin to dance. While holding her tight, Jimmy gropes for Bessie's bankroll in her stocking top. As soon as he has the money, he pushes her roughly away and saunters out.

Bessie returns to the bar and picks up her song, which rises to a crescendo. And the film is over—barely fifteen minutes. This rather sordid tale—yet so well put together—is all we have, in a dimension beyond records and photographs and dim recollections, of this great artist's persona.

To understand the significance of even imperfect films of great jazz artists, one must have seen this example, above all others. Since Bessie Smith was an artist whose personality comes through amazingly well on records, the impact of seeing her on the screen, especially if one has become attached to her music, is even greater than anticipated.

Here she is, for a few moments, immortalized in that unique fashion that is the magic gift of films—a big, strikingly handsome dark woman with a range of facial expressions and a unique presence that communicate emotions fully and directly with the economy of gesture and ease of movement that characterize a great performer; and here is that voice, captured better than on any record, with more than an inkling of its enormous power. This, in a fleeting glimpse, and yet complete, *is* Bessie Smith as she really was.

After the elation, of course, comes the anger at the shameful waste of such a talent—what an actress she could have been if given the chance. And why wasn't that chance given?

This is a theme that runs throughout our story, and the lesson hasn't yet been learned.

Murphy's Ellington film, starring a sleek, youthful Duke and dancer-actress Fredi Washington, also has a sentimental story. She is a dancer, in love with the struggling young bandleader. Both work in a place closely resembling the Cotton Club. She has a heart condition, but Ellington has written a new piece that features her.

One sees Ellington, Miss Washington, and trumpeter Arthur Whetsol putting finishing touches to "Black and Tan Fantasy" in Ellington's room. The janitor and a comic moving man arrive to repossess the piano but are bribed off with a bottle. Comes opening night at the club and a brilliantly photographed band sequence, in which young Johnny Hodges, Harry Carney, Cootie Williams, and other famous-to-be Ellingtonians can easily be recognized.

The girl comes on for her dance, against Ellington's pleadings. She dances. Ellington worries. She falters. She collapses. Pandemonium. The manager insists that the band keep playing. Ellington refuses and quits.

The girl, on her deathbed, is surrounded by the musicians and other friends. In a feeble voice, she requests, "Play the 'Black and Tan Fantasy,' Duke." With Whetsol, trombonist Joe "Tricky Sam" Nanton, and clarinetist Barney Bigard featured, and the Hall Johnson Choir again on hand, the piece is played, ending with the *Funeral March* quote and the girl's death.

I have described these two films at some length because they both remain extraordinary and because, in many ways, they are typical, in story line, of what was to come: sentimental melodrama with a touch of comedy—this was to be the recipe for many films when Hollywood turned "serious" about jazz.

In other ways, however, these early films were far from typical. Few subsequent short subjects had a story line; they were simply filmed stage presentations in which, more often than not, the featured band was saddled with several vocalists and dancers or acrobats. The results were often self-conscious and unintentionally funny, but one or two band numbers, and scattered solos, made up for the stiffness and the unimaginative photography.

This was one of the uses to which films put jazz, but this kind of short subject is no longer made. The others can be broken down into basic categories, which I will list and briefly examine.

Related to the shorts was the aforementioned and still current use of jazz artists in cameo performances within the loose framework of film musicals. Some use was (and is) also made of jazz as non-featured atmosphere, chiefly for nightclub scenes in dramatic pictures, a habit inherited by television.

Sometimes a famous jazz performer would be utilized not only musically and incidentally but also in a bit acting part tied in with the story line; Louis Armstrong was the first and most frequently used performer in this as in so many other categories.

The fifth, and most notorious, way in which jazz has been used on the screen is the dramatic film with a jazz theme, either a faintly recognizable biography of a famous musician or a purely (and always thoroughly) fictitious screenplay with a jazz setting.

An exceptionally rare form is the jazz documentary, a straightforward or arty presentation in which the music is in the spotlight, or else an attempt is made at historical or critical illumination of the music.

The final category of visual film jazz is the Negro film: either an all-Negro, all-star production for the general market or a film made exclusively for the "race" market.

Last, and really a subject unto itself, is the use of jazz purely as musical underscoring for a film with little or no jazz aspects in story or content.

To begin with the short subjects, many of these were produced, especially in the '30s. Most well-known name bands made at least one, and such bands as those of Artie Shaw, Jimmy and Tommy Dorsey, Charlie Barnet, Stan Kenton, etc., made several. In these, aside from normal period interest, famous sidemen can often be seen at the beginning of their careers (sporting the hairstyles of the day).

Of more generic interest are the shorts by Armstrong, Ellington, Fats Waller, and Count Basie, plus some films made by more obscure or forgotten bands. In the latter category are the bands of Eubie Blake, Noble Sissle, and Claude Hopkins.

Armstrong and his 1930 band appeared in *Rhapsody in Black and Blue*, a comedy short in which they are seen in a dream sequence, clad in leopard skins and floating in a sea of soap bubbles. Despite the hokum, Armstrong has a chance to play some fantastic trumpet, notably in a whirlwind version of "Shine," with a staggering display of high notes. This is Armstrong on the threshold of world fame.

The great trumpeter and singer's only other short was also slightly surrealistic. It was a Max Fleischer cartoon, in which Louis's face, disembodied, chases a cartoon creature through the jungle, singing, "I'll be glad when you're dead, you rascal you," his first great hit. At the end, Louis and the entire band are seen in a brief shot.

The year 1930 also brought an interesting short made by a fine band that never recorded, the Elmer Snowden band, which at that time included trumpeter Roy Eldridge and trombonist Dickie Wells. Both can be seen and heard soloing on "Bugle Call Rag" in this opus, called *Smash Your Baggage*, which is otherwise taken up mainly by song-and-dance routines. The film predates Eldridge's recording career by a full four years and thus has a special interest on this count alone.

Ellington, who always benefited from intelligent management, made two interesting shorts in the early '30s. The first, *Bundle of Blues*, dates from 1933. The dancer, Bessie Dudley, is a good one, and the tunes—heard in versions quite different from recordings issued at the time—are "Lightnin'," "Rockin' in Rhythm," "Bugle Call Rag," and "Stormy Weather" (featuring vocalist Ivie Anderson).

The second, and more ambitious, Ellington short, *Symphony in Black*, received an Oscar nomination in 1935. It purports to introduce a major Ellington work, commissioned by "the philharmonic" (of course, a fiction), which depicts various aspects of Negro life in the United States. The music includes pieces known from other contexts ("Ducky Wucky," "Merry-Go-Round," and "Saddest Tale"), as well as material heard nowhere else and segments that were later incorporated in *Reminiscing in Tempo*.

But the most notable element of the picture is the brief appearance of a young and astonishingly beautiful Billie Holiday, who, in a cameo about unrequited love, sings the blues (she, like Bessie, is knocked to the ground by a faithless lover). Since this great artist was to be seen only in two other films, a short with Count Basie's sextet (ca. 1950) and the 1947 feature film *New Orleans*, this brief, early glimpse is among the treasures of jazz in films.

A subcategory of the shorts was the "soundies," films of approximately three-minute duration, made for coin-operated machines in penny arcades. Fats Waller made at least four of these with his fine small group in 1940 or '41, doing such famous numbers as "Ain't Misbehavin'," "Honeysuckle Rose," and "The Joint Is Jumpin'." These films also had a line of chorus girls and dance interludes.

Basie, too, made several soundies (unfortunately, after Lester Young's departure), as did Ellington, Gene Krupa (with Eldridge and Anita O'Day), and, undoubtedly, other jazz artists.

Cameo spots for jazz performers in Hollywood musicals were not infrequent.

Cab Calloway had several; he and his 1933 band do "Reefer Man" in the W. C. Fields comedy *International House* and also were seen in one of the first of the annual *Big Broadcast* films, variety shows with thin story lines. Ellington pioneered in this category, with two featured numbers and background sequences in the 1930 Amos 'n' Andy vehicle *Check and Double Check*. A swinging "Old Man Blues" is the standout (as an ironic sidelight, Juan Tizol, a Puerto Rican, is made up in heavy blackface so as not to contrast with the rest of the band; it only makes him much more obvious).

In 1934 Ellington had spots in two major films, *Murder at the Vanities* (starring Carl Brisson and Kitty Carlisle) and *Belle of the Nineties* (starring Mae West). In the former, the band disrupts the performance (by an orchestra in eighteenth-century costumes!) of Liszt's *Hungarian Rhapsody No. 2* with its jazz version, *Ebony Rhapsody*.

In Miss West's film, the band was heard and seen to better advantage, both as featured pit band behind the star's vocal on "Memphis Blues," and in an after-hours session, draped around Miss West as she sings "My Old Flame." The band appeared (doing "I Want to Be a Rug-Cutter") in *Hit Pa-*

rade of 1937 and in *Reveille with Beverly*, a 1943 all-star compendium starring Ann Miller as a girl disc jockey spinning "hot platters" for the boys in uniform (doing "Take the A Train"—on a train, yet).

Basie was similarly featured in *Stage Door Canteen* and *Hit Parade of 1943* and, much more recently, in Jerry Lewis's *Cinderfella*. The Jimmie Lunceford band's only known movie appearance was in *Blues in the Night* (Elia Kazan portrays a clarinetist who wants to "play hot").

Benny Goodman was seen, with big band and/or small groups, in a number of films, most notably the 1937 *Hollywood Hotel*, in which, with Teddy Wilson, Lionel Hampton, and Gene Krupa, the clarinetist headed the first integrated musical performance on the U.S. screen.

Jack Teagarden was featured (with Mary Martin and Bing Crosby) in *Birth of the Blues* and also appeared with his big band in a number of '40s "B" pictures, among them one with the unlikely title *Twilight on the Prairie*.

Expatriate American jazzmen were sometimes seen in French films. Among these, in the '30s, were pianist Herman Chittison (in *Pepe Le Moko*) and trumpeter Bobby Martin's band, with drummer Kaiser Marshall (*L'Alibi*); in the '50s, trumpeter Bill Coleman appeared in *The Respectful Prostitute* and *Printemps à Paris*, while soprano saxophonist Sidney Bechet was seen in two mysteries, *Serie Noire* (with the great Erich Von Stroheim) and *Blues* (with Viviane Romance).

Bechet's reference to his work in these films in his autobiography, *Treat It Gentle*, sums up an attitude that must have been shared by many of his fellow jazzmen through the years:

"I suppose they weren't the best films ever made, but in both of them, I got to play some music the way I like, and I don't care how the hell it comes about—that's what I'm there for, and that's what I want to do."

Louis Armstrong had several cameo bits unrelated to story line in *Artists and Models*, *Dr. Rhythm*, *Every Day's a Holiday* (another Mae West film; Armstrong leads a street parade, doing "Jubilee," while Miss West plays the drums, riding in an open carriage), *Pillow to Post*, *Atlantic City*, and *Jam Session* (Louis is a bartender).

But the acting talent of this musical genius was too obvious even for Hollywood to overlook. Thus, Louis acted as well as played in *Pennies from Heaven* (with Bing Crosby) and *Goin' Places* (in which singer Maxine Sullivan also was featured) in the '30s and, later, in *The Strip*, *Glory Alley*, and *High Society*.

Cab Calloway had good acting parts in Al Jolson's 1936 *The Singing Kid* and in the recent *The Cincinnati Kid*, which also includes a New Orleans–style funeral parade. Wingy Manone was featured in Crosby's *Rhythm on the River* (1940), and Ivie Anderson and members of the Ellington band performed in the famous "Gabriel" sequence in the Marx Brothers' *A Day at the Races* (1937).

In the '50s Ella Fitzgerald sang a little and acted quite a bit in *Let No Man Write My Epitaph* and was cast in the same vein in *Pete Kelly's Blues*, which also featured Peggy Lee and some quite decent Dixieland music.

Jazz as background atmosphere crops up in numerous films, new and old. For an early example, an excellent unidentified Negro big band plays "Dinah," in *Taxi*, a 1932 James Cagney vehicle. Coleman Hawkins and his 1945 small group are seen in a mystery, *The Crimson Canary*. In 1952 Jack Teagarden, in the unlikely company of reedman Jimmy Giuffre, trumpeter Shorty Rogers, and clarinetist Bob Keene, appeared in *The Glass Wall*, while clarinetist Buddy DeFranco made music in *The Wild Party*, decidedly a B picture.

Olsen and Johnson, the zany comedy team, spotted Slim Gaillard in *Hellzapoppin'* (he also made several other films) and Jimmy Rushing in the sequel, *Funzapoppin'*. Clarinetist Jimmie Noone made his only film appearance in *Streets of New York*, a vehicle for the East Side Boys, a rival film company's answer to the Dead End Kids; and altoist Benny Carter, who usually is involved in scoring pictures, can be seen in *The Snows of Kilimanjaro* and *The View from Pompeii's Head*.

Trombonist Roswell Rudd and clarinetist Kenny Davern are in the Dixieland band that can be heard (but barely seen) in *The Hustler*; Gerry Mulligan and Art Farmer, among others, were on view in *I Want to Live!* and *The Subterraneans* (Mulligan also acting in the latter), while Charles Mingus, of all people, pops up in Frank Sinatra's *Higher and Higher* (holding a saxophone) and in Bing Crosby and Bob Hope's *The Road to Zanzibar*. Kid Ory and his band, with whom Mingus once worked, provide barroom atmosphere in *Crossfire*, a fine 1947 film.

But the pioneer in this field, as well as in jazz recording, was the redoubtable Original Dixieland Jazz Band. The group appeared in a 1917 two-reel comedy, *The Good for Nothing*, filmed at Reisenweber's restaurant in New York City. (H. O. Brunn, in his book, *The ODJB*, claims this was a Chaplin picture, which is an error.) Other jazz bands appeared in silent pictures, but this is a subject a bit too esoteric for these concerns.

The ODJB, as re-created in 1936 (with all the original members excepting pianist Henry Ragas, who was dead), was the subject of the first jazz documentary, a 1937 installment of *The March of Time*.

A clip from this film was seen in the same long-lived and influential series' *Music in America* (1944). This workmanlike survey of classical, popular, and jazz musics had a surprisingly strong jazz segment, including a glimpse of pianist Art Tatum at work on Fifty-second Street, one of only two film appearances by the master pianist; a glimpse of drummer Dave Tough with an Eddie Condon group; and Benny Goodman and his band.

Perhaps the best jazz film, from an artistic standpoint, was made in the same year. Gjon Mili, the famous photographer, and Norman Granz, a young film editor, joined forces in the production of *Jammin' the Blues*, a short subject featuring tenorists Lester Young (his only film) and Illinois Jacquet, trumpeter Harry Edison, drummers Jo Jones and Big Sid Catlett, guitarist Barney Kessel, pianist Marlowe Morris, bassist Red Callender, and singer-dancer Marie Bryant.

A slow blues, a fast blues, and "On the Sunny Side of the Street" (featuring Young and Miss Bryant) comprise the picture. There is a dance sequence, but it is remarkably photographed and integrated with the music, which is superb throughout. Young is much in evidence, both visually and aurally, coming through on the screen in the same startling way Bessie Smith did, and Catlett is also large as life.

Mili is a great photographer, and he was fascinated with jazz. His use of strong contrast in lighting and his careful composition of individual frames recalls the still photograph rather than the work of a man thinking in cinematic terms, and sometimes he gets too tricky, but while these considerations keep the film from being perfectly realized, it is as close to a masterpiece as exists in the genre.

More ambitious in scope is *Jazz on a Summer's Day*, the feature-length, Technicolor film shot at the 1958 Newport Jazz Festival. This, too, was directed by a famous photographer, Bert Stern, who specializes in still fashion work, with much help from Aram Avakian.

Not surprisingly, the film was a bit flashy in visual approach and emphasized entertainment and theatrical values (Chuck Berry and Big Maybelle in place of some of the considerably more jazz-oriented and important artists available), but there was much good music and photography, notably Louis Armstrong dueting with Jack Teagarden. This film was more widely distributed than any other jazz movie and on this count alone marks a milestone in jazz film history.

An excellent documentary, with music and biographical commentary, is the Belgian Yannick Bruynoghue's *Big Bill's Blues*, starring Big Bill Broonzy.

A documentary, *Jazz Dance*, was made on location at the Central Plaza in New York City in the mid-'50s and features pianist Willie "The Lion" Smith, cornetist Jimmy McPartland, clarinetist Pee Wee Russell, trombonist Jimmy Archey, bassist Pops Foster, and drummer George Wettling. It has had some theater showings but is rather amateurish in quality. Nevertheless, it is the only film showing Smith and Russell, two important musicians.

The only propaganda film involving jazz is the 1950s documentary *The Cry of Jazz*, made in Chicago and featuring Sun Ra. There is little music but much talk (simulated living-room discussion) about the nature and meaning of jazz. The film, with a definite black nationalist tone, is, in its own way, as muddled an approach to the subject as Hollywood at its worst and was not widely shown.

We have now reached the *pièces de résistance* in this survey, the "jazz dramas." One central point concerning them: neither the dramatized biographies nor the original stories can be cited for accuracy and care.

To take a typical example, there is *The Rat Race*, a 1957 Tony Curtis–Debbie Reynolds movie written by Garson Kanin. The hero, Curtis, is purportedly a "jazz" musician (he reads *Down Beat* on the bus to New York, doubles on an arsenal of reeds and is heard playing once) and sounds like a watered-down, vintage Bud Shank.

The jazz in the picture is jazzy indeed: pianist Joe Bushkin and tenorist Sam Butera portray two thieving musicians, who steal our hero's horns during a rehearsal that is unlike any rehearsal any living musician ever will attend or conduct, and that's about all.

But to indicate the level of accuracy, a further incident from this epic: Curtis gets a job (on the phone) as an *alto* saxophonist, his chick buys him a *tenor*, and on the job, he is seen playing *baritone* (the bandleader happens to be Gerry Mulligan, and *he* is playing tenor). That kind of thing is about par for the course.

Consider the biographies: *The Benny Goodman Story*, *The Glenn Miller Story*, *The Fabulous Dorseys*, *The Gene Krupa Story*, *The Five Pennies* (the Red Nichols story), and *St. Louis Blues* (the W. C. Handy story).

Of these, only the Dorsey picture had some degree of authenticity, mainly because the battling brothers portrayed themselves, doing excellent acting jobs. Thus, though the story was often nonsensical, there was a touchstone of reality. This picture contains the only other screen appearance of Art Tatum (aside from a glimpse in *The March of Time*), in a jam-session sequence with trumpeter Ziggy Elman, drummer Ray Bauduc, and the brothers.

The Miller story (with James Stewart, a personality as unlike Miller as could be, in the title role) was partially redeemed by a jam-session sequence with Louis Armstrong, Trummy Young, and the All Stars. Miller himself, and his band at its peak of fame, can be seen in *Orchestra Wives*, a picture with little jazz content but a fair sampling of Miller's style.

Goodman, as portrayed by Steve Allen, also lived a screen life somewhat removed from reality. But there was, at least, a considerable amount of good music, with flashes of Kid Ory, Teddy Wilson, Buck Clayton, Harry

James, Lionel Hampton, and a host of ex-Goodmanites. Wilson gave a particularly good acting performance. (In feature films, all music is dubbed. Ziggy Elman's featured solo was actually played by Mannie Klein; this is typical, as we shall see.)

Krupa, played by Sal Mineo, fared worse in terms of scripting and historical accuracy. Bix Beiderbecke, who died in 1931, walks into a 1935 party. Bobby Troup portrays Tommy Dorsey. (A little closer was Shelly Manne as Dave Tough, a role he also played in *Five Pennies*.) Roy Eldridge was sorely missed, but Anita O'Day took care of what little business was offered her.

By far the most unreasonable of these bio-pics was *Five Pennies*, in which Danny Kaye played Red Nichols. The only thing the two men share is hair color, and about the only thing the script had in common with Nichols's life and career was his name. Again, Louis Armstrong supplied the only redemption, carving Nichols gently but definitively, and singing a jolly "Saints" with Kaye. As for the rest, let us merely point out that Nichols was conscientious and diligent to the point of peevishness but is shown as being a crazy cutup who consistently gets himself fired from studio gigs for his antics. Of course, he is dedicated to "jazz" to the point of being unable to force himself to stick to an arrangement. Ah, Hollywood! But the film did trigger a comeback for Nichols.

Handy, played by Nat Cole (who had a number of good, non-jazz acting parts in other films), was also made into more of a jazzman than he ever was or claimed to be, and the script had next to nothing in common with the life of this earnest, eminently respectable businessman-musician. Eartha Kitt and Pearl Bailey provided good entertainment, but for jazz fans, the participation of Barney Bigard, trombonist George Washington (a good actor), and trumpeter Teddy Buckner (a Hollywood veteran, and Armstrong's stand-in for several films) was more to the point. Handy did not live to experience the film, which perhaps was fortunate.

That is the extent to which Hollywood has concerned itself with biographies of jazz artists (though there was *The King of Jazz*, in 1930, starring Paul Whiteman, of course—without Bix Beiderbecke). No *Louis Armstrong Story*, no *Duke Ellington Story*, no *Charlie Parker Story*, and no likelihood that a major studio will ever do any of these. Persistent rumors of Bessie Smith and Billie Holiday bio-pictures have failed to materialize, and an independently produced film loosely based on Parker's life, with Dick Gregory in the lead, has not been released.

Armstrong had his innings, however, in *Satchmo the Great*, a documentary originally made for television but later released as a film. Edward R. Murrow narrates, and Armstrong reminisces about New Orleans days and is seen on the road and backstage, in concert in Europe, at Lewisohn Stadium with Leonard Bernstein, and, most interestingly, in Africa. Though not very imaginatively done, the film is an honest job, and the Armstrong personality comes across.

Armstrong was also featured in two Hollywood musicals concerned with jazz, *New Orleans* (1947) and *A Song Is Born* (1948). The former, a trite soap-opera story, has the virtues of the trumpeter with a fine small group that comprised Ory, Bigard, guitarist Bud Scott, pianist Charlie Beal, bassist Red Callender, and drummer Zutty Singleton and has Billie Holiday's only major film appearance—predictably, in the role of a chambermaid. Her unaccompanied blues singing is worth the whole picture, which, by the way, also spots Woody Herman's band in the finale—as well as, of course, a "symphony" orchestra.

Song, a Danny Kaye movie, had a good acting part for Benny Goodman and featured an impressive array of name jazz talent. Armstrong, Tommy Dorsey, Charlie Barnet, Lionel Hampton, and pianist Mel Powell were on hand, as well as Buck and Bubbles, pianist Page Cavanaugh, and the Golden Gate Quartet. But almost the best jazz in the film came as background to a nightclub scene, in which Benny Carter, trombonist Vic Dickenson, Singleton, and Bigard could be seen and heard. The story, dealing with "jazz history," was mostly pleasant nonsense.

When Hollywood, on rare occasions, got serious about jazz, the results were, to say the least, disappointing. *Syncopation*, a 1940 film starring Jackie Cooper, Bonita Granville, Adolphe Menjou, and Todd Duncan, cast Rex Stewart in the role of a trumpet player patterned, to some rather vague extent, on King Oliver.

Typically, Stewart's trumpet solos were soundtracked by Bunny Berigan (whose sole known film appearance is in an early '30s Fred Rich short), and there was an all-star jam sequence based on the results of a *Saturday Evening Post* swing poll.

This conglomeration featured Harry James, Jack Jenny, Charlie Barnet, Joe Venuti, Alvino Rey, Eddy Duchin (!), Bob Haggart, and Gene Krupa. Duchin's solo was played by Howard Smith, and Benny Goodman, who couldn't make the gig, pre-recorded his solo, which was simulated on camera by a stand-in with his back to the audience. Connee Boswell and our old friends, the Hall Johnson Choir, were also on hand. The story was silly.

Young Man with a Horn, starring Kirk Douglas as an ill-fated trumpeter, and loosely based on the Dorothy Baker novel loosely based on Bix Beiderbecke's life, had little to offer in the way of musical value. Harry James, playing well, soundtracked Douglas's trumpet simulations, and Jimmy Zito, a competent studio man, did the ghosting for Juano Hernandez, whose moving performance as the Negro trumpeter who inspires and befriends the hero was the best thing in the film.

The rest, excepting a brief jam-session sequence, was strictly Hollywood, with Doris Day on hand as romantic interest. Once again, jazz had been submerged in phony trappings.

A few months ago, *A Man Called Adam*, a jazz film with more promise than most, was released but quickly withdrawn. I did not see it, except in the form of unedited sequences in the cutting room. This, however, was enough to indicate that, in spite of a somewhat melodramatic story, the film, starring Sammy Davis, Jr., was an honest effort with meaningful things to say about a jazzman's life. Louis Armstrong turned in a fine acting performance and played very well (with his All Stars); Nat Adderley sound-tracked Davis's trumpet, and Benny Carter composed and arranged the music, using first-class New York musicians for the soundtrack.

One hopes that the picture has been only temporarily withdrawn (the reviews, ignorant of jazz matters, were generally negative in criticizing the story line and some acting) and that it will be better promoted when it reappears. But, in spite of its virtues, this, by all odds, is still not the great jazz film that could be made.

Perhaps *Adam*'s lack of initial success was rooted in its predominantly Negro cast, though all-Negro films, in the past, have occasionally been commercially successful.

The earliest, and most famous, of these was King Vidor's 1929 *Hallelujah*, which contained plenty of spiritual and gospel singing, but no jazz and only a little blues, ably handled by singer Victoria Spivey and a rough-and-ready small band.

In 1942 an all-Negro film with more jazz emphasis, *Stormy Weather*, was released. It starred dancer Bill Robinson and Lena Horne, and featured Cab Calloway and his band, but its true star was Fats Waller.

Waller had a bit part in the 1935 *King of Burlesque* (he played an elevator operator and did one number, "I've Got My Fingers Crossed"), but in *Stormy Weather*, he was better used. With a band, which had Benny Carter (not seen on screen) on trumpet, Slam Stewart on bass, and Zutty Singleton on drums, he did "Ain't Misbehavin'"; an instrumental, "Moppin' and Boppin'"; and accompanied blues singer Ada Brown in "That Ain't Right."

In addition, Waller stole every dramatic scene in which he appeared and made such an impact that he was slated to be featured in other major films. Unfortunately, death intervened. While much of *Stormy Weather* is now dated, Waller's performance continues to shine brightly.

The next year, another all-star Negro production, *Cabin in the Sky*, was made. It starred Ethel Waters, and the story, a fantasy, was considerably more "Tommish" than *Stormy Weather*. However, it did have Armstrong in an acting role (as a devil), and it did have a good deal of Duke Ellington and his orchestra, notably in a swinging, never-recorded "Goin' Up." (Miss Waters also has starred in several films without jazz content.)

Armstrong and Ellington joined forces in a more recent venture, *Paris Blues*, for which Ellington also wrote a beautiful score. The story is about two jazz musicians (Paul Newman and Sidney Poitier, ghosted by trombonist Murray McEachern and tenorist Paul Gonsalves) and their loves and, as jazz films go, was better than most. Armstrong is featured, again, in a jam session.

This brings to an end the survey of jazz seen in films. There remains the matter of jazz scores, concerning which there is room only to provide undetailed comments.

Ellington, in addition to *Paris Blues*, wrote a first-rate score for *Anatomy of a Murder*, which worked well in the film and is good enough to stand on its own as music. Last year, Ellington was commissioned to score a Frank Sinatra vehicle, *Assault on a Queen*. The results did not compare with his two earlier ventures, but the film is so ridiculous that it was almost an insult to Ellington to ask him to do the job.

Some of the best jazz scores by U.S. musicians have been for foreign films. These include Miles Davis's improvised score for the French *Elevator to the Gallows*, Duke Jordan's for *Les Liaisons Dangereuses* (with Art Blakey and Thelonious Monk on screen), Blakey's for *The Disappearing Women*, Kenny Dorham's for *Witness in the City* (also French), Chico Hamilton's for *Repulsion*, and Sonny Rollins's for the current *Alfie* (both British). Hamilton also scored, and was seen in, *The Sweet Smell of Success*. West Coast jazz (remember?) had its innings in *The Wild One* (Leith Stevens, assisted by Shorty Rogers) and *The Man with the Golden Arm* (Elmer Bernstein, with Rogers and Shelly Manne on screen).

John Lewis has composed two excellent scores, for *No Sun in Venice*, a French mystery, performed by the Modern Jazz Quartet, and *Odds Against Tomorrow*, a heavy U.S. melodrama, performed by a studio orchestra that included Milt Jackson and Bill Evans. Charles Mingus did *Shadows*, a semi-experimental film, and Erroll Garner (with Leith Stevens) did *A New Kind of Love*, a 1963 romantic comedy starring Joanne Woodward.

A special case is the film version of *The Connection*, Jack Gelber's play about narcotics addicts. This was, more or less, a filmed stage play and employed the original cast and Freddie Redd's score as performed by a quartet including pianist Redd and altoist Jackie McLean, both of whom had fat acting parts as well.

Several musicians with a jazz background have written film scores of straight movie music with few or no jazz elements, among them Lalo Shifrin, André Previn, John Mandel, and Quincy Jones. Britain's Johnny Dankworth, who also has numerous scores to his credit, generally keeps the jazz flavor in; one of his best jobs was *Sapphire*.

That, by and large, is the record, so far, of jazz in films. It is certain that discoveries of valuable material remain to be made—recently, Norman Granz unearthed some Charlie Parker–Coleman Hawkins footage and is searching for the soundtrack, and collectors like Baker and Smith periodically come up with new finds.

As for the future use of jazz in films, the prognosis is none too hopeful. Dedicated amateurs generally have little real knowledge of either art, and when the professionals get into the act, commercial considerations always seem to override the artistic. Television, so far, has, not taken up the challenge and is content with routine endeavors reminiscent of Hollywood in the '30s. One outstanding exception was the 1957 *The Sound of Jazz*, never shown again and nearly scrapped some years ago. It had Billie Holiday, Lester Young, and many others.

Perhaps a film record of the great players now alive will be made before it is too late. That is a project with which such establishments as the Institute of Jazz Studies, the New Orleans Jazz Museum, and, if they ever awaken to jazz, the major foundations might well concern themselves.

The wedding of jazz and film offers unique possibilities. It is tragic that so little has been done to realize them and that so many opportunities are now forever lost. Yet, we must be thankful to have the few glimpses of the past that do exist. To preserve and protect them should be the first consideration.

(1967)

Much jazz footage has been added in the thirty-five years since my pioneering—and incomplete—effort. So much that only highlights can be mentioned here. First, the feature films. Attempted biographies of Billie Holiday (*Lady Sings the Blues*, 1972) and Charlie Parker (*Bird*, 1988) failed to bring their subjects to life. Though Diana Ross made a musically and dramatically appealing effort and Forest Whitaker tried hard, both films suffered from melodramatic scripts rife with inaccuracies and absurdities (such as the jam session in *Bird*). The hero of Bertrand Tavernier's *'Round Midnight* (1986), a composite of Lester Young and Bud Powell, was fully realized in Dexter Gordon's brilliant performance, which earned him an Oscar nomination; Gordon further served the film by cleansing the script and his own lines of anything that struck him as false and incongruous, and despite its sentimentality and typically French anti-American touches, the film stands as the best jazz film drama yet made. Woody Allen's *Sweet and Lowdown* (1999) also has a fictitious hero, an American guitarist who worships and shares some character traits with Django Reinhardt, well portrayed by Sean Penn (guitar by the great Howard Alden). Himself a semi-pro musician, Allen has considerable jazz insight (his jazz persona is captured in *Wild Man Blues* [1997], a documentary of a European tour by his New Orleans–style band) and has made good use of jazz in almost all his films, many of them scored by Dick Hyman.

Robert Altman sincerely admires jazz, and in *Short Cuts* (1993) elicited a brilliant performance from Annie Ross, cast as a jazz singer, also made good use of her music as a linking device. His *Kansas City* (1996), a gangster melodrama, was widely hailed for its prominent use of jazz, but though Altman grew up in the film's locale, his attempted re-creation of a legendary jam-session cutting contest between Lester Young (Joshua Redman) and Coleman Hawkins (Craig Handy) was unintentionally hilarious. Pianist Geri Allen, however, brought dignity and historical accuracy to her portrayal of Mary Lou Williams. Spike Lee's *Mo' Better Blues* (1990), primarily set in a Brooklyn jazz club, spotted much good music and some excellent performances, notably by Branford Marsalis (hilarious in a dramatic cameo in Danny DeVito's *Throw Momma from the Train*, and also prominent in a documentary about Sting).

A great deal more has been accomplished in the field of documentaries. Five years in the making, Bruce Ricker's *Last of the Blue Devils* (1979) lovingly observes a visit by Count Basie to the Kansas City black musicians' union's cozy club room—the centerpiece of a nostalgic recapitulation of the city's days of jazz glory. Basie's and Joe Turner's early morning exit, arm in arm, is pricelessly authentic. Charlotte Zwerin's *Straight, No Chaser* (1989), in which Ricker had a production hand (much footage came from a German documentary, and Clint Eastwood lent his support and name), stands as one of the finest portraits of a major jazz figure. Thelonious Monk is seen at work in concert and the recording studio, on the road, and strolling in his neighborhood, and there is thankfully little of talking heads. The late Tom Reichman's *Mingus* (1968) caught the great man on a downward curve, but Don McGlynn's *Triumph of the Underdog* (1997) gives a more balanced view. McGlynn has also made films about such varied subjects as Glenn Miller, Art Pepper, Louis Prima, Horace Parlan, and Teddy Edwards. Interesting subjects have included Joe Albany (*A Jazz Life*), Illinois Jacquet (*Texas Tenor*), and Louis Armstrong, whose 1970 Newport birthday tribute, fleshed out with excellent interview footage, became *Salute to Louis* (1972), a George Wein production. The great Benny Carter was not fully captured in *Symphony in Riffs* (1989), and Yudd Yalkut's *Portrait of Pee Wee Russell* (1998) shows us the clarinetist as painter.

The capture of vintage jazz greats I expressed hope for in 1967 came about to some extent in two films by Britain's John Jeremy, *Jazz Is Our Religion* (1972) and *Born to Swing* (1973), and Louis Panassié's *L'Aventure du*

Jazz (1970), but was most fully, and most originally realized more recently, in Jean Bach's *A Great Day in Harlem* (1995), which uses the famous 1958 *Esquire* magazine photo of fifty-eight jazz greats gathered on a Harlem street as a trigger for recollections by survivors (musicians, photographers, organizers, kibitzers, etc.), filled out with film and still footage shot by, pre-eminently, Milt Hinton. It was nominated for an Oscar and should have won. Hinton is the subject of a posthumous documentary unveiled in 2003. Speaking of unveiling: In 1996, Norman Granz decided to share with the world the hitherto unseen sequel to *Jammin' the Blues*. Filmed in 1950 at Gjon Mili's New York studio (so noisy that simulation to pre-recorded music was required), it included footage of Charlie Parker, hitherto captured only on a segment from a 1951 daytime television show, *Stars over Broadway*, discovered by the late film collector David Chertok, where he performs "Hot House" with Dizzy Gillespie and the show's house trio. Now, in one of the last of the many good deeds Granz did for jazz, we also have a much more relaxed Bird, in the company of Coleman Hawkins, Hank Jones, Ray Brown, and Buddy Rich—as well as some precious Lester Young. Fleshed out with other clips from Granz's archives, these treasures are part of a video called *Improvisation*.

Jazz on film has also become the subject of a growing literature. The first was Donald Meeker's *Jazz in the Movies* (1972, revised 1981), a detailed listing. While taking in much more, Thomas Cripps's *Slow Fade to Black: The Negro in American Film* (1977), had jazz in its perspective. German researcher Klaus Strateman produced impressive surveys of Louis Armstrong and Duke Ellington in films and on television, and Krin Gabbard brought contemporary intellectual notions into play in *Jammin' at the Margins*. We've come a long way since my little essay!

Jazz and Television

On the face of it, jazz and television seem made for each other. One of television's great strengths is its immediacy—the sense it gives a viewer of being there. It is a medium made for events, and every jazz performance is an event. (It might be argued, and rightly so, that any musical performance is an event; but the charisma of a Rubinstein or Bernstein or the drama of the "Ode to Joy" in a great concert hall filled to capacity notwithstanding, there is a very special dimension to jazz.)

The secret is the music's spontaneity, which, when combined with high artistic quality, conveys the feeling of being present at a unique moment of creation. To cite an example that ought to be known to everyone interested in our subject: the moment when Roy Eldridge begins his unexpected second chorus on "Fine and Mellow," during the Billie Holiday sequence from *The Sound of Jazz*, unarguably the show that has come closest to capturing the essence of jazz through television cameras.

Unfortunately, such magic moments have been the exception rather than the rule, and the synergistic potential in the relationship between jazz and television has largely gone unrealized. Nevertheless, during the nearly forty years since jazz was first featured regularly on TV, a multitude of jazz images have flickered across millions of screens. Most of them have vanished; a few have been fixed on film or videotape. The potential for preservation has, of course, increased enormously with the age of VCRs, and so has the marketability of what is preserved. What the qualitative impact of these new conditions will be remains to be seen, but a quantitative increase in jazz programming is bound to occur, since special-interest presentations are no longer subject to mass-market pressures.

It will be interesting to observe what happens. Meanwhile, it may come as a surprise even to jazz aficionados how much already has happened, though the survey that follows can make no claims to completeness. Rather, it is a modest attempt to harness some facts about a fascinating aspect of a medium which itself remains relatively unexplored from the perspective of historical research. Considering the tremendous importance of television as a medium of communication, it is surprising how little attention jazz historians, critics, and journalists have paid to the fate of jazz on the home screen, but they are not alone in this display of cultural provincialism.

It is perhaps fitting that the first reference to jazz on TV I have been able to uncover involves an artist who would have been ideally suited to the new medium if he had lived longer. This is Thomas "Fats" Waller (1904–1943), who, while on tour in England in 1938, was the subject of a BBC program emanating from London's Alexandra Palace. Waller is said to have responded with delight to his image on the tiny monitor screens during the broadcast, a sentiment surely shared by the chosen few who saw the show.

The earliest instance of jazz on American TV seems to be the CBS transmission of four Town Hall Jazz Concerts (the famous series produced by Eddie Condon) beginning in April 1942 and brought to a sudden end by wartime restrictions imposed by the FCC. Condon credits a CBS executive, Worthington Minor, with making these pioneering broadcasts possible, and comments that the shutdown was no great loss: "There were probably about three people watching us on three-inch screens."

Condon was again a pioneer when the screens had grown a bit bigger and were watched by sizable audiences. A weekly show hosted by the guitarist was seen during 1948 on New York's WPIX. When that station failed to pick up Condon's option, he moved with pleasure to NBC, where *The Eddie Condon Floor Show* enjoyed a longish run despite the absence of sponsors—and on Saturday nights at that.

A considerable amount of audio from these shows has survived, but no kinescopes seem to exist. I saw a few of the shows, and recall freewheeling camera work and a relaxed atmosphere typical of Condon. Though this witty, articulate musician was most closely identified with Chicago-style jazz and its subsequent New York incarnations, his shows were by no means stylistically narrow. The excellent house band was graced with the presence of drummer Big Sid Catlett, who worked hand in glove with pianist Joe Bushkin, bassist Jack Lesberg, and Condon himself when he moved from emceeing to the guitar chair. Bobby Hackett, Billy Butterfield, and Wild Bill Davison were among the incumbent trumpets; Cutty Cutshall manned the trombone; and Ernie Caceres and Peanuts Hucko were the reedmen. The guests were drawn from the front ranks of the music world and included Louis Armstrong, Jack Teagarden, Roy Eldridge, Charlie Shavers, Sidney Bechet, Billie Holiday, Gene Krupa, Buddy Rich, Artie Shaw, Hot Lips Page, James P. Johnson, Ella Fitzgerald, Buck and Bubbles, Billy Eckstine, and a host of others. The finale was almost always an unrehearsed jam-session blues, and Condon, a born ad-libber, was the perfect host. The spontaneity that characterizes the surviving music from these shows was something that the nature of early, pre-tape TV made possible. Later, this ambience became quite rare.

The formats that were to rule TV for decades, and indeed to a large extent have survived to the present, took shape during the '50s. Music presentations were part and parcel of variety shows (television, it can be said, considerably prolonged the life of vaudeville) such as *The Ed Sullivan Show* and, with a somewhat thicker veneer of "culture," the *Bell Telephone Hour*; shows of similar content hosted by a celebrity (Perry Como, Dinah Shore); the "specials"; and the mixture of celebrity interviews, comedy, and variety of which the original *Tonight* show, hosted by Steve Allen, was the prototype.

To Allen—a man of many parts, some of which related directly to music (songwriter and pianist)—must go the credit of making jazz part of regular television fare. He established high standards for popular music presentation with his attractive "house" duo of singers Eydie Gorme and Steve

Lawrence, supported by a good team of musicians, and his featured guests were not only stars of proven mass popularity but also first-rate jazz artists like Art Tatum, Erroll Garner, and Billie Holiday. Though Allen didn't shy away from playing a duet with Tatum, he treated his jazz guests with respect and admiration, giving his audiences the sense that they were seeing something special. Allen remained loyal to jazz throughout his career; in the '70s, his musical director was vibraharpist Terry Gibbs.

Sullivan generally stuck to the biggest names—Benny Goodman, Count Basie, Duke Ellington, and above all Louis Armstrong. His show emphasized production values, and the atmosphere was seldom sufficiently relaxed to result in great jazz performances. Armstrong, however, always came through on TV, and sometimes a premise that might not seem promising would yield spectacular results—I'll never forget what Armstrong did on a Sullivan show with "Beautiful Dreamer," complete with strings and a choir, and I hope that this wonderful moment survives somewhere.

Armstrong was ubiquitous on TV, not only in the '50s, but until the very last days of his life. His appearances must number in the hundreds, and include every kind of program, from innumerable telethons (another TV format that made frequent use of jazz) to Como, Crosby, Dean Martin, Danny Kaye, *Hollywood Palace*, *Shindig*, Jackie Gleason, Garry Moore; Allen and his successors Jack Paar and Johnny Carson, and the *Tonight* clones, Merv Griffin, Mike Douglas, Dick Cavett, and David Frost; Pearl Bailey, Herb Alpert, and, in one of his very last appearances, Johnny Cash, with whom Armstrong did a moving re-creation of a recording he'd made with Jimmie Rodgers in 1933.

Fittingly, Armstrong was the first jazz figure to get a special of his own, the 1956 *Satchmo the Great*. It was the outgrowth of a segment on Edward R. Murrow's prestigious interview show *See It Now*, included footage filmed in Europe and Africa, and was subsequently edited for release as a documentary film.

Armstrong also loomed large in three rather notorious 1958–59 jazz specials sponsored by Timex, a watch manufacturer. These shows represented a considerable investment and achieved very respectable ratings. Thus, one might have expected them to be greeted by the jazz community as welcome proof that the frequently repeated adage "Jazz doesn't sell" was untrue, but the shows were almost universally condemned, and with some justification.

These large-budget all-star "spectaculars" suffered from a disease endemic to the medium—overkill. Instead of giving the artists requisite elbow room to perform at their best, the producers opted for a circus-like format that specialized in truncated individual efforts (few solos of more than a chorus in length), unlikely combinations of performers (non-jazz singer

Jaye P. Morgan and Armstrong), and Barnum & Bailey finales in which everyone was thrown together helter-skelter. The names were impressive; the music mostly was not.

Yet, there were moments. Armstrong and Dizzy Gillespie, in their only known joint appearance, came up with a too-short but delightful "Umbrella Man" on the third Timex show, which also offered a glimpse of Coleman Hawkins and Roy Eldridge. But what had been a musical highlight of the run-through—Armstrong performing with the Duke Ellington orchestra in a piece put together on the spot by Ellington that pitted Armstrong against the four trumpeters in the band with inspired results—was jettisoned when singers Dakota Staton and Ruth Olay were added to the cast at the last moment. All that remained, under the final crawl, was Armstrong soaring above the Ellington band in a fragment of "Perdido"—an appropriately ironic title, under the circumstances.

Thus, Timex became a word synonymous with what too often went wrong with jazz on TV: show-business values taking precedence over artistic considerations, and the music being cheapened by not being allowed to stand on its own feet. (The intrusive Timex hosts were Allen, Garry Moore, and Jackie Gleason.)

Thirteen years later, Timex revisited jazz and proved that it had learned nothing in the interim. Its 1972 *All Star Swing Festival*, taped in Carnegie Hall before an invited audience, was again overloaded with performers given insufficient time to prove themselves, burdened with a banal script and an intrusive host (Doc Severinsen, dressed to kill any semblance of good taste), and shot in the most unimaginative manner. In addition to the bands of Count Basie and Duke Ellington, Ella Fitzgerald, Joe Williams, the Dave Brubeck Quartet, and what proved to be the final reunion of the original Benny Goodman quartet (augmented by bassist George Duvivier), the show crammed in a so-called tribute to Louis Armstrong, which wasted the talents of no less than ten performers, including Earl Hines (one chorus), Dizzy Gillespie (one chorus), Bobby Hackett (16 bars), Max Kaminsky (16 bars), Barney Bigard (16 bars), and host Severinsen, who took a full chorus of "Sleepy Time Down South." Miss Fitzgerald, who'd already been featured with Basie and in two numbers with her own trio, was also squeezed into this travesty. Thus, a sponsor who had managed to discomfit Armstrong while he was living now gave short shrift to his memory.

Ironically, the inspiration for the Timex spectaculars had come from a show that to this day represents the acme of jazz on TV, the aforementioned 1957 *The Sound of Jazz*. Produced by Robert Herridge for the CBS Sunday series *The Seven Lively Arts*, with critics Whitney Balliett and Nat Hentoff as artistic advisers and Jack Smight as director plus a handpicked crew, this show remains a landmark. Excellence of direction and technical work aside, the reason was startlingly simple: Herridge had the guts and integrity to give the artists free rein, to trust them to do what they did best. The stellar cast responded to the respect with which they were treated with superb performances in the most unselfconscious way. Because they were allowed to concentrate on the music, the music in turn became concentrated to a degree uncommon even in a recording studio, let alone a television or film environment. To use an old jazz expression, they "took care of business" in no uncertain way. Permitted to dress as they wished and to wander about on the set as they pleased while not performing, the musicians brought to the show a special dimension of relaxed ease. Smight took brilliant advantage of the performers' reactions to each other, like the benign amazement registered by Count Basie while listening to Thelonious Monk (and Coleman Hawkins's pride in his erstwhile protégé during the same sequence), or Billie Holiday's loving response to Lester Young's fey and beautiful chorus on "Fine and Mellow."

The single superfluous element in the show was John Crosby's well-meant and earnest commentary, and it is clear that he felt eminently expendable. To a slightly lesser degree, the same can be said for the pre-recorded comments by some of the performers regarding their feelings about music. But these are very small blemishes on the timeless visage of a masterpiece.

Herridge was given his own program, *The Robert Herridge Theater*, by CBS the following year, and for it he produced two further jazz shows. One, which featured the great tenor saxophonist Ben Webster with a more than able supporting group, and the then highly regarded but in retrospect somewhat superficial Ahmad Jamal Trio, was an excellently made piece, but not much more than that, excepting Webster's lovely "Chelsea Bridge." The other, *The Sound of Miles Davis*, was remarkable—and a coup. Davis, then at his first height of fame, had steadfastly refused offers to appear on TV, feeling that the medium was not to be trusted, but *The Sound of Jazz* convinced him that he'd be in good hands with Herridge.

The program is in two parts. The first features Davis's now legendary quintet of the day, with John Coltrane, Wynton Kelly, Paul Chambers, and Jimmy Cobb playing "So What?" at self-chosen length. The music is brilliant and the camera work as fluid and natural as in *The Sound of Jazz*. The second part presents Davis with a large ensemble arranged for and conducted by Gil Evans, in a seamless performance of three numbers, "The Duke," "Blues for Pablo," and "New Rhumba." The musicians are seated in the round, allowing the cameras great freedom of movement, and the results are spectacular. Davis, whose subsequent TV appearances have been infrequent, was never better served by the medium. Now that he has long since abandoned the musical approach he employed in 1959, the value of this document becomes even greater.

Herridge, a maverick, never found a permanent niche in televisionland. Just before his sudden death in 1981, he was making plans to produce another jazz program. It is a great pity that this was not to be, but his name will command respect as long as people care about jazz. (It is worth mentioning that CBS did not choose to preserve their copy of the kinescope of *The Sound of Jazz*; had it not been for Herridge's own copy, this show would now be a lost masterpiece.)

The Timex mistakes, fortunately, were not the sole legacy of *The Sound of Jazz*, which, by the way, was greeted with almost unanimous critical praise. It is not likely that *The Subject Is Jazz*, produced and distributed by NBC for educational purposes in 1958, or *Art Ford's Jazz Party*, broadcast live on Channel 13 (then a small independent station in Newark and not yet the home of WNET), would have come about without the inspiration of Herridge's work. In their very different ways, both programs belong with the memorable output of the decade.

The Subject Is Jazz, with Gilbert Seldes as host and Marshall Stearns and Leonard Feather as expert advisers, was, among other things, Billy Taylor's first major foray into television. Already known as an uncommonly articulate spokesman for jazz, the young pianist made his presence felt on the show as leader of the house band and musical director. This band also included a then quite unknown Doc Severinsen, Ivy League in attire and sporting a crew cut; reedman Tony Scott; trombonist Jimmy Cleveland; and drummer Ed Thigpen. The show's approach was historical, its scripting rather stilted, and its host awkward by today's TV standards. But some of the programs, notably the one about the blues, hold up rather well, and all contain excellent moments of music. Still, there is too much pedantic talk at the expense of music (these were half-hour shows), and a general aura that reveals why the term "educational television" fell into disuse as the years went by. But this was an important show in the respect it showed for the music, and in the mere fact that it acknowledged jazz as a proper "educational" subject.

Jazz Party was not educational in tone or intent. It did not have the brilliant camera work of Herridge's shows. But it had a wholly appealing and effective looseness and informality, and the services of some of the greatest jazz players in the world. Art Ford, already a veteran disc jockey with a fine track record in jazz (for example, his WNEW *Saturday Night Swing Session*, a live radio program), was friendly with many musicians and able to obtain their services, sometimes at very short notice. There was a sort of house band, which often included vibraharpist Harry Sheppard, guitarist Mundell Lowe, pianist Marty Napoleon, and bassist Vinnie Burke. Guests seen with some regularity were pianist Willie "The Lion" Smith, trumpeter Charlie Shavers, and saxophonist Georgie Auld, but it was the special guests that sparked the shows (Shavers aside, for he was a TV natural and always a spark plug). Among these were players seldom seen in those days, like violinist Stuff Smith, drummer Sonny Greer, and trumpeter Cootie Williams. Pee Wee Russell was on hand at times, as was Coleman Hawkins. On one memorable show, Hawkins and Lester Young played together. Buck Clayton was also a frequent guest.

Obviously, the focus of the show was on swinging mainstream jazz, though a few boppers and traditionalists dropped in from time to time. I was an avid watcher of this show and have many fond memories of it, reinforced by viewing surviving kinescopes and hearing bootlegged audio portions; it was, by the way, one of the very first TV programs to be simulcast in FM stereo. Its keynote was informality; station breaks and commercials sometimes were delayed in the heat of the improvised happenings, and Ford never panicked when the musicians took their time deciding what the next number should be. His was a relaxed and unflappable presence, and he had almost as much fun as the players did.

There were times when things didn't quite jell, but that didn't matter, because when they did, the sparks would fly, as in a trumpet duel between Shavers and Clayton on "This Can't Be Love," or an "Air Mail Special" with Cootie Williams in savage form. Or, for an entirely different mood, Billie Holiday, voice worn, body emaciated, yet managing to create music of searing power. Roy Eldridge, Dinah Washington, Big Joe Turner, and Benny Goodman also appeared on this delightful program, which even made a trek to New Orleans, but faded when the station changed hands.

Ford attempted to sell his concept to NBC, but they wanted scripting and rehearsals, and it's perhaps just as well that they didn't manage to straitjacket it. A show like this possibly could not be done today—the pool of musicians who can play well together informally is dwindling. Still, it would be worth trying. *Jazz Party* captured something of the essential spirit of the music and proved that jazz on television works very well without planning every note and camera angle, or forever relying on organized groups to perform.

It was not only in New York that local programming drew on the resources of jazz in the '50s. Boston, then a good town for the music, had several programs of excellence, among them WBZ's *From Storyville*, which presented artists, often big names, who performed at the famous nightclub operated by George Wein of Newport Jazz Festival fame. WGBH had *John McLellan's Jazz Scene*, hosted by the columnist and disc jockey and featuring intelligent interviews with major musicians, and (in 1958) *Jazz Meets the Classics*, hosted by Fr. Norman O'Connor, the "Jazz Priest," and for a while distributed on WNET.

In Los Angeles, pianist-singer-songwriter Bobby Troup produced and hosted *Stars of Jazz* with considerable success, so much so that ABC picked it up for network dissemination. As so often happens, and with all kinds of shows, *Stars of Jazz* did not long survive transplantation into the big time, though it was a tightly produced little show, with the emphasis on singers and what was then called "West Coast jazz." The program did enjoy a very respectable run, from July 1956 to December 1958, the last few months on network.

A notable "special" of the decade was *A Drum Is a Woman*, a 1957 Duke Ellington concoction presenting a fanciful, mythical interpretation of the origin and history of jazz. It utilized the incomparable Ellington orchestra, a spoken narration by the leader, and a troupe of dancers featuring Carmen De Lavallade and Tally Beatty—and, if memory serves, some rather dreadful decor. Not well received by jazz fans, who wanted to hear more from the soloists and were not bowled over by the narration and the dancing, it was a chapter, and an interesting one, in Ellington's imaginative but ultimately unsuccessful attempts to create a theatrically viable music drama.

Another famous bandleader, Benny Goodman, was featured in a well-promoted 1958 special, *Swing into Spring*, sponsored by Texaco. With guest instrumentalists Teddy Wilson and Red Norvo, guest singing stars Ella Fitzgerald, Peggy Lee, and Jo Stafford, and a spin-off LP for Columbia, the show was not as successful as its sponsor no doubt anticipated, perhaps because the band, put together for the occasion, could not compare to the glories of past Goodman units. By all accounts, the medley performed by the three ladies was the highlight of a show that somehow failed to ignite.

It is of passing interest to note that CBS's *Camera Three*, a Sunday morning experimental show (then as now, culture and prime time seldom met), presented a dramatization of the life of Charlie Parker, with musician Tony Scott as one of the speakers—there was no acting as such. (This series also presented *Accent on Jazz*, a conversation between André Previn and poet John Ciardi.) Parker himself made his only known TV appearance on a daytime variety show produced by the Du Mont Network, *Stars on Broadway*, from which a kinescope survives. It is the only audiovisual documentation of one of the greatest musicians in jazz history.

Television was most effective, however, in making a star of the modestly gifted New Orleans clarinetist Pete Fountain, featured on *The Lawrence Welk Show* from 1957 to 1959. Often the butt of jokes among jazz people, Welk's show is one of the biggest success stories in the history of music on television, and he faithfully featured Dixieland jazz on his show. One of Fountain's successors was Peanuts Hucko, who didn't cash in from the exposure. Also in Welk's band were jazz trumpeter George Thow, a Dorsey Brothers alumnus, and the excellent trombonist Bob Havens.

One cannot take leave of the '50s without mentioning the most prominent use of jazz on TV during the decade—as underscoring for various successful crime series. These included *Peter Gunn*, *M-Squad*, *Richard Diamond*, *The Lawyers*, *Pete Kelly's Blues*, and *Bourbon Street Beat*, the latter two the only ones in which jazz musicians were also seen on screen. Composer-arrangers for these epics included Henry Mancini, Benny Carter, André Previn, Elmer Bernstein, Johnny Mandel, and Pete Rugolo. Endless debates in the jazz press pondered whether the linking of jazz music and crime would prove harmful to the jazz image. Much of the music was excellent, and no permanent damage to jazz seems to have resulted.

During the '50s, many key decision makers in the television industry, and many of the medium's most prominent performers, were of a generation whose taste had been shaped during the '30s, when jazz was a popular musical form. Big bands meant something quite tangible to this generation, and early in the decade it was possible to mount a series, *America's Greatest Bands*, hosted by none other than Paul Whiteman. It is no coincidence that most of the jazz we have surveyed thus far was of a kind that would appeal to this generation, on both sides of the screen.

Things changed in the '60s, but only gradually as far as jazz on TV is concerned. The rise of public television created more opportunities for jazz exposure, with less emphasis on swing-era veterans and big names. Local stations could produce low-budget jazz series that lent themselves to nationwide distribution. One of the first and best of these was San Francisco's *Jazz Casual*, produced and hosted by critic-columnist Ralph Gleason, who among other things was able to persuade John Coltrane to make a rare TV appearance on his show with his famous quartet. However, Coltrane declined to be interviewed. (Gleason was a very visible host, and an interview with the featured performer was built into the show's format.)

In 1967, Gleason was instrumental in the production for PBS of a first-rate Ellington documentary, *Love You Madly*. In addition to the customary performance sequences, it captured Ellington on the road, at rehearsal, composing in a hotel room late at night, and performing his *Sacred Concert* at San Francisco's Grace Cathedral. It was a rare instance of presenting a jazz figure on TV as something more than just a performing artist.

Ellington generally fared well on TV from the '60s on. A frequent guest, with or without his band, on major shows, he was also the subject of a well-made *Bell Telephone Hour* special that included nonperformance elements and focused on his global touring. In 1969, Ellington's seventieth birthday was celebrated with a party at the White House, and this received considerable media coverage, including a United States Information Service featurette. Near the end of his life (he died in 1974), Ellington participated in a tribute produced by Quincy Jones that had rather little to do with the core of his music, but showed the respect in which he was held by contemporary black performers. In a sense, it was a preview of things to come, such as a 1982 "tribute" that was remarkable for not containing a single note of anything resembling authentic Ellington music, in which it wasn't so different from the Broadway hit musical *Sophisticated Ladies*. Fortunately, Ellington's many preserved film and TV appearances ensure that an accurate visual record of his legacy will be available to posterity.

Public television also utilized the new phenomenon of the jazz festival as a vehicle for programming. In 1967, the Monterey Jazz Festival yielded three performance shows and a fourth, the most interesting by far, devoted to rehearsals, backstage ambience, and interviews. Surprisingly, the Newport Jazz Festival, though giving birth to a successful film (*Jazz on a Summer's Day*, 1958), was not often used for TV purposes, except by the Providence, Rhode Island, public station, which sometimes taped afternoon "workshop" events and bits and pieces of evening concerts. George Wein, the festival's producer, was himself responsible for the production of a lengthy documentary of the 1970 tribute to Louis Armstrong, but this was conceived and executed as a film project, though portions from it were later used on TV. One such instance, and a memorable one, was the two-hour special *Satchmo!* produced by WNET in 1979, which employed no narration but used interview footage with Armstrong made for the Wein project to link the varied performance segments most effectively.

The often controversial Charles Mingus joined forces with choreographer Elio Pomare for a 1966 PBS special, *Blues from the Ghetto*, in which the dramatic and even theatrical dimensions of his music were tellingly wedded to dance. The same year brought a rather peculiar tribute to the Harlem of the 1920s, in which Ellington was the sole performer who had been active in that decade. Otherwise, *The Strollin' Twenties* had a script by Langston Hughes, some singing by Joe Williams, and was co-hosted by its producer, Harry Belafonte, and Sidney Poitier.

Commercial TV was by no means a wasteland for jazz. With much hoopla and early use of color, NBC assembled the 1961 special *Chicago and All That Jazz*, an honest but flawed attempt to present accurate jazz history in an entertaining manner. A truly impressive array of veteran performers was brought together. While a re-creation of the Original Dixieland Jazz Band relied entirely on competent studio musicians, with ancient vaudevillian Blossom Seely added for the second number, a very plausible New Orleans group was entrusted with the music of King Oliver and Jelly Roll Morton. It consisted of trumpeter Red Allen, trombonist Kid Ory, clarinetist Buster Bailey, pianist Lil Hardin Armstrong, guitarist Johnny St. Cyr, bassist Milt Hinton, and drummer Zutty Singleton—all but Hinton had worked with Oliver and Morton. A Chicago-style group also bore the

stamp of authenticity. It reunited trumpeter Jimmy McPartland, tenor saxophonist Bud Freeman, pianist Joe Sullivan, and Eddie Condon and Gene
Krupa, who all had recorded together in 1927, and added such early associates as clarinetist Pee Wee Russell (whose craggy face and bemused expression made him a TV natural) and trombonist Jack Teagarden, with bassist
Bob Haggart the sole ringer.

The program also made use of archival film footage, some of it quite rare,
such as a silent glimpse of Bix Beiderbecke, and clips of Louis Armstrong
and singers Bessie and Mamie Smith. One effective moment was the transition from boogie-woogie pianist Meade Lux Lewis on film to his "live" presence in the studio. But there were problems. Some of the older performers
simply were no longer playing well. Singers and dancers distracted from the
music, though a jitterbug turn by the former kings of Harlem's Savoy Ballroom, Al Minns and Leon James, was delightful—if incongruously matched
to the strains of "Fidgety Feet," a Dixieland number. The old tendency to
cram too many numbers and too many performers into one show raised its
head, and Gene Krupa, much against his wishes, was overexposed during
the interminable finale. But flaws and all, this was at least an attempt to take
jazz history seriously, and the production was first-class.

NBC's *The Ragtime Years* was also lavishly produced, and preceded the
revival of serious and popular interest in this musical style. It marked the
first major TV appearance of Eubie Blake, who became more famous
the longer he lived (well into his nineties, he charmed Johnny Carson et al.
as a frequent guest). The talents of pianists Ralph Sutton and Dick Wellstood were employed, and Hoagy Carmichael was a knowledgeable if loquacious host. On public TV, the special gifts of historian-performer Max
Morath were well showcased in the 1960 *The Ragtime Era*. A mixture of history and nostalgia informed a segment of *David Brinkley's Journal* titled *The
Decline of Dixieland*.

On CBS, the problem of too much talent crammed into too little time
cropped up on a 1963 installment of *The International Hour* called *American
Jazz*. It featured the Count Basie band, Stan Getz with large ensemble and
small group, Jack Teagarden, Teddy Wilson, the then little-known Muddy
Waters and his blues band, singers Carmen McRae and Lurlean Hunter,
and the popular vocal group Lambert, Hendricks & Ross. Less crowded
and thus more effective was a special edition of Dinah Shore's show aired
late in 1963, with Frank Sinatra, gospel singer Bessie Griffin, and a stellar
jazz group made up of saxophonists Ben Webster and Gerry Mulligan, pianist Jimmy Rowles, bassist Leroy Vinnegar and drummer Mel Lewis.
(Miss Shore offered free copies of this show to the United States Information Service for overseas use.)

Sinatra was the cornerstone of the excellent 1967 *A Man and His Music
Plus Ella Plus Jobim*. If not strictly speaking a jazz show, it offered superb

work by the principals, with Sinatra at his most tasteful and relaxed. Miss Fitzgerald (one of the most frequently seen jazz attractions on TV) was seldom if ever better presented than here, especially in a duet sequence with Sinatra. Low-keyed, relying entirely on the best in American popular song, and with strong support from uncredited but first-rate studio jazz players, this show was an example of music on TV at its rare best.

Another essentially non-jazz show nevertheless worth mentioning is the 1960 *An Evening with Fred Astaire*, in which, at the star's specific request, jazz trumpeter and singer Jonah Jones was well featured, and Astaire showed his jazz roots, both as a dancer and singer. Benny Goodman, still a drawing card, was featured on a special segment of *The Bell Telephone Hour*, in performance at the 1967 Comblain de la Tour Jazz Festival in Belgium.

Jazz also cropped up in unexpected places. On *Captain Kangaroo*, an entire week in 1960 was devoted to explaining and exposing jazz, and also in the kiddie sector, jazz bassist (and natural comedian) Chubby Jackson hosted *The Little Rascals*. This show enjoyed some success, and on one segment of it the host managed to lead an eighteen-piece bebop band. Jackson's erstwhile Woody Herman Herd associate, Terry Gibbs, was musical director of the short-lived ABC series *Operation Entertainment*; his good friend Steve Allen produced the 1963 *Jazz Scene U.S.A.*

It was Allen who had first introduced jazz into the special TV mixture that he pioneered on *Tonight*. By the mid-'60s, all the shows spawned by this program featured house bands with a heavy jazz contingent. While seldom featured on their own, these bands provided first-class support for musical guests and entertained studio audiences during warmings and commercial breaks. A host of well-known jazz musicians made a good living from such work for many years, but in 1985, the sole surviving remnant is the band on Johnny Carson's *Tonight Show*. Carson, a jazz fan, not infrequently features jazz guests, and his regulars include Buddy Rich, Clark Terry (an alumnus of the show's band), Dizzy Gillespie, and Pete Fountain, as well as many singers. Aside from Rich, they play but are not allowed to talk. For a brief while in the early '80s, Carson featured cameo appearances by members of the band, and thus one got to see veteran trumpeter Snooky Young, drummer Ed Shaughnessy, and saxophonists Ernie Watts and Pete Christlieb as welcome and unexpected bonuses between the jokes and gossip. More recently, the young trumpeter Wynton Marsalis has appeared on Carson, but one of the major jazz moments in the show's history came when substitute host Bill Cosby gave Sonny Rollins the chance to present an unaccompanied, purely improvised, and stunning tenor saxophone solo—surely a first on commercial network TV.

Even more unlikely, but much less successful from any standpoint, was the appearance, on *The Ed Sullivan Show* in its waning years, of a group of self-styled spokesmen for the cause of jazz on television, organized into a group called the Jazz and People's Movement. They achieved this visibility after disrupting a rehearsal of the Merv Griffin show, elbowing their way onto Dick Cavett's program (where they talked rather than played; the discussants included Freddie Hubbard and Cecil Taylor), and picketing the networks. Their Sullivan spot was one of the most bizarre moments in the history of jazz on TV. An obviously ill-at-ease Sullivan introduced the group (it had the final slot on the program), which included Charles Mingus, Archie Shepp, and Rahsaan Roland Kirk, the astonishing blind multi-instrumentalist who, under better circumstances, could have been a tremendously effective TV performer. As it turned out, the ad hoc group's single number, which showed no signs of having been rehearsed, was a musical and visual shambles, perplexing even seasoned jazz listeners and viewers. An opportunity to strike a blow for the cause of jazz on commercial TV dissolved into hot air.

Diametrically opposed to such absurd posturing was the dignified and moving use of jazz in commemoration of Robert Kennedy. It came on the day after television had achieved one of its finest moments in covering the agonizing journey of the train that carried the assassinated senator's body to Arlington, and was the brainchild of WCBS-TV program director Ned Cramer, who realized that jazz would be the most appropriate musical language for a tribute to a great American statesman and public figure. He enlisted the aid of Ethel Burns and Ralph Curtis, producer and director of the station's Saturday afternoon program *Dial M for Music*, and its host, Fr. Norman O'Connor (this was an excellent show in its own right).

On short notice, this team put together a superb two-and-a-half-hour program (one of the longest jazz shows ever seen on TV) called *A Contemporary Tribute*. Interlaced with literary quotations ranging from Aeschylus to Dylan Thomas, an array of musicians and singers performed with unflagging inspiration. The show began and ended with Joe Williams singing Duke Ellington's "Come Sunday." Other performers included the Modern Jazz Quartet, alone and accompanied by the CBS Orchestra; the Thad Jones–Mel Lewis orchestra; Horace Silver's quintet; the Woody Herman band; pianist Bill Evans with his trio, in solo, and accompanied by the studio orchestra; Johnny Hodges accompanied by Duke Ellington and bassist Jeff Castleman in "Passion Flower"; and singers Felicia Sanders and Amanda Ambrose. I do not know if a tape of this marvelous show survives.

By the 1970s, the presentation of jazz on television settled into familiar patterns. The bulk of TV jazz was produced for public stations and consisted of performances by organized groups taped before audiences, either in nightclubs or at festivals, or in the studio in simulated club settings. These series, usually of thirteen programs, might emanate from almost anywhere, including such off the beaten path locales as Rochester, New

York, or Minneapolis. The quality of the music was generally good, with performers drawn from the front ranks of jazz. The quality of the productions was variable, ranging from reasonably inventive visual work and good audio to dull and static images accompanied by poor sound. Sometimes, brief on-camera interviews with the leading performer might be included, but mostly the fare was unadorned musical performance, with minimal introductions by a host—usually a local disc jockey.

One of the better of these series, which won a local Emmy but never was picked up by PBS, was Chicago's *Jazz Alley*, hosted by pianist Art Hodes, an engaging talker as well as a fine player. It focused on traditional small-group jazz, featured such guests as Eddie Condon, Pee Wee Russell, and Bud Freeman, and was set in a realistically simulated club, complete with bar and bartender. It was produced and directed by Robert Kaiser, who also directed and co-produced (with this writer) the 1970 PBS series *Just Jazz*, which included the only known TV appearance of tenor saxophonist Gene Ammons, the only U.S. TV appearance of his expatriate fellow tenorist Don Byas, and the last appearance of Coleman Hawkins, taped just weeks before his death in 1969 and aired in a memorial setting.

Kaiser later directed the black music series *From Jumpstreet*, conceived by Charles Hobson and hosted by singer Oscar Brown, Jr. Designed as a "telecourse," it also functioned as straight entertainment with an educational component. Several of the programs focused on jazz, with performers including Dizzy Gillespie, James Moody, Jackie McLean, the Tuxedo Jazz Band from New Orleans, Roy Eldridge in what turned out to be his final TV appearances (he was seen in two shows) as a trumpeter (he suffered a heart attack in 1980, which precluded further playing), and singer Carmen McRae. Here, the musicians had a welcome opportunity to talk (something many if not most jazz artists do very well), but the performances were often average rather than inspired.

Several nostalgia specials were produced for PBS by its New York station, WNET. These mainly featured singers (some of them well beyond their best years, others still excellent) associated with the '30s, '40s, and '50s. One, a big-band special, was sadly lacking in jazz content and leadenly produced and directed; but all these shows have become proven fund-raising devices for public stations.

A major achievement by public television was the two-part, three-hour tribute to legendary talent spotter and veteran record producer John Hammond, produced by Chicago's WTTW and directed by Ken Erlich (who also was responsible for other jazz and blues programs of high quality before making the move to commercial TV, where he has directed several Grammy Awards shows). The Hammond special brought together an impressive array of performers ranging from Benny Goodman and Benny

Carter to George Benson and Bob Dylan, and was a consistently interesting and intelligently paced and presented program, mixing talk and music well.

When PBS, in collaboration with the National Endowment for the Arts' media program, sought advice from a large and representative sector of the jazz community for an ambitious and well-funded project to produce a truly innovative and state-of-the-art series of jazz programs, a lot of interesting ideas were expressed. The decision to open bidding from various PBS member stations for the plum may have been democratic, but the end result was less than the big talk and big dollars led one to expect.

A joint proposal from two powerful stations, New York's WNET and Los Angeles's KCET, was eventually underwritten. What emerged after prolonged labor was a four-part series, *Jazz in America*, in essentially the same old live performance format, with bits of talk and backstage ambience mixed in. Its centerpiece was *Dizzy Gillespie's Dream Band*, taped during two concerts at New York's Avery Fisher Hall. It had its moments—inevitably, considering the artists on hand—but suffered from uneven sound, routine cinematography, and less than brilliant editing. In the end, it was Gillespie's warm and vibrant personality and inspired playing that held it together. The series' three other programs presented club performances by Gillespie and two of his Dream Band guests, Max Roach and Gerry Mulligan, with no innovation in evidence.

The initially much-hailed advent of cable TV has thus far failed to make much of a difference in jazz programming, but its existence as yet another outlet for shows of less than mass appeal holds promise for the future. The ill-fated CBS Cable was planning a major jazz series when it went under; what it did produce in the field was a more than usually inept Count Basie concert show, with some historical film footage and interview material inserted, and a considerably livelier feature on singer Betty Carter (also the subject of a good independent production, thus far without takers).

ABC's Arts and Entertainment Network occasionally features jazz, and recently presented a good profile of trumpeter Wynton Marsalis, also a more than accomplished classical musician. Among independent productions seen on cable is the series *Women in Jazz*, a combination of film clips and live performances hosted by Carmen McRae and Marian McPartland and produced and directed by Burrill Crohn, who is co-producing, with film collector and historian David Chertok, a forthcoming series on the history of jazz for the videocassette market; an excellent profile of guitarist Tal Farlow, produced and directed by Lorenzo Di Stefano; and an intriguing documentary about the up-and-down life of pianist Joe Albany.

We have yet to discuss the treatment of jazz on TV outside the United States. Needless to say, jazz has long enjoyed great acceptance in many

European countries and in Japan, as well as in other parts of the globe. It is impossible here to even begin to scratch the surface of what represents a vast output of programs, but a few points can be made and a few shows cited.

European television is by and large a government-supported enterprise, and the commercial considerations that rule the U.S. roost are thus eliminated. Almost from the start, jazz has been part and parcel of Western European TV programming, and many countries have supported permanent staff jazz ensembles, and annual festivals and workshops, sometimes over periods of many years—even decades.

What I have seen of European TV programs has generally been excellent both in content and execution. Danish television produced a first-rate documentary on the great tenor saxophonist Dexter Gordon while he was a resident of Copenhagen. It integrates performance, interview material, and glimpses of Gordon as instructor at a summer jazz camp and bicycle-riding citizen of Copenhagen. The Danes also did a heartfelt profile of another great expatriate tenor player, Ben Webster, and sent a team to the U.S. to produce a series on jazz in America, which I have not had the opportunity to see. Quite recently, Miles Davis was seen on Danish TV, performing a specially commissioned work by Palle Mikkelborg on the occasion of receiving a coveted Danish music prize, which Davis was the first jazz figure to receive.

Holland is another small country with a long and honorable tradition of jazz programming that includes the sponsorship of an annual jazz festival in Laaren. The Dutch also profiled Ben Webster, who lived in Amsterdam for some years before making the move to Copenhagen, and produced a major documentary on Don Byas, a resident of Europe since 1946, climaxing in his first return visit to his homeland in 1970 and his appearance at the Newport Jazz Festival.

West Germany, with its several networks, has produced much in the way of jazz and has been particularly hospitable to the avant-garde. Among the many German producers involved in jazz, one might cite the late Hans Betberg, whose annual *Jazz Workshop* for NDR resulted in some truly imaginative and original music-making, and Joachim Berendt, a leading jazz writer responsible for many televised jazz summit meetings and encounters between American, European, and Third World musicians. A German TV crew came to the United States in the mid-'60s to film a magnificent documentary on Thelonious Monk, managing to capture many human and artistic facets of this elusive and mystifying genius. Many hours were shot in the production of this one-hour special, and this invaluable footage is now in the hands of an experienced and responsible U.S. production team direly in need of funding to preserve and re-edit the decaying materials.

A non-BBC British production widely seen in the U.S. on public TV during 1980 was the fifteen-episode history of American popular music named after director Tony Palmer's book, *All You Need Is Love*. While it contained much of jazz interest, including interviews and newly taped as well as archival performances, it proved that the title's sentiment is not enough. Confusing transitions, irritating lack of identification of people prominently seen and heard on screen, and the ambition to bite off more than such a program can reasonably be expected to chew or digest, made viewing *All You Need Is Love* an often frustrating experience, though its interview footage in particular should prove useful for future cannibalization.

Thelonious Monk was also intelligently presented on French TV, and that country, with its long tradition of intense interest in jazz, has also produced much of value. In France, as elsewhere in Europe, a real problem is archival protection and preservation. Much invaluable jazz footage has been irretrievably lost as shows were "wiped" for the reuse of videotape, mandated by limited funding.

In Britain, the BBC does not produce sufficient jazz to satisfy the local aficionados, but from an American standpoint, a great deal has been accomplished. In 1968, the BBC presented the Louis Armstrong All Stars in concert with sympathy, imagination, and first-rate sound, to cite one among many achievements. Quite recently, a fascinating Billie Holiday documentary, *The Long Night of Lady Day*, co-produced for BBC and his own TBC Releases by filmmaker John Jeremy, was seen in the United States on the Bravo cable pay service, which also produces a U.S. program, *Jazz Counterpoint*, hosted by Billy Taylor.

I have not seen more than mere glimpses of Japanese TV jazz productions, but it can be assumed that the high standards of excellence so characteristic of that country's approach to the presentation and recording of jazz hold true for TV as well. Presumably, the Japanese also pay more attention to preservation than other countries, so it is likely that a treasure trove of TV jazz materials exists there, so far untapped by outsiders.

The proliferation of new technologies and outlets affecting the medium of television, not least the proliferation of VCRs, is bound to have an impact on its relationship to jazz. If nothing else, increased production of minority-interest programming seems assured.

Quantity of production and reasonable marketability being givens, it now behooves those involved in the creation of jazz materials for the TV medium to attend to quality. Routine presentations of performances are of value for their documentation of gifted performers, but that tends to be all. While creative imagination is sometimes confused with trickery or superficial effects, it only takes one look at *The Sound of Jazz* to understand what the word "quality" really means, and how seldom it is applicable to jazz as seen on TV.

While it might be fun (and good for the music's popularity) to see some jazz MTVs, this approach is not what is needed for jazz to assume its rightful place in the audiovisual world. What is needed are respect, sensitivity, creative handling of the medium's potentials, and, above all, faith in the inherent ability of gifted jazz performers to communicate with an audience. It is that faith, readily enforced by witnessing what these artists do on any given night, that has been responsible for the best of jazz on television and will ensure more to come—with or without commercial breaks.

(1985)

As it turned out, cable TV has not been much of a boon to jazz. BET held promise but turned out mostly reruns and promotional stuff generated by record companies, though there've been such good things as the Jacksonville Jazz Festival shows (the annual event was produced by a local TV station). In 1989, a cable show, *Jazz Vision*, hosted by Ben Sidran, presented Geri Allen, Carla Bley, Sun Ra, and the World Saxophone Quartet, among others. The Knowledge channel gave us a mixed but interesting 1998 bag in *World Jazz*.

But one of the best jazz shows was a network one, NBC's *Night Music* (1989–90), hosted by saxophonist David Sanborn. It presented a true cross section of the music, from Slim Gaillard to Sonny Rollins to John Zorn. PBS's *American Masters* series has included much jazz, most of it later available on home video: Louis Armstrong ("Satchmo," a spin-off from Gary Giddins's book), Charlie Parker (ditto), Benny Goodman, Miles Davis, and Sarah Vaughan, among others. And my piece failed to mention the excellent, Iowa-originated PBS series, *Jazz from the Maintenance Shop*, which ran intermittently from 1979 through the middle of the next decade and presented, in a nightclub-like setting, Bill Evans, Dexter Gordon, Phil Woods, and other notables, and BBC's *Jazz 625*, a mid-'60s series that became available on home video some thirty years later—including some great Erroll Garner.

Much that is mentioned in the postscript to "Jazz on Film" was sooner or later seen on TV, but by far the most significant made-for-television jazz production of recent times was Ken Burns's monumental *Jazz*, an eighteen-hour-long history of the music, first shown on PBS in 2001. Some six years in the making, the series generated an unprecedented amount of media attention for jazz and also spawned a surprisingly successful series of CDs. In the manner of his *Baseball*, Burns presented the jazz story against a backdrop of American history, with an emphasis on race relations. His heroes were Louis Armstrong and Duke Ellington.

Characteristically, reaction in jazz circles to Burns's epic was embarrassingly myopic. Writers and fans complained about the absence of personal favorites, too little attention paid to the music of recent times, and other provincial concerns. To be sure, and as one would expect in a work of such scope and length, *Jazz* had its weak spots, but its narrative strengths and the respect and dignity it accorded its subject far outweighed the negatives. (Disclaimer: I was a consultant to *Jazz*.)

Jazz soon became available on the home market, both in traditional videotape and in the new DVD format, which established itself even quicker than the CD. Even before its advent, an astonishing amount of jazz material, historical and contemporary, had become available for home consumption. While television—network, public, and cable—continues to neglect jazz, one can now readily stage one's own jazz festivals at home.

A final note: Not long after television had established itself as a medium, the early demise of radio was predicted. Nothing of the sort, of course, has happened, and while jazz on the airwaves has had its ups and downs, one must mention the extraordinary longevity of Marian McPartland's *Piano Jazz*, a weekly program syndicated by National Public Radio that first aired in 1979. The charm and musical acumen of the hostess and the astonishing array of guests, encompassing the spectrum of pianists but also including arrangers, composers, singers, and players of other instruments, combine to make this show a model for intelligent presentation of jazz.

Not by Choice

Like New Orleans in the old days, New York has its share of part-time musicians. The difference, though, is that the New Yorkers are not semi-pros by choice. It is necessity and the weirdness of the music business in the United States that causes Manzie Johnson, Louis Bacon, and Bennie Green to drive cabs, and Happy Cauldwell to work for the Civil Service and Walter Johnson for the Post Office. "I never had two bank accounts as a musician. In fact I never had one. My family is eating, and I'm not complaining," said Manzie Johnson, sitting in his cab outside the Metropole. He told us that he was to play a gig with Happy Cauldwell at Small's Paradise on a Sunday in early May, and we kept that in mind.

The occasion was a fashion show and dance, from 5 to 9 p.m. Small's has a large bar in front, with a cozy bandstand, and generally features small and swinging combos. Chris Columbus played a week there recently. In the back there is a large, pleasantly lighted and well-decorated club, with a good-sized dance floor and a bandstand that can accommodate a full band. There are some early Picassos on the wall—the only decor of its kind we have ever observed in a jazz club.

The band was playing to a well-dressed crowd, not just because it was a fashion show. Harlem is perhaps the only part of Manhattan where Sunday is still a day unlike all others. Many people here work a six-day week, and more go to church. The band Happy Cauldwell had assembled consisted of himself on tenor sax. Manzie on drums, Eddie Williams on alto, Archie Johnson on trumpet, and Lou Taylor at the piano. They played a waltz or two and a few cha-cha-chas and answered a request for "Tequila," a rhythm-and-blues number. They played behind the fashion show, ballad medley–style, soft and pretty. But there was plenty of room for swinging out.

Happy Cauldwell, a small man, gray-haired and distinguished, has not recorded since 1940. Prior to that, his output was sporadic and never gave him much room. To many jazz fans, he is a name on a Louis Armstrong record; to historians, an early follower of Coleman Hawkins. But many musicians who heard him then, including Coleman himself, insist that he played that way independently of Hawk, and the man we heard that afternoon was certainly no imitator. Perhaps to prove it, Happy played "Body and Soul" as his only feature, and played it quite his own way. The tone is reminiscent of middle-period Hawkins, if with a rougher edge, and the structure of his improvisations rhapsodic. But there comparisons must end. Happy has his own story to tell, and it merits wider hearing.

Manzie Johnson's drums made us forget there was no bass and made us realize how few drummers today have a thoroughly educated foot. Here was a beat one could feel, a drummer who found just the right thing to do for each soloist and knew how to swing a band at any tempo. Eddie Williams has a pure Carter-like tone and reminds of Tab Smith, with traces of the Bird. (Is there any altoist who has not absorbed a bit of Parker?) Lou Taylor comped well and played pleasantly melodic solos with a Garner hue. But it was the trumpet, Archie Johnson, who was the unexpected discovery. With a big, full tone and excellent range, Archie gave punch to the ensembles and built climactic endings on the jumpers. Louis and Roy are reflected in his playing, and no wonder. They are his favorites. But when we asked about Lips Page, whose memory he had elicited, Archie became eloquent. When Lips felt right, he said, every trumpet player in the house had better watch out, "including *everybody*."

The musicians all apologized for their poor form, as they called it, and would not accept praise. Manzie hinted he might give up playing. "It's too cruel," he said. "You manage to forget how much you love to play, and then you get a gig and begin to get that old feeling back, doing what you want to do and know you can do well, and then it's all over. In a good year, you get maybe twenty-five gigs." This year, there had been only half a dozen so far. "It's too cruel, man. It's better not to play at all." The others agree, but we know that they'll go on. They still dance in New York, and for dancing you need music with a beat. Archie wanted to know why the government doesn't subsidize jazz. "Other countries support their native art forms," he said. And he wondered why a band like Duke Ellington's ("That band has more stories to tell than any other band in the world") has to stay on the road playing one-nighters, three-quarters of its library lying fallow. There was no note of complaint in any of this, just anger and puzzlement. Why isn't there room for a man to do what he loves to do, giving others the benefit of his talent?

(1958)

Cats and Categories

Almost twenty years ago, the co-editors of the *Jazz Record Book*, Messrs. Smith, Ramsey, Rogers, and Russell, made a pungent critical observation. "You can't," they said, "put cats into categories." Nobody paid much heed to this maxim. Yet, during the past six weeks, its wisdom has repeatedly impressed itself upon us.

Consider Coleman Hawkins. Since leaving the Metropole, Hawk has played at the Sutherland in Chicago, a room generally reserved for "modern" names. Here the ageless master found himself in the company of the Three Sounds, a group of young musicians, and was pleased, especially with the pianist, Gene Harris. Some weeks later, Coleman had a weekend gig in Pennsylvania and brought along trumpeter Booker Little, recently with Max Roach, bassist Paul Chambers, and drummer J. C. Heard. A Monday night in New York found him at the Five Spot, where United Artists' enterprising jazz A&R man, Tom Wilson, was recording an album on location. The assembled group, led by Randy Weston, contained the aforementioned Paul Chambers, drummer Roy Haynes, and trumpeter Kenny Dorham. (Singer Brock Peters of *Porgy and Bess* fame was a perhaps expendable addition for one number.) To watch Coleman Hawkins at work in this outpost of modernism was a joy. There was, for one thing, the authority with which he handled his music and horn, which matched the authority of his sound. This was a combination rehearsal, recording date, and public performance—no easy task. There were some arrangements by Randy and one by Billy Strayhorn. The climate was melodic. There was a waltz, of course: Randy is sometimes affectionately referred to as "the waltz king of modern jazz." It swung, and was pretty. The rapport between Hawk and Randy was perfect, and it was good to see Randy's face, which reflects his moods while he plays, light up when Hawk came up with one of those things he unfolds when he has the chords set in his mind.

Hawk had arrived in New York on Monday morning by plane from Chicago, hadn't slept, and hadn't put away a good meal since then. Yet he was relaxed and glowing. On the bandstand, he appeared intent on the business at hand, yet completely at ease, the horn a natural extension of his mind and body. In contrast, Dorham, a tall, well-built young man who once boxed in the Golden Gloves, seemed to be a little in awe of his trumpet. He handled it gingerly, a little cautiously, as if it were a strange chick. And the music he produced was pale contrasted with that of Coleman Hawkins. If Hawk could be termed the father of this assembly, he was also its most youthful member; in the strength and virility of his playing, the freshness of his ideas, and the conviction of their presentation. That is not meant to imply that the others were slouches, far from it. And while Hawkins's contribution stood out, it was also a homogeneous part of the whole. In other words, it was jazz.

The categorizers, the ones who are in constant search for the latest, have a new hero. His name is Ornette Coleman, a twenty-nine-year-old Texan whose proving ground was California. Coleman, his close associate Don Cherry, and his rhythm team, Charlie Haden on bass and Billy Higgins on drums, made their New York debut at the Five Spot in mid-November. Well publicized by the jazz media (*Jazz Review* has practically sanctified him; *Down Beat*, with great caution, confined itself to a page of photographs), the Colemans had a capacity house to welcome them, including several noted critics. One of their new LPs is called *The Shape of Jazz to Come*, with disarming modesty. All this did not dispose this listener to jump for joy, but he was pleasantly surprised.

Whatever else Ornette Coleman may be, one cannot doubt the sincerity of his music. It is fiercely individualistic, and makes no concessions to conventions, not even to those of modern jazz. His tone—he is quoted as striving for a *vox humana* quality—is strident but not unpleasant. It is, pardon the expression, hot. That he takes his cue from Charlie Parker is unquestionable—but this is no imitator. Coleman's cohorts are obviously in full sympathy with his aims, and the unison work between his alto and Don Cherry's miniature cornet (we have been told it was made in Pakistan and is one of four such instruments extant) is thrilling because it sounds so free, yet obviously requires the greatest discipline. Both bass and drums support the horns well, albeit in the "free" style of post-bop jazz. The boys are serious, but not in the professional (and vastly annoying) manner of Miles Davis. There are occasional smiles. And—what do you know?—at the end of the set Ornette Coleman makes an announcement in traditional style: "Thank you, ladies and gentlemen—and now we present the great Benny Golson–Art Farmer Jazztet—let's bring them on with a big hand." One is not used to this at the Five Spot, and can only hope that blasé Manhattan will not destroy this heartening lack of sophistication.

All this having been said, there is serious doubt that this music represents "the shape" of jazz to come. Coleman's approach borders on free improvisation, and there is a very good reason why this style of playing has almost always been confined to musical exercises, primarily among would-be virtuosos. It is too unfocused to engender anything but monotony and eventual boredom. The Coleman-Cherry unison lines are in key, although they skip and slide around it. Coleman then enters with a prolonged improvisation that generally starts out like a string of roman candles but soon fizzles—as soon, in fact, as he gets away from the basic "theme" (somehow, most of the thematic material has a south-of-the-border flavor). What remains fascinating is Coleman's use of shifting rhythmic patterns; often quite unexpected. As he goes on, the "oriental" overtones increase, aided by the nasal sound of his plastic alto sax (Bird had one for a while). In other words, he plays too long—the universal affliction of the generation of jazzmen who grew up without the discipline of big-band and three-minute record work. Cherry, a man so slight of build that one feels relieved he doesn't play a full-grown horn, gets a nice sound but cannot match the leader in invention or intensity. He is undoubtedly the only hornman who can play unison with Ornette Coleman.

They are at their best in the blues. There is that about the blues: when you play it, you can't get too far away from the roots of jazz, no matter what. On the blues, Coleman occasionally comes close to that vocal quality he wants, a quality reflected in his own rather hoarse and husky speaking voice. It is to be hoped that these musicians will not remain in isolation, playing-wise. It seems they have decided to settle in New York, where the climate is more fertile if less rarified, and where their playing may achieve more discipline and concentration. But it is likely that, whatever may happen, this music is not the jazz of the future but a sincere and somewhat raw attempt to chart new tributaries. Eventually, the essence will be distilled and merge with the basic current of jazz. And that's more than enough for any new idea.

To close this dissertation against cats in categories, take a recent modern concert at Town Hall. The program featured Coleman, Cecil Taylor, Monk (with standby Charlie Rouse and temporaries Scott LaFaro, bass, and Elvin Jones, drums—Jones sounding more at home here than in his regular spot with Harry Edison), Ernestine Anderson, the Jazztet, and John Coltrane. It came to a close with Zoot Sims, Bob Brookmeyer, Coltrane, Pepper Adams, Milt Hinton, and Art Taylor being put through their paces by Count Basie at the piano. What else but "One O'Clock Jump" (it was 1:15 a.m.)? It was amazing. Basie set the tempo and played a few choruses of down-home piano—and everything began to rock. We have never had the pleasure of hearing Art Taylor swing more—nor of hearing Coltrane play such straightforward (and we don't mean simpleminded) and booting tenor.

Zoot of course loves to swing, and Dr. Pepper was feeling no pain. The proceedings were kept in constant motion by Mr. Basie, who, along with Duke, must be the Number One Band Pianist in jazz. The audience, whose prior behavior had been properly concert-like, came to their feet with a resounding yell for more—not at all cool-like. And did it make everybody feel good? Zoot and Brookmeyer came marching backstage à la Hamp, playing the closing riff—Art Taylor, sweating somewhat, wore a wide smile (a rarity), and Monk, who had been digging from the sidelines, was glowing. Whatever all this may or may not prove, we think that in his heart of hearts every jazz musician knows that there is no better feeling than reaching people and making them happy—not only and always, but every so often—and when it comes to that, the champs are not the yearlings. Even the house manager at Town Hall, who recently dropped the curtain on George Shearing, knows that. As he said to Count: "We were running overtime when you went on, but I couldn't do that to *you*, Mr. Basie." That's practical criticism at its best.

(1958)

The Conover Controversy

Just prior to the first jazz event at the Kennedy Center, Hollie West, jazz critic and columnist for the *Washington Post*, launched a strongly worded attack on Willis Conover, jazz consultant to the Center and producer of the festival held September 24–26.

West suggested that Conover wears too many hats and wields too much power. He pointed out that Conover is in charge of the Voice of America's jazz program, "a paid consultant to the Kennedy Center . . . a paid consultant to the National Endowment for the Arts [and in addition] a member of the jazz subcommittee for the State Department cultural presentations, chairman of the White House Record Library Commission, and unofficial adviser to the White House on jazz."

Unfortunately, West couched his arguments in racial terms, and in a follow-up piece in the *Post*, conceded that "the emotional issue of race has clouded the question of Conover's role and authority at the Kennedy Center." (West had called for Conover's resignation from his position there.) West then reiterated most of his criticisms, also calling into question Conover's qualifications as a jazz authority.

A week later, in an interview in the *New York Times*, Conover gave his side of the story (West had mentioned in his second article response from "many readers," but his paper published none of it). Conover also discussed his feelings concerning the attack with *Down Beat*, and provided copies of statements in his support by several members of the Kennedy Center Advisory Panel.

Rather than examining at length the charges and countercharges, let us briefly survey Conover's record.

He came to the Voice of America in 1954 as a part-time assistant to the man then in charge of the limited jazz program (himself a part-timer). Within a few years, the greatly expanded Conover-produced jazz program had become the VOA's most popular broadcasts, especially in countries where jazz was in official disfavor and records impossible to acquire. And Conover not only broadcast records covering the whole jazz spectrum; he also arranged for location recordings of major festivals and concerts.

When the National Endowment for the Arts and Humanities was founded, there was no provision for jazz. Almost alone, Conover pushed and maneuvered for jazz behind the scenes, and eventually, in the face of opposition from the classical music establishment, was able to form a jazz advisory panel. Initially, allocations to jazz were negligible, but Conover continued to fight, and this year's jazz allocation promises to be tenfold that of 1969.

Until Duke Ellington's seventieth birthday was celebrated at the White House, no American jazz figure had been comparably honored. It was Conover who suggested the idea and followed through, and he was also able to arrange for less conspicuous jazz events at the White House.

As for the Kennedy Center, there is good reason to believe that without efforts by Conover there would be no jazz panel or jazz program there. (After the initial three-day festival, reviewed in this issue, a series of concerts began with Bill Evans [Oct. 22] and continues with a New Orleans and Ragtime Festival [Nov. 7], Duke Ellington [Dec. 26], The MJQ [Jan. 9], Earl Hines [Feb. 6], Dizzy Gillespie [Feb. 13], Gil Evans [March 19], and a blues festival [April 9].) Nor would a number of jazz artists have been invited to participate in the Center's prestigious Founding Artists project.

Since West brought up the matter of money ("paid consultant," etc.), it seems fitting to reveal that for producing Kennedy Center jazz events, Conover is paid the munificent sum of $75 per concert, and for his services to the Endowment, a grand per diem of $50 when the jazz panel meets (which is about three days a year).

These facts and figures, we believe, speak for themselves. The point is that in every instance, Conover acquired his "positions of power" for the benefit of jazz.

He may not, as West implies, be a great jazz scholar, though his knowledge of the music is probably as broad and well-grounded as that of any "expert," command of technical jargon aside.

He may also, as West implies, sometimes have used his "power" to hire and/or aid musicians whose work he likes. Who wouldn't have? But he has also demonstrably rendered similar services to musicians for whose art he has little or no personal empathy.

Beyond doubt, there are people whom Conover has alienated in the course of his activities. He would not be human if it were otherwise. But he has been anything but dictatorial and inflexible in his exercise of influence, and to our knowledge has never used his position for devious or self-serving purposes. If he has gotten some personal recognition and a few little side gigs out of his years of hard and largely unpaid (or underpaid) labor, so what?

What jazz needs is more Willis Conovers, black and white, not more useless infighting or racial red herrings. Hollie West is an outstanding jazz journalist who has rendered meritorious service to the music. His motives in this affair we know to be sincere. Yet it is not possible to find merit in his attack on Conover.

The case should be closed, the animosities forgotten, and the forces speedily regrouped to carry on in unity the good fight for what really matters: jazz power.

(1971)

Integrating Jazz

More than a decade before Jackie Robinson made his debut with the Brooklyn Dodgers, jazz began to level its playing fields. Benny Goodman (not yet dubbed "King of Swing") had already recorded with the brilliant African-American pianist Teddy Wilson, most notably in a trio context (with the Goodman band's drummer, Gene Krupa, as the third man), when he was persuaded to present the trio in a public performance.

The persuading was done by Helen Oakley, a young jazz writer and activist, who was a leading figure in the Chicago Rhythm Club, which was sponsoring a series of innovative Sunday afternoon jazz concerts at the

Urban Room of the Congress Hotel. The first of these featured the Good-man band, the second that of Fletcher Henderson, whose arrangements were a significant part of the Goodman repertory. Goodman and Krupa had "sat in" with the Henderson musicians during that event, in what was a pretty daring experiment in public integration for early 1936, and it was in part due to this precedent that Goodman agreed to bring Wilson in for the second Rhythm Club concert by his band, on Easter Sunday, but only after the hotel's manager, Harry Kaufman, had approved.

Any apprehension among those involved was literally blown away once the trio took the stage. "The three of us," Goodman recalled, "worked to-gether as if we had been born to play this way," and the audience's response mirrored the musicians' enthusiasm. Then and there, Goodman decided to make the trio a permanent part of his musical organization, a move ce-mented by Kaufman's insistence that Wilson should remain for the dura-tion of the Congress engagement.

Some four months later, during a stay in Los Angeles, Goodman was told about an amazing vibraharpist by some of the musicians in his band. He stopped by the little club where Lionel Hampton was working late one night and was so taken with what he heard that he unpacked his clarinet and, according to Hampton, "we jammed about two or three hours." The next night, Goodman returned with Wilson, Krupa, and other Goodman-ites, and this time, they jammed until sunrise, and then the clarinetist in-vited Hampton to record. As any student of jazz history knows, the trio now became a quartet.

Looking back in 1979, during an interview with bassist-historian Milt Hinton, Wilson described his and Hampton's reception as "a tremendous success. As a matter of fact, it was an asset, racial mixing. The interest . . . was tremendous, and the public was so for the thing that not one negative voice in any audience did we ever get." Hinton inquired about problems within the band, and the pianist responded that his experience had been "completely different from Jackie Robinson's [who had] tremendous prob-lems with baseball players, [while] we were like brothers, the whole outfit. Everybody knew what was happening. And the band, there were Southern-ers in it . . . and there were Jews and Christians . . . Goodman was Jewish, and some of the guys were Italians. . . . But the whole thing was as solid as a family, the Goodman thing. We were all there, just like brothers."

All, of course, was not sweetness and light. In terms of public accommo-dations while touring, for example, segregation continued to be the norm. But as Wilson points out, he and Hampton "went along with the tide the way it was because we had opened up a door already, a giant crack." And that door "gradually opened of its own accord, opened wide as we have today. But that was the first cracking of the door."

That crack in the door was not some magic Open Sesame; it would take years, even decades, before equality was achieved within jazz, especially when it came to economics. The highest-paying location jobs, the opportunities for steady and secure work in the radio studios or in theater pits, continued to favor whites, and well into the 1950s, the musicians' union maintained many segregated locals, with a lower scale for blacks. Nevertheless, jazz was an arena unique in American public life, where blacks and whites interacted as equals, and in which blacks more often than not served as role models and inspirations to whites.

"White," of course, is a colorless term, and when it comes to jazz, a pretty meaningless one. The non-African-American jazz musicians came from a variety of ethnic backgrounds, but the great majority was drawn from what is presently dubbed minorities. The children of Irish, Italian, and Jewish immigrants, growing up in the inner cities of America, heard, responded to, and helped to shape the emerging language of jazz—itself maybe the prime product of the now unfashionable cultural "melting pot" that in its day was a totem of democracy. The very essence of jazz could be described as a model democracy, for it depends on finely attuned interaction within a delicate balance between discipline and freedom.

Is it a coincidence that Jewish-American bandleaders were in the vanguard of the integration of jazz? Artie Shaw, who in 1938 engaged Billie Holiday to sing with his up-and-coming band, and later featured two of the greatest trumpeter-singers in jazz, Oran "Hot Lips" Page and Roy Eldridge, with successive editions of his by then top-ranked orchestra, undoubtedly gave more thought to the social and political overtones of such moves than Goodman, a less intellectually inclined man. And it is true that Goodman was often prodded by his adviser (and eventual brother-in-law) John Hammond, who was a political activist. Goodman himself always insisted that all his hirings were based on musical judgment, and just that.

Yet perhaps the most perceptive assessment of Goodman's attitude came from a man who understood him better than most, the pianist-arranger Mel Powell (born Epstein), who joined Goodman at the tender age of eighteen and later went on to become a Pulitzer prize–winning composer and a great teacher (his *Mission to Moscow* is certain to be a highlight of the concert). Powell joined the Goodman band not long before the great guitarist Charlie Christian, the third of Goodman's black stars, left due to ill health, and served while its ranks included ex-Ellington trumpeter Cootie Williams, bassist John Simmons, and the fabulous Big Sid Catlett on drums. "Benny," Powell said, "was one of the very, very few white people I've known who had not a fiber of racism in him. He was absolutely, authentically color-blind. . . . One of the real giveaways to his outlook was that he could be as rude to a black man as to a white man. He did not get patronizing or suddenly gentle. Not at all. And I always found that admirable."

In terms of the breakthrough decade of the 1930s, Goodman's Carnegie Hall concert of January 16, 1938, can be seen as a landmark in the public integration of jazz. Not only was the quartet well featured, but there were also some very special guests. As luck would have it, both Duke Ellington and Count Basie and their bands were in town. Ellington sent his greatest stars, Cootie Williams, alto and soprano saxophonist Johnny Hodges, and baritone saxophone champion Harry Carney. Basie came himself, and brought along the sublime Lester Young (a great personal favorite of Goodman's), the trumpeter Buck Clayton, and those backbones of his famed rhythm section, guitarist Freddie Green and bassist Walter Page. The Ellingtonians performed one of their specialties, and Hodges and Carney stuck around for the jam session with the Basie contingent, Goodman, Harry James, and Krupa. It was a sterling example of swing solidarity, and if Artie Shaw had been in the house, it would serve even better to tie together the elements of tonight's program.

Sixty years after that memorable event, jazz continues to be a major factor in the often frustratingly slow but nonetheless steady journey toward the realization of the American Dream. As Thelonious Monk once put it: "Jazz and freedom go hand in hand. That explains it. There isn't any more to add to it. If I do add to it, it gets complicated. That's something for you to think about. You think about it and dig it. You dig it."

Amen.

(1998)

"Titans of the Tenor Sax"

While the original format of this concert—to present Coleman Hawkins, Zoot Sims, Sonny Rollins, and John Coltrane as representatives of important and influential tenor saxophone styles—was promising, the promise was not kept. Instead of a concert, this Lincoln Center event was a chaotic, rambling, pointless "happening" seemingly designed to frustrate the audience and embarrass those artists who had come to play. If an enemy of jazz had plotted to make the music and the performers appear absurd and irresponsible, he couldn't have been more successful. To attend this event was an experience that made one doubt one's own sanity.

It got under way with a brief but excellent set by Sims, accompanied by the rhythm section of the Clark Terry–Bob Brookmeyer quintet (Roger Kellaway, piano; Bill Crow, bass; Dave Bailey, drums). Though Sims failed to adjust the microphone, and much of his work thus was barely audible, he produced a series of swinging choruses on Al Cohn's "Mama Flosey," warming up the audience and the rhythm team. He followed with George Handy's pretty ballad "The Trouble with You Is Me," playing with warmth, taste, and feeling. Sims closed with an up-tempo version of "The Man I Love," swinging in a relaxed and authoritative manner that was almost a definition of his Lester Young–based but personal style. Kellaway contributed a stomping, inventive solo, and Crow, a sturdy timekeeper not often heard in solo, held the spotlight for two excellent choruses. Sims was followed by Terry and Brookmeyer, who did "Straight, No Chaser." The hornmen's work was swinging and humorous but seemed to lack their customary sparkle. This interlude, however, had no relation to the evening's tenor theme.

Next, Coleman Hawkins, looking the picture of a jazz patriarch with his flowing, grizzled full beard, joined the quintet. Immediately adjusting the mike (he was the only saxophonist of the night to do so), he launched "In a Mellotone" with a few well-chosen notes, instantly capturing the audience with his rich, golden, powerful sound. Hawk unrolled seven flowing choruses, a tapestry of sound and rhythm that made his appearance the evening's undisputed highlight, though the great man was not at the top of his form. Having made his mark, Hawkins begged off to enthusiastic applause, impervious to demands for more. (He had been contracted to do just one number.)

Emcee Dave Lambert, apparently slightly bewildered, remained on stage to sing "Hackensack" with the band and scatted with spirit, imagination, and wit. Lambert is a delightful performer; nevertheless, this was a rather anticlimactic ending to the first half of what still appeared to be a concert presentation.

The second part began with the entrance of Rollins's rhythm section (John Hicks, piano; Walter Booker, bass; Mickey Roker, drums), introduced by Lambert, who ended with "and now, Sonny Rollins!" Nobody appeared. Undaunted, Lambert tried again. Still no Rollins. Lambert vanished into the wings, and after a few suspenseful moments Rollins emerged, dressed in a black turtleneck polo shirt, dark slacks, and brown shoes. Horn in mouth, he produced a long, held note while walking on stage. He had in tow an unannounced guest, Yusef Lateef.

The two tenors launched "Sonnymoon for Two," and Rollins gave Lateef the first solo. While he played (and very well), Rollins sauntered about the stage, occasionally testing the acoustics with fitting phrases from his horn. But when the time came for his solo, two or three tentative notes were all that happened. Hicks, expectantly, comped for an uneventful 12 bars, then started a solo of his own. Meanwhile, Rollins had wandered across the stage. He now alerted the rhythm section for a downbeat, began "Hold 'Em Joe," abandoned the tune after a few bars, changed the tempo, began to play "Penthouse Serenade," changed the tempo again, and then played half a chorus of "Three Little Words." While the rhythm section vamped, Rollins concluded this lightning "medley" with thank-yous to the audience and the musicians. Then, with Lateef again in tow, he backed out into the wings, playing a tentative riff. The entire performance had lasted less than ten minutes. Rollins returned briefly, quieting the cries for "more," to announce that he would be back later, with Coltrane.

After the confused sidemen had finally collected themselves sufficiently to leave the stage, Lambert announced Coltrane's group. Bassist Jimmy Garrison and drummers Rashied Ali and J. C. Moses caused no great surprise, though the group's new pianist, Alice McLeod Coltrane, did. But that was nothing compared to what was still to come: Pharoah Sanders, the Ayler brothers, and, a bit later, altoist Carlos Ward.

Sanders made his entrance carrying a large brown shopping bag subsequently found to contain tambourines, maracas, and other more exotic rhythmic accoutrements. Coltrane, appearing relaxed and happy, gave his minions time to group themselves on stage while Garrison played nimble, flamenco-like solo bass. Coltrane then intoned "My Favorite Things" on soprano. A few restrained choruses were to be the sole reference to this point of departure during the following thirty-five minutes. Coltrane soon yielded the solo spot to Sanders, who launched a gargling banshee wail that he sustained for the duration of his "solo." It was a grotesque display of willful ugliness. Sanders never touched the keys of his horn and was content with overblowing, creating no musical pattern of any kind, either melodic or rhythmic.

When it came to screaming, however, Sanders met his match in Albert Ayler, whose noises at least had some movement. Squeaking and squealing at lightning speed, he gave a convincing musical impression of a whirling dervish seized by St. Vitus's dance. Trumpeter Don Ayler came to bat next. Because he played with his horn's bell pointed at the floor, most of his solo was inaudible. (Philharmonic Hall's poor acoustics, the racket set up by the two drummers, and the occasional "backgrounds" provided by the reeds didn't help.) What was decipherable seemed to be a series of rapid spurts of disjointed notes played with considerable frenzy but little else.

Ward's ensuing alto solo seemed a model of logic and restraint by comparison, though he didn't do much more than string together phrases taken from Coltrane and Ornette Coleman. He received no tangible assistance from the rhythm section—the two drummers never approached Elvin Jones in terms of excitement and drive, though certainly exceeding him in decibel count. Ward now yielded to the Ayler brothers, who fashioned a weird duet, a bit like the screaming contests little children indulge in and scarcely more pleasing to the ear.

After this quaint interlude Coltrane took to the mike and began to chant "Om-Mani-Padme-Hum" in a gentle singsong (while the other soloists played, he had occasionally joined the fray, three maracas in one hand). Coltrane concluded the set with a few relaxed moments of tenor. In this context his playing sounded positively classic, but this was restrained Coltrane by any standard. The stunned audience collected its wits sufficiently to offer mild applause and scattered booing.

After this display, one wonders what has happened to Coltrane. Is he the prisoner of a band of hypnotists? Has he lost all musical judgment? Or is he putting on his audience? Whatever the answer, it was saddening to contemplate this spectacle, unworthy of a great musician. It was not unlike watching Joe Louis wrestle, but then, Louis did that because he needed money. Coltrane, contracted for five pieces, undoubtedly paid his guests himself. It is conceivable that Coltrane, an earnest and responsible man, has been persuaded that it is his duty to give musicians who presume to be his followers (though their music indicates nothing of the kind, aside from certain superficial mannerisms) the opportunity to be heard. For the last six months or so, Coltrane has hardly made a single appearance without some member of the extremist faction. Thus people who come to hear Coltrane are confronted with spectacles such as that which took place at Philharmonic Hall.

If Coltrane has an obligation, real or imagined, to the people he insists on carrying on his coattails, does he not also have an obligation to his audience? They come to hear him, not those others. They don't hear him. Will they come back? Coltrane is playing a dangerous game in which the risks are all his. The others, the have-nots, have nothing to lose.

As for Rollins, one must assume that he intended to play with Coltrane but was scared off by the circus that ensued. His own set was hardly commensurate with his stature as a great player, but at least his guest was a man who can play his horn. As for the Aylers and Sanders, they made a mockery of the term "titans" in the concert's title. No one would envy these players the bookings they can get on the strength of their own work and following, but to ride on the reputation of others is deception.

(1966)

In Defense of "Commercialism"

I s art divisible from life—should it be? But what is life in 1970? Indeed, what is art?

    Don't wince. My tongue is in my cheek. Or is it? Everything is ambiguous these days. Take record reviewing, the record business, record reviewers, readers of record reviews, and jazz.

Most records made by jazz artists these days are pretty much like the two under scrutiny here, in one way or another. That is to say, they are not "pure" jazz albums, but attempts to present players usually identified with jazz in terms considered compatible with what is called "today's music."

Which means: tunes, rhythms, and areas of sound bought by today's record public. More specifically, hits of the day or blues/soul/rock-flavored melodies, played with a pronounced beat, usually in some variant of contemporary dance rhythm and tempo, often using an organ and/or electronically flavored instrumentation, with sometime additives including strings, brass riffs, or vocal backing, and generally within airplay length.

More and more such records are among the fewer and fewer albums made by jazz players these days, and it ain't likely to subside, this trend. For one thing, it sells records, at least sometimes. For another, it seeks and finds its audience not among dedicated jazz followers but among people who buy records for fun—listening at home with a groove going, dancing at parties—and there's more of the latter, friend—plenty more.

Remember when even people who didn't care about or particularly like jazz had at least a few Miles Davis, Dave Brubeck, Chet Baker, or Stan Getz records at home—and later maybe a Cannonball or Ramsey Lewis? No room here to go into why, but that fringe bought a lot of records. That fringe is gone.

The jazz fringe audience today maybe buys Miles—right now, anyway. It buys blues—phony and real, new and reissued. It probably buys a token Coltrane LP, perhaps a Billie Holiday. The rest is rock—and maybe some sides like these, Junior Mance's *With a Lotta Help from My Friends*, and Ray Bryant's *MCMLXX*, both on Atlantic. Especially if the buyers are into black culture—not the kind you hear demands made for, but the kind that exists because there is demand for it.

The records we're talking about are bought by people whose libraries also include James Brown, Aretha, King Curtis, Ray Charles oldies, and, if they're hip, some contemporary blues, like B. B. King. There are a lot of people out there like that, and they buy a lot of records.

Now, people who review records for this magazine are, in varying degrees, serious about jazz. They may like some contemporary popular music, and even praise it, but they don't much like records like the ones we're talking about. Why? Because they are conditioned to think of jazz musicians as "artists" who, if they are not playing "pure" jazz of one sort or another, must be suspected of compromising their talents. Either they've sold out, or they're being pressured by the record companies, or maybe they were not "real" artists to begin with, the argument goes.

The reviewers also feel, and with good reason, that they are writing for people who want their jazz straight and are likely to share these prejudices against "commercialism."

There certainly are standpoints from which such attitudes are justified: personal esthetics, high artistic standards, notions of a grander design. But is art divisible from life? Are such concepts not perhaps too idealistic and insufficiently realistic when applied to jazz in the marketplace?

Not to say that commercialism is good enough for jazz because jazz isn't on that high a level anyway. Not in the least. But to say that the music in its highest forms could never have survived—not even have come into being— if not for the existence of an environment in which fine distinctions between art and entertainment were not commonly made, or even relevant.

The reviewers who put down today's commercial jazz are almost all in greater or lesser awe of the music's legacy, as handed down on records. Until the late 1930s, however, not one single jazz record was made to sell as art, or even as jazz. Some of the most beautiful jazz records ever cut were quite simply made for entertainment—for dancing, for casual listening, as versions of hit tunes.

How many lovers of jazz now remember that working in even the best big bands of the swing era (Ellington and a very few others excluded) meant, for the dedicated *jazz* player, a compromise with his true ambitions, and that the romantic jazz fans of that day much admired those "fugitives" from the big bands who played "the real jazz" for peanuts in the few joints that would book it? (In retrospect, the ones who didn't flee were not necessarily less dedicated.)

And you don't even need history to make the point: how many of the "pure" jazz albums of the past decade were made by players who, for daily bread, played all kinds of "commercial" music?

The point is: jazz is a music, but is also *a way of playing*, and it has always been fascinating to see how adaptable to a variety of playing situations jazz musicians have been. Even Thelonious Monk used to play for dances and revival meetings. That he doesn't have to do that now is only as it should be. That not every jazzman, not even every great jazzman, can always write his own musical ticket is *not* as it should be—but if we lived in a perfect world, who'd need record reviews?

Compromise with the necessities of life does not always inhibit artists. Indeed, no artist was really free to create as he pleased until art became a luxury—and you only need to visit your nearest gallery of contemporary art to see how much that has improved matters.

It goes against the intellectual's grain, no doubt, but isn't it one of the great achievements of jazz that it has been an intrinsic part of popular music, first in this country and soon elsewhere as well, for five decades or more? Despite the fact that it is an art, or because it is? Ponder that, and ask yourself if it isn't a measure of a musician's strength and identity as an artist that he can make silk purses out of sow's ears, and if it isn't an axiom that if you have something of your own to say, it will come through no matter what? If you can play, there are many ways to play yourself. And who the hell says that "art" must always be pure and holy and profound? Me, I'd rather tap my foot to some soul jazz, organs, electric bass, and all, than be hectored by some no-blowing poseur's naked ego trip. One may be a commercial cop-out, the other serious art—but don't bet on it. These are ambiguous times.

(1970)

Index

Credit Acknowledgments

All of the essays in this collection have been previously published.

"Reminiscing in Tempo" in *Jazz: A History of America's Music* (Alfred A. Knopf, 2000)

"Portrait of the Artist as a Young Man" in *Portrait of the Artist as a Young Man* (Columbia/Legacy, 1994)

"Introduction" in *Satchmo: My Life in New Orleans* (DaCapo Press, 1986)

"A Sixty-fifth Birthday Interview" in *Down Beat* (1965)

"Chicago Concert" in *Chicago Concert* (Columbia Records, 1980)

"Satchmo and the Critics" in *The Village Voice* (2001)

"V.S.O.P." in *Louis Armstrong: V.S.O.P.* (Epic Records, 1969)

"Review of *Louis Armstrong: An American Genius* by James Lincoln Collier" in *Annual Review of Jazz Studies* (1985)

"Review of *Louis Armstrong: An Extravagant Life* by Lawrence Bergreen" in *Los Angeles Times Book Review* (1997)

"Louis and Duke: The Great Summit" in *The Great Summit* (Roulette, 2001)

"Ellington at Philharmonic Hall" in *Down Beat* (1966)

"Billy Strayhorn in Concert" in *Down Beat* (1965)

"Early Ellington" in *Early Ellington* (Bluebird, 1989)

"The Ellington Era" in *Listen: A Music Monthly* (1963)

"Ellington: 1927–1940" in *Jazz* (1964)

"Ellington: 1944–1946" in *Duke Ellington: The Centennial Edition* (RCA Victor, 1999)

"Far East Suite" in *Down Beat* (1967)

". . . And His Mother Called Him Bill" in *Down Beat* (1968)

"Seventieth Birthday Concert" in *Down Beat* (1970)

"Ellington at the Whitney" in *Ellington at the Whitney* (Impulse, 1995)

"Concert of Sacred Music" in *Down Beat* (1966)

"James Reese Europe" in *The New York Times* (1989)

"Paul Whiteman" in *Down Beat* (1968)

"Hot Lips Page" in *Jazz Journal* (1962)

"Eddie Condon" in *Down Beat* (1965)

"Earl Hines" in *Down Beat* (1965)

"Roy Eldridge: 'Little Jazz'" in *Down Beat* (1971)

"Roy Eldridge: 'Little Jazz' for the Ages in *Jazz Times* (1989)

"Bunny Berigan" in *Bunny Berigan* (RCA Victor, 1972)

"Lionel Hampton" in *Down Beat* (1965)

"Jo Jones" in *Down Beat* (1965)
"Milt Hinton" in *Jazz Times* (2000)
"Vic Dickenson" in *Ralph Sutton and Vic Dickinson* (Chazz Jazz, 1985)
"Dizzy Gillespie" in *Down Beat* (1965)
"Clark Terry" in *Down Beat* (1967)
"Billy Taylor" in *Down Beat* (1971)
"Miles Davis" in *The Complete Prestige Recordings* (1980)
"Miles in Motion" in *Down Beat* (1970)
"Charlie Mingus" in *BMI's World of Music* (1979)
"Gene Ammons" in *Gene Ammons* (EmArcy, 1976)
"Dinah Washington" in *Dinah Washington* (EmArcy, 1976)
"Bill Evans" in *Down Beat* (1964)
"Paul Desmond" in *Down Beat* (1965)
"Bob Brookmeyer" in *Down Beat* (1967)
"Dick Wellstood" in *Down Beat* (1967)
"Ornette Coleman" in *Down Beat* (1965)
"Charlie Haden" in *Down Beat* (1967)
"Freddie Hubbard" in *Down Beat* (1966)
"Warren Vaché" in *Down Beat* (1983)
"Ma Rainey" in *Ma Rainey* (Milestone Records, 1974)
"Benny Goodman and Jack Teagarden" in *Benny Goodman and Jack Teagarden in New York* (Decca, 1992)
"Fats Waller" in *The Early Years, Part 1* (Bluebird, 1995)
"Art Tatum" in *God Is in the House* (Onyx, 1974)
"Hot Lips Page: After Hours in Harlem" in *Hot Lips Page: After Hours in Harlem* (Onyx, 1974)
"Coleman Hawkins" in *Body and Soul* (Bluebird, 1986)
"Ben Webster" in *The Complete Ben Webster on EmArcy* (EmArcy, Japan, 1986)
"Jack Teagarden" in *Think Well of Me* (Verve, 1998)
"Pee Wee Russell" in *Memorial Album* (Prestige, 1969)
"Bobby Hackett" in *That Da-Da Strain* (Portrait, 1988)
"Ella Fitzgerald" in *75th Birthday Tribute* (Decca, 1993)
"Lester Young" in *Pres in Europe* (Onyx, 1974)
"Charlie Parker" in *First Recordings!* (Onyx, 1974)
"Thelonious Monk" in *'Round Midnight* (Milestone, 1982)
"Sarah Vaughan" in *Send In the Clowns* (Pablo, 1981)
"Sonny Stitt" in *Sonny Stitt and Friends* (Chess, 1998)
"Dexter Gordon" in *Settin' the Pace* (Savoy, 1998)
"Jimmy Rowles/Stan Getz" in *The Peacocks* (Columbia, 1978)
"John Coltrane" in *Bye Bye Blackbird* (Pablo, 1982)
"Tommy Flanagan" in *Jazz Poet* (Timeless, 1990)
"Martial Solal" in *Improvise Pour France Musique* (Disque JMS, 1994)
"Ruby Braff/Dick Hyman" in *Ruby and Dick Play Nice Tunes* (Arbors, 1994)
"Dick Hyman" in *Gulf Coast Blues* (Stomp Off, 1986)
"Dave McKenna" in *This Is the Moment* (Portrait, 1988)
"Svend Asmussen" in *June Night* (Doctor Jazz, 1983)
"Joe Lovano" in *Universal Language* (Blue Note, 1992)
"Bessie Smith: The World's Greatest Blues Singer" in *Down Beat* (1970)

"The Original Dixieland Jazz Band" in *Down Beat* (1969)

"The Chicagoans: 1928–1930" in *Down Beat* (1968)

"Earl Hines: A Monday Date/Quintessential Recording Session" in *Down Beat* (1971)

"Art Tatum: Piano Starts Here" in *Down Beat* (1968)

"Jimmie Lunceford: Lunceford Special" in *Down Beat* (1968)

"Count Basie: Basie's Beat" in *Down Beat* (1966)

"Thad Jones–Mel Lewis Live at the Village Vanguard" in *Down Beat* (1968)

"Benny Carter: The King" in *Jazz* (1976)

"Lester Young: The Pres/Pres" in *Metronome* (1961)

"Dexter Gordon: The Panther" in *Down Beat* (1971)

"Lee Konitz: Duets" in *Down Beat* (1969)

"Houston Person: Trust in Me" in *Down Beat* (1968)

"Barry Harris: Magnificent" in *Down Beat* (1970)

"Jaki Byard: Solo Piano" in *Down Beat* (1970)

"Wes Montgomery: Down Here on the Ground" in *Down Beat* (1968)

"Erroll Garner at the Village Gate" in *Down Beat* (1965)

"Erroll Garner at Carnegie Hall" in *Down Beat* (1967)

"Bud Powell" in *Down Beat* (1964)

"Bill Evans" in *Down Beat* (1967)

"Cecil Taylor" in *Down Beat* (1966)

"Harry Edison" in *Jazz Journal* (1976)

"Dizzy Gillespie" in *Down Beat* (1970)

"Miles Davis" in *Down Beat* (1966)

"Jazz at the Philharmonic" in *Down Beat* (1967)

"Phil Woods" in *Down Beat* (1967)

"Ira Sullivan/Sonny Stitt" in *Jazz Journal* (1977)

"Joe Turner" in *Jazz Journal* (1977)

"Ornette Coleman at the Five Spot" in *Metronome* (1961)

"Ornette Coleman at the Village Vanguard" in *Down Beat* (1965)

"Mary Lou Williams/Cecil Taylor" in *Jazz Journal* (1977)

"Newport 1960" in *Jazz Journal* (1960)

"One Night in Birdland" in *One Night in Birdland* (Columbia Records, 1977)

"Lester Leaps In" in *Jazz Journal* (1958)

"Eubie Blake in Session" in *Jazz Journal* (1958)

"Jazz Goes to Washington" in *Musical America* (1962)

"Swinging at the White House" in *Down Beat* (1969)

"The Blues Comes to Ann Arbor" in *Down Beat* (1969)

"Breakfast with Champions" in *Down Beat* (1971)

"Woody's Fortieth" in *Jazz Journal* (1977)

"Trumpet Encounter" in *Jazz Journal* (1977)

"Return to Birdland" in *Radio Free Jazz* (1978)

"Recorded Jazz" in *The Oxford Companion to Jazz* (2000)

"Discography: The Thankless Science" in *Down Beat Music* (1966)

"The Commodore Story" in *The Commodore Story* (Commodore, 1997)

"The Hot Record Society" in *The Complete HRS Recordings* (Mosaic, 2000)

"The Birth of Blue Note" in *The First Day* (Blue Note, 1992)

"Notes on Keynote Sessions" in *The Complete Keynote Recordings* (EmArcy, 1986)

"Review of *The Essential Jazz Records, Volume 1: Ragtime to Swing*" in *Annual Review of Jazz Studies* (1988)

"A New Standard for Reissues" in *Down Beat* (1983)

"Hot Chocolates" in *Hot Chocolates* (Smithsonian Records, 1978)

"Jazz and Dance" in *Program Notes* (Dexter Gordon Memorial Concert, Denmark, 1998)

"Jazz on Film" in *Down Beat Music* (1967)

"Jazz and Television" in *Program Notes* (Jazz and TV exhibit, Museum of Broadcasting, 1985)

"Not by Choice" in *Jazz Journal* (1958)

"Cats and Categories" in *Jazz Journal* (1958)

"The Conover Controversy" in *Down Beat* (1971)

"Integrating Jazz" in *Program Notes* (Smithsonian Jazz Repertory Orchestra Concert, 1998)

"'Titans of the Tenor Sax'" in *Down Beat* (1966)

"In Defense of 'Commercialism'" in *Down Beat* (1970)